TRAVELER'S GUIDE TO

ALASKAN CAMPING

Alaska and Yukon Camping With RV Or Tent

Sixth Edition

Mike and Terri
Church

ROLLING HOMES PRESS

Published by
Rolling Homes Press
161 Rainbow Dr., #6157
Livingston, TX 77399-1061
www.rollinghomes.com

Printed in the United States of America
First Printing 2014

Publisher's Cataloging in Publication

Church, Mike.
Traveler's guide to Alaskan camping : Alaska and Yukon camping
    with RV or tent / Mike and Terri Church–Sixth Edition
    p.cm.
    Includes index.
    Library of Congress Control Number: 2013920210
    ISBN 978-0982310151

    1. Alaska–Guidebooks. 2. Camping–Alaska–Guidebooks. 3. Recreational Liv-
ing–Alaska–Guidebooks. 4. Camping Sites, Facilities, etc.–Alaska–Guidebooks. I.
Church, Terri. II. Title. III. Alaskan Camping

F902.3C.48 2014   2013 920210
917.9804/52–dc21

*This book is dedicated
to the memory of our grandparents,*

MURIEL AND CARL JOHNSON

Muriel and Carl lived most of their lives in Fairbanks, Alaska. They fished, hunted, dug clams, and picked wild berries every year and enjoyed Alaska to its fullest. Our love of Alaska, the outdoors, and camping came from them.

Other Books by Mike and Terri Church
and
Rolling Homes Press

Companion to Alaskan Camping

Traveler's Guide To
Mexican Camping

Traveler's Guide To
Camping Mexico's Baja

Pacific Northwest
Camping Destinations

Traveler's Guide To
European Camping

RV and Car Camping
Vacations in Europe

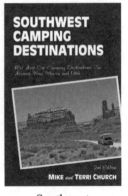

Southwest
Camping Destinations

A brief summary of the above books is provided on pages 484 to 487

Rollinghomes.com has updated information for each of our books which comes from information submitted by others and also from our travels between editions. This information is updated until we begin the process of researching and writing a new edition. Once we start the research process there is just no time to update the website and the new information goes in the next edition. Just go to our Website at www.rollinghomes.com and click on the *Oneline Updates* button to review updates.

Warning, Disclosure, and Communication With The Authors and Publishers

Half the fun of travel is the unexpected, and self-guided camping travel can produce much in the way of unexpected pleasures, and also complications and problems. This book is designed to increase the pleasures of Alaskan camping and reduce the number of unexpected problems you may encounter. You can help ensure a smooth trip by doing additional advance research, planning ahead, and exercising caution when appropriate. There can be no guarantee that your trip will be trouble free.

Although the authors and publisher have done their best to ensure that the information presented in this book was correct at the time of publication they do not assume and hereby disclaim any liability to any party for any loss or damage caused by errors, omissions, or any other cause.

In a book like this it is inevitable that there will be omissions or mistakes, especially as things do change over time. If you find inaccuracies we would like to hear about them so that they can be corrected in future editions. We would also like to hear about your enjoyable experiences. If you come upon an outstanding campground or destination please let us know, those kinds of things may also find their way to future versions of the guide or to our Internet site. You can reach us by mail at:

Rolling Homes Press
161 Rainbow Dr., #6157
Livingston, TX 77399-1061

You can also communicate with us by sending an Email through our Website at:

www.rollinghomes.com

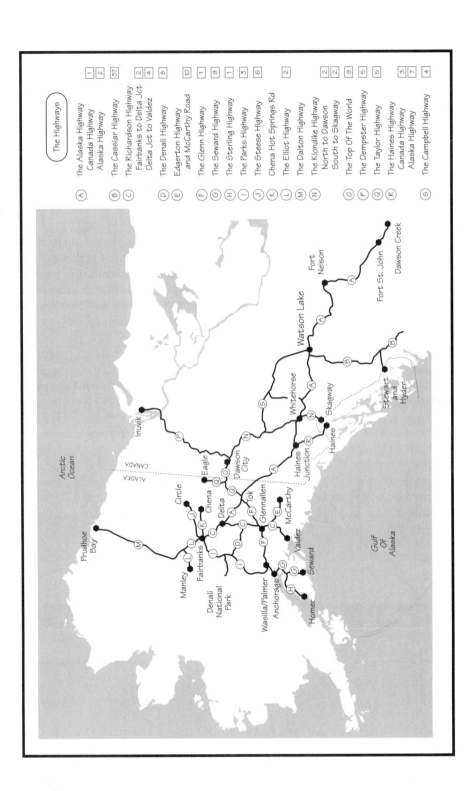

The Highways

Ⓐ	The Alaska Highway	1
	Canada Highway	2
	Alaska Highway	37
Ⓑ	The Cassiar Highway	
Ⓒ	The Richardson Highway	
	Fairbanks to Delta Jct	2
	Delta Jct to Valdez	4
Ⓓ	The Denali Highway	8
Ⓔ	Edgerton Highway	10
	and McCarthy Road	
Ⓕ	The Glenn Highway	1
Ⓖ	The Seward Highway	9
Ⓗ	The Sterling Highway	1
Ⓘ	The Parks Highway	3
Ⓙ	The Steese Highway	6
Ⓚ	Chena Hot Springs Rd	
Ⓛ	The Elliot Highway	2
Ⓜ	The Dalton Highway	
Ⓝ	The Klondike Highway	
	North to Dawson	2
	South to Skagway	2
Ⓞ	The Top Of The World	9
Ⓟ	The Dempster Highway	5
Ⓠ	The Taylor Highway	5
Ⓡ	The Haines Highway	
	Canada Highway	3
	Alaska Highway	7
Ⓢ	The Campbell Highway	4

TABLE OF CONTENTS

INTRODUCTION

For most people Alaska is the dream camping destination. No wonder! There is just no other destination with the same combination of accessibility, scenery, wildlife, outdoor activities, history, facilities, and support. Any camping trip to Alaska, whether in an RV or on foot, along the road system or a remote river, for sightseeing or for fishing, is bound to be the trip of a lifetime.

We've been traveling extensively in an RV for many years now. We've camped around the U.S., Canada, Mexico, Central America, Europe, and Australia. There are lots of places to go and lots to see, but it seems that each year finds us back in Alaska.

We do have a few more Alaska connections than most people. One of us, Mike, was born and raised in Fairbanks. His family arrived there in 1906, fresh from Dawson City and the gold rush there–his grandmother was one of the few children born in Dawson City during the gold rush. There's an Alcan connection too–his mother first came to Alaska in 1947 over the highway, a year before it officially opened to civilian traffic. He's lived in Fairbanks, Anchorage, Cooper Landing, Kenai, Homer, Nenana, Tok, and even Denali Park. Terri arrived in Alaska the day after she graduated from college and lived and worked in Fairbanks, Kenai, and Anchorage for over ten years. We're full-timer RV travelers now, but the state continues to draw us back.

Mike was introduced to camping by his grandparents, both true sourdoughs. His earliest camping experiences were travels along the Richardson between Fairbanks and Anchorage in the fifties, the campground most nights was a gravel pit and dinner was a grayling from a nearby stream. Very few summers since then have gone by without at least one camping vacation somewhere in the state.

Traveler's Guide to Alaskan Camping is one of seven guidebooks we have written. The others are very similar in some ways to this one. They are *Traveler's Guide to European Camping, RV and Car Camping Vacations in Europe, Traveler's Guide to Mexican Camping, Traveler's Guide to Camping Mexico's Baja, Pacific Northwest Camping Destinations,* and *Southwest Camping Destinations.* The seven volumes are the key to a world of travel fun! We hope you will join us.

A L A S K A

A NICE BOONDOCKING SPOT NEAR WORTHINGTON GLACIER

Chapter 1

Why Camp Alaska?

Each year tens of thousands of people head out to camp in Alaska. Some are RVers who drive their rigs up the Alaska Highway. Some are Alaska residents who have waited through the long winter for breakup and summer days of fishing, hiking, floating rivers and enjoying the great outdoors. Others are nature lovers and adventure campers from around the world drawn to some of the most spectacular wilderness anywhere.

There are probably as many reasons to camp Alaska as there are people who do it, but here are a few.

The Attractions

The State of Alaska holds so much wilderness that it is difficult to even grasp its immensity. There are 587,878 square miles in Alaska and over 700,000 residents. That works out to almost a square mile for each person. That's a lot of country with few people, especially when you realize that most of the people are in the cities. As you drive Alaska's highways you'll often cover miles and miles without sighting another person. Leave the road system and you're really alone. The pure solitude is sometimes almost overwhelming, but it's an experience to be treasured in today's world.

Scenery-wise Alaska is unbeatable. Southeast Alaska has deep blue fjords surrounded by steep mountains and glaciers. The Interior's tree-covered hills march into the distance bathed by the light of the midnight sun. Icy Mt. McKinley looms above you as it rises to 20,320 feet from its nearly-sea level base. Beauty is everywhere you look.

Want to see wildlife? Alaska has big animals like grizzly bears, caribou, and moose

EVERYONE LOVES A PUFFIN!

and small ones like beavers and porcupines. Along the coast you can spot whales and sea otters. Each spring millions of birds migrate to Alaska for your viewing pleasure, over 300 species are present. Most appreciated by novice birdwatchers seem to be bald eagles, which are actually common in some areas, or perhaps the puffins that can easily be seen from the tour boats that visit nesting islands from Seward and Homer.

Outdoor sports enthusiasts go crazy in Alaska. The fishing is world class and much of it can be accessed from the road system. Ocean kayakers can explore Southeast Alaska, Prince William Sound, Kodiak Island, and the fjords of the Kenai Peninsula. If you prefer rivers you should be aware that Alaska is home to over twenty designated National Wild and Scenic Rivers, and most are truly wild and scenic. There is an extensive system of hiking trails on the Kenai Peninsula and there are many other trails north of Fairbanks and in Southeast Alaska. You can also hike where there are nothing but animal trails in places like Gates of the Arctic National Park and Lake Clark National Park.

Speaking of national parks–Alaska has nine of them plus two historical national parks. And that's just the beginning. There are national parks, national monuments, national preserves, national forests, and wildlife refuges. And the State of Alaska has its own huge state parks. Almost all of this land is easily accessible to outdoors enthusiasts although they may have to hitch a ride on a boat or airplane to get there.

The wilderness isn't the only attraction in Alaska. There's history too. Gold has played an important part in the history of the state; you can hike the Chilkoot Trail, float the Yukon, or visit famous gold-mining areas like Dawson City, Nome, Circle, or the Fortymile Country.

The Alcan Highway was one of the greatest engineering and construction projects of its time, a drive along it is the best way to appreciate the accomplishment. All along the highway you'll find museums and historical markers. It would be fun even if there weren't hundreds of fishing steams, lots of opportunities to spot wildlife, and gobs of beautiful scenery.

There's another huge engineering project in Alaska that has been in the news over the last 40 years–the Trans-Alaska Oil Pipeline. The arguments over oil in Alaska are still hot. During your visit you can see for yourself if the oil facilities on the North Slope seem to be scaring the caribou, whether the 800-mile pipeline is really an eyesore, and walk the beaches of Prince William Sound to assess the visible damage.

The truth is that there is enough to do and see in Alaska to bring you back each year for many years. The few things we've described above are just the beginning, you need to come and see for yourself.

Why Camp?

It is hard to understand how anyone would visit Alaska and not camp. Along the highways and in the wilderness there is no better way to appreciate the country. If you spend your time riding a tour bus and staying in hotels you'll soon find yourself wondering what all the excitement is about. After all, most people really don't come to Alaska for the restaurants, hotels, and souvenir shops. An important part of the Alaska experience has always been the freedom to do your own thing, and a guided tour doesn't really give you that.

Camping doesn't have to mean roughing it. Modern RVs provide a lot of comfort. Screens on the windows mean that you aren't at the mercy of mosquitoes while you cook, eat, relax and sleep. Furnaces and comfortable beds mean you'll sleep well and wake to a warm rig. Sophisticated plumbing systems mean you can take a hot shower every day. Uncrowded roads make driving an RV a snap, and there's no better wildlife-viewing platform than the high seats of an RV. If you don't have your own RV or if you don't want to drive it up the Alaska Highway you can easily rent an RV in Alaska and spend a week or two exploring the state.

You don't really even need an RV to enjoy the camping along Alaska's road system. It's easy to pack a tent, sleeping bags, and camping equipment into the trunk of a car and hit the road. Most of the state is plenty warm enough for you to be comfortable during June, July, and August. Just make sure you have a good tent that is rain and bug proof, and sleeping bags that will keep you warm down to 40° F or so if you run into an unusually cold night.

If you want to visit the country away from the road system camping is really your only viable alternative. Oh sure, you could stay in one of those $4,000 per week fishing lodges, but how much fun could that be? Most of the state is accessible using either aircraft or boats, and the only real costs for a camper are equipment, food and transportation. There is one additional alternative, the state and federal governments own many small cabins scattered around the state, and they rent them out for a very reasonable fee. They're nothing fancy, really just a high-class form of camping, so we don't feel guilty about mentioning them in this book about camping. See Chapter 14 - *Camping Away From the Road System* for more information.

The Alaska Grand Tour

One of the best ways to show you what Alaska has to offer is to outline an itinerary for an RV trip to Alaska. This is the Full Monty, the mother of all road trips, a drive to Alaska on the Alaska Highway. It is a full tour of most of the roads of Alaska and much of the Yukon, and a return by Alaska State Ferry through Southeast Alaska.

Set aside as much time as possible for this tour, we wouldn't even attempt it in less than two months. Below we lay it out in 50 days, but you'll add some days for relaxing or choose some interesting side trips. Timing is essential, you want to do this between May 15 and September 15. Just one of the suggested week-long side trip additions would make this a two-month trip.

If you have only a week or two for a vacation in Alaska there is no problem. Just fly into Anchorage, rent a car or RV, and head for the Kenai Peninsula or Denali National Park. Rental vehicles are also available in other towns including Fairbanks and Whitehorse. See Chapter 2 for information about RV rental outfits.

You also don't need much time to visit off-the-road destinations in Alaska. Visiting most of them involves only doing your research by mail or on the Web, flying a commercial carrier to a departure city or town, and then using a charter airplane or boat to get into the bush. All of this can be easily arranged by telephone and you can prob-

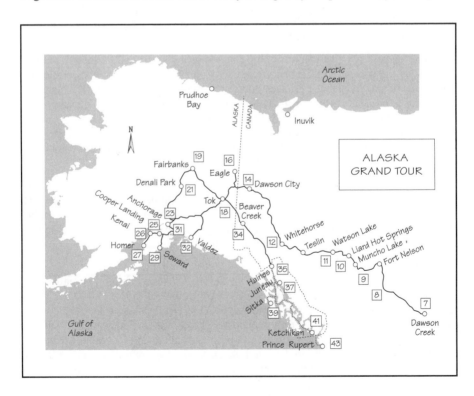

ably be camping on your first day in Alaska. See Chapter 14 for more information.

You will notice that much of the time in the itinerary below is actually spent getting to and returning from Alaska. We allow a full two weeks just for getting to the beginning of the Alaska Highway and returning home from Prince Rupert. This isn't unreasonable, take a good look at a map.

The itinerary below can be modified, a couple of ideas suggest themselves. Many visitors do not venture south to Anchorage and the Kenai Peninsula. They limit the Alaska portion of their visit to Fairbanks, Denali Park, and perhaps Valdez. This would cut about a week off our itinerary. We wouldn't do it, but you can.

Another possible change is to drive both ways and not use the ferry system for your return. If you return on the Cassiar Highway you won't have to drive the same highway both ways and will see some new country.

A word of warning here. It will be necessary to plan ahead and make reservations for the Alaska State Ferry portion of this trip long before you leave home. See Chapter 13 for more information about the ferries. It might also be worthwhile to make camping and bus reservations at Denali Park before leaving home, see Chapter 9 for information about this.

As you read through the itinerary you can refer to the Table of Contents in the front of this book and the Index at the back to find more detailed information about routes, destinations, activities, and campgrounds.

Days 1 to 7 - Getting to Dawson Creek – We used to say that you are on your own getting to Dawson Creek but this is no longer the case. Now we have another book that you might find useful: *Pacific Northwest Camping Destinations*. It covers Washington, Oregon, and Southern British Columbia up to the point where this book takes over.

For some folks from the southern U.S. it will probably take more than a week to get to Dawson Creek. Figure three days from Seattle (817 miles or 1,318 km) if you've come up the west coast and three days from Great Falls in northern Montana (875 miles or 1,411 km) if you come from east of the Rockies. You'll probably wish you had more time for both of these routes, there are lots of interesting stops and side trips. In Dawson Creek stock up on groceries and make sure your rig is in tip-top condition.

Day 8 - Dawson Creek to somewhere between Fort St John and Ft Nelson – between 140 miles (226 km) and 216 miles (348 km), 3 to 4.5 hours – The road is excellent between Dawson Creek and Fort Nelson, good fast paved two-lane road. Be sure to start watching for wildlife, there are both bears and moose in the area. We recommend stopping short of Fort Nelson for your first night on the highway. Staying outside the town will get you in to the spirit of traveling the highway, and it will also save you money since Fort Nelson campgrounds are more expensive than those along the highway to the south. Your choices are Pink Mountain, Sikanni River, Buckinghorse River, or the Prophet Airstrip. It's best not to get into the habit of just traveling from town to town on the highway, the roadhouses and remote campgrounds along the way are a truly unique part of RVing the north. They're a part of the adventure.

Day 9 – Destination somewhere between Ft Nelson and Muncho Lake – Between 203 miles (327 km) and 298 miles (481 km) depending upon choice of overnight stops, between 5 and 7.5 hours driving time – You'll want to stop in Fort Nelson to buy fuel, visit the museum and perhaps make some grocery purchases. Then head west. Between Fort Nelson and Muncho Lake the highway climbs into the Rocky Mountains. The road is fine, you just won't be able to make great time because it climbs and descends and has more curves and hills than the road farther south. There are several good campgrounds, some nice no-hookup places and some roadhouses with hookups. They include Tetsa River Campground Regional Park, Tetsa River Services and Campground, Summit Lake Provincial Campground, 115 Creek, Toad River Lodge, The Poplars Campground and Café, and the three campgrounds along Muncho Lake.

Day 10 – Destination Liard River Hot Springs – Between 35 miles (56 km) and 131 miles (211 km) depending upon where you start the day, 1 to 4 hours – Get an early start for the best chance to see animals along the road. Liard Hot Springs makes a great overnight stop with a nice provincial park, a roadhouse with hookups, and, of course, the hot springs. You should get there in plenty of time to spend some time in the pools.

Day 11 – Liard Hot Springs to Watson Lake – 130 miles (210 km) - In Watson Lake visit the Signpost Forest and the visitor center's Alcan exhibit, you might also attend a show at the Northern Lights Centre. You can spend the night in Watson Lake, or, if you've become accustomed to the advantages of camping between towns, move on up the road a bit.

Day 12 and 13 - Watson Lake to Whitehorse - 270 miles (435 km), 7 hours – The highway is excellent and you'll make good time. Stop and spend some time in Teslin, perhaps visit the George Johnson Museum. In Whitehorse you have many campgrounds to choose from and you might as well spend two days here in the capital of the Yukon Territory. There's lots to see and do. See the sternwheeler *Klondike* and cruise through Miles Canyon. Don't forget to stock up on groceries here, you won't be seeing big stores again for a while.

In Whitehorse you'll have to check at the visitor center to see how the weather has been on the Top of the World and Taylor Highways near Dawson City. If it has been raining a lot it's probably best to continue on the Alaska Highway toward Tok and consider driving the Top of the World Highway from Tok on your return. We'll assume the weather has been good, and we'll head north from Whitehorse.

Day 14 and 15 - Whitehorse to Dawson City - 327 miles (527 km), 7 hours – The road to Dawson City is excellent so you can easily drive through in one day if you get an early start. Don't forget to stop at the overlook for the view of Five Finger Rapids. With the long days this far north you'll probably have lots of energy left when you get to Dawson, so make an evening of it and visit Diamond Tooth Gertie's gambling hall. That should put you in the proper mood to spend the following day exploring Dawson and the creeks.

If you have an extra week you can use it here. Drive the Dempster Highway up across the Arctic Circle to Inuvik. Driving out and back on this 456 mile (735 km) gravel road will let you visit some of the most remote country you've ever seen.

IN WHITEHORSE YOU CAN VISIT THE STERNWHEELER KLONDIKE

🚐 Day 16 and 17 - Dawson City to Chicken or Eagle - 144 miles (232 km), 5 hours – This trip over the Top of the World Highway and then up to Eagle on the Taylor Highway is your first real taste of gravel unless you drove the Dempster. It also finally brings you to Alaska! The Taylor portion of the route is a small road so take it easy. Enjoy the wilderness. Spend a day relaxing in little laid-back Eagle and take the historic tour, it's one of Alaska's most enjoyable. Those with RVs over 35 feet should head for Chicken first, then perhaps take a day trip in the tow car to Eagle.

🚐 Day 18 - Eagle or Chicken to Tok - 173 miles (279 km), 6 hours – You'll return to the Alaska Highway today. Tok has the highest per capita number of RV spaces in the state, it's the first Alaskan town most Alaska Highway travelers reach. The most important thing to do here is visit the Tok Visitor Centers.

🚐 Day 19 and 20 - Tok to Fairbanks - 206 miles (332 km), 5 hours – Today you'll follow the Tanana River downstream to Alaska's second-largest city. We've allotted two days for Fairbanks, it probably won't be enough. Don't miss everyone's Fairbanks favorite–a cruise on the riverboat *Discovery*. The University Museum here is one of the best in the state.

Here's another place you can easily add a week to your trip, or even two weeks. Several roads lead north from Fairbanks including the Dalton Highway to the North Slope and Prudhoe Bay. The Steese, Chena Hot Springs, and Elliott Highways are all worth a look-see, this is also excellent hiking and canoeing country.

🚐 Day 21 and 22 - Fairbanks to Denali Park - 121 miles (195 km), 2.5 hours – If you've made reservations you can camp in the park. Otherwise you'll probably be perfectly happy in one of the many campsites outside the park entrance. The thing you must do here is take a shuttle-bus trip into the park at least as far as Eielson Visitor's Center. Denali Park is probably the best place you will ever visit for observing grizzly bears up close. Cross your fingers for a clear day to see the mountain.

🚐 Day 23 and 24 - Denali Park to Anchorage - 237 miles (382 km), 5 hours – Today's trip is a cruiser, down through Broad Pass and across the Mat-Su Valley on Alaska's best roads. You'll actually have some four-lane freeway going into Anchorage. Anchorage is the best place in the state to get any maintenance problems fixed and stock up on supplies. During your layover check the sporting-goods stores to see which spots are hot on the Kenai Peninsula and pick up some fishing tackle.

Anchorage is one of the most livable cities anywhere. This is your chance to visit a good restaurant and explore the town. Wander around Town Square and 4th Avenue, all decked out with flowers, and perhaps catch a performance in the Alaska Center for the Performing Arts or tour the new Alaska Native Heritage Center. Treat yourself to a night out at an outstanding restaurant.

🚐 Day 25 - Anchorage to Cooper Landing - 101 miles (163 km), 3 hours – Drive down scenic Turnagain Arm and make sure you stop at Portage Glacier. In Cooper Landing, if you've timed it right, you can "combat fish" at the mouth of the Russian River and fill your icebox with red salmon. If not just enjoy some of Alaska's best scenery. Hikers will find what may be the finest trails in the state leading into the mountains nearby. There's also an excellent float trip down the Upper Kenai.

🚐 Day 26 - Cooper Landing to Kenai - 57 miles (92 km), 1.5 hours – Avoid the Soldotna fishing crowds and stay in Kenai. Visit the historic Russian church and perhaps see some beluga whales chasing salmon below the bluff. Ask at your campground or the information center about clam tides, you might have arrived at the perfect time for a clamming expedition.

🚐 Day 27 and 28 - Kenai to Homer - 97 miles (156 km), 2.5 hours – Today's drive brings you to another scenic highlight, Homer. You can camp in town or out on the bustling spit. Either way consider a halibut fishing trip or a bird-watching cruise out to Gull Island and Halibut Cove or Seldovia.

🚐 Day 29 and 30 - Homer to Seward - 173 miles (279 km), 4 hours – A day of backtracking and a chance to see the things you missed on the way down to Homer. Perhaps a visit to Ninilchik or a pause to wet a line in one of the many world-famous fishing rivers along the route. In Seward the silver salmon may be running or you might take a cruise into the Kenai Fjords National Park to see whales, sea otters, puffins, and glaciers.

🚐 Day 31 - Seward to Anchorage - 126 miles (203 km), 3 hours – Back to Anchorage to stock up and prepare for the drive south.

Here's something to consider. The Alaska State Ferry runs from Whittier to Valdez several times each week. You can save yourself two days and about 350 miles of driving by taking this ferry. It will cost more than making the road trip but it's a lot easier and just as scenic.

THE KENAI PENINSULA IS WORLD FAMOUS FOR ITS BIG SALMON

Glennallen

Day 32 and 33 - Anchorage to Valdez - 304 miles (490 km), 7 hours – A long day of driving through beautiful country will bring you to Valdez. See the huge oil tankers, fish for salmon or take a scenic cruise across Prince William Sound to Columbia Glacier.

Day 34 - Valdez to Beaver Creek - 399 miles (644 km), 9 hours – Another very long day of driving. To shorten it a bit you could stay at any of the campgrounds between Tok and Beaver Creek. On the other hand, like a horse heading home you may want to spend a long day on the road.

Day 35 and 36 - Beaver Creek to Haines - 336 mile (542 km), 8 hours – You drive south along Kluane Lake, through Haines Junction, and then across the Chilkat Pass to tidewater at the head of the Inside Passage. This is the last day on the road for a week, you'll let the ferry captain do the driving as far as Prince Rupert. During

A SHORT DRIVE SOUTH OF KETCHIKAN TAKES YOU TO THE SAXMAN TOTEM PARK

your layover day in Haines take the water taxi up the Lynn Canal to Skagway and spend the day touring this gold rush town.

Day 37 and 38 - Ferry to Juneau, 4.5 hours – Use your time in Juneau to explore Alaska's capital. If you have the time consider a cruise to Glacier Bay National Park or Tracy Arm or a helicopter flight to the top of the nearby ice field.

Day 39 and 40 - Ferry to Sitka, 9 hours – You've seen Alaska's present capital, now wander around the former capital of Russian America. Don't miss the Sheldon Jackson Museum.

Day 41 and 42 - Ferry to Ketchikan, 19 hours cruising time plus possible time in port in Petersburg and Wrangell – Consider booking a stateroom for this segment of your ferry trip. Ketchikan is Alaska's totem pole center. You also might take a cruise or sightseeing flight to Misty Fiords National Monument, your last chance to visit really pristine wilderness before leaving the state.

Day 43 - Ferry to Prince Rupert, 6 hours – You'll save yourself a bundle by leaving Alaska through Prince Rupert rather than riding the ferry all the way to Bellingham.

Day 44 to 50 - Drive home – From Prince Rupert to Seattle is 1,035 miles, Prince Rupert to Great Falls is 1,235 miles. Both routes are paved all the way.

Once you reach home you can start planning next year's trip.

Chapter 2

Details, Details, Details

Animals (Wildlife)

For most visitors to Alaska the wildlife is a huge attraction. During even a road trip to the state you are likely to see grizzly bears, black bears, moose, caribou, stone and Dall sheep, mountain goats, and perhaps even a musk ox. In addition to these large mammals Alaska has some of the best bird-watching opportunities anywhere, over 350 species are present. Marine mammals including whales, sea otters, and seals are common in many saltwater areas easily accessible on short sightseeing cruises. You can even watch fish at the many salmon-spawning viewing sites.

Be sure to bring along a set of binoculars and perhaps a spotting scope. These are particularly useful for birders but will also help you spot and enjoy watching larger animals.

You can see more wildlife while driving if you: 1. Watch closely and don't drive too fast; 2. Plan to be on the road in the early morning and late evening when animals are most active; 3. Get away from the road system by hiking or using air or water transportation.

As you drive along make sure to keep an eye on the brush line along the road. During the spring (May, June) and during berry season (July and August) there are often bears feeding in the wide cleared open areas next to the highways. RVers have an advantage over those driving passenger cars since they have an elevated seating position. Stop often to check likely habitats. Moose are often browsing in the water near the shores of lakes along the road. Bears are sometimes seen on gravel bars along rivers. It is often possible to see bears, sheep and goats on grassy mountainsides with

SOMETIMES THE ANIMALS DO CROSS DIRECTLY IN FRONT OF YOUR VEHICLE

a pair of binoculars. If you aren't proactive in your wildlife watching you'll only see the few animals that cross directly in front of your vehicle.

You'll see more animals if you schedule your driving in the early morning and late evening. That's when animals are most active. With the long daylight hours during June and July it would actually be possible to see wildlife during the entire night, but a nighttime driving schedule would probably be going a little overboard. Perhaps early starts and late stops with an afternoon nap thrown in makes more sense.

There are some outstanding places to see wildlife in the state and on the routes north, here are a few. In both **Stone Mountain Provincial Park** and **Muncho Lake Provincial Park** along the Alaska Highway both stone sheep and caribou are often spotted. Just outside Hyder, Alaska near the Cassiar Highway is **Fish Creek** where you can see both brown and black bears as well as bald eagles during the August salmon runs. **Haines, Alaska** is world famous for its congregation of bald eagles during the late fall along the Chilkat River but it's also a good place to see grizzlies along the short Chilkoot River outside town. On a bus ride into **Denali Park** it would be unusual not to see several grizzlies as well as assorted caribou, sheep, and smaller animals. A boat tour from Seward into the **Kenai Fjords National Park,** from Valdez or Whittier out into **Prince William Sound,** or from Juneau into **Glacier Bay** in Southeast Alaska will probably net you a whale spotting or two, not to mention sea otters, puffins, sea lions, dolphins, and perhaps seals. Even as you just drive the highways, you're bound to see a moose or two and even the occasional bear.

There's another side to the wildlife in the North. Some of it presents a certain amount of danger, particularly large animals like bears and moose. Bears are attracted by food so proper food and garbage handling procedures are important when camping. Tent campers will want to keep food in vehicles, in the food storage lockers provided at many campgrounds, or suspended from trees. In the tundra country where this isn't possible make sure to cache your food far from your tent or use bear-proof containers. Garbage containers in campgrounds are now often bear proof, if they aren't you should consider the location of garbage containers when choosing your campsite.

Many people consider the presence of grizzlies an indicator of true wilderness. They are widespread in Alaska and quite common in many places. Grizzlies can be extremely dangerous since they are big, fast, and sometimes aggressive. On the other hand, fishermen often share streams with grizzlies and hikers in some places often find themselves with bears as visitors in camp. You'll find pamphlets about the proper way to handle yourself in bear country at many information offices. Thousands of people spend time in the northern wilderness with no problems, you just have to take care and do things properly. See Chapter 14 for a more thorough discussion of bear safety.

Border Crossings

It is very possible that your Alaska camping trip will involve several border crossings. These are generally uneventful but there are a few things you should bear in mind.

A passport or equivalent travel document is required for U.S. or Canadian citizens crossing into the U.S. Canada does not require a passport to enter Canada but does require some documentation. As a practical matter, however, you'll have to get back into the U.S. so you will have to have the US documentation anyway, and that's accepted for travel into Canada too. Passport equivalent travel document include NEXUS cards, U.S. Passport Cards, and Enhanced Drivers Licenses. Most people, however, will be using passports. If you have children along it is very important to have certified copies of their birth certificates and permission letters from parents if they are not yours. Passports may not be required for children under 16 years of age if they are under adult supervision, but you should check with Canadian and U.S. government agencies to make sure that you have exactly what is required if you are traveling with children.

For your vehicle you'll want the following: registration, up-to-date license tags, and proof of insurance. Make sure you have your vehicle registration with you and if you are not the legal owner a signed statement that it is OK to take it out of the country. You can get a Canadian Nonresident Interprovince Motor Vehicle Liability Insurance Card from your insurance company. It is likely that you will not have to show any of these documents but having them on hand is definitely nice if you are asked for them. You might also check with your insurance broker to see if your windows are covered against gravel dings.

Guns are always a problem going into Canada and it is best not to bring one. Rifles and shotguns are sometimes allowed, pistols never are. If you must bring a firearm prepare before heading for the border. For more information contact Canadian Firearms Centre, 239 Wellington, Ottawa, Canada ON K1A 0H8; (800) 731-4000. There is a link on our website: www.rollinghomes.com.

Many people like to carry pepper spray for defense against bears. This often presents a problem at the Canadian border. Spays designed for defense against people definitely aren't allowed. With bear spray the border agent has quite a bit of discretion so be polite. A good way to avoid problems is to just wait until you are in Canada before buying bear spray, it's readily available there.

Dogs, cats, or small animals need a recent rabies vaccination and a certificate stating so from a veterinarian. Your veterinarian will probably know all about this.

Both Canada and the U.S. have regulations about importing certain things (like souvenirs) made of restricted animal parts like ivory and hides. Unfortunately the regulations are not the same so some things purchased in Canada can't come into the U.S. and vice versa. Check this if possible before purchase.

Finally, when crossing into Canada you must theoretically have enough money on hand to get where you are going and back out of Canada. There are no hard and fast rules. We've never had problems carrying bank cards that allow us to get cash along the way. You probably won't even be asked unless you look to the customs officer like you might not have enough cash to get by.

For more information about border crossing details and requirements please check the Alaska Links page of our website, www.rollinghomes.com. The internet is a good source of information but links frequently change, our Alaska Links page has several border information links and we keep them up to date.

Budget

Each person has his or her own idea of an acceptable standard of living so there is no one budget for every person. On the other hand, if you are camping you are not at the mercy of the local tourist economy like a traveler staying in hotels. In Alaska, you'll save a lot of money by camping. Here are some guidelines that should help.

The Canadian dollar has appreciated against the U.S. Dollar in recent years. This has driven prices up for U.S. travelers and in this book has pushed many Canadian campgrounds into a higher price category than in the prior edition. Still, Canadian campgrounds are now generally priced about like those in the US even if gas and food prices are not. The value of the U.S. and Canadian dollars were almost the same when this book was researched.

In general, transportation is a big part of the price of things along the highways and in Alaska. Fuel, groceries, and services get more expensive as you get farther into the bush. This applies along the Alaska Highway too. Expect prices on remote sections of the roads to be much higher than in Dawson Creek or Whitehorse. Fill your tanks and buy your groceries in the larger towns. See also the *Fuel Cost* section in this chapter.

Alaskan prices are much more reasonable in larger towns than in years past. Fuel is more expensive than in the Lower 48, but cheaper than in Canada. Groceries too are reasonable. Although most are shipped from the Lower 48 there is lots of competition in the big cities like Anchorage, Fairbanks, Kenai and Juneau. In other places prices are higher, transportation and lack of competition become more important.

Many visitors to Alaska will want to go on some commercial tours, things like sightseeing cruises or perhaps a float trip. You can save 50% on many of the available tours throughout the state if you have an Alaska TourSaver coupon book. See the *Tours and the Great Alaska TourSaver* section of this chapter for more about this.

Campfires

A campfire is a big part of a cheerful and enjoyable campsite. Fortunately, you'll have lots of opportunities to have a campfire while camping in the North. Virtually all governmental campgrounds in both Alaska and Canada have fire pits or rings. Many privately operated campgrounds outside towns have them too. We've included information about whether a campground has fire pits in the individual campground descriptions.

A very nice feature of the government campgrounds in the Yukon is free firewood. It is usually dry but seldom split, bring along an axe. In Alaska and British Columbia free firewood is no longer provided. Many campgrounds, however, have it for sale.

Wilderness campers will find that the forested areas of southcentral and central Alaska have lots of dry downed wood, the best is usually in the form of dead spruce. Campfires are perfectly acceptable in these areas if extreme care is taken not to start a wild fire. Stoves still work best for cooking. Make sure your fire is on mineral, not vegetable soil. Gravel bars in rivers are the best place for fires, they are generally scoured clean by the high water each spring.

In Southeast Alaska there may be plenty of wood but it is often too wet to burn. In the far west and north there are often no trees so firewood is scarce. Campers in these areas will have to rely on portable stoves.

Campgrounds

Throughout the areas covered in this book you will have a choice: government or privately-operated campgrounds. In general you can expect government campgrounds to have more scenic locations with more land per camper. They also almost always provide picnic tables and fire pits. On the other hand, toilets are almost always vault toilets and there are seldom hookups or showers.

In Alaska you will find that government campgrounds are run by either the State of Alaska, the United States Forest Service (USFS), the United States Fish and Wildlife Service (USF&W), the National Parks Service (NPS), the Bureau of Land Management (BLM), or one of the local governments. Information about all of the Alaskan governmental campgrounds run by all of these organizations and their related public lands are available from four Alaska Public Lands Information Centers located in Anchorage (Anchorage APLIC, 605 W. 4th Ave., Suite 105, Anchorage, AK 99501; 907 644-3661 or 866 869-6887), Fairbanks (Fairbanks APLIC, 101 Dunkel St., Suite 110, Fairbanks, AK 99701; 907 459-3730), Tok (Tok APLIC, 1314 Alaska Hwy. (PO Box 359), Tok, AK 99780; 907 883-5666 or (888) 256-6784), and Ketchikan (Southeast APLIC, 50 Main St., Ketchikan, AK 99901; 907 228-6220). While similar, there are some differences between these government campgrounds. Note that the *Campground Index* at the back of the book identifies the campground type.

State of Alaska campgrounds are scattered throughout the state virtually wherever there are highways. They usually charge a fee, most commonly between $10 and $15 per night, per party. Many of their campgrounds are now run by independent contractors as the state tries to improve services and cut costs. One of these, in Fairbanks, has electrical hookups. Others, north of Anchorage, take reservations.

The United States Forest Service (USFS) operates the second highest number of campgrounds in Alaska. These are in Chugach National Forest on the Kenai Peninsula near Anchorage and in the Tongass National Forest in Southeast Alaska. They vary in quality, a few have been upgraded recently with large sites, paved roads, and handicapped facilities – Russian River near Cooper Landing and Williwaw near Portage Glacier are two of the upgraded ones. Some also accept reservations including Williwaw, Ptarmigan Creek, Trail River, Cooper Creek, and Russian River. Call (877) 444-6777 for reservations or visit www.recreation.gov on the Internet. Daily camping fees usually run from $14 to $18 and there is usually a 14 day limit. Wilderness tent camping outside the developed campground areas is also allowed in these forests.

The National Park Service (NPS) has more parkland in Alaska than in all of the rest of the country, but they have very few developed campgrounds. The only ones connected to the road system are those in Denali National Park, one tent-camping area at the Exit Glacier near Seward, and one near Skagway at the foot of the Chilkoot Trail. There are also walk-in tent campgrounds in Glacier Bay National Park & Preserve and Katmai National Park & Preserve. The National Park Service also manages the Klondike Gold Rush National Park which has campgrounds along the Chilkoot Trail and the Sitka National Historical Park which has no camping at all. Wilderness camping is allowed throughout the national parks, monuments, preserves and national wild rivers throughout the state with some restrictions.

The Bureau of Land Management manages campgrounds on federal lands not controlled by other agencies. In Alaska these include campgrounds along the Dalton Highway Pipeline Corridor and those along National Wild Rivers like the Gulkana and the Fortymile. In recent years many have been upgraded and have large sites, handicaped-accessible vault toilets, and even dump stations.

The U.S. Fish and Wildlife Service (USF&W) manages 16 national wildlife refuges with 77 million acres in Alaska. In Alaska their nicest campgrounds are in the Kenai National Wildlife Refuge, they also have a couple between Tok and the border on the Alaska Highway.

The Yukon Territory maintains many campgrounds along roads throughout the territory. They are usually fairly large and located near water. The usual facilities include vault toilets, picnic tables, fire pits and free firewood. There are also often picnic shelters and children's playgrounds. A few years ago a new payment system was put into effect that required you to buy vouchers elsewhere before visiting these campgrounds. This system has been modified to allow payment at the campgrounds, you no longer must have the vouchers. Most Yukon campgrounds cost $12 Canadian. These territorial campgrounds usually have a 14-day limit.

British Columbia Provincial Campgrounds are located along the roads throughout the Province. They usually provide about the same amenities as the campgrounds in the Yukon Territory although many are upgraded with paved roads and parking pads. Firewood is usually not provided. You pay at the campground in British Columbia.

There are many excellent commercial campgrounds in Alaska. Most have electricity, sewer, and water hookups as well as modern restrooms with flush toilets and hot showers. When you are visiting one of the urban areas in the North, private campgrounds are usually much more conveniently located than government ones.

Private campgrounds in both Canada and Alaska are in competition primarily with the government which has free land and can impose hard-to-meet and expensive restrictions upon private owners. Among these are dump station requirements, charges for signage, and just plain taxes. We suggest that you give the private campground operator a break whenever possible. Here's an example. Don't dump your holding tanks at a rural campground when you could just as conveniently do so later in the day at a campground or dump station hooked up to a municipal sewage system. Holding tank discharge is difficult and expensive for a remote campground to handle, many campgrounds must pay big bucks to have their dump station contents pumped out and hauled away.

Camping Reservations

We generally do not bother with reservations for a campground in the evening. On the other hand, we're generally happy with almost any campsite at the end of a long day and we usually travel in a small rig. If you want the best campsites (like along the water) or if you are planning to visit one of the most popular destinations during a busy part of the season (like when the salmon are running) you can call ahead to make a reservation. In the campground section we make a note when campground reservations are a good idea. You will also find campground telephone numbers and addresses there. As you travel along you'll quickly realize whether you need reservations or not, it just depends upon how many people are traveling at the same time you are.

Camping Vehicles and Tents

You can camp in Alaska, the Yukon, and British Columbia in any kind of rig, or without one if you like.

If you are planning to camp in the back country away from the roads you will be tent camping. You can also comfortably tent camp from the trunk of a car or when bicycling. A tent with a floor and good bug screens is essential. Have some kind of waterproof fly for rainy periods, they can last for many days. A plastic sheet with poles and guy ropes is very useful around the campsite during long rainy periods. A dark-colored tent is nice to block out the light during those summer periods when it never really gets dark. You may be surprised at how hard it is to sleep in the daylight. Consider bringing some kind of blindfold for sleeping. A large water container is useful in campgrounds. Bring an axe if you plan to burn wood, that in the campgrounds is often not split. If you are tough it is possible to tent camp all year, but the best months are June, July, and August.

Pickup campers and vans are very popular with Alaska residents. They let you use all of the campgrounds and also find good free camping spots. Their small size and maneuverability is a big plus when you get a little off the beaten track. An additional thing to keep in mind - charges on the ferries are based upon vehicle length.

Motorhomes, trailers, and fifth-wheels have to be the most comfortable camping vehicles. If you are driving the highway just to visit don't buy a special rig for Alaska camping since virtually anything will work as long as it is durable and in good condition. Most major roads are paved and high mountain passes are actually uncommon. If you want to travel the few long gravel highways you probably won't want to be pulling a trailer since flying gravel can be hard on them. If you have a trailer or fifth-wheel consider bringing along a tent for use while exploring the gravel roads like the Dalton Highway, Dempster Highway, or the roads north of Fairbanks. Any kind of rig provides big advantages in bug protection and extends the comfortable season for camping.

Caravans

RV caravan tours to Alaska are very popular. They generally start in the U.S. or perhaps Dawson Creek and spend many weeks driving up the Alaska Highway or the Cassiar, exploring the state, and then returning by either road or ferry. There are lots of variations.

A typical caravan tour is composed of about 20 rigs. The price paid generally includes a knowledgeable caravan leader in his own RV, a tail-gunner or caboose RV with an experienced mechanic, campground fees, many meals and tours at stops along the way, and lots of camaraderie. Many people love RV tours because someone else does all the planning, there is security in numbers, and a good caravan can be a very memorable experience. They aren't for everyone, however.

Remember that there will be a lot of costs in addition to those covered by the fee paid to the caravan company including fuel, insurance, maintenance, ferry charges, and groceries. We hear a lot of good things about caravans, but also many complaints. Common problems include caravans that do not spend enough time at interesting places, delays due to mechanical problems with other rigs in the caravan, and poor caravan leaders who do not really know the territory. A badly run caravan can be a disaster.

We've given the names, addresses and phone numbers below of some of the leading caravan companies. Give them a call or write a letter to get information about the tours they will be offering for the coming year. Once you have received the information do not hesitate to call back and ask questions. Ask for the names and phone numbers of people who have recently taken tours with the same caravan leader scheduled to be in charge of the tour you are considering. Call these references and find out what they liked and what they didn't like. They are likely to have some strong feelings about these things.

Adventure Caravans, 125 Promise Lane, Livingston, TX 77351-0855; 800 872-7897 and 936 327-3428.

Alaskan Discovery RV Tours, 645 G. Street #542, Anchorage, AK 99501; 800 842-7764.

Fantasy RV Tours, 6655 W. Sahara Ave., Suite E-102, Las Vegas, NV 89146; 800 952-8496.

Cash and Credit Cards

There are really only two currency problems that you are likely to run into during a trip to Alaska. The first is that cash and perhaps credit cards are the preferred tender in the cities and along highways. Cash machines are easy to find in larger towns but not available in all of the small ones. Credit cards (Master Card and Visa) are almost always accepted for gas and in restaurants. You should let your credit card company know where you will be traveling before you leave home so they won't cancel your card when use it on the road. You should also probably keep a cash stash (say $200) available for emergencies. Out of state checks are unlikely to be accepted anywhere.

The second challenge is Canadian currency, and it isn't really much of a challenge. Don't convert money on a transaction-by-transaction basis, it will cost you a lot. Instead, stop at a bank or cash machine when you reach a sizeable town after crossing the border to get a Canadian cash fund. Cash machines will accept your U.S. card and they give a good exchange rate. Check with your bank card issuer before leaving home to make sure it will work in Canada, sometimes special PIN numbers (personal identification numbers) are needed for international use.

CB Radio

A CB radio can be useful for emergencies and for communication between rigs if you are traveling as part of a group. No standard frequency is used for communications in Alaska but channel 9 and 11 are used for emergencies. If those don't work try 14 and 19. Channel 19 is the frequency used by truckers on the Dalton Highway.

Children

One of the nice things about an Alaska outdoors trip is that the summer visitors season coincides with the summer school recess. An outdoors vacation is perfect for children of all ages and present opportunities for all types of activities.

One thing to keep in mind is that distances can be long and the driving sometimes a little boring. Remember, the Alaska Highway was originally described as miles and miles of miles and miles. The scenery is sometimes spectacular but there will also be many driving hours to fill with activities.

Clothing

For RV campers it is important to bring warm clothing like sweaters, jackets, and long underwear so that you are comfortable outdoors on cloudy days and in the evening. Otherwise you will spend little time outside and miss the pleasures of the evening campfire or stroll. A really heavy coat probably isn't necessary, instead have things you can layer to suit your activities and the temperature. You don't want to spend all of your time indoors while visiting this premier wilderness area. There are also some more specific things you should bring along.

Don't forget your bathing suit for Liard Hot Springs, and others. Also some lakes. People commonly swim at Big Lake in the Mat-Su and at Harding and Birch Lakes near Fairbanks. Shorts can be useful when the temperatures rise over 70° F and the mosquitoes are temporarily somewhere else.

DISTANCE TABLE

Miles (upper‑right of each pair) · Kilometers (lower‑left of each pair)

The chart lists point‑to‑point distances among the following 24 locations (shown along the diagonal):

Anchorage · Calgary · Chena Hot Springs · Circle · Dawson City · Dawson Creek · Delta Junction · Denali Park · Eagle · Fairbanks · Fort Nelson · Fort St. John · Gakona · Haines · Haines Junction · Homer · Inuvik · Prince Rupert · Seattle · Skagway · Tok · Valdez · Watson Lake · Whitehorse

Kilometer distances (lower‑left triangle), read to each preceding city:

From \ To	Anchorage	Calgary	Chena H.S.	Circle	Dawson City	Dawson Creek	Delta Jct	Denali Park	Eagle	Fairbanks	Fort Nelson	Fort St. John	Gakona	Haines	Haines Jct
Calgary	3478														
Chena Hot Springs	675	3579													
Circle	837	3574	345												
Dawson City	829	2813	731	894											
Dawson Creek	2592	882	2494	2657	1967										
Delta Junction	547	3125	256	419	475	2238									
Denali Park	382	3476	293	456	828	2590	353								
Eagle	807	3070	708	871	232	2199	2396	805							
Fairbanks	576	3281	98	261	635	2198	158	195	610						
Fort Nelson	2136	1336	2038	2201	456	1512	1782	2135	1744	1940					
Fort St. John	2668	958	2418	2581	76	1892	2162	2515	2124	2320	380				
Gakona	304	3167	499	662	518	2281	243	573	496	401	1826	2206			
Haines	1248	2716	1150	1312	931	1831	894	1246	998	1051	1375	1755	937		
Haines Junction	1006	2457	908	1071	671	1586	652	1001	741	810	1150	1510	696	245	
Homer	364	3841	877	1040	1032	2795	750	584	1009	779	2719	507	333	1525	1029
Inuvik	1604	3507	1505	1668	774	2661	1249	1602	1006	1407	2204	2584	1293	2273	1825
Prince Rupert	2584	2486	2418	2648	1919	1137	2230	2582	2151	2368	592	212	2948	1188	1591
Seattle	1364	4068	869	3175	1420	3183	982	3487	3724	1771	1391	3610	3169	1922	1592
Skagway	3920	1188	3822	3985	3255	1315	3566	3919	3487	3724	1391	2719	3610	217	720
Tok	203	3680	877	1040	1032	2795	584	1009	779	1525	2017	2597	192	884	599
Valdez	1340	2486	1241	1404	700	1599	932	1358	1212	1604	1525	2373	541	1484	1243
Watson Lake	237	3714	911	1074	1066	2829	784	618	1043	813	2231	2753	137	1191	1204
Whitehorse	2233	1509	2135	2297	1586	1116	1879	2231	1984	1818	1182	1608	2017	478	94

Kilometer distances (continued), to the remaining preceding cities:

From \ To	Homer	Inuvik	Prince Rupert	Seattle	Skagway	Tok	Valdez	Watson Lake
Inuvik	2597							
Prince Rupert	2280	2924						
Seattle	1076	2056	459					
Skagway	1129	884	853	892				
Tok	192	1294	1969	980	599			
Valdez	1129	858	1674	1418	145	404		
Watson Lake	192	1294	1220	1530	855	145	855	
Whitehorse	979	766	1542	151	731	692	596	174

Sample mile distances (upper‑right triangle) from the chart include, to Whitehorse: Anchorage 724, Calgary 1436, Chena Hot Springs 663, Circle 764, Dawson City 327, Dawson Creek 895, Delta Junction 495, Denali Park 723, Eagle 471, Fairbanks 602, Fort Nelson 612, Fort St. John 848, Gakona 531, Haines 251, Haines Junction 90, Homer 950, Inuvik 758, Prince Rupert 881.

Kilometers

Rain gear is a necessity. Southcentral and Southeast sometimes have long periods of rainy weather and you'll have to get out in it if you want to be active.

Bring hiking boots. Also consider rubber break-up boots or some kind of waterproof hiking boots for hiking in wet areas. Trails in much of Alaska can be very wet. Fishermen will want hip boots or waders.

Hikers and bikers have special requirements. See Chapter 14 for more about this.

Distances

As you plan your camping trip to Alaska and as you drive the highways you have to remember that the distances can make for some long driving days. It is difficult to cover over 300 miles in a reasonable day of driving. We've included a mileage chart nearby (page 32) so that you can find the mileage information you need in one place.

Driving and Road Conditions

Most of your driving in northern Canada and Alaska will be on two-lane roads. For safety's sake you should leave your headlights on at all times to enhance the visibility of your rig to traffic approaching from the other direction. In the Yukon, the Northwest Territories, and some roads in Alaska and British Columbia this is the law. Experiments have shown that the use of headlights on two-lane roads does reduce the accident rate substantially, on dusty gravel roads it's even more important.

In both Alaska and Canada the use of seatbelts is mandatory. Radar detectors are illegal in the Yukon Territory.

Frost heaves are a unique road hazard in Alaska and the Yukon. They are caused by both permafrost and the constant freezing and thawing of water in the gravel underlying the pavement. After being bounced off the ceiling by the first couple you hit you'll learn to keep a sharp lookout for them. We've seen them so bad that we had to unhook our tow car and drive it separately to save the hitch.

You can find road condition reports on the internet (see links from www.rolling-homes.com) and also get them by telephone: Alaska (while in the state) 511 or 866 282-7577, Yukon Territory 867 456-7623 or toll free (while in the Yukon) 877 456-7623.

Dump Stations

There are plenty of dump stations to fill your needs while visiting the North Country but in remote areas they are not as common as you might sometimes wish. In Canada you'll find them marked as sani-dumps. It is important to plan ahead so you don't find yourself with a full holding tank miles from the nearest place to empty it.

In general, remember to always empty your tanks when you are in a town. More heavily populated areas have sewage treatment plants and can deal with sewage more easily than can operators in remote areas who either depend upon cesspools and drainage fields or pay high charges for pumping services.

Few government campgrounds have dump stations. Private campgrounds allow visitors to dump, usually for a fee. This is a reasonable charge, in remote areas operators often have to pay high pump-out fees on a per gallon basis. If you aren't staying in the campground you should help pay the fee.

Many gas stations also have dump stations and some communities provide them too. At the end of each of the campground chapters in this book is a listing of dump stations not located in campgrounds.

Fishing

Everyone knows that Alaska offers a wide selection of fishing opportunities. Along the Alaska Highway and throughout the Interior rivers, streams, and lakes have grayling, lake trout, and even salmon. Southcentral Alaska offers many river fishing hot spots, especially along the Parks Highway near Wasilla and on the Kenai Peninsula in the Soldotna area. Both Seward and Valdez are known for their saltwater salmon fishing and Homer is a big halibut charter center. Every Southeast destination mentioned in this book offers at least saltwater fishing possibilities.

The best fishing tends not to be right along the highways, especially if you are not fishing for salmon. A fly-out fishing trip should be a part of any fisherman's trip to Alaska. A time-honored technique for catching fish along streams crossing the highways is to walk some distance up or downstream from the road to reach less easily accessed waters. On the other hand, I can remember many occasions when I've hooked a fish on the first cast into a pool directly under the highway bridge.

Fishermen from outside Alaska will find that trout and salmon fishing may require a new assortment of tackle. Local knowledge is essential and tackle is available almost everywhere since fishing is such a popular recreational pursuit. The best prices, however, are in the larger cities. It would be worth your time to pick up one of the readily available Alaska fishing guidebooks before leaving home to make sure you bring the right poles, reels, and other expensive equipment. See the *Travel Library* section of this chapter for some suggestions. You can buy terminal tackle once you reach the area where you plan to fish. A small boat or canoe can be very useful, particularly if you enjoy lake fishing.

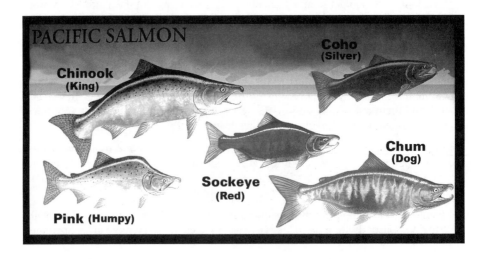

British Columbia, the Yukon, and Alaska all require resident and non-resident fishing licenses. Additional licenses are required in some parks, for example, there is a Canadian National Park license required for fishing in Kluane National Park. Licenses can usually be issued by tackle stores, a good excuse to go in and ask questions. Regulation booklets are readily available for all areas where licenses are sold and at Tourist Information offices. See our website, www.rollinghomes.com, for links for buying Alaska licenses and links to Alaska fishing information.

Free Camping (Boondocking)

Many RVers love to find a free campsite. The thrill of spending the night parked without paying anyone a fee is hard to deny. If you love to free camp and successfully find good parking spots in the Lower 48 there is no doubt you'll love Alaska. Many Alaska campers never use a formal campground.

On the other hand, we prefer formal campgrounds for many reasons. They are safer because there are usually many fellow campers around. You never have to get up in the middle of the night to answer a trooper's knock and be told to move on. Garbage is usually properly handled so that it won't attract bears. Alaska's campgrounds don't cost much, particularly the government ones, and they are often in a much more attractive and scenic location than any free pull-off. Campgrounds also provide picnic tables, toilets, firewood, fire pits, and sometimes showers.

It is probably a fact of life that if you spend a night camping outside a campground you are breaking some kind of law. It may be a trespass law, it may be a vagrancy law, it may be something else. That doesn't necessarily mean that anyone will care. We often see people camping on city streets, in parking lots, or on pull-offs along the road. The key is to be low profile, don't make a pest of yourself, and don't obstruct traffic.

In general, the farther you are from civilization the easier it is to find free camping spots. In the less populated areas of the state no one is likely to care if you pull off the road at a good looking spot next to a river or on an abandoned section of road. Just make sure not to park in places where there are no-parking signs, don't block access, and avoid private property.

There are a couple of unusual free camping possibilities in the cities of Whitehorse and Soldotna. For several years the Whitehorse Walmart has allowed self-contained RVers to park overnight in their parking lot. In Soldotna the Fred Meyer store actually encourages RVers to park in their lot, they have even installed dump stations. The situation at these stores could change at any time due to political pressure from RV park owners or a change of heart of store management. Anchorage is a good example, the Walmarts there were not allowing camping last time we visited..

Fuel Cost

Both gasoline and diesel are readily available throughout Alaska and the Yukon but prices vary widely and change often. You'll find that we have included relative gas and diesel price graphs near the beginning of many chapters. These graphs show gas prices relative to those in Anchorage and Seattle that we observed during the summer of 2013. We have shown prices as a percent of prices in Anchorage, Alaska during the same period. The price in Anchorage averaged $3.96 for gas, $4.17 for diesel. Alaska gas and diesel prices tend to be slightly higher than those in the Lower 48.

The graphs should be of interest because they show the effect of transportation costs. In general, large cities with good transportation services have better prices. If you have a large rig it makes sense to take a look and plan your fill-ups accordingly.

How Much Time is Required for a Visit to Alaska

The time you'll need for an Alaska trip depends upon your starting point, of course. For an Alaska resident a weekend is plenty of time for a visit to a salmon stream or hiking trail. For an RVer from the Lower 48 much more time is required. Remember, it is quite a journey from most places to Dawson Creek which is just the beginning of the Alaska Highway. Dawson Creek is 817 miles north of Seattle, Washington and 875 miles north of Great Falls, Montana.

If you are planning to drive the Alaska Highway and want to see at least part of the state give yourself at least three weeks from the time you reach Dawson Creek. It takes most people about a week to drive the highway to Anchorage or Fairbanks. After driving that far you deserve to have some time to explore and relax. Most caravan companies allow at least 5 weeks for their guided trips and they don't visit all areas of the state. Our itinerary in Chapter 1 requires a good two months if you don't want to exhaust yourself. Three months would be better.

The quickest and most relaxing way for a non-resident to visit Alaska is to rent an RV in one of the major towns. Take a look at the *Motorhome and RV Rentals* section in this chapter for more information. With a rental you can have an enjoyable trip even if you only have a week available for your visit.

Information by Mail, Phone or the Internet - Prepare for Your Trip

It is always a good idea to know as much as you can about a destination before you go. Knowing what to expect makes planning easier and increases your appreciation of the new places you see and the things there are to do.

There is a great deal of information available about Alaska, the Yukon, and British Columbia. Computer users should visit our website, www.rollinghomes.com, for links to many sources of information about Alaska, the Yukon, and British Columbia. Most websites include an address if you prefer to have some printed materials mailed to you. Finally, the *Travel Library* section of this chapter and our Website contain information about an excellent selection of books about many aspects of visiting Alaska and the Yukon.

Here are some places to write for general information about the state and the roads north:

Alaska Public Lands Information Center, 605 W. 4th Ave., Suite 105, Anchorage, AK 99501; 907 644-661 or 866 869-6887.

Alaska Travel Industry Association, 2600 Cordova Street, Suite 201, Anchorage, AK 99503: 907 929-2842.

Alaska Wilderness Recreation and Tourism Association, 2207 Spenard Rd., Anchorage, AK 99503; 907 258-3171.

Department of Tourism and Culture, Government of the Yukon, Box 2703, Whitehorse, Yukon, Canada Y1A 2C6; 800 661-0494.

Insects and Other Pests (Like Bears)

Alaska and the Yukon are famous for their mosquitoes. They also both are home to two other northland pests–white sox and no-see-ums. On the positive side, there are no poisonous snakes. Bears, both blacks and browns, often fall into the pest category, particularly around campgrounds, dumps, and fishing streams. Even the shy and slow-witted moose can sometimes be a problem.

Mosquitoes, white sox and no-see-ums are not present in all locations and at all times. Many variables including the amount of standing water, the severity of the winter, the time of the season, and the strength of the breeze make a big difference. When you pick a campsite it pays to stay away from puddles and swampy areas and pick a site with at least the possibility of a breeze.

Mosquitoes are present throughout the summer. They appear as soon as the weather begins to get warm in May and last until the hard freezes in September. They are at their worst in the early season just after breakup. Scientists say that only the females will attack you, but it seems to us that they must all be females. It actually takes a mosquito about a minute to poke into you, inject the saliva that keeps your blood from being too thick to suck, and begin drawing blood. It is the saliva that causes the mosquito prick to itch afterwards.

White sox are also known as black flies in other places, the ones in Alaska have white on their legs. They are present from midsummer until freezing. Their bite is actually worse than that of a mosquito.

No-see-ums are very small and travel in swarms. They tend to land and then crawl under your clothing. Any breeze at all will keep them down, and you can probably outrun them at even a walking pace since they are slow fliers. Their bite is every bit as bad as a white sox and they are present during about the same period.

If you use the proper techniques these flying pests can be dealt with and you can enjoy the outdoors. When they are present you should wear clothing that covers your arms and legs. Some people think that dark colored clothing attracts them.

Anti-insect products containing DEET (diethyl-meta-toluamide) or citronella work best. There is some question about DEET's safety, it is pretty powerful stuff. Be aware that DEET is a solvent and will soften and damage things like plastic fishing lines and plastic watches. Citronella isn't as effective but does not have these problems. We use DEET. Some folks also swear by Skin-So-Soft, an Avon skin cream which wasn't even designed to repel insects but has a cult following.

Another essential product to have along is an anti-itch product, often these are combined with an antiseptic. Once you receive the inevitable bite an anti-itch cream will help you forget about it and reduce the scratching and swelling that results.

It is very important to have good insect screens on your rig and on your tent. You must have some retreat to get away from the bugs when they are really bad, and they will occasionally be very bad. Tent campers should have a head net. They may look funny but when you need them they are priceless and allow you to lead an almost normal life while setting up camp, preparing food, or even while hiking.

Bears can be a problem in camp, particularly if you don't take the proper precautions. They are attracted by food so there are two rules that you should always follow. Do not feed them and keep a very clean camp. All food items must be inside a rig or hung out of reach away from the tent and campsite. Cook away from your tent, never cook in your tent. Make sure your tent is clean if you have done so in the past. Dispose of trash well away from the tent and campsite. Camp away from trash barrels. In the wilderness watch for bear trails, especially along streams and beaches and do not set up your tent near them. Dogs seem to attract bears so it is best not to have one along in bear country. For much more about bear safety see *Chapter 14 – Camping Away From the Road System* in this book.

Moose can be dangerous. They seem slow-moving and stolid but they are huge, can cover ground quickly, and when riled sometimes protect themselves by trying to stomp their foe. Don't get too close when taking pictures and be careful around mothers and calves. They often stomp dogs and bears, they can do the same to you. Dogs and moose don't mix well, dogs often harass moose and cause real problems, don't let your dog run loose.

Internet Sites

Every day there are more and more internet sites devoted to Alaska, the Yukon, and B.C. They are a great way to familiarize yourself with the North Country before leaving home. Rather than trying to list them all here we have set up our own Website: **www.rollinghomes.com**. On it you will find links to other Websites with a lot of good information.

We have another use for our Website. As a small publisher we can only afford to update our travel guides on a three to five year cycle. In order to keep the books more current we publish updated information on the Web. Our site has pages for each of our books with updates referenced by page number. We gather information for these updates ourselves and also depend upon information sent in by our readers and others. This information is only posted on the Website until we issue a new edition, once the new edition comes out we remove the page and post updates only for the new book.

Laundry

Finding a place to do your laundry won't be a problem in Alaska and the Yukon. Almost all privately-owned RV parks have coin-operated clothes washing equipment. If you are camping in government campgrounds you will be able to find a public laundromat with little problem. Even the smallest communities usually have a laundromat since many locals don't have running water or electricity. Laundromats also often have shower facilities, this is good to know if you frequent government campgrounds or free camp.

Mail

Alaska, the Yukon, and British Columbia all have excellent mail service. Outlying areas have slightly slower service than you may be accustomed to, add a couple of days for towns along the highways. Even outlying villages off the road system often have frequent airmail service since aircraft are their only link to the outside world.

In the U.S. just have your mail sent to General Delivery of a town you expect to visit. Some of the important zip codes are as follows: Anchorage 99510, Fairbanks 99701, Juneau 99801, Ketchikan 99901, Kenai 99611, Homer 99603, Seward 99664, Valdez 99686, Tok 99780, Denali National Park 99755.

Motorhome and RV Rentals

If you don't have your own rig for an Alaska trip you can always rent one. This is an extremely popular way to visit Alaska. Here are some of the rental outfits. Note that some are located in Alaska while others are in British Columbia, Alberta, or the Yukon Territory. Reserve your rental RV as early as possible, many companies are fully booked by the time the camping season arrives. Often there is an early booking discount. The rental company listing below is only a starting point. All of these companies will send you an information pack if you request information. When you receive the packages take a look at the following items to compare them.

- Types of rigs including age
- Rates
- Mileage charges
- Required deposits
- Insurance coverage and related extra charges
- Pick up and drop off procedures, times, and locations
- Availability of one-way rentals
- Extra charges for housekeeping and linen packages
- Limitations on where you can take the rig, and extra charges for gravel roads
- Pets allowed?

A & M RV Center, 2225 East 5th Avenue, Anchorage, AK 99501; (907) 279-5508, (800) 478-4678, Website: www.GoRV.com.

ABC Motorhome & Car Rentals, 3875 Old International Airport Rd., Anchorage, AK 99502; (800) 421-7456, (907) 279-2000, Website: www.abcmotorhome.com.

Adventures in Alaska RV Rentals, 1145 Shypoke Dr., Fairbanks, AK 99709; (907) 458-RENT, Website: www.adventuresAkRV.com.

Alaska Motorhome Rentals, 9085 Glacier Highway, Ste 301, Juneau, AK 99801; (800) 323-5757, Website: www.alaskarv.com.

Alldrive Canada Inc., 1908 10th Ave. S.W., Calgary, Alberta, Canada T3C 0J8; (403) 245-2935, Website: www.alldrive.com.

Canadream Campers, 2510-27 Street NE, Calgary, Alberta T1Y 7G1, Canada; (888) 480-9726, (403) 291-1000, Website: www.canadream.com.

Clippership Motorhome Rentals, Inc., 5401 Old Seward Highway, Anchorage, AK 99518; (800) 421-3456, (907) 562-7051, Website: www.clippershiprv.com.

Fraserway RV Rentals, 9039 Quartz Road, Whitehorse, Yukon, Y1A 4Z5; (800) 661-2441, (867) 668-3438, Website: www.fraserwayrvrentals.com.

Go North Alaska Travel Center, PO Box 60147, Fairbanks, AK 99706; (907) 479-7272, (866) 236-7272, Website: www.gonorth-alaska.com.

Go West Motorhome Rentals, 32 Fawcett Road, Coquitlam, B.C., Canada, V3K 6X9; (604) 528-3900, (800) 661-8813, Website: www.go-west.com.

Great Alaskan Holidays, 9800 Old Seward Highway, Anchorage, AK 99515; (888) 225-2752, (907) 248-7777, Website: www.greatalaskanholidays.com.

Murphy's RV Inc., 5300 Eielson St., Anchorage, AK 99518; (888) 562-0661, (907) 562-0601, Website: www.alaskaone.com/murphyrv.

Northern Lights and the Midnight Sun

One of the reasons that Alaska has a special ambiance is the far northern location. The midnight sun and the northern lights are manifestations of this.

During June and July the days are very long. Baseball games are played at midnight, people are full of energy and work and play until all hours of the night. Most Alaskans love this, for them it helps make up for the long, dark winter. You'll probably like it too, but many people have trouble sleeping in broad daylight. Either take along something to cover your eyes when you are sleeping or cover the windows of your rig with something to keep out the light, many people use aluminum foil. Tenters may find that a dark-colored tent helps.

The longest day of the year is June 20 or 21. It is known as the summer solstice. On that day a person standing on the Arctic Circle would be able to see the sun all night long if the terrain were perfectly flat. As a practical matter, people from Fairbanks go to the summits north of town where they have some altitude and are guaranteed the sun for their summer solstice celebration even though they really aren't as far north as the Arctic Circle.

One reason to plan a late trip to Alaska is the northern lights. You won't be able to see them unless it is dark at night, and for campers that means September.

There's a great exhibit on northern lights at the University of Alaska museum in Fairbanks. There's also a theater devoted to shows about the northern lights in Watson Lake, Y.T. Either of them provides a good introduction.

To see the northern lights you'll need a clear dark night. They do not appear every night but if you keep an eye open you'll eventually have a good sighting. They'll be toward the north and are usually best after midnight. The best area for northern light observations along the road system is the band stretching from Fairbanks to Fort Nelson.

BRING ALONG A CAMERA TO CAPTURE ALL THE GREAT PHOTOGRAPHY SUBJECTS

Photography

Wildlife, scenery, and outdoor sports, all make great photography subjects. If you're traveling by RV bring your gear. If you have to carry it in a backpack you'll have to pack lighter, but don't forget a camera.

Definitely bring along a telephoto. A tripod is very useful for telephoto photography, especially at low light levels. You'll also want a medium length lens that can be hand held since wildlife often won't stick around while you set up your tripod. For dark blue skies use a polarizing filter.

Propane

You'll have no problem finding propane throughout the North Country. All larger towns have several sources and virtually every smaller town also has some place where you can fill up. Just ask at the campground for advice. Plan ahead so that you don't run out while far from civilization.

Public Transportation

There's a variety of public transportation in the North. Many of the larger towns have bus systems that work great for getting around while staying at a campground on the outskirts of town. A limited number of busses ply the highways. State ferries connect the towns of southeast Alaska and also run to Kodiak, Cordova and out the Aleutian Chain. And in the bush you might find that public transportation will take the form of a small airplane.

The cities of Anchorage, Fairbanks, Whitehorse, Juneau and Ketchikan all have public bus systems. Many of the city campgrounds are on or near a bus route.

While intercity busses are infrequent in Alaska and the Yukon it is possible for travelers without their own wheels to get around. In places where there is enough demand service is available, although often in the form of vans able to carry only a few passengers. Bus service offerings tend to change frequently, just as airline service offerings do. Check with information centers for more details about available bus transportation.

Small vans provide service along several routes. Probably the most interesting are runs from Anchorage and Fairbanks to Denali National Park, from Fairbanks up the Dalton Highway, and from Glennallen to McCarthy. You will be able to find information about these and other van operations locally.

The Alaska Railroad offers some interesting transportation options. The railroad is very tourist-friendly, they have excellent schedules for sightseeing and also can arrange tours at the destinations. Trains run between Anchorage and Fairbanks with stops in Talkeetna and at Denali National Park. They also run to Seward and to Whittier from Anchorage. Contact the railroad at (800) 544-0552 or (907) 265-2494, Website at www.alaskarailroad.com.

Air transportation in Alaska is widespread and easy to find. Airlines flying modern jets provide scheduled service between larger cities. From the larger cities smaller operators flying light aircraft provide both scheduled and charter flights to any village with a safe airstrip and to a huge selection of lakes and rivers large enough for a float-equipped airplane. If you are bound for a remote campsite it is generally more economical to fly a scheduled operator to a hub town or village near your eventual destination and then charter a small aircraft for a short flight. More information about access to remote locations is included in Chapter 14 of this book.

Telephones

The good news is that phones in Alaska and Canada use much the same system that is used in the Lower 48. You can direct dial in and out of Canada and Alaska using the normal area code and seven-digit number format. It is not necessary to use an international country code when calling Canada from the U.S. or the U.S. from Canada. The area code for all of Alaska is 907, for all of the Yukon it is 867, and for all of British Columbia except the Vancouver area it is 250.

Telephone rates are more expensive than those in the Lower 48. Sometimes, especially in remote areas you will notice an echo or delay because telephone signals are bounced off a satellite.

We have found that some U.S. calling cards will not work in Canada. Before entering Canada you should call your service provider and make sure your card will work in Canada, and particularly in remote areas of the Yukon along the highway. If it doesn't, the answer is a prepaid pin card, they are available pretty much wherever they might be needed.

You'll find cell phones work in most of the larger towns in Northern British Columbia, the Yukon and Alaska; but service along the highways outside of built-up areas is not available. Each of our campground descriptions has a cell phone symbol if cell service is available in that location.

Digital cell service, for Internet access, it also limited to the towns. Both AT&T and Verizon now service Alaska.

Time Zones

All of Alaska except the very western islands of the Aleutian Chain are in one time zone and use Alaska Time. This is one hour earlier than Pacific time as used on the West Coast of the U.S. and Canada. The Yukon is on Pacific Time also. British Columbia has two time zones, Pacific time is used in most areas but the far eastern area of the Province including the part of the Alaska Highway from Dawson Creek north to Fort Nelson is on Mountain Time. Alaska, the Yukon, and British Columbia all observe daylight saving time.

Tourist Information Offices

Tourist information is very easy to find throughout Alaska, the Yukon, and British Columbia. Any town of even moderate size seems to have a tourist office, we've tried to give their locations and phone numbers in the city descriptions included in the campground chapters of this book. The U.S. government and the Alaska government also have information offices in various locations, usually related to government-owned lands like national forests and state and national parks. You'll find addresses and phone numbers throughout the book. To easily find them go to the index and look for entries under the following headings: Visitor Information, local; Alaska Public Lands Information Center; BLM addresses; NPS addresses; State of Alaska addresses; USF&W Service addresses; and USFS addresses. As a practical matter, if you can't figure out the governmental agency that can answer your question it is best to call one of the Alaska Public Lands Information Centers, if they can't answer your question they can direct you to the proper agency.

Tours and the Great Alaskan TourSaver

Even though camping visitors to Alaskan destinations tend to be "do-it-yourselfers", there are occasions when you'll want to let someone else do the driving. Popular tours include sightseeing trips to Mt. McKinley, day-trip cruises through the Kenai Fjords National Park, float trips of many Alaskan rivers, and fishing expeditions. Many of the destination descriptions in this book suggest possible tours.

Any resident of or visitor to Alaska should be aware of the Great Alaskan Tour-Saver coupon book. The book costs $99.95 and is full of two for one deals on tours throughout Alaska. You need only take advantage of the deals a time or two to save the cost of the booklet. If you have one you'll find yourself using it a lot. The books are available at Carrs or Safeway supermarkets or on a website: www.toursaver.com. Take a look at the website to see what coupons are included or ask to see one when you visit your first Safeway or Carrs in Alaska.

Travel Library

One of the best things about traveling in your own vehicle is that you have plenty of room for a library. Your appreciation of the country will be much improved by a little background reading and the availability of a few reference books as you travel.

The **Milepost** (Morris Communications Corporation; Augusta, GA; 2013, ISBN 978-1892154309) is the bible of Alaska highway travel with a new edition issued each year. It contains a wealth of information about services, history, sights, and just about everything else. It also has mile-by-mile logs of all of the routes to and in Alaska. The one drawback to the Milepost is that almost all commercial facilities mentioned are advertisers who write their own descriptions. Enough said.

Off-highway campers have their own Milepost, *The Alaska Wilderness Guide* by the Milepost editors (Morris Communications Corporation; Augusta, GA; 2005; ISBN 978-1892154200).

Probably the best history of the Klondike gold rush readily available is *The Klondike Fever: The Life and Death of the Last Great Gold Rush* by Pierre Berton (Martino Fine Books, Eastford, CT.; 2010; ISBN 978-1578989645). First published in 1958 this book continues in print today, which is a real testimony to its quality. The author grew up in Dawson City and, until his death, was one of Canada's foremost historians.

As you sit beside your campfire in the evening you'll probably find you have lots of light for reading. Make sure to have a copy of the **poems of Robert Service** on hand. His ballads of the gold rush days have a special resonance when you visit the far North and they are widely available in bookstores in the Yukon and Alaska.

In a place like Alaska, especially away from the roads, you'll need maps. A good place to start is DeLorme Mapping's *Alaska Atlas & Gazetteer* (ISBN 978-0899332895) which has 1:300,000 and 1:1,400,000 scale topographic maps covering the entire state. Later you'll want to get maps that show more detail for hiking or when you get away from the highway.

There are two excellent guides to hiking in Alaska. The classic is *55 Ways to the Wilderness in Southcentral Alaska* by Helen Nienhueser and John Wolf (The Mountaineers; Seattle, Washington; 2002; ISBN 978-0898867916). *Hiking Alaska* by Dean Littlepage (Falcon Press Publishing Co., Inc.; Helena, Montana; 2006; ISBN 978-0762722372) is a another favorite and covers the entire state.

A good guide to floatable Alaska rivers is *The Alaska River Guide: Canoeing, Kayaking, and Rafting in the Last Frontier* by Karen Jettmar (Menasha Ridge Press; 2008; ISBN 978-0897329576).

Fishermen will need a guide showing techniques and other information about Alaskan fishing. Readily available is *The Highway Angler: Fishing Alaska's Road System* by Gunnar Pedersen (Fishing Alaska Publications; Anchorage, Alaska; 2007; ISBN 978-1578333660) and also *Alaska Fishing: The Ultimate Angler's Guide* by Rene Limeres and Gunnar Pedersen (2005; ISBN 978-1929170111) .

The ultimate guide to Alaska's government lands is the encyclopedic *Wild Alaska: The Complete Guide to Parks, Preserves, Wildlife Refuges, and Other Public Lands, Second Edition* by Nancy Lange Simmerman and Tricia Brown (The Mountaineers; Seattle, Washington; 1999; ISBN 978-0898865837).

You'll find links for purchasing many of these books and others on our Website, www.rollinghomes.com.

Units of Measurement

Alaska uses the same measurement systems as the Lower 48–miles, gallons, and degrees Fahrenheit. Canada does not, there you have to deal with kilometers, liters, and degrees Celsius.

Here are a few conversion factors and tricks to help you cope.

One kilometer is about .62 miles. For converting miles to kilometers divide the number of miles by .62. For converting kilometers to miles multiply the kilometers by .62. Since kilometers are shorter than miles the number of kilometers after converting will always be more than the number of miles, if they aren't you divided when you should have multiplied or multiplied when you should have divided.

For liquid measurement it is usually enough to know that a liter is about the same as a quart. When you need more accuracy, like when you are trying to make some sense out of your miles per gallon calculations, there are 3.79 liters in a U.S. gallon.

Here are a few useful conversion factors:

  1 km = .62 mile
  1 mile = 1.61 km
  1 meter = 3.28 feet
  1 foot = .3 meters
  1 liter = .26 U.S. gallon
  1 U.S. gallon = 3.79 liters
  1 kilogram = 2.21 pounds
  1 pound = .45 kilograms
  Convert from °F to °C by subtracting 32 and multiplying by 5/9
  Convert from °C to °F by multiplying by 1.8 and adding 32

Vehicle Preparation and Breakdowns

Vehicle preparation for the trip north runs the gamut. Some people do nothing more than change the oil. Others definitely go overboard. We tend to take the middle road. It is important to have a rig that will not go haywire on you and force you to make expensive repairs (not to mention incur an expensive tow bill) in an isolated location.

Make sure that your tires are in very good shape and that you have a spare. Consider carrying two spares if you plan to spend a lot of time on gravel roads like the Dalton Highway (Prudhoe Bay Haul Road) or the Dempster. Make sure that you have a good jack and tire wrench that will work on your rig, some new motorhomes do not come with either. Even if you don't want to change a tire on one of the huge rigs yourself you should at least have the tools to let someone help you and a spare tire of each size used by your rig or rigs. Big rigs sometimes don't have the space for a mounted spare, consider bringing along a much lighter and easier-to-pack unmounted one. It's a lot easier to get that tire mounted than to wait for a week while the tire you need is shipped in.

Do a complete systems check before you leave home. If you have a nagging problem with something in your vehicle, say a balky refrigerator or a leak of some kind make sure to fix it before heading north. It is bound to get worse during a long trip and repairs are definitely not cheaper up north.

Bring jumper cables and small tool kit. Spares are usually not necessary but if you know of some filter or essential part that is particularly difficult to find you might want to bring an extra along so that you are not faced with a long delay in a remote location. If a part isn't essential you can sometimes get your rig to a place where parts are available, we once drove over 500 miles in second gear to reach Whitehorse when an electronic part in our motorhome's transmission went south near Muncho Lake.

Emergency road service insurance is very worthwhile even if it is only for the peace of mind. Towing charges can be very high, especially in remote areas. Make sure your plan will cover you in northern Canada and Alaska and on remote roads.

Gravel roads are probably the hazard requiring the most vehicle preparation. Fortunately, you're really likely to run into few of them if you keep to the main highways. The Alaska Highway and the Cassiar Highway are paved for the entire distance although there are likely to be some unpaved sections where upgrades and road repairs are underway. The only other gravel most people are likely to encounter is the Klondike Loop between Dawson City and Tok. More aggressive travelers will see gravel if they drive the Taylor Highway north to Eagle, the Denali Highway between the Tangle Lakes and the Parks Highway, the Nabesna Road, the McCarthy road to McCarthy, the Dalton Highway to Prudhoe Bay, the Dempster Highway from Dawson City to Inuvik, and the roads north of Fairbanks to Circle and Manley Hot Springs. Read on if you plan to travel these roads.

The way you drive on gravel directly affects the damage you will receive from flying rocks. Most damage from rocks is done by you when you run in to a flying rock thrown into the air by someone else. Your forward speed makes all the difference. You'll find that if you slow to about 35 mph (55 kph) when a car passes you in either direction you will reduce rock damage by about 90%. That's our estimate, but it's close. Be particularly alert when on freshly finished seal coat before it is swept. Speeds tend to be high on these very smooth sections of highway, but there's lots of loose gravel so windshields are often damaged.

There are a few things that can easily be done to cope with dust on gravel roads. You may already know the spots where dust leaks into your RV. Consider using duct tape to seal leaky storage compartments and doors while underway. It also helps to have a positive air pressure inside your vehicle, turn on your dash heater or air conditioner fan and close your windows to do this.

Even if you drive carefully you may expect at least a little rock damage. The large front windshields of RVs are particularly vulnerable. They are virtually impossible to protect so drive carefully and make sure you have insurance. We make sure that we get small dings repaired when we reach Anchorage or Fairbanks so cracks won't spread. Forward facing windows on trailers, campers and motorhomes (not windshields) can be protected with cardboard and tape. The cardboard covering may also help you sleep in the midnight sun.

Rocks can also hit your headlights. You can buy inexpensive protectors in auto shops that will save your headlights. Radiators also sometimes get hit by rocks, you can protect them with metal screening. This has always seemed like overkill to us but many people do it. We've had no radiator problems due to leaving ours unprotected. Diesel pushers should consider screening for radiators, they seem to be much more vulnerable than rigs with front-mounted radiators.

Plumbing and dump fixtures on RVs are often made of plastic and hang down where flying rocks from the tires will easily hit and break them. Consider carrying extras or building rock deflectors. We find that wrapping them with fiberglass insulation and duct tape is effective and easy, but not very pretty. Don't forget the copper pipes and valves of your propane system. They can be covered with insulation or a rubber hose that has been split for installation and then taped.

Vehicles that are being towed are particularly vulnerable to rocks thrown up by the towing vehicle. Use cardboard or plywood shields on the front of trailers and fifth-wheels. Fit your tow vehicle with good mud flaps and cover the nose of a towed car with something to protect it from flying rocks. Don't worry about how it looks, you'll save it from a lot of damage. If you don't want to do this consider unhooking and driving the car separately when you reach a stretch of gravel.

Gravel sections of the Alaska Highway are often treated with chemicals to keep the dust down. You should wash your RV after traversing these areas because the chemicals are corrosive, many campgrounds provide washing facilities. Don't forget the underside of the vehicle.

In "the old days" travelers on the Alaska Highway seemed to often get leaks in their gas tanks from flying rocks. This isn't likely today since there are so few miles of gravel. A quick fix used then was to rub the outside of the puncture with a bar of soap, it often worked until you could reach a repair shop.

Water

It is easy to fall into the trap of thinking that drinking water in a place as huge and unspoiled as Alaska must be safe. This is not exactly the case, you must be just as careful about your drinking water in the North as you would be in the Lower 48.

Giardia (causes beaver fever) and other contaminants are wide-spread in Alaska, even in places far from the nearest settlement. Use a filter or water treatment on all surface water. This is likely to be a problem only if you are camping away from the road system since good pure water is available at almost all private campgrounds and many government ones. We have noted, however, that Yukon Government campgrounds often post a notice that their water must be purified. You should do so if posted.

Campgrounds may have good water but getting the water into your rig at a government campground may be difficult. Many have hand pumps or faucets that cannot be used with a hose. Your only solution may be to pump water into a container and then fill your vehicle's water tank using a funnel. If you plan to camp solely at government campgrounds you will probably want to add a bucket and funnel to your equipment list. For more about water treatment see Chapter 14.

When to Camp - The Season and Weather

This book is primarily aimed at the summer camper. Most camping facilities are open from break-up in the middle of May until freeze-up sometime in September or early October. Many government campgrounds close in September but many others stay open until the snow flies. Actually, most of the RVing traffic from warmer climes disappears during the first part of September and only local hunters are in the campgrounds until snow and cold force them to close.

June, July, and August are the most popular camping months, the high season. There are few mosquitoes in May but things haven't really dried out from break-up in many areas. The end of the month is often OK. The ice in many lakes does not go out until mid-May. Things start to turn green in June and in many areas this month has the least rain. July is the warmest month, the Fairbanks area can see 90° F, Anchorage residents are happy with 70°. August sees the days start to grown shorter and the temperature fall just a little. September is the fall, trees quickly turn yellow and "termination dust"–snow– begins to appear on the hills. By the end of the month in the Interior the leaves are gone and the hard freezes have started.

Southcentral - The best weather in the Anchorage area including the Susitna Valley and the Kenai Peninsula is June–July and August have a little more rain. Expect 50° to 70° F in Anchorage, slightly warmer on the Kenai Peninsula and in the Mat-Su Valley. The Anchorage bowl can sock in for long periods, if it does just head for the Kenai or the Interior.

Interior - The weather is pretty good in the Interior during all three high-season months. Fairbanks often has temperatures in the 70° to 80° F range. There's more rain in the summer than snow in the winter but the Interior is fairly dry. Expect a few rainy periods but many days of clear or partly-clear weather with perhaps a rain shower or two. August and early September is our favorite time in the Interior. Temperatures start to fall but aren't bad if you have a heated RV for getting up in the morning, campgrounds are virtually empty, the northern lights are out at night, and the trees are beautiful.

Southeast - Expect rain in Southeast. If you get lucky and have a few days of sunshine consider yourself blessed. The scenery is spectacular when the sun shines. Temperatures in southeast are mild, say 45° to 60° F during most of the summer. Rainfall patterns are important. June is the driest month with rainfall increasing through the summer until October, which is the wettest month. Also note that rainfall is heaviest in the south and lightest in the north.

Chapter 3

How To Use The Destination Chapters

Chapters 4 through 14 of this book contain information about the many camping destinations available to you in Alaska and along the Alaska and Cassiar Highways. Chapters 4 through 13 covering campgrounds along the highways, are all similarly arranged. Each covers the campgrounds along a major highway route. Chapter 14 on *Camping Away from the Road System* follows a different self-explanatory format, this chapter does not apply to it.

Introductory Road Map

Each of the campground chapters begins with a road map. The map shows a lot of information that will allow you to use it as an index to find campgrounds as you travel. The map shows the route covered in the chapter and also the most important towns. Many towns along the route have their own maps which are placed later in the chapter and show in-town campground locations. Dotted lines outline areas outside towns that have their own campground location maps. These two types of maps together cover all areas along the road system.

Introductory Text

Each chapter starts with an **Introduction** giving important information about the route or routes covered in the chapter. Usually there is something of the history of the route and the area, a description of the lay of the land, and a summary of the highlights. These might be important towns, unusual geographical or physical features, or outstanding destinations of one kind or another.

In Alaska outdoor activities are a primary attraction. We have discovered, however, that it is very easy to miss an area's outdoor attractions if you don't have a handy guide. For this reason we've included information about four different kinds of outdoor activities that we think will be popular with our readers: Fishing; Boating Rafting, Canoeing, and Kayaking; Hiking and Mountain Biking; and Wildlife Viewing. Our intention is not to try to replace the many individual guides that are published about each of these activities, we just want you to be aware of each area's attractions. If you are interested you can look farther for more detailed information. We've included references in many places to help you do just that. Some of the books listed in Chapter 2 will also be helpful.

In this section you'll find that we have included gas and diesel price charts. These charts show fuel prices we observed during the summer of 2013. We have shown prices as a percent of prices in Anchorage Alaska at the same time. The charts aren't there to tell you exactly how much fuel will cost, they're to help you predict the places that may have the lowest prices. These charts should help you plan your fill-ups.

Route and Town Descriptions

Following the introductory material in each chapter is the **Routes, Towns, and Campgrounds** section. In addition to the campground overview maps described below this section has a few paragraphs of text describing each route or town. We've described the local attractions and also included information about the location and phone number of the visitor center in each town if there happens to be one.

Our descriptions of the destinations and routes in this book are intended to give you an idea of what the city or region has to offer. They are by no means complete, you will undoubtedly need additional guides during your visit. Local visitor centers in Alaska and along the roads north are essential stops, they have lots of interesting materials and usually are staffed by knowledgeable locals.

We have given population and altitude information for each major town. These are our estimates. Population figures are constantly changing and sometimes they reflect artificial political boundaries, we've just tried to give you some idea ahead of time of what you can expect by giving you our best estimate based upon many different sources. The altitudes are also estimates, some are based upon the local airport altitude which may be somewhat different than the altitude of the central business district, we've tried to correct for this.

We've also included many mileage figures. Mileages are the best way to fix locations along the roads in the north but they are often not 100% accurate for several reasons. Most northern roads have mileposts placed along them and these mileposts are used to determine location. It would be prohibitively expensive to change them all each time a road is straightened and shortened. You will find that many older establishments along the Alaska Highway list addresses based upon historical mileposts that are twenty or more miles different than today's mileposts, which are really kilometer posts. Another problem is that many of the mileposts are missing for one reason or another.

If you examine guidebooks to rural Alaska and the roads north you will see that each has slightly different mileage numbers as each tries in its own way to cope with the problems. We've done the same and no doubt you will find some of our figures that do not quite agree with your own odometer. This may be because we usually round to the nearest mile or kilometer. None of this should cause you any big problems, the north is pretty empty and if you are close to a destination you will usually have no problem finding it.

As everyone knows the U.S. uses miles and Canada uses kilometers. We've tried to use miles when we are writing about Alaska and kilometers when we are writing about Canada. When we give distances (not Mileposts or Kilometerposts) we usually give both miles and kilometers. That's because some users of this book will have odometers marked in miles and some will have them marked in kilometers.

Campground Overview Maps

Each important city or town and each region between the towns has its own campground overview maps. These maps are designed to do two things: they quickly show you the lay of the land and the campgrounds that are available, and if you examine them more carefully they will help you drive right to the campground you have decided to use.

There are two different types of campground overview maps. The first is a city map. Each city map is associated with a written description of the city and a listing of the campgrounds in that city. The second type is an area map. These usually show the road between two cities and each is associated with a description of that road and also a listing of the campgrounds on that road. Campgrounds are not shown on two different maps. In some cases a campground that might be shown along the road between towns is instead shown on a town map. This happens when we think the campground is a good place to stay for a visit to the town even though it might be located a short distance down the road.

While the maps are for the most part self-explanatory here is a key.

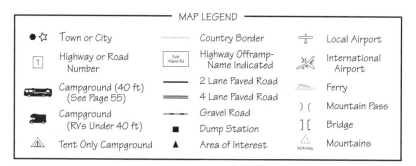

One thing you will not find in our campground descriptions is a rating with some kind of system of stars, checks, or tree icons. Hopefully we've included enough in-

Campground Descriptions

Each campground section begins with location or address and telephone number, if applicable. While it is not generally necessary to obtain campground reservations in Alaska you may want to do so for some very popular campgrounds. This is particularly true in areas where people congregate to wait for ferries or where weekend crowds from nearby cities are likely to plug the campgrounds.

One thing you will not find in our campground descriptions is a rating with some kind of system of stars, checks, or tree icons. Hopefully we've included enough information in our campground descriptions to let you make your own analysis.

We've included limited information about campground prices. The price you pay depends upon the type of rig you drive, the number in your party, your use of hookups, and sometimes even the time of year.

Generally you can expect that tent campers will pay the least. Throughout the north the prices charged by commercial campgrounds for both tenters and dry sites are heavily influenced by the prices charged in the many government campgrounds. Usually the commercial price is a dollar or two more than local government campgrounds because commercial campgrounds generally have additional amenities like showers and dump stations.

RV charges depend more upon the hookups used than the size of the rig. Expect dry sites to cost a few dollars more than a space in a government campground, electricity will add a few dollars, and a sewer hookup a few more.

There is one more important factor. In remote locations hookups and dump station use can be more expensive than in a city. Electricity is sometimes generated on site, this can be a costly proposition. Dump stations in remote areas are often septic systems, sometimes everything you dump must be pumped out by the operator and trucked away. This also is an expensive operation. We always try to dump our tanks in a town with a city sewer system, it's better for the environment and it saves everyone a lot of trouble and money.

We've grouped the campground fees into the following categories in our campground descriptions:

FREE	Free	$$$ $$$	Over $25 and up to $30
$	Up To $5	$$$ $$$$	Over $30 and up to $35
$$	Over $5 and up to $10	$$$$ $$$$	Over $35 and up to $40
$$$	Over $10 and up to $15	$$$$ $$$$$	Over $40 and up to $45
$ $$$	Over $15 and up to $20	$$$$$ $$$$$	Over $45 and up to $50
$$ $$$	Over $20 and up to $25	Over $50	Over $50

These prices are in U.S. dollars. They are summer (high season) prices for an RV with 2 people using a basic 30-amp full hookup site if available. Some campgrounds charge more for pull-thrus, hi-amp hookups, and waterfront or view sites. In government campgrounds the prices are for an RV. Note that in many government campgrounds there is only one price.

You'll find that this book has a much larger campground description than most guidebooks. We've tried to include more information so you can make a more informed decision about which one you want to pick for your stay.

Campground icons can be useful for a quick overview of campground facilities or if you are quickly looking for a particular feature. The following is a key to the symbols used in this book.

No Tents – Most of the campgrounds in this book accept both RVs and tents. If the campground is for tents only we say so in the text. If an RV campground does not accept tents or we feel that it is not suitable for tents we show the no tents symbol.

20 Amp Electric – Only basic 15 or 20 amp service is available. Most low amp electrical hookups have 20 amp breakers but occasionally you'll find a 15 or even a 10-amp circuit.

30 Amp Electric – Some 30-amp service is available, there is no 50-amp. 20-amp sites are usually available too.

50 Amp Electric – Some 50-amp serviced sites are available. Usually 30-amp sites are also available, and perhaps 20-amp sites too.

No Drinking Water – A few campgrounds listed have no drinking water and we use a no water symbol for them. If water is provided, even if it is posted as non-potable or if it is a stream or lake, we do not use the symbol. Most water officially provided at campgrounds is fine unless otherwise posted, we don't purify water from pumps or taps unless it is posted as non-potable. However, water from streams and lakes should always be treated if used.

Sewer – Sewer drains are available at some or all of the sites. Note that in the far north drains can be a real maintenance problem due to very cold winter temperatures and permafrost, many campgrounds do not have them.

Dump – Indicates the campground has a dump station (sani-station) available.

Flush Toilets – We show a toilet symbol if a campground has flush toilets. If there are no toilets of any kind we say so in the text. The rest of the camp-grounds listed have what we've identified as outhouses, pit toilets, or more modern and less smelly vault toilets.

Showers – Hot showers are available. There may be an extra fee for showers, usually in the form of coin box that takes quarters or loonies (Canadian one-dollar coins).

Laundry – The campground has user-operated washers.

Telephone - A telephone is available. It may be either a pay phone or a courtesy phone in the office.

Cell Phone Signal – There is a usable cell phone signal at the campground.

TV – Television hookups are available at some or all of the sites.

Wi-Fi – Indicates that Wi-Fi (wireless internet) is available in the campground. Wi-Fi access is the fastest growing amenity offered by campgrounds today. If this is important to you don't hesitate to ask before making a reservation or perhaps call ahead as you approach your destination to determine the current offerings of the campgrounds you are considering. For many people this is the most important factor in choosing between campgrounds.

Free Wi-Fi – Wi-Fi is not only available – it's free. Since Wi-Fi is such a new thing many campground owners are feeling their way on this. We're finding that many that charged at first are now offering it for free, but also that some that originally didn't charge now are. If you appreciate free Wi-Fi you should let campground operators know it.

Playground – There is a playground for children with swings, slides and the equivalent or there are horseshoes, a play field, or provisions for some other type of sport.

Campfires – Campfires are allowed, usually at individual sites but sometimes at a central fire pit. Plan on either bringing firewood along with you or buying it at the campground. These days you won't be able to pick wood off the forest floor either because it is prohibited or because there have been too many folks there ahead of you. Cutting standing trees is never permitted. Temporary fire bans are sometimes in effect.

Restaurant – We show a restaurant symbol if there is one at the campground or if one is within close proximity.

Swimming – The swimming symbol is used if any swimming is available. Since few campgrounds have swimming pools (usually just the few hot springs) this probably means lake swimming. The lakes in Alaska are usually only warm enough for swimming in July and early August, and even then only if you're young or very tough. There are seldom lifeguards so caution is advised.

Hiking – We show a hiking symbol if there are hiking trails near the campground. This could mean there is a short nature trail or it could mean that a long cross-country trail starts nearby. Generally we try to say which it is.

Fishing – We show a fishing symbol if fishing is possible within close proximity.

Handicap – The wheelchair symbol indicates that at least partial handicapped access is provided, often it just means that the vault toilets have large doors and room to maneuver a wheel chair. These provisions vary considerably, you should call the information number listed for the campground or the operating organization to get more details if this is a consideration for you.

Vehicle Washing Area – The vehicle wash symbol means that there is an area for washing rigs. This may be a pressure system or just a hose.

Good Sam – Many campgrounds give a discount to members of the Good Sam Club. We include the symbol only if they are official Good Sam Campgrounds. We find that the standards required for listing by Good Sam mean that in general these campgrounds stand out as having decent facilities, good management, and relatively fair prices. For club information call (866) 205-7451 or see the Good Sam website at www.goodsamclub.com.

Escapees – Our Escapee symbol means that discounts are given to members of the Escapee RV Club. Call (888) 757-2582 or (939) 327-8873 for more information or see their website – www.escapees.com.

Passport America – Passport America discount cards are accepted. Most campgrounds offering this discount also will sell you the card.

FMCA – Discounts are available to FMCA members. Call (800) 543-3622 for more information if you own a qualifying motorhome, or check the website at www.fmca.com.

Coast to Coast – This is a Coast to Coast park.

 40 Foot RVs – Our Big Rig symbol means that there is room for coaches to 40 feet to enter the campground, maneuver, and park. Usually this means that we've seen them do it. The driver we saw may have been a better driver than most so exercise caution. If you pull a fifth-wheel or trailer you'll have to use your own judgment of how your RV handles compared with a coach. You may have to park your towing vehicle or toad off-site. If you drive an even larger 45-foot coach or really large fifth-wheel you can at least use our symbol as a starting point in making your campground decisions. There's often more in the write-up itself about this, and we'll also usually mention pull-thrus if available. Always evaluate the campground and assigned space yourself before attempting to maneuver and park, the final decision is yours. A properly trained outside spotter is essential, most RV mishaps seem to occur during the parking phase.

GPS (Global Positioning System) Location Coordinates

You will note that we have provided a GPS location for all of the campgrounds. GPS is a modern navigation tool that uses signals from satellites. Most of them will let you enter the coordinates we have given for the campgrounds in this book into the receiver so that it can tell you exactly where the campground lies in relation to your position. While we think our location descriptions and maps are the best in the business, you can fall back on the GPS information if you don't find them adequate (or if you think the GPS is more fun).

If you don't have a GPS receiver already you certainly don't need to go out and buy one to use this book. On the other hand, if you do have one bring it along. If you are finding that our readings are not entirely accurate you should check to see which Map Datum your machine is set to use. The coordinates in this book are based upon the World Geodetic System 1984 (WGS 84) datum. We use the pure decimal format for our GPS listings. We think it's the easiest format to use with modern digital mapping systems. Your GPS should let you select this format, there's usually a choice under Settings or on the screen where you actually enter coordinates.

Finally, if you are going to go on a hike or boating trip from the campground and use the GPS as a tool to help you return **do not use** our readings. Take your own reading before leaving the campground to ensure accuracy.

Dump Stations

At the end of each chapter we have included a listing of dump stations that are not located in campgrounds. We have visited these locations to confirm their availability and GPS readings are included in the text.

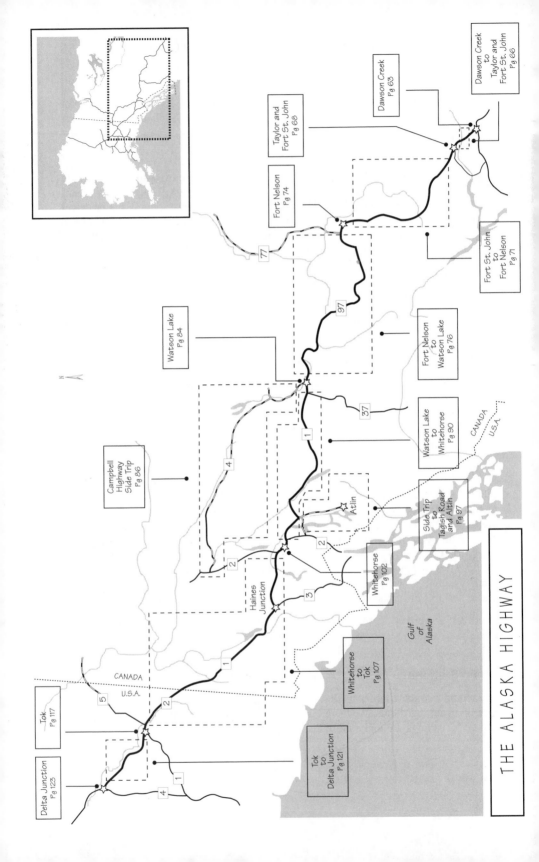

THE ALASKA HIGHWAY

Atlin

CANADA
U.S.A.

Haines Junction

CANADA
U.S.A.

Gulf of Alaska

77

97

37

4

1

2

2

3

5

2

1

4

Chapter 4

The Alaska Highway

INTRODUCTION

For many years the Alaska Highway (the Alcan) has held a special place in the hearts of adventurous highway travelers. This major highway was constructed through virtually unexplored wilderness during World War II. It opened a huge and fascinating territory—Alaska, the Yukon, and Northern British Columbia—to anyone who could climb into a vehicle and drive north.

The Alaska Highway begins at Dawson Creek in British Columbia. Just getting to Dawson Creek is an adventure. From Seattle the driving distance to Dawson Creek is 815 miles, from Great Falls, Montana it is 867 miles. Information about the routes to Dawson Creek could fill several guidebooks, unfortunately there is not room for it here. For the most part you can be confident that the roads leading north to Dawson Creek are paved and services adequate and not hard to find.

We'll start our coverage at Dawson Creek. Some folks may decide to follow one of the other routes north: the Cassiar Highway (Chapter 5 in this book) or the ferry routes through the Inside Passage (Chapter 13 in this book).

Highlights

The Alcan (Alaska-Canada Highway), now called the **Alaska Highway**, is itself an interesting destination. Construction of the highway from Dawson Creek to Delta, Alaska was undertaken during World War II to provide a supply route to Alaska in case the Japanese gained control of water routes. Construction was begun in 1942 with little prior exploration of some remote portions of the route chosen. In fact, planned routings were only approximations and construction techniques to deal with permafrost and swampy terrain had not yet been developed. U.S. Army construction crews punched a narrow, rough, and almost impassible road through the mountains and tundra from Dawson Creek to Delta, Alaska in eight months. Since that time crews have been continuously upgrading the road. Anyone planning to drive the Alaska Highway should read one of the many books that have been written about the project.

As you travel along the highway you will find many information boards commemorating events during road construction. You'll also see many historic signposts with original Alcan mileages on them. They are of little use today for navigation since road mileage has changed, but they designate important spots along the road. There are also several museums covering the highway construction along the route north, including ones in Dawson Creek, Fort Nelson, Watson Lake, and Whitehorse.

There are eight towns along the Alaska Highway. These are **Dawson Creek**, **Fort St. John/Taylor**, **Fort Nelson**, **Watson Lake**, **Teslin**, **Whitehorse**, **Tok**, and **Delta Junction**. These towns are the best place to buy provisions and get repair work done if you need it. They also have interesting histories, museums, and good campgrounds. Each is covered in more detail later in this chapter.

During the early years of the highway many roadhouses were built to provide services for Alcan travelers. These facilities generally boasted gas pumps, a repair shop, a café, cabins or rooms, and often a campground. Many of them have closed over the years as the highway has improved and drivers cover many more miles than they could in early years. Still, many remain open and they are an interesting place to spend the night. When you do so, visit the café and talk to the owners and locals. You'll get a real feel for what it's like to live along the highway. Excellent examples of these, and a few less historic but similar facilities, include Sikanni River Campground and RV Park (Fort St. John to Fort Nelson section), Tetsa River Services and Campground (Fort Nelson to Watson Lake section), Toad River Lodge (Fort Nelson to Watson Lake section), Rancheria Lodge and RV Park (Watson Lake to Whitehorse section), Cottonwood RV Park and Campground (Whitehorse to Tok section), and Discovery Yukon Lodgings (Whitehorse to Tok section). We highly recommend overnights at these places to form a memorable impression of the historic Alcan Highway lifestyle.

You'll find miles and miles of virtually empty country along the highway but the section of road through the Rocky Mountains between Fort Nelson and Watson Lake stands out. There are two British Columbia Provincial Parks along this segment of road: **Stone Mountain Provincial Park** and **Muncho Lake Provincial Park**. Both have campgrounds and offer opportunities to view wildlife including caribou and stone sheep.

At Km 765 of the highway, about 213 km (132 miles) south of Watson Lake is **Liard Hot Springs**. Liard has a wilderness pool where you can soak in the hot spring water (there's just a little sulfur smell) with changing rooms at the pool. There's a pebbled bottom and benches in the water. There's also a provincial campground and a commercial campground nearby. Seems like everyone traveling the highway stops here for at least a quick dip.

As you travel along the highway keep an eye peeled for wildlife. Moose are likely to burst from the underbrush and cross in front of you. If one does, watch out. There's often a calf or two following along behind. Bears are often spotted feeding in the cleared areas along the road. This isn't a zoo so animals aren't guaranteed, but if you keep your eyes open you will see them.

The Road and Fuel

The Alaska Highway stretches about 1,350 miles from Dawson Creek in British Columbia to Delta Junction in Alaska. Along the way it crosses the Rocky Mountains and passes through the province of British Columbia, the Yukon Territory, and the state of Alaska. The road is without a doubt one of the most interesting in North America. It is also very long.

The entire length of the Alaska Highway is now paved. This doesn't mean you won't find stretches of gravel. The road is constantly being upgraded and repaired and you are bound to run into patches of dirt and gravel. All road work has to be done during the summer when temperatures are above freezing so road work follows the same pattern each year. As early as possible in the spring (May) sections of road are torn up and work commences. By fall the road has to be ready for winter so by late August and September many of the places that were bad in the early summer have been finished or temporarily surfaced. We find that the highway is often in its best condition in early September.

Mileage markings along the highway can be confusing. The road was originally marked in miles. It was longer then, between Dawson Creek and the Alaska border

MUCH OF THE ALASKA HIGHWAY HAS BEEN STRAIGHTENED AND WIDENED

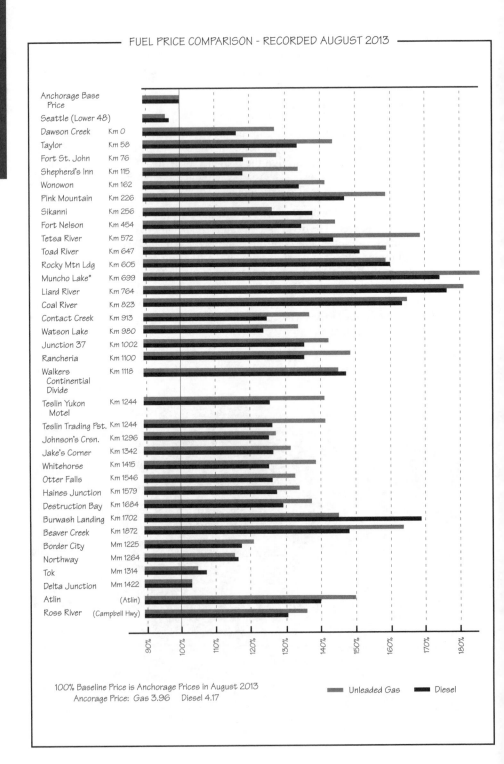

FUEL PRICE COMPARISON - RECORDED AUGUST 2013

100% Baseline Price is Anchorage Prices in August 2013
Ancorage Price: Gas 3.96   Diesel 4.17

Unleaded Gas   Diesel

the road was originally 1,971 kilometers (1,222 miles) long, now it is about 53 kilometers (33 miles) shorter. Many establishments along the road still use their original milepost locations as an address (they're usually called Historic Miles) and there are occasional historic milepost monuments along the road for tourism purposes.

Today the entire Canadian portion of the road has been re-posted with kilometer markers. In both British Columbia and the Yukon the kilometer posts are located on the right side of the road going north. In British Columbia there's one every 5 kilometers, in the Yukon they're usually every two kilometers. Only recently were the Yukon mileposts brought into agreement with those in B.C. so you'll find some confusion in older guides. We use actual kilometer post readings to designate locations of Canadian campgrounds in this chapter. Sometimes the Historic Mile figure is also given because it's the mailing address used by many establishments.

At the Alaska border things change. Alaska uses miles, of course. They also use the original Alcan mileage as a starting point at the border. Although the border is now about 1,189 miles from Dawson Creek, mileposts at the Alaska border start at 1,222. We use mile markings that conform to those you will find along the road. In a few cases they may be slightly different than the actual driving distance since there has also been some straightening of the road in Alaska and mileposts are not always updated.

As a practical matter you'll find that all of this makes little difference. When you are on the road it is easy to find things you are watching for, a few kilometers or miles one way or another will make less difference than you might think.

Fishing

One of the joys of traveling on the Alaska Highway is the many opportunities to wet a line at the many rivers and streams that cross the highway. Often fishing isn't great near the road but a little hike will change your luck.

Remember, along this highway you are in British Columbia, the Yukon Territory, and Alaska. Each has its own licensing requirements and regulations. Also, in Canada the fishing is good in several of the parks you pass through, and they have their own requirements. See the *Fishing* section of Chapter 2 in this book for more information.

Between Dawson Creek and Fort Nelson try the **Peace River** (Km 53) for grayling and Dollies; **Charlie Lake** (Km 80) for walleye, and perch; the **Sikanni Chief River** (Km 256) for grayling, northern pike, and Dollies; the **Buckinghorse River** (Km 278) for grayling; **Beaver Creek** (Km 328); and the **Prophet River** (Km 349) for Dollies and grayling.

From Fort Nelson to Watson Lake try the **Tetsa River** (Km 551) for grayling and Dollies; **Summit Lake** (Km 598) for lake trout, rainbows, and grayling; **115 Creek** and **MacDonald Creek** (Km 615) for grayling and Dollies; **MacDonald River** (Km 628) for grayling and Dollies; **Racing River** (Km 641) for Dollies and grayling; **Toad River** (Km 672) for grayling and Dollies; **Muncho Lake** (Km 701) for lake trout, rainbows, Dollies, and grayling; the **Trout River** (Km 733) for grayling; the **Liard River** (Km 763) for northern pike, grayling and Dollies; **Iron Creek Lake** (Km 922) for stocked rainbows; **Hyland River** (Km 937) for lake trout, grayling and Dollies; and finally, **Watson Lake** for lake trout and grayling.

From Watson Lake to Whitehorse are the **Upper Liard River** (Km 991) for grayling and Dollies; the **Rancheria River** (Km 1,063) for grayling and Dollies; **Morley Lake and River** (Km 1,204) for lake trout, northern pike, and grayling; **Teslin Lake** (Km 1,244) for lake trout, grayling and northern pike; the **Teslin River at Johnson's Crossing** (Km 1,296) for lake trout, northern pike, grayling, and king salmon in the fall; **Squanga Lake** (Km 1,316) for northern pike, grayling, whitefish, and lake trout and nearby Salmo Lake is stocked with rainbows; **Marsh Lake** (Km 1,370) for lake trout, northern pike, and grayling; and **Wolf Creek** (Km 1,408) for grayling. Several lakes near Whitehorse are stocked with rainbows including the **Hidden Lakes** and **Chadden Lake**.

Between Whitehorse and Tok try **Pine Lake** (Km 1,572) for lake trout, grayling and pike; huge **Kluane Lake** (from Km 1,644 to Km 1,730) for lake trout, grayling, and northern pike; **Edith Creek** (Km 1,782) for grayling; **Pickhandle Lake** (Km 1,802) for lake trout, grayling, and Dollies; **Deadman Lake** (Mile 1,249) for northern pike; and **Moose Creek** and the **Chisana River** on the Northway Road (from Mile 1,264) for northern pike.

Hiking and Mountain Biking

We think that the best hiking along the Alaska Highway is in Canada's **Kluane National Park** near Haines Junction. The main Kluane National Park Visitor's Center (PO Box 5495, Haines Junction, Yukon, Y0B 1L0; (867) 634-7207) is in Haines Junction and has maps and information as well as hiking guidebooks. There's also a visitor's center farther north at **Tachal Dahl** (formerly Sheep Mountain, Km 1,649) at the south end of Kluane Lake. You must sign in and out at a visitor center when hiking at Kluane so the rangers know who is out in the park. Some good trails are the 85-km **Cottonwood Trail** from the Kathleen Lake Campground (See Chapter 12 - *Skagway and Haines*) back to the road at Dezadeash Lodge near Dezadeash Lake, the 15-km **Auriol Loop Trail** from 6 km south of Haines Junction on the Haines Highway (Km 239), the 24-km **Alsek Pass Trail** from near Km 1,589 of the Alaska Highway just northwest of Haines Junction, and the **Slim River Trails** near Kluane Lake that start near the Tachal Dahl Visitor Center at Km 1,649 of the Alaska Highway. Many of these trails are mining trails or roads leading to old remote mining sites.

Wildlife Viewing

As you head north from Dawson Creek on the highway you should begin to get into the habit of actively watching for wildlife. Most of the north is not a zoo or park with large numbers of animals waiting near the roadside for you to happen by and see them. On the other hand, there are many more animals than most people see, it is quite easy to drive right by and miss them.

You may have a chance to try your spotting skills early in the trip. In spring and summer watch the bushes in the cleared area back to the tree line along the road. There are often bears, sometimes grizzlies, feeding there. Many people don't notice them.

In **Stone Mountain Provincial Park** near Summit Lake at Km 598 caribou and stone sheep are often present.

Near **Muncho Lake** at about Km 727 there are often stone sheep on the road, there are mineral licks nearby. If you follow the short trail here your chance of spotting animals is even better.

In Kluane National Park at Km 1,649, at the south end of Kluane Lake, Dall sheep are often visible on **Tachal Dahl** (formerly Sheep Mountain). There's a visitor center there with a viewing scope. The sheep are in the area in the spring and fall.

THE ROUTES, TOWNS, AND CAMPGROUNDS

DAWSON CREEK
Population 12,000, Elevation 2,200 feet

Dawson Creek is the kick-off point for a drive up the Alaska Highway. Don't confuse this town with Dawson City, the gold rush town located on the Yukon River north of Whitehorse. Dawson Creek is well equipped to provide groceries and vehicle supplies. Don't be deceived by the small population figure above, Dawson Creek really serves as an important services town in the agricultural Peace River Block with a population of over 50,000 people. It has several supermarkets as well as a Walmart and Canadian Tire.

You'll want to visit the **Dawson Creek Visitor Information Centre** (900 Alaska Avenue, Dawson Creek, B.C., V1G 4T6; 250 782-9595) for information about sights

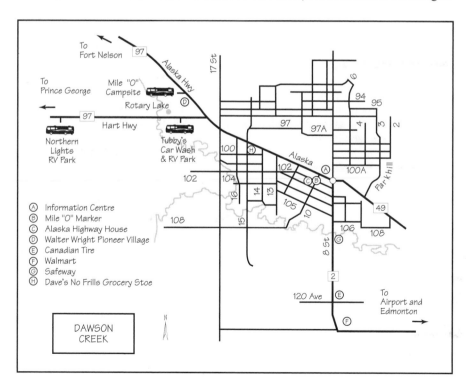

Ⓐ Information Centre
Ⓑ Mile "0" Marker
Ⓒ Alaska Highway House
Ⓓ Walter Wright Pioneer Village
Ⓔ Canadian Tire
Ⓕ Walmart
Ⓖ Safeway
Ⓗ Dave's No Frills Grocery Stoe

DAWSON CREEK

THE ALASKA HIGHWAY

THE "TRUE" MILE ZERO OF THE ALASKA HIGHWAY

and campgrounds north along the highway. It is located near the intersection of Highway 49 and Highway 2 near the center of town. They can also give you information about road conditions farther north. It is in a complex called the NAR (Northern Alberta Railways) Park which also houses the **NAR Railway Station Museum** and which concentrates on the area's agricultural and natural history and the Alcan. There's lots of room to park even the largest rig. In the same complex is the **Dawson Creek Art Gallery**. In the parking lot is the Mile Zero Cairn, claimed to be the true Mile 0 of the Alaska Highway. You're probably more familiar with the second Mile 0 Marker in town, it's a short two-block stroll away. You want to take a photo of each before mounting your expedition north.

While visiting the Mile 0 Marker in town it's worth the time to take a stroll around. A walking guide with a map can be obtained at the Dawson Creek Visitor Information Centre. It details the locations of the many murals painted on downtown buildings. It's also well worth your time to visit the new **Alaska Highway House**, a museum about the building of the Alaska Highway, which is located on the corner downtown next to the Mile 0 Marker.

If you have a little more time in Dawson Creek you might want to visit the **Walter Wright Pioneer Village** at the **Mile 0 Rotary Park**, there are historic buildings from before the highway was constructed. The park is located near the intersection of the Hart and Alaska Highways.

The **Dawson Creek Golf and Country Club** (250 782-9155), an 18-hole, par 72 course is almost adjacent to the Mile 0 RV Campsite and has a restaurant.

Dawson Creek hosts the **Dawson Creek Fall Fair Exhibition and Rodeo** in early August.

There are three campgrounds in Dawson Creek and many more north as far as Fort St. John. Most of Dawson Creek's big box stores are located off Highway 2, the road that leaves Dawson City to the south toward Grand Prairie and Edmonton.

Dawson Creek Campgrounds

NORTHERN LIGHTS RV PARK

Address:	Box 2476, Dawson Creek, B.C. V1G 4T9
Telephone:	(855) 782-9433, (250) 782-9433
Email:	nlrv2010@gmail.com
Website:	www.nlrv.com

GPS Location: 55.76639 N, 120.29083 W, 2,300 Ft.

If you are approaching Dawson Creek from the direction of Prince George this is the first RV park you'll see. It's hard to see well from the road but this is an excellent facility with views over Dawson Creek to the east.

There are about 90 sites, a large proportion of them are large pull-thrus with room for RV combos to 60 feet and slide-outs. Most are full hookup sites with 50-amp service and TV hookups. Sites have picnic tables and grass strips separate them. There are some fire pits and also a tenting area. Restrooms are modern with spotless individual rooms and free showers. There is a convenience store, a laundry and also a dump station. Wi-Fi coverage is excellent. The campground stays open all year.

The Northern Lights is located on the south side of Highway 97S from Prince George about 2.4 km (1.5 miles) west of its intersection with the Alaska Highway, Highway 97N.

MILE O RV CAMPSITE (CITY OF DAWSON CREEK)

Address:	1901 Alaska Avenue (PO Box 2383), Dawson Creek, B.C. V1G 4T9
Telephone:	(250) 782-2590
Email:	mile0rvpark@gmail.com
Website:	www.mile0park.ca

GPS Location: 55.76949 N, 120.25883 W, 2,200 Ft.

This city campground makes a convenient overnight stop in Dawson Creek. It is only open during the summer season, from May 1 to September 15, so it's a traveler's campground with few if any long-term residents.

This is a large grassy park-like campground with scattered shade trees. Camping spaces are widely separated off wide gravel drives and have picnic tables. Most of the 80 sites are back-ins but 13 are pull-thrus that will accommodate combos to 80 feet. Most of these are not level and may challenge you. A variety of utility combinations are available including full, partial, or no hookups. There is also a dump station. The combination restroom, laundry, and kitchen shelter building is older but well maintained and there are free showers. A picnic shelter makes things more comfortable for tenters. Wi-Fi is good only near the office so take that into account when selecting a site. There is an outdoor swimming pool (really a cement pond called Rotary Lake) nearby as well as the Walter Wright Pioneer Village outdoor museum.

A paved walking trail can be accessed from the grounds of Tubby's RV Park across the highway and there's a golf course just north of the campground.

The campground is on the west side of the Alaska Highway just north of its junction with Highway 97 from Prince George.

▣ TUBBY'S CAR WASH AND RV PARK

Address:	1913-96 Ave., Dawson Creek, B.C. V1G 1M2
Telephone:	(250) 782-2584, (866) 720-2584
Email:	info@tubbysrvpark.com
Website:	www.tubbysrvpark.com

GPS Location: 55.76611 N, 120.26034 W, 2,200 Ft.

Tubby's is very easy to spot from the highway. They have a 4-bay vehicle wash out front, one of the bays will accommodate big RVs.

The campground has at about 90 campsites, most have full hookups. The camping area is a large gravel lot. There are a variety of hookup options including full-hookups (20 and 30 amp). Pull-thrus are available and some sites are as long as 45 feet. There are some fire pits, the campground has newly renovated restrooms (showers cost extra) and laundry, also a dump station. There's a paved city bike or walking path that begins at the campground. Tubby's is open all year and has a large number of long-term occupants.

Tubby's is one of the two campgrounds located near the junction of the Alaska Highway (Hwy. 97N) and the Hart Highway (97S). It is .5 km (.3 miles) west of the junction on the south side of the Hart Highway.

FROM DAWSON CREEK TO TAYLOR AND FORT ST. JOHN
76 Kilometers (47 Miles)

When the US Army arrived in Dawson Creek to begin building the Alcan there was already a small road north to Fort St. John. Unfortunately there were several rivers along the road with no bridges so the first order of business was to hurry up and get supplies north to Fort St. John before the ice melted.

Today the road is excellent and the bridges are all in so the hour-long drive north is uneventful. You might want to take a short side trip at Km 26 to visit the old curved wooden Kiskatinaw Bridge. This is the only original timber bridge remaining along the Alaska Highway. The access road is part of the original highway and is no longer on the main route.

Dawson Creek to Taylor and Fort St. John Campgrounds

▣ FARMINGTON FAIRWAYS GOLF AND RV RESORT

Address:	5764 Hwy 97 North, Farmington, B.C. V0C 1N0
Telephone:	(250) 843-7774
Email:	farmingtonfairways@hotmail.com
Website:	www.farmingtonfairways.com

GPS Location: 55.85833 N, 120.39611 W, 2,500 Ft.

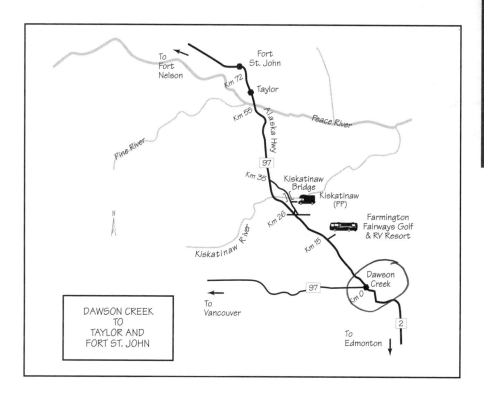

To Fort Nelson

Fort St. John

Km 72

Taylor

Km 55

Peace River

Pine River

Alaska Hwy

97

Km 35

Kiskatinaw Bridge

Kiskatinaw (PP)

Farmington Fairways Golf & RV Resort

Km 26

Kiskatinaw River

Km 15

Dawson Creek

Km 0

97

To Vancouver

To Edmonton

2

DAWSON CREEK TO TAYLOR AND FORT ST. JOHN

Here's a one-of-a-kind stop along the Alaska Highway, a combination campground and golf course. The course is 9 holes, and there is also a driving range and a licensed clubhouse. RVers staying at the campground get a greens-fee discount.

There are actually two campgrounds here. One is a 26-site RV campground that has large pull-thru sites with electrical and water hookups. Sites will accommodate RV combos to 65 feet and are located in an open area near the clubhouse. There is also a camping area with no hookups set in a wooded area nearby. This camping area has 28 sites, some large enough for big RVs, and has picnic tables and fire pits. Facilities include a portable-type building housing restrooms with free showers and a laundry. There is also a dump station.

The Farmington Fairways in located near Km 15 of the Alaska Highway on the east side of the highway.

🚐 KISKATINAW PROVINCIAL PARK CAMPGROUND

Location:	4.7 Kilometers On Old Alaska Highway Loop Which Leaves The Alaska Highway Near Km 26
Info:	(250) 843-0074
Website:	www.env.gov.bc.ca/bcparks/explore/parkpgs/kiskatinaw/

GPS Location: 55.95806 N, 120.56194 W, 1,900 Ft.

The Kiskatinaw River Bridge is a popular sightseeing stop for visitors traveling the Alaska Highway. This is the only original wood bridge still in use and is interesting because it curves as it crosses high above the river. The campground is right next to the bridge.

This government campground offers 28 back-in sites on a rather narrow gravel access loop. The gravel sites are well-separated in poplar and spruce trees and some are right along the river. Some sites are actually 45 feet long but because access is difficult and maneuvering room very limited this campground is best for RVs to 35 feet. All sites have picnic tables and fire pits, there are vault toilets and a water pump.

To reach the campground you must drive 4.7 km (2.9 miles) along a paved section of the old Alcan which leaves the new road near Km 26. The campground entrance is on the right just before you reach the bridge. There is also access to the bridge and campground from Km 35 at the other end of the loop of old road, the distance is 5.0 km (3.1 miles). Both routes are decent but there is about a half-mile of gravel if you use the northern entrance.

TAYLOR AND FORT ST. JOHN
Population Taylor 1,500, Fort St. John 19,000, Elevation 2,300 feet

You'll drive through the town of Taylor about 21 km (13 miles) south of Fort St. John and just north of the Peace River bridge at Km 55. This is a nicely laid out town with several huge industrial complexes including a gas processing plant and a pulp mill.

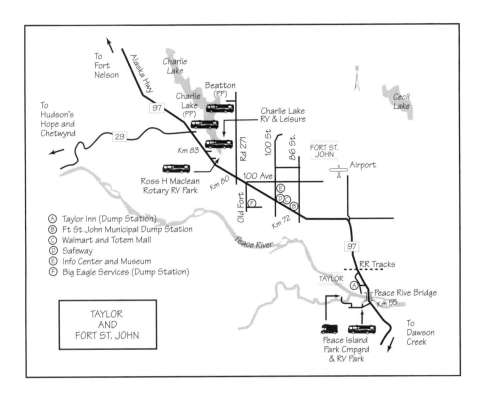

Fort St. John was originally a fur trading post known as Rocky Mountain Fort, settled in 1794. It's the oldest non-First Nation town in British Columbia. Today gas and oil are the biggest industries. The largest oil and gas field in British Columbia is nearby. Fort St. John is growing rapidly and now is a larger town with more stores and service facilities than Dawson Creek. However, it has a much poorer selection of RV parks.

The **Fort St. John-North Peace Museum** at Centennial Park covers the town's history as a fur trading center as well as the construction of the Alaska Highway. Nearby is the excellent **Visitor Info Center** (9324-96 St., Fort St. John, B.C. V1J 6V5; 250 785-3033 or 877 785-3033).

The drive to the **W.A.C. Bennett Dam** is a popular side trip from Fort St. John. Drive north on the Alaska Highway to Km 83 and then on Highway 29 west through Hudson's Hope to the dam. The total distance one-way is 99 km (61 miles). This huge earth-filled dam provides 40% of British Columbia's electricity and forms Williston Lake. Pilots who have flown the "trench" will be familiar with this long, skinny lake, British Columbia's largest. Tours of the power station are available. Another dam nearby, the **Peace Canyon Dam**, has self-guided tours. The town of **Hudson's Hope** is an old fur trading center and has a museum with exhibits related to the dinosaur fossils found in the area.

Taylor and Fort St. John Campgrounds

🚐 PEACE ISLAND PARK CAMPGROUND AND RV PARK

Location:	West Side Of Hwy. At South End Of Peace River Bridge
Address:	Box 300, Taylor, B.C. V0C 2K0
Telephone:	(250) 789-9295
Email:	info@districtoftaylor.com
Website:	www.districtoftaylor.com/peaceislandpark.shtml

GPS Location: 56.13158 N, 120.67380 W, 1,300 Ft.

The crossing of the Peace River has always been problematic. Rafts were used to move road-building equipment after an ice bridge went out during the spring thaw of 1942. Several timber bridges were built and washed out before a suspension bridge was finished in 1943, but that bridge collapsed in 1957. The current bridge looks pretty solid but you might keep an eye on it from this campground.

There are actually two campgrounds here. Near the highway is an RV park section in a large flat lot. This has 60 long paved pull-thrus and back-ins off gravel loop access roads in large grassy fields. There are 30-amp hookups as well as picnic tables and fire pits but no water or sewer hookups. There's a hand-operated water pump. Restrooms are vault toilets and nearby is a playground and boat launch.

The second campground entrance is beyond the one for the hookup campground, off the same access road but farther from the highway. It sits on an island in the river and is reached by a causeway from the south. This area has large playing fields and picnic areas and also 40 campsites. They have picnic tables and fire pits and there are outhouses. There are no hookups but there is a hand-operated water pump. Firewood is available from the camp hosts in both sections.

The access road to the campground is very near the south end of the Peace River

Bridge near Km 55 of the Alaska Highway. After leaving the highway you'll immediately pass the RV park on your right, if you continue straight at .6 km (.4 miles) you'll come to the entrance to the second area. Turn right and follow the driveway through the trees and across the causeway to the park.

BEATTON PROVINCIAL PARK CAMPGROUND

Location:	East Side Of Charlie Lake
Info:	(250) 787-1893
Res.:	(800) 689-9025 or
	https://secure.camis.com/Discover camping/
Website:	www.env.gov.bc.ca/bcparks/explore/parkpgs/beatton/

GPS Location: 56.33328 N, 120.95111 W, 2,200 Ft.

Beatton is not right next to the highway, you must drive around the south side of Charlie Lake to reach this campground which is located on the east shore of the lake. In addition to swimming, boating and fishing in the lake (walleye and northern pike) this park has miles of cross-country ski trails that double as hiking trails in the summer.

The campground has 37 paved back-in sites off paved access roads, some to 45 feet although access for large RVs can be difficult at some sites. Like other B.C. provincial parks this one offers picnic tables and fire pits at each site, vault toilets, and water. Camping sites are set in trees and some are along the lake. There is also a nearby boat-launching ramp. Stays here are limited to 14 days.

The paved road to the park (Beaton-Montney Rd 271) leaves the Alaska Highway near Km 80. Head north for 7.7 km (4.8 miles), then turn left and drive another mile to the park entrance on the left.

ROSS H MACLEAN ROTARY RV PARK

Address:	Mile 52 Alaska Hwy, Ft. St. John, B.C. V1J 4H8
Telephone:	(250) 785-1700
Email:	office@rotaryrvparkfsj.com
Website:	www.rotaryrvparkfsj.com

GPS Location: 56.27667 N, 120.95500 W, 2,200 Ft.

With a tall chain-link fence surrounding it this must be the most secure campground on the Alaska Highway. It has spacious grassy areas between sites and good facilities and is a popular campground, particularly for larger rigs. There is a nearby boat ramp for fishermen interested in the walleye that Charlie Lake is known for, and also a nearby playground. It's also near the highway so road noise can be a problem.

The Rotary RV Park has 69 sites. A few are full hookups but most are electric and water or electric only sites. Some are pull-thrus and there is lots of room to maneuver and park RV combos to 100 feet. Each site has a picnic table. There are also tent sites. Restrooms are spic-and-span and have showers (small fee). There is also a laundry, a dump station (extra charge), and a community fire pit. Free Wi-Fi reaches the sites.

To reach the campground just turn east off the highway near Km 82. You can see the campground from the highway.

CHARLIE LAKE RV AND LEISURE

Address: Historic Mile 52 (Box 55),
              Charlie Lake, B.C. V0C 1H0
Telephone: (250) 787-1569

GPS Location: 56.28333 N, 120.96833 W, 2,300 Ft.

This campground is mostly filled with residential campers but usually has some spaces for travelers. The campground is near but not on the shore of Charlie Lake. There are about 45 sites. Most are back-in RV spaces with full hookups but there are 6 nice tent sites and a few pull-thrus and also some sites with only electricity. A few sites will take RVs to 40 feet but maneuvering room is tight and leveling is often difficult. Small trees provide decent separation. Some sites have picnic tables and fire pits. The restrooms have showers (small fee) and there is a laundry area. Canoes are available for rent. The facility is open all year.

The campground is located east of the Alaska Highway near Km 83.

CHARLIE LAKE PROVINCIAL PARK CAMPGROUND

Location: West Shore Charlie Lake Near Km 83
              Alaska Hwy.
Info: (250) 787-1894
Res.:   (800) 689-9025 or
              https://secure.camis.com/Discover camping/
Website: www.env.gov.bc.ca/bcparks/explore/parkpgs/charlie_lk/

GPS Location: 56.30583 N, 121.00389 W, 2,500 Ft.

This large provincial campground is convenient to the highway and very nice, it also takes reservations. It has paved access roads and large back-in gravel sites. There are 57 of them, set in a grove of trees. Many of the sites exceed 50 feet in length and there is quite a bit of maneuvering room. Each has a picnic table and fire pit, there are vault toilets and a picnic/kitchen shelter and children's playground. A 2-kilometer (1.2-mile) trail leads to the lake and there is even a dump station (extra fee). There's also a boat launch and picnic area at the lake, but access is from another road just to the east of the campground entrance. There is a 14-day stay limit in this campground.

FROM FORT ST. JOHN TO FORT NELSON
381 Kilometers (236 Miles)

The section of the Alaska Highway between Fort St. John and Fort Nelson is in excellent condition. The road skirts the eastern edge of the Rocky Mountains as if waiting for the chance to leave the plains and climb toward the west. When the troops arrived to build the Alaska Highway in 1942 there was only a winter road between Fort St. John and Fort Nelson and it was not deemed suitable for an upgrade to an all-weather road. Instead the road was moved westward into the foothills of the Rockies where the terrain was better drained and the road easier to build.

During the mid-summer berry season keep an eye on the cleared area along the highway. We've spotted many bears, both blacks and browns, along this section of highway feeding on the berries, or even on the grass in the spring.

Just 9 kilometers (6 miles) north of Fort St. John near Km 81 (Mile 51) is Charlie

THE ALASKA HIGHWAY

Lake. There are two provincial park campgrounds here and two private ones. The lake is famous for its walleye fishing. We've included these Charlie Lake campgrounds under the Fort St. John heading above since they are so close.

North of Charlie Lake you'll find miles of empty highway with the occasional tiny settlement. These include Wonowon at Km 163 (Historic Mile 101, get it?), Pink Mountain at Km 226, Sikanni Chief at Km 256 and Prophet River at Km 365. Most of these settlements have little more than a roadhouse and perhaps a campground.

Recently the region from Fort St. John to Fort Nelson has been a beehive of activity due to development of natural gas in the region. Several of the campgrounds have been converted to industrial camps for workers using Atco-type portable units or perhaps just RVs. The campgrounds we list continue to cater primarily to RV travelers. You may spot a few additional places in this section that we do not list where you could spend the night but the traveler's campgrounds provide a more pleasant experience.

Fort St. John to Fort Nelson Campgrounds

PINK MOUNTAIN CAMPSITE AND RV PARK

Address:	Historic Mile 143 (Box 26), Pink Mountain, B.C. V0C 2B0
Telephone:	(250) 772-5133
Email:	lory@northwestel.net

GPS Location: 57.03997 N, 122.50994 W, 3,700 Ft.

Behind an old log building housing a post office, very small grocery, liquor store, and gift shop with gas out front you'll find a variety of campsites (about 30 of them) set in pine and spruce trees. Although some appear to have full hookups they are pretty old with questionable sewer and water connections. Some are long pull-thrus, there are also some good tent sites. This campground has a dump station and laundry. Water is very mineralized and can stain clothes and fixtures. The campground is off the grid so it generates its own power.

You'll spot the campground on the west side of the Alaska Highway near Km 226 across from the Pink Mountain Motor Inn.

SIKANNI RIVER CAMPGROUND AND RV PARK

Address:	Historic Mile 162 (Box 4), Sikanni River, B.C. V0C 2B0
Telephone:	(250) 772-5400
Email:	jackie.allen@northwestel.net

GPS Location: 57.23806 N, 122.69389 W, 2,600 Ft.

Coming from north or south watch carefully as you approach the Sikanni River because you won't see the campground until you're almost past as you highball down the hill and cross the river. The scenic riverside location and friendly owners make this a good stop.

This campground has about 30 sites along the edges of a large gravel area near the river. Some have full hookups and some are pull-thrus to 60 feet, there are also tent sites. Sites have picnic tables and fire rings. There are showers, flush toilets, and a

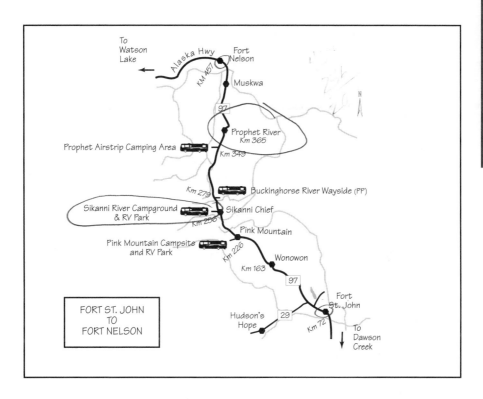

laundry, as well as a dump station. A small store can supply camping supplies and snacks and there are also rental cabins. Wi-Fi is a hot spot at the office.

Sikanni River RV Park is located on the north shore of the Sikanni River near Km 256 (Historic Mile 162) of the Alaska Highway.

BUCKINGHORSE RIVER WAYSIDE PROVINCIAL PARK CAMPGROUND

Location:	Near Km 279 Of The Alaska Highway
Info:	(250) 772-4999
Website:	www.env.gov.bc.ca/bcparks/explore/parkpgs/buckinghorse_rv/

GPS Location: 57.38306 N, 122.84556 W, 3,300 Ft.

The Buckinghorse River campground has 33 back-in spaces next to the Buckinghorse River. They are not separated, this is really more of a parking lot than a campground. Some sites are long enough for RVs to at least 45 feet without being in the way. Access to this park is an in-and-out road with a turnaround at the end so rigs with a tow can take a look without worries. The camp sites are some distance from the highway and are along a creek that has some grayling so this is a good place to overnight. Don't let the industrial crew camp north of the entrance discourage you, it has little or no effect on the campground. A nice feature is the Buckinghorse River Lodge across the highway which has a cafe, firewood, and phone. They also manage the campground. Sites have picnic tables and fire pits and there are vault toilets and a hand-operated water pump. There is a 14-day stay limit for this campground.

THE ALASKA HIGHWAY

▄ PROPHET AIRSTRIP CAMPING AREA
(FORMERLY PROPHET RIVER PROVINCIAL PARK)

Location: Near Km 349 Of The Alaska Highway

GPS Location: 57.97111 N, 122.77528 W, 1,900 Ft.

This former provincial park continues to get a lot of use even though it is no longer maintained as a campground or park. An airstrip near the highway is sometimes used in fire season and the campground can be active when it is in service. It has both back-in sites with parking on grass and long pull-thrus to 60 feet. Some sites have rock fire rings. Facilities include occasionally serviced outhouses. The Prophet River is nearby and you can follow a trail down to take a look or maybe wet a line.

Watch carefully for a side road with no sign on the west side of the highway near Km 349. It's easy to miss.

FORT NELSON
Population 4,000, Elevation 1,400 feet

Little Fort Nelson has become something of an economic center in recent years. Before the construction of the Alaska Highway the population of this fur town was fewer than 500 people. Today the town is a trade center for the McConachie Creek agricultural subdivision as well as a service center for the very active natural gas development activities in the area. It's also home to the northern-most traffic light in B.C.

Fort Nelson visitors usually take in the **Fort Nelson Heritage Museum** which has displays about local history, wildlife, vehicles, and the construction of the Alaska Highway.

There are two supermarkets in town for groceries and two good-sized campgrounds.

Fort Nelson Campgrounds

▄ THE BLUEBELL INN

Address:	4203 50ᵗʰ Ave S (Box 931), Fort Nelson, B.C. V0C 1R0
Telephone:	(250) 774-6961
Email:	bluebellinn@northwestel.net
Website:	www.bluebellinn.ca

GPS Location: 58.80190 N, 122.68020 W, 1,300 Ft.

This campground is located behind a modern motel in the center of Fort Nelson. There are 42 campsites, both back-in and pull-thrus to 60 feet. These are large sites on gravel with full hookups including 30-amp power. They have picnic tables and there is one fire pit. A restroom building in the middle of the camping area offers flush toilets and showers and out front there's a laundry, a convenience store and gas pumps. Restaurants are nearby. There's free Wi-Fi at the hotel which is sometimes usable in the campground.

The Blue Bell Inn is on the south side of the highway in central Fort Nelson, it's across from the A&W.

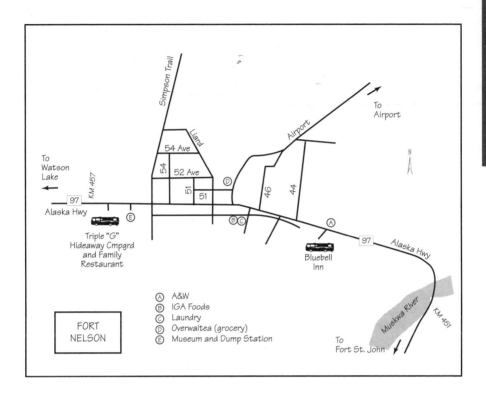

TRIPLE "G" HIDEAWAY CAMPGROUND AND FAMILY RESTAURANT

Address:	5651 Alaska Highway, Ft. Nelson, B.C. V0C 1R0
Telephone:	(250) 774-2340
Email:	tangle@shaw.ca
Website:	www.tripleghideaway.com

GPS Location: 58.80444 N, 122.72056 W, 1,300 Ft.

Located in the western outskirts of Ft. Nelson this campground is right next door to the museum and across the street from the town's recreation center.

Sites include long pull-thrus to 60 feet, star-burst back-ins, and others, some 130 in all. Most sites are full hookups with 30-amp power and many have TV, but there are also sites with just electricity and water and some with no hookups. There's an on-site restaurant and a gift shop. Showers are available and there is also a laundry, a pressure RV wash (extra cost), and a dump station. Electrical hookup are available all winter long.

As you enter Ft. Nelson on the Alaska Highway from the west watch for the Triple "G" on the right.

FROM FORT NELSON TO WATSON LAKE
532 Kilometers (330 Miles)

The miles from Fort Nelson to Watson Lake are some of the most scenic along the Alaska Highway. The road climbs through the Rocky Mountains and reaches the highest point of the highway near **Summit Lake** at Km 597–4,250 feet. The road is paved but narrow in some places and drivers shouldn't expect to make the same kind of speeds that were possible in the Dawson Creek to Fort Nelson section.

When army crews started cutting the Alaska Highway west from Fort Nelson toward Watson Lake the route through the mountains had not been surveyed. In fact, the route had not even been scouted on foot. There was some concern that there might not even be a suitable route through the mountains. Some quick work including getting help from local trappers and bush pilots was necessary. One of the toughest challenges on this part of the highway was building the section of road along Muncho Lake near Km 725.

There are three Provincial Parks between Fort Nelson and the Yukon border. The first of these (heading north) is **Stone Mountain Provincial Park** near Km 597. You cross the highest pass along the whole highway here right next to a beautifully located campground along Summit Lake. There are several hiking trails in the vicinity and you stand a good chance of seeing stone sheep or caribou here.

You'll pass through **Muncho Lake Provincial Park** from Km 655 to Km 737 of

STONE SHEEP ARE ALMOST ALWAYS PRESENT IN STONE MOUNTAIN PROVINCIAL PARK

the Highway. The road runs along the shore of this long, deep lake for about 11 kilometers (7 miles). There are two provincial campgrounds and also a commercial campground. The lake has huge lake trout. Watch for stone sheep along the highway just north of the lake, they are attracted by mineral licks in the area and are often on the road. There's a short trail to the mineral licks at Km 727 to view the mineral seeps and perhaps see sheep or caribou.

Liard River Hot Springs Provincial Park is near Km 765. There is a provincial campground and a commercial campground nearby. The hot pool at the springs has temperatures to 110° F. Almost everyone stops here for a dip. There is a half-mile boardwalk to the pool. It has become common to see bison along the highway near the Liard River.

After Liard Hot Springs the road gets better and you can cruise into Watson Lake at a good clip. A point of interest is **Contact Creek** at Km 909 (Historic Mile 588) where crews working west from Fort Nelson and east from Whitehorse hooked up when building the Alaska Highway.

The highway crosses into the Yukon Territory at Km 906. It crosses and re-crosses the border 7 times before reaching Watson Lake although some of these crossings are not marked. If you have a GPS you can spot the crossings since the border is at 60 degrees north latitude.

Fort Nelson to Watson Lake Campgrounds

TETSA RIVER CAMPGROUND REGIONAL PARK

Location: At The End Of A 2 Km (1.2 Mile) Road
                  Leaving The Alaska Hwy. Near Km 551
Res and Info: (250) 321-3321
Website: www.britishcolumbia.com/parks/?id=170

GPS Location: 58.65385 N, 123.94208 W, 2,100 Ft.

This former provincial campground is located far enough from the highway for peace and quiet but close enough for convenience. Grayling and Dolly Varden fishing in the river here is good. It's a well-run and managed park, virtually indistinguishable from a provincial park.

There are 25 large back-in sites suitable for RVs to 45 feet, many overlooking the river. This is a wooded campground with separated sites having the normal picnic table and fire pit. The campground has vault toilets and there's also a grassy tent-camping area. There's a hand-operated water pump. When a host is camping on-site firewood is available for purchase.

The road into the campground leaves the highway near Km 551. Follow the gravel road a distance of about 2 km (1.2 miles).

TETSA RIVER SERVICES AND CAMPGROUND

Address: Historic Mile 375 Alaska Highway (Box 238),
                  Fort Nelson, B.C. V0C 1R0
Telephone: (250) 774-1005
Email: tetsariverlodge@gmail.com
Website: www.tetsariver.com

GPS Location: 58.65222 N, 124.23556 W, 2,600 Ft.

THE ALASKA HIGHWAY

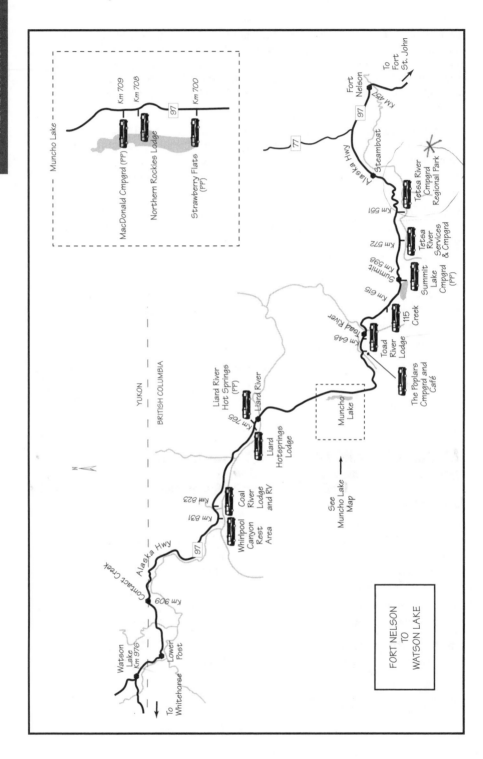

Muncho Lake

Km 709　MacDonald Cmpgrd (PP)
Km 708　Northern Rockies Lodge
97
Km 700　Strawberry Flats (PP)

To Fort St. John
Km 457
Fort Nelson
97
77
Steamboat
Alaska Hwy
Tetsa River Cmpgrd Regional Park
Km 551
Tetsa River Services & Cmpgrd
Km 572
Summit Km 598
Summit Lake Cmpgrd (PP)
Km 615
Toad River
115 Creek
Km 648
Toad River Lodge
The Poplars Cmpgrd and Café

YUKON
BRITISH COLUMBIA

Liard River Hot Springs (PP)
Liard River
Km 765
Liard Hotsprings Lodge

Muncho Lake

See Muncho Lake Map

Coal River Lodge and RV
Km 823
Whirlpool Canyon Rest Area
Km 831

97
Alaska Hwy

Contact Creek
Km 909

Watson Lake
Km 976
Lower Post
To Whitehorse

N

FORT NELSON
TO
WATSON LAKE

Tetsa River Services is a popular stop along this section of the highway. The lodge here is also pretty well known for the baked goods it sells, In fact, they claim to be the Cinnamon Bun Center of the Galactic Cluster. Coffee is available to go with those buns. There's also a nice selection of books and other souvenirs.

The lodge has 30 campsites in all. Many have no hookups and are suitable for both tent and RV use. Those with RVs to about 40 feet will find about seven or eight locations where they can hook up to electricity (15 amp, generator on site, no power for a time during the night) and water and there is a dump station. Some sites are pull-thrus. Showers are available, gas is sold, and there are even some rooms for rent.

The operation is located on the south side of the highway near Km 572.

SUMMIT LAKE PROVINCIAL CAMPGROUND

Location: Near Km 598 Of The Alaska Hwy.
Info: (250) 265-4710
Website: www.env.gov.bc.ca/bcparks/explore/parkpgs/summit_lk/

GPS Location: 58.65111 N, 124.65083 W, 4,200 Ft.

This striking campground is located in high alpine country in Stone Mountain Provincial Park. Its site is at the east end of Summit Lake very near the highway. This pass is the highest point of the Alaska Highway, 1,295 meters (4,250 feet). You'll probably think that it seems much higher. Several excellent hiking trails leave the road from the vicinity of the campground and caribou are often present nearby.

There are 34 sites that are separated but since there are no trees here they are not really very private. Road noise is a problem and the weather can be harsh since the altitude is high and this is a pass. On the other hand, in good weather it's hard to pass this place up. Sites have picnic tables and fire pits and the campground has vault toilets and a hand-operated water pump, some sites will take RVs to 45 feet and they are well separated. There's also a boat launch but fishing in the lake and on MacDonald Creek running by the campground is poor due to the cold water.

115 CREEK REST AREA

Location: Near Km 615 Of The Alaska Highway

GPS Location: 58.71750 N, 124.91333 W, 3,000 Ft.

This is nothing more than a wayside along the highway. At one time it was actually a campground but the outhouses, tables, and fire pits have all been removed. All that remains are the cement slabs where the tables once were and sometimes a dumpster. Still, it is a popular place for RVs to spend the night, people apparently became attached to the place back when it really was a campground. There is room for about 5 RVs to parallel park here. You can fish in 115 Creek and MacDonald Creek and caribou and moose are often seen in the vicinity. A very scenic large beaver dam is located on the river behind the campground.

The wayside is completely unmarked, it is just east of 115 Creek bridge on the south side of the highway.

THE ALASKA HIGHWAY

TOAD RIVER LODGE IS ONE OF THE BEST PLACES TO STAY ALONG THE HIGHWAY

TOAD RIVER LODGE

Address:	Historic Mile 422 Alaska Highway
	(Box 7780), Toad River, B.C. V0C 2X0
Telephone:	(250) 232-5401, (855) 878-8623
Email:	Travel@ToadRiverLodge.com
Website:	www.ToadRiverLodge.com

GPS Location: 58.84694 N, 125.23167 W, 2,300 Ft.

The camping facilities at Toad River Lodge are much improved over the last few years. This is now one of the best places to stay between Fort Nelson and Watson Lake, an excellent roadhouse. In the café take a look at the ceiling, it is covered by one of the largest hat collections anywhere. There are reported to be nearly 8,000 of them.

There are 25 RV spaces, four are pull-thrus to 70 feet with 30-amp outlets, water, and TV. Others are back-in sites, some with full hookups, some with electricity and water, and some with no hookups at all. The ones at the back of the property overlook Reflection Lake. Two tent sites on grass with a table also overlook the lake. Power is generated on-site but noise is minimal, there are free showers, a laundry, a dump station, free firewood, a café, and a gas station. Note that the water here is mineralized and poor for drinking and can stain washed clothes and fixtures. It's best to arrive with enough water in the tanks for your needs.

The lodge is located near Km 647 of the Alaska Highway.

THE POPLARS CAMPGROUND AND CAFÉ

Address: Box 30, Toad River, B.C. V0C 2X0
Telephone: (250) 232-5465

GPS Location: 58.85139 N, 125.31083 W, 2,500 Ft.

Not far down the road from Toad River is another great campground. The Poplars is a pleasant RV campground located in magnificent mountain country.

There are 45 pull-thru sites, some are big full-hookup sites with 30-amp power suitable for RV combos to 70 feet located in a cleared area at the top of the campsite. Others are back-in sites in the trees. Most sites have picnic tables and fire rings. Restrooms have hot showers and there is also a café. Power comes from a generator. Note that this campground often opens later in the season than most along the highway, there doesn't seem to be a set date.

The Poplars is located near Km 652 (Historic Mile 426) of the Alaska Highway.

STRAWBERRY FLATS CAMPGROUND –
MUNCHO LAKE PROVINCIAL PARK

Location: Km 700 Of The Alaska Highway
Info: (250) 776-7000
Website: www.env.gov.bc.ca/bcparks/explore/parkpgs/muncho_lk/

GPS Location: 58.94750 N, 125.76972 W, 2,700 Ft.

This is a nice provincial campground on the shore of Muncho Lake. The 15 sites are separated and many are on the lakeshore. These are back-in sites off an in-and-out road with a turning circle at the end. All have picnic tables and fire pits and many are suitable for RVs to 40 feet. There are vault toilets, a drinking water system, and a dock.

NORTHERN ROCKIES LODGE

Address: Mile 462 (Box 8-M), Muncho Lake, B.C. V0C 1Z0
Telephone: (250) 776-3481 or (800) 663-5269
Email: info@northernrockieslodge.com
Website: www.northernrockieslodge.com

GPS Location: 59.00889 N, 125.77194 W, 2,700 Ft.

You can't miss this beautiful log lodge on the shores of Muncho Lake even if you aren't looking out for it. In addition to the hotel they sell gas, have a restaurant and bakery, and also operate an active bush-flying operation off the lake out front.

There are also about 30 RV camping sites here. There are back-ins and pull-thrus (to 70 feet), a few with full hookups. The lodge also offers flush toilets and showers, a laundry, and a dump station. Wi-Fi is available in the lodge lobby but not at the sites. Power is generated on site, check your site for noise before accepting it.

The lodge is located at Km 708 (Historic Mile 462) of the Alaska Highway.

MACDONALD CAMPGROUND – MUNCHO LAKE PROVINCIAL PARK

Location: Near Km 709 Of The Alaska Highway
Info: (250) 776-7000
Website: www.env.gov.bc.ca/bcparks/explore/parkpgs/muncho_lk/

GPS Location: 59.02000 N, 125.77250 W, 2,700 Ft.

This lakeside campground has 15 back-in separated spaces located along the lake. Some are suitable for RVs to 45 feet. Like Strawberry Flats, these sites too are on an out-and-back road with a turnaround at the end. They have picnic tables and fire pits. The campground also has vault toilets, a hand operated water pump, and a boat ramp.

LIARD RIVER HOT SPRINGS PROVINCIAL PARK

Location:	Near Km 765 Of The Alaska Highway
Info:	(250) 776-7000
Res.:	(800) 689-9025 or
	https://secure.camis.com/Discover camping/
Website:	www.env.gov.bc.ca/bcparks/explore/parkpgs/liard_rv_hs/

GPS Location: 59.42583 N, 126.10278 W, 1,500 Ft.

Almost everyone traveling the highway stops at Laird Hot Springs for a soak, even if only for a short time. The outdoor pools are just the right temperature and a great place to meet other travelers. In addition to the campground there is a large parking lot next to the quarter-mile boardwalk out to the springs and another across the highway. There's a $5 per person or $10 per vehicle fee to just park and use the pools, campground users are not charged for the pools, just for camping.

The provincial campground is located right near the beginning of the boardwalk to the springs. There are 53 well-separated back-in sites, each has a picnic table and fire pit. Some sites will take RVs to 40 feet. There are vault toilets and a hand water pump. While there are no showers you can always take a dip in the springs which have lots of water flow and only a slight sulfur smell. It's best not to wear your jew-

ENJOY A SOAK IN THE NEWLY REMODELED LIARD RIVER HOT SPRINGS

elry out to the pools, silver items tarnish rapidly in the water. This is a very popular campground, arrive early in the day or make reservations if you plan to stay here during late June, July, and early August. When the campground is full it is possible to RV camp in the day-use parking area or across the highway in an overflow area, the price is the same as the campground.

LIARD HOTSPRINGS LODGE

Address:	Historic Mile 497 Alaska Highway, Liard River, B.C. V1G 4J8
Telephone:	(250) 776-7349 or (866) 939-2522
Email:	manager@liardhotspringslodge.com
Website:	www.liardhotspringslodge.com

GPS Location: 59.42528 N, 126.10611 W, 1,600 Ft.

If you are looking for a campground with hookups in the Liard Hot Springs area this is the place. And the lodge usually doesn't fill up as fast as the provincial park does. The downside is that you'll have to pay to visit the hot springs.

There are about 35 RV sites located in a clearing a short distance behind the gas pumps and garage. Twenty have electric and water hookups and are pull-thrus, some suitable for RVs to 40 feet. There are another thirteen back-in sites with electricity and water hookups. Grass separates the sites. Some picnic tables are available and some sites have fire pits. There is also a tent camping area in trees nearby. Power is generated on-site. There is a dump and water fill station as well as a cafe, a small grocery store, gas sales, and guest rooms.

Liard Hotsprings Lodge is located near Km 765 of the Alaska Highway, about .2 km (.1 mile) from the hot springs parking lot.

COAL RIVER LODGE AND RV

Location:	Historic Mile 533, Alaska Highway, B.C.
Address:	D. Rogers, 9515 – 95 Ave, Ft. St. John, B.C. V1J 1H7
Telephone:	(250) 776-7306 (May-Sept), (250) 785-8775 (Off season)
Email:	d_rogers@telus.net
Website:	www.coalriverlodge.com

GPS Location: 59.65779 N, 126.95278 W, 1,500 Ft.

This roadhouse-style operation has fuel, a cafe, lodging and a campground. It's off the grid so power is from a generator. There are 12 sites suitable for RVs to 45 feet with electricity (20-amp outlets) and water in a gravel lot next to the other facilities. These are side-by-side pull-thrus with rails between the sites. Restrooms have flush toilets and showers and there is a laundry. Free Wi-Fi is available in the lodge, not at the sites. The Coal River Lodge is at Km 823 of the Alaska Highway.

WHIRLPOOL CANYON REST AREA

Location:	Near Km 831 Of The Alaska Highway

GPS Location: 59.62444 N, 127.08500 W, 1,600 Ft.

This small rest area is a popular boondocking spot. It has about 8 sites, a couple are large enough for big rigs. However, if there are big RVs already here you'll probably have to back out as maneuvering room is limited. There are no amenities other than a dumpster. One small site is very scenic and overlooks the Mountain Portage Rapids of the Liard River. The road into the campsite is sometimes unmarked, it is on the south side of the highway and is only about 200 meters long so you can walk in and look around before committing yourself.

WATSON LAKE
Population 800, Elevation 2,250 feet

Watson Lake serves as the trade center for the southeastern Yukon. The little town is located near the junction of the Cassiar Highway and the Alaska Highway.

Watson Lake is also at the junction with the gravel-surfaced **Campbell Highway** running northwest to meet the Klondike Loop at Carmacks. We describe the Campbell Highway as a side trip below.

Probably the most famous sight in Watson Lake is the **Signpost Forest**. Started by a G.I. during the construction of the Alaska Highway the original signpost has grown to a true forest with over 75,000 signs. You can put one up yourself if you wish. In fact, it's really a good idea to bring one along when you head north just for the purpose. Right next to the signpost forest is the **Alaska Highway Interpretive Center** (867 536-7469) with information about attractions throughout the Yukon. Watson Lake also has another attraction, the **Northern Lights Space and Science Centre**. This is a domed theater featuring northern lights shows. If you feel like stretching

DON'T FORGET TO BRING A SIGN TO ADD TO THE 75,817 (2013) SIGNS AT WATSON LAKE

THE ALASKA HIGHWAY

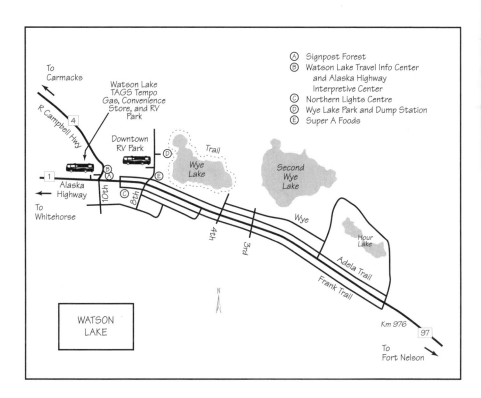

your legs after a long day on the road you might want to follow the nature trail around **Wye Lake**. It's a good trail with boardwalks to let you get closer to the birds.

Watson Lake has two decent campgrounds in or near town. In addition, to the west is a government campground and two commercial ones near the junction with the Cassiar Highway. These last three are included in the next section. There are also small supermarkets and some vehicle repair facilities. For repairs, however, we recommend waiting for Whitehorse if at all possible.

Watson Lake Campgrounds

DOWNTOWN RV PARK

Address:	103 Lake Street, Watson Lake, Yukon Y0A 1C0
Telephone:	(867) 536-2646
Email:	atannock@hotmail.com

GPS Location: 60.06333 N, 128.70639 W, 2,300 Ft.

For convenient access to central Watson Lake the Downtown RV Park is a decent choice. The lack of ambiance here–the park is basically a large gravel lot–is mitigated by Wye Lake which is located just across the road and is encircled by a walking and nature trail. You can easily walk from the campground to buy groceries or visit Watson Lake's biggest attractions: the Signpost Forest and Northern Lights Centre.

The Downtown has about 80 full-hookup sites (20 and 30 amps). There are back-ins and pull-thrus to 70 feet. There are clean restrooms with flush toilets and showers and a very popular large area with hoses to wash down your RV with no fee. There is also a laundry. There's free Wi-Fi available in the office.

The campground is well-signed in the middle of Watson Lake. It sits about a block north of the highway. Turn north next to the Super A Foods, a small supermarket east of the signpost forest.

WATSON LAKE TAGS TEMPO GAS, CONVENIENCE STORE, AND RV PARK

Address: 107 Campbell Hwy., Watson Lake, Yukon Y0A 1C0
Telephone: (867) 536-7422 or (867) 536-2051

GPS Location: 60.06399 N, 128.71788 W, 2,300 Ft.

This was the newest campground in Watson Lake and deserved to be one of the most popular. Unfortunately, the service station/convenience store building out front burned down in the spring of 2013. It was being rapidly rebuilt when we visited and the facility should be open again for the 2014 season. The description below describes the facility before the fire and as it is expected to be when reopened.

Both the location and facilities are good. The park is across the street from the info centre and Signpost Forest and just a short stroll from Wye Lake. Although the camping area is similar to that at the Downtown RV Park nearby, it's more protected with trees surrounding the area.

There are 40 sites in a gravel lot behind the convenience store. These are big back-in and pull-thru sites. They have 30-amp hookups and the pull-thrus also have sewer hookups. RV combos to 60 feet will find plenty of room to park and maneuver. A nice dedicated restroom building also has clothes washers and dryers, and there is a convenience store with snack bar out front as well as an additional laundromat there too. Free Wi-Fi can be received in the park.

As you pass through Watson Lake look for the Tempo gas station on the corner near the Signpost Forest. The campground is behind it.

CAMPBELL HIGHWAY SIDE TRIP
582 Kilometers (361 Miles)

The partly paved Campbell Highway runs northwestward from the center of Watson Lake to connect to the Klondike Highway near Carmacks. Navigation is easy, the road is pretty well marked with kilometer posts. They start in Watson Lake and end near Km 582 at the junction with the Klondike Highway near Carmacks. Note that fuel is hard to come by along the Campbell. Always fill up at Watson Lake or Carmacks before starting your drive.

There are two towns along the route. From the south the first is Ross River (population 350). It is reached using a short 10 km (6 mile) access road from Km 358. This is primarily a First Nation town, it serves as a supply center and is a popular put-in point for folks floating the Pelly River. Ross River has two small grocery stores and both gas and diesel are available. A ferry operates across the Pelly here and offers access to the North Canol Road which continues another 232 km (144 miles) north to the Northwest Territories border, where it is blocked. Check locally for road conditions if you plan to drive farther north.

The other town is Faro, built to service a huge open pit lead and zinc mine nearby. Unfortunately the mine is now closed and the town is suffering as a result. The population in the early 1980s was over 2,000, now it's about 400. It too is reached via a short 10 km (6 mile) access road, this one from near Km 414. The town has a nice municipal campground with hookups and also a territorial one on a lake just outside town. There's a visitor center and museum (PO Box 580, Faro, Yukon, Y0B 1K0; 867 994-2728) here and you can't miss the huge red ore truck which serves as a monument welcoming you at the entrance to town. Faro has a grocery store and restaurant but fuel is sometimes not available so be prepared.

The truth is that most residents of Faro and Ross River use the northwest end of the highway toward the Klondike Hwy. so that's the best section of road. The distance between Ross River and Carmacks is 137 miles (221 km) Most of it is paved with a few short gravel stretches. From Ross River to Watson Lake is 226 miles (364 km). Much of this section is unpaved. Even if paving isn't important to you the road from Watson Lake to Ross River is not as well-built or maintained as the section from Ross River west to Carmacks. It can be quite rough although in good weather it's certainly passable with most RVs. It's a good idea to check road conditions locally in Watson Lake or Carmacks before tackling the Campbell Highway.

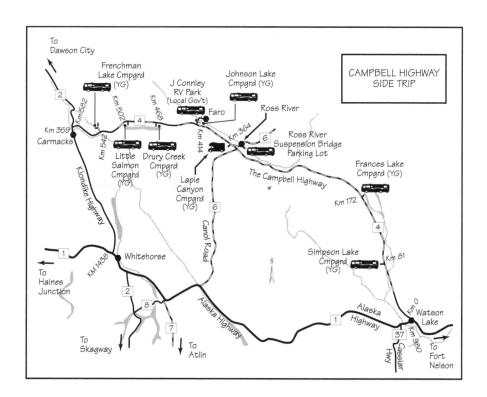

THE ALASKA HIGHWAY

Campbell Highway Campgrounds

SIMPSON LAKE CAMPGROUND (YUKON GOV.)

Location: Km 81 Of The Campbell Hwy.
Telephone: (867) 667-5648

GPS Location: 60.67761 N, 129.22874 W, 2,300 Ft.

This is a small 10-site campground on the shore of Simpson Lake. Some sites here are very large including two very long pull-thrus. Sites are off a loop access road and have picnic tables, fire pits, vault toilets, a boat launch, kitchen shelter, playground, free firewood, and a swimming beach.

Access to the campground is via a 1.5 km (.9 mile) access road from near Km 81 of the Campbell Hwy.

FRANCES LAKE CAMPGROUND (YUKON GOV.)

Location: Km 172 Of The Campbell Hwy.
Telephone: (867) 667-5648

GPS Location: 61.40995 N, 129.63073 W, 2,500 Ft.

Frances Lake is a beautiful large lake. The wide gravel beach next to the campground provides evidence that it's large enough to get lots of wave action. Many of the 25 sites here overlook the lake and folks pull their boats up right in front of the RVs. Sites here are all back-ins, but some are as long as 50 feet. They have picnic tables and fire pits, a hand water pump and vault toilets, free firewood, a kitchen shelter, and a boat ramp.

The access road for the campground leads 1.6 km (1 mile) east from near Km 172 of the Campbell Highway.

ROSS RIVER SUSPENSION BRIDGE PARKING LOT

Location: Ross River, Yukon

GPS Location: 61.98683 N, 132.44839 W, 2,200 Ft.

On the shore of the Pelly River just north of town is a gravel lot near the pedestrian suspension bridge where overnight RV parking is allowed. There are no services. To get there just drive right through town until you reach the river.

LAPIE CANYON CAMPGROUND (YUKON GOV.)

Location: Km 364 Of The Campbell Hwy.
Telephone: (867) 667-5648

GPS Location: 61.98332 N, 132.60590 W, 2,500 Ft

The campground at scenic Lapie Canyon has about 18 sites. Some are pull-thrus as long as 100 feet but narrow access roads and lack of maneuvering room make this a campground for RVs to 35 feet. Sites have picnic tables and fire pits and there are outhouses, a kitchen shelter, and free firewood. Trails lead from the campground to viewing spots overlooking the small canyon.

The campground entrance is near Km 364 of the Campbell Hwy, just west of the Lapie River bridge.

J. CONNLEY RV PARK (LOCAL GOV.)

Location: Faro, Yukon
Telephone: (867) 994-2288, (867) 994-2728

GPS Location: 62.23073 N, 133.35381 W, 2,400 Ft.

Just across from the Faro visitor center and museum is a very nice little municipal campground. There are 15 sites. Some are back-ins and some pull-thrus to 50 feet. Some sites have full-hookups. There are restrooms with showers and a laundry. Each site has a picnic table and a fire pit, there is also a dump station and free firewood. Internet access is possible at the visitor center.

As you come into Faro you'll spot a big red dump truck parked on the left side of the road. It's a permanent fixture. Take the right turn just beyond and in .6 km (.4 mile) you'll spot the campground entrance on the left, just opposite the log visitor center.

JOHNSON LAKE CAMPGROUND (YUKON GOV.)

Location: Off The Faro Access Road
Telephone: (867) 667-5648

GPS Location: 62.20733 N, 133.38635 W, 2,300 Ft.

This is a 15-site campground along the shore of Johnson Lake near Faro. Sites are off a loop access road and include pull-thrus near the lake to 70 feet. They have picnic tables and fire pits and the campground has vault toilets, free firewood, and a boat ramp.

From Km 414 of the Campbell Highway follow the Faro access road north for 3.5 km (2.2 miles). Turn right at the campground sign, the road also provides access to the Faro airport, and follow it .6 km (.4 miles) to the campground.

DRURY CREEK CAMPGROUND (YUKON GOV.)

Location: Km 468 Of The Campbell Hwy.
Telephone: (867) 667-5648

GPS Location: 62.19812 N, 134.38503 W, 2,100 Ft.

This campground is located just off the highway where Drury Creek flows into Little Salmon Lake. It's an exceptionally nice campground with ten sites, some are pull-thrus as long as 100 feet and many are right along the lake. They have picnic tables and fire pits, other amenities include vault toilets, free firewood, kitchen shelter, and a boat launch.

LITTLE SALMON CAMPGROUND (YUKON GOV.)

Location: Km 502 Of The Campbell Hwy.
Telephone: (867) 667-5648

GPS Location: 62.18203 N, 134.96611 W, 2,100 Ft.

This is another campground on Little Salmon Lake. This one has 15 sites and can easily take RVs to 45 feet. Turnaround room is limited however, most coaches with tow cars would probably have to unhook before leaving the campground. The sites have picnic tables and fire pits, there are also vault toilets, free firewood, a kitchen shelter, and a boat ramp.

THE ALASKA HIGHWAY

FRENCHMAN LAKE CAMPGROUND (YUKON GOV.) $$$
Location: Km 543 Of The Campbell Hwy.
Telephone: (867) 667-5648

GPS Location: 62.11709 N, 135.71039 W, 1,900 Ft.

This is one of three campgrounds accessible off the same side road. The others are Nunatak and Tatchun Lake, both some distance beyond Frenchman Lake on a road that isn't nearly as good.

Frenchman Lake has 15 sites arranged around a large gravel lot. There's parking for RVs of any size due to this arrangement. Sites have picnic tables and fire pits, there's also free firewood, vault toilets, and a boat launch.

From Km 543 of the Campbell Highway follow the signs on the road to the north for 5.5 km (3.4 miles) to the campground.

FROM WATSON LAKE TO WHITEHORSE
455 Kilometers (282 Miles)

The Alaska Highway between Watson Lake and Whitehorse is an excellent paved two-lane road with long flat straight stretches, particularly near Whitehorse.

The road actually crosses the Continental Divide as it gently climbs up through the Rancheria Valley and then descends along the Swift River. It then follows the shores of two large lakes through the upper Yukon basin: Teslin Lake and Marsh Lake.

At Km 1,002, about 21 kilometers (13 miles) west of Watson Lake is the junction with Highway 37, the **Cassiar Highway**. The Cassiar is an alternate route for many people traveling to Alaska and is covered in Chapter 5 in this book.

At Km 1,120 the highway crosses the **Continental Divide**. The waters to the east drain into the Arctic Ocean, those to the west into the Yukon.

The small town of **Teslin** at Km 1,244 is the only community of any size along the highway between Watson Lake and Whitehorse. Teslin has a large RV park, restaurants, and service stations. There's also a store in the village of Teslin just off the highway. Teslin has a population of about 500 and has one of the largest First Nation populations in the Yukon. The town has an interesting museum, the **George Johnston Museum**, which is well worth a stop. Another attraction is the **Tlingit Heritage Center**.

There are a few more campgrounds, both government and commercial, along the shore of **Teslin Lake**. This huge lake has excellent fishing for lake trout and near inlets and near the outlet you will find grayling and pike.

At Km 1,341 is **Jake's Corner**. From here Yukon Highway 8 (the Tagish Road) leads 55 kilometers (34 miles) west to a junction with the Skagway-Whitehorse road (Klondike Highway 2) at Carcross. Just 2 kilometers (1 mile) down the Tagish Road is another junction, this one with Yukon Highway 7 to Atlin. Both the Tagish Road and Atlin are covered as a side trip below.

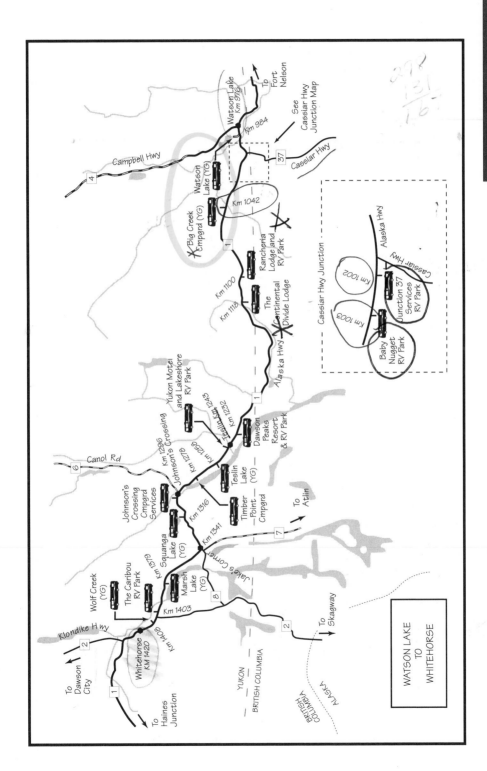

WATSON LAKE
TO
WHITEHORSE

Watson Lake to Whitehorse Campgrounds

WATSON LAKE CAMPGROUND (YUKON GOV.)

Location: Near Km 984 Of The Alaska Highway
Telephone: (867) 667-5648

GPS Location: 60.09000 N, 128.82056 W, 2,300 Ft.

If you are heading north this is probably the first Yukon government campground you will have a chance to visit, and it's a good one.

There are about 55 sites off two circular drives. Twelve are large pull-thrus, some can take RVs to 45 feet. All sites are well separated with lots of big trees and natural vegetation, they have picnic tables and fire pits. Free firewood is provided and there are vault toilets. None of the campsites are actually next to the lake but there is a day-use area with a boat launch at the lake. Trails connect the lake with the campground.

To reach the campground you head north on a gravel road from near Km 984 of the Alaska Highway. This is about 4 km (2.5 miles) west of central Watson Lake. At 2.1 km (1.3 miles) the road bends right and at 6.1 km (3.8 miles) reaches the campground.

JUNCTION 37 SERVICES RV PARK

Address: Historic Mile 649 Alaska Highway (Box 172), Watson Lake, Yukon
Telephone: (867) 536-2794
Email: Yukonglenn@yahoo.ca

GPS Location: 60.02471 N, 129.06081 W, 2,400 Ft.

Travelers coming north on the Cassiar Highway meet those traveling the Alaska Highway at a junction near Km 1,002 of the Alaska Highway, about 21 kilometers (13 miles) west of Watson Lake. On the corner is a large establishment with two service stations (only one in use), propane sales, repair shop, cafe, motel, small grocery store and an older RV park. When we last visited the place was pretty quiet with not much being open except the RV park and one gas station. This may not be a permanent situation.

There are about 50 camping sites located on gravel in a partially treed area south of the other facilities. Twenty-six sites have full hookups (20 and 30 amp), some are pull-thrus to 70 feet, there is lots of room for big RVs. There are quite a few trees separating sites and some have picnic tables and a few have fire rings. Restrooms with showers are available in the Atco-type motel compound as is a laundry area. There's also a dump station.

BABY NUGGET RV PARK *Stayed here*

Address: Historic Mile 650 Alaska Hwy. (Box 850), Watson Lake, Yukon Y0A 1CO
Telephone: (888) 536-2307 or (867) 536-2307 (Summer), (250) 494-0131 (Winter)
Email: nuggetcityyukon@gmail.com
Website: www.nuggetcity.com

GPS Location: 60.02778 N, 129.08250 W, 2,400 Ft.

The Baby Nugget is a large newer RV park. It has been built with big RVs in mind,

THE ALASKA HIGHWAY

there are acres of maneuvering room. The whole operation here is known as Nugget City, It includes The Northern Beaver Post Gift Shop, Northern Beaver Post Cottages, Wolf It Down Restaurant (specializing in Buffalo steaks and burgers), and Baby Nugget RV Park.

There are about 80 RV sites, most of them are very large pull-thrus, some exceeding 100 feet, with 15, 30 or 50-amp outlets. Most also have water and there is a dump station. Restrooms are nice and have good showers and a laundry. There's also a vehicle washing facility. Free Wi-Fi is available at the buildings near the entrance.

The campground is on the Alaska highway .8 km (.5 mile) west of its junction with the Cassiar Highway. It is 22 km (14 miles) west of Watson Lake, near Km 1,002.

▤ BIG CREEK CAMPGROUND (YUKON GOV.)
Location: Km 1,042 Of The Alaska Highway
Telephone: (867) 667-5648

GPS Location: 60.15865 N, 129.70672 W, 2,600 Ft.

This is a pleasant campground next to Big Creek with most of the 15 sites arranged around a small loop road. If hookups, a shower house, and internet aren't important to you this is a good alternative to the commercial parks in and near Watson Lake. Any size RV is OK here as many sites are pull-offs along the gravel drive. Sites have picnic tables and fire pits. There's also a water pump, handicapped accessible vault toilets, free firewood, and a cooking shelter.

▤ RANCHERIA LODGE AND RV PARK
Address: Historic Milepost 710 Alaska Highway, Yukon Territory, Canada Y0A 1A0
Telephone: (867) 851-6456
Email: bouch1@telus.net
Website: www.rancherialodgeyukon.com

GPS Location: 60.08806 N, 130.60361 W, 2,900 Ft.

Rancheria is a traditional roadhouse. There are the usual gas pumps, cafe, cocktail lounge, and motel. In the trees to the west is a nice little campground. The lodge is off the grid and generates its own power.

Rancheria has about 40 camping sites. Some sites are pull-thrus to 50 feet. Many sites have electric hookups and there is a dump and water fill station. RVs to 40 feet can use this campground if they maneuver carefully. There are trees and natural vegetation separating sites and one of the sites overlooks the river. The restrooms are older but have free showers. Wi-Fi is only available in the café.

Rancheria is located near Km 1,100 of the Alaska Highway.

▤ THE CONTINENTAL DIVIDE LODGE
Address: Historic Mile 721 Alaska Highway (General Delivery), Swift River, Yukon Y0A 1C0
Telephone: (867) 851-6451
Email: raley@telusmail.net
Website: www.continentaldividelodge.com

GPS Location: 60.07912 N, 130.91416 W, 3,200 Ft.

The Continental Divide is a roadhouse-style campground with good modern sites for big rigs. There are 24 sites behind the roadhouse. Fifteen are pull-thrus to 90 feet with 30-amp outlets. There are also no-hookup sites. There's a dump station, a laundry, and showers. Wi-Fi is free and reaches the sites but this is a satellite system so service can be slow. Electricity is generated on-site. They also offer gas and have a café, a bakery, a pub, and free firewood. The Rancheria River runs right behind the campground but cannot be seen from the sites. They are located at Km 1,118 of the Alaska Highway.

⛺ DAWSON PEAKS RESORT & RV PARK

Address:	Box 80, Teslin, Yukon Y0A 1B0
Telephone	(867) 390-2244 or (866) 402-2244
Email:	info@dawsonpeaks.ca
Website:	www.dawsonpeaks.ca

GPS Location: 60.11028 N, 132.55278 W, 2,300 Ft.

Dawson Peaks Resort stands out as one of the better places to stay along this section of the Alaska Highway. They have a very good restaurant, a gift shop, and a pleasant RV park.

The campground has 28 sites, some have 30-amp power, others 15. Several are pull-thrus to 60 feet but maneuvering room can be tight, drivers of really big RVs should park by the restaurant (which is easy in and out for any size RV) and walk into the camping area to take a look. The sites are located in trees and natural vegetation and situated above the lake. Picnic tables and fire rings are at each site and firewood is provided. A small road leads down to a boat ramp and dock. There is a dump station and showers (extra fee) are available. Wi-Fi reaches some sites from the restaurant, but not all.

Watch for the Dawson Peaks near Km 1,232 (Historic Mile 797) of the Alaska Highway.

⛺ YUKON MOTEL AND LAKESHORE RV PARK

Address:	Box 187, Teslin, Yukon Y0A 1B0
Telephone:	(867) 390-2575
Email:	yukonmotel@northwestel.net
Website:	www.yukonmotel.com

GPS Location: 60.16778 N, 132.70861 W, 2,300 Ft.

The Yukon Motel in Teslin is a large modern facility with a motel, a very popular restaurant, cocktail lounge, gas station, post office, and wildlife museum. It sits near the bridge on Nisutlin Bay.

Below the restaurant in a large open flat area near the water is a large RV park. There are about 70 sites. Forty are pull-thrus to 60 feet. Most sites offer electricity (20 or 30 amp) and water, there are also a few dry sites. Restrooms have flush toilets and showers and there is a laundry, a dump station, and a vehicle wash. Wi-Fi is a hot spot at the coffee shop. There is a dump station, it can also be used by non-guests with a fuel fill-up.

The campground is located near Km 1,243 (Historic Mile 804) of the Alaska Highway in the small town of Teslin.

298

 TESLIN LAKE CAMPGROUND (YUKON GOV.)
   Location: Near Km 1,258 Of The Alaska Highway
   Telephone: (867) 667-5648

GPS Location: 60.23250 N, 132.91056 W, 2,300 Ft.

This is a government campground set in trees overlooking Teslin Lake. There are 27 spaces, six are long parallel-types that are good for RVs to 45 feet. Of course there are picnic tables, fire pits, vault toilets, a picnic shelter, water pump, and free firewood. Fishing in the lake is good for lake trout, and you can hike the beach. There is a boat launch, but it's a short distance north of the campground.

TIMBER POINT CAMPGROUND
   Location: Near Km 1278 Of The Alaska Highway

GPS Location: 60.37466 N, 133.11928 W, 2,300 Ft.

This is a new campground in a large grassy field overlooking Teslin Lake next to the owner's house. Camp sites are not delineated, park where you like but watch for soft spots. There are picnic tables, free firewood, and outhouses. Wi-Fi comes from the house. While the campsite itself is not directly next to the lake there's a short trail to the beach.

JOHNSON'S CROSSING CAMPGROUND SERVICES

   Address: Km 1296 Alaska Highway,
                  Johnson's Crossing, Yukon Y1A 9Z0
   Telephone: (867) 390-2607
   Website: www.johnsoncrossing.ca

GPS Location: 60.48306 N, 133.30722 W, 2,300 Ft.

Johnson's Crossing is a roadhouse in a historic location with a pretty good campground. The roadhouse building houses a souvenir shop and small grocery store as well as a bakery (specializing in cinnamon rolls) and restaurant. It sits on the shore of the Teslin River near Teslin Lake and offers good grayling fishing in the river and lake fishing for lake trout nearby.

The campground is set in trees with separated sites. There are about 35 sites, many of them are pull-thrus to 40 feet. Full hookup (30 amp), partial hookup, dry, and tent sites are available. Fire rings and picnic tables are provided and there is also a dump station. A wash house has flush toilets and pay showers.

The roadhouse is located near Km 1,296 of the Alaska Highway and is open all year.

SQUANGA LAKE CAMPGROUND (YUKON GOV.)
   Location: Near Km 1,316 Of The Alaska Highway
   Telephone: (867) 667-5648

GPS Location: 60.44722 N, 133.60250 W, 2,700 Ft.

This small government campground has 16 vehicle spaces, one is a pull-thru. There are also some tent sites. Some larger sites in this campground are suitable for RVs to 40 feet. None are on the lake. If you're towing and want to check the campground out there is a loop so you can turn around. The campground has picnic tables, fire pits, free firewood, vault toilets, a picnic shelter, a water pump, and a boat launch. You can fish here for pike, grayling, and rainbows.

■ MARSH LAKE CAMPGROUND (YUKON GOV.)

Location: Near Km 1,379 Of The Alaska Highway
Telephone: (867) 667-5648

GPS Location: 60.55891 N, 134.44677 W, 2,200 Ft.

This large government campground has 41 separated sites off 2 loop roads. Nine are pull-thrus and 4 are tent sites. Many sites are suitable for RVs to 40 feet. Many are nicely set near the lake shore. There are picnic tables, fire pits, vault toilets, free firewood, and a picnic shelter.

■ THE CARIBOU RV PARK

Address: Km 1403 Alaska Highway, Whitehorse, Yukon Y1A 7A1
Telephone: (867) 668-2961
Email: caribourvpark@northwestel.net
Website: www.caribou-rv-park.com

GPS Location: 60.59792 N, 134.85256 W, 2,500 Ft.

The Caribou is located south of Whitehorse but near enough that you can easily drive in to see the sights. The campground has a wilderness feeling although it's conveniently located next to the highway. This is a smaller campground, run by the owners.

There are 27 large sites with 30-amp electricity and water hookups. Most are closely-spaced pull-thrus to 60 feet. There are also many dry and tent sites, most in trees. Those treed sites have fire pits and firewood is available. Restrooms with showers are individual rooms with toilet, sink and shower. There is also a laundry. The campground has a dump station, a dishwashing station for tent campers and a vehicle washing station for RVers. Wi-Fi is free but there is a charge for heavier use. There's also a restaurant called the Wolf's Den next to the campground that specializes in Swiss dishes but also has North American favorites. The campground has quite a bit of undeveloped property and there are some short hiking trails.

The entrance road for the Caribou is located near Km 1,403 (Historic Mile 904) of the Alaska Highway. That's 16 km (10 miles) south of the southern access road into Whitehorse.

■ WOLF CREEK CAMPGROUND (YUKON GOV.)

Location: Near Km 1,408 Of The Alaska Highway
Telephone: (867) 667-5648

GPS Location: 60.60752 N, 134.94392 W, 2,400 Ft.

Wolf Creek Campground has 37 vehicle sites and additional tent sites arranged off a loop in a treed valley not far from Whitehorse. Eleven of the sites are pull-thrus and many sites will take RVs to 40 feet. They are gravel sites off a gravel access road. Wolf Creek runs right through the middle of the campground. There are picnic tables, fire pits, free firewood, a playground, water pumps, picnic shelters, and vault toilets. A hiking trail runs for three miles to a vista over the river.

157
52
105
14
55
160 Km
92
252 Km
nope

THE ALASKA HIGHWAY

✘ SIDE TRIP TO TAGISH ROAD AND ATLIN ⚐
55 Kilometers (34 Miles)

At Km 1,342 of the Alaska Highway another road, Yukon Highway 8 (the Tagish Road), leads 55 kilometers (34 miles) west to a junction with the Skagway-Whitehorse highway (Klondike Highway 2) at Carcross. Just 2 kilometers (1 mile) down the Tagish Road is another junction, this one with Yukon Highway 7 to Atlin.

If you are bound for Skagway Highway 8 provides a shortcut. The entire road is paved. There are three campgrounds along this road. They are described below.

The road south to Atlin follows the shore of Little Atlin Lake and then Atlin Lake. It's very scenic and a road suitable for any RV. Much is now paved. Last time we visited paving was finished or underway for 52 km (33 miles) of the 92 km (57 mile) total distance.

The town of **Atlin** is a destination in itself, in fact Atlin has been promoted as a tourist destination since at least 1917. In those days visitors would arrive on boats. The route was from Carcross across Tagish Lake and up Taku Arm, by railroad on a 3.2 km (2 mile) line from Taku Landing to Scotia Bay, and then across Atlin Lake. The **MV Tarahne**, which you will see on the shore in Atlin, was used for this run.

The population of Atlin is about 400 people. This was originally a gold rush town.

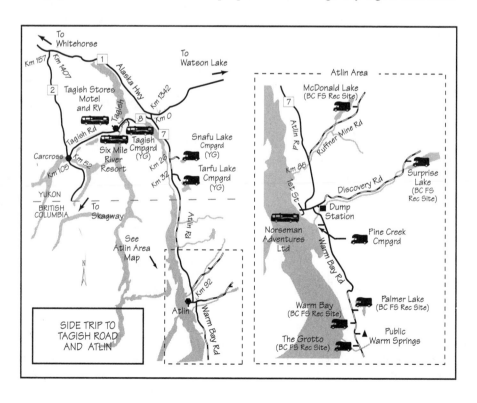

The first rush was in 1899 and gold was mined here using dredges for many years after that. To get oriented you'll want to visit the **Tourist Information Center** at the **Atlin Historical Museum** at the corner of Third Street and Trainor Avenue (PO Box 365, Atlin, B.C., V0W 1A0; 250 651-7522). Other attractions in town include the **Globe Theatre** and the **MV Tarahne**.

Exploring the roads to outlying destinations near Atlin can be fun if you have a suitable vehicle. Five B.C. Forest Service campgrounds are located on these roads, see the campground descriptions below for detailed information about access to them. Here's a general description.

You can drive out **Discovery Road** about a mile to the **Pioneer Cemetery** near the airport. Beyond are tailing piles from mining operations, some are being actively reprocessed and mined. There is a public **gold-panning area** on Spruce Creek Road. To get there drive out Discovery Road for 5.8 km (3.6 miles) and turn right onto Spruce Creek road, the panning area is 1.4 km (.9 mile) down this road. It is possible to drive out Discovery Road to the dam on **Surprise Lake**, a distance of 19 km (12 miles) from town. Just beyond is a B.C. Forest Service campground, described below. **Warm Bay Road** runs south for 26.7 km (16.6 miles) past Pine Creek Campground and provides access to three small B.C. Forest Service campgrounds, described below. Also out this road is **Warm Spring** at Km 23.3 (Mile 14.5) which is a small warm swimming hole. Warm Bay Road cuts off Discovery road to the south just a short distance outside town. Finally, you can drive out **Ruffner Mine Road** where you'll find another small B.C. Forest Service campground, also described below. The Ruffner Mine Road leaves Hwy 7 about 10.2 km (6.3 miles) north of Atlin and heads inland.

Atlin has a campground in town with hookups and another with no hookups not far out of town, both are listed below. Also listed below are small B.C. Forest Service campgrounds with very limited facilities on the small outlying roads that are suitable for smaller RVs. There is a well-signed primitive dump station about 4 km (2.5 miles) out of town on Discovery Road.

Tagish Road and Atlin Campgrounds

TAGISH CAMPGROUND (YUKON GOV., MANAGED BY CARCROSS FIRST NATION)

Location: Km 20.4 Of Hwy. 8 (The Tagish Road)
Telephone: (867) 821-4251

GPS Location: 60.31633 N, 134.25583 W, 2,200 Ft.

The Tagish Campground has 35 sites. In the trees are a variety of back-in and pull-thru sites, some are suitable for large RVs to 40 feet. In an open gravel lot next to the highway are seven very large pull through sites. Sites have picnic tables and fire pits and there are vault toilets as well as a kitchen shelter. This campground is located near the Six Mile River channel between Marsh Lake and Tagish Lake, there is a boat ramp.

The campground is located on the south side of the highway some 20.4 km (12.7 miles) from Jake's Corner at Km 1,342 of the Alaska Highway. It is just east of the Tagish River Bridge.

☐ TAGISH STORES MOTEL AND RV

Location:	Km 22 On Hwy. 8
Address:	(PO Box 101), Tagish, Yukon Y0B 1T0
Telephone:	(867) 399-3032
Email:	kurt.gantner@yukontagishstores.com
Website:	www.yukontagishstores.com

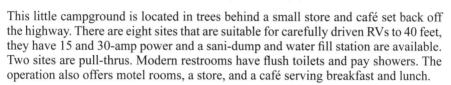

GPS Location: 60.30806 N, 134.27250 W, 2,200 Ft.

This little campground is located in trees behind a small store and café set back off the highway. There are eight sites that are suitable for carefully driven RVs to 40 feet, they have 15 and 30-amp power and a sani-dump and water fill station are available. Two sites are pull-thrus. Modern restrooms have flush toilets and pay showers. The operation also offers motel rooms, a store, and a café serving breakfast and lunch.

The campground is located on the north side of the Tagish Road at Km 22 in the settlement of Tagish. This is 22 km (14 miles) from Jake's Corner at Km 1,342 of the Alaska Highway, just a short distance west of the Tagish River Bridge.

☐ SIX MILE RIVER RESORT

Location:	Km 22 on Hwy. 8
Telephone:	(867) 399-4121
Email:	info@sixmileriverresort.com
Website:	www.sixmileriverresort.com

GPS Location: 60.30901 N, 134.2716 W, 2,200 Ft.

This recently opened RV park is located along the Six Mile River between Tagish Lake and Marsh Lake. There are seven RV sites with electricity and water for rigs to 35 feet as well as tent sites. Amenities include rooms, restaurant, and restrooms with flush toilets and showers. There are also canoe, kayak and skiff rentals and a community fire pit.

You'll find the resort entrance along the Tagish Highway. It's just west of the Tagish Bridge and across the highway from the Tagish Stores Motel and RV, described above. This is 22 km (14 miles) from Jake's Corner at Km 1,342 of the Alaska Highway, just a short distance west of the Tagish River Bridge.

☐ SNAFU LAKE CAMPGROUND (YUKON GOV.)

Location:	Km 26.2 Of The Atlin Road
Telephone:	(867) 667-5648

GPS Location: 60.13444 N, 133.80889 W, 2,500 Ft.

This campground has 10 sites next to Snafu Lake. Sites have picnic tables and fire pits and there are outhouses and a boat ramp. Due to the access road, small sites, and limited maneuvering room this campground is only suitable for RVs to about 30 feet or small trailers. Access is via a 1.3 km (.7 mile) dirt road from Km 26.2 of the Atlin Road.

☐ TARFU LAKE CAMPGROUND (YUKON GOV.)

Location:	Km 32.1 Of The Atlin Road
Telephone:	(867) 667-5648

GPS Location: 60.06361 N, 133.75444 W, 2,500 Ft.

This campground has 10 sometimes poorly defined sites arranged in pines and aspens near Tarfu Lake. Due to the access road and uneven sites it is probably only suitable for RVs to about 30 feet. There are picnic tables at some sites and fire pits. Outhouses are provided. The campground is on a hillside above Tarfu Lake and has a boat ramp. The access road is narrow and rough, it leads 3.7 km (2.3 miles) east from Km 32.1 of the Atlin Road.

NORSEMAN ADVENTURES LTD.

Address:	Box 184, Mill Street, Atlin B.C. V0W 1A0
Telephone:	(250) 651-7535 or (604) 823-2259 (Winter)
Email:	vig@uniserve.com
Website:	www.atlin.net/norseman/

GPS Location: 59.56890 N, 133.70308 W, 2,200 Ft.

Norseman Adventures is a campground and simple marina in Atlin. The campground has a beautiful situation on the lakeshore, there are 14 sites with electricity (either 15 or 30 amp) and water hookups. Some sites have picnic tables and all are suitable for any size RV since sites are long back-ins on solid gravel above the beach. The only restroom is a portable toilet so there are no showers. Although the campground does not have a dump station there is one outside town. Birdwatchers will love the marsh across the street.

When you arrive in Atlin just make your way down to First Street near the lake and then follow it south until it curves to the right, you'll see the campground on the lakeshore.

THE VIEW FROM THE NORSEMAN ADVENTURES LTD CAMPGROUND IS UNFORGETABLE

PINE CREEK CAMPGROUND
Location: Km 2.2 Warm Bay Road
GPS Location: 59.56056 N, 133.66639 W, 2,300 Ft.

The Pine Creek Campground is a community campground in a forest setting with 12 vehicle sites off two loops as well as 6 tent sites. Each site has a picnic table and fire drum or ring, restrooms are outhouses. Firewood is usually provided. It is suitable for RVs to about 30 feet.

To reach the campground drive out Discovery Road for about .3 km (.2 miles) and turn right on Warm Bay Road. You'll see the campground on your right 2.2 km (1.4 mile) from the turn.

SURPRISE LAKE BC FOREST SERVICE RECREATION SITE
Location: Km 18.7 Discovery Road
GPS Location: 59.63186 N, 133.42049 W, 3,000 Ft.

The Surprise Lake campground has five sites with picnic tables and fire rings. There are also outhouses and a primitive boat launch area. The campground is on the north shore of Surprise Lake with one site near the road and four more in an open area near the lakeshore. Surprise Lake is a large lake known for its grayling fishing.

To reach the campground head out Discovery Road for 18.7 km (11.6 miles). The entrance is on the right about .5 km (.3 mile) beyond the bridge at the foot of the lake. The road to the lake is good gravel but the we recommend the campground only for small RVs to 25 feet because the campground access road is narrow and steep.

PALMER LAKE BC FOREST SERVICE RECREATION SITE
Location: Km 18.7 Warm Springs Road
GPS Location: 59.43763 N, 133.58310 W, 2,300 Ft.

This small campground has only two sites. They are next to the lake and suitable for RVs to about 30 feet. Watch for soft spots. There are picnic tables, fire pits and an outhouse. This is a free user-maintained campground. Palmer Lake is good for canoes and kayaks, it has pike and whitefish.

Follow directions to Pine Creek Campground, then continue another 16.5 km (10.2 miles) to the campground, it's on the left. Warm Bay Road is paved for the first 8.2 km (5.1 miles), then is good gravel beyond.

WARM BAY BC FOREST SERVICE RECREATION SITE
Location: Km 22.1 Warm Springs Road
GPS Location: 59.41087 N, 133.57758 W, 2,200 Ft.

The Warm Bay Campground is next to a gravel beach on Atlin Lake. It has 5 sites, most are suitable for RVs to 30 feet. There are picnic tables, fire rings, and outhouses; and small boats can be launched directly across the solid gravel beach. This is a free user-maintained campground.

Warm Bay is named for the nearby Warm Springs, a short distance inland. To get there drive to Km 23.7 of Warm Springs Road, about 1.6 km (1 mile) beyond the campground, the entrance road is on the left. The springs surface in a nice little pool in a meadow, the water is slightly warm, not hot. There is one picnic table and an old outhouse.

To find Warm Bay Campground follow directions to Pine Creek Campground, then continue another 19.9 km (12.3 miles) to the campground, it's on the right. Warm Bay Road is paved for the first 8.2 km (5.1 miles), then is good gravel.

⛺ The Grotto BC Forest Service Recreation Site

Location:　　Km 25.8 Warm Springs Road

GPS Location: 59.38337 N, 133.55698 W, 2,400 Ft.

This small camping area has two vehicle sites and a walk-in tent site. There are picnic tables and fire pits. A beautiful stream runs by the sites, it forms a small arc around the tent site. The area is known as Grotto because of the stream running through rock formations in the forest. Sites are suitable only for small RVs to about 25 feet. This is a free user-maintained campground. Note that the Warm Springs, described above in the Warm Bay Campground listing, is nearby.

Follow directions to Pine Creek Campground, then continue another 23.6 km (14.6 miles) to the campground, it's on the right. Warm Bay Road is paved for the first 8.2 km (5.1 miles), then is good gravel.

⛺ McDonald Lake BC Forest Service Recreation Site

Location:　　9.7 Km Ruffner Mine Rd.

GPS Location: 59.71154 N, 133.57831 W, 3,000 Ft.

This is another small campground set along a remote lake. There are five sites with picnic tables and fire pits as well as an outhouse. Boats can be launched from a primitive ramp. McDonald Lakes are known for their grayling fishing.

From near Km 85 of Hwy. 7 (the Atlin access highway) Ruffner Mine Road heads east. It's a good gravel road for the first 7.1 km (4.4 miles), then it narrows and becomes soft surfaced as it crosses marshy areas. The campground is on the left at 9.7 km (6.0 miles). It is not suitable for large and heavy rigs. The extremely poor access road means this is a campground for tenters in small high-clearance vehicles, vans, and pickup campers.

Whitehorse
Population 24,000, Elevation 2,300 feet

Whitehorse is the capital of the Yukon Territory and by far the largest town with about 60% of the territory's population. This is the best place along the Alaska Highway for vehicle repairs, banking, grocery shopping, and acting like a tourist.

Whitehorse was founded during the Klondike gold rush. The section of river upriver from town, Miles Canyon and the White Horse Rapids, was so dangerous that two rail trams were built around it to portage the boats and goods of the prospectors floating down to Dawson City. This was also the head of navigation of the Yukon, a natural place for a town. Large steamboats could go no farther although other steamboats plied the waters of the lakes upstream. Very soon the railroad from Skagway tied Whitehorse to the sea and cemented Whitehorse's position as the supply center

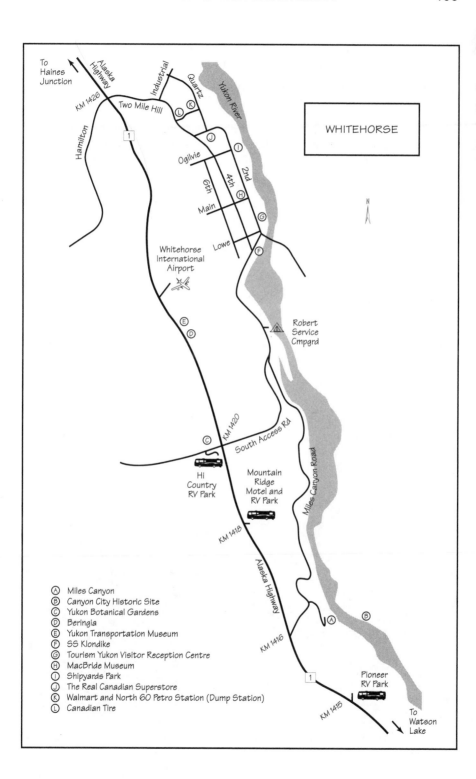

To Haines Junction

Alaska Highway

KM 1426

Two Mile Hill

Harmilton

Industrial

Quartz

Yukon River

Ⓛ Ⓚ

Ⓙ

Ⓘ

Ogilvie

6th

4th

2nd

Ⓗ

Main

Ⓖ

Lowe

Ⓕ

Whitehorse International Airport

WHITEHORSE

N

Ⓔ

Ⓓ

Robert Service Cmpgrd

Ⓒ

KM 1420

South Access Rd

Hi Country RV Park

Mountain Ridge Motel and RV Park

Miles Canyon Road

KM 1418

Alaska Highway

KM 1416

Ⓐ

Ⓑ

1

Pioneer RV Park

KM 1415

To Watson Lake

Ⓐ Miles Canyon
Ⓑ Canyon City Historic Site
Ⓒ Yukon Botanical Gardens
Ⓓ Beringia
Ⓔ Yukon Transportation Museum
Ⓕ SS Klondike
Ⓖ Tourism Yukon Visitor Reception Centre
Ⓗ MacBride Museum
Ⓘ Shipyards Park
Ⓙ The Real Canadian Superstore
Ⓚ Walmart and North 60 Petro Station (Dump Station)
Ⓛ Canadian Tire

for the Yukon. For a long time, though, Dawson City remained the capital of the territory, only in 1953 was the government moved to Whitehorse.

The large **Tourism Yukon Visitor Reception Centre** is located on 2nd Avenue and Lambert Street and offers parking for RVs (Box 2703, Whitehorse, Yukon, Y1A 2C6; 867 667-3084). The town is well supplied with interesting things to see and do. Those aimed specifically at the tourist trade include the excellent **Frantic Follies Vaudeville Revue** at the Westmark Hotel, the **MV Schwatka** tour of Miles Canyon, the **Yukon Botanical Gardens**, and the **SS Klondike** restored riverboat. Tickets and transportation to most of these are available at RV parks. You might also find the town's museums to be interesting. The **MacBride Museum** is located downtown and has gold rush-era exhibits. The **Yukon Transportation Museum** at the airport covers the full range of transportation in the Yukon. Finally, **Beringia**, also near the airport, has displays covering the ice age era when this particular region was ice free and home to woolly mammoths. After all those museums you might find a visit to the Yukon's only brewery to be inviting, the **Yukon Brewing Company** offers tours and samples (867 668-4183).

An interesting hike is the one to Canyon City. Drive to Km 1,416 of the Alaska Highway and follow the Miles Canyon Road .5 km (.3 Mile) to a Y and then turn right to a parking lot. A trail leads to a suspension bridge across **Miles Canyon**. Turn right on the far side of the river and in another 1.7 km (1.1 mile) you'll come to the site of the gold rush town of **Canyon City**. Boats coming down river offloaded here and trams carried passengers and goods downstream past the rapids. Not much remains

ONE OF THE WORLD'S LARGEST WIND VANES IS IN FRONT OF THE WHITEHORSE AIRPORT

THE ALASKA HIGHWAY

except the site and the former tram grades. If you enjoy walking you'll find that the hike above covers only part of a well developed trail system along both sides of the river upstream of central Whitehorse, the **fish ladder** on the right bank is accessible from this trail and the float planes on **Schwatka Lake** are also interesting.

Whitehorse has two **golf courses** that are open to the public: Meadow Lakes Golf and Country Club (867 668-4653) with 9 holes and Mountain View Club with 18 holes (867 633-6020).

There is enough to see and do in Whitehorse to justify several days of visiting. Whitehorse is also something of a crossroads so you may find yourself here more than once. From Whitehorse the Klondike Highway leads south to Skagway and the Klondike Loop leads northward to Dawson City. The Alaska Highway and this chapter lead west toward Haines Junction and Alaska.

Whitehorse Campgrounds

See also Caribou RV Park, page 96; Wolf Creek Campground, page 96, and Takhini Hot Springs, page 357.

PIONEER RV PARK

Address:	91091 Alaska Highway, Whitehorse, Yukon Y1A 5V9
Telephone:	(867) 668-5944
Res.:	(866) 626-7383
Email:	info@pioneer-rv-park.com
Website:	www.pioneer-rv-park.com

GPS Location: 60.64958 N, 135.02064 W, 2,400 Ft.

The Pioneer is a very large and popular RV park located some four miles from downtown Whitehorse. There are about 150 sites with something to please almost everyone. Sites include full and partial hookups (30-amp outlets), pull-thrus to 70 feet, back-ins in the trees, and dry or tent sites. Especially nice are some large electric/ water sites in the trees behind and above the park. TV hookups are available, free (quantity limited) Wi-Fi reaches the lower sites and some of the upper, and there are two dump stations. Other amenities include showers; laundry; small grocery store; a recreation hall; breakfast service; gas, diesel and propane sales; a gift shop; a pet wash room: and a RV wash facility. You can get tickets here for most of the tours and attractions in Whitehorse and bus service into town is available.

The campground is located near Km 1,415 of the Alaska Highway. This is 4.5 km (2.8 miles) south of the highway's junction with the South Access Road to downtown Whitehorse, about 6.5 km (4 miles) from downtown Whitehorse.

MOUNTAIN RIDGE MOTEL AND RV PARK

Address:	Mile 91297 Alaska Highway (PO Box 34027), Whitehorse, Yukon Y1A 7A3
Telephone:	(867) 667-4202, (888) 667-4202
Email:	info@mtnridge.ca
Website:	www.mtnridge.ca

GPS Location: 60.67472 N, 135.05250 W, 2,400 Ft.

The small Mountain Ridge Motel has 12 pull-thru sites with full hookups. These are large sites for RV combos to 60 feet. Three have 30-amp service and the remainder have 20 amp. There are two restrooms with showers and a laundry accessible to those camping in the sites. The Mountain Ridge Motel is located near Km 1,418 of the Alaska Highway. This is 1.1 km (.7 mile) south of the South Access Road junction. It is open all year long.

HI COUNTRY RV PARK

Address:	91374 Alaska Highway, Whitehorse, Yukon Y1A 6E4
Telephone:	(867) 667-7445 or (877) 458-3806
Email:	hicountryrv@polarcom.com
Website:	www.hicountryrvyukon.com

GPS Location: 60.68336 N, 135.06025 W, 2,400 Ft.

This is a good Whitehorse campground. It is close enough to town for convenience and has campsites with trees and decent facilities.

The Hi Country has about 130 sites. They are set in spruce and pines and are fairly close together, but small trees and shrubs separate most of them. There are a variety of sites. Large pull-thrus to 50 feet with full hookups including TV are available as well as water and electric back-ins and dry sites in trees. All sites have picnic tables and fire pits. They have good restroom facilities with showers, a laundry, a convenience/tourist shop, pressure vehicle washing facilities, and a dump station. Firewood can be purchased. Bus transportation in to town is available from a stop out front.

The Hi Country is located just off the Alaska Highway. Turn west (away from town) at the intersection of the Alaska Highway with Robert Service Way (South Access Road) near Km 1,420. In just a short distance turn left into the access road to the campground.

ROBERT SERVICE CAMPGROUND

Address:	Box 33137, Whitehorse, Yukon Y1A 6S1
Telephone:	(867) 668-3721 (summer)
Email:	rsc@klondikeer.com
Website:	www.robertservicecampground.com

GPS Location: 60.70117 N, 135.04751 W, 2,100 Ft.

Whitehorse has a tent-only campground located within easy walking distance of downtown. The Robert Service Campground has about 65 tent sites set in the woods near the river. Sites have picnic tables and fire pits. Even though this campground is intended for tent campers, small RVs (vans and pickup campers) are accommodated, they assign you a tent site with a parking slot nearby. There are flush toilets and showers (extra charge), a small coffee shop with a few baked goods and Wi-Fi (for a fee), firewood , and a picnic shelter.

To reach the campground from downtown walk or drive south along the river. You'll end up on what is called the South Access Road and soon see the campground sign on the left.

FROM WHITEHORSE TO TOK
639 Kilometers (396 Miles)

The Alaska Highway from Whitehorse to Tok is paved, but much of it is in poor condition. This is where you will meet the nemesis of road maintenance in the north, the frost heave. Frost heaves are the result of building roads across permafrost, and they are virtually impossible for road builders to conquer. These unpredictable dips and mounds mean that you must often hold your speed down, especially if you are driving a large RV or pulling a trailer. The road gets better each year but it pays to stay alert.

Because of the condition of the road it is important to take it easy on this section of highway. You might consider covering it in two days rather than one. We like to overnight at one of the campgrounds near beautiful Kluane Lake.

Almost immediately after leaving Whitehorse you will come to the junction with Highway 2 north to Dawson City. This road, known as the Klondike Loop, is covered in Chapter 11 of this book.

Continuing west the next important settlement is **Haines Junction** at Km 1,579. Watch yourself in Haines Junction, if you aren't alert you'll end up on the road to Haines rather than the Alaska Highway to Tok. The 245 kilometer (152 mile) long Haines Highway is covered in Chapter 12 of this book. Haines Junction serves as the jump-off point for expeditions into Kluane National Park. This small town of about 800 has the **Kluane National Park Visitors Center** (PO Box 5495, Haines Junction, Yukon YOB 1L0; 867 634-2345), as well as stores, restaurants, gas stations, and RV parks.

From Haines Junction the highway gradually climbs over 3,280 foot **Bear Creek Summit** and then descends to skirt the west side of emerald green **Kluane Lake**. Near the southwest shore of the lake at Km 1,649 is Kluane Park's **Tachal Dahl** visitor center where Dall sheep are often seen in the spring and fall.

Kluane Lake is the largest lake in the Yukon and there are two communities–**Burwash Landing** and **Destruction Bay**–and several campgrounds along its length. The lake's unusual color is caused by glacial silt suspended in the water and reflecting the sky.

After Kluane Lake the road deteriorates somewhat because of swampy ground and permafrost. Construction and reconstruction is constant here and you may run into sections of gravel. On the other hand, there are also some sections of brand-new beautiful highway.

At Km 1,871 is the little town of **Beaver Creek**. This is the site of the Canadian border station and also of several hotels and a good RV park.

You reach the **Alaska border** at Km 1,903 (Historic Mile 1221.8). At the top of the hill is the U.S. border station and customs. There is usually little or no delay.

At this point distance markers change again. Now you're back in the U.S. and the markers are mileposts again. They start at the border at 1221.8 and continue to count

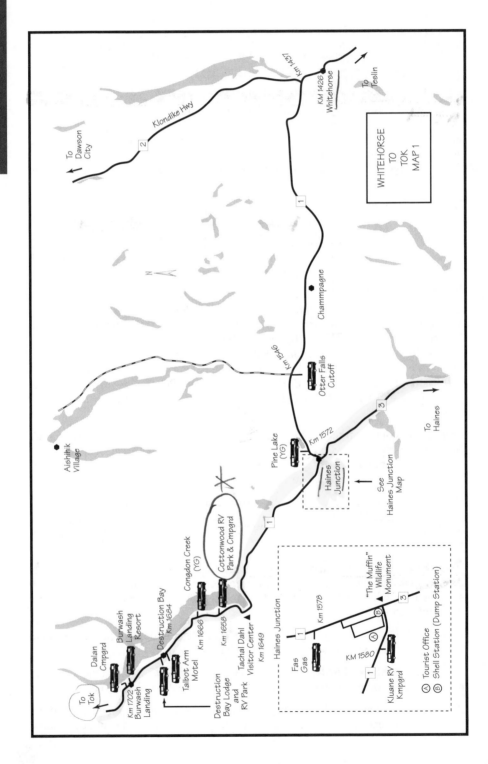

up until reaching Delta Junction, the end of the Alaska Highway.

With recent improvements to the Alaska Highway on the Canadian side you may not notice much difference in the road on the Alaska side. Not many years ago crossing the border brought pure bliss, smooth pavement after more than 1,200 miles of gravel. From the border you can reach the first Alaska town of any size, Tok, in a little over an hour and a half, the distance is 92 miles (148 km).

Whitehorse to Tok Campgrounds

OTTER FALLS CUTOFF

Address:	Mile 995 Alaska Highway (Box 5450), Haines Jct., Yukon Y0B 1L0
Telephone:	(867) 634-2812
Email:	info@otterfallscutoff.com
Website:	www.otterfallscutoff.com

GPS Location: 60.85443 N, 137.03420 W, 2,300 Ft.

The Otter Falls Cutoff is a combination gas station, grocery store, restaurant, and RV park along a section of the highway that doesn't have many other establishments of any kind, including campgrounds. It's a good place to stay if you want to take a side trip to see Otter Falls, 28.6 km (17.4 miles) up Aishihik Road. These falls are the ones that were shown on the back of the old Canadian five-dollar bill. That road isn't suitable for large RVs.

There are about 50 sites. Most have either 20 or 30-amp electrical outlets and water, a few also have sewer. There are also some sites without power next to the trees, these are also used as tent sites. A central area has fire pits and some picnic tables. Showers are available for a fee and there is a playground. There is also a dump station. A bird watching trail runs quite a distance into the woods at the back of the campground and there is fishing nearby.

The Otter Falls Cutoff is at the junction with Aishihik Road at Km 1,546 of the Alaska Highway. This is 121 Km (75 miles) west of Whitehorse and 33 kilometers (20 miles) east of Haines Junction.

PINE LAKE CAMPGROUND (YUKON GOVERNMENT)

Location:	Km 1,572 Of The Alaska Highway
Telephone:	(867) 667-5648

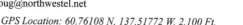

GPS Location: 60.79914 N, 137.48838 W, 2,200 Ft.

This government campground is located just outside Haines Junction, gateway to the Kluane National Park. There are 42 sites here, 6 are pull-thrus (to 60 feet, but narrow), and some of the back-ins are long (to 50 feet, and wider). All sites have picnic tables and fire pits and are well-separated with spruce trees and other natural vegetation. There are vault toilets, a covered kitchen and picnic area, a water tap, a boat launch, free firewood, and swimming in Pine Lake for the hardy.

FAS GAS

Address:	PO Box 5345, Haines Junction, Yukon Y0B 1L0
Telephone:	(867) 634-2505
Email:	vandoug@northwestel.net

GPS Location: 60.76108 N, 137.51772 W, 2,100 Ft.

About the first thing you see when you approach Haines Junction from the White-horse direction is a Fas Gas station on the north side of the road. They have 21 RV spaces with electricity and water hookups in an open area next to the station. There are a few picnic tables. Nine sites are pull-thrus to 45 feet. There is also a sani-dump. The price of an overnight stay includes a water fill-up and a holding tank dump. This facility recently changed hands so you might find some changes when you visit.

◼ KLUANE RV KAMPGROUND

Address:	Box 5496, Haines Junction, Yukon Y0B 1L0
Telephone:	(867) 634-2709 or (866) 634-6789
Email:	kluanerv@northwestel.net
Website:	www.kluanerv.ca

GPS Location: 60.75275 N, 137.52111 W, 2,000 Ft.

This is the largest full-service RV park in Haines Junction. There are about 100 spaces, most are pull-thrus to 60 feet and there is lots of room for parking and ma-neuvering since these are in a large open gravel field. Additional sites are located in a wooded area. Full hookup, partial hookup, and dry sites are available, as are tent sites. There are some picnic tables but not at most sites. The Kluane has restrooms and pay showers (individual rooms) in the main building as well as a small store and laundry. TV hookups are available and there is also a dump station, a vehicle wash, and a service station with gas, diesel, and propane. Wi-Fi doesn't reach the sites, you must use it in or near the main building. A good 5 km (3 mile) hiking trail leads from the campground.

The campground is located at Km 1,580 of the Alaska Highway, about 1.1 km (.7 mile) west of the junction.

◼ COTTONWOOD RV PARK AND CAMPGROUND

Address:	Historic Mile 1067 Alaska Highway, Destruction Bay, Yukon Y0B 1H0
Telephone:	(867) 841-4066
Email:	glen.brough@sympatico.ca
Website:	www.yukonweb.com/tourism/cottonwood/

GPS Location: 61.08780 N, 138.53503 W, 2,600 Ft.

 The Cottonwood is one of our favorite stops along the Alaska Highway. It is a beauti-ful campground in a beautiful location.

The campground must have at least 50 camping sites of various types scattered along the shore of Kluane Lake. The small trees and shrubs that occur naturally in the area separate the sites, much like in a government campground. About 30 sites have electricity and 20 of these also have water hookups. The electric-only sites are on the waterfront while many of the water and electric sites are pull-thrus to 40 feet. Sites have fire pits and picnic tables. The restroom building has flush toilets and free showers. Power here is produced by a generator but the noise is almost impossible to hear from the camping sites and the generator operates 24 hours. There are also two rental cabins, a small grocery and gift store, a laundry, Gopher Golf (mini golf), and dump and water fill stations.

The campground is located at Km 1,658 of the Alaska Highway, about 26 km (16 miles) south of Destruction Bay and on the shore of Kluane Lake.

THE COTTONWOOD RV PARK IS A BEAUTIFUL CAMPGROUND IN A BEAUTIFUL LOCATION

CONGDON CREEK CAMPGROUND (YUKON GOVERNMENT)

Location:	Near Km 1,666 Of The Alaska Highway
Telephone:	(867) 667-5648

GPS Location: 61.15240 N, 138.55099 W, 2,700 Ft.

Congdon Creek is a large government campground adjoining Kluane Lake. There are some 80 spaces usually open, some are pull-thrus. They are well separated and set in spruce and alder, many are along the lakeshore. All have fire pits and picnic tables. Sites here are mostly large, it's a good campground for today's large RVs. In fact, RVs are preferred during some periods, bears can be a problem from mid July until September. Tents are usually allowed, but a sign at the entrance warns that bears like the local soap berries and may create problems and closures. The campground also offers vault toilets, free firewood, kitchen shelters, hand-operated water pump, playground and a boat launch.

TALBOT ARM MOTEL

Address:	Box M, Destruction Bay, Yukon Y0B 1H0
Telephone:	(867) 841-4461
Email:	talbotarm@northwestel.net
Website:	www.talbotarm.com

GPS Location: 61.25176 N, 138.80442 W, 2,700 Ft.

The Talbot Arm is a motel and restaurant with gift shop and gas sales. At the north end of the motel building there are about four usable RV sites with electricity but no water or sewer. Water is available, however, as is a dump station, and there are showers and restrooms.

The Talbot Arm is on the west side of the Alaska Highway near Km 1684.

DESTRUCTION BAY LODGE AND RV PARK

Address:	Historic Mile 1,083 Alaska Highway (PO Box 48), Destruction Bay, Yukon Y0B 1V0
Telephone:	(867) 841-5332 or (867) 841-4332
Email:	d-baylodge@northwestel.net or yukoneze@yahoo.ca

GPS Location: 61.25334 N, 138.80820 W, 2,700 Ft.

The camping slots at this facility occupy a large gravel lot beside and behind a lodge and restaurant that is often not open. There are 27 pull-thru sites to 80 feet with water and electric (30-amp) hookups. There are also 16 back-ins with 20-amp and water hookups and space for dry camping. Restrooms are individual rooms with toilet and free shower. There is also a laundry and a dump station. RV washing is allowed at your site.

Destruction Bay Lodge is near Km 1,684 of the Alaska Highway.

BURWASH LANDING RESORT

Address:	Historic Mile 1,093 Alaska Highway, Burwash Landing, Yukon Y0B 1V0
Telephone:	(867) 841-4441
Email:	blresort@northwestel.net

GPS Location: 61.35772 N, 138.99736 W, 2,600 Ft.

This old-time resort on the shore of Kluane Lake has 6 back-in (or pull-in) sites with electricity (20 amp) and water hookups situated along the water next to a restaurant/bar/lodge. The site is an open gravel area and visitors to the lodge park in pretty much the same lot. Since this is just a gravel lot any size RV will fit although larger RVs will be a bit of a parking obstacle. There's also a nice grass covered tent camping area away from the parking lot making this one of the best tent-camping campgrounds in the area. There are picnic tables in the tent area. Showers are available in the lodge for an extra fee and the restaurant is popular with locals and travelers. The Wi-Fi is only useable in the lodge. There's also a dump station.

To reach the camping area turn in at the sign near a gas station near Km 1,701. Drive down to the lake, a distance of about .5 km (.3 miles).

DALAN CAMPGROUND

Location:	Km 1702 Alaska Highway

GPS Location: 61.36543 N, 138.99959 W, 2,600 Ft.

Formerly a Yukon Government campground and then run by the Kluane First Nation, this campground may soon be closed. When we visited no fee was being charged and there was no signage, but the gate was open and facilities were clean and useable. The entry road is mostly unpaved, it's about 1.2 km long. There are 24 separated sites, three are large pull-thrus and there are back-ins to 45 feet. Several sites are

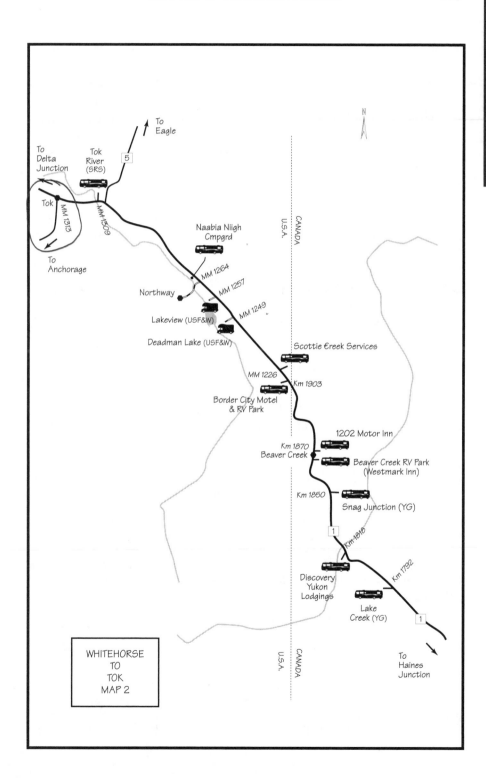

To Eagle

To Delta Junction

Tok River (SRS)

5

Tok

MM 1313

MM 1509

To Anchorage

Naabia Niigh Cmpgrd

MM 1264

MM 1257

Northway

MM 1249

Lakeview (USF&W)

Deadman Lake (USF&W)

Scottie Creek Services

MM 1226

Km 1903

Border City Motel & RV Park

1202 Motor Inn

Km 1870
Beaver Creek

Beaver Creek RV Park (Westmark Inn)

Km 1850

Snag Junction (YG)

1

Km 1818

Discovery Yukon Lodgings

Km 1792

Lake Creek (YG)

1

To Haines Junction

N

CANADA
U.S.A.

U.S.A.
CANADA

WHITEHORSE
TO
TOK
MAP 2

near the lake shore. There are picnic tables, fire pits, free firewood, hauled-in water, outhouses, a covered picnic shelter, and even a dump station.

The 1.2 km (.7 mile) access road leaves the Alaska Highway near Kilometer 1,702. It's not currently marked for the campground, but is the first road north of the entrance for Burwash Landing Resort. It has a sign for Burwash Heights Subdivision. Drive .4 km (.2 mile) down the road and turn left into the campground entrance road.

LAKE CREEK CAMPGROUND (YUKON GOVERNMENT)

Location: Near Km 1,792 Of The Alaska Highway
Telephone: (867) 667-5648

GPS Location: 61.85617 N, 140.15171 W, 2,300 Ft.

This 28-site government campground has large separated sites, thirteen are pull-thrus, some to 70 feet, and several border the creek. There are picnic tables, fire pits, free firewood, vault toilets, a kitchen shelter, and a hand water pump. The road through the campground has a turn-around loop at the end so it's easy to take a look.

DISCOVERY YUKON LODGINGS *Stayed here* (FORMERLY WHITE RIVER RV PARK) *on way back*

Address: Historic Mile 1169 Alaska Highway, Yukon Y0B 1A0
Telephone: (867) 862-7408
Email: info@discoveryyukon.com
Website: www.discoveryyukon.com

GPS Location: 61.98527 N, 140.53778 W, 2,300 Ft.

Just south of the White River Bridge you'll spot a park-like camping area in trees to the south of the highway. Arranged around the grounds is a collection of vintage heavy equipment, much of it actually used in constructing the Alcan.

Discovery Yukon Lodgings offers a large RV and tent camping area. Sites are set in a grassy area to the east of the old lodge buildings, many trees provide some shade but the area is really pleasantly open. There are about 50 pull-thru sites with full hookups and 30-amp power as well as many more no hookup or tent sites. Some sites are as long as 60 feet. Some picnic tables are provided, there is a dump station, and also showers. Wi-Fi coverage in the RV area is very good. A central campfire area is active most nights, the owners take a lot of pleasure sharing their knowledge of the region. Sometimes they even take folks out in a classic WWII era truck for a tour, often including a bear sighting. The RV park is located at Km 1,818 of the Alaska Highway.

SNAG JUNCTION CAMPGROUND (YUKON GOVERNMENT)

Location: Near Km 1,850 Of The Alaska Highway
Telephone: (867) 667-5648

GPS Location: 62.23923 N, 140.68630 W, 2,300 Ft.

Snag Junction is a small government campground with 15 separated back-in and parallel-parking sites. Some are near a small lake and all have picnic tables and fire pits. A few sites stretch to 55 feet and there is a circular drive if you want to pull in and take a look without unhooking. There are vault toilets, free firewood, and a kitchen shelter.

186 miles from HJ

BEAVER CREEK RV PARK (FORMERLY WESTMARK INN AND RV PARK)

Address:	Historic Mile 1,202 Alaska Highway (PO Box 59), Beaver Creek, Yukon Y0B 1A0
Telephone:	(867) 862-7501

GPS Location: 62.38247 N, 140.87499 W, 2,600 Ft.

If you've been looking for 50-amp power and big sites you'll appreciate this campground although you'll have to use the dump station since sites have no sewer. There are 67 nicely-spaced sites here with electric (30 and 50 amp) and water hookups. Over half of them are large pull-thrus to 60 feet. Sites also have picnic tables and barbecues. Three tent sites with grass are at the back of the RV park. There are showers and flush toilets in the washrooms, there's also a laundry, a mini-mart, gas sales, and a dump station. There is Wi-Fi in the office/minimart/laundry building.

Watch for the campground just north of the Westmark Inn in Beaver Creek.

1202 MOTOR INN

Address:	Mile 1202 Alaska Highway, Beaver Creek, Yukon Y0B 1A0
Telephone:	(867) 862-7600, (800) 764-7601 (US), (800) 661-0540 (Canada)
Email:	1202motorinn@northwestel.net
Website:	www.1202motorinn.ca

GPS Location: 62.38725 N, 140.87336 W, 2,200 Ft.

The 1202 seems to be the most popular stop in Beaver Creek, their bakery, gift shop, and gas station are always busy. They also offer a basic campground. It is traditionally open all winter.

There are about 20 electric only sites. Ten are pull-thrus to 60 feet at the back of the property, the others are small back-ins along the side. Some sites have picnic tables. There is also a water fill area and a dump station. Wi-Fi is available inside the lodge, but can't be received in the camping area.

The campground is located in the town of Beaver Creek at Mile 1202 of the Alaska Highway, Km 1872. It's the place with the Fas Gas Plus sign.

BORDER CITY MOTEL & RV PARK

Address:	Mile 1,225 Alaska Highway, Alaska
Telephone:	(907) 774-2205
Email:	info@bordercitylodge.com
Website:	www.bordercitylodge.com

GPS Location: 62.66420 N, 141.05811 W, 1,900 Ft.

1225
1169
/55

Border City is the first stop north of the Alaska border. This is a large roadhouse with gas station, motel, and gift shop. In a field to the south, not far from the road, are 40 large pull-thru sites with 30-amp outlets and water suitable for RV combos to 80 feet. There are flush toilets and showers, and a dump station. Wi-Fi is free but can only be received close to the main building.

The motor inn is located at Mile 1,225 of the Alaska Highway, 3.7 miles (6 km) north of the U.S. Customs station.

SCOTTIE CREEK SERVICES

Location:	Mile 1,226 Alaska Hwy., HC 63 Box 1226, Tok, Alaska 99780
Telephone:	(907) 774-2009
Email:	scottiecreekenterprises@gmail.com

GPS Location: 62.67033 N, 141.06097 W, 1,900 Ft.

This gas station, convenience store, liquor store, and gift shop is on a hillside overlooking the highway and the Border City Lodge and offers no-frills sites with full hookups. The eight sites are on a flat area above and behind the station with large-rig access possible. Restrooms are in the main building.

DEADMAN LAKE CAMPGROUND (USF&W)

Location:	Near Mile 1,249 Of The Alaska Highway
Info:	(907) 883-5312

GPS Location: 62.88887 N, 141.54146 W, 1,800 Ft.

This is a small campground and the entrance is very easy to miss. The roads and spaces have recently been improved, it is suitable for RVs to 30 feet. A circular drive lets you turn around if you drive in for a look. There are 15 separated sites set in black spruce along Deadman Lake. Sites have picnic tables and fire pits and there are vault toilets. A screened picnic shelter is provided and there is sometimes a host. Water is hauled in. There's a boat ramp and dock and the lake is good for pike, there's also a nature trail. This is prime mosquito country. There's a 14-day stay limit. Leave the highway at about Mile 1,249 and follow the gravel and dirt road for 1.2 miles (1.8 km) to the campground.

LAKEVIEW CAMPGROUND (USF&W)

Location:	Near Mile 1,257 Of The Alaska Highway
Info:	(907) 883-5312

GPS Location: 62.96449 N, 141.64082 W, 1,800 Ft.

Another very small public campground, this one on Yarger Lake. There are 11 sites and little maneuvering room but there is a tight circular drive. A 30-foot RV is about the max for this campground. Sites have picnic tables and fire pits, and there is a vault toilet and a hand water pump. None of these sites are directly on the lake. There is a 14-day stay limit. The entrance road here is about .3 miles (.5 km) long.

NAABIA NIIGH CAMPGROUND

Address:	PO Box 476, Northway, AK 99764
Telephone:	(907) 778-2297

GPS Location: 63.01001 N, 141.80196 W, 1,800 Ft.

This facility is much more than a campground. It is a gas station, a small store, a laundry, and an unusual gift shop featuring authentic Athabascan birch bark and bead creations.

Behind and below the store there are 20 older back-in sites to 50 feet. Fifteen sites have full hookups (20 and 30 amp), the others have no utilities. Some sites have picnic tables and fire pits. Flush toilets and showers are located up in the laundry.

The campground is located at Mile 1,264 of the Alaska Highway.

Tok River State Recreation Site

Location: Near Mile 1,309 Of The Alaska Highway
Info: (907) 883-3686

GPS Location: 63.32557 N, 142.83165 W, 1,700 Ft.

This state campground has been modernized and is now quite nice. There are 43 sites off a circular drive. Many are tent sites but five sites are pull-thrus and are suitable for larger RVs and others are nice back-ins. Most sites are separated by vegetation. There are picnic tables and fire pits, as well as vault toilets and a boat ramp. This campground sometimes has a host and firewood available.

Tok
Population 1,300, Elevation 1,650 feet

If you are coming in to Alaska on the Alaska Highway Tok is your first Alaska town. It will probably be the last you'll see on the way home too. You'll find that Tok is a very RV friendly town with 8 RV parks. You'll find pretty much all services available here with RV parks, restaurants, stores, and repair facilities.

The **Tok Mainstreet Visitor Center** (907 883-5775) is located in a large log building in the northeast quadrant of the intersection of the Alaska Highway and the Tok Cutoff. This is an important stop, you can pick up a ton of information about the whole state. Nearby, just to the east, is the **APLIC** or **Alaska Public Lands Information Center** (PO Box 359, Tok, AK 99780; 907 883-5666). It concentrates on public lands (parks, etc.) and you can also try to make Alaska State Ferry Reservations, although you probably should have done that long before you left home.

The **APLIC** is one of four in the state, the others are in Fairbanks, Anchorage, and Ketchikan. There is so much federal and state land in Alaska that the governing organizations–eight different ones including the National Parks Service, the Bureau of Land Management, the U.S. Fish and Wildlife Service, and the State of Alaska–have set these information centers up in an attempt to make it easy for people to find all the information they need in one place. The information centers are a good place to start, but often it is necessary to actually go to the governing organization for all the information you need. This center caters more to highway travelers than the others and may not be the best place to look for information about off-highway camping possibilities. See Chapter 14 - *Camping Away From the Road System* for more information.

There aren't a lot of tourist attractions in Tok, but one you might enjoy is called **Mukluk Land**. Covering nine acres it's a collection of interesting stuff. Call it exhibits or call it junk, there's something for everyone. In addition to the exhibits there are also things to do like gold panning and mini golf. Mukluk Land it on the south side of the road leading toward Fairbanks, it's 2.8 miles (4.5 km) from the junction with the Glenn Cutoff to Anchorage.

In Tok you must make an important decision. Will you continue up the Alaska Highway to Fairbanks or will you turn south toward Valdez and Anchorage? An amazingly large number of people head for Fairbanks and never see the southern part of the state. Don't be one of them. See it all. You've come a long way.

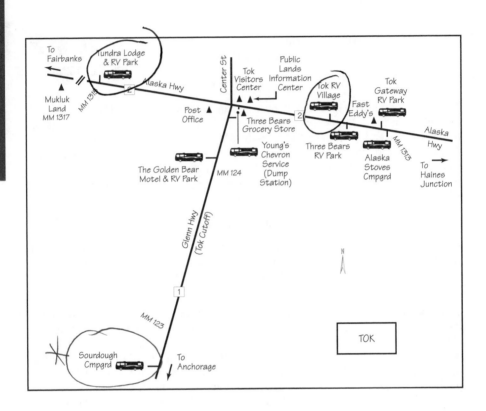

Tok Campgrounds

🚐 Tok Gateway RV Park

Address:　PO Box 482, Tok, AK 99780
Telephone:　(907) 883-4411
Email:　edyoung@aptalaska.net

GPS Location: 63.33420 N, 142.95460 W, 1,600 Ft.

One of the first campgrounds you'll see in Tok is hidden behind a salmon bake restaurant on your right as you enter town from the direction of the border. The name is somewhat misleading as the salmon bake no longer operates. Instead, there's Fast Eddy's Restaurant next door.

There are 39 pull-thru or back-in sites set in a grove of spruce trees. Some are full-hookup, others are partial or tent sites. A modern restroom building has showers and flush toilets and there is a dump station. The campground has no Wi-Fi but Fast Eddy's does.

The Gateway is on the north side of the Alaska Highway near Mile 1,313. It is 1 mile (1.6 km) east of the intersection of the Tok Cutoff and the Alaska Highway, the first campground you reach when approaching Tok from Canada. Check in at Fast Eddy's restaurant just to the west.

ALASKA STOVES CAMPGROUND

Address:	Milepost 1315 Alaska Hwy, Tok, AK 99780
Telephone:	(907) 883-5055
Email:	info@alaskanstovescampground.com
Website:	www.AlaskanStovesCampground.com

GPS Location: 63.33278 N, 142.94991 W, 1,600 Ft

This is a small rustic campground set in spruce next to the Tok airstrip. It's on the far side of the highway from the Tok Gateway RV Park described above. It's quite popular with bike travelers arriving from the direction of the border but RVers are welcome too. There's a paved bike trail running on in to town and a restaurant across the highway.

The campground is becoming a little more sophisticated each year. There are four sites with power but no water or sewer and another four being added. Some of these are pull-thru sites. There are also sites with no hookups. The campground has a dump and water fill station and a new restroom building with showers and laundry. The largest sites are about 35 feet long, but the owner says a 40-footer will fit (but it's tight). There's also a small tent that is used as a hostel or bunkhouse.

The Alaska Stoves Campground is well-signed on the south side of the highway near Mile 1,313, on the far side of the road from Fast Eddie's Restaurant.

THREE BEARS RV PARK

Address:	PO Box 189, Tok, AK 99780
Telephone:	(907) 883-5370

GPS Location: 63.33360 N, 142.96242 W, 1,700 Ft.

The Three Bears is a nicely laid out and conveniently located campground tucked behind a sporting goods store. There are 25 sites, they are pull-thrus to 40 feet with grass separating them. There are eight full service sites with 30-amp power, the rest have water and electricity. Parking and maneuvering room for big RVs is more than adequate. The washrooms have flush toilets and free showers and there is a dump station. The sporting goods store out front is small but surprisingly good.

Watch for the Three Bears on the south side of the Alaska Highway .9 miles (1.5 km) east of the intersection with the Tok Cutoff.

TOK RV VILLAGE

Address:	Mile 1313.4 Alaska Hwy. (PO Box 739), Tok, AK 99780
Telephone:	(907) 883-5877 or (800) 478-5878
Email:	tokrv@apalaska.net
Website:	www.tokrv.net

GPS Location: 63.33489 N, 142.96550 W, 1,700 Ft.

The Tok RV Village is without a doubt the most popular place to stay in town. It's a large campground and has modern facilities. Most caravans stay here.

The campground has about 160 sites. There are all types of sites including lots of 70-foot pull-thrus as well as tent and no-hookup sites. Some but not all sites have fire pits, some have television hookups. This campground has scattered spruce trees but is mostly open. The campground offers free showers to overnighters, a laundry, and a gift shop which also has a few RV supplies. There is a dump and water-fill station. Wi-Fi is available, a limited but relatively generous amount of useage is included at no extra charge. Recently added are rental cabins out front.

The campground is located at Mile 1,313 of the Alaska Highway, about .8 miles (1.3 km) east of the intersection with the Tok Cutoff.

YOUNG'S CHEVRON SERVICE

| Address: | PO Box 167, Tok, AK 99780 |
| Telephone: | (907) 883-2821 |

GPS Location: 63.33530 N, 142.98540 W, 1,700 Ft.

This Chevron station offers one of the best deals for RVs in Tok. They have about 10 large back-in sites in back of the station, some with picnic tables but no hookups. If you fill up at the station you can stay for free, you can also dump at their dump station. They also have a vehicle washing station, and limited groceries and fast-food items in their store. And then there's the Grumpy Griz Café next door.

The station is on the south side of the highway just east of the junction of the Glenn and Alaska highways, it's across from the visitor centers.

THE GOLDEN BEAR MOTEL AND RV PARK

Address:	PO Box 500, Tok, AK 99780
Telephone:	(907) 883-2561 or (866) 883-2561
Email:	alaskagoldenbear@gmail.com
Website:	www.alaskagoldenbear.com

GPS Location: 63.33109 N, 142.99163 W, 1,700 Ft.

The Golden Bear has about 45 sites in an older campground that has not been modernized for today's larger rigs. Many sites are pull-thrus, some to 40 feet, but access and site width are cramped. Full-hookup, water and electric, and dry sites are offered. Power is 20 amp. There are also tent sites. The campground sits in a grove of spruce trees and sites have picnic tables. Flush toilets and showers in an old building are included in the price of your site. This campground also offers a laundry, dump station, and a restaurant. There's a big TV in the lounge and free coffee in the morning. Wi-Fi from the motel reaches some of the sites

The campground is located just south of the intersection of the Tok Cutoff and the Alaska Highway on the west side of the highway.

SOURDOUGH CAMPGROUND

Address:	One Prospector Way (PO Box 47), Tok, Alaska 99780
Telephone:	(907) 883-5543
Email:	contact@sourdoughcampground.com
Website:	www.sourdoughcampground.com

GPS Location: 63.31141 N, 143.00427 W, 1,700 Ft.

The Sourdough is a little farther from the center of town than the other Tok campgrounds and is on the road to Anchorage so many Fairbanks-bound travelers never even see it until they return home after a visit to Southcentral. That's too bad since this is the most interesting of the Tok campgrounds. The owners here make a big effort to entertain and introduce new visitors to the state. Breakfast and dinner are available as well as an evening campfire get-together often featuring entertainment by local artists and a pancake toss (don't ask, you'll have to see it). This is one campground where you'll know you're appreciated.

The Sourdough is a medium-sized campground with about 80 camping sites in a fairly dense patch of spruce. Parking pads are gravel and have picnic tables. Both 20 and 30-amp outlets are offered, and sites are available with various combinations of electrical, water, and sewer hookups as well as without any services at all. Some 90 foot pull-thrus are available, also a tent-camping area with sawdust surfaces. There is a gift shop, a laundry, and a coin-operated high-pressure vehicle wash. Showers are free. There is a dump station. Free Wi-Fi is available and reaches most sites.

To reach the campground take the Tok Cutoff toward Anchorage from central Tok, the campground is about 1.5 mile (2.4 km) from the intersection on the right at Mile 122.8.

TUNDRA LODGE AND RV PARK

Address:	PO Box 760, Tok, Alaska 99780
Telephone:	(907) 883-7875
Email:	tundrarv@aptalaska.net

GPS Location: 63.33890 N, 143.01724 W, 1,700 Ft.

The Tundra is a good RV park that probably suffers a little for business because it is on the far side of Tok and folks coming in to town from the east just don't see it in time. It has a very pleasant and spacious camping area with good facilities, and an excellent price compared with the places to the east.

This is a large park. There are some 80 widely-spaced sites here: pull-thrus to 90 feet, full-hookups, partial hookups, and dry. Twenty, 30, and 50-amp electricity is available. All are in a nice setting with many trees, they also have picnic tables and fire pits with wood. Showers are free and there is a laundry, a vehicle wash, a dump station, and even a cocktail lounge and meeting room. Wi-Fi is available in the main building.

The campground is located at Mile 1,315 of the Alaska Highway, about .8 miles (1.3 km) west of the junction with the Tok Cutoff.

FROM TOK TO DELTA JUNCTION
108 Miles (174 Kilometers)

From Tok the Alaska Highway follows the wide Tanana Valley northwest to Delta Junction. The road is excellent, the entire trip takes less than two hours. At Delta Junction the Alaska Highway ends. The Richardson Highway runs north 98 miles (158 km) to Fairbanks and south 266 miles (429 km) to Valdez.

Tok to Delta Junction Campgrounds

MOON LAKE STATE RECREATION SITE

Location:	Mile 1,332 Alaska Highway
Info:	(907) 883-3686
Website:	dnr.alaska.gov/parks/aspunits/northern/moonlksrs.htm

GPS Location: 63.37584 N, 143.54421 W, 1,600 Ft.

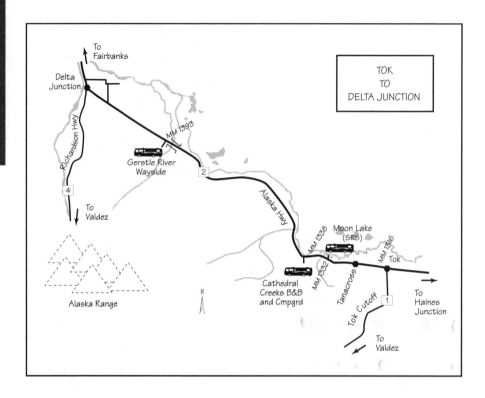

This campground is located alongside Moon Lake, a pretty little swimming lake just off the highway. There are 15 back-in sites near the water with picnic tables, fire pits, and vault toilets. They are suitable for RVs to about 40 feet. The short access road comes to a T at the lakeshore, then short drives with parking sites go each way, each has a turnaround at the end. Water is from a hand pump, there's a boat launch, and firewood can be purchased. Locals park their float airplanes along the shore so you can get a good look (but don't touch). There is a swimming beach here too. The campground has a 15 day stay limit. The short access road leads north from the Alaska Highway just east of Mile 1,332, about 18 miles (29 km) west of Tok.

🚐 Cathedral Creeks B&B and Campground

Address:	HC 62, Box 5035, Delta Junction, AK 99737
Telephone:	(907) 883-4455
Email:	cmbentele@yahoo.com
Website:	www.cathedralcreeks.net

GPS Location: 63.38510 N, 143.74548 W, 1,600 Ft.

This is a small bed and breakfast located along an old section of the Alaska Highway a short distance south of the new road. It's out of the way and not well known, but is a pleasant place, particularly in a small rig.

There is a lawn area for tent campers and also for parking two or possible three rigs to

25 feet. In this area you can get electricity with a cord strung from the house. There's also room for rigs to about 35 feet to park on the old highway with no hookups. Larger rigs would fit, of course, but may have trouble turning around since there's is not room to do a 180 without some backing. Showers are available and there's a central fire pit in the lawn area. Rental rooms are offered and meals can be arranged.

The access road goes south from Mile 1338.4, there's a sign along the highway.

GERSTLE RIVER WAYSIDE   FREE

Location: Alaska Highway At Mile 1,393,
About 29 Miles East Of Delta Junction

GPS Location: 63.81919 N, 144.92858 W, 1,400 Ft.

This wayside has a large gravel circular drive that is back off the highway. In the center are a picnic shelter, tables and a fire pit. Vault toilets are provided.

Watch for the entrance road just west of the Gerstle River at Mile 1,393 of the Alaska Highway, about 29 miles (47 km) east of Delta Junction.

DELTA JUNCTION
Population 1,000, Elevation 1,200 feet

Delta Junction started as a construction camp on the old Richardson Highway before the Alaska Highway was built. The surrounding country has become an important agricultural area.

Delta is known for the **bison** that were transported into the area in the 1920s. There are now over 400 of them and they roam pretty much where they want to. You may be fortunate enough to see some, a popular place to try is the overlook at Mile 241 of the Richardson Highway about 25 miles south of town. On one our recent trips a large herd of them blocked us as they crossed the highway about five miles east of Delta on the Alaska Highway, no doubt headed for some local farmer's grain field. Watch out for them along the road, a collision with a bison will do your RV no good.

The Delta Junction Visitor Center (907 895-5068) is located at the Y where the Alaska Highway meets the Richardson. Just to the south is the **Sullivan Roadhouse Museum**. This roadhouse was moved to its present location from a nearby army gunnery range, it's a very worthwhile stop.

Rika's Roadhouse, 9 miles north toward Fairbanks, was constructed at a ferry crossing of the Tanana River. This, like the Sullivan Roadhouse, was one of the original Richardson Highway roadhouses and is today a state park. A walk around the grounds is rewarding, there's a restaurant and a gift shop. You can even camp in the parking area.

Delta Junction has several campgrounds in the vicinity and makes a good overnight stop. Some are actually on the Richardson Highway but are included here because they are close enough to Delta to be considered when spending the night here.

Delta Junction Campgrounds

DELTA STATE RECREATION SITE

Location: Delta Junction, Alaska
Info: (907) 451-2695
Website: dnr.alaska.gov/parks/units/deltajct/deltasrs.htm

GPS Location: 64.05330 N, 145.73642 W, 1,200 Ft.

This is a pleasant and convenient state campground. It is located right next to the Delta airport, a real plus for us aviation lovers. If you happen to be flying the Alaska Highway this is a convenient camping spot.

There are 25 spaces off a gravel loop road, maximum RV size here would be about 35 feet. The campground is set in a grove of trees but there is still plenty of light. There are picnic tables and fire pits and wood bundles can be purchased. A water tap is provided and there are vault toilets.

The campground is located along the east side of the Richardson Highway in Delta about 1.1 miles (1.8 km) north of the intersection of the Alaska Highway and Richardson Highways.

SMITH'S GREEN ACRES RV PARK

Address: Milepost 268 Richardson Highway,
                 Delta Junction, AK 99737
Telephone: (907) 895-4369 or (800) 895-4369
Email: sgarvpark@gmail.com
Website: www.smithsgreenacres.com

GPS Location: 64.06523 N, 145.74126 W, 1,200 Ft.

This motel and RV park has the best facilities in Delta Junction.

There are about 80 sites of all types: pull-thrus, full utilities (20 or 30-amp electric), electric and water, dry, and even tent sites. They cover a large field with a few trees and some grass. There are also a few permanently-located RVs near the rear of the campground. Some pull-thru sites will take combos up to 80 feet long. The services building houses restrooms with free showers and a laundry. There is also a dump station and water fill station.

Watch for this campground on the east side of the road about 1.5 miles (2.4 km) north of the junction of the Richardson and the Alaska Highway. The Richardson mileage is 268.

CLEARWATER STATE RECREATION SITE

Location: East Of Delta Junction On Clearwater Rd.
Info: (907) 451-2695
Website: dnr.alaska.gov/parks/units/deltajct/clearwtr.htm

GPS Location: 64.05250 N, 145.43276 W, 1,200 Ft.

This campground is located on what is known locally as the Delta Clearwater (to distinguish it from another nearby river which is also known as the Clearwater). It is a very clear river offering good grayling fishing. The campground is a popular access point for river boaters, there is a boat ramp.

There are 17 sites, two of them are large pull-thrus and another is a large parallel-

THE ALASKA HIGHWAY

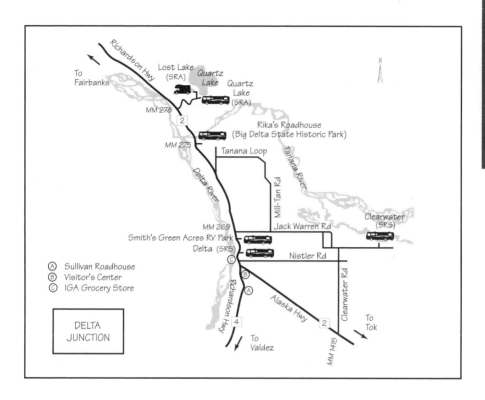

style parking site. They have picnic tables and fire pits and decent separation and surrounding vegetation with trees. There are vault toilets and a hand-operated water pump. Firewood can be purchased from the host.

There are two ways to access this campground. The first is the paved Clearwater Road from the Alaska Highway at mile 1,415, about 7 miles (11.3 km) east of the Alaska Highway-Richardson junction in Delta. Follow signs about 8.5 miles (13.7 km) to the campground. The second is the Jack Warren Road, also paved, which leaves the Richardson near Mile 268, about 2 miles (3.2 km) north of the Alaska Highway-Richardson junction in Delta. Follow signs about 11 miles (17.7 km) to the campground on this road.

RIKA'S ROADHOUSE
(BIG DELTA STATE HISTORICAL PARK)

Location: Mile 275 Richardson Highway
Telephone: (907) 451-2695
Website: dnr.alaska.gov/parks/aspunits/northern/bigdeltashp.htm

GPS Location: 64.15476 N, 145.84211 W, 1,000 Ft.

You should stop and take a look at Rika's Roadhouse even if you don't want to camp here. This restored roadhouse, built in 1913, was one of the originals along the old Valdez to Fairbanks trail. A ferry crossed the very dangerous Tanana River at this point. There is a self-guided tour, a museum, a restaurant, and also a gift shop. The

Trans-Alaska oil pipeline crosses the Tanana just down the road.

The camping area is really just the parking lot for the park. There are nine large back-in sites in the gravel lot labeled for RV parking. The state website says there are 25 sites, so apparently it's OK to park in some sites not marked. A few sites have picnic tables and fire pits and there are nearby vault toilets. There is also a dump and water-fill station nearby (extra charge).

The roadhouse is located near Mile 275 of the Richardson just south of the bridge over the Tanana. A short road leads back to the roadhouse from the highway.

🚐 Quartz Lake Campground
(Quartz Lake State Recreation Area)

Location:	Mile 278 Of The Richardson Highway
Info:	(907) 451-2695
Website:	dnr.alaska.gov/parks/units/deltajct/quartz.htm

GPS Location: 64.19780 N, 145.82612 W, 800 Ft.

This is a nice campground on a popular area lake. Quartz Lake gets warm enough for swimming and is also a popular fishing lake. There are also some local hiking trails.

There are two camping areas here. The primary campground is in the trees above the large lakeside parking lot. It has 16 back-in sites, some to forty feet. They have picnic tables and fire pits and the area has a vault toilet and water pump. When this fills the large parking lot has sites that are set aside as an overflow area. There are 55 spaces designated for RV parking, units to 45 feet are fine. It has a few picnic tables, fire pits, and vault toilets. There's a campground host and firewood is sold.

The campground is located about 2.7 miles (4.4 km) from the Richardson Highway on a paved road. The access road leaves the highway at about Mile 278, about 11 miles (17.7 km) north of Delta Junction. You'll drive across the pipeline which dives underground to pass under the campground access road, this is a good place to get a picture of it.

🚐 Lost Lake Campground
(Quartz Lake State Recreation Area)

Location:	Mile 278 Of The Richardson Highway
Info:	(907) 451-2695
Website:	dnr.alaska.gov/parks/units/deltajct/quartz.htm

GPS Location: 64.19581 N, 145.84035 W, 800 Ft.

Near the Quartz Lake Campground is another much smaller one, the Lost Lake Campground. Trails lead between the two. These are stocked lakes so fishing can be good.

This campground has 12 medium to short sites with some large enough for 30-foot RVs. They are normal state campground back-in type sites with picnic tables and fire pits. There are vault toilets and a hand-operated water pump.

You come to this campground before reaching the Quartz Lake Campground. Follow the access road from Mile 278 of the Richardson Highway about 11 miles (17.7 km) north of Delta Junction. The Lost Lake Campground is at mile 2.3 (3.7 km) of the paved access road.

ALASKA HIGHWAY DUMP STATIONS

Dump stations (called sani-dumps in Canada) are sometimes hard to find in the north. Even when you do find one you will probably have to pay to use it because handling sewage in an area with few sewer systems can be expensive. Plan ahead by dumping when you can, preferably when in a larger town that has a sewer system. Many of the campgrounds listed in this book have dump stations, you can usually pay to use them even if you aren't staying at the campground. Many service stations also have dump stations, particularly if they have an associated camping area.

Here are additional sites not associated with campgrounds:

In **Dawson Creek** there's a dump station at the city's Mile 0 RV Campsite.

In **Taylor**, between Dawson Creek and Ft. St. John, there's a city dump station off the street behind the Taylor Inn (*GPS Location 56.15224 N, 120.68375 W*).

In **Ft. St. John** there is a city dump station near Km 72 (Mile 45) on the right at 86th Street as you drive north (*GPS Location 56.23009 N, 120.82248 W*).

Also in Ft. St. John there's a dump station at Big Eagle Services, a car, truck and RV wash facility. To get there turn south off Hwy. 97 onto Old Fort Road near Km 75, drive south for .5 km (.3 miles), you'll see the facility on the left (*GPS Location 56.24158 N, 120.87325 W*), the sani dump is on the south side of the building.

In **Fort Nelson** there is a municipal dump station at the Fort Nelson Heritage Museum on the Alaska Highway at the west end of town (*GPS Location 58.80443 N, 122.71715 W*).

Watson Lake has a city dump station at Wye Lake Park across from Downtown RV Park (*GPS Location 60.06591 N, 128.70469 W*). Also easily accessible is a free dump station at Junction 37 Services, the service station at the junction of the Cassiar and Alaska Highways (*GPS Location 60.02471 N, 129.06081 W*).

In **Atlin** you can dump at the city sewage lagoon at a gravel pit 4 km (2.5 miles) east of town on Discovery Road (*GPS Location 59.58969 N, 133.64084 W*).

In **Whitehorse** there's a dump station at the North 60 Petro Station next to the Walmart parking lot (*GPS Location 60.73226 N, 135.06830 W*).

In **Haines Junction** try the Fas Gas at the east entrance to town (*GPS Location 60.76108 N, 137.51772 W*), it's free if you fill up or overnight. Also Haines Junction Shell which is on the corner where the highway to Haines cuts off to the south (*GPS Location 60.75311 N, 137.51204 W*).

In **Tok** Young's Chevron at Mile 1,314.1 of the Alaska Highway has an easily accessible dump station (*GPS Location 63.33508 N, 142.98726 W*) which is free if you fill up with fuel.

In **Delta Junction** there is an easily accessible state-operated dump station behind Rika's Roadhouse (*GPS Location 64.15461 N, 145.83705 W*). There's a $5 charge.

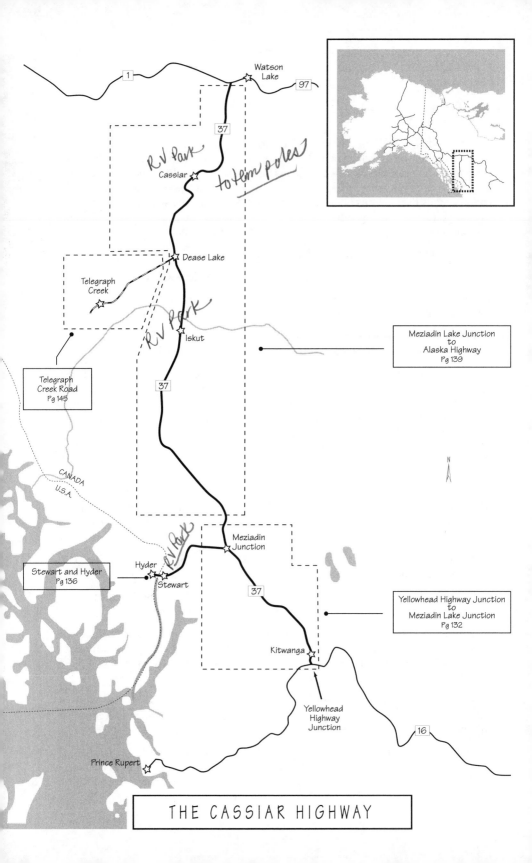

THE CASSIAR HIGHWAY

Chapter 5

The Cassiar Highway

INTRODUCTION

The Cassiar follows a route north much closer to the coast than the Alcan or Alaska Highway. Actually the Cassiar route was one of those considered during World War II when plans were being made to build the Alcan. At that time there was fear that the Cassiar route was too close to the coast and therefore might be in danger from the Japanese. Because the Cassiar Highway wasn't completed until 1972 it is the newest route to Alaska and therefore something of an adventure. Although it is now all paved you will find that fuel and supply stops can be a little far apart. On the other hand, wildlife is sometimes more plentiful than on the Alaska Highway and the scenery is great!

Highlights

The area around the junction of the Yellowhead Highway (Hwy. 16) and the Cassiar Highway (Hwy. 37) has a number of interesting First Nation (American Indian) attractions. The reconstructed village of **'Ksan** is adjacent to the first campground listed below, 'Ksan Campground. See the directions to that campground to find the village. At the southern end of the Cassiar is the village of **Gitwangak** which is home to a fine collection of totem poles. The town of **Gitanyow** about 21 km (13 miles) to the north also has a large group of totem poles. Near Kitwanga, off a circle road 4.3 km (2.7 miles) north of the Cassiar-Yellowhead junction is **Kitwanga Fort National Historic Site (Battle Hill)**, a First Nation fortified village site. It's just beyond the Kitwanga Centennial Park Campground, see instructions for how to find that campground below.

One hundred fifty-seven kilometers (97 miles) north of the beginning of the Cassiar a paved road runs west for 62 scenic kilometers (38 miles) to the coastal towns of **Stewart, British Columbia** and **Hyder, Alaska**. There's a drive-up glacier en route (the **Bear Glacier**) and when you reach the coast you'll find two entirely different kinds of towns: orderly Canadian Stewart and the tiny Alaskan bush town of Hyder. Even better, just outside Hyder when the fish are running is one of the better places to see bears in all of Alaska. The road to Stewart and Hyder is excellent, don't miss this side trip.

The Road and Fuel

The Cassiar Highway runs 724 kilometers (449 miles) north through the wilderness from the Yellowhead Highway (Hwy. 16) near the small town of Kitwanga to join the Alaska Highway near Watson Lake in the Yukon Territory. It is a good alternate route to the Alaska Highway. From Prince George the distance to the Alaska border is 200 km (124 miles) shorter via the Cassiar than via the Alaska Highway from Dawson Creek. If you do choose to drive the Cassiar to Alaska you will still drive much of the Alaska Highway, the two roads join near Watson Lake.

The Cassiar is now paved for the entire distance. Many truckers now use the Cassiar rather than the longer and sometimes slower Alaska Highway so it is clear that the Cassiar is a viable alternate to the southern portion of the Alaska highway.

The Cassiar remains less traveled than the Alaska Highway and has fewer service stops. You should be well prepared when traveling and plan ahead, don't run out of fuel or neglect to bring a spare tire.

Distance and location markings along the Cassiar are in kilometers. Posts are placed every 5 kilometers. The kilometer posts are not necessarily accurate, they have not always been corrected for mileage changes due to road straightening. Campground

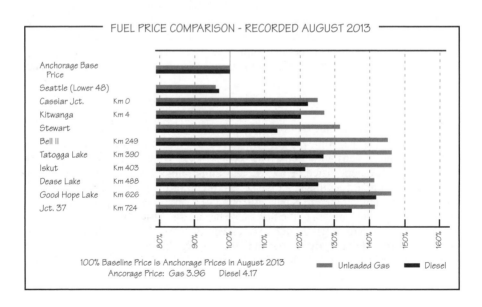

FUEL PRICE COMPARISON - RECORDED AUGUST 2013

Anchorage Base Price		
Seattle (Lower 48)		
Cassiar Jct.	Km 0	
Kitwanga	Km 4	
Stewart		
Bell II	Km 249	
Tatogga Lake	Km 390	
Iskut	Km 403	
Dease Lake	Km 488	
Good Hope Lake	Km 626	
Jct. 37	Km 724	

100% Baseline Price is Anchorage Prices in August 2013
Ancorage Price: Gas 3.96   Diesel 4.17

Unleaded Gas   Diesel

locations in this book are based upon the kilometer posts. They start at the junction with the Yellowhead Highway in the south and increase heading north.

Fishing

The Cassiar Highway passes over or along many rivers, lakes and streams. Many of them offer excellent fishing. Take the time to stop and give a few a try. Several of the campgrounds listed in this section are on lakes with fishing possibilities. See the individual campground listings for more information. As always, don't hesitate to ask the locals for fishing tips. Most of this route is within British Columbia and fishing licenses are required.

Wildlife Viewing

One of the best reasons to visit Hyder is to see the bears. When the salmon are running from the middle of July until early September there are a lot of them around, both blacks and grizzlies. The best place to see them is at **Fish Creek**, a 5 km (3 mile) drive on a good gravel road on the far side of Hyder. A viewing platform was constructed in 2001 at Fish Creek by the U.S. Forest Service and rangers are on-site making observation easier and safer.

The northern section of the Cassiar also offers wildlife-viewing possibilities. We've often seen stone sheep near the road near Km 618, and if you are traveling in the early spring you may see woodland caribou along the section of road between Dease Lake and the Alaska Highway. All along the highway watch the ditches and cleared

HYDER'S VIEWING PLATFORM IS ONE OF THE BEST PLACES TO SEE BEARS IN ALASKA

THE CASSIAR HIGHWAY

areas out to the tree line, black bears are common and grizzlies not uncommon in spring and also later in the summer during berry season.

THE ROUTES, TOWNS, AND CAMPGROUNDS

FROM YELLOWHEAD HIGHWAY JUNCTION TO THE MEZIADIN LAKE JUNCTION
157 Kilometers (97 Miles)

The Cassiar Highway leaves the Yellowhead Highway some 481 kilometers (298 miles) west of Prince George and 243 kilometers (151 miles) east of Prince Rupert. It immediately crosses the Skeena River Bridge and in just .3 kilometers (.2 miles) a road goes east to Gitwangak which is home to a fine collection of totem poles. If you find these interesting there's another group at Gitanyow along a short road from the highway about 21 km (13 miles) to the north.

Three kilometers (2 miles) north of Gitwangak you'll come to Kitwanga. This is the home of the **Kitwanga Fort National Historic Site (Battle Hill)** and has a modern RV park and a very small free community campground.

From Kitwanga the road runs north through gently rolling scenic country with a few lakes to big Meziadin Lake and its provincial campground at Km 155. The cutoff going west to Stewart and Hyder is at Km 157.

VISIT A FIRST NATION CEDAR HOUSE AT THE 'KSAN HISTORICAL VILLAGE

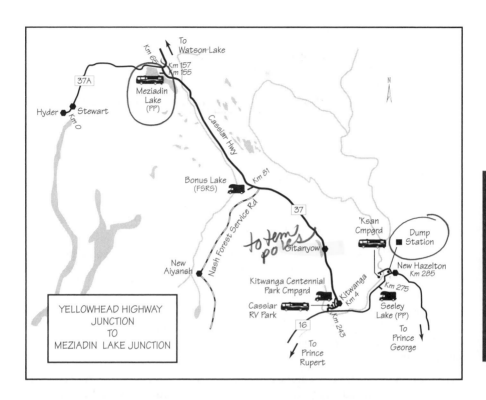

THE CASSIAR HIGHWAY

Yellowhead Highway Junction to the Meziadin Lake Junction Campgrounds

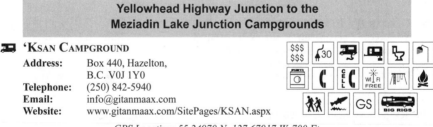

🚐 **'KSAN CAMPGROUND**

Address:	Box 440, Hazelton, B.C. V0J 1Y0
Telephone:	(250) 842-5940
Email:	info@gitanmaax.com
Website:	www.gitanmaax.com/SitePages/KSAN.aspx

GPS Location: 55.24970 N, 127.67917 W, 700 Ft.

While not really on the Cassiar Highway, this campground is located near the southern end. It sits at the confluence of the Skeena and Bulkley Rivers near historic Old Hazelton, also right next to the 'Ksan Historical Village and Museum which has totem poles and traditional First Nation cedar houses. With these two attractions so near, and such a nice campground, it makes a good place to spend the night before heading north on the Cassiar.

The campground has 60 spaces. Thirty are large pull-thru sites to 90 feet with 30-amp outlets, water, and sewer arranged in a large grassy field broken up by grass-covered mounds, very attractive. Picnic tables and fire pits are provided at some sites. There are also many tent and no-hookup sites, some in a loop with individual sites separated by thick natural vegetation. There is a restroom building with showers, laundry machines, and a dump station. Firewood is available. You can walk along the river the half-mile to Old Hazelton.

To reach the campground leave the east-west Hwy. 16 near Km 284, there is a visitor center with sani-dump on the corner. Go north on the paved road, you'll cross an impressive single-lane suspension bridge at 1.6 km (1 mile), pass through a populated area, and at 7.4 km (4.6 miles) you'll see the campground entrance on your left, this is also the entrance to the historical village. Old Hazelton is straight ahead.

≡ SEELEY LAKE PROVINCIAL CAMPGROUND

Location:	Near Km 275 Of Hwy. 16
Info:	(250) 638-8490
Website:	www.env.gov.bc.ca/bcparks/explore/parkpgs/seeley_lk/

GPS Location: 55.19667 N, 127.68833 W, 1,000 Ft.

This small provincial campground is conveniently located right next to the highway. Seeley Lake is adjacent although bushes obscure the view.

Sites here are back-ins. A narrow access road makes this campground appropriate for RVs to about 35 feet although some sites would actually take 40-footers. This is a loop road that exits onto the highway a few hundred feet east of the main entrance. There are 20 sites, all have fire pits and picnic tables, some have tent pads. Restrooms are vault toilets and there is a hand water pump. There is an overlook near the sites that allows great views of the lake and the mountains beyond, there's also a day use area near the campground entrance. There is a 14-day maximum stay at this campground.

Watch for the campground sign near Km 275 of Hwy. 16 about 33 km (21 miles) east of the Yellowhead Highway - Cassiar Highway junction. It's on the south side of the highway.

≡ CASSIAR RV PARK

Address:	PO Box 301, Kitwanga, B.C. V0J 2A0
Telephone:	(250) 849-5799, (888) 678-7275
Email:	enquiries@cassiarrv.ca
Website:	www.cassiarrv.ca

GPS Location: 55.11472 N, 128.03362 W, 700 Ft.

This RV park is the first of a thin line of campgrounds along the Cassiar. It has decent facilities and is especially popular with folks returning from the north. To many pulling in here feels like arriving back in civilization.

The campground has parking in three separate areas. There are 30 full-hookup spaces with 30-amp outlets in an area near the office and restrooms, some are pull-thrus. Overlooking the office on a small hill to the right are 7 double pull-thrus making up 14 sites with 20-amp outlets and water. Another large area beyond the office has another 16 or so sites, some with 20-amp outlets. Many sites are large enough for any size RV, some to 80 feet, and access is easy. There is well-clipped grass throughout the campground and also some tent sites. There's a dump station and a high-pressure vehicle wash. Campfires are allowed in a few designated areas. The office is the Wi-Fi hotspot, nearby sites may have a strong enough signal for use. There's also a trail from the RV park to a salmon-counting station on the Kitwanga River. The distance is less than a mile.

From the Cassiar Highway at Km 4 drive .6 kilometer (.4 miles) west on Barcalow Rd. The campground is on the left.

KITWANGA CENTENNIAL PARK CAMPGROUND
   Location: Across From Dollops Gas Station On Kitwanga Valley Rd.
                     GPS Location: 55.11287 N, 128.02339 W, 700 Ft.

This is a simple community-run campground in Kitwanga. There are 12 small back-in sites in a grove of trees with no utilities. Vault toilets are provided as well as a covered picnic shelter, tables, fire pits, and free firewood. We found the campground in very good condition on our last visit. It is suitable for RVs to about 30 feet. Stays are limited to three days. There are a number of walking trails in this community, access to them is easy from the campground.

Easiest access is from Km 4.2 of the Cassiar. Follow Kitwanga Valley Road left for .6 kilometer (.4 mile) to the Dollops service station, the campground is across the street.

BONUS LAKE RECREATION AREA   FREE
   Location: Near Km 81 Of The Cassiar Highway
                     GPS Location: 55.60915 N, 128.61973 W, 1,100 Ft.

This is a small forest service recreation site with three picnic tables, a fire ring, an outhouse, and a dock located on little Bonus Lake. It is not far off the highway, a convenient and inexpensive place to spend the night. Access to the sites is down a narrow road with a short but fairly steep ramp down to the parking area and there is little room to turn around so it is not suitable for RVs over about 25 feet.

MEZIADIN LAKE PROVINCIAL PARK
   (B.C. GOVERNMENT)
   Location: Km 155 Of The Cassiar Highway
   Telephone: (250) 638-8490
   Website: www.env.gov.bc.ca/bcparks/explore/parkpgs/meziadin_lk/
                     GPS Location: 56.08971 N, 129.30390 W, 800 Ft.

Meziadin Lake campground is located on the shores of huge Meziadin Lake near the junction where the Stewart/Hyder road meets the Cassiar. This is one of the prettiest of British Columbia's provincial park campgrounds with sites right on the waterfront. The lake has good Dolly Varden and rainbow trout fishing and the campground has a boat ramp. Bears are common at this campground so don't leave food outside your rig and dispose of garbage properly. This is an unusual B.C. provincial park in that it has Wi-Fi, a convenience store, and soon will even have power to some sites.

There are now 66 spaces at Meziadin Lake with many along the lake. The remaining sites are above and behind the lakefront ones, most of these have views. Sites are off a loop so a drive-through with a tow is no problem, some sites reach 60 feet in length. The roads here are paved but site surfaces are gravel. Facilities include the boat ramp, picnic tables, fire pits, wheelchair access vault toilets, a small store during the busiest part of the summer, Wi-Fi (extra fee), and a hand pump for water. There is a 14-day annual stay limit in this campground.

The campground is located west of Highway 37 near Km 155.

STEWART AND HYDER

Population Stewart 700, Hyder 100, Elevation sea level

The 65 kilometer (40 mile) road that descends from the Cassiar Highway down to Stewart and Hyder on the coast is one of the most scenic in British Columbia. The entire distance is paved and grades are no problem for even the largest rigs. At about Kilometer 24 (Mile 15) is an overlook with excellent views of the **Bear Glacier** just across the valley on the far side of a lake. Near the coast the highway threads its way through Stewart, laid out in an organized grid pattern, and then follows the shore of the Portland Canal, a 90-mile-long fjord, a mile or so to the border and little Hyder. There is no U.S. border post or inspection going into Hyder but there is a Canadian post when you return to Stewart.

Much larger Stewart with its paved streets is the best place for purchasing supplies and has a gas station and decent-sized grocery store. There is also a town dump station. Funky Hyder is more interesting with gravel streets, several bars and souvenir stores and an excellent bear-viewing area from the middle of July to early September during the chum (dog salmon) and pink salmon run on Fish Creek about 5 kilometers (3 miles) outside town.

If you have a smaller RV or a tow car consider making the drive to the Salmon Glacier overlook, out beyond the Fish Creek bear-viewing area. The overlook is 37 kilometers (23 miles) on gravel from Hyder but the view of the glacier is spectacular.

AN EXCELLENT VIEW OF BEAR GLACIER ON THE ROAD TO STEWART AND HYDER

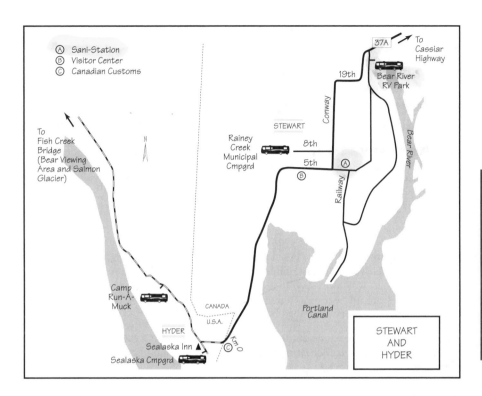

Check at the information center in Stewart for an excellent pamphlet that describes the route.

Stewart and Hyder Campgrounds

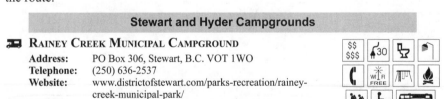

RAINEY CREEK MUNICIPAL CAMPGROUND

Address:	PO Box 306, Stewart, B.C. V0T 1W0
Telephone:	(250) 636-2537
Website:	www.districtofstewart.com/parks-recreation/rainey-creek-municipal-park/

GPS Location: 55.93860 N, 129.99808 W, Near Sea Level

This is a popular and inexpensive camping option in Stewart/Hyder. It is conveniently located in town, you can easily stroll downtown. The many campers staying in this campground each summer are a big boost to the local economy. The office people are excellent sources of information about the area.

The campground has about 85 RV sites and an additional area for tent camping. Sixty-five of the RV sites offer electricity, some 20 amp and some 30 amp. Sites and maneuvering room in this campground can be tight, some sites reach 45 feet in length but exercise caution. Picnic tables and fire pits are provided and there is a dish-washing area and two covered picnic shelters. One water fill station services the campground. There is no dump station in the campground, instead, campers use one provided by the city several blocks away on Fifth Ave. Restrooms are in a cement block building and are well-maintained and clean. The showers are coin-operated. Wi-Fi is available at a hot spot in a kitchen shelter. Stewart's downtown area is within walking distance and there are tennis courts, a hiking trail, and a playground adjoining the campground.

As you enter downtown Stewart watch for 8th. Turn right and follow this street to where it ends against the mountain. That's where the campground entrance is located.

⛟ BEAR RIVER RV PARK

Address:	PO Box 97, Stewart, B.C. V0T 1W0
Telephone:	(250) 636-9205
Email:	bearriver@xplornet.com
Website:	www.stewartbc.com/rvpark

GPS Location: 55.95247 N, 129.97777 W, 100 Ft.

This is an established RV park with a few permanently-located units. It also has many sites available for travelers. Sites have 30-amp outlets, water, and sewer and TV hookups, as well as picnic tables. There are both pull-thru and back-in sites, some to 80 feet. Restrooms with showers (coin-op) are located in an ATCO-type building, fires are allowed in a few designated places. Tents are prohibited because bears are often present.

The campground is located near the entrance to Stewart from the east. Coming in to town from the east you'll cross a bridge over the river and just beyond is a left turn signed for the campground.

IT'S ALWAYS FUN TO VISIT THE FUNKY LITTLE ALASKAN TOWN OF HYDER

THE CASSIAR HIGHWAY

🚐 SEALASKA CAMPGROUND

Address: 999 Premier Avenue (PO Box 33),
                  Hyder, AK 99923
Telephone: (250) 636-2486 or (888) 393-1199
Website: www.sealaskainn.com

GPS Location: 55.91112 N, 130.02058 W, Near Sea Level

This campground is a decent place to stay in Hyder if you don't need hookups.

After crossing the border into Hyder you will come to a T in the road. Just half a block or so to the left is the Sealaska Inn. You can check in to the campground in the bar. Just to the left of the hotel is the camping area. Parking is on grass and there's maneuvering and parking room for large RVs. There are no hookups or defined sites but picnic tables and fire pits are provided. A building with laundry, showers, and flush toilets sits out front and there is a covered picnic shelter with tables and a wood stove provided for the use of tent campers. With a good computer you can use Wi-Fi in the camping area.

🚐 CAMP RUN-A-MUCK

Address: PO Box 150, Hyder, Alaska 99923
Telephone: (250) 636-9006 or (888) 393-1199
Email: camprunamuck@usa.net
Website: www.sealaskainn.com

GPS Location: 55.92023 N, 130.03181 W, 100 Ft.

For hookups in Hyder there is one choice. This is Camp Run-a-Muck. The name of the campground overstates the case, actually this is usually a pretty well-run place.

Campsites for larger RVs are in a large gravel area along the road north out of town toward Fish Creek and Salmon Glacier. There are about 60 sites, many pull-thrus, with 30-amp outlets and water. Some sites extend to 70 feet. Picnic tables and fire pits are provided. Smaller sites are located back in the trees, many of these also have electricity and water. Campers must use the dump station in Stewart but there is a building with restrooms, coin-op showers, and a laundry.

When you enter Hyder you'll drive past the few gift shops and bars on the main road and come to a T. Turn right and drive about a half-mile. The campground is on the left, you can't possibly miss it.

FROM THE MEZIADIN LAKE JUNCTION TO THE ALASKA HIGHWAY
567 Kilometers (352 Miles)

In past years this section of road had a few segments with gravel surface, but now it is entirely paved other than some short sections where each year upgrades continue.

There are really only a few small population centers along this section. One is little Iskut (population about 300) at Km 405 and the other Dease Lake at Km 487. Both have small grocery stores. Iskut sits between the **Spatsizi Wilderness Provincial Park** to the east of the highway and **Mount Edziza Provincial Park** to the west, both are becoming popular wilderness destinations and along the highway are a string of lakes that are excellent for fishing and canoeing.

THE CASSIAR HIGHWAY

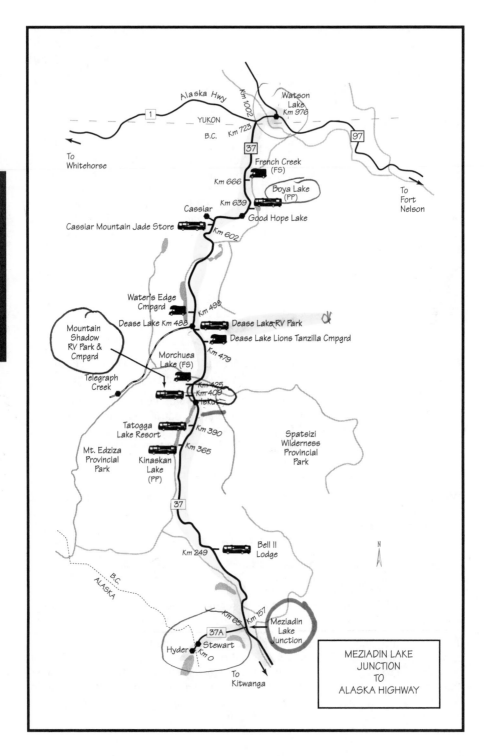

An interesting side trip from the Cassiar at the town of Dease Lake is the **Telegraph Creek Road**. We describe the route and its campgrounds later in this chapter.

Meziadin Lake Junction to the Alaska Highway Campgrounds

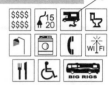

BELL II LODGE

Location:	Km 249 Hwy. 37N
Telephone:	(250) 275-4770 or (888) 499-4354
Email:	info@bell2lodge.com
Website:	www.bell2lodge.com

GPS Location: 56.74331 N, 129.79343 W, 1,800 Ft.

The Bell II is a very modern roadhouse and upscale lodge. In the winter it is used for heliskiing but in the summer it relies on highway traffic and has a nice RV park.

There are 10 large gravel pull-thru sites with full hookups (15 amp) and a few additional ones with no hookups. Sites stretch to 60 feet. There are also five back-in camping sites with no services suitable for smaller RVs or tent campers. Restrooms are new and have showers. The hotel also has a restaurant, a coffee shop, a small store with gifts and sundries, and gas sales. Wi-Fi is available but very expensive.

The location of the lodge at Km 249 is about 93 km (58 miles) north of the junction with the road out to Stewart and Hyder.

**KINASKAN LAKE PROVINCIAL PARK
   (B.C. GOVERNMENT)**

Location:	Km 365 Of The Cassiar Highway
Info:	(250) 638-8490
Website:	www.env.gov.bc.ca/bcparks/explore/parkpgs/kinaskan_lk/

GPS Location: 57.53013 N, 130.18424 W, 2,800 Ft.

Kinaskan Lake is a beautiful lakeside campground with much more separation between sites and privacy than is found at the next lakeside park to the south - Meziadin Lake. Rainbow trout fishing in the large lake is an attraction here (during late summer) as is the Mowdade Trail to volcanic Mt. Edziza Park to the west. Some visitors even swim in the lake.

The campground has 50 spaces, many of them exceeding 50 feet, and also many along the lake. They are all back-ins. All have the customary picnic table and fire pit, some also have separate tent pads. The access road has a loop at the end so vehicles with a tow do not need to unhook to take a look. The campground has vault toilets, a water pump, firewood for sale, and a boat launching ramp. There is a 14-day stay limit at the campground.

TATOGGA LAKE RESORT

Address:	Box 59, Iskut, B.C. V0J 1K0
Telephone:	(250) 234-3526
Email:	tatogga1@yahoo.ca
Website:	www.tatogga.ca

GPS Location: 57.71109 N, 129.99190 W, 2,800 Ft.

Despite the name this establishment seems less like a resort than a traditional roadhouse. The log restaurant building is tastefully decorated with moose antlers. They

CRUISING THE CASSIAR HIGHWAY

also sell gas. Hiking, fishing, and canoeing excursions are available, including fly-in trips.

Behind the buildings located along the highway is a large field with campsites that slopes down toward Tatogga Lake. There are about 40 sites, most of them offer 20 or 30-amp electricity and water hookups. Some pull-thrus extend to 75 feet. A restroom building near the campsites offers flush toilets and showers. There is a dump station as well as a boat ramp. This camping area is showing its age, the hookups have been around a long time and don't receive much TLC. Wi-Fi is a hot spot in the restaurant building.

The resort is located on the west side of the Cassiar Highway near Km 390.

 MOUNTAIN SHADOW RV PARK AND CAMPGROUND

Address:	Box 3, Iskut, B.C. V0J 1K0
Telephone:	Summer (250) 234-3333,
	Winter (415) 328-8768
Email:	info@mtshadowrvpark.com
Website:	www.mtshadowrvpark.com

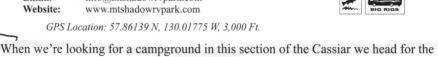

GPS Location: 57.86139 N, 130.01775 W, 3,000 Ft.

When we're looking for a campground in this section of the Cassiar we head for the Mountain Shadow RV Park. It's a meticulously laid out and maintained facility with both large pull-thru sites and secluded back-ins. Views to the west are spectacular and a short trail takes you to a small lake which offers rainbow trout fishing and bird watching.

The campground has two different camping areas. For large RVs there are 10 spacious pull-thrus to 80 feet and water and electricity (20 or 30-amp) hook-ups. In the same area are another 10 large back-ins with water and electricity. Smaller rigs and tent campers will appreciated the 11 back-in spaces in trees, three with electrical hook-ups. There are fire pits in this area. All sites have picnic tables. Showers (no extra charge) are available, there are flush toilets, and there is a dump station. The park also has two rental cabins and a gift shop.

A wide and well-maintained entrance road leads down a gentle slope to the campground from near Km 408 of the Cassiar Highway. Watch for the sign on the west side of the highway.

MORCHUEA LAKE FOREST SERVICE CAMPSITE   FREE
    Location: Near Km 425 Of The Cassiar Highway

        GPS Location: 57.98459 N, 130.06335 W, 3,100 Ft.

This is a small forest service recreation site with a few picnic tables, fire rings, an outhouse, and a boat ramp. It is near the highway and is suitable for RVs to 30 feet.

DEASE LAKE LIONS TANZILLA CAMPGROUND $$$
    Location: Km 479 Of The Cassiar Highway

        GPS Location: 58.36890 N, 129.91230 W, 3,000 Ft.

This little campground is a government-style place but operated by the local Lions Club. It sits on the bank of the Tanzilla River just east of the highway.

There are 16 back-in sites with tables and fire pits. These are individual separated sites, parking is on gravel under pine trees and some sites are right on the river. The campground is suitable for RVs to about 30 feet. Firewood is available for an extra charge.

DEASE LAKE RV PARK
    Address: PO Box 129, Dease Lake,
                   B.C. V0C 1L0
    Telephone: (250) 771-4666
    Email: dlrvpark@hotmail.com

        GPS Location: 58.43276 N, 129.98584 W, 2,700 Ft.

Large RV owners will appreciate this campground. Although it is little more than a large gravel lot filled with RV sites there is lots of room and the surface is solid and well drained.

There are about 35 sites, 29 are large pull-thru sites suitable for RVs to 60 feet. All have electricity (30 amp) and water and about half also have sewer hookups. There are also a number of large back-in sites, also with power and water hookups. The tiled bathrooms have flush toilets and showers. There is also a dump station and a vehicle wash station. Wi-Fi is a hot spot at a picnic shelter but does reach some sites.

The campground is located on the east side of the Cassiar near the Telegraph Creek Road junction in the community of Dease Lake near Km 488.

THE CASSIAR HIGHWAY

WATER'S EDGE CAMPGROUND

Address:	PO Box 217, Dease Lake, B.C. V0C 1L0	
Telephone:	Campground (250) 771-4055, Home (250) 771-3392	
Email:	cwphillips99@hotmail.com	
Website:	www.watersedgecampground.ca	

GPS Location: 58.51819 N, 130.03707 W, 2,500 Ft.

This is a private campground that is much like a provincial forest service campground. It has no hookups. The back-in sites along the shore of Dease Lake are fairly long, but we recommend RVs only to about 35 feet due to limited maneuvering room. Some larger rigs do use them however. They have picnic tables, fire pits, an outhouse and Wi-Fi. The owner lives on the property in the summer. Wi-Fi is a hotspot at the office but reaches nearby sites. Power for that is generated on site.

The campground is on the west side of the highway near Km 498. There's a wide quarter-mile-long gravel road down to the lake shore and then a large gravel area to turn around. Sites are off a loop with limited maneuvering room so it's best to walk the final few feet to the sites to take a look before parking. There's also a boat ramp.

CASSIAR MOUNTAIN JADE STORE

Location:	Km 602, Cassiar Hwy., B.C.
Telephone:	(250) 239-5233
Email:	info@jadecity.com
Website:	www.jadecity.com

GPS Location: 59.24951 N, 129.65086 W, 3,100 Ft.

The Cassiar Mountain Jade Store is a popular stop. You can see large jade boulders being reduced to jewelry-sized pieces and visit the friendly store. Camping without hookups is possible here in an open gravel area with a dedicated outhouse. Because it's just a gravel lot it can take any size RV. There's also tent camping in the nearby trees. Shower and a laundry room are available.

Cassiar Mountain Jade Store is on the west side of the highway near Km 602.

BOYA LAKE PROVINCIAL PARK
(B.C. GOVERNMENT)

Location:	Km 639 Of The Cassiar Highway
Info:	(250) 638-8490
Website:	www.env.gov.bc.ca/bcparks/explore/parkpgs/boya_lk/

GPS Location: 59.36866 N, 129.10646 W, 2,300 Ft.

The farthest north provincial park campground along the Cassiar is on the shores of crystal clear Boya Lake. On a clear day this lake is a beautiful bright blue, great for photos. Unfortunately the fishing is very poor in the lake. The nearby Dease River does have grayling.

The campground has 42 sites. They're off two loops. To the right as you enter is a loop with six sites, several on the water. To the left is an out-and-back spur with a turnaround at the end. It also has lakeside sites. Some sites reach 60 feet in length. All sites are gravel surfaced off gravel roads and have picnic tables and fire pits. Some also have dedicated tent pads. There are vault toilets, firewood, water faucet, a dock, and a boat ramp. There's a hiking trail along the lake shore and to the river.

WATCH JADE BOULDERS REDUCED TO JEWELRY SIZE PIECES ON A VISIT TO JADE CITY

The maximum stay here is 14 days.

The 2.4-kilometer (1.5-mile) entrance road heads east from near Km 639 of the Cassiar Highway. This is about 93 kilometers (57 miles) south of the junction of the Cassiar and the Alaska Highway.

🚐 **FRENCH CREEK FOREST SERVICE CAMPSITE**
   Location: Near Km 666 Of The Cassiar Highway

FREE

   GPS Location: 59.59396 N, 129.21977 W, 2,200 Ft.

This is a small forest service recreation site with a few picnic tables, fire rings, and an outhouse. It's located along French Creek. While it is near the highway it is only suitable for RVs to about 30 feet. The access road does form a loop through the campground so it's possible to drive in and look, but over the years maintenance at this campground has been irregular to nonexistent and sometimes the road is narrow because bushes encroach from the sides.

The campground is on the east side of the highway near Km 666.5. This is .8 km (.4 mile) south of the French Creek Bridge. Last time we visited there was a new sign marking the road.

TELEGRAPH CREEK ROAD
113 Kilometers (70 Miles)

The community of Dease Lake marks the junction with a cutoff to **Telegraph Creek** on the Stikine River. The original route into the Cassiar area was along this road from Telegraph Creek, the Stikine is a navigable river and was traveled by large sternwheelers almost to Telegraph Creek from the mouth near Wrangell, Alaska. Now the 113 kilometer (70 mile) gravel road is used to go the other way, it is suitable for small to medium rigs only and is a bit of an expedition. If you want to drive this road check first in Dease Lake for information about road conditions.

Today's Telegraph Creek has a population of about 300. It's primarily a Tahltan First Nation village and is a popular access point to the Stikine River. The de facto tourist center in town is the Stikine Riversong, a café and lodge on the riverfront (www. stikineriversong.com, 250 235-3196). The Riversong actually occupies the former Hudson's Bay post here and is a good source of information, not to mention the food. They also offer jetboat tours up through the Grand Canyon of the Stikine and canoe and kayak rentals.

The road to Telegraph Creek goes west from the Petro Canada station in Dease Lake. In just 1.6 km (1 mile) you'll come to a T where you turn left. From here it's 111 km (69 miles) to Telegraph Creek. There are 5.2 km (3.2 miles) of pavement and then the road turns to dirt and gravel. At Km 69 the road descends into the river canyons and continues to climb and descend until you reach Telegraph Creek. It's very scenic, a great drive. Many of the hills are marked as 20% so you'll want to be sure you have plenty of power and good brakes. We don't recommend the trip for trailers or for

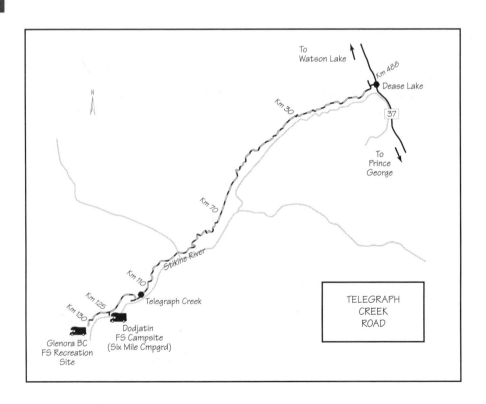

motorhomes over 30 feet because of the grades, some sharp switchbacks, and the occasionally poor road surface. We also recommend avoiding it in wet conditions.

Telegraph Creek Road Campgrounds

The campgrounds in this area are former B.C. Forest Service campgrounds. For the most part they are unmaintained with just a few picnic tables and fire pits remaining although they do have outhouses. These campgrounds are used by the locals as fishing camps during much of the summer.

DODJATIN B.C. FOREST SERVICE CAMPSITE
(SIX MILE CAMPGROUND)

Location: 10 Km (6.2 Miles) Beyond Telegraph Creek

GPS Location: 57.86820 N, 131.28664 W, 600 Ft.

This campsite is used primarily as a fishing camp and has many permanent structures constructed of plywood and visqueen. There are some nice sites with picnic tables and fire pits along the water as well as an outhouse.

The campground is just beyond Dodjatin Creek Bridge, about 10 km (6.2 miles) beyond Telegraph Creek.

GLENORA B.C. FOREST SERVICE RECREATION SITE
Location: 18.7 Km (11.6 Miles) Beyond Telegraph Creek

GPS Location: 57.83636 N, 131.39004 W, 500 Ft.

Glenora is used primarily as a fish camp and parking area for the pickups of folks using the boat launch area here. There are a few picnic tables and also an outhouse. Parking is in a large grassy field – along with those pickups. If you walk downstream along the bank you'll find a trail leading up a bluff. This is the location of the first Hudson's Bay post here, nothing remains but the scenic location.

Glenora is at the end of the road, 18.7 km (11.6 miles) beyond Telegraph Creek.

CASSIAR HIGHWAY DUMP STATIONS

Before you start north you might want to take advantage of the free sani-dump at the Infocentre in the **Hazeltons** at Km 284 of Highway 16 *(GPS Location: 55.24746 N, 127.59376 W)*. It's some 42 kilometers (26 miles) east of the junction of Highway 16 and the Cassiar Highway. The Infocentre is on the corner where Highway 62 goes north to Old Hazelton.

Most of the dump stations along the Cassiar (called sani-dumps in Canada) are in private campgrounds. We've noted those campgrounds offering dump stations with an icon, expect to pay a fee if you aren't staying at the campground, and sometimes if you are.

There is one important exception. The town of **Stewart** has a free city-operated dump and water station with excellent access *(GPS Location 55.93611 N, 129.98645 W)*. See the Stewart map in this book on page 137 for help locating it.

THE CASSIAR HIGHWAY

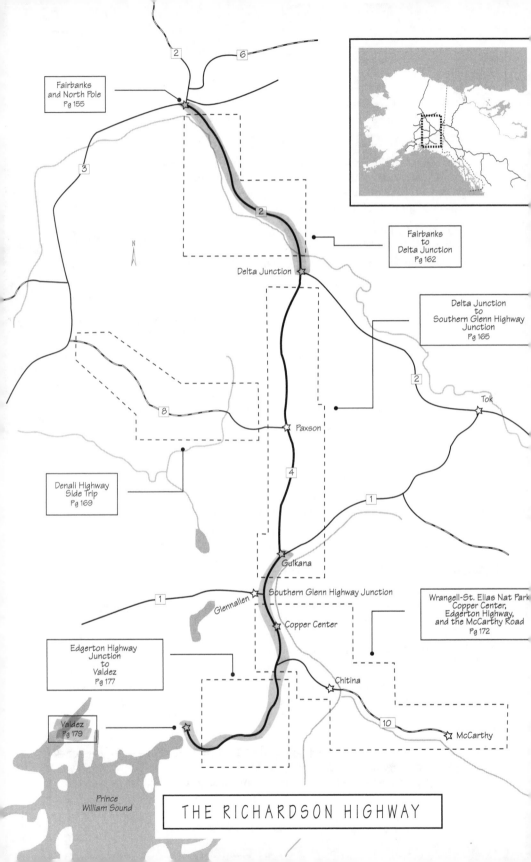

Delta Junction

Paxson

Tok

Gulkana

Southern Glenn Highway Junction

Glennallen

Copper Center

Chitina

McCarthy

Valdez

Prince
William Sound

THE RICHARDSON HIGHWAY

Chapter 6

The Richardson Highway

INTRODUCTION

The Richardson is Alaska's oldest major highway. It runs from tidewater at Valdez to Fairbanks in the interior. The Richardson is also one of the state's most scenic highways with natural scenery including distant mountain peaks, wide interior valleys, overhanging glaciers, and mountain passes.

In this guide we'll cover the Richardson from north to south. This may seem strange at first. After all, the highway mileposts go from south to north. We think most people will first drive most of this road from north to south so that's the way we laid things out.

You are likely to travel only segments of the Richardson. If you've driven the Alaska Highway from the south you'll probably join it at Delta Junction near Mile 266 and drive north to Fairbanks. Alternately, you may drive the Richardson for only a few miles between the two segments of the Glenn Highway on your way to Anchorage. If you decide to visit Valdez you'll drive quite a bit of the Richardson, including some of its most scenic sections.

Highlights

The cities at each end of the Richardson, **Fairbanks** and **Valdez**, are two of the most popular destinations in the state. They're very different, of course, most people will want to see them both.

The **Trans-Alaska Oil Pipeline** has been a top Alaska news story for many years. You'll have lots of chances to see it while driving the Richardson since the pipeline parallels the highway for most of its length. There will be times when you can't see the pipeline from the highway but it is usually not far away. There are viewing areas and displays at Mile 215, Mile 88, and Mile 65. You'll probably also spot Pump Station 9 at Mile 258, Pump Station 10 at Mile 219, and Pump Station 12 at Mile 65.

The Richardson began as a gold rush trail to Eagle, Alaska even before Fairbanks was founded. Very soon, however, most people traveling along it were following a new left fork toward Fairbanks. In 1910 the road was upgraded to allow the use of automobiles. Roadhouses were built along the road at approximately 10 mile (16 km) intervals (one day's travel before automobiles) by private individuals. Most roadhouses disappeared but a few remain. **Rika's Roadhouse** at Mile 275 just north of Delta Junction is now a state park and makes an interesting stop. In Delta the **Sullivan Roadhouse** is an excellent little museum. This roadhouse was moved to its present location from an army gunnery range.

The Richardson will give you several opportunities to take a good look at glaciers. The best of the bunch is the **Worthington Glacier** at Mile 30 just north of Thompson Pass. Paved handicapped-accessible paths lead to an overlook near the glacier.

As Denali National Park gets more and more crowded the National Park Service would like us to visit Alaska's other national park with road access. This is the **Wrangell-St. Elias National Park**. Unfortunately, opportunities for access to Wrangell-St. Elias National Park are limited. There are two driving routes, the Nabesna Road (from Mile 60 of the Tok Cutoff - See Chapter 7 - *The Glenn Highway*) and the Edgerton Highway and McCarthy Road (from Mile 83 of the Richardson), but both are rough and not really suitable for larger RVs. We cover the Edgerton Highway and McCarthy Road in more detail later in the chapter.

The Road and Fuel

The Richardson Highway was once the major route into the interior of the state. Until the Alaska Railroad from Seward to Fairbanks was finished in 1923 the choice was between the Richardson Highway and riverboat down the Yukon. Much later, in 1971, the Parks Highway opened. Today most Anchorage to Fairbanks traffic follows the Parks so the Richardson is not really heavily traveled.

All of the Richardson is paved. Most is pretty good road but not up to the same standards as the much newer Parks Highway. There are some sections of road that have permafrost problems. Most of the wear and tear of the pipeline construction years along this route has been repaired.

The Richardson Highway, from Fairbanks to Valdez, is 368 miles (594 km) long. Mile markers along the highway count up from just outside Valdez to Fairbanks. We'll travel in the opposite direction in this chapter, from Fairbanks to Valdez.

Fishing

In Alaska timing is an important part of catching fish, particularly salmon. You can't catch fish if they aren't there. Salmon arrive in runs and may be entirely absent the rest of the time. For timing purposes there are two regions traversed by the Richardson Highway: the Tanana Valley and Prince William Sound/Copper Valley. In general the Tanana Valley salmon arrive later because they have

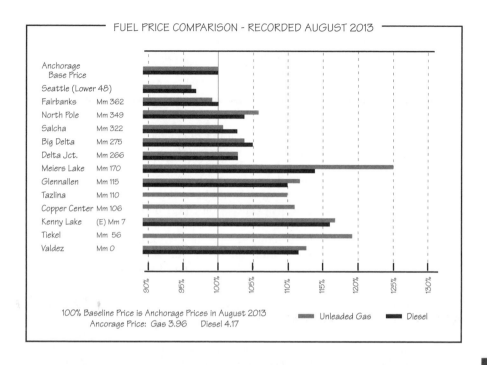

FUEL PRICE COMPARISON - RECORDED AUGUST 2013

Anchorage Base Price	
Seattle (Lower 48)	
Fairbanks	Mm 362
North Pole	Mm 349
Salcha	Mm 322
Big Delta	Mm 275
Delta Jct.	Mm 266
Meiers Lake	Mm 170
Glennallen	Mm 115
Tazlina	Mm 110
Copper Center	Mm 106
Kenny Lake	(E) Mm 7
Tiekel	Mm 56
Valdez	Mm 0

100% Baseline Price is Anchorage Prices in August 2013
Ancorage Price: Gas 3.96   Diesel 4.17

Unleaded Gas   Diesel

farther to travel from the ocean. In the Tanana Valley July is the king month, in the Copper Valley they show up in the middle of June while in salt water it's early June. Copper Valley reds are present from late June to the end of August, Copper Valley silvers are present from the middle of August until the middle of September. In Valdez expect pinks in July and August with a July peak and silvers just a little later with an August peak.

Many of the good fishing locations near Fairbanks are actually north of town. See Chapter 10 - *North of Fairbanks* for information about them.

From Fairbanks to Paxson most of the fishing along the Richardson Highway is lake fishing. A small boat is a big help. Try the **Chena Lakes** (Mile 347) for rainbows and silvers, **Lost Lake** (off a side road at Mile 306) for rainbows, **Birch Lake** (Mile 306) for rainbows, **Quartz Lake** (Mile 278) for rainbows, **Fielding Lake** (Mile 200) for lake trout and grayling, and **Summit Lake** (Mile 195) for grayling and lake trout.

At Paxson (Mile 185) the Denali Highway heads west toward Denali Park and the Parks Highway. Along the Denali try fishing **Ten Mile Lake** (Mile 10) for lake trout and grayling, **Denali-Clearwater Creek** (Mile 18) for grayling, the **Tangle Lakes** (at about Mile 21) for grayling and lake trout, **Clearwater Creek** (Mile 56) for grayling, and **Brushkana Creek** (Mile 104) for grayling.

Back on the Richardson Highway and heading south from Paxson try **Paxson Lake** (Mile 175) for grayling and lake trout; **Dick Lake** (Mile 173) for grayling; **Meiers Lake** (Mile 170) for grayling; **Gillespie Lake** (Mile 168) for grayling; **Sourdough Creek** (Mile 147) for grayling in the creek and also access to the Gulkana River;

THE RICHARDSON HIGHWAY

trails to the **Gulkana River** (Mile 146.5, 141.4, 139.6, 136.7, 129.3, and 129.1) for kings, reds, rainbows, and grayling; the **Gulkana Highway Bridge** (Mile 126.9) for kings, reds, grayling, and rainbows; the **Klutina River** at Copper Center for kings, reds, grayling and Dollies; the **Squirrel Creek gravel pit** (Mile 80) for grayling and rainbows; the **Little Tonsina River** (Mile 65) for Dollies; **Worthington Lake** (Mile 28) for rainbows; **Blueberry Lake** (Mile 24) for rainbows and grayling; and **Robe River** (Mile 5) for Dollies and reds using flies.

At Mile 83 the Edgerton Highway leads east to Chitina, the Copper River, the McCarthy Road, and eventually, McCarthy. The Copper River near Chitina is the scene of one of Alaska's most interesting fisheries, the salmon dip-net fishery. It is open only to Alaska residents and special permits are required. Big nets with handles over 20 feet long are used to catch fish in water that is just too silt-laden to be fished using other methods. It's fun to just watch. Other fishing possibilities along the road are **Liberty Falls** (Mile 25) for grayling, **Second Lake** (Mile 36) for rainbows and grayling, **First Lake** (Mile 37) for rainbows and grayling, **Chitina Lake** (Mile 39) for grayling, **Strelna Creek** (Mile 15, McCarthy Road) for Dollies, **Lou's Lake** (Mile 26, McCarthy Road) for silvers and grayling, and **Long Lake** (Mile 45, McCarthy Road) for grayling, lake trout, silvers, and Dollies.

Valdez is the top sport fishing destination on Prince William Sound. This is a great place to join a charter operator for a day of salmon fishing. Valdez also has some of the best and easiest beach fishing for pinks and silvers in Alaska at **Allison Point** near the **Solomon Gulch Hatchery** on Dayville Road. There are three different fishing derbies with prizes in Valdez. Dates vary slightly from year to year but the Halibut Derby runs all summer, the Pink Salmon Derby is in July, and the Silver Salmon Derby is in August. Check out the rules before you go fishing, you must follow them to win.

A large proportion of the campgrounds along the Richardson are in locations that offer fishing possibilities. This is a little surprising since most people don't think of this area of Alaska as being a top fishing destination. See the campground descriptions for more information.

Boating, Rafting, Canoeing, and Kayaking

When Fairbanks residents head out for a day of swimming, water skiing, and fun on the water they generally end up at **Harding Lake** (Mile 321, Richardson Highway) or **Birch Lake** (Mile 306, Richardson Highway). The **Chena Lakes Recreation Area** (Mile 347, Richardson Highway) is dedicated to non-powered boats and aquatic sports. North of Fairbanks there are several possibilities for river float and canoe trips, see Chapter 10 - *North of Fairbanks*, for information.

Between Delta Junction and the Gakona Junction there are two popular floatable rivers–the north-flowing **Delta River** and the south-flowing **Gulkana River**. Both are designated Wild and Scenic Rivers and are administered by the BLM (Glennallen District Office, PO Box 147, Glennallen, AK 99588; 907 822-3217). A Delta River trip starts by crossing the Tangle Lakes from a put-in at the Tangle Lakes Campground at Mile 21 of the Denali Highway. From the lakes the float is mainly Class II with a portage around a falls. The first take-out is at Mile 212 of the Richardson Highway. This trip is suitable for canoes, kayaks, and rafts. The **Gulkana River** has several different forks and possible routes, but the most popular float is from Paxson Lake (Mile 175, Richardson Highway) to take-outs at Sourdough Campground (Mile 148, Richardson Highway), Poplar Grove (Mile 137, Richardson Highway with 1-mile trail) or the Richardson Highway Bridge (Mile 127, Richardson Highway). You can also put in at Sourdough Campground to avoid the worst stretches of white water. Water is mostly Class II and a portage is required around Canyon Rapids. The Gulkana is a well-known fishing stream offering excellent red and king fishing during their respective runs. Rafts, kayaks, and canoes (only for good canoeists) are suitable. Both of these rivers have long stretches that are remote from road access and can be dangerous. If you plan to float them prepare yourself with adequate research and make sure you have the proper experience and equipment.

Several large lakes along this stretch of road are also popular with boaters. They are **Fielding Lake** (Mile 200), **Summit Lake** (Mile 195), and **Paxson Lake** (Mile 175).

Visitors to the Wrangell-St. Elias National Park will find that commercial operators offer whitewater rafting on rivers in the park including the **Chitina River**, the **Kennicott River**, and the **Nizina River**. Some of these rivers can be pretty challenging and entrance and exit points are often not obvious or easy to reach. Commercially guided tours are the best way to float them.

Valdez sits on the shore of the Valdez Arm which leads out into **Prince William Sound**. These waters are some of the best in the world for ocean kayaking. Possible routes are numerous and range from a day trip on the Arm to something much longer, say a 150 mile (242 km) crossing to Whittier. Several state marine parks with tent campsites are within a day's paddle of Valdez. Use of a charter vessel to drop you far out can save many days of paddling if you want to explore some of the more remote reaches of the sound.

Hiking and Mountain Biking

Most good hikes in the Fairbanks area are north of town. See Chapter 10 - *North of Fairbanks* for information about them. One exception is Creamers Field, formally known as **Creamer's Field Migratory Waterfowl Refuge**. The refuge is located on the northern outskirts of Fairbanks along College Road. There is a 2 mile (3 km) guided nature trail with observation platforms. The best months for observing waterfowl are April, May, and August.

The entire **Denali Highway** has become a popular mountain bike route. One hundred and fourteen miles (184 km) of gravel are hard going on a touring bike, but mountain bikes have no problems and traffic is minimal. There are also some high-country hiking routes from the highway. This is a popular hunting area and there are many off-road vehicle trails, many are not very good for hiking because the wheeled vehicles tend to tear up the tundra leaving a muddy mess. Some of the best hikes are away from the trails. The **Landmark Lake** hike from Mile 25 follows an old dirt road 2.4 miles (.4 km) to Landmark Gap Lake, you can catch grayling in the lake and hike the surrounding hills. The route in is suitable for hiking or mountain bikes. From Mile 37 just west of **Maclaren Summit** (4,086 ft.) you can hike north on an old vehicle trail through a region of small lakes and big views. Go as far as you want across the open tundra, the first part of the trail is fine for mountain bikes. Mountain bikers will also like the 12 mile (19 km) **Maclaren River Road** heading north for 12 miles (19 km) from Mile 43 to the Maclaren Glacier.

There are several decent trails in the Wrangell-St. Elias National Park accessible from the Edgerton Highway and the McCarthy Road. Two trails lead from the Nugget Creek Road near Mile 13.5 of the McCarthy Road. **Dixie Pass** is an 11 mile (18 km) strenuous back-packing trip that takes at least three days. Much of the route is not on well-defined trail, you must have good maps and route instructions before attempting it. The **Nugget Creek Trail** is easier to follow since it follows an old mining road. The 15 mile (24 km) trail is also suitable for mountain bikes and leads to an old mining works and an unmaintained park cabin overlooking the Kuskulana Glacier.

At the end of the McCarthy Road there's a parking lot where you can camp in your RV or tent, from there you must either walk or catch a shuttle the 1 mile (1.6 km) to McCarthy and 5 miles (8 km) to Kennecott. A mountain bike comes in very handy here for transportation since you must cross a foot bridge to reach the towns from the parking lot. From Kennecott there are at least three trails for strenuous day hikes or easy overnighters: **Bonanza Mine Trail**, **Jumbo Mine Trail**, and **Root Glacier Trail**. Portions of these trails can be done on mountain bikes.

Mountain bikers might want to try the **Bernard Creek Trail** at Mile 79 of the Richardson. The BLM recommends this 15 mile (24 km) road southeast to Kimball Pass and it looks good on the map. There's another similar road called the **Klutina Lake Trail** from about Mile 101 of the Copper Center Bypass section of the Richardson that goes west for 25 miles (40 km) up the Klutina River to Klutina Lake.

In Valdez the most popular hike is probably the **Solomon Gulch Trail**. The trail starts across from the Solomon Gulch Fish Hatchery on Dayville Road. The 1.3 mile (2.1 km) trail climbs steeply to the Solomon Creek power plant dam and offers great views of the town of Valdez across Port Valdez.

Wildlife Viewing

Bird lovers will love **Creamer's Field.** It is located just north of Fairbanks, there are nature trails and a visitor's center with displays and volunteers to answer questions and lead hikes. Spring and fall are the best times to visit because the area is full of migrating waterfowl. The visitor center telephone number is (907) 452-5162.

Almost **anywhere along the Richardson** you are likely to suddenly spot a moose, maybe when you least expect them. Keep your eyes peeled. Isolated caribou are also often spotted on portions of the road passing through the Alaska Range. Also watch along streams for signs of beaver.

Bison were introduced into the Delta Junction area in 1928. They did well, today there are over 400 of them and there is an annual hunt to keep the numbers in check. The huge animals can be a problem, they love the grain that is grown by the farmers around Delta Junction and no fence seems to keep them out of the fields. The **Delta Junction State Bison Range** has been set aside for them but they tend to go where they want. In early summer you can often see them on the flats near the Delta River from viewpoints between Mile 265 and Mile 241. A pair of binoculars will help you spot them.

The **Denali Highway** is an excellent place to spot animals, perhaps because the country is so open and the traffic so sparse. The Nelchina Caribou herd is present during the fall. Caribou and grizzly bears tend to stick to the wide-open areas, watch for moose and black bears where there are trees. Long sections of the road run along gravel eskers left by retreating glaciers. These raised sections of road overlook ponds offering some great birding. It pays to stop occasionally and examine the lakes and open country with a pair of binoculars.

Wrangell-St. Elias National Park is accessible from the Richardson Highway by following the Edgerton Highway east to McCarthy. There's lots of game in this largest of U.S. national parks including Dall sheep, mountain goats, brown and black bear, moose, caribou, and even bison. Viewing the animals, however, isn't quite as easy as in Denali Park. There's no long road through the park with vistas in all directions as there is at Denali. Watch for animals along the McCarthy access road, you're likely to see a moose or two. To really see animals in this park, however, you need to get out and hike away from the roads or take a sightseeing flight.

In Valdez make sure to stop at the **Crooked Creek salmon spawning area** which is just outside town along the highway. From Valdez you can access the waterways of **Prince William Sound** on charter boats, cruise boats, ferries, or even with a kayak. The sound is home to Steller sea lions, seals, sea otters, orcas, gray and humpback whales, eagles, and a virtually unlimited number of marine birds, shorebirds, raptors, and ducks.

THE ROUTES, TOWNS, AND CAMPGROUNDS

FAIRBANKS AND NORTH POLE
Population 32,000 (metro area 98,000), Elevation 440 feet

Fairbanks may be only Alaska's second largest town but there is no doubt that the interior city is a more popular destination among Alaska Highway RVers than much larger Anchorage. This may be because Fairbanks appreciates its RVing visitors. There are lots of things to do in the area and many good RV parks. Fairbanks serves as a gateway to both the Denali Park area (121 miles (195 km) south on the Parks Highway) and the roads extending to the north, one as far as Prudhoe Bay (see Chapter 10 of this book). For RV travelers from the south Fairbanks may also be more popular than Anchorage because its summer weather is much nicer. There's a lot less rain in the interior and evenings never really get dark because of the midnight sun.

Fairbanks is the older of the two largest Alaska cities. The town was founded in 1901 and soon became a supply center for nearby gold fields. Gold continues to be mined in the area. Today Fairbanks is still a supply center, but now the area served includes most of Interior Alaska and the North Slope.

The new **Morris Thompson Cultural and Visitor Center** in downtown Fairbanks (101 Dunkel Street, (907) 459-3700) is a place where you can find information about

THE POPULAR RIVERBOAT DISCOVERY

the entire northern part of the state. It combines the former Fairbanks Visitor Information Center, the Alaska Public Lands Information Center, and a native cultural center in one location. You'll find a number of interesting dioramas, native art demonstrations and a theater here in addition to the information resources.

Pioneer Park, the town's historical theme park, makes a good afternoon's destination that can easily stretch into the evening. On the grounds you'll find several museums, the stern wheel riverboat Nenana, historical displays, souvenir shops, and a salmon-bake restaurant.

After seeing the riverboat at Pioneer Park you'll probably want to take a ride on one. The most popular attraction in Fairbanks has got to be the **Riverboat Discovery**. This sternwheeler makes twice daily trips down the Chena to the Tanana and is usually packed with visitors enjoying an extremely well-done trip including a stop at Old Chena Indian Village.

On the campus of the University of Alaska you'll find one of the most interesting museums in the state. The **University of Alaska Museum of the North** has displays about gold mining, natural history, the Alaska Highway, mastodons and dinosaurs, the northern lights, and lots more. You don't want to miss it! The museum has recently been greatly expanded, doubling in size. Nearby you'll find the University's **Georgeson Botanical Gardens**, these experimental gardens are a great place to see big vegetables and beautiful flowers.

A big part of the history of Fairbanks and Alaska is gold mining. Near Fairbanks are areas that have been extensively mined using huge floating dredges that left rows and rows of gravel "tailing piles". North of town out the Steese Highway is the Goldstream area around the little town of Fox. There you'll find **Dredge No. 8**. It is a great introduction to Alaskan gold mining, done by the same folks who run the Discovery III sternwheeler.

Fairbanks has 3 golf courses: Chena Bend (907 353-6223) has 18 holes and is located on Fort Wainwright but is open to the civilian public, Fairbanks Golf Course (907 479-6555) has nine holes and the North Star Golf Club (907 457-4653) has 18 holes. All of these courses are open to the public.

There are several interesting celebrations and events during the summer in Fairbanks. **Golden Days** during the middle of July is when the city celebrates its past with a parade and other events lasting five days. The **Tanana Valley State Fair** is held during the first half of August. That makes it easier for most visiting RVers to attend than the Alaska State Fair in Palmer at the end of the month. Both feature huge vegetables.

Fairbanks Campgrounds

CHENA RIVER WAYSIDE STATE RECREATION SITE

Location:	221 University Ave., Fairbanks, AK 99707
Info:	(907) 452-7275
Website:	dnr.alaska.gov/parks/aspunits/northern/chenariversrs.htm

GPS Location: 64.83932 N, 147.81058 W, 400 Ft.

This is a state campground right in the middle of Fairbanks, it has a convenient location and is very popular. Two large supermarkets are within easy walking distance. This campground is privately managed and electrical hookups are available.

There are 59 back-in vehicle sites well separated with trees and natural vegetation, some to 50 feet. Eleven have 30-amp electrical hookups and water. There are also 5 tent sites. All have picnic tables and fire pits. There are flush toilets but not showers. The campground also has a boat ramp and a dump station. It's free if you're staying at the campground, otherwise there is a five dollar charge. A host is usually on site. There is a 5 day camping limit during the June 10 to August 10 high season, otherwise the limit is 15 days. Wi-Fi is available only in a small area near the host's space.

Access to this campground has changed in the last few years. Best access is now on Washington Drive from Airport Way. Washington is the stoplight between the ones on University Way and Market Street. Go north on Washington from Airport Way for a block, turn left on Geraghty Ave, and you'll see the campground entrance on the right in a short distance.

RIVER'S EDGE RV PARK AND CAMPGROUND

Address:	4140 Boat St., Fairbanks, AK 99709
Telephone:	(907) 474-0286 or (800) 770-3343
Email:	rvpark@riversedge.net
Website:	www.riversedge.net

GPS Location: 64.83944 N, 147.83446 W, 400 Ft.

One of the nicer and more popular campgrounds in Fairbanks is the River's Edge. It

THE RICHARDSON HIGHWAY

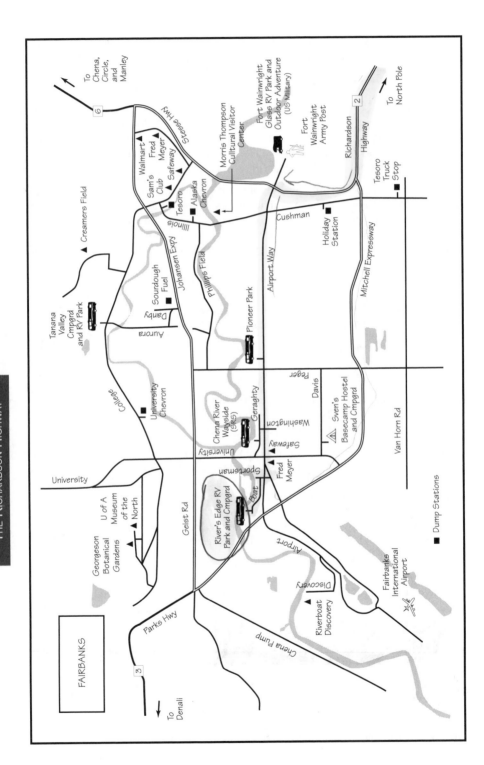

sits on the south bank of the Chena River, has lots of grass and trees and specializes in arranging tours.

The campground has about 190 sites. There are a variety of types: full and partial hookups, pull-thrus to 60 feet, dry sites for vehicles and also tent sites. All have picnic tables. The restrooms offer flush toilets and free showers, there is a coin-op laundry, a gift shop, and a nice riverside restaurant. There is also a vehicle wash station and dump and water-fill stations. Reservations are recommended.

The campground is located just off Airport Way, one of Fairbanks' main arterials. Turn onto Sportsman's Way across from the Fred Meyer store, immediately turn left on Boat Street, and then watch for the campground on the right.

PIONEER PARK

Location: Just Off Airport Way At Peger Road
Telephone: (907) 459-1087
Email: pioneerpark@co.fairbanks.ak.us
Website: co.fairbanks.ak.us/pioneerpark/visitor_information/rv_visitors.htm

GPS Location: 64.83750 N, 147.77417 W, 400 Ft.

The Pioneer Park city-run historical park offers dry camping in its huge parking lot. Lots of people take them up on it. There are no hookups although there is a potable water outlet along the south border of the parking lot. RV parking slots are located at both the east and west ends of the parking lot. Either portable toilets are provided or you are allowed to use the restrooms inside the park. Sometimes there is even a host at this camping area. Check in at the Riverboat Nenana inside the park or talk to the host if he's on-site. There's a four day limit for campers here. During the busy part of the summer there is a salmon bake located at the park.

Pioneer Park is centrally located just off Airport Way near the Peger Road intersection.

TANANA VALLEY CAMPGROUND AND RV PARK

Address: 1800 College Rd., Fairbanks, AK 99709
Telephone: (907) 456-7956
Email: info@fairbankscampgroundandrvpark.com
Website: www.fairbankscampgroundandrvpark.com

GPS Location: 64.86464 N, 147.75933 W, 400 Ft.

The Tanana Valley Fair is a popular area attraction during the first or second week of August. Don't try to stay in this campground that week without reservations, the place is very busy. At other times, however, the campground makes a convenient and pleasant base.

There are about 55 camping sites with picnic tables and fire pits. They are set in a grove of trees and have pretty good separation. RVs to 40 feet can park in some spaces with careful driving. There are also some tent sites reserved for hikers and bikers. The campground has flush toilets, free showers, a dump station, and a coin-op laundry. There is free Wi-Fi in the area of the office but use is limited to 10 minutes at a time. There are usually conscientious and helpful hosts at this campground and firewood for sale. There is convenient bus service along College Road to downtown and the university. Creamer's Field is also close by.

The campground is located at the Tanana Valley Fairgrounds on College Road. From the Parks Highway take the Geist Road exit and head east to University Ave., a distance of 1.5 miles (2.4 km). Turn left on University and drive north for .4 miles (.6 km) to College Road, turn right on College Rd. and drive 1.7 miles (2.7 km). You will see the campground entrance on your left.

SVEN'S BASECAMP HOSTEL AND CAMPGROUND

Address:	3505 Davis Rd., Fairbanks, AK 99709
Telephone:	(907) 355-7088
Email:	info@svenshostel.com
Website:	www.svenshostel.com

GPS Location: 64.82716 N, 147.80790 W, 500 Ft.

If you've ever stayed at a hostel you know that it offers an experience much different than a normal campground. For tent campers this hostel makes a convenient place to stay, and perhaps to meet other travelers. It's a tent campground only, vehicles are parked in a lot.

The camping area here is small, there's just room to pitch a few tents under trees at the edge of the property. Amenities include restrooms with coin-op showers, a kitchen area, free Wi-Fi, a game room, and a community campfire area. You can rent bikes and canoes. Private rental cabins, and a teepee are also available. Since this is a small facility it may be full, call in advance for a reservation.

From Airport Way travel south on University Ave. for .6 miles (1 km) and turn left on Davis Road. You'll see the campground on the right almost immediately.

FORT WAINWRIGHT GLASS RV PARK AND OUTDOOR ADVENTURE – U.S. MILITARY

Location:	Fort Wainwright

This is a campground on Fort Wainwright. It is only open to active military personnel, National Guard personnel, reservists, retired military, and Department of Defense employees. Reservations can be obtained by calling (907) 361-6350. The campground has 27 RV spaces with electric and water, water only, or no hookups and also tent sites. A laundry, and showers are also available.

North Pole and Badger Road Campgrounds

RIVERVIEW RV PARK

Address:	1316 Badger Road, Fairbanks, AK 99705
Telephone:	(907) 488-6392 or (888) 488-6392
Email:	riverview@acsalaska.net
Website:	www.riverviewrvpark.net

GPS Location: 64.83244 N, 147.51740 W, 400 Ft.

The Riverview is a large and well-maintained campground with a quiet location along the Chena River several miles outside Fairbanks.

The campground has about 160 spaces, many are pull-thrus to 60 feet. Full utility hookups are offered including 30 and 50-amp electric and cable TV. Spaces are separated by grass and some trees. Picnic tables are provided. There is also a tent area. Individual shower rooms provide privacy. The campground sits behind a gas station

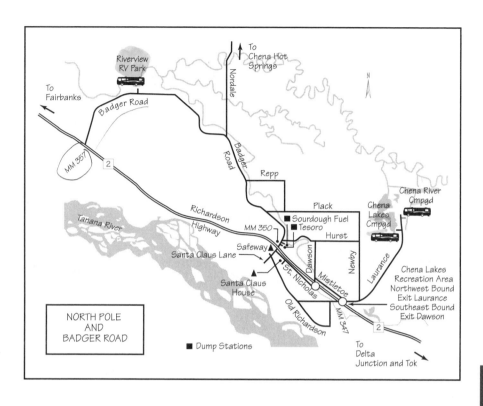

and convenience store with the same ownership and also has a gift shop. Other features include a small 3-hole pitch-and-putt golf course and a vehicle wash.

The Riverview is located on Badger Road. The best access route is from the Richardson Highway near Mile 357. Follow Badger Road for 2.7 miles (4.4 km), you'll see the campground on the left.

Chena Lakes Recreation Area

Address:	3780 Laurance Road, North Pole, AK 99705
Telephone:	(907) 488-1655
Email:	parks@co.fairbanks.ak.us
Website:	www.chenalake.com

GPS Location: 64.75392 N, 147.21861 W, 500 Ft.

One of the big disasters in modern Alaskan history was the almost complete flooding of Fairbanks by the Chena River in 1967. To prevent this from happening again a major flood-control project was undertaken. Huge dikes were built to divert flood water, and some of the gravel came from what is now the Chena River Lakes Recreation Area. Built by the Corps of Engineers and managed by the North Star Borough this is one of the best camping areas in the Fairbanks region and certainly one of the best deals.

There are actually two campgrounds in the recreation area. One is the Lake Park with

The Richardson Highway

45 sites and the other is the River Park with 33 sites. There are also additional tent sites including some on a small island in Chena Lake. Both camping areas offer large back-in and pull-thru wilderness-type sites with good separation by trees and natural vegetation. Roads and sites are gravel although those designated as handicap-access-able are paved. Some sites reach 100 feet. Sites have picnic tables and fire pits. There are vault toilets and hand-operated water pumps. The recreation area also has a dump and water-fill station and firewood for sale as well as boat ramps, covered picnic areas, playgrounds and playfields, and swimming beaches. There are also extensive paved bike trails and a fish-counting operation which monitors salmon ascending the Chena River. Stays are limited to 5 nights out of every 30.

Coming from the east take the exit at Mile 347 signed for Chena Lakes and follow Laurance Road to the right for 2.6 miles (4.2 km) to the recreation area entrance gate. Coming from Fairbanks you must exit closer to the city at the Dawson Road/Busby Road Exit, cross to the north side of the highway, and follow signs eastward to the exit mentioned above at Mile 347.

FROM FAIRBANKS TO DELTA JUNCTION
98 Miles (158 Kilometers)

Between Fairbanks and Delta Junction the Richardson follows the north bank of the Tanana River. Much of the time the river is not visible from the highway. The Ta-

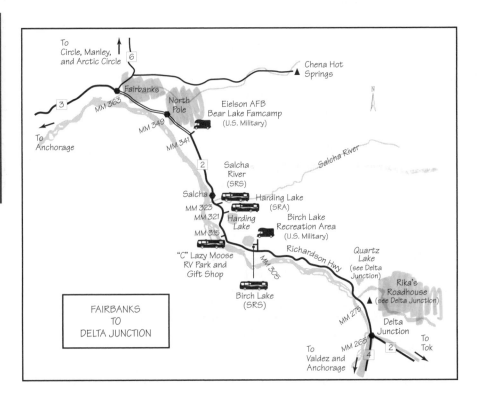

nana is a very dangerous, muddy, fast-moving river that carries tons of mud and silt. Where it does adjoin the road it is often a problem because it threatens to wash out the highway as it unpredictably tries to change course.

For the first 25 miles (40 km) or so the Richardson is a new four-lane divided highway. You'll cruise past Fairbanks's southern suburb, North Pole, at Mile 349, about 14 miles (23 km) from Fairbanks. Most people stop in North Pole to visit **Santa Claus House** where you can pick up a toy or Christmas ornament and arrange to have Santa send a letter to someone back home. Twenty-five miles (40 km) from Fairbanks you'll see the long runway at Eielson Air Force Base on your left, watch for a long line of KC-135 tankers, F-16s, or even more exotic aircraft during the occasional Red Flag training exercises.

At Eielson the road narrows down to two lanes and stays that way all the way to Valdez. For most of the distance to Delta Junction you'll have low bluffs on your left and the river on your right. At Mile 275 the road crosses the Tanana. The Trans-Alaska Oil Pipeline crosses at this same spot, you can't miss it.

Just south of the river crossing, at Mile 275 is the entrance road to the **Big Delta State Historical Site and Rika's Roadhouse**. This is one of the few remaining roadhouses along the Richardson and a good place to stop and stretch your legs. Delta Junction is just 9 miles (15 km) farther south.

Delta is where the Alaska Highway from the Lower 48 officially ends, so see Chapter 4 - *The Alaska Highway* for information about Delta Junction and its campgrounds.

Fairbanks to Delta Junction Campgrounds

EIELSON AFB BEAR LAKE FAMCAMP – U.S. MILITARY

Location: Eielson Air Force Base

This is a campground on Eielson Air Force Base. It is only open to active military personnel, National Guard personnel, reservists, retired military, and Department of Defense employees. Reservations can be obtained only for active duty on order personnel at Eielson. Contact Eielson Famcamp, 354 SVS/SVRO, 3112 Broadway Avenue, Unit 6B, Eielson AFB, AK 99702-1885 (907 377-1317). The campground has 18 RV spaces with electric and water hookups and 8 tent sites. A laundry, dump site and showers are also available.

SALCHA RIVER STATE RECREATION SITE

Location:	41 Miles (66 Km) South Of Fairbanks On The Richardson Highway
Info:	(907) 451-2695
Website:	dnr.alaska.gov/parks/units/salcha.htm

GPS Location: 64.46781 N, 146.92386 W, 700 Ft.

Designed primarily to be a boat-launching area for the clear-running Salcha River, this recreation site also allows camping. There is a huge gravel parking lot with about 60 sites where camping is allowed and also 2 designated campsites along its borders. The recreation site has a few of the customary picnic tables and fire pits, there are vault toilets and a hand-operated water pump. North of the parking lot there's access to a large gravel bar along the river where many people camp in RVs and tents. Vault toilets are provided for this area too. Watch out for soft spots! The boat ramp can be a busy place, particularly on weekends. Stays here are limited to 15 days.

The access road for this area is at Mile 323 of the Richardson Highway, just southeast of the bridge over the Salcha.

Harding Lake State Recreation Area

Location:	44 Miles (71 Km) From Fairbanks
	Off The Richardson Highway
Info:	(907) 451-2695
Website:	dnr.alaska.gov/parks/units/harding.htm

GPS Location: 64.43746 N, 146.87975 W, 800 Ft.

Harding Lake is one of the few large lakes near Fairbanks, it is surrounded by cabins owned by local residents. The Harding Lake State Recreation Area gives the rest of us access to the lake. The recreation area offers a large beach with swimming, picnicking, sports fields and hiking trails as well as camping. Weekends can be crowded because Fairbanks is so close.

This campground has about 78 back-in vehicle camping sites off two loops as well as a walk-in camping area for tents. These vehicle sites are wilderness sites with surrounding natural vegetation and trees. Some are large enough for RVs to about 45 feet. They are situated back from the lake and have no views. Sites have picnic tables, fire pits and dish-water drains. The campground has vault toilets. Other facilities include a dump station, a water-fill station, and a boat ramp. There are also some overflow camping spaces for busy weekends. Stays here are limited to 15 days.

The paved access road to the campground leaves the Richardson Highway at Mile 321. It will lead you about .6 mile (1 km) to the campground.

"C" Lazy Moose RV Park and Gift Shop

Address:	Mile 315 Richardson Highway,
	Salcha, AK 99714
Telephone:	(907) 488-8141
Website:	www.clazymooserv.com

GPS Location: 64.36516 N, 146.87596 W, 800 Ft.

The Lazy Moose is a RV park on the banks of the Tanana River between Harding and Birch Lake. There are 28 sites with back-ins and pull-thrus to 60 feet with both full and partial hookups. Some are along the river. Restrooms have flush toilets and pay showers and there is a laundry and also a dump station. Check in at the gift shop out front or at the pay station if the gift shop is closed.

The campground is on the south side of the highway at Mile 315.

Birch Lake State Recreation Site

Location:	On The East Shore Of Birch Lake
Info:	(907) 451-2695
Website:	dnr.alaska.gov/parks/units/birch.htm

GPS Location: 64.31516 N, 146.64553 W, 700 Ft.

This small state recreation area is very popular on weekends during the summer because it gives access to one of the best lakes for swimming and water sports near Fairbanks.

There are 17 back-in spaces for RVs to about 40 feet as well as an additional separate tent sites. The RV spaces are really just slots in the parking lot but they're long. There's a swimming beach, some picnic tables, a hand-operated water pump, vault toilets, a rental cabin, and a boat ramp. Maximum stay is 15 days.

Access is from a short access road that leaves the Richardson near Mile 305.2.

BIRCH LAKE RECREATION AREA – U.S. MILITARY
Location: Mile 305 Richardson Highway

There is a military campground on Birch Lake, about 55 miles (89 km) outside Fairbanks. It is only open to active military personnel, National Guard personnel, reservists, retired military, and Department of Defense employees. Reservations can be obtained at 354 SVS/SVRO, 3112 Broadway Street, U-6, Eielson AFB, AK 99702-1875 (907 377-1317). In addition to cabins the area has 29 RV spaces with 30-amp electric hookups and 14 tent spaces. Water is available and there are restrooms and showers.

FROM DELTA JUNCTION TO THE SOUTHERN GLENN HIGHWAY JUNCTION
151 Miles (244 Kilometers)

Driving south from Delta Junction you'll pass through **Fort Greeley**, probably without even noticing. The fort was closed in 2001 but reactivated as a national missile defense site in 2002.

At Mile 244 there is a pull-off and overlook that in good weather offers views of three Alaska Range peaks to the southwest. These are **Mount Deborah** (12,339 ft.), **Mount Hess** (11,940 ft.), and **Mount Hayes** (13,832 ft.). This viewpoint is also a popular place to glass for the **Delta bison herd**.

The Richardson soon begins climbing through the Alaska Range to **Isabel Pass**. This 3,284 foot crossing is very gradual, you'll hardly know when you reach the top at Summit Lake at Mile 198. Before reaching the summit watch for pipeline Pump Station Number 10 at Mile 219. Also watch for the **Gulkana Glacier** at Mile 197. The summit is where the watersheds of the Yukon River and the Copper River meet.

From Summit Lake the road gradually descends to the Paxson Junction with the Denali Highway at Mile 185. The Denali Highway is discussed in a following section in this chapter.

Another important junction, this time the North Junction with the Glenn Highway (also called the Tok Cutoff), is at Mile 128. For 13 miles (21 km) the Glenn and the Richardson are the same highway, then at Mile 115 is the South Junction where the Glenn heads west through Glennallen to Anchorage.

Delta Junction to the Southern Glenn Highway Junction Campgrounds

DONNELLY CREEK STATE RECREATION SITE
Location: Near Mile 238 Of The Richardson Highway
Info: (907) 451-2695
Website: dnr.alaska.gov/parks/units/deltajct/donnelly.htm

GPS Location: 63.67418 N, 145.88412 W, 1,800 Ft.

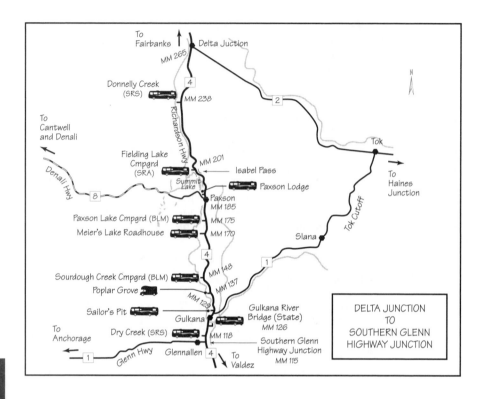

Donnelly Creek campground is one of the older ones operated by the state. Still, this small campground makes a good place to spend the night along a section of road that doesn't have many places to stay.

There are 11 back-in and one pull-thru site arranged around a loop road, one site has been filled with a host's cabin. Spaces are well separated in willows and white spruce but many are small, RV size is limited to about 35 feet in these formal sites. All have fire pits and picnic tables. The campground has vault toilets and a hand operated water pump. There's also an area for overflow camping and for folks with big rigs. Stays are limited to 15 days.

Watch for the campground near Mile 238 of the Richardson Highway on the west side of the road.

FIELDING LAKE STATE CAMPGROUND

Location:	Near Mile 200 Of The Richardson Highway
Info:	(907) 875-4599
Website:	dnr.alaska.gov/parks/units/deltajct/fielding.htm

GPS Location: 63.19474 N, 145.64979 W, 3,000 Ft.

Fielding Lake Campground sits near the shore of a large lake offering good lake trout and grayling fishing. There are a few private cabins in and near the campground vicinity. This lake is situated above the tree line in Isabel Pass so the surroundings are a little barren and unprotected from the weather. Ice often remains on the lake into July. However, the views in this region can be spectacular.

There are about 17 sites here, not all of them well defined. Many are side-by-side sharing small parking areas. All are along a stream that runs into the lake. Any size RV will find maneuvering and parking room. Fire pits, picnic tables, and a vault toilet are available. There is also a boat ramp. Stays here are limited to 15 days.

To reach the campground follow the gravel road which leaves the Richardson Highway near Mile 200 for 1.6 miles (2.6 km). The condition of this entrance road varies but even large RVs should always be able to negotiate it.

PAXSON LODGE

Location:	Mile 185.5 Richardson Hwy., Crossroads of AK 8 and AK 4
Telephone:	(907) 822-3330

GPS: 63.03012 N, 145.49762 W, 2,700 Ft.

The Paxson Lodge has been in its current location since the fifties, before that it was across the highway. This place is an old-timer and has seen better days. It sits at a strategic location where the Denali Highway meets the Richardson Highway. When the Denali Highway was the only access highway to Denali Park this was an important place.

There has been a campground, mostly used as a residential camp by construction workers, behind the lodge for some time. There are about 20 sites, some back-in and some pull-thru, with full hookups. Flush toilets are located in the lodge building, One of the motel rooms may be available for showers if you ask. Non-guests can dump for $5.

The lodge is located at Mile 185.5 of the Richardson Highway on the west side. It's at the intersection of the Richardson and Denali Highways.

PAXSON LAKE BLM CAMPGROUND

Location:	Near Mile 175 Of The Richardson Hwy.
Info:	(907) 822-3217

GPS Location: 62.88471 N, 145.48630 W, 2,600 Ft.

This large campground is popular with RVers because it offers nice large spaces, some are even pull-thrus. There is also a dump station. Paxson Lake is quite large and offers lake trout, grayling, and even red salmon fishing. Many people float the Gulkana River from here to the Sourdough Campground described below. Note that the dump station here is open to folks from outside the campground and that there is no fee to use it.

The campground has 40 vehicle spaces off two loops, 8 of these are pull-thrus, some to 70 feet. There is also a nice tent-camping area near the lake. Spaces are well separated with many spruce trees. They have fire pits and picnic tables but are not located along the lake shore. This campground has vault toilet, and a dump station, but only hand-pump water. There is also a boat ramp. The time limit for this campground is fourteen days.

THE RICHARDSON HIGHWAY

From Mile 175 of the Richardson Highway follow a wide gravel access road west for 1.6 miles (2.6 km) to the campground.

MEIERS LAKE ROADHOUSE

Address:	Mile 170 Richardson Highway
	(HC72, Box 7190), Delta Junction, AK 99737
Telephone:	(907) 822-3151
Email:	tina@meierslake.com
Website:	www.meierslake.com

GPS Location: 62.81693 N, 145.49667 W, 2,700 Ft.

This roadhouse operation occupies a site along an empty stretch of highway near a lake known for its grayling fishing. If you don't need hookups it's a decent stop.

There are some 10 very large pull-thru and back-in RV sites located behind the road-house. They have informal fire rings and some have old wire spools that serve as tables. There are showers (substantial extra fee), a laundry, some grocery items, gas, a restaurant, and a lounge. Wi-Fi is available only in the lodge.

The roadhouse is on the west side of the highway at Mile 170.

SOURDOUGH CREEK BLM CAMPGROUND

Location:	Near Mile 148 Of The Richardson Hwy.
Info:	(907) 822-3217

GPS Location: 62.52744 N, 145.51826 W, 2,000 Ft.

This large campground is located along the Gulkana River and is a take-out point for people floating from Paxson Lake and a put-in point for people planning to float the lower river. A large area is set aside for parking RVs belonging to boaters. Fishing in the Gulkana and Sourdough Creek for grayling, rainbows and king salmon is quite good.

The campground itself has 42 sites. These are large sites suitable for big RVs, eight are pull-thrus, some to 70 feet. Even the back-ins reach 45 feet. The sites are separated by natural vegetation including black spruce and have picnic tables and fire pits. There are vault toilets, a nature trail, a boat launch, and a covered picnic area. The campground usually has a host and firewood is available. There is a 14 day stay limit.

POPLAR GROVE

Location:	Mile 137 Richardson Highway
Telephone:	(907) 822-3476
Website:	permits.ahtna-inc.com

GPS Location: 62.39524 N, 145.37944 W, 1,800 Ft.

The gravel Poplar Grove road leads .3 miles (.5 km) from the Richardson Highway to a parking lot where folks leave their cars and then walk a trail down to the Gulkana River to fish. The road and parking area belong to Ahtna Inc (the regional native corporation) and there are fees for their use. RVs often overnight in the parking lot although it is not large. This parking area is best for smaller RVs because the turn-around could be difficult and so there is room for other users. Tent campers can find decent locations nearby.

The access road leaves the Richardson near Mile 137, a sign marks it as Gulkana River Trail Road.

Sailor's Pit
Location: Mile 129 Richardson Highway
Telephone: (907) 822-3476
Website: permits.ahtna-inc.com

GPS Location: 62.29978 N, 145.36328 W, 1,500 Ft.

This is a popular access point for fishing the Gulkana River. It's run by Ahtna, Inc., the regional native corporation. Parking here has been in a large gravel pit but roads have now been built and a few camping slots placed in the trees between the pit and the river. There are portable toilets but the only water is from the river.

Access is via a good gravel road suitable for any vehicle that leaves the Richardson near Mile 129 and leads down the hill to the west and the Gulkana River.

Gulkana River Bridge State Right of Way
Location: Mile 126.5 Richardson Highway

GPS Location: 62.26711 N, 145.38592 W, 1,500 Ft.

During fishing season you're likely to spot lots of RVs camped in a large gravel lot to the east and south of the Richardson's bridge over the Gulkana River. These campers are parked on a state right of way and there is no charge. Facilities are minimal, limited to some port-a-potties and garbage dumpsters. Rigs park where they like, tent campers sometimes find a spot in the willows along the river but these areas can be muddy so many just pitch in the gravel lot. The beach works good as a launch, fairly large boats are launched from trailers here.

Access is via a paved access road. It's the first road that leaves the Richardson Highway (about 100 yards) south of the bridge over the Gulkana at about Mile 126.5.

Dry Creek State Recreation Site
Location: Mile 118 Of The Richardson Hwy.
Info: (907) 259-4123
Website: dnr.alaska.gov/parks/aspunits/matsu/drycreeksrs.htm

GPS Location: 62.15290 N, 145.47129 W, 1,600 Ft.

Dry Creek campground is conveniently located just north of the junction of the Glenn and Richardson Highways at Glennallen. It's managed by a private contractor.

There are 50 well-separated vehicle sites at this campground. Most are back-ins off three loops (some sites to 45 feet) and one area has eight pull-thrus as long as 70 feet. There are also some walk-in tent sites. All sites have picnic tables and fire pits. There are vault toilets and water is hauled in to the campground. Maximum stay here is 15 days.

The campground is located just west of the highway across from the Gulkana Airport, it is near Mile 118 of the Richardson Highway. This is three miles (5 km) north of the junction with the Glenn Highway at Glennallen.

DENALI HIGHWAY SIDE TRIP

The Denali Highway runs from Paxson at Mile 185 on the Richardson Highway to the Parks Highway at Mile 210. This is a distance of 135 miles (218 km), only the

GREAT SCENERY ON THE DENALI HIGHWAY

eastern-most 21 miles (34 km) are paved. Before the Parks Highway was finished the Denali Highway served as an access route to Denali National Park, today the road is little-used and traversed mostly by outdoors-oriented travelers. In the fall it is a popular hunting area but all summer the road is used almost exclusively by wildlife watchers, fishermen, hikers, canoeists, and scenery lovers. It really doesn't serve as a preferred route to anywhere else.

There are two formal BLM campgrounds along the highway but there are many more places where an RVer can just pull over and spend the night. The route covered is mostly high plateau dotted with lakes, fishing in many of them is good and it's easy to see birds and other wildlife with binoculars. Maclaren Summit at Mile 35 is the second-highest highway pass in the state (4,086 ft.), second only to Atigun Pass on the Dalton Highway.

Denali Highway Campgrounds

TANGLE LAKES CAMPGROUND (BLM)

| Location: | Mile 21 Denali Highway |
| Info: | (907) 822-3217 |

GPS Location: 63.04968 N, 146.00719 W, 2,900 Ft.

The Tangle Lakes Campground is located in high country with little in the way of trees. In good weather the vistas are wonderful. The campground is often used as a starting point for floats of the Delta River which is a designated a National Wild and Scenic River.

THE RICHARDSON HIGHWAY

This campground has recently been totally rebuilt. There are now 40 sites, 12 of those are pull-thrus and 4 are walk-in tent sites. They have picnic tables and fire pits and some have pads for tents. The campground sometimes has a host, firewood is sold, and there are hand pumps for water, vault toilets, and a boat ramp. A nice mile-long hiking trail leads along the hillside above the lake. There's even Wi-Fi, available for a fee from Copper Valley Wi-Fi. The only fly in the ointment is that the campground is no longer free. Maximum stay here is 14 days.

Tangle Lakes Campground is located on the north side of the Denali Highway near the end of the pavement at Mile 21.

➡ CLEARWATER CREEK WAYSIDE

Location: Mile 56 Denali Highway

GPS Location: 63.04148 N, 146.88144 W, 2,900 Ft.

The Clearwater Creek Wayside has lots of room for RVs to park overnight and they commonly do exactly that. There is a vault toilet, 2 picnic tables, and 2 metal fire pits. It's a very scenic location.

➡ BRUSHKANA CAMPGROUND (BLM)

Location: Mile 105 Denali Highway
Info: (907) 822-3217

GPS Location: 63.29042 N, 148.06290 W, 2,600 Ft.

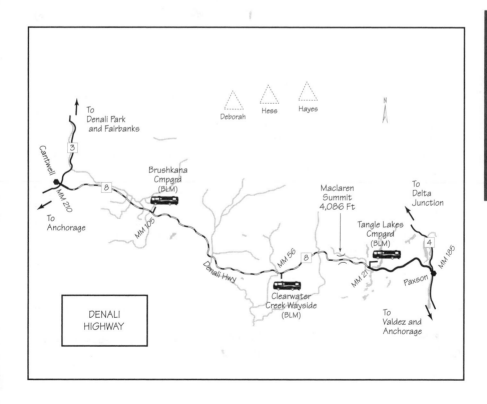

DENALI HIGHWAY

The Brushkana Campground has about 18 back-in RV and tent sites off a loop road as well as an overflow area suitable for RVs. In all there are 22 numbered sites. Some will take RVs up to 45 feet. Sites have picnic tables and fire pits, there are vault toilets and water faucets. You can fish for grayling in Brushkana Creek and the Bruskana Creek Trail leaves from the campground. Maximum stay here is 14 days.

Other Camping Possibilities

The Denali Highway runs through remote country. It has dozens of gravel pull-offs and easily accessible parking sites near the highway. RVers commonly overnight on these, particularly those along the unpaved section.

WRANGELL-ST. ELIAS NATIONAL PARK, COPPER CENTER, EDGERTON HIGHWAY AND THE McCARTHY ROAD

32 Miles (52 Kilometers) on the Richardson from the Glennallen Junction to the Edgerton Junction

At Mile 106.6 of the Richardson Highway you'll find the access road to the **Wrangell-St. Elias National Park Visitor's Center** (Mile 106, Copper Center, AK 99573; 907 822-7250). The visitor center is not in the park, it's near Copper Center so that it is more accessible to the public, and because you need to stop and get information before heading for the park. The ranger here can fill you in on the park which has very limited road access. The two access roads are the Nabesna Road off the Tok Cutoff (see Chapter 7 - *The Glenn Highway*) and the Edgerton Highway at Mile 83 of the Richardson (see below).

Just a bit farther south is an old town, **Copper Center**, which was founded in 1896 as a government agricultural experimental station. The main road now bypasses Copper Center, if you want to drive through town turn east at the junction at Mile 106 for the Old Richardson Highway. Near Mile 100 (off the Old Richardson loop) are the two entrances to an inner loop road which runs through old Copper Center. Copper Center now has a population of about 500 and has several interesting stops including, the **George Ashby Memorial Museum**, the log **Chapel on the Hill**, and a couple of king and red salmon fishing-oriented camping areas along the Klutina River which runs into the Copper River here.

The Copper Center loop rejoins the Richardson Highway at Mile 100. Soon there's another junction, this one with the **Edgerton Highway** at Mile 83. The Edgerton provides access to McCarthy and the Wrangell-St. Elias National Park. Think of the road as having two sections. The first is the Edgerton Highway. It is a 35 mile (56.5 km) paved highway running through Kenny Lake and Chitina and then crossing the Copper River on a good modern bridge. At Chitina the paving ends and at the Copper River the McCarthy Road begins. The **McCarthy Road** is an unpaved 58 mile (94 km) narrow dirt and gravel road following an old railway roadbed. Occasionally spikes from the old railroad have been known to work loose and puncture tires. The road is not suitable for large RVs but pickup campers, vans, and RVs to 30 feet are fine. A van shuttle service runs from Glennallen to McCarthy and is an excellent way to get to McCarthy if you don't want to drive. Check at the park visitor's center in Copper Center for information. There are several small commercial campgrounds and camping areas along the McCarthy Road and near its end.

At the end of the McCarthy road is a parking lot and from the parking lot there is a walking bridge across the Kennicott River to McCarthy and Kennecott. Shuttle vans pick people up on the far side of the river. The distance to McCarthy is about a mile (1.6 km), Kennecott is about 5 miles (8 km) distant.

McCarthy, with a population of about 50, is the service center for this area. You'll find lodging, a restaurant or two, and guide services in McCarthy.

Kennecott is the reason for the development in this area. From 1910 to 1930 this was the location of a huge copper mine. Ore was transported to tidewater at Cordova along the railroad that formed the base for the road you traveled to get here. Red-painted buildings remain and are being restored (they're mostly off limits) and there is a lodge. There's also a National Park Service visitor center and rangers lead some informational tours. Hiking trails lead up the adjoining Kennicott Glacier and up the mountainside above the structures.

Wrangell-St. Elias National Park, Copper Center, Edgerton Highway and the McCarthy Road Campgrounds

🚐 KING FOR A DAY CAMPGROUND AND OTHER
       KLUTINA RIVER FISHING CAMPGROUNDS

Location:	Along The Klutina River Near Mile 101 Of The Richardson Highway
Address:	PO Box 372, Copper Center, AK 99573
Telephone:	(907) 822-3092
Email:	king4day@alaska.net
Website:	www.kingforadaycharters.com/

GPS Location: 61.95205 N, 145.31807 W, 1,100 Ft.

There are three of these campgrounds. They are used by fishermen fishing the Klutina River, well known for its runs of king and red salmon. These places are located between the old and new Richardson Highway routes, a short distance, along the banks of the river. The campgrounds are known as King For a Day Campground, Grove's Klutina River King Salmon Charters and Fish Camp, and Klutina Salmon Charters. Keep in mind that the single-minded object of pretty much everyone in these campgrounds is to catch fish, there's not a lot of concern about the amenities. When the fish are running they're crowded, when there are no fish they're likely to be closed. The peak weekend is July 4 but all of late June and July is busy.

King for a Day Campground has the nicest facilities. It has about 50 sites suitable for RVs, some next to the river, some with electrical hookups. There are even a few full-hookup sites at this campground and sites for RVs to 45 feet. There is a dump station and water fill as well as recreation room, showers, laundry, and fishing charters. The location and contact information in the title block above is for this campground. It is located next to the new Richardson Highway near Mile 101, fourteen miles (23 km) south of the southern junction of the Richardson with the Glenn.

Nearby, next to the river on the old highway, are Groves Klutina River King Salmon Charters (907 822-5822) and Klutina Salmon Charters Campground (907 822-3991). Groves is much more basic with a few electrical hookups and showers while Klutina

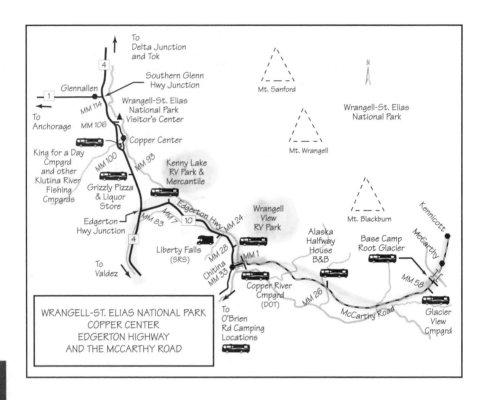

Salmon Chargers is similar to King for a Day. Room for big RVs can be scarce and access can be difficult, walk in to check them out before taking in a big RV. You can reach these campgrounds by driving the Copper Center Bypass or by taking a short good gravel road between the Bypass and the Richardson that runs from the entrance of King for a Day Campground toward the east.

🚐 Grizzly Pizza and Liquor Store

Location: Mile 92 Richardson Hwy

GPS Location: 61.84357 N, 145.23177 W, 1,500 Ft

Grizzly Pizza is a roadhouse-style restaurant bar. It has about five back-in sites for rigs to about 30 feet off to the side with electricity and water hookups. There's a restroom when the bar is open, and showers are available for a fee. There's Wi-Fi in the bar.

Watch for the roadhouse on the west side of the Richardson between Mile 92 and 93.

🚐 Kenny Lake RV Park and Mercantile

Location: Mile 7.2 Edgerton Hwy.
Telephone: (907) 822-3313
Email: knnylake@cvalaska.net
Website: www.kennylake.com

GPS Location: 61.73594 N, 144.95226 W, 1,300 Ft.

Kenny Lake Mercantile is located on the Edgerton Highway between Chitina and the Richardson Highway. It is a well-run fairly modern roadhouse-style facility with restaurant, laundry, hotel, groceries and campground. This is a good place to base your RV when catching the shuttle or driving a tow car into McCarthy. It also serves campers not staying in the park since it has pay showers, a dump station (fee) and water fill (fee) that are available for drive-ins.

There are 20 camping spaces. Ten are back-in sites with electrical hookups (30 amp) in the cleared yard near the store and laundry/shower building. There is lots of room for RVs to and exceeding 60 feet since these are back-ins off a large gravel parking lot. Nine others are large pull-thru camping sites with no utility hookups set in trees in a secluded area nearby, these make excellent tenting sites or big no-hookup RV sites. The restrooms and coin-op showers share a building with the laundry and cafe. There's also a grocery store and a gift shop in separate buildings as well as gas and diesel pumps. Wi-Fi can be used from the RV sites nearest the store. Both a dump station and water-fill station are provided, there is no charge for those staying in the park.

This campground is on the north side of the Edgerton Highway some 7.2 miles (11.6 km) from its junction with the Richardson Highway.

LIBERTY FALLS STATE RECREATION SITE

Location:	Mile 24 Of The Edgerton Hwy.
Info:	(907) 823-2223
Website:	dnr.alaska.gov/parks/aspunits/matsu/libertyflsrs.htm

GPS Location: 61.62224 N, 144.54757 W, 1,200 Ft.

This very small campground is probably most suitable for tent campers. It sits in a small canyon next to the highway with a creek running through. Little Liberty Falls forms the centerpiece of the campground.

There are 7 tent camping sites, some with platforms located on a sloping hillside. For vehicles there are three back-in sites in trees. Although two sites will take big RVs the access roads are narrow and sites not level, we don't recommend this campground for RVs over 30 feet. Also note that the bridge in the middle of the campground is limited to 8 tons. There are picnic tables, fire pits, vault toilets and a water pump. Stays here are limited to 15 days.

Watch for the campground on the south side of the Edgerton Highway near Mile 24. There are two entrances with the access road looping through the campground.

WRANGELL VIEW RV PARK

Address:	PO Box 3, Chitina, AK 99566
Telephone:	(907) 823-2255
Email:	chitina_native@cvinternet.net

GPS Location: 61.58346 N, 144.43654 W, 700 Ft.

This is an RV park owned and operated by the Chitina Native Corporation. It is usually unattended. There are 11 sites situated off a gravel lot. Ten are full-hookup sites. RVs to 45 feet should have no problems parking. There are 50 amp outlets. The only restrooms are portable toilets, not always provided.

The campground is on a short access road from Mile 29 of the Edgerton Hwy, about 5 miles (8 km) north of Chitina.

**DEPARTMENT OF TRANSPORTATION
COPPER RIVER CAMPGROUND**

Location: East End Of Copper River Bridge On The Edgerton Hwy.

GPS Location: 61.52775 N, 144.40455 W, 500 Ft.

This small camping area on the banks of the Copper River is extremely popular when the salmon are running, any other time you're likely to be here by yourself.

There are about 12 sites with picnic tables and fire pits located in a grove of cottonwoods. During the fishing season this campground can be packed with rigs and tents everywhere. The campground has few amenities but does offer vault toilets. There is plenty of room for big RVs.

To find the campground follow the Edgerton Highway to Chitina, through town, and across the Copper River Bridge. The campground is on the south side of the highway just after the bridge near what would be Mile 35 of the Edgerton except that this part of the highway is called the McCarthy Road.

O'BRIEN ROAD CAMPING LOCATIONS

FREE (or) $$$

O'Brien Road splits south from the highway's right-angle turn as it passes through Chitina. The road soon is running along above the Copper River and there are several pull-offs popular with RV campers during the dip-net season. Camping is only allowed on the road right-of-way. Measuring from the cut-off in town it's 1.9 mile (3.1 km) to the first pull-off (GPS Location 61.49083 N, 144.45929 W) and 2.2 mile (3.6 km) to the second pull-off (GPS Location 61.48848 N, 144.46173 W). No facilities are provided.

In 2.7 miles (4.4 km) (GPS Location 61.47247 N, 144.45513 W) the road descends steeply to a parking area where O'Brian Creek enters the Copper River and where overnighting is allowed. There's a portable toilet there. The fee is $15 for 24 hours. The descent is very steep and large RVs are not suitable.

ALASKA HALFWAY HOUSE B & B

$$$

Address: PO Box 68, Chitina, AK 99566
Telephone: (907) 259-4300
Website: www.alaskahalfwayhouse.com

GPS Location: 61.45520 N, 143.76736 W, 1,500 Ft.

This friendly B&B has 3 RV sites and 4 tent sites. It's a truly beautiful location with mountain views and a river running alongside the property. The owner is enthusiastic and friendly. Wildlife frequently visits the property and there are opportunities for hiking, birdwatching and photography.

The RV parking locations are carefully situated and are large enough for any RV. There are no hookups. The tents sites are separated to insure privacy. Restrooms are outhouses. There's an outdoor shower near the river, the water is heated in a solar bag. It is possible to have the owners prepare breakfast with advance notice.

The campground is located at Mile 26.7 of the McCarthy Road.

GLACIER VIEW CAMPGROUND

Location:	One-half Mile (.9 Km) From The End Of The McCarthy Road
Telephone:	(907) 554-4490 Summer, (907) 441-5737 Winter
Email:	glacierviewcampground@ak.net
Website:	www.glacierviewcampground.com

GPS Location: 61.43550 N, 142.95936 W, 1,400 Ft.

Just a half-mile (.9 km) from the end of the McCarthy Road is a commercial campground. It has 20 back-in sites separated by sparse natural vegetation. They are located on a loop road and well separated, most have picnic tables and fire rings. Some sites will take big rigs. The campground also has outhouses, showers, and a simple restaurant. Bikes are rented to make the trip to McCarthy and Kennecott and tires are repaired. You can park a car in the lot here for the day for free, overnight parking requires payment of a small fee.

BASE CAMP ROOT GLACIER

Location:	At The End Of The McCarthy Road

GPS Location: 61.43454 N, 142.94333 W, 1,400 Ft.

When you reach the end of the road to McCarthy you can't drive into town. Instead you must park and walk across a footbridge. The land where you park is privately owned, in the summer of 2013 the charge was $10 per day to park and $20 to camp for the night. Facilities are minimal, there are outhouses and a public telephone. In addition to the gravel parking lot there are some campsites in the trees above the parking lot on the south side of the road.

FROM THE EDGERTON HIGHWAY JUNCTION TO VALDEZ
83 Miles (143 Kilometers)

From the Edgerton Highway junction the Richardson continues south through the Copper River Valley.

At Mile 29 a short side road leads to a parking lot and overlook for the **Worthington Glacier**, an easy place to get very close to a glacier.

The road crosses **Thompson Pass** at Mile 26. Thompson is only 2,678 feet high but seems higher. The huge snowfall here means that the vegetation is truly alpine. After the pass the road descends steeply and passes through scenic **Keystone Canyon** to end, according to the mileposts, four miles (6 km) short of Valdez. This is because the entire town of Valdez was moved to a new site after the 1964 Good Friday earthquake. Continue straight ahead to the new townsite.

Edgerton Highway Junction to Valdez Campgrounds

SQUIRREL CREEK STATE RECREATION SITE

Location:	Near Mile 80 Of The Richardson Hwy.
Info:	(907) 822-5932
Website:	dnr.alaska.gov/parks/aspunits/matsu/squircksrs.htm

GPS Location: 61.66670 N, 145.17637 W, 1,600 Ft.

A small campground with nice sites and offering some fishing for grayling where

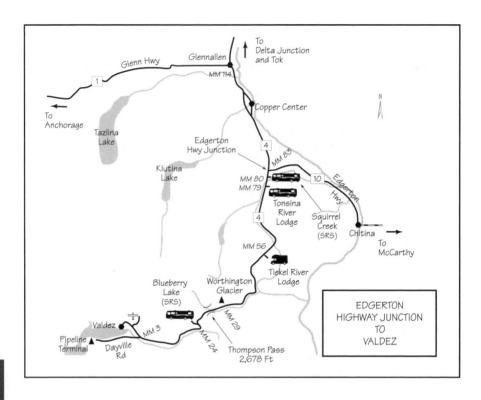

THE RICHARDSON HIGHWAY

Squirrel Creek empties into the Tonsina River. There are also stocked fish in the gravel pit next to the campground. In the middle of the summer it's a popular swimming hole too.

There are about 25 sites of various types, some are around a gravel lot and others are individual separated sites. Many will take large rigs. Take a look on foot before driving into any blind entrances if you have a large RV, you might have to back out. The area has cottonwood trees and some sites are along Squirrel Creek. They all have fire pits and picnic tables, there are vault toilets and a hand-operated water pump. The camping time limit here is 15 days.

The campground is situated just east of the Richardson Highway near Mile 80.

🚐 TONSINA RIVER LODGE

Address:	Mile 79, Tonsina, AK 99573
Telephone:	(907) 822-3000
Email:	tonsinalodge@gmail.com
Website:	www.tonsinariverlodge.com

GPS Location: 61.66176 N, 145.18039 W, 1,600 Ft.

This lodge offers RV and tent camping in addition to a bar, restaurant (Mangy Moose Saloon and Cantina), a liquor store, ATM, laundry, airstrip, spa, convenience store, rooms and gas and diesel sales.

Campsites are well away from the road. There are 10 large RV sites in an open field, some full hookup. There's also plenty of room for no-hookup RV parking. Tenters are welcome to pitch on grass in the open field, and tent camping here is free.

The lodge is on the east side of the highway near Mile 79, that's not far south of the Squirrel Creek Recreation Site.

TIEKEL RIVER LODGE

Location:	Mile 56 Richardson Highway
Telephone:	(907) 822-3259
Email:	info@tiekelriverlodge.com
Website:	www.tiekelriverlodge.com

GPS Location: 61.38362 N, 145.23651 W, 1,500 Ft.

This roadhouse-style facility is located on the banks of the Tiekel River. They offer a restaurant and gas. The campground area has six sites near the river. Some have electric and water hookups. They are suitable for RVs to about 30 feet and tents. Wi-Fi is available only in the restaurant.

The lodge is on the east side of the Richardson Highway near Mile 56.

BLUEBERRY LAKE STATE RECREATION SITE

Location:	Near Mile 24 Of The Richardson Highway
Info:	(907) 262-5581
Website:	dnr.alaska.gov/parks/aspunits/kenai/blueberrylksrs.htm

GPS Location: 61.12086 N, 145.69840 W, 2,100 Ft.

This is a small campground, fairly close to Valdez, with a spectacular location. It sits below the summit of Thompson Pass, surrounded by mountains and meadows. Little Blueberry Lake adjoins the campground. Bears are frequently seen nearby.

There are 15 sites off a paved loop. Some sites are right along the lake. Sites reach as long as 45 feet. Stunted alders are the primary local vegetation. Fire pits, picnic tables, roofed shelters, vault toilets, and a water pump are available. There's a 15 day limit at this campground.

Watch for the .8 mile (1.3 km) access road near Mile 24 of the Richardson Highway.

VALDEZ
Population 4,000, Elevation sea level

Since the Exxon Valdez oil spill in 1989 this little town has become very well known. Most people even know how to pronounce it now (Val-DEEZ). Before the pipeline the town may have been best known for its tremendous winter snowfall which sometimes exceeds 40 feet.

The oil spill wasn't the first disaster to strike Valdez. In 1964 the town was virtually destroyed during the Good Friday Earthquake. The present town is brand new, not much is left of old Valdez which was four miles (6.5 km) to the east.

The top summer attraction in Valdez seems to be the fish. Three fishing derbies run throughout the summer: the Halibut Derby for most of the summer, the Pink Salmon

TOURING PRINCE WILLIAM SOUND ON A CRUISE BOAT OUT OF VALDEZ

Derby at the end of June and most of July, and the Silver Salmon Derby in August. You can easily charter a boat, use your own, or fish from the beach. Fishermen practically fill Valdez's many campgrounds during the summer.

The **Valdez Visitor Center** is at 104 Chenega Street, (907 835-4636). You'll see that the new version of Valdez built after the earthquake doesn't have a traditional downtown area, things are pretty spread out for such a small town.

Valdez is a port for the **Alaska Marine Highway**. From here you can catch a ferry to Cordova or Whittier. That's one way to get out on Prince William Sound but a better way is one of the many cruise boats that work out of Valdez. The most popular destination is no doubt the **Columbia Glacier**.

The **Valdez oil terminal** is located across the Port Valdez from the town. You can easily see the huge oil storage tanks and usually a loading tanker from the Valdez waterfront.

The museum here is the **Valdez Historical Museum** (217 Egan Drive). It has displays on the history of the area, the local natives, the oil pipeline, and the oil spill.

Valdez is a small town but very busy during the summer. Tourism, fishing, and pipeline activities are all happening at the same time. There are lots of camping slots in Valdez and also, for such a small town, an adequate service infrastructure including a medium-sized supermarket.

Valdez Campgrounds

🚐 EAGLE'S REST RV PARK

Address:	139 E. Pioneer (PO Box 610), Valdez, AK 99686
Telephone:	(907) 835-2373 or (800) 553-7275
Email:	rvpark@alaska.net
Website:	www.eaglesrestrv.com

GPS Location: 61.13139 N, 146.34597 W, Near Sea Level

Valdez's largest RV park is also probably its best promoted. You'll undoubtedly run into pamphlets and cards singing its praises long before you reach Valdez. It is also likely to be the first place you see when you reach town. That's OK because this is a friendly and well-run campground.

The Eagle's Rest has about 200 vehicle spaces and also a grassy area for tents. The vehicle area is a large gravel lot with little landscaping, much like practically every other campground in Valdez. There are back-ins and pull-thrus to 70 feet. Full hook-up (20/30 and 50-amp power), partial, and dry sites are available, as are many small rental cabins. The central office building has restrooms with showers, two laundries, and a fish cleaning area. There's also a Tesoro gas station right in the campground with a convenience store as well as a free dump station near the Tesoro. Propane is

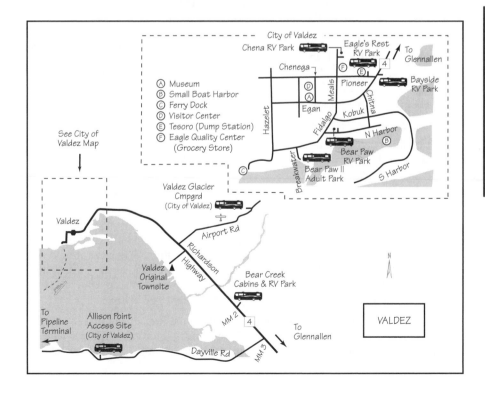

available and the town's main supermarket is next door. This campground is one of the farthest from the waterfront, but still within easy walking distance.

As you enter Valdez on the Richardson Highway watch for the Eagle's Rest on the right.

▣ BAYSIDE RV PARK

Address:	230 E. Egan Drive (PO Box 466), Valdez, AK 99686
Telephone:	(907) 835-4425 or (888) 835-4425
Email:	bayside1@cvinternet.net
Website:	www.baysiderv.com

GPS Location: 61.13055 N, 146.34388 W, Near Sea Level

The Bayside is one of the newer RV parks in Valdez. This is not a waterfront campground but it is within walking distance of the boat harbor. There are water views across an undeveloped open area to the east. The personable owner actively manages this campground and are very willing to offer fishing and sightseeing tips.

Like most Valdez campgrounds this is a large gravel lot with lots of room to maneuver. The campground has about 110 vehicle spaces. Seventy-five are full-service sites and 35 are pull-thrus to 50 feet. Most sites have 30-amp power but a few offer 50 amp. There are also TV hookups. Nice individual restrooms have showers and there is a dump station. Propane is available.

You can't miss the Bayside. As you arrive in Valdez on the Richardson Highway you'll see the campground on your left as you enter town.

▣ BEAR PAW RV PARK

Address:	101 North Harbor Dr. (PO Box 93), Valdez, AK 99686
Telephone:	(907) 835-2530
Email:	bearpaw@valdezak.net
Website:	www.bearpawrvpark.com

GPS Location: 61.12696 N, 146.34976 W, Near Sea Level

The Bear Paw is conveniently located just across the road from the small boat harbor. If you are in Valdez to take advantage of the available fishing charters this is a good base.

The campground is a large fenced gravel lot. With 70 sites it's large, but not quite as huge as a couple of the other campgrounds in town. It was the first of the big RV parks in Valdez. There are a variety of site types, some are pull-thrus to 60 feet. Electricity is 30 amp and there are full hookup, electric only, and dry sites available. Some sites have cable TV and there's also a dump station. The campground has restrooms with showers in private rooms and is convenient to a laundry, restaurants, charter boat operators and central Valdez. The same owners also operate an adult park and an adult tent camping area nearby, they're described below.

The easiest way to find the campground is to follow the Richardson into town until you see Fidalgo. Turn left on Fidalgo and drive .1 mile (.2 km) to the corner with N. Harbor Dr. The Bear Paw is on the corner on the left.

◼ BEAR PAW II ADULT PARK

Address:	300 Wyatt Way, Valdez, AK 99686
Telephone:	(907) 835-2530
Email:	bearpaw@valdezak.net
Website:	www.bearpawrvpark.com/adult_park.html

GPS Location: 61.12476 N, 146.35520 W, Near Sea Level

The Bear Paw Adult Camper Park is nicely located right on the water at the entrance to the Valdez small boat harbor. While not quite as convenient as the other Bear Paw campground the scenic location easily compensates.

There are about 30 back-in spaces to 40 feet in this park. They have 30-amp electricity, sewer, water and TV hookups. There are picnic tables and a dump station. There is also a tent camping area in a small grove of alders behind the park with tent platforms, picnic tables, and fire pits. Reservations are recommended. Restrooms with showers are available.

To find this campground follow the Richardson into town until you see Fidalgo. Turn left here and drive .1 mile (.2 km) to the corner with N. Harbor Dr. The Bear Paw is on the left, you check in here. Then continue toward the water on Fidalgo for another .2 miles (.3 km) until you see a small street (Breakwater) going left. Turn here and you'll soon come to a dead end at the water with the campground to your left.

◼ CHENA RV PARK

Address:	101 E Chena St., Valdez, AK 99686
Telephone:	(907) 378-6165
Email:	e.bart@hotmail.com
Website:	www.chenarv.com

GPS Location: 61.13315 N, 146.34808 W, Near Sea Level

This small RV park is simple but popular. There are 10 full-hookup RV sites suitable for large rigs but no restrooms. Sites have picnic tables and there is a community fire pit.

As you enter Valdez turn right on East Pioneer Drive. Drive .2 mile (.3 km), one long block, to Meals Ave. Turn right here and drive north for .1 mile (.2 km). That's three blocks. Turn right on Chena and into the park.

◼ BEAR CREEK CABINS AND RV PARK

Location:	Mile 2 Richardson Hwy
Address:	PO Box 122, Valdez, AK 99686
Telephone:	(907) 835-2723
Email:	bigbear@bearcreekcabinsrvpark.com
Website:	www.bearcreekcabinsrvpark.com

GPS Location: 61.09978 N, 146.21663 W, 100 Ft.

This RV park is located out past the old Valdez townsite. The access road is off the highway but campsites are a bit back off the road.

This is a large campground with 70 sites. Most of them have water and electric hookups and there is a dump station. These are wide sites and most are long enough for any RV. There are both pull-thru and back-in sites and they have picnic tables and

THE RICHARDSON HIGHWAY

rock fire rings. There's a small laundry and restrooms with flush toilets and showers. There are also rental cabins. A paved bike path runs along the highway all the way to town.

The campground is located near Mile 2 of the Richardson Highway on the north side of the road. That makes it about six miles (10 km) from town.

⛺ ALLISON POINT ACCESS SITE (CITY OF VALDEZ)

Location: Near The Trans Alaska Pipeline Terminal Across From Valdez
Telephone: (907) 835-2282

GPS Location: 61.08277 N, 146.32861 W, Near Sea Level

This campground's reason for being is salmon fishing. Either pink or silver salmon can be caught from the shore during their respective runs. There is a salmon hatchery nearby, that's why there are so many fish here.

Fifty-one back-in parking lot spaces, some to about 45 feet, line the road for a half-mile. Some, on the ocean side of the road, are pretty nice sites with excellent views across the fiord to Valdez. There is no separation between adjoining parking slots. Vault toilets are provided and drinking water is hauled to the campground. There is also a host.

The camping area is located along the access road to the pipeline terminal across the bay from Valdez. To get there follow Dayville Road from Mile 3 of the Richardson Hwy. The campground lines the road from Mile 4.6 to Mile 5 of the Dayville Road.

⛺ VALDEZ GLACIER CAMPGROUND (CITY OF VALDEZ)

Location: 2.3 Miles (3.7 Km) On Valdez Airport Rd.
Address: 1200 Airport Rd, Valdez, AK 99686
Telephone: (907) 803-3695

GPS Location: 61.13858 N, 146.20480 W, 300 Ft.

This very large government campground has been upgraded in recent years with the addition of electrical hook-ups, showers, and flush toilets. It serves as the military campground in the area but is open to the public too.

There are 108 camping spaces arranged off gravel access roads. Twenty-one are large back-ins with electrical service. Other sites have no hookups but some will easily handle RVs to 45 feet, 14 are pull-thrus. Other sites are best for small RVs or tent campers. Each space has a picnic table and fire pit. There are vault toilets as well as basic modern restroom buildings with flush toilets and showers. A dump station is available. Most of the vegetation is cottonwood or alder and spaces are well separated.

The campground is located past the airport on the paved Airport Road that leaves the Richardson Highway about 3.4 miles east of town near the Old Valdez townsite. You'll pass the airport at .8 mile (1.3 km) and find the campground at 2.3 miles (3.7 km).

RICHARDSON HIGHWAY DUMP STATIONS

Travelers in Alaska should try to use dump stations in larger cities, on the Richardson that means Fairbanks and Valdez. Many of the campgrounds in this chapter have dump stations or sewer hookups. There is generally a fee, particularly if you are not staying at the campground, which is only fair.

Among the many gas stations in Fairbanks with dump stations available to customers are the Holiday station at 2300 South Cushman Street (*GPS Location 64.82539 N, 147.71463 W*), University Chevron at 3245 College Road (*GPS Location 64.85783 N, 147.79724 W*), Alaska Chevron at 333 Illinois Street (*GPS Location 64.84890 N, 147.71873*) which charges $10 or $5 with fill-up, the Tesoro at the corner of Illinois and College Road (64.85377 N, 147.71571 W), Sourdough Fuel off the Johansen Expressway (*GPS Location 64.85277 N, 147.75057 W*), and the Tesoro Truck Stop at Cushman and Van Horn Road (*GPS Location 64.81386 N, 147.71025 W*). Most of these stations are free but a fill-up would be considerate.

In **North Pole** there is a dump station at the Tesoro station at 3392 Badger Road (*GPS Location 64.75954 N, 147.34926 W*). This is just north of the main North Pole exit, on the opposite side of the highway from the McDonalds and the Safeway store. There is also one at the nearby Sourdough Fuel station (*GPS Location 64.76174 N, 147.34660 W*).

See Chapter 4 - *The Alaska Highway* for Delta Junction dump stations.

Between Delta Junction and Glennallen there are two dump stations along the road. The Paxson Lodge (*GPS Location 63.03012 N, 145.49762 W*) has a dump station where you can dump for a fee. The Paxson Lake BLM Campground (*GPS Location 62.88471 N, 145.48630 W*) has a free dump station which folk not staying in the campground are welcome to use.

See Chapter 7 - *The Glenn Highway* for Glennallen dump stations.

In **Valdez** most campgrounds have dump stations, there's also one at the Tesoro at Eagle's Rest RV Park (*GPS Location: 61.13141 N, 146.21663 W*). It's free.

THE RICHARDSON HIGHWAY

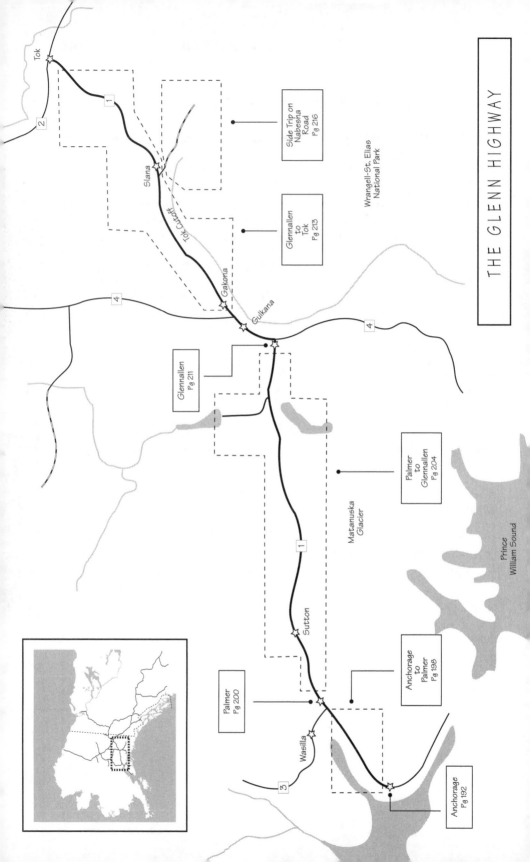

THE GLENN HIGHWAY

Tok

Slana

Tok Cutoff

Gakona

Gulkana

Wrangell-St. Elias National Park

Side Trip on Nabesna Road
Pg 216

Glennallen to Tok
Pg 213

Glennallen
Pg 211

Palmer to Glennallen
Pg 204

Matanuska Glacier

Prince William Sound

Sutton

Palmer
Pg 200

Wasilla

Anchorage to Palmer
Pg 198

Anchorage
Pg 192

Chapter 7

The Glenn Highway

INTRODUCTION

The Glenn Highway runs northeast 189 miles (305 km) from Anchorage on the shores of Cook Inlet to meet with the Richardson Highway near Glennallen. It then follows the Richardson north just 14 miles (23 km). Leaving the Richardson again at Gakona Junction the Glenn becomes the Tok Cutoff and crosses the northern Copper River country, threads through Mentasta Pass, and meets the Alaska Highway at Tok, a distance of 125 miles (202 km). The entire Glenn Highway from Anchorage to Tok is 328 miles (529 km) long.

If you are starting your trip in Anchorage, the Glenn to the Gakona Junction is the first part of one of two possible routes to Fairbanks. If you have driven up the Alaska Highway, the Glenn is your quickest route from Tok to Anchorage and the Kenai Peninsula.

Highlights

The Glenn highway starts in **Anchorage**, the state's largest town and commercial center. Visitors from outside the state shouldn't skip a visit to Anchorage, your trip to Alaska isn't complete until you've seen this city that is so different from the rest of the state.

The **Matanuska Valley** is Alaska's most successful agricultural area. In recent years it has also become something of an Anchorage suburb. This large area north of Knik Arm is usually known as the Mat-Su Valley because it combines the valleys of two rivers, the Matanuska River in the east and the Susitna River in the west. The Glenn

Highway travels through the Matanuska Valley while the Parks Highway (see Chapter 9 - *The Parks Highway*) cuts off to head up the Susitna Valley.

As the Glenn climbs out of the Matanuska Valley you'll have a chance to see some very scenic country. A highlight is the Matanuska Glacier descending out of the Chugach Mountains to the south and visible from scenic viewpoints near the highway.

Once you reach the Glennallen area and turn north you'll have some great views of the mountains of the Wrangell-St. Elias National Park to the southeast. You'll find more about this park in Chapter 6 - *The Richardson Highway*. One of the access roads to the park is the Nabesna Road which leaves the Tok Cutoff near Mile 60. The road and its campgrounds are described in a section at the end of this chapter.

The Road and Fuel

The Glenn Highway was only a rough trail until World War II. Then it was improved to connect the military bases in Anchorage with the Alcan. Until the Parks Highway was completed in 1971 the Glenn was Anchorage's only connecting road to the rest of the state and the Lower 48.

From Anchorage to Tok is a distance of 328 miles (529 km), a long drive but possible in a long day. The entire highway is paved but it is all two-lane road except for a short segment near Anchorage. Many sections have permafrost problems and larger rigs are forced to drive slowly to stay in one piece.

Mileposts on the Glenn Highway run from south to north, but there are three segments of them. From Anchorage to the junction with the Richardson Highway near Glennallen they run from 1 to 189. Then there is a short section of the Richardson Highway with mileposts indicating the distance from Valdez. Back on the Tok Cutoff mileposts start at the south end at 1 and run up to 125 at Tok.

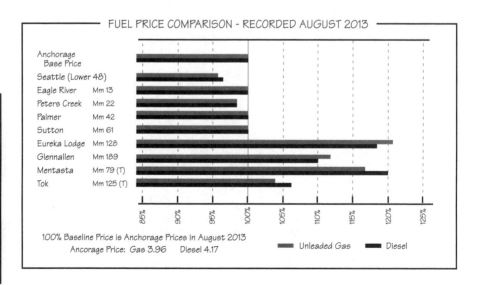

FUEL PRICE COMPARISON - RECORDED AUGUST 2013

100% Baseline Price is Anchorage Prices in August 2013
Anchorage Price: Gas 3.96   Diesel 4.17

Unleaded Gas   Diesel

Fishing

Ship Creek, almost in downtown Anchorage, is the second most popular fishing site in the state with only the Russian River receiving more angler/days of fishing pressure. The best campground for fishing here is Anchorage Ship Creek RV Park which is within walking distance.

Many lakes in the Matanuska Valley are stocked with rainbow trout. See Chapter 9 - *Parks Highway* for more information about other fishing lakes in the Matanuska Valley, but also consider spending the night at one of the three campgrounds near the **Kepler-Bradley Lakes State Recreation Area**. You'll find stocked rainbow trout in the lakes.

Lake Louise is a large lake reached by paved road from the Glenn Highway at Mile 160 and offers campers with their own boats the opportunity to catch large lake trout and grayling. The State's Lake Louise Recreation Area with the Lake Louise and Army Point Campgrounds is right on the lake.

As you drive up the Glenn Highway you may want to wet a line in one or another of the many small streams and lakes along the road. Here are a few to try: **Moose Creek** (Mile 55), **Granite Creek** (Mile 62), **Kings River** (Mile 66), **Chickaloon River** (Mile 78), **Long Lake** (Mile 85), **Mendeltna Creek** (Mile 153), **Gergie Lake and Arizona Lake** (Mile 155), **Mae West Lake** (by 1-mile trail from Mile 169), **Tolsona Lake** (Mile 170), **Tolsona Creek** (Mile 173), **Moose Creek** (Mile 186), the **Gulkana River** (access trail at Mile 123 of the Richardson), the **Gakona River** (Mile 1 of the Tok Cutoff), **Tulsona Creek** (Mile 15 to 18 Tok Cutoff), **Sinona Creek** (Mile 35 Tok Cutoff), **Chistochina River** (Mile 35 of the Tok Cutoff), **Ahtell Creek** (Mile 61 Tok Cutoff), **Carlson Creek and Lake** (Mile 68 Tok Cutoff, trail 2.5 miles up creek to lake), **Mable Creek** (Mile 76 Tok Cutoff), and **Mentasta Lake** (Mile 81.5 on the old Slana-Tok bypass). In the low country expect Dollies and rainbows, in higher country you are more likely to find grayling.

Boating, Rafting, Canoeing, and Kayaking

Anchorage is a waterfront city but don't expect to see many small boats on the Inlet out front. Cook Inlet is notoriously dangerous with a tidal range of near 30 feet, extremely cold muddy water, and frequent strong winds from nearby passes. Much farther south, off the Kenai Peninsula and in Kachemak Bay many people do use small boats on the Inlet but even there extreme caution is the rule.

The glacial **Eagle River** near Anchorage is a convenient and popular canoe, kayak and rafting river just outside Anchorage. Commercial rafting companies run the river. Access is from near the Eagle River Visitor Center and there are several take-out points. The first portion of the float is Class I, but Class II and Class III rapids near Eagle River require caution. Check with Chugach State Park personnel for more information. The Eagle River Campground sits on the river and is used as a take-out point by rafters, but note that it is just below the Class III Campground Rapids. There's a marked takeout just above the rapids and a trail to help you tote your boat. After the campground the river passes under the Glenn Highway, do not continue past this point because the river becomes very dangerous.

The **Knik River** near Palmer is a braided river running from Knik Glacier for about 26 miles (42 km) to Knik Arm. This is a Class I - II glacial river with access to the upper river off the Knik River Road. The operators of the Mt. View RV Park run jet boat tours up the river. There are also commercial rafting tours of the Knik River.

Commercial raft tour companies run raft excursions on the glacial **Matanuska River** from Chickaloon which is near Mile 76 of the highway.

Lake Louise is a very large lake in the Copper Valley region west of Glennallen. It connects to Susitna Lake and Tyone Lake. Fishing and water sports are both popular on the lake, you can stay at the Lake Louise Recreation Area campgrounds on the lakeshore.

Hiking and Mountain Biking

Anchorage has one of the best systems of bike paths in the country, there are 135 miles (218 km) of paved trails. Don't miss the chance to explore them on foot or on a bike. The best is the **Tony Knowles Coastal Trail** which runs along the shore of Cook Inlet from Westchester Lagoon past the airport and connects with miles of cross-country ski trails in Kincaid Park. This trail has been designated a National Recreation Trail. Other trails connect at Westchester Lagoon and lead downtown or east to the University and Russian Jack Park. In fact, bike trails lead out along the Glenn Highway past Eagle River.

Chugach State Park just outside Anchorage has some of the best hiking and mountain bike trails in the state. The mountainous terrain means mostly dry trails and great views over Anchorage and Cook Inlet. There are access points to the trails in Anchorage's Upper Hillside area as well as from Eklutna Lake and the Eagle River Visitor Center. An excellent place to camp while taking advantage of the park is the Eklutna Lake Campground. See Chapter 14 - *Camping Away From The Road System* for more information about Chugach State Park.

Wildlife Viewing

The city of **Anchorage** offers an amazing variety of wildlife viewing opportunities. Hikers on the bike trails, particularly the Tony Knowles Coastal Trail, will see a variety of birds. Chances of meeting a moose are pretty high, there are thought to be about 1,000 of them living in Anchorage, as well as about 50 black bears and another 10 or so brown bears. Bird lovers will also want to visit Potter Marsh, see Chapter 8 - *The Kenai Peninsula* for more information. During the summer it is often possible to see white beluga whales chasing salmon and hooligan from the Resolution Park viewing platform overlooking Cook Inlet at the corner of 3rd and L Street.

To get warmed up (especially if you have kids along) visit the **Alaska Zoo** for guaranteed sightings of Alaska wildlife. Head out the Seward Highway and take the O'Malley offramp. Turn toward the mountains and watch for the entrance on the left side of the road.

Chugach State Park's **Eagle River Visitor Center** has wildlife displays, videos about local wildlife, and you can often see Dall sheep on the mountainsides. There's also a nature trail. Along more remote trails in **Chugach State Park** you may see both

A MOOSE OBEYING THE TRAFFIC SIGNS IN ANCHORAGE

brown and black bears, moose, goats, bald eagles, and sharp-shinned hawks. You reach the visitor center by exiting the Glenn Highway at Mile 13 and then following the paved Eagle River Road for just over 12 miles (19 km). For more about Chugach State Park see Chapter 14 - *Camping Away From the Road System.*

Just a little farther from Anchorage the **Eklutna Lake Valley** and surrounding hillsides, also inside Chugach State Park, is a good place to see Dall sheep, moose, and perhaps even mountain goats if you are willing to hike the trails leading into the mountains from the campground.

The **Palmer Hay Flats** are a good place to watch ducks and moose. Access is via the frontage road on the south side of the Parks Highway accessed via the Trunk Road exit at Mile 36 of the Parks Highway. That's just west of where the Glenn Highway now exits northbound.

In the Matanuska Valley there is another quite unusual animal viewing stop. The **Musk Ox Farm** (Mile 50.1 Glenn Highway; 907 745-4151) has a herd of almost 80 domestic musk oxen. They're being raised for their hair (called qiviut and harvested by combing the animals) and as a tourist attraction. There is a visitor's center and opportunities for photographing the oxen. Fairbanks also has a musk ox farm but your only chance of seeing a musk ox from the road in Alaska is on the Dalton Highway, a much longer drive.

As you travel up the Glenn Highway stop to search for Dall sheep on the mountainside at **Sheep Mountain**. It's on the north side of the road from about Mile 106 to

Mile 113. You may also recognize that this extremely scenic stretch of road is used as a location for many cover photos on publications about driving or RVing in Alaska.

As you cross the high open country between Mile 115 and Glennallen keep your eyes peeled for caribou, this is part of the range of the **Nelchina herd**.

THE ROUTES, TOWNS, AND CAMPGROUNDS

ANCHORAGE
Population 300,000, Elevation near sea level

Anchorage is by far the largest town in Alaska, almost half of the state's population lives here. Many visitors to the state avoid Anchorage because they see no reason to spend time in a place that is much like any medium-sized western city in the Lower 48.

The fact is that Anchorage has its own charm. It sits on a point of land bounded on two sides by water and on the third by the Chugach Mountains. The city/borough (they're one entity) covers 1,955 square miles, about the same area as the state of Delaware. This largest city in Alaska is really not far from the surrounding wilderness, the huge Chugach State Park overlooks the city from the east and offers hiking trails, wildlife, and mountains to 8,000 feet.

Anchorage's weather, due to the city's location along the ocean and near several mountain passes, tends to be much cooler and cloudier than the weather in the Interior around Fairbanks. A temperature of 70° F is a heat wave in this part of the state. The dry summer month is June. July and August get quite a bit of rain.

Even though Anchorage is the largest town in the state you will find driving to be very easy. Locals complain, but the morning and evening rush hours are really quite short and roads are plentiful and wide. The large stores in the suburban area outside downtown Anchorage have huge parking lots and lots of room to maneuver. The large grocery chains are Carrs and Safeway (both actually now owned by Safeway), you'll also find Walmart, Sam's Club, Fred Meyer, Costco, and Barnes & Noble. The city has a bus system called the People Mover (Ride Line information number is 907 343-6543) and most city RV parks are on the routes. The downtown Transit Center is at 6th and G Street. There's a special lot for RV parking downtown. It's north of the Howard Johnson's on Third Ave. between A and C Streets.

Anchorage's central downtown area along 4th Avenue seems to have been almost totally dedicated to summer tourism. On the corner of 4th and F Street is the **Log Cabin Visitor's Information Center** (524 W. 4th Ave., Anchorage, AK 99501; 907 274-3531). This little sod-roofed cabin looks like a prospector's shack decked out with flower baskets, you can find information at the center about almost anything to do with Anchorage. A walking tour route starts at the information center, you can get a map inside. Across the street and on the next block is the **Alaska Public Lands Information Center** (605 West Fourth Avenue, Suite 105, Anchorage, AK 99501; 907 644-3661) one of four similar centers with exhibits and information about public land and parks (both national and state owned) all around the state. The others are in

THE GLENN HIGHWAY

Tok, Fairbanks, and Ketchikan. Near these two Anchorage information centers you will find many small shops and a mall complete with a Nordstrom's and a Penny's.

An important downtown site is the **Anchorage Museum** (entrance at 625 C Street; 907 929-9200). It has excellent historical, cultural and art exhibits, as well as a planetarium. Another good museum is the **Heritage Library Museum** located in the Wells Fargo Bank Building at the corner of Northern Lights and C Street (907 265-2834). It has displays of Alaska paintings and native artifacts.

The Anchorage International Airport is a busy place, but even busier (in terms of landings and takeoffs) and more interesting during the summer is the nearby **Lake Hood Seaplane Base**. With over 800 takeoffs or landings in a peak summer day it is the busiest water airfield in the world and a great place to find a bush pilot to fly you out into the real Alaska. It can be fun to find a quiet place to park along the lakeshore and watch the constant coming and going of small aircraft, particularly on Friday evening or Sunday afternoon on a good-weather summer weekend. On the south shore of the lake you'll find the **Alaska Aviation Heritage Museum** (4721 Aircraft Dr.; 907 248-5325).

A relatively new addition to the Anchorage scene is the **Alaska Native Heritage Center** (907 330-8000), a 26-acre first-class facility with exhibits and programs about native culture throughout the state.

Anchorage is known for its **bicycle and walking paths**. They run through many wooded areas of town as well as along the shore of Cook Inlet from downtown to

GREAT VIEW OF ANCHORAGE'S SKYLINE FROM THE COASTAL BIKE TRAIL

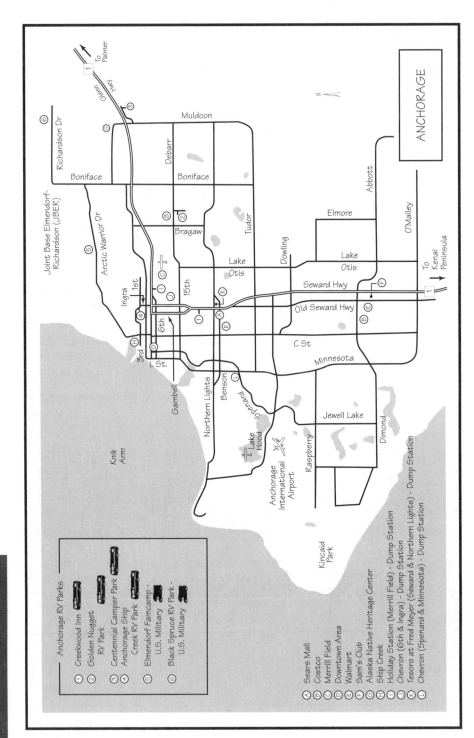

well past the airport. Get out and stretch your legs, walkers often see a moose or two along the trail.

Those interested in catching a salmon have an opportunity to do so right in Anchorage. **Ship Creek** has good runs of king and silver salmon and is within a mile of the central downtown area. The king run is in June, the silver run is in late August and early September. There's a king salmon derby in June, a silver salmon derby in August. Even-numbered years (like 2014 or 2016) also bring a run of pink salmon. This is shoulder-to-shoulder combat fishing at its best (or worse) but can be amazingly productive. At least drive down and take a look.

Anchorage has six golf courses. The Anchorage Golf Course (3651 O'Malley Road; 907 522-3363) has 18 holes. Tanglewood Lakes Golf Club (11801 Brayton Drive; 907 345-4600) has 9 holes. Russian Jack Springs Park (5200 DeBarr Rd.; 907 343-6992) is a 9-hole course with Astroturf greens. Two military courses are open to civilians: Eagleglen Golf Course (907 753-0213) is an 18-hole Air Force course and Moose Run Golf Course (907 384-6675) is two 18-hole Army courses.

If you are planning to fly to Alaska and rent an RV Anchorage is your best choice for a base. See Chapter 2 for a listing of RV rental companies. Almost all direct flights into Alaska (except those into Southeast) stop first in Anchorage. From here you can hit the road and head south for the scenery and fishing of the Kenai Peninsula or north to Denali Park or the Copper River Valley. RVers who have driven a RV up the highway will find that Anchorage has the most complete and reasonably-priced collection of service facilities available anywhere in Alaska or the Yukon.

Anchorage Campgrounds

🚐 **CREEKWOOD INN**

Address:	2150 Seward Hwy., Anchorage, AK 99503
Telephone:	(907) 258-6006 or (800) 478-6008
Email:	information@creekwoodinn-alaska.com
Website:	www.creekwoodinn-alaska.com

GPS Location: 61.20117 N, 149.86834 W, 100 Ft.

The Creekwood has a convenient central location near Anchorage's Sullivan Arena and next to the Chester Creek bike trails. These trails will lead you down Chester Creek to Cook Inlet and then either downtown or along the inlet past the airport. They're one of Anchorage's nicest features. Creekwood Inn is one of the few Alaska campgrounds open year-round, as a result it has quite a few older permanently-located units.

All of the 57 slots in this campground are back-in, most to about 40 feet. Most sites have full hookups with 30-amp outlets and cable TV although a few have only electricity and water. There are a few back-in sites with electricity and water located directly off the side street that will take 45-foot rigs and don't require driving into the park. There is a central services building with bathrooms, showers and laundry. The motel office can book excursions and tours. RVs over 35 feet long will find this campground a tight fit, sites are very tightly spaced. Reservations are recommended.

The campground is most easily reached by driving south on Gambell Street from just east of the downtown area. Gambell is the street that becomes the Seward Highway farther south. Gambell crosses 15th and descends into the Chester Creek Valley, you will see the Sullivan Arena on your right. As the road begins to ascend you will see the Creekwood Inn on your right. From the south you'll have to go north to 15th and return toward the south to enter the park.

GOLDEN NUGGET RV PARK

Address:	4100 DeBarr Road, Anchorage, AK 99508
Telephone:	(907) 333-5311 or (800) 449-2012
Email:	Christinel@mgi-alaska.com
Website:	www.goldennuggetrvpark.com

GPS Location: 61.20874 N, 149.80050 W, 200 Ft.

The Golden Nugget is a huge RV park. Some folks think the campground's location across the street from the Costco store is its best feature, but it is also conveniently close to the 9-hole golf course (Astroturf greens) at Russian Jack Park and the city's bike-trail system. The campground also has good city bus service to downtown.

The campground has 215 RV sites, most are full hook-ups about 45 feet long. Some sites are pull-thrus, many have room for large RVs. There are picnic tables at the sites. The restrooms are well-maintained and clean with free showers and there is also a huge laundry and free Wi-Fi. A covered community lounge area is used many evenings for entertainment events. The campground is open all winter.

The campground is located near the corner of Bragaw and DeBarr. One possible access route would be to take the Muldoon Road exit from the Glenn Highway. Travel south on Muldoon Road to DeBarr, then west on DeBarr. You will cross the Boniface Parkway and then climb and descend a small hill, just after descending the hill you will see a Costco store ahead on your right, the campground is on your left. Turn left on Hoyt Street and then right into the campground.

CENTENNIAL CAMPER PARK
(MUNICIPALITY OF ANCHORAGE)

Address:	8300 Glenn Highway (Box 196650), Anchorage, AK 99519
Telephone:	(907) 343-6986
Email:	bishiptl@muni.org
Website:	www.muni.org/departments/parks/pages/camping.aspx

GPS Location: 61.22833 N, 149.72256 W, 300 Ft.

Centennial Park is a Municipality of Anchorage campground. Government campgrounds tend to offer more greenery and Centennial Park is no exception. While most sites are not overly large they are well-separated and there are lots of trees. This is also the least expensive formal campground in town.

During the summer of 2013 the park was adding electrical hook-ups to 25 of their sites and these should be ready for the 2014 season.

The campground offers 88 spaces for vehicle campers and also large grassy areas for tents. There are no hook-ups other than the electricity being added to 25 sites. Six sites are large pull-thrus to 60 feet, the rest are medium-sized back-ins to about 35 feet. Restrooms are very basic but do offer showers for no extra fee. There is also a dump station. Campfires are allowed in this campground which is unusual in Anchorage. City bus service is available. The bike trail to Eagle River is just across the Glenn Highway. There is a fourteen day stay limit.

To reach Centennial Park head south on Muldoon Road from the Glenn Highway interchange. Almost immediately turn left onto Boundary Ave., the first turn south of the highway. From there it is easy to follow signs for about a half-mile to the campground.

ANCHORAGE SHIP CREEK RV PARK

Address:	150 N. Ingra Street, Anchorage, AK 99501
Telephone:	(907) 277-0877 or (800) 323-5757
Email:	info@bestofalaskatravel.com
Website:	www.bestofalaskatravel.com

GPS Location: 61.22220 N, 149.86906 W, 100 Ft.

Ship Creek is the closest RV park to downtown. Visitors interested in the central tourist area will love the fact that they can walk there in about ten minutes. The downside is that the campground is near the railroad yards so there's quite a bit of related wheel rumble and whistle noise here.

There are about 130 campsites, most are back-in spaces with full hookups and 30-amp power to 40 feet although there are a handful of pull-thrus to 60 feet. An area is also provided for tent camping. The campground itself is a large gravel area below a bluff which blocks much of the southern sun. There is lots of room for big RVs. Some picnic tables are provided. The restrooms are in reasonably good condition with showers and there is a laundry.

If you are arriving on the Glenn Highway from the north zero your odometer as you pass the Muldoon Road freeway interchange at the entrance to town. Continue for 4.5 miles (7.2 km) to Ingra Street (the sixth stoplight the last time we were in town). Turn right on Ingra and go three blocks to the stop sign at the bottom of the hill. Turn left and you will see the campground entrance on your left.

ELMENDORF FAMCAMP – U.S. MILITARY

Location:	Formerly Elmendorf Air Force Base, now JBER

This is a military campground on Joint Base Elmendorf-Richardson, in the section that was formerly Elmendorf Air Force Base. It is only open to active military personnel, National Guard personnel, reservists, retired military, and Department of Defense employees. No reservations are accepted. The contact address is SVS, RE: Elmendorf FAMCAMP, 3 SVS/SVRO, Bldg. 7301, 13th Street, Elmendorf AFB, AK 99506-5000; (907) 552-2023. The campground has 60 RV sites with electricity and water hookups and 10 tent sites. Laundry, playground, dump, and showers are available.

BLACK SPRUCE RV PARK – U.S. MILITARY

Location:	Formerly Fort Richardson, now JBER

This is a military campground on Joint Base Elmendorf-Richardson, in the section that was formerly Fort Richardson. It is only open to active military personnel, National Guard personnel, reservists, retired military, and Department of Defense employees. No reservations are accepted. The contact address is Outdoor Rec. Center, Bldg. 794, Davis Hwy. between 2nd and 5th Streets, Fort Richardson, AK 99505-

6600; (907) 384-1476. The campground has 40 full-hookup RV sites and 5 sites with electricity and water hookups. There are also 5 no-hookup sites at Upper Otter Lake Campground. Both showers and a dump site are available.

FROM ANCHORAGE TO PALMER
42 Miles (68 Kilometers)

From Anchorage a four-lane divided highway runs north through a region of rolling hills between the Chugach Mountains and Knik Arm. The Anchorage suburb of **Eagle River** is at Mile 13, it has a population of about 22,000. Eagle River has supermarkets and restaurants. The paved Eagle River Road runs back into the Chugach Mountains for 13 miles (21 km) to the **Chugach State Park Nature Center**. Trails lead from the center into the park.

At Mile 31 the highway crosses the Knik River and enters the Matanuska Valley. At a junction at Mile 34 you must exit the highway to remain on the Glenn Highway. If you don't do this you'll be on the Parks Highway. You could follow this road to Denali Park and for the shortest route to Fairbanks. See Chapter 9 - The *Parks Highway* for information about the route. However, for the Glenn Highway go ahead and exit.

A few miles after leaving the Parks Highway the road reaches Palmer at Mile 42.

Anchorage to Palmer Campgrounds

EAGLE RIVER CAMPGROUND
(CHUGACH STATE PARK)

$$$

Location:	Near Mile 12 Glenn Highway
Res and Info:	(907) 694-7982
Website:	dnr.alaska.gov/parks/aspunits/chugach/eaglerivercamp.htm

GPS Location: 61.30627 N, 149.57131 W, 300 Ft.

This large state campground is said to be one of the most popular in Alaska. That's understandable considering its location near the largest city in the state. This is one of the few state campground in Alaska that accepts reservations, about half the sites can be reserved. Many visitors to Anchorage find that this campground makes a reasonably inexpensive base compared to the campgrounds in the city. The campground is situated along the Eagle River near the Glenn Highway. Don't be put off by signs at the access off-ramp for both the municipal landfill and a correctional center, neither are evident from the campsites.

This large campground has 57 spaces including eight walk-in tent sites. The sites are off a loop road. Most RV sites are back-ins to 45 feet. There's also an overflow area with 10 more sites. All interior roads and parking pads are paved and sites have picnic tables and fire pits. The camping sites are well-separated and there are lots of trees and natural area. Toilets are vault type. There is a large dump station facility and water is available at the station for RV fill-ups. There is an extra $5 charge for use of the dump station, even if you are staying in the campground. Use by outsiders is fine. The campground is run by a private contractor, it has a 4-day limit and there is usually a host who sells firewood.

Take the Hiland Road Exit from the Glenn Highway near the 12 mile marker. The

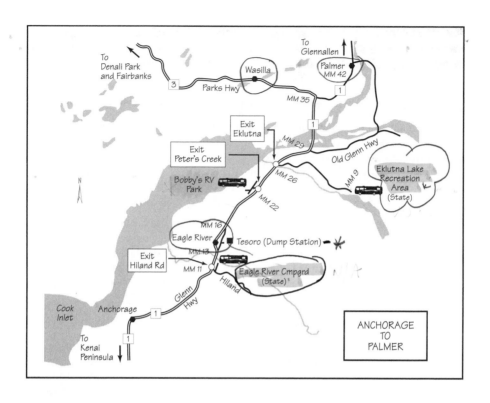

campground access road entrance is right at this interchange. The road runs north along the east side of the highway for about 1.4 miles (2.3 km) to the campground.

🚐 Bobby's RV Park

Address:	20940 Glennway Dr., Chugiak, AK 99567
Telephone:	(907) 688-2487

GPS Location: 61.40969 N, 149.44771 W, 400 Ft.

This small campground is conveniently located near the Glenn Highway with easy frequent bus connections into Anchorage. There are 26 spaces, 14 have full hookups with 20, 30, or 50-amp outlets. Eight more have electricity. There are also a few grassy tent sites. The only restroom facilities are portable toilets.

To reach the campground take the South Peters Creek exit from the Glenn Highway near the 22 mile (36 km) point. The campground is on the west side of the freeway, Almost immediately as you head west the road T's, turn left at the T and drive about a tenth of a mile, the campground will be on your right.

🚐 Eklutna Lake Recreation Area (Chugach State Park)

50 sites
1st come
1st served

Location:	Mile 9 Eklutna Lake Road
Info:	(907) 345-5014
Website:	dnr.alaska.gov/parks/units/chugach/eklutna.htm

GPS Location: 61.41008 N, 149.15017 W, 1,100 Ft.

This very nice state campground near Anchorage is located high in the Chugach mountains. It's a wilderness campground easily accessed by big RVs. The campground sits next to Eklutna Lake, source of drinking water and hydroelectric power for Anchorage. There are several good hiking and biking trails from the campground leading into the surrounding Chugach State Park.

Eklutna Lake Campground has been upgraded to modern standards. Roads and sites are paved and some sites are as long as 45 feet. There are 49 back-in sites, 1 pull-thru, and 8 walk-in tent sites in the normal campground area. An additional 15 back-in sites for RVs to 30 feet are on the day-use area loop. Sites have picnic tables and fire pits. Restrooms are modern vault toilets and there is a hand-operated water pump. There is also a walk-in boat launching area (for canoes and kayaks) and kayak rentals. The campground has a 15-day limit and there is usually a host.

Access to the campground is via the Eklutna Road which leaves the old Glenn Highway just east of the Eklutna exit from the 26 mile (42 km) point of the new Glenn Highway in Eagle River. The paved access road is nine miles (15 km) long, the last seven miles (11 km) are narrow but easily driven in any RV.

PALMER
Population 5,900, Elevation 250 feet

Palmer was founded in 1916 as a stop on the newly constructed Alaska Railroad and served as the supply center and rail head for the surrounding area. In 1934 the Matanuska Valley around Palmer was the destination for 202 families from depressed areas in the Lower 48, the U.S. government moved them to the Matanuska Valley to take advantage of the area's obvious agricultural potential. Today's Palmer is surrounded by both farms and residential areas that stretch westward through the valley to and beyond Wasilla on the Parks Highway.

The **Mat-Su Visitor's Center** (7744 E Visitors View Court, Palmer, Alaska 99645; 907 746-5000) is actually located just off the Parks Highway at about Mile 36. This is very near the junction of the Glenn and Parks Highways. Palmer also has its own visitor's center, the **Palmer Visitor Center** (Palmer Chamber of Commerce, 723 S Valley Way, Palmer, Alaska 99645; 907 745-8878) in town near the railroad tracks at South Valley Way and East Fireweed. It has a gift shop and a small museum describing the valley's agricultural history. There are also public gardens showcasing locally grown vegetables. If you are in the area during the week before Labor Day (the last week in August) be sure to visit the **Alaska State Fair** and take a look at some of the really big prize-winning vegetables that result from the long summer daylight hours.

Golfers will be glad to hear that Palmer has a course. The 18-hole **Palmer Golf Course** (907 745-4653) is located behind the State Fairgrounds on Inner Springer Road which leaves the Glenn Highway at about Mile 40 and is open from 6 a.m. to 11 p.m.

A very interesting side trip from the Palmer area is **Hatcher Pass**. There's more about Hatcher Pass and the Independence Mine in Chapter 9 - *The Parks Highway*, but one of the best access routes is Fishhook Road which heads west from the Glenn Highway at Mile 49.5 near Palmer.

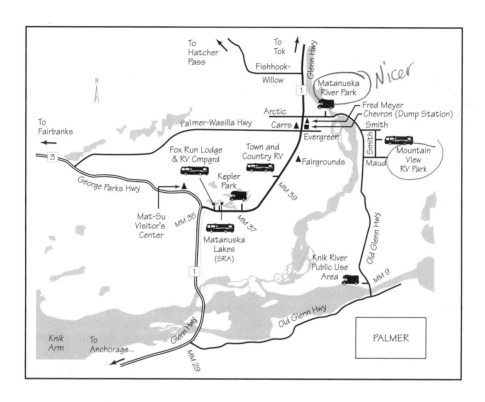

Palmer Campgrounds

🚐 **MOUNTAIN VIEW RV PARK**

Address: 1405 N Smith Rd, Palmer, AK 99645
Telephone: (907) 745-5747 or (800) 264-4582
Email: info@mtviewrvpark.com or star1@mtaonline.net
Website: www.mtviewrvpark.com

GPS Location: 61.59472 N, 149.02523 W, 300 Ft.

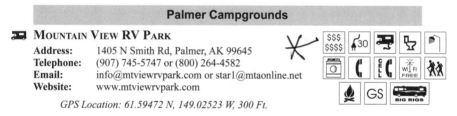

This large and friendly park in the quiet countryside east of Palmer offers an unusual attraction, boat tours up the nearby Knik River.

The campground has about 110 spaces, many are pull-thrus to 60 feet with 30-amp electricity, water, and sewer. Parking is on grass, in fact the entire campground is a large open field, perhaps not as attractive as a treed area but a popular feature here since it means fewer mosquitoes and lots of sunshine. There's also lots of room for big RVs. A designated tent-camping area is provided. Another popular feature at this campground is the many individual bathrooms, each with toilet, sink and shower. There is also a coin-operated laundry and a community fire pit with wood supplied by the campground. There's also an expresso shop in the office area.

To drive to the campground follow Arctic Avenue east from its junction with the Glenn Highway just outside Palmer near Mile 42. This takes you along the route of the Old Glenn Highway, it used to swing much closer to the mountains than the current routing across the hay flats to Anchorage. Follow the highway east for 2.8 miles (4.5 km), then turn left onto Smith Road, drive .6 miles (1 km), and turn right. You'll see the campground on your left in .3 mile (.5 km).

 MATANUSKA RIVER PARK (MATANUSKA-SUSITNA BOROUGH)

$$$	30			

Location: Mile 17 Old Glenn Highway
Telephone: (907) 745-9578
Website: www.matsugov.us/communitydevelopment/recservices/parks/matanuska-river-park

GPS Location: 61.60870 N, 149.09031 W, 300 Ft.

This is a nice campground operated by the local borough. The 101-acre park is more than a campground, there are hiking trails along the Matanuska River, playing fields, and a picnic area.

There are two camping areas. One is an open grassy area with back-in slots for about 40 RVs. A few of these sites will take RVs to 35 feet. The RV sites have 30-amp outlets. The other area has about 45 back-in slots along winding roads through a forested area with picnic tables and fire pits, a traditional government-type Alaska campground with no hookups. Only rigs to 30 feet are allowed in this area. Both sections can be used by tenters. Restrooms near the upper hookup section have flush toilets and coin-operated showers. Water is available and there is a dump station. There is a $5 fee to use the dump station even if you're staying in the campground.

Follow Arctic (Old Glenn Highway) east from its intersection with the Glenn Highway near Palmer, the campground entrance is on the left at .9 miles (1.5 km).

KNIK RIVER PUBLIC USE AREA

FREE			

Telephone: (907) 269-8552
Website: www.knikriver.alaska.gov

GPS Location: 61.50706 N, 149.03528 W, 100 Ft.

This is a large gravel beach area along the Knik River near the Knik River Bridge on the old Glenn Highway. Campers are welcome to park and spend the night. Tent campers usually pitch at the edge of the tree line where there is some earth making a better base than the gravel covering the remainder of the area.

This area is part of the Knik River Public Use Area and there are no amenities. Restrictions include a 14 day limit and a ban on rigs over 10,000 pounds without authorization from the management agency (Alaska Department of Natural Resources).

You'll find the parking area east and south of Palmer. From Palmer follow Arctic Street east from its junction with the Glenn Highway just outside Palmer near Mile 42. After 9.3 miles (15 km) you'll see the bridge ahead and can turn right into the parking area.

TOWN AND COUNTRY RV

Address: Mile 39.5 Glenn Hwy., Palmer, AK 99654
Telephone: (907) 746-6642 or (907) 746-7275
Email: rvpark@mtaonlin.net

GPS Location: 61.57109 N, 149.15135 W, 200 Ft.

This is a newer campground located just south of Palmer on the Glenn Highway. It has 28 large pull-thru sites to 65 feet with electricity and water, 21 of them offer sewer. There is also a dump station. Grass separates the sites and a grassy area is set aside for tent campers. A central building houses restrooms with free showers and a laundry.

The campground is located near Mile 39 of the Glenn Hwy. near the state fairgrounds. You can easily spot the campground from the highway, it's on the west side.

🚐 KEPLER PARK

Location: Mile 37.4 Glenn Highway, Palmer, AK 99645
Telephone: (907) 745-3053
Website: www.keplerpark.com

GPS Location: 61.55189 N, 149.19971 W, 100 Ft.

The campground has a variety of sites. Above the office near the highway are five back-in slots for RVs to about 35 feet. There are no hookups. Along the lake near the office are about 10 sites that are most suitable for tent campers or small RVs. Across the bridge in front of the office and up a narrow road on a ridge are another 20 larger sites in trees. They seem to be suitable for rigs to about 25 feet. Restrooms here are portable toilets and outhouses. Pedal boats and other small watercraft are available for rent when an attendant is present.

Kepler Park is located just off the Glenn Highway near Mile 37.

🚐 MATANUSKA LAKES STATE RECREATION AREA

Location: Mile 36 Of The Glenn Highway
Res and Info: (907) 746-4644
Website: dnr.alaska.gov/parks/aspunits/matsu/keplerbradlksra.htm

GPS Location: 61.55164 N, 149.22776 W, 200 Ft.

The Matanuska Lakes have long been a popular fishing destination. There are ten designated camping sites. Sites 1 to 6 are in trees and best for tent campers. Sites 7 through 10 are at the back or east side of the large gravel parking area. They are back-in sites with no size restrictions. There are vault toilets, picnic tables and fire pits, hiking trails, a water faucet, and, of course, the lakes. A host is usually on site and may have canoes available for rent.

The entrance to the Matanuska Lakes SRA is off the Glenn Highway near Mile 36. This is just east of the entrance to the Fox Run Campground.

🚐 FOX RUN LODGE AND RV CAMPGROUND

Address: 4466 S. Glenn Hwy, Palmer, AK 99645
Telephone: (907) 745-6120
Email: foxrunrv@mtaonline.net
Website: www.foxrunlodgealaska.com

GPS Location: 61.55189 N, 149.23151 W, 200 Ft.

This campground is situated next to Matanuska Lake, part of the Kepler-Bradley lake complex. Much of this area is part of a state recreation area with stocked lakes and hiking trails.

The campground has 29 sites, 22 are full-hookup, most with 30-amp outlets but

some with 50 amp. Many are pull-thrus to 60 feet. There is also a tent-camping area. Showers and laundry machines are available. Boats can be rented and propane is sold.

The campground is located at Mile 36 of the Glenn Highway.

FROM PALMER TO GLENNALLEN
147 Miles (237 Kilometers)

After Palmer the highway begins to wind its way through a mountain pass and climb toward the Copper River Valley. At Mile 101 is the Matanuska Glacier State Recreation Site which has a viewing area overlooking the **Matanuska Glacier**. For a closer look at the glacier you can drive in to the private Glacier Park, which allows no-hookup RV and tent camping. For many miles along the highway there are spectacular views to the south of the Chugach Range. The mountains to the north are the Talkeetna Mountains.

After climbing out of the Matanuska Valley the road runs through **Tahneta Pass** and across 3,322-foot **Eureka Summit**, then through a high plateau region with hundreds of little lakes and scattered black spruce trees. Many of the lakes have good fishing but they're difficult to access. There is a paved road that runs north for 17 miles (27 km) from Mile 160 to **Lake Louise** which has excellent fishing and two state campgrounds.

Once you pass the Lake Louise junction you'll start to see the Wrangell Mountains ahead. From left to right the peaks are **Mount Sanford** (16,237 feet), **Mount Drum** (12,010 feet), and **Mount Wrangell** (14,163 feet). All of them are in the Wrangell-St. Elias National park. See Chapter 6 - *The Richardson Highway* for more about this park. The road reaches Glennallen at Mile 187.

Palmer to Glennallen Campgrounds

PINNACLE MOUNTAIN RV PARK

Address:	Mile 70 Glenn Highway, 26616 Glenn Hwy, Sutton, AK 99674
Telephone:	(907) 746-6531
Email:	pinnaclepeak@mataonline.net
Website:	www.pinnaclervandcafe.com

GPS Location: 61.74460 N, 148.65972 W, 700 Ft.

This roadhouse-type campground is located along the Glenn Highway near Sutton. In addition to the campground the roadhouse offers a café, groceries and a laundry.

There are 42 campsites. Twelve are large pull-thrus on gravel and grass next to the lodge building. These sites have 30-amp electrical and water, some have sewer. Other campsites are in the trees behind, some are pull-thrus with electricity, others are smaller sites without services. Some sites have picnic tables, there are restrooms with showers and a dump station. Wi-Fi can be used from the sites nearest the café, and in the café too, of course.

The campground is located right on the Glenn Highway at Mile 69.7.

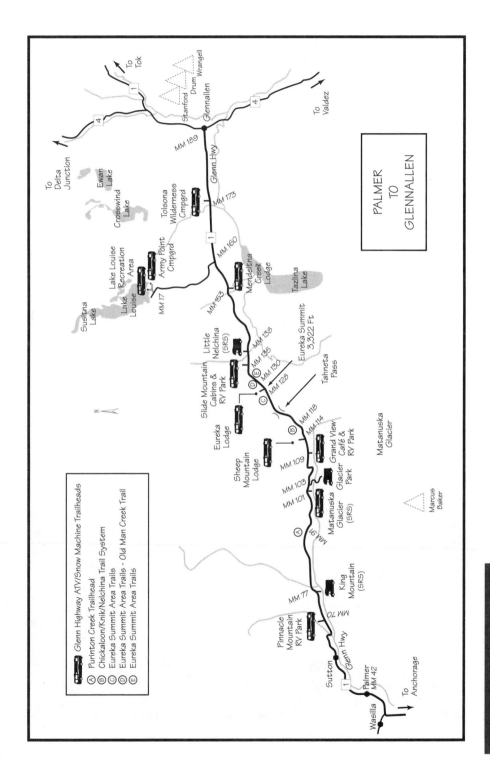

PALMER
TO
GLENNALLEN

Glenn Highway ATV/Snow Machine Trailheads

(A) Purinton Creek Trailhead
(B) Chickaloon/Knik/Nelchina Trail System
(C) Eureka Summit Area Trails
(D) Eureka Summit Area Trails - Old Man Creek Trail
(E) Eureka Summit Area Trails

KING MOUNTAIN STATE RECREATION SITE

Location: Mile 76 Glenn Highway
Res and Info: (907) 746-4644
Website: dnr.alaska.gov/parks/aspunits/matsu/kingmtnsrs.htm

GPS Location: 61.77560 N, 148.49443 W, 900 Ft.

An excellent state campground for smaller RVs along this section of the Glenn Highway is King Mountain. There are some 22 smallish back-in sites suitable for RVs to about 30 feet in a wooded setting next to the milky Matanuska River. Campers often spot rafts full of river runners passing by. Sites have picnic tables and fire pits and there are vault toilets and a water pump. This campground also has a kitchen/picnic shelter with some walk-in tent sites nearby. Reservations are available through the campsite concessionaire, the phone number is listed above. There is a 7-day stay limit at this campground.

MATANUSKA GLACIER STATE RECREATION SITE

Location: Mile 101 Of The Glenn Highway
Info: (907) 745-5151
Website: dnr.alaska.gov/parks/aspunits/matsu/matsuglsrs.htm

GPS Location: 61.80028 N, 147.81534 W, 1,800 Ft.

This recreation site gets lots of visitors because it offers a viewpoint with exceptional views of the Matanuska Glacier. Many tour busses and passing motorists make the stop. A nature trail follows the bluff so you can stretch your legs.

There are also 9 vehicle camping sites for RVs to about 30 feet. The sites are located

EXCELLENT VIEW OF MATANUSKA GLACIER

off a loop and are well separated with vegetation and have picnic tables and fire pits. Camping is also allowed in the overlook parking lot, this area will take any size RV and the price is a little lower. There are nine pull-through spaces in the parking lot for RVs. The campground has modern vault toilets in both locations and a water pump in the campground area. The stay limit here is 14 days.

Watch for the recreation site on the south side of the Glenn Highway near Mile 101.

▦ GLACIER PARK

Location:	Road From Mile 102 Of The Glenn Highway
Telephone:	(907) 745-2534 or (888) 253-4480
Email:	blueice@mtaonline.net

GPS Location: 61.79304 N, 147.79720 W, 1,500 Ft.

Glacier Park is a unique private operation. They have an impressive road that descends from the highway to the flat bench near the Matanuska Glacier. You leave the highway near Mile 102 and descend to a gatehouse area at about .8 miles (1.3 km). Here you'll find a gift shop. To pass on to the glacier overlook you must pay a fee of $20.00 per person. To overnight costs another $15 per person. The overlook is at 3.1 miles (5 km) and is popular for picnics. From the parking area it is possible to walk to the rapidly retreating glacier.

Camping facilities at Glacier Park are limited. At the overlook it is possible to dry camp in the parking area if you have an RV. There are picnic tables and portable toilets but this is an exposed location with often blustery weather. Near the gatehouse complex there is a small tent camping area suitable for tents with picnic tables, fire pits, and portable toilets. Road conditions here are changeable. Those with RVs should call first and check with the owners about access and parking.

⛟ GRAND VIEW CAFÉ & RV PARK

Address:	HC03 Box 8484, Palmer, AK 99645,
Telephone:	(907) 746-4480
Email:	info@grandviewrv.com
Website:	www.grandviewrv.com

GPS Location: 61.79862 N, 147.60880 W, 2,400 Ft.

This campground has a spectacular location next to the highway in a high mountain pass. You can often spot Dall sheep from the campsites.

The campground has 26, sites, 19 are large pull-thru sites to 60 feet and 7 are back-ins. All are situated on a big gravel bench next to the highway. They are all either full hookup or water and electric sites, some with 30-amp power and some with 50 amp. There are picnic tables, a community fire pit, showers, a dump station, a laundry and a café. The campground is located near Mile 110 of the Glenn Highway and is easy to spot from the road.

⛟ SHEEP MOUNTAIN LODGE

Location:	Mile 113.5 Glenn Highway
Address:	17701 Glenn Hwy., Sutton, AK 99674
Telephone:	(907) 745-5121 or (877) 645-5121
Email:	info@sheepmountain.com
Website:	www.sheepmountain.com

GPS Location: 61.81220 N, 147.49865 W, 2,800 Ft.

THE GLENN HIGHWAY

The Sheep Mountain Lodge is well known for its great views, excellent restaurant and nice rental cabins and spa. Now they've added five back-in sites and one pull-thru RV site adjacent to the parking lot out front. These sites have 30-amp outlets and picnic tables and have grass separating the sites. Wi-Fi is useable in the restaurant. You can pay extra for a shower in the immaculate restrooms, for laundry service, or to soak in the hot tub.

The lodge is located on the north side of the highway near Mile 113.5 of the Glenn Highway.

🚐 GLENN HIGHWAY ATV/SNOW MACHINE TRAILHEADS

There are a number of large parking areas along the Glenn Highway between Mile 91 and Mile 132. These are commonly used by folks running their off road vehicles on the extensive trail systems in this area. These people often overnight in RVs in the lots, why not join them? Here are locations for a few of the parking areas, it's not a complete list.

Near Mile 91 – Purinton Creek Trailhead – *GPS Location 61.80464 N, 148.08780 W, 2,300 Ft.* – Large gravel pull-off next to highway.

Near Mile 118 – Chickaloon/Knik/Nelchina Trail System – *GPS Location 61.85013 N, 147.38465 W, 3,300 Ft.* – Paved lot, vault toilets.

Near Mile 128 – Eureka Summit area trails - *GPS Location 61.89421 N, 147.33256 W, 3,100 Ft.* – Large pull-off, some separation from highway.

SOME OF THE BEST VIEWS IN THE STATE ARE ALONG THE GLENN HIGHWAY

THE GLENN HIGHWAY

Near Mile 130 – Eureka Summit area trails, Old Man Creek Trail - *GPS Location 61.95961 N, 147.12554 W, 3,300 Ft.* – Large gravel lot.

Near Mile 132 – Eureka Summit area trails - *GPS Location 61.98529 N, 147.07868 W, 3,200 Ft.* – Large gravel lot.

EUREKA LODGE

Address: HC01 Box 2240, Glennallen, AK 99588
Telephone: (907) 822-3808
Email: info@eurekalodge.com
Website: www.eurekalodge.com

GPS Location: 61.93780 N, 147.17340 W, 3,300 Ft.

The Eureka Lodge is a center for activities related to the extensive trail system in the high country around Eureka Summit. They're also a good spot to spend the night if you're traveling through.

They have 10 back-in hookup electric-only sites. The sites are off a large maneuvering area so any size rig is OK. The sites overlook a small lake out back. There's also lots of room for dry camping. The facility has a restaurant and bar, a gas station, and some cabins. There are no showers and the only restrooms are in the restaurant.

The lodge is on the north side of the highway near Mile 128.

SLIDE MOUNTAIN CABINS AND RV PARK

Address: HC01 Box 2439, Glennallen, AK 99588
Telephone: (907) 822-5864 or (907) 822-3883
Email: slidemountaincabins@gmail.com
Website: www.slidemountaincabins.net

GPS Location: 61.98846 N, 147.01273 W, 2,800 Ft.

This is a newer facility with cabins and good RV sites in wide open country where the highway climbs toward Glennallen. It's a nice place.

There are 15 RV sites here. Ten are long back-ins on grass with 30-amp outlets to 45 feet, five are long gravel pull-thrus separated by grass and rail fences with 50-amp outlets to 75 feet. The tent camping area has a covered and screened picnic shelter with a fireplace. There are flush toilets and showers, water is in short supply but available for showers. There are no sewer drains or dump station. Free Wi-Fi internet access is available at the office.

The campground is on the north side of the highway near Mile 135.

LITTLE NELCHINA STATE RECREATION SITE

Location: Mile 138 Of The Glenn Highway

GPS Location: 61.98974 N, 146.94659 W, 2,500 Ft.

This little state recreation site is tucked into a small canyon near the highway. It's a former state campground now not being maintained, but still in pretty good shape. Access is via a short stretch of the old highway that was abandoned during road-straightening construction.

There are 8 sites in this camping area. Several of them are along the creek in spruce and cottonwoods. Most are fairly small and are back-ins or tent sites. There are out-

THE GLENN HIGHWAY

houses and a raft launching area. The picnic tables have disappeared and there is no drinking water other than the creek, but this isn't a bad place to stop for the night if you have a RV up to about 25 feet long

The campground isn't right on the main road. Instead, it's off an old section of the highway that has been bypassed by the new highway. There's no sign, you turn onto the old section of road, which is still paved, near Mile 138 and drive about a hundred yards to the camping area entrance.

MENDELTNA CREEK LODGE

Address:	HC01 Box 2560, Glennallen, AK 99588
Telephone:	(907) 822-3346
Website:	www.mendeltnacreeklodge.com

GPS Location: 62.04864 N, 146.53849 W, 2,300 Ft.

This roadhouse-style operation offers cabins and gas sales and a restaurant in an old but beautifully built lodge building out front.

There are at about 80 camping spaces in a large gravel lot behind the restaurant and cabins. Trees break up the large expanse of the campground. Many sites are pull-thrus. Serviced sites have either electricity or electricity and sewer, there is also a dump station and water fill hose. Some sites are along the Little Mendeltna, a small stream running along the side of the campground. There are picnic tables and some sites have circles of rocks forming fire rings. The laundry/shower building has flush toilets and showers.

The campground is located on the south side of the Glenn Highway near Mile 153. This is about 30 miles (48 km) from Glennallen and near the half-way point if you are driving between either Tok or Valdez and Anchorage.

LAKE LOUISE STATE RECREATION AREA
LAKE LOUISE AND ARMY POINT CAMPGROUNDS

Location:	Mile 17 Lake Louise Road, Leaves Glenn Highway At Mile 160
Info:	(907) 441-7575
Website:	dnr.alaska.gov/parks/aspunits/matsu/lklouisesra.htm

GPS Location: 62.28167 N, 146.54275 W, 2,500 Ft.

Lake Louise is a huge lake that is very popular year-round, which is surprising considering its remote location. In the summer fishing, especially for lake trout, is popular. In late summer the water is warm enough for swimming (you've got to be tough) and water sports. During the fall this is a popular hunting area and in the winter this can be great snow machining and ice fishing country.

There are two modern state campgrounds located right next to each other on the southwest shore of the lake with 58 camping spaces. They really make up one large campground. Most of the sites here are marked back-ins in gravel parking areas but a few sites are singles separated by vegetation. The trees in the area are very small dwarf species or shrubs so don't expect a lot of privacy even if you get one of the separated spaces. There are picnic tables and fire pits. Other offerings are vault toilets, water pumps, a boat launching area, and a walking trail between the two campgrounds and out to Army Point and the ridge behind. The beach is stones and mud but still popular. There is a 14-day limit here.

To reach the campgrounds you follow Lake Louise Road north from near Mile 160 of the Glenn Highway. The campgrounds are at Mile 17. This road is now paved for the entire distance, but many frost heaves make it slow going for big rigs.

TOLSONA WILDERNESS CAMPGROUND

Address:	PO Box 23, Glennallen, AK 99588
Telephone:	(907) 822-3865
Email:	camp@tolsona.com
Website:	www.tolsona.com

GPS Location: 62.11362 N, 145.97456 W, 2,000 Ft.

One of the best spots to stop for the evening or a week along the whole Glenn Highway is the Tolsona Wilderness Campground. This is a commercial campground with the advantages and ambiance of a government campground. It is also located almost a mile from the highway so road noise is entirely absent.

Tolsona is a large campground, there are some 80 sites. Most are back-ins but there are also a few pull-thrus to 60 feet. Large rigs can have difficulty maneuvering and the long sites are narrow. About 40 of the sites have electricity (20, 30 or 50 amps) and water hookups. The remainder are dry. All sites are on the banks of Tolsona Creek which runs right through the campground, and which has grayling. Campsites are well-separated and the campground is wooded with white spruce. Each site has a picnic table and fire pit. There are restrooms with flush toilets and inexpensive coin-op showers, a laundry, a dump station and water fill site, and even playing fields. Wi-Fi is included and can be received at sites in the neighborhood of the office.

The .8 mile (1.3 km) long gravel access road leaves the Glenn Highway near Mile 173. This is about 13 miles (21 km) west of Glennallen.

GLENNALLEN
Population 500, Elevation 1,450 feet

Glennallen occupies a strategic position just west of the south junction of the Richardson and Glenn highways. It serves as the supply center for the huge but sparsely populated Copper River Valley and has lots of government offices including the Bureau of Land Management, State Troopers, and Fish and Game. You'll find that the services are strung along the highway and include RV parks, grocery stores, restaurants, and gas stations. The **Copper River Valley Information Center** is located right at the junction of the Glenn and Richardson Highways.

Glennallen Campgrounds

CARIBOU HOTEL

Address:	P.O. Box 329, Glennallen, AK 99588
Telephone:	(907) 822-3302
Email:	info@caribouhotel.com
Website:	www.caribouhotel.com

GPS Location: 62.10737 N, 145.53710 W, 1,400 Ft

The Caribou Hotel, along the highway in Glennallen, has 14 pull-thru side-by-side

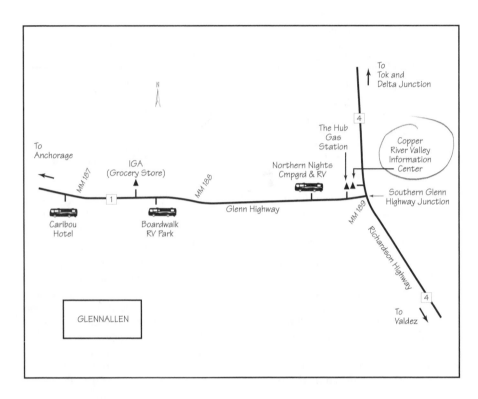

sites in the parking lot out front. They are full-hookup sites with 50 amp power. Restrooms with showers are located off the lobby and there is a restaurant.

The hotel is located on the south side of the highway in Glennallen about 2 miles (3.2 km) west of the Glenn's junction with the Richardson Highway.

▣ BOARDWALK RV PARK
Telephone: (907) 822-4420

GPS Location: 62.10723 N, 145.51589 W, 1,500 Ft.

Self-contained campers who like to keep things simple, and who like a good deal, will like this place. The campground has 10 pull-thru sites. There are 30-amp electric water, and sewer hookups. There is also a dump station (fee is $5). All are set on a gravel lot behind a small office building. Watch for the campground on the south side of the highway in Glennallen about 1.3 miles (2.1 km) west of the Glenn's junction with the Richardson Highway.

▣ NORTHERN NIGHTS CAMPGROUND AND RV
Address:	Mile 188.7 Glenn Hwy. (PO Box 528), Glennallen, AK 99588
Telephone:	(907) 822-3199 Summer, (907) 929-5220 Winter
Email:	darlene528@gmail.com
Website:	www.northernnightscampground.com

GPS Location: 62.10776 N, 145.48641 W, 1,600 Ft.

This campground is actively managed by its owners and offers a good combination of features for travelers.

The campground has 26 sites set in a spruce grove. The gravel sites are well separated for a commercial campground and many are pull-thrus for RV combos to 80 feet. Only a few back-in sites offer sewer but the pull-thrus have electricity and water hookups and there are no-hookup sites. A dump station is located on the exit road and is available to those not staying in the park for an extra fee. Nice tent sites with parking pads and some tent platforms are located in the rear of the campground. All sites have fire rings and tables. A computer is available for email and there is Wi-Fi included in the price.

The campground is located on the north side of the Glenn Highway in Glennallen .3 miles (.5 km) west of the intersection of the Glenn and Richardson Highways.

FROM GLENNALLEN TO TOK
139 Miles (224 Kilometers)

From Glennallen the Glenn and Richardson are the same road for 14 miles (23 km) northward to the Gakona junction. From there a section of road runs northeast to Tok, it is commonly called the Tok Cutoff.

For many miles the Tok Cutoff runs along high ground overlooking the **Copper Riv-**

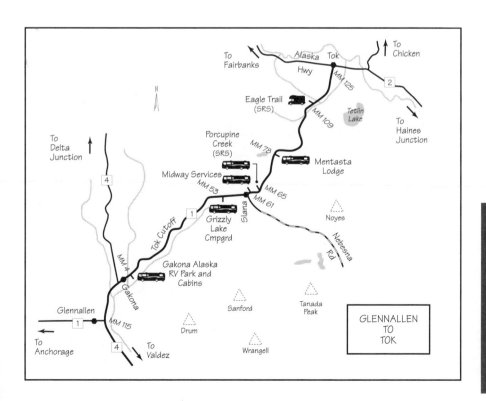

THE GLENN HIGHWAY

er. At higher points there are great views toward the southeast and the **Wrangell-St. Elias National Park** and **Mt. Drum** (12,010 feet) and **Mt. Sanford** (16,237 feet). At Mile 60 there is a junction with the **Nabesna Road**. See the section near the end of this chapter for information about sights and camping along the road.

After passing the Nabesna Road the highway runs through **Mentasta Pass** and crosses the 2,234-foot summit to pass through the Alaska Range from the Copper River drainage into the Tanana and Yukon drainage. The road reaches Tok junction at Mile 125 where it joins the Alaska Highway some 93 miles (150 km) from the Alaska border. See Chapter 4 - *The Alaska Highway* for information about Tok.

Glennallen to Tok Campgrounds

GAKONA ALASKA RV PARK AND CABINS

Address:	PO Box 299, Gakona, AK 99586
Telephone:	(907) 822-3550
Website:	www.gakonarvpark.com

GPS Location: 62.30857 N, 145.23297 W, 1,500 Ft.

This campground has 48 sites, 24 are pull-thrus to 60 feet sitting on a large open gravel area next to the Copper River. Full service (20, 30 and 50 amp), water and electric, electric only, and dry sites are available. An older restroom building has flush toilets and showers and there is a laundry and dump station. Other attractions include a playground, some picnic tables, and fire pits.

The entrance road to the campground is on the Tok Cutoff some 4.2 miles (6.8 km)

A NICE CAMPSITE ALONG THE LAKE AT THE GRIZZLY LAKE CAMPGROUND

northeast of the junction of the Richardson and the Tok Cutoff (Gakona Junction).

GRIZZLY LAKE CAMPGROUND

Address:	PO Box 340, Gakona, AK 99586
Telephone:	(907) 822-5214
Email:	grizzlylake1@cvinternet.net

GPS Location: 62.71288 N, 144.19782 W, 2,500 Ft.

This small RV Park and cabin resort occupies a scenic site near the Tok Cutoff on a small lake with great views toward the Wrangell-St Elias Park to the south. They have parking with no hookups for RVs and tent sites. Five smaller parking slots are down by the lake, other back-in and pull-thru sites to 60 feet are near the entrance. They have flush toilets and showers. Cabins are also offered and there are boat rentals. Watch for the sign and entrance road on the east side of the highway near Mile 53 of the Tok Cutoff.

MIDWAY SERVICES

Location:	Mile 61 Tok Cutoff, Gakona, AK 99586
Telephone:	(907) 822-5877
Email:	jaycapps@hotmail.com

GPS Location: 62.71863 N, 143.96107 W, 2,500 Ft.

This is a rural grocery store with some camping options. There is room for about three RVs to park in the area in front of the store with electrical outlets, tents can pitch here too. There is no charge for the RV parking or tent camping, just a $10 charge if you hook up to electricity. The owners also have a converted school bus, much like the famous bus north of Denali Park that was featured in the movie *Into the Wild*. It too was at one time located far out in the boonies, but now you can drive right up to it. They often let friendly tent campers stay in it for free. Inside the main building are restrooms, showers, a laundry, a computer for internet access, and a grocery store. There's good fishing nearby, particularly for grayling.

PORCUPINE CREEK STATE RECREATION SITE

Location:	Near Mile 64 Of The Tok Cutoff
Info:	(907) 822-3973
Website:	dnr.alaska.gov/parks/aspunits/matsu/porcksrs.htm

GPS Location: 62.72781 N, 143.87105 W, 2,400 Ft.

This small state campground has 12 sites. Three are in an open gravel area and are pull-off type, the remainder are back-ins to 60 feet. Each site has a picnic table and fire pit. There are vault toilets and a water pump. The time limit here is 15 days.

MENTASTA LODGE

Address:	HC 01, Box 585, Mentasta, AK
Telephone:	(907) 291-2324
Email:	Mentastalodge@starband.net
Website:	www.mentastalodge.com

GPS Location: 62.88856 N, 143.67903 W, 2,300 Ft.

The Mentasta Lodge has a restaurant, a bar, a store and a motel. There are also about 20 back-in RV sites located north of the lodge near the highway. These are big sites off a wide gravel drive so big rigs will fit fine. These sites have electrical and water hookups, and there is a dump station. The lodge also offers pay showers and a laundromat. Gas is sold here too, and there is free Wi-Fi in the restaurant.

The campground is Mile 78 of the Tok Cutoff and is on the east side of the road.

EAGLE TRAIL STATE RECREATION SITE

Location:	Near Mile 109 Of The Tok Cutoff
Info:	(907) 883-3686
Website:	dnr.alaska.gov/parks/aspunits/northern/eagletrailsrs.htm

GPS Location: 63.16372 N, 143.19850 W, 2,000 Ft.

Eagle Trail is a large and pleasant state campground. It celebrates the Eagle Trail, built from Valdez to Eagle (and including a telegraph line) to improve communications with the gold fields. A short trail nearby follows portions of the Eagle Trail and a connecting trail climbs to a nice overlook. The park has recently been rebuilt and now will accommodate modern large RVs.

The campground has about 35 sites including 5 for tents. They are arranged in 4 wheel-like groups with some pull-thrus to 60 feet and many back-in sites for RVs to about 45 feet. There is good separation between sites and they are set in a wooded area. All have picnic tables and fire pits. There are vault toilets and a water pump as well as a picnic area with a shelter. The campground has a 15 day limit.

SIDE TRIP ON NABESNA ROAD

The Nabesna Road runs eastward from Mile 60 of the Tok Cutoff for 45 miles (73 km) into the Wrangell-St. Elias National Park and Preserve to the former gold-mining town of Nabesna. The road is paved for just 4 miles (6.5 km), it is decent gravel to Mile 29, then it deteriorates further with some sometimes dicey stream fords. The section to Mile 29 is usually suitable for carefully driven RVs. There are no park facilities other than a few rest area/campsite/trailheads, some with vault toilets, along the road but the scenery is spectacular. There are several good fishing lakes and also some hiking possibilities. You should be aware that this is a wilderness highway and fuel is not available.

The friendly Slana Ranger Station is located about a quarter-mile in. It's open from 8 AM to 5 PM during the summer, the telephone number is 907 882-7401. They can fill you in on road conditions and hiking and camping possibilities. They have a very useful printed log of the highway which includes historical data, campsites, sightseeing facts, hiking and ATV trails, and even information about fishing lakes.

Most campsites along the road have few amenities. In addition to those listed below which are specifically identified as campsites by the Park Service there are a number of gravel pits that provide excellent locations for boondocking in self-contained RVs.

Nabesna Road Campgrounds

HART D RANCH (DOUBLE TREE RV PARK)

Address:	.5 Mile Nabesna Road, Slana, AK 99586
Telephone:	(907) 822-3973
Email:	dehart@hartd.com
Website:	www.hartd.com

GPS Location: 62.70774 N, 143.96886 W, 2,200 Ft.

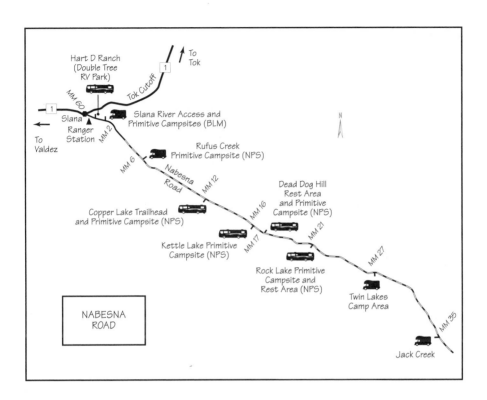

This is the home of long-time Alaskan bronze sculptor Mary Frances Dehart. She has displays of bronze sculptures, prints, photos and embroidery items for sale. There are a B&B and campground on the very well-kept grounds. The campground has about 40 sites, some are pull-thrus with electricity, water, and sewer hookups to 60 feet. Others have only water and sewer. They are nicely arranged and separated by vegetation and trees. Maneuvering room is a little tight but big RVs do use this campground. There is a dump station and very nice restrooms are available with showers. Wi-Fi is useable near the office.

To reach the campground follow the Nabesna Road east from near Mile 60 of the Tok Cutoff. At .5 miles (.9 km) turn left into the post office parking lot and continue on through to the campground. If no one is at the campground office (a residence) try going next door to the post office, the owner often is running it too.

SLANA RIVER ACCESS AND PRIMITIVE CAMPSITES (BLM)

FREE

Location: Mile 1.7 (Km 2.7) Of Nabesna Road

GPS Location: 62.70587 N, 143.94429 W, 2,200 Ft.

This is a parking area next to the Slana River. There are no facilities but it's a pleasant location. The .2 mile (.3 km) access road is narrow and maneuvering room is limited so this place is best for RVs to 30 feet. Driving eastward you'll cross the Slana River bridge at Mile 1.5. The unmarked entrance road is the first left after the bridge.

RUFUS CREEK PRIMITIVE CAMPSITE (NATIONAL PARK SERVICE)

Location: Mile 6.1 (Km 9.8) Of The Nabesna Road

   GPS Location: 62.65962 N, 143.84357 W, 2,300 Ft.

Rufus Creek Campsite has room for parking 2 RVs to 30 feet. There's a picnic table and a fire pit. Rufus Creek has decent fishing for Dollies.

**COPPER LAKE TRAILHEAD AND PRIMITIVE CAMPSITE
(NATIONAL PARK SERVICE)**

Location: Mile 12.2 (Km 19.7) Of The Nabesna Road

   GPS Location: 62.61694 N, 143.68440 W, 2,600 Ft.

Copper Lake Trailhead has one picnic table and a fire pit, there's room to park four or five RVs to 40 feet.

**KETTLE LAKE PRIMITIVE CAMPSITE
(NATIONAL PARK SERVICE)**

Location: Mile 16.6 (Km 26.8) Of The Nabesna Road

   GPS Location: 62.58451 N, 143.56794 W, 2,900 Ft.

There's one site here with a picnic table and fire pit. Large RVs will fit.

**DEAD DOG HILL REST AREA AND PRIMITIVE CAMPSITES
(NATIONAL PARK SERVICE)**

Location: Mile 17.2 (Km 27.7) Of The Nabesna Road

   GPS Location: 62.573676 N, 143.53500 W, 3,000 Ft.

This rest area has one of the few vault toilets along the highway. There's a picnic table, a fire pit, bear-proof garbage bins and enough space for parking several large RVs.

**ROCK LAKE PRIMITIVE CAMPSITE AND REST AREA
(NATIONAL PARK SERVICE)**

Location: Mile 21.1 (Km 34) Of The Nabesna Road

   GPS Location: 62.56328 N, 143.41714 W, 3,200 Ft.

Rock Hill has a picnic table, a fire pit, bear-proof garbage bins and a vault toilet. A large RV can park here. It overlooks a beautiful lake with the Wrangell Mountains visible in the background.

**TWIN LAKES CAMP AREA
(NATIONAL PARK SERVICE)**

Location: Mile 27.8 (Km 44.8) Of The Nabesna Road

   GPS Location: 62.52983 N, 143.25900 W, 3,100 Ft.

Twin Lakes is the largest of the campgrounds along the Nabesna Road. Some site will take RVs 35 feet. There are vault toilets, fire pits, and bear-proof garbage bins. Fishing here is for grayling.

JACK CREEK (NATIONAL PARK SERVICE)
   Location: Mile 35.3 (Km 56.9) Of The Nabesna Road

GPS Location: 62.45169 N, 143.08696 W. 2,900 Ft.

Jack Creek has 2 picnic tables and a vault toilet. There is room for up to three vehicles. There are game trails for hiking and fishing in Jack Creek for grayling.

GLENN HIGHWAY DUMP STATIONS

Many of the campgrounds in this chapter have either dump stations or sewer hookups. In most cases use of the dump stations is either restricted to people staying at the campground or requires payment of a fee. Try to empty your holding tanks in one of the larger cities where proper sewer treatment is guaranteed and isn't a financial burden to the campground owner.

In **Anchorage** many gas stations have dump stations available to customers. Here are some of them: Holiday at 1500 East 5th Ave. on the north side of Merrill Field (*GPS Location 61.21693 N, 149.85401 W*); Chevron at 6th and Ingra (832 East 6th Ave.) (*GPS Location: 61.21611 N, 149.86809 W*); Tesoro in the Fred Meyer parking lot in the southeast quadrant of the intersection of the Seward Highway and Northern Lights (2811 Seward Highway) (*GPS Location 61.19480 N, 149.86694 W*); Chevron in the northwest quadrant of the intersection of Spenard and Minnesota (3608 Minnesota) (*GPS Location 61.18737 N, 149.91403 W*).

In **Eagle River** there's a dump station at the Tesoro on the east side of the highway at 12139 Old Glenn Highway (*GPS Location 61.32955 N, 149.56616 W*).

In **Palmer** go to Palmer Chevron, 439 West Evergreen (*GPS Location 61.60001 N, 149.12115 W*). The station here is often difficult to access due to congestion.

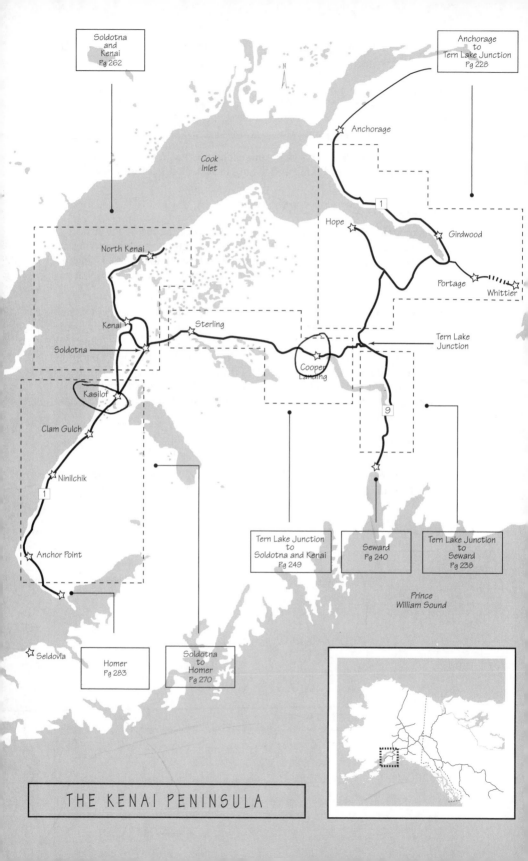

N

Cook
Inlet

Anchorage

Hope

Girdwood

North Kenai

Portage

Whittier

Kenai

Sterling

Tern Lake
Junction

Soldotna

Cooper
Landing

Kasilof

1

9

Clam Gulch

Ninilchik

1

Anchor Point

Prince
William Sound

Seldovia

THE KENAI PENINSULA

Chapter 8

The Kenai Peninsula

INTRODUCTION

The one region in Alaska with the most to offer campers is undoubtedly the Kenai Peninsula. This huge wilderness playground, almost an island, has something for everyone.

The Kenai is the most popular place in the state for campers from Anchorage. The state's largest city is home to the state's largest group of campers, and on weekends during the summer they head south every Friday night and usually return on Sunday evening. There are many camping sites on the Kenai but they can be crowded on weekends. Anchorage campers should make reservations when possible so they have a comfortable spot to park while enjoying the peninsula.

It you are not tied to a Monday to Friday job you can easily arrange to enjoy the Kenai during the week when it isn't very crowded. When the weekend comes you can be comfortably parked in a beautiful campsite and watch the weekenders arrive with a cocktail (or fishing pole) in your hand. Many people arrange for extra vacation days in the summer for this very reason.

The busiest time of the season is late June and July when both king and red salmon are running in the lower Kenai and the rivers south toward Homer. During that period don't forget than many campgrounds, including almost all commercial campgrounds and many Forest Service campgrounds, take reservations. See the individual campground listings for more information.

THE KENAI PENINSULA

Highlights

Three major population centers are located on the Kenai Peninsula, these are **Seward, Kenai-Soldotna**, and **Homer**. Each of them has many campgrounds and is covered in more detail below.

The **Seward Highway** is a designated National Forest Scenic Byway. Attractions along the way like **Turnagain Arm**, the **Alyeska Ski Area**, **Portage Glacier**, **Turnagain Pass**, **Kenai Lake**, and the **Exit Glacier** are excellent reasons to make this drive.

Much of the Peninsula is federal or state land. While there you can visit **Chugach National Forest**, **Kenai Fjords National Park**, the **Kenai National Wildlife Refuge**, and the **Kachemak Bay State Park**. If you like the outdoors you'll love the Kenai Peninsula. It's one of the best places in Alaska to find beautiful scenery, fishing, hiking, canoeing, kayaking, and just about anything you want to do in the outdoors.

The Road and Fuel

Two highways combine to give access to the Kenai Peninsula. From Anchorage the only route to the south is the **Seward Highway**. The Seward Highway is very scenic and has been designated a National Forest Scenic Byway. This two-lane paved road hugs the cliffs along Turnagain Arm until reaching Girdwood, then circles around the end of Turnagain to climb into the mountains onto the Kenai Peninsula proper. Ninety-two miles (148 km) from Anchorage the peninsula's second highway, the Sterling Highway, branches off to the west. The Seward Highway continues south, eventually ending at Seward on the south coast. By law headlights are required to be on at all times along this road.

The **Sterling Highway** leads west from its junction with the Seward Highway. After some 11 miles (18 km) it leaves the mountains and crosses the flatlands until reaching Soldotna near the west coast of the Kenai Peninsula. The highway then follows the coast south to Homer, ending at the point of the Homer Spit.

From Anchorage to Seward along the Seward Highway is a distance of 127 miles (205 km). Mileposts along the Seward Highway start in Seward and run north to Anchorage. Several important side roads lead off from the Seward Highway including the Alyeska Highway (Mile 90), the Portage Valley Highway (Mile 79), and the Hope Highway (Mile 57). From Mile 90 at Girdwood to Mile 7 about 6 miles from Seward there is no gas available on the Seward Highway so be prepared. If you find yourself running low you can turn west on the Sterling Highway at Mile 37 and drive 8 miles to buy gas at the Sunrise Inn or nearby Cooper Landing.

The Sterling Highway from Tern Lake Junction to Homer is 143 miles (231 km) long. Mileposts along this highway are confusing because they start in Seward which is not even on the highway. Tern Lake Junction, the highway's starting point, is at Mile 37. Mileposts count up from there. Important side roads off the Sterling Highway include the Skilak Lake Loop (Mile 58 and Mile 75), the Swanson River Road (Mile 83 in Sterling), and the Kenai Spur Road (Mile 94).

The highway designation system used on these two roads is also confusing because the names and numbers do not designate the same stretches of roads. Highway 1

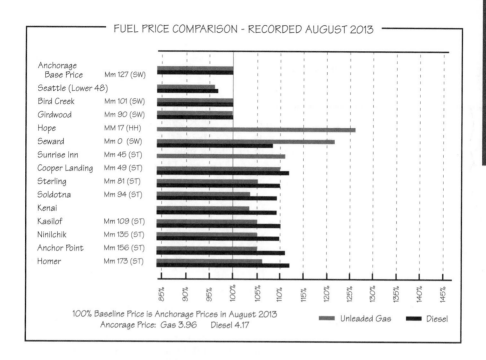

FUEL PRICE COMPARISON - RECORDED AUGUST 2013

Anchorage Base Price	Mm 127 (SW)
Seattle (Lower 48)	
Bird Creek	Mm 101 (SW)
Girdwood	Mm 90 (SW)
Hope	MM 17 (HH)
Seward	Mm 0 (SW)
Sunrise Inn	Mm 45 (ST)
Cooper Landing	Mm 49 (ST)
Sterling	Mm 81 (ST)
Soldotna	Mm 94 (ST)
Kenai	
Kasilof	Mm 109 (ST)
Ninilchik	Mm 135 (ST)
Anchor Point	Mm 156 (ST)
Homer	Mm 173 (ST)

85% 90% 95% 100% 105% 110% 115% 120% 125% 130% 135% 140% 145%

100% Baseline Price is Anchorage Prices in August 2013
Ancorage Price: Gas 3.96   Diesel 4.17

■ Unleaded Gas   ■ Diesel

includes the Seward Highway from Anchorage to Tern Lake Junction and then the Sterling Highway to Homer. The Seward Highway from Tern Lake Junction to Seward is known as Highway 9.

Fishing

Probably the most popular attraction on the Kenai is the fishing. You have lots of choices: king salmon on the world famous Kenai River and other streams, halibut out of Homer or Deep Creek, silver salmon in Seward, red salmon at the Russian River, trout from dozens of lakes and streams. The truth is that there are excellent fishing opportunities on the Kenai during the entire summer. The fish are almost everywhere so we'll only mention the highlights.

The possibilities for catching salmon start almost as soon as you start down the Seward Highway from Anchorage. **Indian Creek** (Mile 103) and **Bird Creek** (Mile 101) have heavy runs of pink and silver salmon in July and August. Remember, Cook Inlet pinks only run in large numbers during even numbered-years like 2012 and 2014. The **Twentymile River** (Mile 81) and the **Placer River** (Mile 78) have an interesting dip net fishery for hooligan in May. It's as much fun to watch as it is to fish.

Seward is best-known for its silver salmon. You can catch them from the beach or from boats during August. The Seward Silver Salmon derby is held during the second week of August. Seward also offers fishing for kings, pinks, halibut, sea-run Dollies, and bottom fish.

When heading down the Sterling Highway from the intersection at Tern Lake the fishing action is dominated by the **Kenai River** all the way to Soldotna/Kenai. There are fish, especially trout and Dollies, in other places, notable Quartz Creek and the lakes of the Kenai Mountains and the Kenai Moose Range, but most people are after big salmon in the Kenai.

The first stop is the **Russian River**. This tributary of the Kenai is fished in two places, the Russian itself and the Kenai where the Russian flows in. The area of the Kenai just below the mouth of the Russian receives extremely heavy fishing pressure. During late June and again in late July fishermen are elbow to elbow flipping flies to red salmon on both side of the river. They wouldn't be there if their chances of catching fish weren't extremely good. Access to the far side of the Kenai away from the road is by ferry from Mile 55 of the Sterling Highway. Silver fishing in the Russian is good in August, so is Dolly and catch-and-release rainbow fishing. Fishing regulations for the Russian can be complicated and different from those for the surrounding area so check them out.

The **Upper Kenai**, from the outlet of Kenai Lake to Skilak Lake, is a beautiful emerald-colored stream 17 miles (27 km) in length. The Sterling Highway runs along it between Mile 48 and Mile 57, then the river turns away from the road and enters a canyon. You can fish from the bank or from a raft or drift boat to reach otherwise inaccessible waters. Fish for reds in late June and late July into August. Silvers appear in August and September and again in October and November. The area is closed to king fishing. This is also a good place to fish for rainbows and Dollies, especially in the fall. Again, the regulations should be checked carefully when fishing this water.

The **Lower Kenai** is the king fishery. It runs 50 miles (81 km) from the Skilak Lake outlet to salt water near Kenai. The Sterling Highway does not run along this river very much, but there is access all along its length using side roads. A lot of the fishing is from boats, this is big water. There are two runs of kings, one in June and the other starting in mid July. There are also two runs each of reds and silver salmon, and there are also Dollies and rainbows. For best results on the lower Kenai hire a guide, they have the knowledge and the boats. No fisherman should visit Alaska and not spend at least a day on a guided Kenai king fishing expedition.

The Kenai River mouth hosts a special fishery for two weeks through the middle of July. This is the Alaska residents-only dip net fishery for red salmon. There's also a dip net fishery at the mouth of the Kasilof River.

From Soldotna the Sterling highway heads south, and along the way it passes over a string of extremely productive rivers flowing west into Cook Inlet. These include the **Kasilof River and Crooked Creek** (Mile 109), the **Ninilchik River** (Mile 135), **Deep Creek** (Mile 137), and the **Anchor River** (Mile 157). All have large state campgrounds near the river and offer fishing for kings and silvers.

There is also a substantial salt water fishery in **Cook Inlet from Ninilchik to Anchor Point**. Along the shore fishermen find kings, pinks, silvers, and even halibut. Charter operators from **Deep Creek** and the **Anchor River** in larger boats offer excellent halibut fishing, they fish some of the same waters as charter boats out of Homer.

Homer is at the end of the road. Most fishermen come to Homer for the halibut. They fish from charter boats and often limit out with two halibut in the ten to thirty pound range. Occasionally a halibut as large as 400 pounds (that's right!) is caught. Homer also has its "fishing hole" near the end of the Spit which is designed just to give tourists a better-than-fighting chance to catch a king or silver. This is a terminal fishery with no place to spawn. Hatchery king and silver fingerlings are released here and come back as adults just to be caught.

Have you ever gone clamming? Digging for razor clams along Cook Inlet beaches is like clamming nowhere else. During the lowest tides (you can't reach the clams any other time) it is easy to get your limit, and the limit is usually 60 clams. You can easily equip yourself for clamming in Soldotna or Kenai, you only need a fishing license, a clam shovel, boots and a bucket. Head for either Clam Gulch or Ninilchik. Once you're on the beach just watch someone who's finding clams, it's easy if you use the right technique. You'll also need a few tips on cleaning those clams. Check around your campground, during the clam tides you'll probably have no trouble finding an expert. A word to the wise, limit your enthusiasm when you're digging, cleaning clams can take longer than digging them and it's not nearly as much fun.

It's important to check fishing regulations carefully because they can be complicated and they do change. The State of Alaska puts out some great little regulation booklets and they're easy to get at sporting goods stores and tourist information locations. Another good source of information is the Alaska Department of Fish and Game (ADF&G) website: www.adfg.state.ak.us .

Boating, Rafting, Canoeing, and Kayaking

The Kenai has an excellent canoe trail system. The Kenai National Wildlife Refuge's **Swanson River Canoe Route** is a multi-day trail passing through lakes and along the Swanson River. Another trail in the moose range, the **Swan Lake Route**, is similar. See Chapter 14 - *Camping Away From the Road System* for information about the canoe routes and this chapter for road-accessible campgrounds along the Swanson River and Swan Lake Roads, the access roads to the canoe system.

A popular rafting trip is a float of the **Upper Kenai**. The section from the Kenai Lake outlet to Jean Creek is primarily a fishing trip but there are sections of Class III water. From Jean Creek to Skilak Lake is Class III water in the Kenai Canyon. Neither section is a place for inexperienced rafters. Your best bet is to float with a commercial operator. They can be found in Anchorage and Cooper Landing. Canoeists also like to float the **Lower Kenai** between Skilak Lake and Jim's landing, the take-out there allows them to avoid rapids below the landing.

Ocean kayakers will find three exceptional areas accessible on the Kenai Peninsula. The first is world-famous **Prince William Sound**. While not really on the Kenai Peninsula we'll mention it here since access is possible via the road to Whittier near Mile 80 of the Seward Highway. **Resurrection Bay** near Seward has excellent kayaking waters, since the **Kenai Fjords** are a long paddle away try catching a lift with a excursion or charter boat operator. Finally, **Kachemak Bay** has miles of relatively protected shoreline across from Homer. All of these areas are further described in Chapter 14 - *Camping Away From the Road System*.

Hiking and Mountain Biking

The Kenai Peninsula has the best selection of good hiking trails in all of Alaska. Probably the best known is the **Resurrection Pass Trail** that runs from Hope to Cooper Landing and then on to Seward. Hiking the whole thing would take over a week. This is a popular mountain bike trail but be careful. Grizzly bears are often on the trail and it is possible to get very close on a bike before you see the bear or the bear sees you, that's a recipe for trouble. Other trails lead to lakes, ridges, and glaciers. Several hiking guidebooks describe hikes in this area, check our Chapter 2 - *Details, Details, Details* for our suggestions. Here are a few of our favorite hikes.

In the Portage Valley the hard-surfaced **Trail of Blue I**ce runs from Black Bear Campground to the Begich-Boggs Visitor Center, a distance of about five miles. It's a wide, flat trail and bicycles are allowed. It's accessible from both Black Bear and Williwaw NFS campgrounds and also provides access to the Williwaw salmon viewing platform. Hanging glaciers on the mountainside are easy to see from the trail.

The **Primrose Trail** from Primrose Campground on Kenai Lake and the **Lost Lake Trail** from Lost Lake Subdivision near Mile 5 of the Seward Highway both go to the same place, a big alpine lake called Lost Lake. The one-way distance from either is 7 miles, you can also make a traverse out of this hike. This trail is open to bikes.

Johnson Pass is usually hiked as a traverse. This is a historic trail that was originally part of a pack route from Seward to Sunrise and Hope. It is also part of the historic

VIEW FROM A HIKING TRAIL IN THE PORTAGE VALLEY

Iditarod Trail. This 23-mile trail is a popular mountain bike route. Trailheads are near Mile 32 and Mile 64 of the Seward Highway.

Across Kachemak Bay from Homer is **Kachemak Bay State Park**. It has lots of hiking trails, see Chapter 14 - *Camping Away From the Road System* for more information.

 ### Wildlife Viewing

Almost as soon as you leave Anchorage heading south you'll come to one of the most-visited bird-watching sites in the state–**Potter Marsh**. Near Mile 117 of the Seward Highway is a boardwalk leading into the marsh. Best viewing is in April and May but all summer long you might spot a variety of ducks, Canadian geese, bald eagles, grebes, loons, yellowlegs, and arctic terns. It's also a salmon spawning area.

Just a little farther south, near Beluga Point (Mile 110) or Windy Corner (Mile 106) along **Turnagain Arm** Dall sheep often come all the way down to the road to pose for pictures. Also keep an eye open for bald eagles along the shoreline and beluga whales offshore when the hooligan or salmon are running, particularly near Bird Creek.

Kenai Fjords National Park, accessible in excursion boats from Seward, is one of the best places in the state to see seabirds and marine mammals. On a typical day trip you might spot whales (humpback, minke, or gray), orcas, Steller sea lions, harbor seals, sea otters, and Dall porpoises. Some trips visit the Chiswell Islands to see colonies of puffins, murres, and kittiwakes. You might even sight mountain goats or bears from the boat. This is also a good place to get away from the crowds, see Chapter 14 - *Camping Away from the Road System*.

The **Kenai Mountains** may seem almost civilized since they are laced with hiking trails, but stay alert. Hikers shouldn't be surprised to see grizzly bears in the high country, not to mention even more common black bears. Valleys often have moose and beaver. A desire to see some wildlife is an excellent reason to get out and do some hiking.

Near the north shore of Kenai Lake at Mile 46 of the Sterling Highway there's a parking area just for viewing sheep and goats with binoculars and spotting scopes. Directly north of the site is **Near Mountain** where Dall sheep are often visible. Across Kenai Lake is **Cecil Rhode Mountain** which sometimes has mountain goats. Also watch for bears a little farther down the mountains.

At the mouth of the Kenai River near the town of Kenai are the **Kenai River Flats**. In April the flats are covered with snow geese migrating to Siberia. There's also a small herd of caribou that uses the flats as a calving area in May. Later in the year birders can see a variety of water birds and ducks as well as several bald eagles. Best viewing is from the Kenai River Access Road. Another attraction here is the beluga whales and harbor seals attracted by hooligan and salmon runs, they may be best seen from the Kenai bluff.

The **Kenai National Wildlife Refuge** used to be known as the Kenai National Moose Range. That should give you some idea of what you should be watching for. It's a huge (2,000,000 acres) flatland covering almost all of the western Kenai Peninsula. You've got to keep your eyes open, the moose in most areas are hunted in the fall so they may be wary. Still, there are so many of them that you're sure to spot some. When heading into the refuge stop at the visitor contact station at Mile 58 of the Sterling Highway for a map and information. The Kenai National Wildlife Refuge Headquarters (USF&W) is near Soldotna on Ski Hill Road (off the Sterling Highway at Mile 98) and has wildlife displays and information (PO Box 2139, Soldotna, AK 99669; 907 262-7021). They also administer the Swanson River and Swan Lake Canoe Trails.

Deep Creek, accessed from the Sterling Highway near Ninilchik at Mile 137 is a popular departure point for halibut fishing. Discarded halibut carcasses along the beach at Deep Creek attract dozens of bald eagles, not to mention lots of seagulls.

Kachemak Bay near Homer also has an excellent place to watch seabirds. **Gull Island** is a short excursion boat or kayak ride away, it is said to be home to some 20,000 seabirds, much like the Chiswell Islands out of Seward. Kayakers and other visitors to the south side of the bay often see sea otters, harbor seals, and Dall porpoises.

Homer is also an excellent place to book a charter flight to **the west side of Cook Inlet** to see grizzly bears. It's probably the best location in the state to see concentrations of bears during the salmon season when they congregate near the coast in large numbers to catch fish. This isn't a cheap trip, but it's worth the money.

THE ROUTES, TOWNS, AND CAMPGROUNDS

FROM ANCHORAGE TO TERN LAKE JUNCTION
90 Miles (145 Kilometers)

The real start of the Seward Highway begins near central Anchorage at the corner of Gambell Street and 5th and 6th Avenues (the Glenn Highway). Gambell (the Seward Highway) heads south, stopping at many stoplights, and then turns into a four-lane expressway until meeting Turnagain Arm near **Potter Flats** at Mile 117. This is where you leave Anchorage's suburbs and abruptly find yourself in what would be considered wilderness in most places.

The highway now runs between cliffs and the rocky edge of muddy **Turnagain Arm**. In recent years this has become a popular if somewhat dangerous wind-surfing area. Stay off the mud flats, they can be like quicksand and the tides come in very rapidly. You're also likely to see climbers on the rocks along the road. Another frequent sight is Dall sheep on the cliffs just above the road or even on the road itself. When the tide is in watch the waves on the right, there are often beluga whales very near the highway. If you see a lot of cars pulled off the road they have probably spotted the whales.

At Mile 90, twenty-five miles (40 km) from Potter Flats is the cutoff to **Girdwood** and the Alyeska Ski Resort. Girdwood is a popular weekend get-away for Anchorage residents and that explains the excellent road from Anchorage to this point. Summer

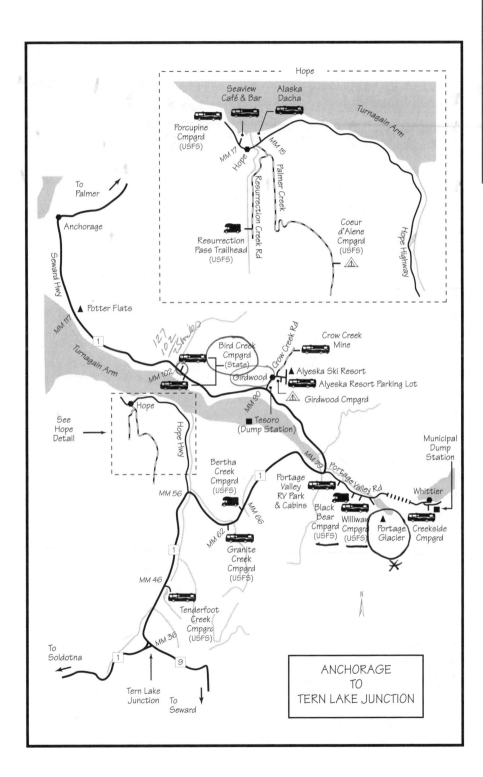

Hope

Seaview
Café & Bar   Alaska
Dacha

Turnagain Arm

Porcupine
Cmpgrd
(USFS)

MM 17   Hope   MM 15   Palmer Creek

Resurrection Creek Rd

Resurrection
Pass Trailhead
(USFS)

Coeur
d'Alene
Cmpgrd
(USFS)

Hope Highway

To
Palmer

Anchorage

Seward Hwy

MM 117

Potter Flats

Turnagain Arm

127
102
23 miles

MM 102

Bird Creek
Cmpgrd
(State)

Crow Creek Rd

Crow Creek
Mine

Girdwood

Alyeska Ski Resort

Alyeska Resort Parking Lot

MM 90   Girdwood Cmpgrd

See
Hope
Detail

Hope

Hope Hwy

Tesoro
(Dump Station)

Municipal
Dump
Station

Bertha
Creek
Cmpgrd
(USFS)

Portage
Valley
RV Park
& Cabins

MM 79   Portage Valley Rd

Whittier

MM 56

MM 66

Black
Bear
Cmpgrd
(USFS)

Williwaw
Cmpgrd
(USFS)

Portage
Glacier

Creekside
Cmpgrd

MM 62

Granite
Creek
Cmpgrd
(USFS)

MM 46

Tenderfoot
Creek
Cmpgrd
(USFS)

MM 36

To
Soldotna

1

9

Tern Lake
Junction

To
Seward

N

ANCHORAGE
TO
TERN LAKE JUNCTION

visitors will find some hiking possibilities and can ride a tram up onto the ski slope for a great view.

At Mile 79 the Seward Highway reaches the Portage Valley Highway. **Portage Glacier**, at Mile 5.5, is one of Alaska's most-visited tourist sites. The **Begich, Boggs Visitor Center** (907 783-2326) has a viewing area, displays, a film, and naturalists. You can also take a boat ride to get a closer view of the glacier which has retreated to the point that direct views are not available from the visitor's center. Along the access road you can see small hanging glaciers above the road and also stop and watch spawning salmon at a viewpoint at Williwaw Creek near Mile 4. There are two good USFS campgrounds along this road.

The Portage Valley Highway runs beyond what is now the turnoff to the Begich, Boggs Visitor Center and provides an access route to **Whittier** on Prince William Sound. This road shares a 2.2-mile single-lane tunnel with a train. Traffic runs one way and is usually allowed through at one-hour intervals unless train traffic interrupts. Any size RV can drive through, the toll is $12 for a passenger vehicle, most RVs pay $35. The toll is only collected eastbound. Check the web site that is linked to our web site at www.rollinghomes.com for more information.

Whittier is a small town located at the head of the Passage Canal, a fjord that connects with Prince William Sound. Whittier was built by the government during World War II and access to Prince William Sound is the attraction here. Alaska state ferries run from Whittier to the Prince William Sound ports of Valdez and Cordova. Cruise companies offer tours from Whittier of the sound. There is a no-hookup camping area suitable for RVs in Whittier.

After passing Portage the Seward Highway begins climbing into the mountains at Mile 75. This long hill has always been a problem area for trucks and RVers because they are forced to slow by the long climb. New passing lanes are making the road much safer. Before long the highway approaches the tree line at not much over 1,000 feet, you can glass for bears on the slopes on both sides.

At a junction at Mile 57 the Hope Highway descends north for 18 miles (29 km) along Sixmile Creek to Turnagain Arm and the old gold-mining town of **Hope**. The virtual ghost town sits at the mouth of Resurrection Creek. There's good pink and silver salmon fishing during July and August and upstream you'll find gold panning possibilities and the trailhead for the Resurrection Pass Trail. Hope has an interesting little museum, the **Hope and Sunrise Historical and Mining Museum**.

After passing the Hope Highway junction the road continues through mountains past Upper and Lower Summit Lakes to the Tern Lake Junction with the Sterling Highway.

Anchorage to Tern Lake Junction Campgrounds

BIRD CREEK CAMPGROUND
(CHUGACH STATE PARK)

Location:	Mile 101 Seward Highway
Info:	(907) 345-5014
Website:	dnr.alaska.gov/parks/aspunits/chugach/birdcreekcamp.htm

GPS Location: 60.97151 N, 149.45966 W, Near Sea Level

Bird Creek is the closest government wilderness campground to Anchorage. It is also conveniently located near Bird Creek, a popular and relatively good fishing spot for pink and silver salmon in July and August. Coastal views of the cliffs and tide flats along Turnagain Arm are spectacular. Bald eagles and Dall sheep are often seen nearby and a paved bike trail runs right next to the campground.

During the summer of 2013 this campground was being completely upgraded and rebuilt. Information about its final design was not available but we're guessing that there will be approximately the same number of sites as in the old campground. This was 28 sites. From what we saw when we toured the construction site it appears that the campground will be much more open than before with fewer trees and that sites will be large and easy to access with big rigs.

There is also a paved lot across the road providing 16 overflow camping spaces for RVs to 40 feet. It sits well above the highway and provides excellent views south across Turnagain Arm to the Kenai Peninsula. It costs slightly less than the formal campground south of the highway and has some picnic tables and fire pits as well as a vault toilet. Stays here are limited to 7 days.

To find Bird Creek Campground just drive south from Anchorage on the Seward Highway. The campground is on the right about 16 miles (26 km) after the highway meets Turnagain Arm just outside Anchorage. It is near Mile 101.

CROW CREEK MINE

Address:	PO Box 113, Girdwood, AK 99587
Telephone:	(907) 229-3105
Email:	crowcreekmine@yahoo.com
Website:	www.crowcreekgoldmine.com

GPS Location: 61.00026 N, 149.08279 W, 600 Ft.

If you are looking for an interesting campsite not far from Anchorage and are willing to do without hookups you will enjoy the Crow Creek Mine. Crow Creek was a working placer mine, it is now a National Historic Site, and offers displays and buildings from early days and the chance to pan for gold. Gold mining here was no joke, Crow Creek was the most productive placer stream in southcentral Alaska with over 40,000 ounces produced since 1896.

The mine allows camping next to the gravel parking lot and also along the entrance road with fire rings and some picnic tables. RVs can park overnight in the parking lot. There are no hook-ups but portable toilets are available and drinking water can be purchased at the gift shop. During the day when the visitor area is open there are flush toilets. The price here is $5 per person, that includes camping and the entrance fee to the visitor area. There are hiking trails nearby. The mine is open from May 15 to September 15.

The Crow Creek Mine is located near Girdwood, home of Alyeska, Alaska's largest ski area. Girdwood is about 42 miles (68 km) southeast of Anchorage off the Seward Highway. Take the Girdwood cutoff near Mile 90 and drive into the valley for 1.9 miles (2.6 km) to the Crow Creek Road which goes left. Follow this gravel road for 3.1 miles (5 km), turn right at the mine entrance road, and you will reach the parking lot in another .4 miles (.6 km). In wet weather this dirt road can be soft, not a good place to be in a heavy rig.

IN THE SUMMER RIDE THE ALYESKA GONDOLA UP THE SKI SLOPE FOR A GREAT VIEW

ALYESKA RESORT PARKING LOT

Address: 1000 Arlberg Ave, Girdwood, AK 99587
Telephone: (907) 754-1111

GPS Location: 60.95873 N, 149.11196 W, 300 Ft.

The Alyeska Ski Resort in Girdwood allows RVs to park in their parking lot during the summer. Five consecutive nights are allowed. This is a paved parking lot and can take any size RV. There are no amenities other than the lodge with its restaurant and other facilities.

Girdwood is about 42 miles (68 km) southeast of Anchorage off the Seward High-way. Take the Girdwood cutoff near Mile 90 and drive up the valley on the Alyeska Highway for 2.9 miles (4.7 km) to the parking lot. The RV parking area is at the far end of the lot. There is a kiosk where you pay by stuffing money into very small slots.

GIRDWOOD CAMPGROUND

Telephone: (907) 783-8146
Email: lazarusjv@muni.org
Website: www.muni.org/Departments/parks/Pages/GWCampground.aspx

GPS Location: 60.96028 N, 149.13843 W, 200 Ft.

The town of Girdwood also has a tent campground. At Fair Park near the baseball diamond there is an 18-site tent campground. The tent sites are scattered in the trees and there is a shared fire pit and covered picnic shelter. No individual fires are allowed at the tent sites. Restrooms are portable toilets. The maximum stay here is 14 days, it's first come, first served.

To reach the campground take the Girdwood cutoff near Mile 90 of the Seward Highway and head up the gentle slope toward Girdwood. After 2.2 miles (3.5 km) turn right into Glacier Creek Drive and you'll reach the campground entrance in another .1 mile (.2 km), just beyond the ball field.

PORTAGE VALLEY RV PARK AND CABINS

Location:	Mile 1.7 Of The Portage Valley Highway
Telephone:	(907) 783-3111 or (877) 477-8243
Website:	www.portagevalleyrvpark.com

GPS Location: 60.80362 N, 148.93302 W, Near Sea Level

This is a private RV park, the only one in the Portage Valley. If you like electrical hookups you might like this campground better than the Forest Service campgrounds farther up the valley.

There are 40 formal sites in this campground as well as an area for dry camping. Thirteen are large pull-thrus and the others are spacious back-ins. There are 30 or 50-amp electrical hookups at some sites as well as lots of room for tent camping and parking without hookups. A portable dump station is available. The campground has showers available, restrooms are a portable toilet. A central covered campfire and barbecue area is very popular and a good place to meet other campers.

To find the RV park, take the Portage Valley Highway near Mile 79 of the Seward Highway (48 miles (77 km) from Anchorage). Drive toward the glacier for 1.7 miles (2.7 km), the campground entrance road is on the right.

BLACK BEAR CAMPGROUND (USFS)

Location:	Mile 3.7 Of Portage Valley Highway
Info:	(907) 522-8368 or (907) 743-9500

GPS Location: 60.78892 N, 148.88921 W, 100 Ft.

Black Bear Campground is a small U.S. Forest Service campground located conveniently near Portage Glacier. It has not been upgraded with paving and large sites like the nearby Williwaw Campground but in addition to the parking spots there are gravel pitching spaces for tents at some sites. The Trail of Blue Ice runs from the campground to the Begich-Boggs Visitor Center providing a nice hike or bicycle ride.

Black Bear is a wooded campground with 13 sites, two are pull-thrus. They're off a fairly tight loop road. This campground is best for tents and RVs to about 25 feet. There are bear-proof food lockers, picnic tables, fire pits, and vault toilets. Maximum stay at the campground is 14 days.

To find Black Bear take the Portage Valley Highway near Mile 79 of the Seward Highway (48 miles (77 km) from Anchorage). Drive toward the glacier for 3.7 miles (6 km), the campground is on the right.

Reserved

✿ 🚐 WILLIWAW CAMPGROUND (USFS)

Location:	Mile 4.1 Of Portage Valley Hwy.
Info:	(907) 522-8368 or (907) 743-9500
Res.:	(877) 444-6777
Website	
For Res.:	www.recreation.gov

GPS Location: 60.78608 N, 148.87560 W, 100 Ft.

This government campground near Portage Glacier has wide paved roads and large paved sites. It sits below overhanging Middle Glacier and is right next to the Williwaw Creek salmon viewing area. The Blue Ice Trail runs right by the campground providing nice hiking or bike access to Begich-Boggs Visitor Center.

There are 60 sites in the campground. Many are pull-thrus and most are large enough for large RVs, even the back-ins reach 50 feet. Sites have picnic tables and fire pits as well as room to pitch tents on level gravel surfaces next to the picnic tables. There is a hand-operated water pump and vault toilets. The campground has a host and amphitheater for campfire programs and reservations can be made. Maximum stay at the campground is 14 days.

You can find Williwaw on the Portage Valley Highway which leaves the Seward Highway at Mile 79 (48 miles (77 km) from Anchorage). The campground is 4.1 miles (6.6 km) from the junction.

🚐 CREEKSIDE CAMPGROUND

Location:	Whittier, Alaska
Telephone:	(907) 472-2670
Website:	www.alaskawhittier.com/campground.php

GPS Location: 60.77065 N, 148.68755 W, 100 Ft.

Whittier has a large gravel campground set above but near the busy port area.

There are about 70 back-in sites in a gravel lot. Willows have been growing over the last few years so there is separation between some sites. They are large, suitable for any size rig, and some overlook a creek. Campfires are allowed in rock rings, there are some picnic tables. Portable toilets are provided. The camping area is open from late May through September depending on the weather. Ask at the parking lot in front for directions to the dump station and water fill at the municipal garages.

After exiting the tunnel continue for 1.4 miles (2.3 km) and turn right just past the unmarked Whittier Creek onto Whittier Street. This is the first possible right as you enter town and is signed for parking and for RV and large vehicle overnight parking. Follow the road for .3 miles (.6 km), and turn right on Glacier Street. Proceed up the hill for .2 miles (.3 km) to the campground entrance. There's an unmanned pay station at the campground.

🚐 BERTHA CREEK CAMPGROUND (USFS)

Location:	Near Mile 65 Of The Seward Highway
Info:	(907) 522-8368 or (907) 743-9500

GPS Location: 60.75117 N, 149.25445 W, 800 Ft.

This is a small government campground in high country near the highway. There are 12 back-in sites off a loop road, a few will take larger RVs to about 35 feet since there are no barriers at the back of the sites but maneuvering room is tight so 30 feet is probably the maximum size RV that should use this campground. Roads are gravel and so are the sites. Picnic tables, fire pits, and bear-proof storage containers are provided. Most sites have room to pitch a tent on a fine gravel surface. There is a hand-pump water well and vault toilets. Maximum stay at this campground is 14 days.

Bertha Creek Campground is located on the west side of the road near Mile 65 of the Seward Highway about 62 miles (100 km) from Anchorage.

🚐 GRANITE CREEK CAMPGROUND (USFS)

Location:	Near Mile 63 Of The Seward Highway
Info:	(907) 522-8368 or (907) 743-9500
Res.:	(877) 444-6777
Website For Res.:	www.recreation.gov

GPS Location: 60.72458 N, 149.29435 W, 600 Ft.

Granite Creek Campground is a 19-site campground located in a spruce and cottonwood forest next to a rushing glacial stream. The long loop road is gravel and so are the widely-spaced sites. Many are located next to the creek. All are back-in sites, they have picnic tables and fire pits. Sites in this campground aren't huge, it's best for rigs to 35 feet. There are no dedicated spaces for tents so pitching is on the parking pad or dirt alongside. The campground has a hand-operated water pump and vault toilets. This campground sometimes has a host and firewood is available. You can make reservations at this campground, see the telephone number and website above. Maximum stay is 14 days.

The access road to the campground leaves the Seward Highway near Mile 63. Drive south on the access road for .8 miles to reach the campground.

🚐 ALASKA DACHA

Address:	19842 Hope Hwy. (Box 129), Hope, AK 99605
Telephone:	(907) 782-3223
Email:	Rochelle@alaskadacha.com
Website:	www.alaskadacha.com

GPS Location: 60.91948 N, 149.62010 W, 200 Ft.

This store, laundry, and campground is located about a mile from the historic Hope town site.

There are 13 camping sites located next to the store. All have 50-amp electrical outlets, some have water and sewer hook-ups also. A few are pull-thrus. Maneuvering room is restricted in this campground but a few sites will take carefully driven large RVs to 40 feet. Although there is no dedicated dump station rigs not staying in the campground can dump at a site for a fee if one is available. Tent campers will find a grassy area with picnic tables. Fires are allowed only in a community area which also has picnic tables. Alaska Dacha has a small grocery store with movie rentals, propane sales, an ATM, a laundry, offers showers, and has an available internet computer as well as Wi-Fi. Reservations are recommended.

The campground is located near Mile 16 of the Hope Highway on the north side of the road. Just past Alaska Dacha the Palmer Creek Road goes left providing access to the Resurrection Trail.

SEAVIEW CAFÉ AND BAR

Address:	PO Box 110, Hope, AK 99605
Telephone:	(907) 782-3300
Email:	seaviewinhope@hotmail.com
Website:	seaviewcafealaska.com/bar.html

GPS Location: 60.92102 N, 149.64429 W, Near Sea Level

For a convenient place to stay when you visit the old gold-mining town of Hope you'll probably want to stay at the Seaview. It is located right at the edge of town, you can take a walking tour right from your campsite.

The Seaview has 21 sites, 15 have 20-amp outlets and water is available. A nice tent camping area with grass to pitch on is also provided, it has a few camp tables and fire rings. There are portable toilets at the campground and a more substantial modern municipal vault toilet close by. The bar and a café are next to the camping area which fronts on the Turnagain Arm flats. The campground is also located right next to the mouth of Resurrection Creek so fishing for pink salmon is extremely handy.

To reach Hope and the Seaview follow the Hope Highway for 17 miles (27 km) from its intersection near Mile 57 of the Seward Highway. The campground is well-signed from the edge of town.

PORCUPINE CAMPGROUND (USFS)

Location:	Mile 18 Of The Hope Highway, The End Of The Road
Info:	(907) 522-8368 or (907) 743-9500
Res.:	(907) 224-3374
Website	
For Res.:	www.recreation.gov

GPS Location: 60.92841 N, 149.65946 W, 100 Ft.

The Porcupine Campground makes a great destination for a weekend trip from Anchorage. The Gull Rock Trail leaves from the campground and pink salmon run in the nearby Resurrection Creek. Restaurants are located a short distance away in Hope. The Resurrection Creek mining area and Resurrection Trailhead are within easy driving distance. The campground has recently been reworked and has more, and larger sites than in the past.

This state campground has 34 sites, most are back-in but there are a few nice pull-thrus. Interior roads are paved as are parking pads. Each site has a picnic table and fire pit and they are well-separated with natural vegetation and trees. The campground has vault toilets and a hand-pump for water. Reservations are possible, see the information above. Maximum stay at the campground is 14 days.

You reach the campground by following the Hope Highway all the way to the end, a distance of eighteen miles (29 km) from the junction with the Seward Highway near Mile 57.

RESURRECTION PASS TRAILHEAD (USFS)

Location:	Near The End Of Resurrection Creek Road
Info:	(907) 743-9500

GPS Location: 60.86948 N, 149.62997 W, 400 Ft.

This is an almost undeveloped campsite that is very popular with gold panners searching for gold in the creek. For the May 15 to July 15 dredging season you can be sure that this campground will be full of prospectors. The rest of the year it is almost empty.

Sites are on either side of the Resurrection Pass trailhead parking lot. There is room for about 10 parties with RVs to about 30 feet to camp under cottonwood trees next to Resurrection Creek. There are no real designated sites but repeated use has resulted in established sites, most have fire rings but no tables. No water is available except that in the creek, all water from lakes and rivers should be treated before use. There are modern vault toilets.

A hundred yards or so down the creek is the parking area for the very popular Resurrection Trail. There are also vault toilets here and many people overnight in this parking area, particularly if they are getting ready to head out on the trail or if they are waiting for a party of hikers.

The Resurrection Creek Road leaves the Hope Highway at Mile 16. This is 1.8 miles (2.9 km) from where the Hope Highway ends at the Porcupine Campground. Drive south on the Resurrection Creek Road following signs for the Resurrection Trail. The only Y is at .7 miles (1.1 km) where the Palmer Creek Road goes left, you want to go right on the Resurrection Creek Rd. From here the road is narrow and rough, it's suitable only for smaller RVs. The Resurrection Pass Trailhead Campground is 4.3 miles (6.9 km) from the Hope Highway junction.

🚐 COEUR D' ALENE CAMPGROUND (USFS)

| **Location**: | Mile 7.7 Palmer Creek Road |
| **Info**: | (907) 743-9500 |

GPS Location: 60.84966 N, 149.53545 W, 1,300 Ft.

This is a little tent-only campground located far up the narrow gravel Palmer Creek Road. There are 6 tent sites with picnic tables and fire pits located fairly close together. The campground has a vault toilet. This is a popular area for hiking and mountain bikes. Maximum stay here is 14 days.

To reach the campground follow the Resurrection Creek Road as it leaves the Hope Highway at Mile 16. In just .7 miles (1.1 km) the road forks, the Resurrection Creek Road goes right and the Palmer Creek Road left. Continue on the Palmer Creek Road and in another 7 miles (11.3 km) you'll reach the campground.

🚐 TENDERFOOT CREEK CAMPGROUND (USFS)

Location:	Near Mile 46 Of The Seward Highway
Info:	(907) 522-8368 or (907) 743-9500
Res.:	(877) 444-6777
Website	
For Res.:	www.recreation.gov

GPS Location: 60.63696 N, 149.49649 W, 1,300 Ft.

This is a very nice recently upgraded campground on the shore of Summit Lake. It sits across the valley from the highway so there is little road noise, a nice feature. Nearby Summit Lake Lodge has a restaurant.

There are 35 separated sites off a loop road, 7 are pull-thrus. Five are walk-in tent sites. Sites are long, some to 55 feet. Each site has a picnic table and fire pit and there are vault toilets and a boat ramp. Some sites are right next to the beach. There is sometimes a host. Maximum stay here is 14 days.

The .5 mile (.8 km) gravel entrance road leaves the Seward Highway near Mile 46, just north of the Summit Lake Lodge.

FROM TERN LAKE JUNCTION TO SEWARD
35 Miles (56 Kilometers)

From Tern Lake the two-lane paved Seward Highway continues toward Seward. At Mile 29 it passes through a small town called **Moose Pass** and then passes the south end of Kenai Lake at Mile 17. Several good USFS campgrounds are located along this stretch of road. Very soon the outskirts of Seward begin to appear.

Tern Lake Junction to Seward Campgrounds

MOOSE PASS ALASKA RV PARK

Location: Near Mile 29 Of The Seward Highway
Telephone: (907) 288-5682

GPS Location: 60.48555 N, 149.36994 W, 500 Ft.

This small commercial RV park has about 30 sites on gravel with small trees separating sites. Small sites and lack of maneuvering room limit its use to RVs to 35 feet.

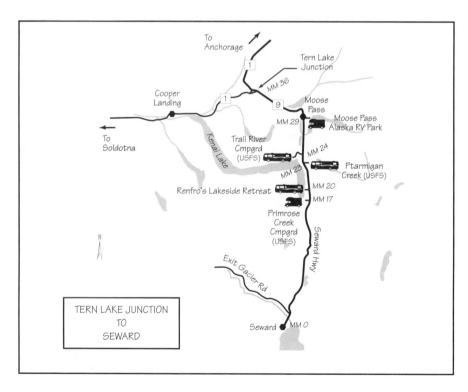

Many sites have 30-amp electrical hookups. There are some picnic tables and fire rings. Tent campers pitch on gravel or sparse grass and weeds. The campground has no showers and the only restrooms are portable toilets. A restaurant is nearby. The campground entrance is on the east side of the highway in Moose Pass, near Mile 29 of the Seward Highway.

TRAIL RIVER CAMPGROUND (USFS)

Location:	Near Mile 24 Of The Seward Highway
Info:	(907) 522-8368 or (907) 743-9500
Res.:	(877) 444-6777
Website	
For Res.:	www.recreation.gov

GPS Location: 60.41659 N, 149.38010 W, 500 Ft.

The Trail River Campground is located along the Lower Trail River and Kenai Lake. Fishing is good for Dolly Varden and rainbows. Reservations are possible, see the information above.

This is a modern forest service campground with large sites. There are about 90 separated campsites arranged off three gravel loops. Sites are gravel and as long as 45 feet, there are even some pull-thrus. A few sites are along the lake. Each site has a picnic table and fire pit, there are vault toilets and hand-operated water pumps. Tenters pitch on fine gravel areas adjacent to the parking pad. This campground also has some large group campsites available and there is a host. Maximum stay here is 14 days.

The 1.2 mile (1.9 km) long entrance road leaves the Seward Highway near Mile 24.

PTARMIGAN CREEK (USFS)

Location:	Near Mile 23 Of The Seward Highway
Info:	(907) 522-8368 or (907) 743-9500
Res.:	(877) 444-6777
Website	
For Res.:	www.recreation.gov

GPS Location: 60.40555 N, 149.36525 W, 500 Ft.

This is another USFS campground that takes reservations. A 3.5 mile long hiking trail to Ptarmigan Lake starts at the campground. There are a total of 16 sites off a gravel loop road. They are separated and have picnic tables and fire pits. Most sites will take RVs to 25 feet, two pull-thrus and 2 back-ins will take 40-footers. There are vault toilets and a hand water pump. A fish-viewing platform is great for watching spawning salmon in Ptarmigan Creek. Maximum stay here varies, it is sometimes as short as 5 days. The campground entrance is on the east side of the Seward Highway near Mile 23.

RENFRO'S LAKESIDE RETREAT

Address:	27121 Seward Highway, Seward, AK 99644
Telephone:	(877) 288-5059 or (907) 288-5059
Email:	renfroslakesideretreat@gmail.com
Website:	www.renfroslakesideretreat.com

GPS Location: 60.35614 N, 149.35325 W, 500 Ft.

Renfro's Lakeside Retreat has a number of cabins along the shore of Kenai Lake as well as RV sites. The Victor Creek hiking trail starts just down the road.

The RV parking is back from the lake in a large gravel lot near the entrance. There are 10 large back-in sites to 60 feet with 30 or 50-amp power and water hookups, six of the sites also have sewer. This is an RV-only resort, no tents are accepted. A restroom and laundry building offers showers. There's access to the lake and there are paddle boats to rent. The entrance is difficult from the south but not bad from the north if you know it is coming. Watch for the sign on the right (from the north) at Mile 19.9.

PRIMROSE CREEK CAMPGROUND (USFS)

| **Location:** | Near Mile 17 Of The Seward Highway |
| **Info:** | (907) 522-8368 or (907) 743-9500 |

GPS Location: 60.34054 N, 149.36795 W, 500 Ft.

Primrose is a small campground located near the southern shore of Kenai Lake. An excellent hiking trail leading to Lost Lake starts from the campground so sites are often filled early in the day. A large parking area at the campground entrance also serves the trail.

There are 8 sites here. They are separated back-ins of various sizes, two are large enough for rigs to 40 feet. Some sites back onto Primrose Creek. There's a turn-around loop so you can drive in with a tow to take a look. Each site has its picnic table and fire pit. There are vault toilets, a food locker, and a boat launch. Maximum stay here is 14 days.

A one-mile access road leaves the Seward Highway near Mile 17 and runs past some private homes to the campground. The first short section is paved, then it turns to gravel.

SEWARD
Population 2,700, Elevation near sea level

Seward was founded in 1903 as an ice-free port which could be the southern end of an Alaska railroad. Private attempts to build one didn't go well until the U.S. government took over in 1915. Construction of a line through newly settled Anchorage to Fairbanks was finished in 1923.

In 1980 the ice fields and coastline to the west of Seward were designated as the **Kenai Fjords National Park**. Gradually the park has attracted more and more visitors. The usual access is on excursion boats making day trips from Seward. Visitors see whales, sea otters, mountain goats, puffins, and other marine birds and animals. The only road access to the park is the Exit Glacier Road which leaves the Seward Highway at Mile 4. The 9-mile road leads to a parking lot, small tent campground, and trails to the glacier. More challenging trails also lead to a view of the Harding Ice Field. The **Kenai Fjords National Park** (PO Box 1727, Seward, Alaska 99664; 907 422-0535) has a visitor center near the boat harbor on Fourth Avenue. They have slide shows and can answer questions and supply information about the park.

Seward's other big attraction, and it's an impressive one, is the **Alaska SeaLife Center** (800 224-2525 or 907 224-6300). This marine laboratory and aquarium was par-

SEWARD AND THE MT. MARATHON RACE IS THE PLACE TO BE ON THE 4TH OF JULY

tially funded by the Exxon Valdez Oil Spill Settlement Fund, it opened in 1998. It's a large facility with first-class displays of Alaska marine mammals, fish, and birds, well worth a visit.

Seward is also well known for its fishing. A very popular and productive **silver salmon derby** is held in the middle of August. Charter operators are easy to find or you can use your own boat for fishing for salmon, rockfish, and halibut.

There are a couple of good hiking trails in the Seward area. The **Mt. Marathon Trail** is the scene of a race on the 4th of July. It goes to the top of 3,022 foot Mt. Marathon and back. For something flatter try the Caine's Head Trails leading south along the coast to **Caine's Head State Recreation Area**.

Seward is a great place to be on the **4th of July**. The Mt. Marathon race is the centerpiece of a great traditional celebration. RVers from all over make special plans to be in Seward on the Fourth.

Seward Campgrounds

BEAR CREEK RV PARK

    Address: 33508 Lincoln St., Seward, AK 99664
    Telephone: (907) 224-5725, (877) 924-5725
    Email: bearcreekrvpk@seward.net
    Website: www.bearcreekrv.com

    GPS Location: 60.18446 N, 149.37287 W, 300 Ft.

Like the Stoney Creek RV Park below, this campground is a full-service place lo-

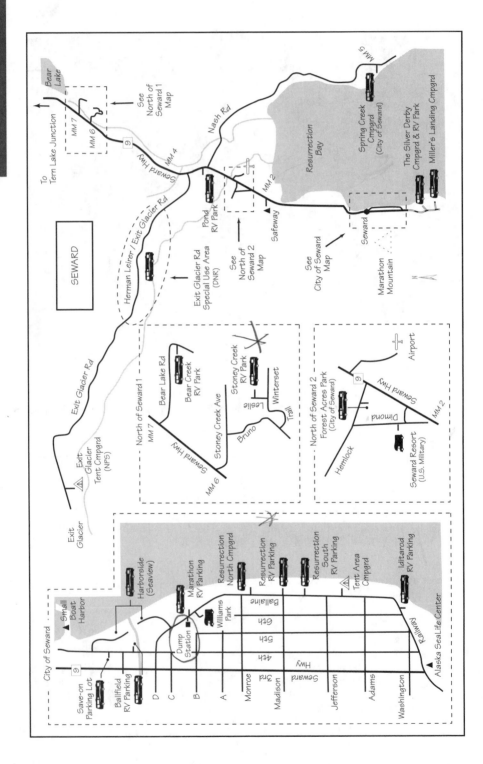

THE KENAI PENINSULA

SEWARD

cated outside of town. It's an older park. There's a state-operated fish weir nearby that can be quite interesting when the salmon are running.

This commercial campground has about 100 sites. There are a variety of site types including full, partial and no-hookup sites. A few spaces are pull-thrus. These are full-hookup sites with 30-amp power and also TV. There are some picnic tables. The campground has flush toilets, showers, a convenience store, a liquor store and tavern, free continental breakfast from June to August, propane sales, an on-site mechanic and a dump station. A community fire pit is provided. Wi-Fi is available in the office lounge area but doesn't reach the sites. They can help you make arrangements for the various tours and boat excursions from Seward.

The campground is located at Mile .3 of the Bear Lake Road. This road leaves the Seward Highway at Mile 6.6 and goes east.

STONEY CREEK RV PARK

Address:	13760 Leslie Place (Box 1548), Seward, AK 99664
Telephone:	(907) 224-6465 or (877) 437-6366
Email:	info@stoneycreekrvpark.com
Website:	www.stoneycreekrvpark.com

GPS Location: 60.18082 N, 149.37831 W, 200 Ft.

The Stoney Creek RV Park is a modern full-service campground in Seward. It's well maintained and excellent for big rigs. The downside is that the location is somewhat remote. It's not near the downtown area.

The campground has about 80 spaces. These are big sites with lots of maneuvering room. They are set in a large gravel lot, some have fire rings. About half the sites are pull-thrus, some to 65 feet. Full-hookup spaces are available with 50-amp power to some and cable TV. The central facilities building has showers, a coin-operated laundry, an upstairs hospitality room, and there is a dump station. There's also a courtesy van available for travel into Seward.

To find the campground take Stoney Creek Avenue east from Mile 6.3 of the Seward Highway north of Seward. Pass over the railroad tracks and at .2 mile (.3 km) turn right on Bruno. Follow Bruno .2 mile (.3 km) as it turns left, crosses the creek and then turns right. Turn left on Winterset (also called Trail) and then in another .2 mile (.3 km) turn left on Leslie Place. The campground is .1 mile (.2 km) down Leslie on the right.

EXIT GLACIER TENT CAMPGROUND (NPS)

Location:	Mile 8.2 Of Herman Leirer Road (Exit Glacier Road)
Info:	(907) 422-0500
Website:	www.nps.gov/kefj/planyourvisit/campgrounds.htm

GPS Location: 60.19125 N, 149.61958 W, 400 Ft.

This is a nice tent-only campground located just outside the entrance gate for the Exit Glacier parking lot. The design is unique and may be a look into the future of government tent campgrounds in Alaska, particularly in areas that have bears.

There are 12 widely-spaced walk-in tent sites set between a parking area and the river. Tents are pitched on finely crushed gravel surfaces. Individual sites have no picnic tables or fire areas. Near the parking area is a covered food preparation area with picnic tables, a fire pit, and a food storage area. To reduce bear problems no food is allowed at the campsites, all food preparation and storage is at the food preparation pavilion. The campground also has handicapped accessible vault toilets and a hand-operated water pump.

To find the campground take the Herman Leirer Road (Exit Glacier Road) which goes west from the Seward Highway near Mile 4, the campground will be on your left at Mile 8.2.

▄▄ Exit Glacier Road Special Use Area (Alaska Department of Natural Resources)

Location: Mile 1.4 Through Mile 3.6 Of Herman Leirer Road (Exit Glacier Road)

GPS Location: 60.16190 N, 149.45021 W, 400 Ft.

Along this section of road there are pull-outs where RV and tent camping are allowed. There is a vault toilet in the area. Parking space is limited and all garbage must be packed out, there is an 8 day limit.

To find this area take the Herman Leirer Road (Exit Glacier Road) which goes west from the Seward Highway near Mile 4. The pull-outs run from Mile 1.4 to Mile 3.6.

▄▄ Pond RV Park

Address: Seward Highway, Mile 3, Seward, AK

GPS Location: 60.14562 N, 149.41686 W, Near Sea Level

This small RV park is also away from central Seward but closer than the two listed above. It's next to the highway but the sites are back behind a small pond. The land has a big cleared area in the back that is sometimes in use as a helicopter landing site. When the helicopters are active the campground is closed, when they are not camping is available.

The campground has no hookups. There are about 25 designated camping sites set in a grove of spruce trees. There is also a large flat gravel lot behind them suitable for any size RV. Designated sites have picnic tables and fire rings, there are outhouses and no showers.

The campground is easy to find. It's on the west side of the Seward Highway north of Seward at about Mile 3.

▄▄ Spring Creek Campground (City of Seward)

Telephone: (907) 224-4055
Website: www.cityofseward.us

GPS Location: 60.08927 N, 149.35665 W, Near Sea Level

This is the most remote of the Seward city campgrounds. It's located along the water near the mouth of Spring Creek on the far side of Resurrection Bay from the town. There's a large open gravel area for parking. No tents are allowed. To get there take Nash Road from Mile 3.2 of the Seward Highway. Follow the road 5.1 miles east (8.2 km), the entrance is on the right just before reaching Ward's drydock. There is a 14 day limit at this park.

THE KENAI PENINSULA

FOREST ACRES PARK (CITY OF SEWARD)

Location:	Mile 2.3 Of The Seward Hwy. On Hemlock Ave.
Telephone:	(907) 224-4055
Website:	www.cityofseward.us

GPS Location: 60.13482 N, 149.42891 W, Near Sea Level

This city campground is located along the highway coming in to Seward. It's easy to miss because the sites are back in the trees. If you are looking for a quiet location away from the waterfront you might like this campground.

There are 42 back-in sites scattered around the park. Most are well separated. There are no hookups although water is available at a faucet. Some sites have picnic tables and fire pits and there is sometimes a host. There are also restrooms without showers, a playground, and tennis courts. Maneuvering room for big RVs is limited although they will fit in a few sites in unmarked open areas. There is a 14 day limit at this park.

Coming in to Seward watch for airport road on your left. Don't turn. In another .3 miles (.5 km) Hemlock Avenue goes right, turn here and then make the first left into the campground. Hemlock Avenue is at about Mile 2.3 of the Seward Highway.

RESURRECTION RV PARKING (CITY OF SEWARD)

| Telephone: | (907) 224-4055 |
| Website: | www.cityofseward.us |

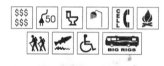

GPS Location: 60.10670 N, 149.43469 W, Near Sea Level

This is the only city-operated campground with hookups, it's also the most crowded. There are 99 back-in sites here to 45 feet, they have either 30 or 50-amp electrical hookups and water. Some of these sites are reserved for groups of 10 or more RVs although they can be used by individual RVs if no groups have reservations. A few sites are reserved for handicapped RVers needing electricity. One of the four rows here is waterfront, those sites have some picnic tables and fire pits along the water. There is an on-site host. A building with flush toilets and coin-op showers is adjacent. A paved walking or bike trail runs along the water in front of the campground. There is a 14 day limit at this park.

To find the camping area just drive south on Third Avenue which is the continuation of the Seward Highway as you enter town. You'll pass Monroe St, turn left at the next corner which is Madison St., the camping area is four blocks directly ahead.

RESURRECTION NORTH CAMPGROUND (CITY OF SEWARD)

| Telephone: | (907) 224-4055 |
| Website: | www.cityofseward.us |

GPS Location: 60.10816 N, 149.43454 W, Near Sea Level

Resurrection North is a small campground with 14 back-in sites. Most sites are short and there is grass so it's popular with tenters but will take RVs too. Amenities include portable toilets, picnic tables and fire pits. Potable water is available near the entrance and the flush toilets and coin-operated showers are nearby. This campground is adjacent to Resurrection, described above, and just to the north. You enter through the same driveway, see the driving directions above. There is a 14 day limit at this park.

RESURRECTION SOUTH RV PARKING (CITY OF SEWARD)

Telephone: (907) 224-4055
Website: www.cityofseward.us

GPS Location: 60.10565 N, 149.43523 W, Near Sea Level

Resurrection South is also adjacent to Resurrection, but to the south. There are 69 back-in sites to 45 feet with no hookups. Some have picnic tables or fire pits and the restrooms building with its flush toilets and showers is nearby. Access it from the Resurrection campground, see the driving directions above. There is a 14 day limit at this park.

TENT AREA CAMPGROUND (CITY OF SEWARD)

Telephone: (907) 224-4055
Website: www.cityofseward.us

GPS Location: 60.10407 N, 149.43520 W, Near Sea Level

Located just south of Resurrection South along the waterfront is a tent-only area. It has 23 sites set on grass, no RVs are allowed. There are picnic tables and fire pits, the restrooms with showers at Resurrection are not far away. Tents are pitched on grass or fine gravel. To get to this campground follow the instructions above to the Resurrection Campground, but rather than entering the campground turn right on Ballaine Blvd. and drive about 300 yards to the south. The entrance is on the left. There is a 14 day limit at this park.

IDITAROD RV PARKING (CITY OF SEWARD)

Telephone: (907) 224-4055
Website: www.cityofseward.us

GPS Location: 60.10133 N, 149.43656 W, Near Sea Level

Iditarod is the smallest of the City of Seward RV parking areas. It is also the most scenic since it sits on the waterfront near the SeaLife Center with fantastic views south over Resurrection Bay.

There are only ten sites here and maneuvering room is somewhat restricted although big RVs seem to find room. Fire rings are located above the beach. This campground usually has a host and there is a 14 day limit.

Easiest access is to follow Third Avenue south all the way to the end, then turn left on Railway Avenue. You'll see the parking area on the right just beyond the parking for the SeaLife Center.

WILLIAMS PARK (CITY OF SEWARD)

Telephone: (907) 224-4055
Website: www.cityofseward.us

GPS Location: 60.11041 N, 149.43719 W, Near Sea Level

Williams Park is a small RV and tent campground, RVs over 20 feet are prohibited and no generator use is allowed. This is a pleasant camping area with grass and trees, it's across the street from the Resurrection RV Camping complex with its flush toilets and showers and next to the city dump station facility. The 31 sites have picnic tables and fire pits and there are portable toilets on site. There is a 14 day limit at this park.

MARATHON RV PARKING (CITY OF SEWARD)

Telephone: (907) 224-4055
Website: www.cityofseward.us

GPS Location: 60.11108 N, 149.43666 W, Near Sea Level

The Marathon RV parking area is along the waterfront across the street from the city's dump station. There are 40 back-in sites here for RVs to 45 feet with rock rings for fires above the beach. A city restroom building is across the road to the north with flush toilets. For easiest access follow the instructions for the Resurrection RV parking area but don't enter. Instead turn left and you'll see Marathon on the right in .3 mile. There is a 14 day limit here.

HARBORSIDE (SEAVIEW) (CITY OF SEWARD)

Telephone: (907) 224-4055
Website: www.cityofseward.us

GPS Location: 60.11232 N, 149.43716 W, Near Sea Level

Harborside is the closest city campground to the small boat harbor. It's in an easy to miss location between the water and the baseball diamond just south of the harbor area. It's split by a stream so there are two entrances.

There are 40 sites, 29 in the north section and 11 in the south. The north section has some portable toilets and isn't far from the harbormaster's building which has flush toilets and showers. The south section is near the city restroom building with flush toilets. Some fire rings are available. Both sections are crowded, large RVs have trouble maneuvering although a few large ones seem to get in. There is a 14 day limit at this park.

Access to the north section is directly from the street next to the small boat harbor and is pretty constricted. The south section entrance is next to the baseball diamond just beyond the small boat harbor area. Drive toward the harbor on Ballaine Road just past the baseball diamond and then take the first left toward the beach to enter.

BALLFIELD RV PARKING (CITY OF SEWARD)

Telephone: (907) 224-4055
Website: www.cityofseward.net

GPS Location: 60.11340 N, 149.43973 W, Near Sea Level

The City of Seward uses this baseball diamond as overflow parking when there are a lot of RVs in town. It's used for both RV and boat-trailer parking and the only amenities are the municipal restrooms to the south. As you enter Seward you'll spot the busy small boat harbor area on the left, the ball park is just beyond. There is a 14 day limit at this park.

SAVE-ON PARKING LOT

Location: Corner Of 4th And Van Buren Street

GPS Location: 60.11445 N, 149.44122 W, Near Sea Level

This gravel lot appears at first to be one of the city-operated parking areas however it's privately owned and small rigs can park here overnight. There are 50 closely-spaced back-in slots and no amenities. Restrooms and shower facilities are nearby at the harbor master's office. A payment board with money slots is located at the entrance.

The campground is located at the corner of 4th and Van Buren Street just south of the small boat harbor and across the street off Fourth Avenue.

The Silver Derby Campground and RV Park

Address:	13750 Well Point Road, Seward, AK 99664
Telephone:	(907) 224-4711 or (907) 491-0771
Website:	www.resres.net/silverderby.html

GPS Location: 60.07457 N, 149.44021 W, Near Sea Level

The Silver Derby is a simple camping area that is located south of Seward toward Lowell Point. There are about 50 sites, most are gravel back-ins and they're well separated by natural vegetation. Sites have rock fire rings but no picnic tables. Most sites are fairly short, but a few that back off a cleared area to the left as you enter will take rigs to 40 feet since you back into them from a central area. There are portable toilets but for showers you must head down the road to Miller's Landing or in to Seward. The beach is accessible from the campground and firewood is for sale.

To reach the Silver Derby drive right through Seward and find the small gravel road that continues to follow the shoreline below the cliffs to the south. This is Lowell Point Road. The campground is 1.8 miles (2.9 km) from the end of the pavement.

Miller's Landing Campground

Address:	Box 81, Seward, AK 99664
Telephone:	(907) 224-5739 or (866) 541-5739
Email:	millerslanding@alaska.com
Website:	www.millerslandingak.com

GPS Location: 60.07086 N, 149.43618 W, Near Sea Level

For something different in the Seward area try Miller's Landing. This beachfront campground looks at first like it was constructed of driftwood collected from the beach, but they have electric hookups, showers, and offer lots of recreational options. You can rent kayaks or small outboard skiffs, ride a water taxi to a remote cove, hike to nearby Cain's Head State Park or Tonsina Creek, or just beachcomb and fish right out front. Best of all, when the fish are running the location is far from the madness of central Seward.

The campground has over 30 sites. There is a line of 15 sites overlooking the beach with 30-amp electrical hookups, picnic tables, and fire rings. Many of these sites slope so leveling is difficult. The remaining smaller sites are in trees back from the water, a few in this area also offer electricity. Water is available but there is no dump station. Flush toilets, showers, and a laundromat are located in a modern building. There is a small store for fishing tackle and you can get lots of advice about things to do and see in the area.

To reach Millers drive right through Seward and find the small gravel road that continues to follow the shoreline below the cliffs to the south. This is Lowell Point Road. The campground is 2.2 miles (3.5 km) from the end of the pavement. Big RVs should have no problem if they take it easy.

🚐 SEWARD RESORT – MILITARY CAMPGROUND
Location: Dimond Rd, Seward, AK

This campground is open to active military personnel, National Guard personnel, reservists, retired military, and Department of Defense employees. **Seward Resort** (PO Box 329, Seward, AK 99664-5000; 907 224-2659) has 40 RV/trailer spaces with electric hookups and 15 tent spaces with showers and a dump station. Coming in to Seward watch for airport road on your left. Don't turn. In another .3 miles (.5 km) Hemlock Avenue goes right, turn here and then after a block turn left on Dimond. You'll soon see the resort on the right. Hemlock Avenue is at about Mile 2.3 of the Seward Highway.

FROM TERN LAKE JUNCTION TO SOLDOTNA AND KENAI
58 Miles (94 Kilometers)

From its junction with the Seward Highway at Mile 37 the Sterling Highway starts west through scenic mountainous country. At Mile 45 it reaches the north edge of Kenai Lake and follows the lakeshore to the lake's outlet, the Kenai River.

The **Kenai River** is world famous for its king salmon. The current record for a Kenai king is 97 pounds. The river flows 17 miles (27 km) from Kenai Lake to Skilak Lake. This part of the river is known as the upper Kenai. The lower Kenai flows from Skilak Lake 50 miles (81 km) to Cook Inlet at Kenai. The river is a playground, it offers fishing for king, red, silver and pink salmon as well as opportunities for both white and flat-water boating.

The Sterling Highway follows the upper Kenai through the **Cooper Landing** area to a junction with the gravel Skilak Lake Road at Mile 58. This section of the Sterling Highway is lined with campgrounds and has probably the most heavily-fished location in the entire state, the Kenai River just below the **Russian River** mouth at Mile 55 of the highway. Even if you don't fish you'll enjoy watching the action during the red salmon runs.

The highway then enters the **Kenai National Wildlife Refuge**. The Skilak Loop Road is a 19 mile (31 km) gravel road that leaves the Sterling Highway at Mile 58 and rejoins it at Mile 75. This road gives access to campgrounds and boat ramps on Skilak Lake at two points and also to a very nice large campground on Hidden Lake.

After the Sterling Highway passes the junction with the Skilak Lake Road it crosses the flat Kenai National Wildlife Refuge and reaches little Sterling at Mile 81. Sterling has a few stores and services, it is located where the Moose River enters the Kenai, another popular fishing spot. Near Sterling, at Mile 83, the 29 mile (47 km) Swanson River Road leads north to the Swanson River and Swan Lake Canoe Routes. Road accessible campgrounds along these roads are included in those listed below. See Chapter 14 for more about the backwoods canoe routes.

After Sterling the highway begins to pass through the outskirts of Soldotna which it reaches at Mile 94.

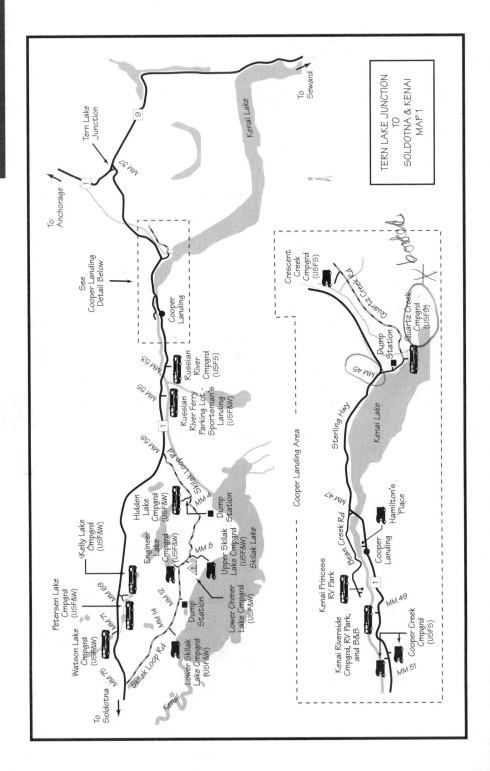

TERN LAKE JUNCTION
TO
SOLDOTNA & KENAI
MAP 1

Tern Lake Junction to Soldotna and Kenai Campgrounds

QUARTZ CREEK CAMPGROUND (USFS)

Location:	Mile .3 Of Quartz Creek Road
Info:	(907) 522-8368 or (907) 743-9500
Res.:	(877) 444-6777
Website	
For Res.:	www.recreation.gov

booked

GPS Location: 60.47891 N, 149.72821 W, 500 Ft.

Quartz is one of the prettiest government campgrounds in Alaska, particularly if you manage to snag one of the few lakefront sites. Altogether there are 45 spacious vehicle sites off two loops and also a tent area next to the lake. Sites are separated and both the parking pads and access roads are paved. There are a few pull-thrus but most sites are back-ins, all sites have picnic tables and fire pits. Tents are pitched on areas with fine gravel, most vehicle sites do have room for tents off the parking pad. Some sites will take 45-foot RVs. Water is available from faucets. An unusual feature here is flush toilets, there are no showers. Also, there's a dump station on the access road. The campground has a boat ramp. Exercise caution boating on Kenai Lake, the wind comes up quickly. There's also a salmon viewing area. Reservations can be made at this campground, see the phone number listed above. Maximum stay here is 14 days for sites that can't be reserved, 5 days for sites that can be reserved.

Turn south on the Quartz Creek Road near Mile 45 of the Sterling Highway. This is right next to the Sunrise Inn. Drive .3 miles (.5 km) on the paved road to the first entrance road. An entrance to the second loop road is another three-tenths mile farther along.

CRESCENT CREEK CAMPGROUND (USFS)

Location:	Mile 2.9 Of The Quartz Creek Road
Info:	(907) 522-8368 or (907) 743-9500

GPS Location: 60.49722 N, 149.67980 W, 600 Ft.

This small government campground is a good base if you plan to hike the good six-mile-long trail up to Crescent Lake or if you want to fish Quartz Creek. There are nine separated back-in sites set in trees. Each site has a picnic table and fire pit. Site size, available maneuvering room, and a 10 ton weight limit on a bridge on the access road limit RV size in this campground to about 30 feet. There are vault toilets and a hand operated water pump. Maximum stay here is 14 days.

To reach the campground take Quartz Creek Road near Mile 45 of the Seward Highway. It's paved for the first .3 miles (.5 km), then turns to gravel. The campground is on the left after 2.9 miles (4.7 km).

KENAI PRINCESS RV PARK

Address:	17225 Frontier Circle, Cooper Landing, AK 99572
Telephone:	(907) 595-1425

GPS Location: 60.49114 N, 149.85016 W, 600 Ft.

Princess Cruises (of Love Boat fame) has several hotels scattered around Alaska where cruise boat passengers stay during the land portion of their Alaska visit. One of these is hidden on a back road in Cooper Landing. This one is different from all the others, it has an RV park. If you stay here you can recover from a hard day of fishing by relaxing in their hot tub or in the hotel lounge.

There are 33 back-in RV spaces to 55 feet. They are separated by grassy areas and have full hookups with 30-amp power. There are restrooms with flush toilets and showers as well as a small convenience store, a laundry, and a dump station. People staying at the RV park are welcome to use the hotel's facilities including restaurant, bar, hot tubs, exercise room, and a computer for email access. Reservations are recommended.

To reach the campground turn north at Mile 47.7 of the Sterling Highway just east of the Kenai River bridge at the outlet of Kenai Lake. Follow paved Bean Creek Road for 2 miles (3.2 km) to the hotel and campground.

⛟ HAMILTON'S PLACE

Address:	Box 569, Cooper Landing, AK 99572
Telephone:	(907) 595-1260
Email:	dodiewilsonak@gmail.com

GPS Location: 60.49003 N, 149.82649 W, 500 Ft.

Hamilton's Place has been in the same location for many years, a handy place to stop in Cooper Landing during the drive between Kenai and Anchorage. Hamilton's is a gas station, restaurant, bar, grocery store, liquor store, tackle shop, and RV park.

There are about 20 back-in sites overlooking the river located behind the buildings along the road. Eight have full hookups, the rest power and water only. There is room for RVs to about 30 feet. Restrooms have coin-operated showers.

The campground is located at Mile 48.5 of the Sterling Highway, .5 miles (.8 km) west of the Kenai River bridge in the community of Cooper Landing.

⛟ KENAI RIVERSIDE CAMPGROUND, RV PARK, AND B&B

Address:	PO Box 774, Cooper Landing, AK 99572
Telephone:	(907) 595-1406 or (888) 536-2478
Email:	info@kenairv.com
Website:	www.kenairv.com

GPS Location: 60.48643 N, 149.86193 W, 400 Ft.

If you are looking for a place with hookups that is convenient to the Upper Kenai and Russian River fishery you'll like the Kenai Riverside. Some folks check in for a month at a time.

There are about 30 sites. Two are long pull-thrus and eighteen are back-ins to 35 feet with 20 and 30-amp electricity in the center of a gravel lot. Additional no-hookup sites are located at the edge of the lot, some with trees nearby. Some of these no hookup sites have picnic tables and some have fire rings. Flush toilets and showers are available and there is a dump station (fee to dump if you're not paying for a site). You can fish from the bank at the campground or arrange a guided float trip.

The campground is located between the river and the road near Mile 50 of the Sterling Highway.

THE KENAI PENINSULA

COOPER CREEK CAMPGROUND (USFS)

Location:	On Both Sides Of The Sterling Hwy Near Mile 51
Info:	(907) 522-8368 or (907) 743-9500
Res.:	(877) 444-6777
Website	
For Res.:	www.recreation.gov

GPS Location: 60.48388 N, 149.88223 W, 400 Ft.

This little Forest Service campground is one of the oldest in the neighborhood and still popular since it's located in one of the most beautiful areas of the state. You can reserve a site here in the area south of the highway, not north of it. There are 26 back-in sites and three tent-only sites. Seven are on a loop near the Kenai River on the north side of the highway and the rest occupy a circular drive on the south side of the road along little Cooper Creek. Several of the sites will take RVs to about 35 feet. Each site has a picnic table and fire pit, there is a water pump, and there are vault toilets on both sides of the road. The campground has a host , firewood is available, and there's a restaurant within walking distance. Maximum stay here is 5 days south of the highway, 14 days north of the highway. It's located at Mile 50.7 of the Sterling Highway.

RUSSIAN RIVER CAMPGROUND (USFS)

Location:	Entrance At Mile 53 Sterling Highway
Info:	(907) 522-8368 or (907) 743-9500
Res.:	(877) 444-6777
Website	
For Res.:	www.recreation.gov

booked

GPS Location: 60.48195 N, 149.94303 W, 400 Ft.

The huge Russian River Campground is one of the most popular in the state, particularly when the red salmon are running in the Russian River. During the red salmon runs, from June 15 to August 20, you are limited to a three-day stay here, reservations are available. The very popular Russian Lakes hiking trail starts from this campground and there is a parking fee for hikers.

Eighty-three separated sites are arranged off a number of circular drives. All access roads and parking pads are paved and some sites are large, a few are pull-thrus to 75 feet. Some back-ins are as long as 35 feet. They all have picnic tables and fire pits. There are vault toilets and some flush toilets, also a dump station. There's a $6 fee to dump if you're not paying for a campsite.

The entrance road for the campground leaves the Sterling Highway near Mile 53. Almost immediately you'll come to the manned entrance kiosk where your fee will be collected and a site assigned.

RUSSIAN RIVER FERRY PARKING LOT – SPORTSMAN'S LANDING (USF&W)

Location:	Near Mile 55 Of The Sterling Highway
Info:	(907) 522-8368 or (907) 262-7021

GPS Location: 60.48538 N, 150.00565 W, 400 Ft.

The most crowded and perhaps the most productive sports fishery in the state of Alaska is located on the Kenai River downstream from the outlet of the Russian Riv-

THE RUSSIAN RIVER CABLE FERRY LETS FISHERMEN WORK BOTH SIDES OF THE RIVER

er. There is a cable ferry located here so fishermen can work both sides of the Kenai. The parking lot at the ferry is a popular dry-camping area. Fishing goes on 24 hours a day although the gate is closed from 9 p.m. to 8 a.m. This is a show not to be missed.

There is probably room for about 80 RVs to park in back-in side-by-side spaces in two areas. One is upstream from the entry gate near the boat launch and the other is downstream at the ferry. There are also a few tent-camping sites. There are vault toilets and fish-cleaning tables but no other amenities. The camping fee is collected at a kiosk on the entrance road when the fish are running. There's a two-day time limit at this campground and there is an additional fee for the pedestrian ferry.

KELLY LAKE CAMPGROUND (USF&W)

Location:	Near Mile 68 Of The Sterling Highway
Info:	(907) 262-7021

GPS Location: 60.52103 N, 150.38934 W, 300 Ft.

Kelly Lake and Petersen Lake Campgrounds are located off the same access road. At .3 miles (.5 km) from the highway if you take the left fork you'll soon arrive at Kelly Lake. There are 4 campsites arranged off a circular gravel parking area next to the lake. The camping area is OK for large RVs since its parking along the side of the open lot. There are picnic tables, fire pits, a hand water pump, vault toilets and a boat ramp. The campground has a 14-day stay limit. The Seven Lakes Trail leaves from the campground and connects with Skilak Road at Engineer Lake Campground, a distance of 4.5 miles (7.3 km). The lake has rainbow trout.

PETERSEN LAKE CAMPGROUND (USF&W)

Location: Near Mile 68 Of The Sterling Highway
Info: (907) 262-7021

GPS Location: 60.52495 N, 150.39765 W, 300 Ft.

Near Mile 68 of the Sterling Highway a small road leads a mile south to two little lakes: Kelly and Petersen. If you take the right at the Y some .3 miles (.5 km) from the highway you're on the short access road to Petersen Lake. There are four sites around the edge of a gravel lot with picnic tables, fire pits, a hand water pump, vault toilets and a boat ramp. Big rigs are fine and there is a 14-day stay limit. This lake also has rainbows.

WATSON LAKE CAMPGROUND (USF&W)

Location: Near Mile 72 Of The Sterling Highway
Info: (907) 262-7021

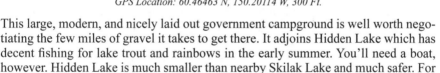

GPS Location: 60.53622 N, 150.46144 W, 300 Ft.

This gravel lot camping area next to little Watson Lake has three sites with picnic tables and fire pits. There's no maximum RV size since parking is in the gravel lot next to the sites. There's also a vault toilet, a water pump, and a boat ramp. The short access road to the campground goes north from near Mile 72 of the Sterling Highway.

HIDDEN LAKE CAMPGROUND (USF&W)

Location: 3.4 Miles (5.5 Km) From The Eastern Junction Of Skilak Lake Loop Road And The Sterling Highway
Info: (907) 262-7021

GPS Location: 60.46463 N, 150.20114 W, 300 Ft.

This large, modern, and nicely laid out government campground is well worth negotiating the few miles of gravel it takes to get there. It adjoins Hidden Lake which has decent fishing for lake trout and rainbows in the early summer. You'll need a boat, however. Hidden Lake is much smaller than nearby Skilak Lake and much safer. For hikers, the short Burney's Trail leaves from opposite site 7 on the Skyview Loop.

There are 43 large well-separated paved sites arranged off paved loop and stub roads. Sites have large picnic tables and fire pits and some are suitable for RVs to 40 feet. Four of them are pull-thrus and nice paved handicapped sites are available. Most sites have a gravel area for pitching tents. There are vault toilets and a dump station. The campground has a host and firewood can be purchased. Down by the lake are a boat launch ramp and a few camping spaces as well as an amphitheater where campfire programs are sometimes offered. The campground also has a 10-space overflow parking area. Stays here are limited to 14 days.

The gravel Skilak Loop Road leaves the Sterling Highway at Mile 58 (eastern junction) and at Mile 75 (western junction). The campground entrance road is 3.4 miles (5.5 km) from the eastern junction and 15 miles (24.2 km) from the western junction.

UPPER SKILAK LAKE CAMPGROUND (USF&W)

Location: 8.1 Miles (13.1 Km) From The Eastern Junction Of Skilak Lake Loop Road And The Sterling Hwy.
Info: (907) 262-7021

GPS Location: 60.43998 N, 150.32050 W, 300 Ft.

The Upper Skilak Lake Campground has a boat launch that is used as a take-out by boats and rafts that float the Upper Kenai River from Cooper Landing. Boating on Skilak Lake is considered very dangerous because winds come up suddenly. This is another first class government campground with paved access roads and parking pads as well as some lakefront campsites.

There are 15 separated vehicle sites and 10 walk-in tent sites with bear-proof food storage boxes. Sites have the normal picnic tables and fire pits. The sites here are small, some will take RVs to 30 feet. There are very nice vault toilets (with skylights) and a hand-operated water pump as well as a covered picnic area and a boat ramp and large boat trailer parking area. There is a host and firewood can be purchased. There is no dump station at this campground but there is one located nearby in the middle of nowhere along the Skilak Loop Road 12 miles (19 km) from the east junction and 8 miles (13 km) from the west junction. Stays here are limited to 14 days.

To reach the campground follow a gravel access road for 2 miles (3.2 km) from a point on the Skilak Loop Road that is 8.1 miles (13.1 km) from the east junction and 10.3 miles (16.6 km) from the west junction.

LOWER OHMER LAKE CAMPGROUND (USF&W)

FREE

Location: 8.2 Miles (13.2 Km) From The Eastern Junction Of Skilak Lake Loop Road And The Sterling Highway

Info: (907) 262-7021

GPS Location: 60.46072 N, 150.31953 W, 400 Ft.

Lower Ohmer is really a tent campground although it is frequently used by RVers with small units. There is room to maneuver and park RVs to 25 feet but the four picnic tables and fire pits are not situated directly adjacent to the parking sites. Amenities include handicap-accessible vault toilets, and a boat launch but no water other than that in the lake. Stays here are limited to 14 days.

The campground is located on the south side of Skilak Lake Road, just west of the intersection with the side road to Lower Skilak Lake Campground about 8.2 miles (13.2 km) from the eastern junction with the Sterling Highway and 10.2 miles (16.5 km) from the western junction.

ENGINEER LAKE CAMPGROUND (USF&W)

FREE

Location: 9.1 Miles (14.7 Km) From The Eastern Junction Of Skilak Loop Road And The Sterling Highway

Info: (907) 262-7021

GPS Location: 60.47397 N, 150.32756 W, 300 Ft.

This campground is an open parking area on the edge of Engineer Lake. There's limited turnaround room, it's best for RVs only as large as 30 feet. There are two sites with picnic tables and fire pits, the area also has a vault toilet, a hand-operated water pump, and a boat launch. Seven Lake Trail connects this campground with the one at Kelly Lake off the Sterling Highway, it's 4.5 miles (7.3 km) long.

The short access road to this campground goes north from the Skilak Lake Road at a point 9.1 miles (14.7 km) from the eastern junction with the Sterling Highway and 9.3 miles (15 km) from the western junction.

⛺ LOWER SKILAK LAKE CAMPGROUND (USF&W)

Location:	13.3 Miles (21.5 Km) From The Eastern Junction Of Skilak Lake Loop Road and The Sterling Hwy.
Info:	(907) 262-7021

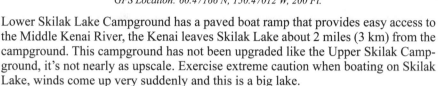

GPS Location: 60.47166 N, 150.47012 W, 200 Ft.

Lower Skilak Lake Campground has a paved boat ramp that provides easy access to the Middle Kenai River, the Kenai leaves Skilak Lake about 2 miles (3 km) from the campground. This campground has not been upgraded like the Upper Skilak Campground, it's not nearly as upscale. Exercise extreme caution when boating on Skilak Lake, winds come up very suddenly and this is a big lake.

The small campground has 6 separated RV sites and 5 beachside tent sites. Some RV sites are suitable for RVs to about 30 feet, most are shorter. They have picnic tables and fire pits, there are handicapped vault toilets and a water pump. The sites all are arranged to be near the lakeshore. Stays here are limited to 14 days.

A 1-mile gravel access road leaves the Skilak Lake Loop Road 13.3 miles (21.5 km) from the eastern junction with the Sterling Highway and 5.1 miles (8.2 km) from the western junction.

⛺ BING'S LANDING CAMPGROUND – KENAI RIVER SRA

Location:	Near Mile 80 Of The Sterling Highway
Info:	(907) 262-5581
Website:	dnr.alaska.gov/parks/aspunits/kenai/bingslandingcamp.htm

GPS Location: 60.52070 N, 150.70415 W, 300 Ft.

Bing's Landing is primarily used by fishermen accessing the middle Kenai River. There is an important boat launching area here, and also a campground. There is bank fishing here as well as a trail to the Kenai River Rapids where you can wade in with boots to fish for salmon as well as Dolly Varden and rainbows when regulations allow.

In the modern campground here there are 35 long back-in sites to 50 feet with picnic tables and fire pits. These sites are nicely separated and there are handicapped-access vault toilets. There's also a covered picnic area and a hand-operated water pump. This campground normally has a host so firewood is available for purchase, and there is a seven day stay limit from May through September.

The access road to Bing's is at Mile 80 of the Sterling Highway.

⛺ REAL ALASKAN CABINS AND RV PARK

Address:	Box 69, Sterling, Alaska 99672
Telephone:	(907) 262-6077
Email:	realalaskancabins@gmail.com
Website:	www.realalaskan.com

GPS Location: 60.52352 N, 150.71018 W, 300 Ft.

This small private campground is nicely designed with trees separating sites and room for larger RVs. It is located near the highway just east of Sterling on the access road to Bing's Landing.

The campground has 33 sites with 30 and 50-amp electricity water and sewer. Four

THE KENAI PENINSULA

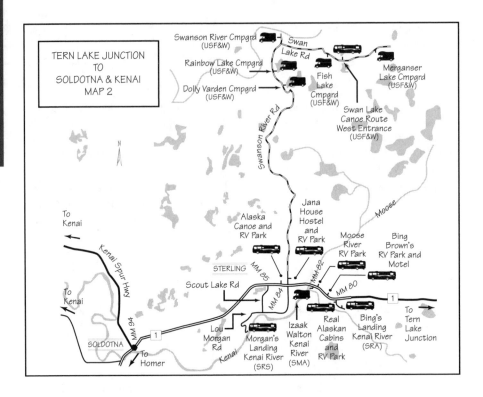

are pull-thrus to 60 feet, the others are long back-ins, some to 55 feet. Access roads and parking pads are gravel separated by trees, natural vegetation and grass; there are even some flowers. There are flush toilets and showers.

To reach the campground just take the road south toward Bing's Landing near Mile 80 of the Sterling Highway, the campground entrance is on the right just a tenth of a mile from the highway.

▨ BING BROWN'S RV PARK AND MOTEL

Address:	PO Box 1039, Sterling, AK 99672
Telephone:	(907) 262-4780
Email:	debbass23@hotmail.com

GPS Location: 60.52721 N, 150.72697 W, 200 Ft.

This old but serviceable and reasonably-priced campground is located behind a motel in the small town of Sterling. It's conveniently close to Bing's Landing so is popular with fishermen. There are about 15 full-hookup sites and about 10 with only electricity as well as a grassy area for no hookup camping or tenting. There are pull-thrus to 60 feet and back-ins to 45. Some picnic tables are provided and there is a central campfire area. Restrooms offer flush toilets and coin-op showers, there is a dump station as well as a laundry, a small store with fishing tackle, and a liquor store.

Bing Brown's is on the north side of the highway near Mile 81 in Sterling.

MOOSE RIVER RV PARK ✓

Address: PO Box 168, Sterling, AK 99672
Telephone: (907) 260-7829

GPS Location: 60.53532 N, 150.74224 W, 200 Ft.

This is a small campground located in the town of Sterling. It has 30 sites, some are pull-thrus to 55 feet. Sites have full hookups. Some sites have a picnic table and there is a central campfire area. Restrooms with showers are in the main building. Wi-Fi is a hotspot, also in the main building.

The campground is easy to find. It's in Sterling on the north side of the highway just east of a Tesoro station at Mile 81.5.

IZAAK WALTON CAMPGROUND – KENAI RIVER SMA

Location: Near Mile 82 Of The Sterling Hwy., In Sterling
Info: (907) 262-5581
Website: dnr.alaska.gov/parks/aspunits/kenai/izaakwalsrs.htm

GPS Location: 60.53613 N, 150.75506 W, 100 Ft.

As the name suggests this is a campground primarily used by fishermen. It is located at the point where the Moose River enters the Kenai in Sterling and is a popular place to fish from the bank for salmon using flies.

The campground has some 31 sites, seven of these are tent sites. Most are short separated paved sites off a paved but narrow circular access road. This is not a good campground for large RVs, a few sites will take RVs to 30 feet (including tow vehicle and trailer) but 25 feet is more comfortable. Picnic tables and fire pits are provided as well as vault toilets and a water pump. There is a host and firewood is available for purchase. There is also a boat launch. The campground has a seven day limit.

This campground is located at the confluence of the Kenai and Moose Rivers in Sterling near Mile 82 of the Sterling Highway. Do not enter with a rig larger than 30 feet (including trailer), there is not sufficient room to park or turn around and unfortunate big rig drivers don't enjoy backing out the long driveway.

JANA HOUSE HOSTEL AND RV PARK

Address: 38670 Swanson River Rd. (PO Box 287), Sterling, AK 99672
Telephone: (907) 260-4151
Email: janamae@hotmail.com

GPS Location: 60.54143 N, 150.79359 W, 200 Ft.

Jana House is a huge building that serves as a hostel. It is located just outside Sterling on the Swanson River Road just a half-mile or so from the Sterling Highway. At one time it was a private school. In addition to the RV sites there are 48 dorm-style beds and 6 private rooms.

Behind the hostel building are ten very large full-hookup RV sites with 60-amp outlets. Pull-thrus are available. The sites are situated on a large gravel lot so there's plenty of room. Picnic tables are provided. RVers can use the bathrooms and showers inside the main building.

THE KENAI PENINSULA

To reach the campground drive north from Mile 83 of the Sterling Highway (just west of Sterling) on the Swanson River Road. After .4 mile (.6 km) you'll see the large hostel building on your right.

⛟ DOLLY VARDEN CAMPGROUND (USF&W)

| Location: | Swanson River Road, 13.4 Miles (21.6 Km) From Sterling Junction |
| Info: | (907) 262-7021 |

GPS Location: 60.70066 N, 150.79810 W, 200 Ft.

Dolly Varden is the largest of the campgrounds along this road as well as the easiest to reach. It has 12 sites off a loop access road. Some sites will take RVs as large as 30 feet, many of them are right along the lake. There are picnic tables and fire pits as well as vault toilets, a hand-operated water pump, and a boat launch.

⛟ RAINBOW LAKE CAMPGROUND (USF&W)

| Location: | Swanson River Road, 14.9 Miles (24 Km) From Sterling Junction |
| Info: | (907) 262-7021 |

GPS Location: 60.71839 N, 150.81829 W, 200 Ft.

Rainbow Lake has 3 sites suitable for RVs to 30 feet. There are fire pits and picnic tables as well as a hand-operated water pump, a vault toilet, and a boat launch.

⛟ SWANSON RIVER CAMPGROUND (USF&W)

| Location: | Swanson River Road, 16.9 Miles (27.3 Km) From Sterling Junction |
| Info: | (907) 262-7021 |

GPS Location: 60.74350 N, 150.80115 W, 200 Ft.

This is a good RV campground and is located only a short distance from the launch point on the Swanson River. There are four RV sites that are very wide but only 30 feet long on a gravel loop access road. Sites have picnic tables and fire pits and there is a vault toilet.

⛟ FISH LAKE CAMPGROUND (USF&W)

| Location: | Swan Lake Road, 19.3 Miles (31.1 Km) From Sterling Junction |
| Info: | (907) 262-7021 |

GPS Location: 60.72791 N, 150.72318 W, 200 Ft.

Fish Lake Campground has only two sites. They have picnic table and fire pits, there is a vault toilet. The parking slots will take RVs to 25 feet.

⛟ SWAN LAKE CANOE ROUTE WEST ENTRANCE (USF&W)

| Location: | Swan Lake Rd., 20.2 Miles (32.6 Km) From Sterling Jct. |
| Info: | (907) 262-7021 |

GPS Location: 60.72304 N, 150.69831 W, 200 Ft.

No picnic tables or fire pits here, but there's a large parking lot and a vault toilet. Eight side-by-side parking lot spaces are designated for RVs only, they'll take any size RV.

⬛ MERGANSER LAKE CAMPGROUND (USF&W)

Location: Swan Lake Road, 22.4 Miles (36.1 Km) From Sterling Junction
Info: (907) 262-7021

GPS Location: 60.73058 N, 150.63927 W, 200 Ft.

This site is on the shore of Merganser Lake. It has a picnic table and fire pit as well as a vault toilet. There's room for an RV to 25 feet to park.

⬛ ALASKA CANOE AND RV PARK

Address: 35292 Sterling Hwy., Sterling, AK 99672
Telephone: (907) 262-2331
Email: alaskacanoe@yahoo.com
Website: www.alaskacanoetrips.com

GPS Location: 60.53732 N, 150.80335 W, 200 Ft.

Just outside Sterling there's a small campground that specializes in information, rental canoes, and ferrying canoeists to and from the various canoe routes in the area. It's a good place to leave your RV while you make a canoe trip. They also rent mountain bikes.

There are 25 sites located behind the main building. Most are full hookup with 20, or 30-amp power. There are also tent sites. While some RV sites are as long as 45 feet we'd say that folks with RVs over 30 feet should take a look before entering, there's plenty of room out front to park and do so. Picnic tables, and fire pits are provided and there is a small store. There are restrooms with flush toilets and showers.

The campground is located on the north side of the Sterling Highway near Mile 84 which is just west of Sterling.

⬛ MORGAN'S LANDING CAMPGROUND – KENAI RIVER SRS

Location: Scout Loop Road From Mile 85 Of The Sterling Highway
Info: (907) 262-5581
Website: dnr.alaska.gov/parks/aspunits/kenai/morgldcamp.htm

GPS Location: 60.50027 N, 150.86643 W, 200 Ft.

This fairly large state campground is another popular access point for the middle Kenai River. The Alaska State Parks headquarters for the district is also located here. There are trails along the riverbank and fishing platforms if you want to try your luck.

There are 39 sites with tables and fire pits. Many are pull-thrus to 90 feet and are off a gravel loop road. The campground has vault toilets, a water faucet, and a host. There's also an overflow area where you can camp for a night while waiting for a standard campsite to open up. Stays here are limited to 7 days in a row and 14 days per calendar month from May to September.

Best access to the campground is from Mile 85 of the Sterling Highway. Follow the Scout Lake Loop Road for 1.6 miles (2.6 km), then turn right on Lou Morgan Road. The campground will appear in another 2.5 miles (4.2 km).

Soldotna and Kenai

Population Soldotna 4,200, Kenai 7,100, Elevation near sea level

Soldotna has grown because of its convenient location near the junction of the Sterling Highway and Kenai Spur Road. The settlement began to grow in the 1940s. The location along the Kenai River didn't hurt either, today the town really hops when the salmon are running. Soldotna has full services including a large Fred Meyer and a Safeway. Right next to the Kenai River Bridge at Mile 96 is the **Soldotna Visitor's Center** (Greater Soldotna Chamber of Commerce, 44790 Sterling Highway, Soldotna, Alaska 99669; 907 262-9814). This is an essential stop, they have the huge 97 pound, 4 ounce world record Kenai king salmon on display (it's mounted, of course).

Kenai, by far the older of these towns, is located well west of the Sterling Highway. To get there follow the Kenai Spur Road for 8 miles (13 km) from near Mile 94 of the Sterling Highway. This intersection is in Soldotna across from the Fred Meyer store. Kenai was originally an Indian village and then in 1791 became the second permanent Russian settlement in Alaska. You will still find signs of the Russians in Kenai in the form of the **Holy Assumption Russian Orthodox Church** with its blue onion dome and also **St. Nicholas Chapel**. Kenai now has big box stores including a large Walmart, Lowe's, and Home Depot; restaurants and other services. The town seems well-clipped and organized compared to upstart Soldotna. Kenai has its own visitor center called the **Kenai Bicentennial Visitors and Cultural Center** (11471 Kenai Spur Highway, Kenai, AK 99611; 907 283-1991).

KENAI'S HOLY ASSUMPTION RUSSIAN ORTHODOX CHURCH

The Kenai-Soldotna area offers several golf courses. **Kenai Golf Course** (907 283-7500) has 18 holes and a driving range. It is located in Kenai next to Oiler Park on Lawton Drive. The **Birch Ridge Golf Course** (907 262-5270) is a nine-hole course and driving range located on the Sterling Highway not far east of Soldotna. **Bird Homestead Golf Course** (907 260-4653) is eight miles (13 km) out on Funny River Road and has nine holes.

A big summer attraction in Kenai is the Kenai River dipnet opening. During this two-week period the town is full of Alaskans attempting to fill their freezers with red salmon for the winter. Even those who are not Alaska residents and therefore do not qualify to fish find the whole thing to be quite entertaining. Folks are allowed to camp on the river banks near the mouth of the river during this time, see the description below in the *Kenai Campgrounds* section.

Both Soldotna and Kenai are well supplied with campgrounds, they're the supply centers for the western Kenai Peninsula.

Soldotna Campgrounds

FRED MEYER PARKING LOT
Location: In Soldotna At Mile 94 Of The Sterling Hwy.

GPS Location: 60.48838 N, 151.05019 W, 100 Ft.

Fred Meyer is a huge and hugely popular grocery and discount store in Soldotna. To the chagrin of local RV park operators and the delight of frugal RVers it also is one of the more popular campgrounds in town since RVs are allowed to park overnight in the lot when there is room. There's no telling how long this situation will last as the commercial and political forces play out.

There is a dump station at the south border of the lot. Next to it is a board where the rules are posted. Stays are limited to 3 days and RV combos longer than 22 feet are directed to park in only certain areas. During busy periods the store sometimes even posts an employee in the lot to assist RVers.

The store is impossible to miss, it is located on the east side of the highway near the point where the Sterling Highway enters Soldotna from the north.

SWIFTWATER PARK (CITY OF SOLDOTNA)
Telephone: (907) 262-5299
Website: www.ci.soldotna.ak.us

GPS Location: 60.48303 N, 151.04170 W, 100 Ft.

The City of Soldotna maintains two RV parks along the Kenai River. This is the smaller of the two. There are 47 spaces, many are pull-thrus or parallel-type spaces. Some will take RVs to 40 feet. Many are along the river bank. Picnic tables and fire pits are provided. There are vault toilets and a boat launch. The campground usually has a host and firewood is sold.

To reach the campground leave the Sterling Highway in Soldotna near Mile 94, this is just south of the Fred Meyer store. Drive east on Redoubt for .5 mile (.8 km), then turn right onto Swiftwater Park Road. You'll reach the park in another .3 miles (.5 km).

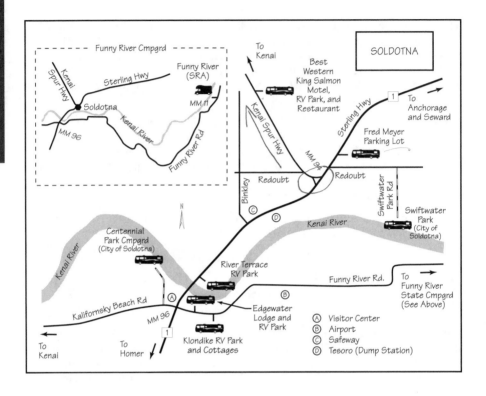

BEST WESTERN KING SALMON MOTEL RV PARK AND RESTAURANT

Address:	35546 A Kenai Spur Hwy. (PO Box 430), Soldotna, AK 99669
Telephone:	(907) 262-5857
Email:	ksalmon@alaska.com

GPS Location: 60.49529 N, 151.06627 W, 100 Ft.

This motel has 39 sites located in a large open gravel lot. Most of the sites are wide pull-thrus to 60 feet, they have electric (20, 30 or 50-amp), water, and sewer hookups. Sites have picnic table but not fire pits. A laundry between the camping area and the motel has restrooms with flush toilets and coin-operated showers, and the motel has a restaurant. Wi-Fi is available at the motel office. To reach the motel just follow the Kenai Spur Road .7 mile (1.1 km) west from its junction with the Sterling Highway at Mile 94. You'll soon see the motel on your right. The campground occupies the next block behind the motel.

RIVER TERRACE RV PARK

Address:	44755 Sterling Hwy. (PO Box 322), Soldotna, AK 99669
Telephone:	(907) 262-5593

GPS Location: 60.47722 N, 151.07861 W, 100 Ft.

The River Terrace is one of the older and better known campgrounds in Soldotna. You can't miss it as you drive across the bridge over the Kenai. It sits right on the river and has been a popular base for fishermen during June, July, and August for many years when the salmon are thick. Unfortunately the campground facilities are old and have seen better days.

The campground occupies a couple of terraces along the river bank. There are about 70 back-in or pull-into sites available, many right along the river. Sites are either full-hookup or electric only (20, 30, and 50 amp). Any size RV can find a site here. There is a dump station. Restrooms have flush toilets and showers are available. Bank fishing is possible, there's even a fishing platform that is wheel-chair accessible. Fishing is the mainstay of this campground, they can help you arrange charters and fish processing. Reservations are recommended during the summer, and you must make them well in advance. Rates in July are about $10 higher than shown above.

The campground is located on the north bank of the river. As you drive south toward Homer it will be on your left just before you cross the bridge over the Kenai River in Soldotna.

EDGEWATER LODGE AND RV PARK

Address:	48798 Funny River Road (PO Box 976), Soldotna, AK 99669
Telephone:	(907) 262-7733 or (800) 392-8560
Email:	edgewaterlodge@sunriseresorts.com
Website:	www.sunriseresorts.com

GPS Location: 60.47485 N, 151.08131 W, 100 Ft.

The Edgewater is Soldotna's camping club campground and is a member of RPI and Coast to Coast. It's tough to get in to this campground if you're not a member unless it's during the shoulder season when the fishermen are gone. Reservations are essential in July and the price is $5 higher than shown above. The local visitor center is right across the highway. In it you'll find the largest king ever caught in the Kenai.

There are 60 large sites in a gravel lot. These are mostly big pull-thrus to 50 feet. Most are full-hookups with 30-amp outlets but a few are water and electricity sites. Amenities include restroom with flush toilets and showers, a laundry, a dump station, and bank fishing along the river just upstream of the bridge.

The campground is located very near the Soldotna bridge over the Kenai. From central Soldotna drive south across the bridge to the stoplight. Turn left here onto Funny River Road and then almost immediately turn left into the campground.

KLONDIKE RV PARK AND COTTAGES

Address:	48665 Funny River Road (PO Box 2568), Soldotna, AK 99669
Telephone:	(907) 262-6035 or (800) 980-6035
Email:	manager@klondikervpark.com
Website:	www.klondikervpark.com

GPS Location: 60.47392 N, 151.07849 W, 100 Ft.

The Klondike is the newest of the Soldotna campgrounds. It's a nice modern RV park with 35 wide full-hookup sites but is not on the riverbank. There are back-in and pull-thru sites to 60 feet. Most have 30-amp power but a few have 50-amp. Wi-

Fi and showers are included in the base price. The campground is open from May 1 to September 1. Reservations are essential and rates are about $10 higher June 15 to July 31.

From central Soldotna drive south across the bridge to the stoplight. Turn left here onto Funny River Road, the campground is on the right in .2 mile (.3 km).

FUNNY RIVER SRA

Info: (907) 262-5581
Website: dnr.alaska.gov/parks/aspunits/kenai/funnyriversrs.htm

GPS: 60.49236 N, 150.86225 W, 200 Ft.

This is a small state campground near the south shore of the Kenai River quite a distance upstream from Soldotna. There are six formal sites here. Three are off a small circular cleared turning area and three are walk-ins near the pay station. RVs of any size can also park along one side of the entrance road in an area indicated by signage. The formal sites have picnic tables and fire-pits but the other parking is provided with no facilities. There are vault toilets and there is a 7 day stay limit.

From central Soldotna drive south across the bridge to the stoplight. Turn left here onto Funny River Road, cross the Funny River at 11.2 miles (6.9 km), the campground is on the left at 11.4 miles (7.1) km), just beyond the 11 mile marker.

CENTENNIAL PARK CAMPGROUND (CITY OF SOLDOTNA)

Telephone: (907) 262-5299
Website: www.ci.soldotna.ak.us

GPS Location: 60.47864 N, 151.08888 W, 100 Ft.

This second campground operated by the City of Soldotna is large. There are about 125 sites set in spruce trees along the Kenai River. Sites have picnic tables and fire pits, many are large enough for the largest RVs. There are vault toilets and a dump stations (big extra charge). The person at the gatehouse kiosk can direct you to the nearby sports center for showers. There is a boat launch at the campground and large areas for parking boat trailers. The campground has lots of riverfront and bank fishing is possible. Reservations are not accepted but there is an overflow camping area where you can stay while waiting for a campsite.

To reach the campground turn onto the Kalifornsky Beach Road from the Sterling Highway at Mile 96. Turn right in just .1 mile into the campground.

Kenai Campgrounds

BELUGA LOOKOUT LODGE AND RV PARK

Address: 929 Mission Ave., Kenai, AK 99611
Telephone: (907) 283-5999
Email: belugarv@belugalookout.com
Website: www.belugalookout.com

GPS Location: 60.55112 N, 151.26550 W, 100 Ft.

For a campground that takes full advantage of Kenai's view across Cook Inlet of the volcanoes of the Alaska Range you can do no better than the Beluga Lookout. High on a bluff overlooking the outlet of the Kenai River this is also a good place to watch for white beluga whales feeding off the mouth of the Kenai.

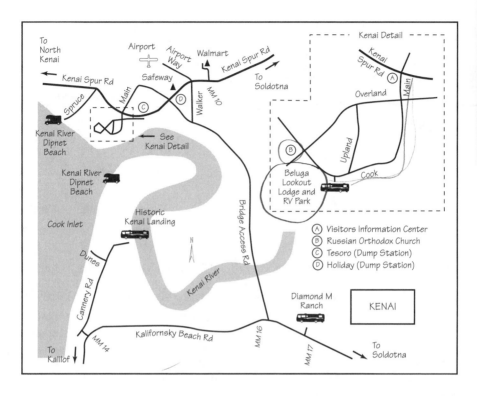

The campground has 65 full-hookup spaces (20, 30, and 50 amp) occupying a large open lot at the top of a bluff overlooking Cook Inlet. Sites have picnic tables and many are as long as 55 feet but they are narrow and maneuvering room is tight. Cable-TV hook-ups are available. There are showers and flush toilets and a coin-op laundry. The restaurants, sights, and shopping of central Kenai are within walking distance. Reservations are essential at this park and rates are $10 higher during dipnet season during the last half of July.

To find the campground follow Main Street south from the visitor information center and turn right on Cook Drive. The campground is hard to miss on the lip of the bluff.

🚐 DIAMOND M RANCH RESORT

Address:	48500 Diamond M Ranch Rd, Kenai, AK 99611
Telephone:	(907) 283-9424
Email:	stay@diamondmranch.com
Website:	www.diamondmranch.com

GPS Location: 60.51719 N, 151.19048 W, Near Sea Level

This is a very large and popular campground located south of Kenai. It is a well-managed family-owned campground that offers many additional amenities including van outings to nearby attractions and a paved bike trail along the highway out front.

The campground has about 75 RV sites and 10 tents sites. There are both pull-thrus and back-ins to 60 feet with 20, 30 and 50-amp power and full hookups. Restrooms have flush toilets and free showers. There's also a dump station and a laundry. Fires are in community fire pits and also at some of the RV sites.

The Diamond M Ranch is located off Kalifornsky Beach Road at Mile 16.5. From its intersection with the Sterling Highway just south of Soldotna drive 5.7 miles (9.2 km) west on the Kalifornsky Beach Road. You'll see the campground entrance on your right. Alternately, from Kenai head south on Bridge Access Road to intersect with Kalifornsky Beach Road, a distance of about 3.3 miles (5.3 km). Turn left and you'll see the campground on the left in just .4 miles (.6 km).

HISTORIC KENAI LANDING

Address:	2101 Bowpicker Lane, Kenai, AK 99611
Telephone:	(907) 690-3642
Email:	endofthespit@alaska.net
Website:	www.kenailanding.com

GPS Location: 60.53114 N, 151.25655 W, Near Sea Level

This campground is part of a larger development. It's an historic cannery that is being turned into restaurants, shops, and hotel rooms, not to mention camping out back. It makes an interesting place to camp since it's near the mouth of the Kenai River.

There are 12 back-in RV sites with 30-amp power. They'll take any size RV since they open in to a large gravel maneuvering area. Next door is a walk-in tent area with some trees for about 10 sites with pitching on gravel. There are many additional sites for RVs to park without hookups. Water is available but there is no dump station. Portable toilets are located in the campground. There is a restaurant and a boat launch nearby. Wi-Fi is available at the office but not at the campground itself.

Follow the Bridge Access Road from Kenai south for 3.3 miles (5.4 km) to the intersection with the Kalifornsky Beach Road. Turn right and drive 2.4 miles (3.9 km) to turn right on Cannery Road, this is just beyond the mile 14 marker. Follow Cannery Road 1.3 miles (2.1 km) to the campground.

KENAI RIVER DIPNET BEACHES

Telephone:	(907) 335-6000

GPS Location: 60.54690 N, 151.22139 W, Near Sea Level

The city of Kenai allows and oversees camping on the beaches on both sides of the mouth of the Kenai River during the personal use dipnet opening. This is generally from July 10 through July 31.

On the north shore there is a vehicle parking area and limited RV dry camping area at the end Spruce Street at the beach. Vehicles are allowed on the beach west of this point but not left or upstream. Only four-wheel vehicles should be on the beach, it's easy to get stuck and lose your rig to the big tides. Tent camping is allowed on the beach but only upstream to the left. Access is controlled and there are fees for both parking and camping. Access is via Spruce Drive which goes south from the Kenai Spur Highway .5 mile (1 km) west of the intersection of Kenai Spur and Main Street where the visitor center is located.

On the south shore there is camping near the mouth of the river after a long drive of about one mile (2 km) on a sandy path between the high water mark and the dunes. Again, only four-wheel drive vehicles should attempt this. Here too, access is controlled and there are parking and camping fees. Care is taken to protect the dunes inland of the vehicle access route and camping area. Follow the Bridge Access Road from Kenai south for 3.3 miles (5.4 km) to the intersection with the Kalifornsky Beach Road. Turn right and drive 2.4 miles (3.9 km) to turn right on Cannery Road, this is just beyond mile 14 marker. Proceed another 1 mile (2 km) to Dunes Road and follow it to the beach. There is parking here before you get to the beach or you can use your 4-wheel-drive vehicle to reach the camping area a mile to the north.

Both portable toilets and waste dumpsters are provided. Because there are so many people camping, fishing, and cleaning their catch there are strict rules in effect and they are enforced by both the Alaska Department of Fish and Game and local police. Make sure you know the rules and behave responsibly.

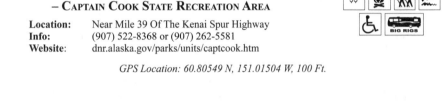

North Kenai Campgrounds

**DISCOVERY CAMPGROUND
– CAPTAIN COOK STATE RECREATION AREA**

Location:	Near Mile 39 Of The Kenai Spur Highway
Info:	(907) 522-8368 or (907) 262-5581
Website:	dnr.alaska.gov/parks/units/captcook.htm

GPS Location: 60.80549 N, 151.01504 W, 100 Ft.

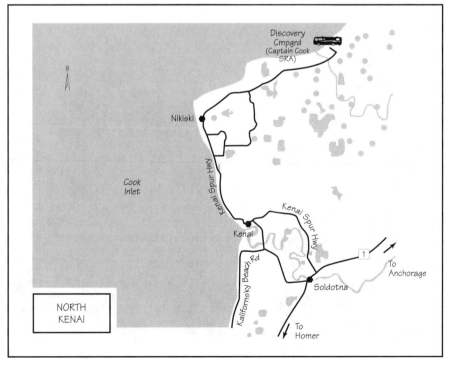

Discovery Campground is a large and very nice government campground located a little off the beaten path. The fishing crowds found throughout the rest of the Kenai seldom venture out to the end of the Kenai Spur Highway although fishing can be good in the nearby river. On the other hand, this makes a good place to stay if you are assigned pick-up duties for someone canoeing the Swanson River. Nearby Stormy Lake is popular for boating and the Cook Inlet beach is easily accessible.

The campground has 53 back-in spaces off a circular access road. RVs to about 45 feet should fit in some of the larger sites. Sites have picnic tables and fire pits, there are vault toilets. The campground sits near the bluff overlooking Cook Inlet and there are hiking paths down to the beach. Stays here are limited to 15 days.

From Kenai drive north 27 miles (43.5 km) on the Kenai Spur Road past the refineries at Nikiski to the end of the road. Turn left and you'll soon see the campground.

FROM SOLDOTNA TO HOMER
85 Miles (137 Kilometers)

From Soldotna the Sterling Highway leads directly south toward Homer. At Mile 109 the road crosses the **Kasilof River** and from Mile 115 near Clam Gulch it never strays far from the bluffs overlooking Cook Inlet. The road can't really run along the water because high tides and storms eat away at the foot of the bluffs and they move to the east a few feet each year. Nonetheless there are access roads to the beach at many places and often there are views across the inlet to the snowcapped volcanoes

THE DEEP CREEK BEACH IS A FUN PLACE FOR CLAM DIGGING

(from left to right): **Augustine** (4,025 ft.), last eruption 2006; **Illiamna** (10,016 ft.); **Redoubt** (10,197 ft.), last eruption 2009; and **Spur** (11,070 ft), last eruption 1992.

At Mile 117 an access road leads west to **Clam Gulch State Recreation Area**. This is the first of several beaches along Cook Inlet where razor clams can be found. The next good one is **Deep Creek** at Mile 137. Tides along here can range 35 feet from low to high water so be careful if you take your RV onto the beach. If you get stuck you may lose it.

As the road continues south it crosses several rivers: the **Ninilchik River** at Mile 135, **Deep Creek** at Mile 137, and the **Anchor River** at Mile 157. Each of these rivers is a popular fishing stream with runs of king and silver salmon as well as Dolly Varden, rainbows, and steelhead. There are lots of campgrounds allowing easy access to the fishing. You might want to note that the road out along the south side of the Anchor River to the beach past the Anchor River state campgrounds and the Kyllonen RV Park is the **westernmost road in North America** that is connected to the road system.

Finally, at Mile 170 the highway crests the bluff overlooking **Kachemak Bay**. Pull off the highway at the developed overlook for one of the most scenic vistas in Alaska. Spread out before you are the Homer Spit, Kachemak Bay, and the snow-covered Kenai Mountains forming a magnificent backdrop.

Soldotna to Homer Campgrounds

DECANTER INN

Address:	PO Box 1089, Kasilof, AK 99610
Telephone:	(907) 262-5917 or (907) 262-5933
Website:	www.decanterinn.com/

GPS Location: 60.34086 N, 151.22727 W, 100 Ft.

The Decanter Inn has been in this location for a long time, there is a little-used RV camping area between the highway and the restaurant and bar.

The campground has 55 sites. Many are back-ins to 35 feet. Two are pull-thrus to 50 feet. The sites have only electrical hookups (30 amp) but there is a dump site and water fill station. Last time we visited electrical outlets were inactive and there were only restroom facilities in the bar/restaurant. The inn overlooks Roque Lake, fishing is possible.

The Inn is located along the Sterling Highway between Soldotna and the Kasilof River, it's on the east side of the road near Mile 107.

JOHNSON LAKE STATE RECREATION AREA

Location:	Near Mile 110.5 Of The Sterling Highway
Info:	(907) 262-5581
Website:	dnr.alaska.gov/parks/aspunits/kenai/johnsonlksra.htm

GPS Location: 60.29667 N, 151.26584 W, 100 Ft.

Johnson Lake is a larger state campground with a nice lake next to the campground and the Clam Gulch beaches not far away. You can catch small rainbows in the lake and there is a boat launch. It makes a good base for those planning to spend some time on the Kenai with visits to both the Homer and Kenai areas.

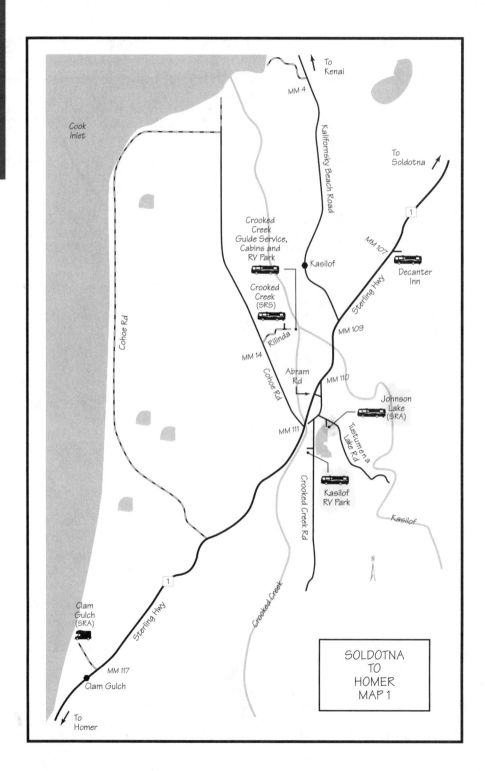

There are about 50 back-in sites off two loops. As you enter the campground the older section is to the right. In 2013 it was being redone so facilities should be similar to the modern ones in the loop to the left. These are large sites, some suitable for RVs to 45 feet. A few sites are along the lake, these go first. There's also a walk-in tent-camping area. Each campsite has a picnic table and fire pit and there are vault toilets and hand-operated water pumps. This campground often has a host and stays are limited to 15 days.

To reach this campground turn east from the Sterling Highway near Mile 110.5 on Abram Road. In .1 mile (.2 km) turn right at the first road you come to. In .3 mile (.5 km) you'll see the Tustamina Lake Road on your left, marked with a large T. Turn left here and in .2 mile (.3 km) you'll see the Johnson Lake campground entrance on your right.

KASILOF RV PARK — *consider this one*

Address:	21377 Crooked Creek Rd (PO Box 944), Kasilof, AK 99610
Telephone:	(907) 262-0418 (Summer), (785) 657-1465 (Winter)
Email:	info@kasilofrvpark.com
Website:	www.kasilofrvpark.com

GPS Location: 60.29057 N, 151.27139 W, 100 Ft.

Near the Johnson Lake State Rec. Area is an excellent little family run RV park. It's not on the main road so many people don't know it's there. This place has a location central to many western Kenai Peninsula attractions with the added advantages of hookups and showers. Johnson Lake is just across the road.

There are 17 sites on a wooded ridge between Crooked Creek and Johnson Lake. These are wooded and separated sites much like a government campground. Twelve of these are pull-thru sites, some to 90 feet. Some sites are full-hookup, others have water and electricity. Restrooms are very clean and have showers. There is also a dump station, a laundry, and a small gift shop. Propane is available. Campfires are in a community fire pit, free firewood is provided. Clamming equipment can be rented here too. Rates are $5 higher in July.

The route to this campground is from Mile 110.5 of the Sterling Highway. Turn east on Abram road. In .1 mile (.2 km) turn right at the first road you come to. In .9 mile (1.5 km) turn left on Crooked Creek Road and you'll see the campground on your right in .5 mile (.8 km).

CROOKED CREEK STATE RECREATION SITE

Location:	1.8 Miles On Cohoe Loop Road
Info:	(907) 262-5581
Website:	dnr.alaska.gov/parks/aspunits/kenai/crookedcreeksrs.htm

GPS Location: 60.32166 N, 151.28809 W, 100 Ft.

This has been a popular campground with fishermen because it is located near a good hole at the confluence of the Kasilof River and Crooked Creek.

There are about 80 camping spaces at the campground. These are side-by-side back-in parking spaces in a gravel parking lot. There's room for RVs to 45 feet. There are also some walk-in tent camping sites in the trees. Fishing is the attraction here, not peaceful enjoyment of an unspoiled setting. Vault toilets are provided and a few sites have picnic tables and fire pits. There's also a host. Stays here are limited to 7 days.

To reach the campground turn west on the Cohoe Loop Road from Mile 111 of the Sterling Highway. The campground access road is on the right at 1.8 miles (2.9 km).

CROOKED CREEK GUIDE SERVICE, CABINS AND RV PARK

Address:	PO Box 601, Kasilof, AK 99610
Telephone:	(907) 262-1299
Email:	crookedcreekrvpark@netzero.com
Website:	www.crookedcreekrv.com

GPS Location: 60.32112 N, 151.28385 W, 100 Ft.

This commercial campground is right next to the Crooked Creek State Recreation Area. Fishing charters are available here for the Kenai, the Kasilof, and Cook Inlet.

The campground has about 60 available full and partial-hookup back-in and pull-thru sites to 70 feet. These are separated sites with trees but laid out in a grid-like pattern. There are also some tent sites. There are flush toilets, showers, laundry facilities, and a dump station. Many sites are occupied by permanently-located RVs, some of which are available as rentals. Out front is an office with a tackle store and restaurant.

To reach the campground follow the directions given for the Crooked Creek State Recreation Site but continue on past the state site entrance for just a short distance.

CLAM GULCH STATE RECREATION AREA

Location:	Mile 117 Sterling Highway
Info:	(907) 262-5581
Website:	dnr.alaska.gov/parks/units/clamglch.htm

GPS Location: 60.23863 N, 151.39666 W, 100 Ft.

The beaches along the west shore of the Kenai Peninsula along Cook Inlet provide some the best razor clam digging in the United States. Clam digging can be really fun and easy if you know how, virtually impossible if you don't. You can find information in many places including at the information offices in Kenai and Soldotna. The Clam Gulch State Recreation Area is probably the best place to come for your introduction to this activity.

There are over 116 back-in side-by-side parking lot type camping spaces on the bluff above the beach. RVs over 30 feet will find maneuvering and parking difficult here if the campground is anywhere near full. This campground is likely to be full on spring and summer weekends with big negative tides, virtually empty otherwise. There is also a tent camping area with grass for pitching tents and a covered pavilion. Picnic tables, fire pits, vault toilets and water are provided. From the campground a steep sand road leads down to the beach. Four-wheel drive vehicles can be used on the beach, no permit is required. Keep in mind, however, that sea salt isn't very good for your vehicle. Most people just walk the beach or use quads, you can find clams directly in front of the campground. That can still be a healthy walk since Cook Inlet tides have a range of over 20 feet and the beach here is practically flat.

THE KENAI PENINSULA

You'll find the quarter-mile road out to the Clam Gulch Recreation Area leaving the Sterling Highway at about Mile 117.

SCENIC VIEW RV PARK

Address: PO Box 39253, Ninilchik, Alaska 99639
Telephone: (907) 567-3909 (seasonal)
Email: scenicrv@yahoo.com
Website: www.scenicviewrv.com

GPS Location: 60.13124 N, 151.53628 W, 300 Ft.

This RV park has an idyllic bluff-top location overlooking the inlet and the mountains to the west. While there's no direct access to the beach here the park is very popular with travelers since the owners love spending their summers with visiting RVers and are full of local information.

The park has 18 back-in sites. Ten are full-hookup and eight partial with electricity and water. Maximum length of sites is 45 feet and most sites are shorter. Parking is on grass and sites are separated by shrubs. Amenities include a dump station, restrooms with flush toilets and showers, laundry, central fire pit, picnic tables, and free Wi-Fi. For fishermen there's a cleaning table, a smoker and a freezer. Clamming equipment can be rented.

The campground is located on the west side of the Sterling highway at Mile 127. There is an overlook area with parking off the highway at the entrance. Park here and walk in to register, there is little turnaround room.

HEAVENLY SIGHTS CHARTERS AND CAMPING

Address: 13295 Sterling Highway, Ninilchik, AK 99639
Telephone: (907) 567-7371 or (800) 479-7371
Email: heavenlysights@msn.com
Website: www.heavenlysights.com

GPS Location: 60.08024 N, 151.62531 W, 100 Ft.

This is a campground run in conjunction with a fishing charter operation. There are 13 full-hookup back-in sites to 40 feet with 30-amp outlets and another ten or so large sites with no hookups. There are also tent sites down a hill toward the bluff. Restrooms have flush toilets and showers, there is a laundry room, and sites have picnic tables and fire pits.

The campground is accessed directly off the Sterling Highway near Mile 132.2. It's on the west side of the road. This is about four miles (6.5 km) north of Ninilchik.

NINILCHIK RIVER CAMPGROUND
(NINILCHIK STATE RECREATION AREA)

Location: Near Mile 134 Of The Sterling Highway
Info: (907) 262-5581
Website: dnr.alaska.gov/parks/units/nilchik.htm

GPS Location: 60.05224 N, 151.65028 W, 100 Ft.

The Ninilchik River Campground is one of three camping areas on the lower Ninilchik River. It is the largest and we think has the most pleasant setting, particularly

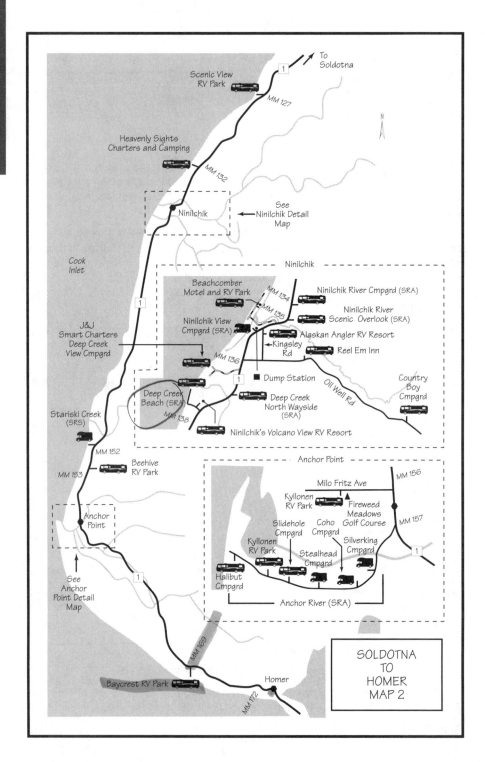

SOLDOTNA
TO
HOMER
MAP 2

when the fish are running and this area becomes a madhouse. There's a short trail from the campground down to the river.

There are 43 sites off two loop roads in a treed area near the highway north of the Ninilchik River. Fourteen of these are walk-in tent sites, the others are back-in vehicle sites, many of them doubles. A few sites are as long as 45 feet. Spaces have picnic tables and fire pits. The campground has a host, vault toilets, and a water faucet. Stays here are limited to 15 days.

Watch for the campground on the east side of the highway near Mile 134 north of the Ninilchik River bridge.

NINILCHIK RIVER SCENIC OVERLOOK CAMPGROUND (NINILCHIK STATE RECREATION AREA)

Location:	Near Mile 134 Of The Sterling Highway
Info:	(907) 262-5581
Website:	dnr.alaska.gov/parks/units/nilchik.htm

GPS Location: 60.04864 N, 151.65341 W, 100 Ft.

The Ninilchik River area needs lots of camping slots when the fish are running and this parking area provides 25 of them. These are long back-in side-by-side spaces in a paved parking lot, they're suitable for any size RV. There are some picnic tables, raised fire pits, vault toilets, and a water pump. Stays here are limited to 15 days. The overlook is just north of the Ninilchik River.

BEACHCOMBER MOTEL & RV PARK

Address:	Box 39367, Ninilchik, AK 99639
Telephone:	(907) 567-3417 or (408) 802-8544 (Winter)
Email:	ball3734@comcast.net
Website:	www.beachcombermotelrvpark.com

GPS Location: 60.05085 N, 151.66946 W, Near Sea Level

This little motel has an enviable location across a small access road from the Ninilchik Beach. Behind the hotel and its 15 back-in sites is the Ninilchik River where you can moor your small boat. Camping sites have full hookups with 30-amp power but there are no restroom or shower facilities for campers. The campground will take RVs to 40 feet. A word of warning: this is a popular place and you are unlikely to find an empty space when the fish are running. Early reservations are recommended. The facility is open from about May 1 through Labor Day.

The Ninilchik Beach Access Road leaves the Sterling Highway near Mile 135. The road goes down the hill for .5 mile (.8 km) to the beach and turns right. The motel is on the right a short distance along the beach road.

ALASKAN ANGLER RV RESORT

Address:	15640 Kingsley Road, Ninilchik, AK 99639
Telephone:	(800) 347-4114 or (907) 567-3393
Email:	aarvresort@yahoo.com
Website:	www.alaskabestrvpark.com

GPS Location: 60.04526 N, 151.66637 W, 100 Ft.

If you like the Ninilchik area but don't want to stay in a government campground there is a good alternative. It's the largest of the fishing-oriented private campgrounds in Ninilchik and has the nicest and most complete facilities. This is a full-service campground and also offers guided fishing trips on Cook Inlet.

The Alaskan Angler has about 65 available sites. Most of these are large back-ins to 60 feet in a large open lot with either full (20, 30 or 50-amp) or partial hookups. They are suitable for any size RV. TV hookups are available, so are temporary telephone hookups. There are also wooded tent and dry sites. The campground has good restroom facilities with coin-op showers, a laundry, a dump station, a gift shop, propane sales, and a fish and clam cleaning area.

The campground is located near Mile 135.4 of the Sterling Highway.

⛺ NINILCHIK VIEW CAMPGROUND
(NINILCHIK STATE RECREATION AREA)

Location:	Near Mile 135.4 Of The Sterling Highway
Info:	(907) 262-5581
Website:	dnr.alaska.gov/parks/units/nilchik.htm

GPS Location: 60.04711 N, 151.67020 W, 100 Ft.

Ninilchik View is a nice wooded state campground located at the top of the bluffs over the Ninilchik beaches. There are 14 separated sites with picnic tables and fire pits as well as vault toilets. A few sites will take RVs to 40 feet but access roads are narrow and turns tight so the campground is best for RVs to 35 feet. A trail leads down to the beach. Stays here are limited to 15 days. There is also a dump and water-fill station off the entrance road to the campground which serves this entire busy area. Watch for the sign marking the campground access road at Mile 135.4 of the Sterling Highway.

⛺ REEL EM INN

Address:	PO Box 39292, Ninilchik, AK 99639
Telephone:	(907) 567-7335, (800) 447-7335 (Summer),
	(907) 345-3887 (Winter)
Email:	fishing@cookinletcharters.com
Website:	www.cookinletcharters.com

GPS Location: 60.03971 N, 151.65000 W, 100 Ft.

This campground is run in conjunction with Cook Inlet Charters, a fish guiding outfit. There are 11 full hookup back-in sites to 40 feet. Restrooms with coin-op showers are available and there is a laundry and a community fire pit. There are also four rental rooms and a rental cabin.

The campground is located at approximately Mile 1 on paved Oil Well Road which leaves the Sterling Highway toward the east in Ninilchik near Mile 136.

⛺ COUNTRY BOY CAMPGROUND

Address:	PO Box 39697, Ninilchik, AK 99639
Telephone:	(907) 252-1365 (Cell)
Website:	www.countryboycampground.com/

GPS Location: 60.02414 N, 151.59363 W, 200 Ft.

Country Boy is a bit off the main road but is a large campground with full services.

The campground has about 50 sites with water, electric and sewer. Some 10 of these

Deep Creek View 136.2

are pull-thrus to 40 feet. There are additional sites without hookups. Any size RV can find room to park here. There are restrooms with flush toilets and free showers as well as a laundry and a restaurant. A number of other rough buildings are scattered around the campground to give it a bit of a wild-west look.

The campground is located at approximately Mile 3.3 on paved Oil Well Road which leaves the Sterling Highway toward the east in Ninilchik near Mile 136.

J & J Smart Charters Deep Creek View Campground

Address:	PO Box 39023, Ninilchik, AK 99639
Telephone:	(907) 567-3320 or (888) 425-4288
Email:	info@smartcharters.com
Website:	www.smartcharters.com

GPS Location: 60.03699 N, 151.69015 W, 200 Ft.

Run in conjunction with a fishing charter operation, this campground sits on the bluff looking out across a beach that is far below.

There are about 30 sites in this commercial campground. They're back-in sites, some large, with 20 or 30-amp service. The large sites can take RVs to 40 feet and have picnic tables and fire pits. Tents pitch in a grassy area. There is a dump station and restrooms with showers. Cabins are also available and tents are welcome.

To reach the campground leave the highway in Ninilchik near Mile 136 of the Sterling highway opposite the fairgrounds on Julia Steik Ave. Follow the gravel road west for .3 mile (.5 km) to a T, turn right and you'll reach the campground in another .1 mile (.2 km).

Deep Creek North Wayside (Deep Creek State Recreation Area)

Location:	Near Mile 137 Of The Sterling Highway
Info:	(907) 262-5581
Website:	dnr.alaska.gov/parks/units/deepck.htm

GPS Location: 60.02973 N, 151.68251 W, Near Sea Level

Deep Creek, like the Ninilchik River just four miles (6.5 km) north, is a popular fishing stream. On both sides of the creek where the Sterling Highway crosses there are open parking lots. The north wayside has 25 spaces and will take RVs to 40 feet. There are some picnic tables and fire pits as well as a vault toilet and hand-operated water pump.

Ninilchik's Volcano View RV Resort

Address:	16867 Sterling Hwy (PO Box 39278), Ninilchik, AK 99639
Telephone:	(877) 418-1953
Email:	linda@ninilchikvolcanoviewrv.com
Website:	www.ninilchikvolcanoviewrv.com

GPS Location: 60.02721 N, 151.69971 W, 100 Ft.

This is another campground associated with a fishing charter operation. It's located on a shelf overlooking Deep Creek and Cook Inlet, the views are spectacular.

The camping sites are arranged along the bluff. There are 23 back-in sites with water and electric hookups as well as dry sites. Sites have fire pits and there are coin-op showers, a laundry, and a dump station. Bluff-side view slots are slightly more expensive, tents are welcome. There's lots of maneuvering and parking room here, any size RV is fine.

You'll see the entrance on the right as you drive down the Deep Creek Beach access road from Mile 137 of the Sterling Highway.

DEEP CREEK BEACH
(DEEP CREEK STATE RECREATION AREA)

$$

Location:	At The Beach At The End Of Deep Creek
	Access Road Near Mile 137 Of The Sterling Hwy.
Info:	(907) 262-5581
Website:	dnr.alaska.gov/parks/units/deepck.htm

GPS Location: 60.03086 N, 151.70288 W, Near Sea Level

Deep creek is a very popular fishing stream but there is another attraction here. Sports fishing guides use the beach next to the creek mouth as a launching ramp for their halibut and salmon boats. These guides go after the same fish as those based in Homer, but the fishing grounds are much closer to Deep Creek. The halibut carcasses on the beach here attract large numbers of Bald Eagles and the clamming is excellent during big minus tides.

The state campground at the mouth of Deep Creek is very well used. There is room for about 75 rigs in back-in parking-lot style sites at this campground. The open gravel sites will take any size RV and parking is somewhat haphazard. Beach-front sites are at a premium, particularly on good clamming weekends. Fortunately there's usually a host here so things are amazingly orderly. The campground has picnic tables, fire pits, vault toilets and a boat-launching ramp into the protected river mouth. Stays are limited to 15 days.

To reach the campground drive down the Deep Creek Access Road from Mile 137 of the Sterling Highway. The road is paved to the beach, then turns to gravel. Turn right when you reach the beach, pass the commercial boat-launching area, and you'll find yourself at the entrance kiosk.

STARISKI CREEK STATE RECREATION SITE

Location:	Near Mile 152 Of The Sterling Highway
Info:	(907) 522-8368 or (907) 262-5581
Website:	dnr.alaska.gov/parks/aspunits/kenai/stariskisrs.htm

GPS Location: 59.84246 N, 151.81257 W, 200 Ft.

Stariski is a small state campground in a pleasant location at the top of the bluff above Cook Inlet. Since this isn't a good fishing base (at least not without a drive) it tends to have a different atmosphere than the busy fishing sites near Ninilchik and Deep Creek some 15 miles (24 km) to the north. Although right above the beach there is no access to it from the campground.

There are 16 sites at Stariski. While some sites are as long as 45 feet the maneuvering room is limited making 35 feet the recommended maximum RV size here. Sites are separated and located in spruce trees. Picnic tables and fire pits are at each site and there are vault toilets. Some sites have grassy areas for pitching a tent. Stays are limited to 15 days.

The campground is on the west side of the Sterling Highway at about Mile 152.

▄▄ BEEHIVE RV PARK

Location:	Mile 153.2 Sterling Highway, Anchor Point, AK
Telephone:	(907) 235-5327, (907) 299-3819, (907) 299-1529
Email:	beehivecampground@gmail.com
Website:	www.beehivecampground.com

GPS Location: 59.82608 N, 151.81877 W, 200 Ft.

This is a small campground along the highway. There are nine full-hookup pull-thru sites and nine back-ins with water and electricity. These are big sites to 60 feet and have picnic tables. There are also two rental cabins. A restroom with coin-op showers and a laundry are available, as well as a fish cleaning area and some fishing tackle..

The RV park is on the east side of the Sterling Highway near Mile 153.

▄▄ FIREWEED MEADOWS GOLF COURSE
(SECOND LOCATION OF KYLLONEN RV PARK)

Location:	Milo Fitz Avenue, Anchor River, AK
Telephone:	(907) 399-3001 (golf course), (907) 235-7762
	or (888) 848-2589

GPS Location: 59.77945 N, 151.84480 W, 300 Ft.

The Fireweed Meadows is a 9-hole golf course with pro shop, a covered driving range, and a small restaurant called the Grille and Pub. It's located in Anchor River. It has five full-hookup back-in RV sites. There is lots of maneuvering room so these sites can take any size RV. The only restrooms are at the restaurant and pro shop when it is open. This campground is run by Kyllonen RV Park which has another location along the Anchor River nearby. See our description below.

To reach the campground turn west on Milo Fitz Avenue in Anchor Point at Mile 156.4 of the Sterling Highway. You'll see the entrance on the left in .3 miles (.6 km).

▄▄ ANCHOR RIVER STATE RECREATION AREA

Location:	Near Mouth Of Anchor River
Info:	(907) 522-8368 or (907) 262-5581
Website:	http://dnr.alaska.gov/parks/units/anchoriv.htm

GPS Location: 59.77114 N, 151.83746 W, Near Sea Level

The Anchor River is another well-known Kenai Peninsula fishing destination. There are runs of king, silver and pink salmon but the river is probably most famous as a steelhead stream. Near the mouth of the river is an excellent state campground. Nearby are several good fishing holes with names like Slide Hole, Dudas Hole, Campground Hole and Picnic Hole. It appears that the Halibut Campground at the end of the road is the farthest west campground on the contiguous road system in North America.

Anchor River State Recreation Area has over 100 sites in five different areas called Silverking, Coho, Steelhead, Slide Hole and Halibut. Many are just side-by-side parking-lot spaces but at the Slide Hole area there are 39 nice back-in sites, some side-by-side parking lot style but others separated by vegetation. There are also 9 tent sites. Some of the RV sites are as long as 40 feet. Picnic tables and fire pits are at the sites and there are vault toilets near all of the campsites. There are also 26 nice back-in sites for RVs and tents at Halibut which is near the beach and away from the river. Some of these will also take 40 foot RVs. Many of the sites in the other areas are also modern large sites and can take larger RVs. Water pumps are available at Slide Hole and at Halibut. Stays are limited to 15 days.

The access road to the campground, the Old Sterling Highway, goes west from to-day's Sterling Highway in the town of Anchor Point near Mile 157. Drive down the hill and across a bridge for .3 miles (.5 km). Note that the clearance height on the bridge is a little over 13 feet so be aware of your height. Take the first right after the bridge onto Beach Road, you will immediately start seeing the campground entrance roads on your right. Slide Hole is the third one and Halibut is at the beach beyond Kyllonen RV Park, discussed below.

KYLLONEN RV PARK

Address:	PO Box 805, Anchor Point, AK 99556
Telephone:	(907) 235-7762 or (888) 848-2589
Email:	kyllonenrvpark@gmail.com
Website:	www.kyllonensrvpark.com

GPS Location: 59.77115 N, 151.86001 W, Near Sea Level

Right in the middle of the state campgrounds near the mouth of the Anchor River is a commercial one. Kyllonen has 27 back-in or pull-in sites to 45 feet, all with full hookups with 20 and 30-amp outlets. Maneuvering room is tight for big RVs. Sites are partially separated and there are flush toilets, coin-op showers, and a laundry. Wi-Fi reaches the sites near the office. There are picnic tables, fire pits, and free firewood is available. There's also espresso and a gift shop.

From Mile 157 of the Sterling Highway follow the old Sterling Highway west down the hill and across the bridge. Note that the clearance height here is a little over 13 feet so exercise caution. Turn right onto Beach Access Road at .3 miles (.5 km), you'll find Kyllonen on your right at 1.2 miles (1.9 km).

BAYCREST RV PARK

Address:	3375 Sterling Highway, Homer Alaska, 99603
Telephone:	(907) 226-2886
Email:	baycrestrvpark@gmail.com
Website:	www.baycrestrvpark.com

GPS Location: 59.65724 N, 151.64058 W, 700 Ft.

The Baycrest undoubtedly has the most spectacular view of any campground in Alaska. RVs park at the lip of a bluff that must be 500 feet high overlooking the mouth of Kachemak Bay and the mountains on the far side.

There are 45 back-in (or pull-in) sites here with picnic tables and lots of maneuvering room. Most are suitable for any size RV. Some have picnic tables and designated areas for campfires. There is a laundry and restrooms with flush toilets and coin-op showers. Out front is a Shell station with propane sales and a burger restaurant. You check in at the Shell station.

The campground is at the top of the long hill that descends into Homer near Mile 169 of the Sterling Highway, watch for the Shell station.

HOMER
Population 5,100, Elevation near sea level

Alaskans often think of Homer as something of an art colony. A combination of a beautiful setting, mild weather, and an isolated end-of-the-road location have combined to make Homer an attractive place to live. The largest part of the economy here, however, is tied to fishing. It's an interesting mix.

Homer spreads over a pretty large area. The central business district occupies a location overlooking Kachemak Bay. Here you'll find the schools, many stores, restaurants, and some RV parks. A 1.5 mile (2.4 km) road runs from town, along Beluga Lake, past many roadside service establishments, to the base of the Spit. Four and one-half miles out on the Spit is another center, this one with a small boat harbor, fish-packing plants, and lots of tourist facilities. The windswept Spit is the scene of lots of action during the summer with hundreds of RVs camped here and there, fishing charter boats heading out to catch halibut, and ferries crossing to the far side of the bay. The **Visitor Center** (201 Sterling Hwy, Homer, AK 99603; 907 235-7740) is located on the Homer Bypass.

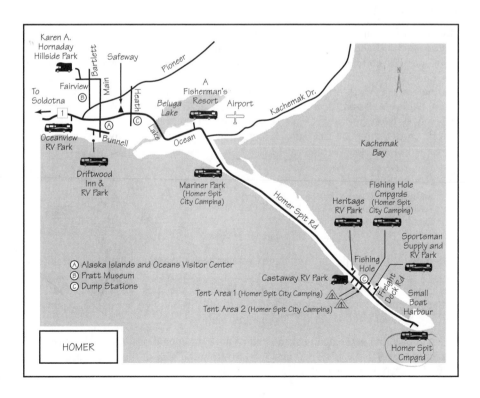

Homer is one of the best places in the state to take a trip out to catch a **halibut**. The limit is two fish, usually these are "chicken" halibut weighing less than 20 pounds, but halibut over 100 pounds are often caught. It's easy to set up a charter at one of the offices on the Spit or at the reception desk of your RV park. There's a halibut derby from May 1 to September 15.

The **Pratt Museum** (3779 Bartlett St., 907 235-8635) has a wide range of exhibits focusing on the natural and cultural history of the Kenai Peninsula. Several remote cameras are monitored here including one on Gull Island and another showing bears on the Alaska Peninsula. In addition, the Pratt is also an art museum.

Homer is home to the headquarters for the **Alaska Maritime National Wildlife Refuge.** There's a great facility, finished in late 2003, the **Alaska Islands and Ocean Visitor Center.** Located overlooking the bay near the western entrance to Homer it's actually a joint facility which includes information about the **Kachemak Bay Research Reserve**. Interactive exhibits cover the huge refuge which includes rugged islands all along the Alaska coast all the way from the tip of the panhandle near Ketchikan to Barrow. The visitor center has displays and programs including guided bird and beach walks. Naturalists from the facility also are on board the state ferry to Seldovia, Kodiak and down the Alaska Peninsula.

An early season event in Homer that is becoming more and more popular is the **Kachemak Bay Shorebird Festival**, in early May. That's when thousands of migrating shorebirds arrive at the flats around Kachemak Bay for a brief stop before heading farther north.

Kachemak Bay and the islands and fjords on the south side across from Homer are a huge attraction. The **Kachemak Bay State Park** covers 350,000 acres with islands, bays, glaciers, and lots of outdoor attractions, see Chapter 14 - *Camping Away From the Road System* for more information. **Gull Island** is home to large numbers of marine birds, a small ferry that runs over to **Halibut Cove** is an excellent way to see them. **Seldovia**, a small town of 300 people, makes a great place to visit if you want to get away from the crowds. The Alaska State Ferry serves Seldovia but most people travel across the bay on smaller commercial passenger ferries or by airplane.

Homer Campgrounds

HOMER SPIT CAMPGROUND

Address:	PO Box 1196, Homer, AK 99603
Telephone:	(907) 235-8206
Email:	pchapple@gci.net

GPS Location: 59.60057 N, 151.41692 W, Near Sea Level

The Homer Spit Campground occupies a waterfront site at the end of the Homer Spit. There are some 120 spaces at this campground, most with 30-amp electrical hookups. There are no-hookup sites along the beach. Some sites will take 40-foot RVs with some careful maneuvering. Flush toilets and pay showers are available, there is a gift shop, a laundry, water fill, and a dump station.

The campground is located near the end of the Homer Spit past the fishing hole and the Salty Dog Saloon. It's 3.9 miles (6.3 km) from the base of the Spit. Watch for the sign, the campground is on the right.

▣ SPORTSMAN SUPPLY AND RV PARK

Address: 1114 Freight Dock Rd., Homer, AK 99603
Telephone: (907) 235-2617 (Summer),
(907) 262-9749 (Winter)

GPS Location: 59.60696 N, 151.43300 W, Near Sea Level

This is a small full-service RV park on the Spit. There's also a tackle shop. The RV park has 10 large back-in spaces with full hookups including 30-amp power. There are picnic tables, restrooms with pay showers and a laundry room. The showers and laundry rooms are also popular with folks camped in other locations on the spit.

The campground fronts on Freight Dock Road. This road goes east off the main Spit road about 3.0 miles (4.8 km) from the base of the Spit, after turning you will see the campground on your left almost immediately.

▣ CASTAWAY RV PARK

Location: Homer Spit, 2.9 Miles From The Base

GPS Location: 59.60970 N, 151.44139 W, Near Sea Level

This is a small campground on the west beach of the spit. There are about 10 back-in sites on gravel (of course) with electrical outlets. RVs to about 35 feet will fit. There are some fire pits and some picnic tables. The city restrooms with flush toilets are across the street and about .2 mile (.3 km) to the south. The campground is 2.9 miles (4.7 km) from the base of the spit, it's on the right.

▣ HOMER SPIT CITY CAMPING ✕

Location: Several Of The Spit Parking Areas And Beaches
Telephone: (907) 235-1583
Website: www.cityofhomer-ak.gov/recreation/campgrounds

GPS Location: Various, See below

The City of Homer lets RVers (any size RV) and tent campers dry camp in several places on the Spit. Watch for signs designating camping and no-camping areas. A fee is charged, the registration office is located on the west side of the highway opposite the fishing hole, that's 3 miles (4.8 km) from the base of the Spit. There's another pay station right next to the fishing hole, as well as a dump station and handicap-accessible restrooms. Several of the private campgrounds on the Spit will provide showers for a fee. Wi-Fi is available over much of the spit too, also for a fee. There's a 14-day limit. The locations of the main city camping areas are as follows:

Mariner Park (*GPS 59.63183 N, 151.49469 W*) This camping spot is near the base of the spit, at about .5 miles (.8 km), on the right. Many parking locations are along the beach looking west. Some spaces have picnic tables and rock fire rings. Portable toilets are provided. The area is suitable for any size RV and also for tenters.

Tent Area 1 (GPS 59.60961 N, 151.441114 W) Looking west (on the right heading out onto the Spit) this is a campground for tents and RVs to 20 feet in length. Some spaces have picnic tables and rock fire rings. It's 2.7 miles (4.4 km) from the base of the Spit.

A SCENIC CAMPING LOCATION ON THE HOMER SPIT

Fishing Hole (*GPS 59.60792 N, 151.43649 W*) This camping area is just past the fishing hole and on the left. It's 3.0 miles (5 km) from the base of the spit. Turn at the dump station. Many sites look out over the water to the east of the Spit. Many sites have picnic tables and rock fire rings and there's a fish cleaning station here too.

Tent Area 2 (*GPS 59.60873 N, 151.44037 W*) This camping area is opposite the fishing hole and on the right. It's 2.9 miles (4.8 km) from the base of the spit, on the right. There are some picnic tables and rock fire rings. It's a beach-front area designated for tents and vehicles up to 20 feet.

HERITAGE RV PARK

Address:	3550 Homer Spit Road, Homer, AK 99603
Telephone:	(907) 226-4500 or (800) 380-7787
Email:	heritagervpark@alaska.net
Website:	www.alaskaheritagervpark.com

GPS Location: 59.61129 N, 151.44338 W, Near Sea Level

This upscale campground on the Homer Spit has some of the nicest facilities we've seen in any campground, it also has one of the highest prices.

The campground has 107 back-in or pull-thru sites to 50 feet. Each site has 20, 30 and 50-amp power, water, sewer, satellite TV, instant-on telephone, modem hookups, and Wi-Fi reaches the sites. Some sites are on the beach which is on the east side of the Spit looking up the bay or overlook the fishing hole which is right next door. Campfires are allowed on the beach in front of the beach sites but not in the park.

There are also nice restrooms, laundry, gift shop and coffee shop. All sites have the same price, about $70 when we last visited.

The campground is located east of the Spit road at about 3 miles (4.8 km) from the base of the spit. You can't miss it.

A FISHERMAN'S RESORT

Address:	1302 Ocean Dr, Homer, AK 99603
Telephone:	(907) 235-1997
Email:	afishermansresort@gmail.com
Website:	www.afishermansresort.com

GPS Location: 59.63921 N, 151.51026 W, 100 Ft.

This is a small RV camping area located away from all the other RV parks in town. It's between the downtown area and the Spit, near the south shore of Beluga Lake.

There are six large back-in sites here. They have full hookup and picnic tables in a sloping site that is terraced to provide flat sites. The RV park sits behind a small lodge that fronts on Ocean Drive.

From central Homer follow the road toward the Spit. You'll cross the causeway at the foot of Beluga Lake and climb the far shore. The road makes a 90-degree left turn and you'll see A Fisherman's Resort on the left in .2 mile (.4 km).

KAREN A. HORNADAY HILLSIDE PARK

Location:	629 Fairview Avenue, Homer, AK
Telephone:	(907) 235-1583
Website:	www.cityofhomer-ak.gov/recreation/campgrounds

GPS Location: 59.65174 N, 151.55427 W, 400 Ft.

The City of Homer operates a campground that is located uphill from the central business area. The Karen A. Hornaday Hillside Park has 31 separated sites set in alders. These are back-in sites and most are pretty small although there are a couple large enough for RVs to 35 feet in an open area near the entrance. Otherwise the campground is best for RVs to 30 feet because maneuvering room is limited. Sites have picnic tables and fire pits. The restrooms in the campground are new vault-style types with handicap access, and there are flush toilets at the ballpark below the campground. The stay limit here is 14 days.

To reach this campground drive north on Bartlett from Pioneer Avenue in central Homer for .3 mile (.5 km). Turn left on Fairview and then right in another .1 mile (.2 km) on Campground Road. The route is fairly well signed.

DRIFTWOOD INN & RV PARK

Address:	135 West Bunnell Ave., Homer, AK 99603
Telephone:	(907) 235-8019
Email:	driftwoodinn@alaska.com
Website:	www.thedriftwoodinn.com

GPS Location: 59.63973 N, 151.54528 W, Near Sea Level

The Driftwood Inn is a hotel with a small RV park that is conveniently located near central Homer. It overlooks the beach which is a good place to walk and, like much of Homer, has a spectacular view of mountains and water. The campground has 19 sites. One is a pull-thru of about 50 feet, the others are back-in or drive-in spaces to 35 feet with electricity (30 amps), water, sewer and TV hookups. There are also tent spaces on grass. The inn has restrooms with showers and a laundry. Prices vary by month and are highest in July, slightly less in June and August, and as shown by the icon above for the rest of the year. The campground is open all year long.

Easiest access is from the Homer Bypass. Turn south on Main Street and then west on Bunnell to the campground entrance.

OCEANVIEW RV PARK

Address:	Mile 172.7 Sterling Hwy., (PO Box 891), Homer, AK 99603
Telephone:	(907) 235-3951
Email:	camp4fun@gci.net
Website:	www.oceanview-RV.com

GPS Location: 59.64174 N, 151.55326 W, 100 Ft.

The first campground you will see when you enter Homer (on the right) is the Ocean-view. This is a large and well organized campground, an excellent place to stay since it has convenient access to downtown, direct access to a good walking beach, and beautiful views of the water and mountains on the far side of Kachemak Bay.

The Oceanview has about 100 spaces. Most are full hookup back-ins or pull-thrus to 45 feet with 30 or 50-amp power and TV hookups. Tent sites are available. The campground has flush toilets and showers as well as a gift shop and laundry. They will help you arrange fishing charters or tours at the office.

KENAI PENINSULA DUMP STATIONS

Because the Kenai Peninsula is such a popular RVing destination it has a better se-lection of dump stations than anywhere else in the state. Many of the campgrounds described in this chapter have their own dump stations, even some of the government campgrounds. Here are some other possibilities.

In **Girdwood** there is a dump station with water at the Tesoro station on the corner of the Seward Highway and the Alyeska Highway near Mile 90 of the Seward Highway (*GPS Location 60.94047 N, 149.17019 W*).

In Whittier there is a dump station with potable water at the municipal garage. There's a $2 charge. *(GPS Location 60.77439 N, 148.68436 W).*

Seward has a nice modern city dump station with potable water and easy access. It is located across the street and just north of the new restrooms and hookup sites of the city waterfront camping area on Ballaine Boulevard (*GPS Location 60.11079 N, 149.43790 W*).

Near the **Quartz Creek Campground** on Kenai Lake, near Mile 95 of the Sterling Highway (*GPS Location 60.48065 N, 149.72841 W*), there's a dump station with water. It's outside the campground and easy to access since it's only a quarter-mile off the main highway. There is a $8 fee.

On Skilak Road in the **Kenai National Wildlife Refuge** there is a first-class dump station at Mile 11.5 about half way between Upper and Lower Skilak Campgrounds (*GPS Location 60.46967 N, 150.39603 W*). Use is free but the water provided is marked as non- potable. It's hard to imagine anyone but users of one of the local campgrounds using it since the Skilak Road is gravel and often very rough. There's also one at Hidden Lake campground (*GPS Location 60.46463 N, 150.20114 W*), also free.

Soldotna has several dump stations to take care of all of you salmon fishing fanatics, here are two of them. The Tesoro 2 Go at 44279 Sterling Highway (*GPS Location 60.48359 N, 151.06509 W*) has a dump station. There's a dump station in the parking lot of the Fred Meyer at 43843 Sterling Highway (*GPS Location 60.48838 N, 151.05019 W*).

In **Kenai** the Tesoro at the junction of Willow and the Kenai Spur Highway (*GPS Location 60.55526 N, 151.2507 W*) has a dump station. So does the Holiday at the junction of the Kenai Spur Highway and the Kenai Bridge Access Road (*GPS Location 60.55736 N, 151.23973 W*).

Lots of people frequent the salmon streams near **Ninilchik**. There's a state-operated dump station near the Ninilchik View State Campground at Mile 135.4 (*GPS Location 60.04642 N, 151.66851 W*) to serve them. The fee is $5.

Finally, in **Homer** the city has a dump station located next to the Homer Bypass near the junction with Lake Street (*GPS Location 59.64241 N, 151.52935 W*) where traffic heading for the Spit turns right to head across the Beluga Lake dam. There's also a city dump station on the Spit, it's on the left about 3 miles (4.8 km) from the base of the Spit just past the fishing hole and next to the city restrooms (*GPS Location 59.60792 N, 151.43649 W*). Both of these municipal stations have water and a $2 fee.

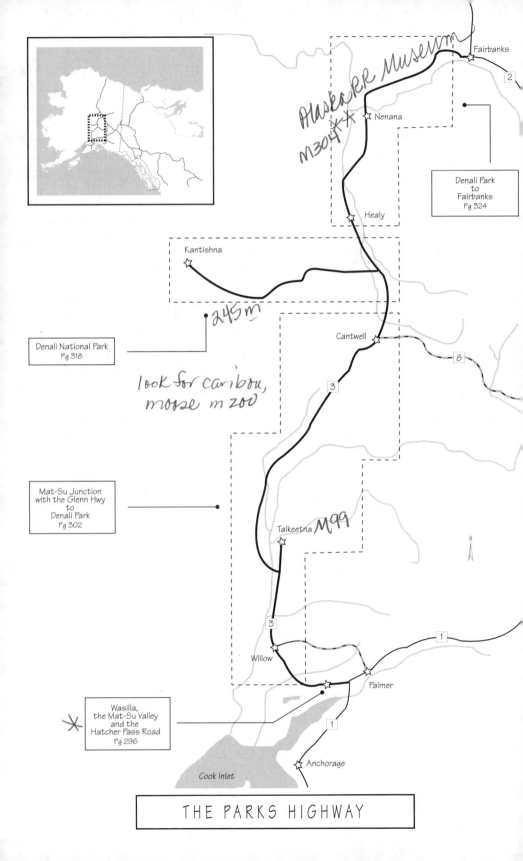

Fairbanks

2

Alaska RR Museum
M304✶✶ Nenana

Denali Park
to
Fairbanks
Pg 324

Healy

Kantishna

245m

Denali National Park
Pg 318

Cantwell

8

3

look for caribou,
moose m 200

Mat-Su Junction
with the Glenn Hwy
to
Denali Park
Pg 302

Talkeetna *M99*

3

1

Willow

Palmer

1

Wasilla,
the Mat-Su Valley
and the
Hatcher Pass Road
Pg 296

Anchorage

Cook Inlet

THE PARKS HIGHWAY

Chapter 9

The Parks Highway

INTRODUCTION

The Parks Highway runs north from a junction on the Glenn Highway about 35 miles (56 km) from Anchorage to the interior city of Fairbanks. This is the state's newest major road. Until 1971 Fairbanks-bound travelers had to travel the Glenn north to Glennallen and then the Richardson through Delta Junction. The Alaska Railroad follows almost the same route as the Parks, but the railroad is seldom within sight of the road.

We'll cover the Parks Highway from south to north. This is convenient for folks who are based in Anchorage or who rent rigs there, probably the larger part of the people who will be using this book.

Highlights

Anchorage's northern suburb, **Wasilla**, is growing rapidly in the Mat-Su Valley. You'll find lots of recreation activities near what has become a weekend playground for many people. They include boating, hiking, fishing, and golf.

The **Hatcher Pass Road** runs for 49 miles (79 km) from near Wasilla through the Talkeetna Mountains to meet the Parks Highway near Willow. You can stop and visit **Independence Mine State Historical Park** or hike above the timber line. The center portion of this road, across Hatcher Pass, is only suitable for smaller RVs.

Denali State Park, not to be confused with Denali National Park, sits astride the Parks Highway south of the Alaska Range. There you'll find some state camp-

THE PARKS HIGHWAY

THE MOST POPULAR ACTIVITY AT DENALI IS A BUS RIDE INTO THE PARK

grounds, high-country hiking trails, and wonderful views of the south face of Mount McKinley.

The most-visited attraction along the Parks Highway must be **Denali National Park**. At Mile 237 the park road leads westward into the park. The most popular activity at Denali is a bus ride into the park interior to see the wildlife. Vehicle access is controlled but there are many vehicle and tent camping sites in the park and nearby.

Fishermen will find lots of action on the Parks Highway. **Many good fishing streams** cross under the highway between Mile 57 and Mile 97. They include the Little Susitna, Willow Creek, Little Willow Creek, the Kashwitna River, Sheep Creek, and Montana Creek. The heavy fishing in these creeks is primarily for salmon.

The village of **Talkeetna** is located on a spur road from Mile 99 of the Parks Highway. Talkeetna is the base for Mt. McKinley climbing expeditions. It also is the base for riverboat salmon fishing expeditions, one of the most popular charter fishing options in the state.

The Road and Fuel

Building the Parks Highway was no easy project. Work started in 1959 and it wasn't until 1971 that it was completed. One of the toughest sections was across permafrost along a long section south of Nenana, you'll be able to identify this section by the heaves and dips in the road. Another challenge, a different kind, was the section through the Nenana Canyon north of Denali Park. The rest of the highway, however, is probably the nicest you'll find in all of Alaska and the Yu-

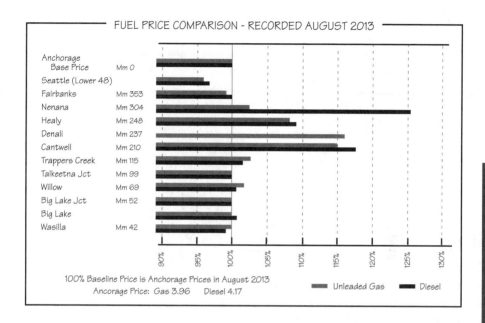

FUEL PRICE COMPARISON - RECORDED AUGUST 2013

Anchorage Base Price	Mm 0
Seattle (Lower 48)	
Fairbanks	Mm 353
Nenana	Mm 304
Healy	Mm 248
Denali	Mm 237
Cantwell	Mm 210
Trappers Creek	Mm 115
Talkeetna Jct	Mm 99
Willow	Mm 69
Big Lake Jct	Mm 52
Big Lake	
Wasilla	Mm 42

100% Baseline Price is Anchorage Prices in August 2013
Ancorage Price: Gas 3.96   Diesel 4.17

Unleaded Gas   Diesel

kon. It was engineered from the beginning for modern traffic and has wide shoulders.

From Anchorage to Fairbanks along a short section of the Glenn Highway and then the entire length of the Parks Highway is 358 miles (577 km), you can easily drive it in one day. It is easy to maintain a constant speed of 60 MPH along virtually the entire distance. Mile markers on the Parks run from south to north. The highway begins at an intersection in the Matanuska Valley 35 miles (56 km) from Anchorage. Mile markers start at 35 at this point.

Fishing

The Matanuska Valley is full of small lakes, many of them stocked. Once established at a campground in the area you might want to check out **Finger Lake**, the **Kepler-Bradley Lakes State Recreation Area, Meirs Lake, Matanuska Lake, Seymour Lake, Nancy Lake**, or **South Rolly Lake** and the other lakes in the **Nancy Lake Recreation Area**. You'll notice that many of the campgrounds in the Mat-Su are near fishing lakes. Fishing in these lakes is best in the spring or fall. A boat is very helpful.

From Mile 57 at the Little Susitna River to Mile 97 at Montana Creek the highway crosses many small rivers flowing into Cook Inlet or the Susitna River that offer outstanding salmon fishing, much of it can be done from the bank without a boat. As in all salmon fishing timing is important. Kings (Chinook Salmon) peak in June, reds (Sockeye Salmon) peak in July, pinks (Pink Salmon) peak in the last half of July, and the first weeks of August are best for silvers (Coho Salmon). Pinks in this watershed only run in significant numbers in even years (2012, 2014, etc.). Salmon runs can't always be accurately predicted, sometimes the fish are early or late (or don't show up). Since the salmon ascend the rivers from the ocean they reach fishing holes downstream before those that are upstream. Information about the status of the salmon runs in this area is easy to obtain, just ask at sporting goods stores, information offices, campgrounds, or even check the newspapers. Fishing regulations may change during the run based upon the quantity of fish in the streams so make sure you stay abreast of the current rules.

Here are some of the streams and locations in the area: **Little Susitna River** (Mile 57) for kings, reds, silvers, pinks, rainbows, Dollies; **Willow Creek Recreation Area** (Mile 71) for kings, silvers, pinks, rainbows, Dollies, and grayling; **Willow Creek** (Mile 71) for kings, silvers, pinks, rainbows, Dollies and grayling; **Little Willow Creek** (Mile 75) for king salmon, pinks, silvers, grayling and rainbows; **Kashwitna Lake** (Mile 76) for stocked rainbows; **Grey's Creek** (Mile 81) for kings, silvers, pinks, grayling, and rainbows; **Kashwitna River** (Mile 83) for king salmon, silver salmon, grayling and rainbows; **Caswell Creek** (Mile 84) walk in for kings, silvers, grayling and rainbows; **Sheep Creek mouth** (Mile 86) kings, silvers, pinks, grayling and rainbows; **Sheep Creek** (Mile 89) for kings, silvers, pinks, grayling and rainbows; **Montana Creek** (Mile 97) kings, silvers, pinks, grayling, and rainbows. Almost all of these fishing hot spots have a campground along the creeks or nearby.

The **Susitna River** is a braided glacial river that is a very popular jet boat river. The Susitna can be dangerous to those who do not know it. You need the right equipment and local knowledge for this river. Charter boat operators offer guided fishing trips on the Susitna from several places including Susitna Landing (Mile 82.5). From Talkeetna jet-boat tours let fishermen access the middle section of the Susitna above Talkeetna and also the **Talkeetna River**. Most fishing from Talkeetna and along the length of the Susitna is in the clear-water rivers that run into the silty Susitna and Talkeetna.

Farther north you might want to try the **Chulitna River** (Mile 133) for grayling, **Troublesome Creek** (Mile 137) for grayling, rainbows and salmon (king fishing not allowed), or **Byers Lake** at Mile 147 for lake trout.

Boating, Rafting, Canoeing, and Kayaking

Big Lake, located in the Mat-Su Valley is probably Anchorage's favorite water-sports destination. It's a large shallow lake that gets plenty warm enough for swimming. Several other nearby lakes are also popular but access isn't as easy for folks who do not have cabins and the lakes aren't as large.

The **Nancy Lake State Recreation Area**, accessible from Mile 67 of the Parks Highway via a 6.6-mile (10.6 km) paved road is a favorite canoeing area. There's a circular 16 mile (26 km) canoe trail through 14 lakes and a longer one than connects with the Little Susitna River. Lakes offer fishing and there are quite a few black bears and other wildlife in the area. The South Rolly Campground is near the starting point of the canoe trail and makes a good base, there are also designated back-country camping sites along the canoe trail.

The **Little Susitna River** also makes a good canoe route. It is 56 miles (90 km) from the Parks Highway bridge at Mile 57 to a take-out at the end of the Little Susitna Access Road off Knik Road. You can connect into the Nancy Lakes canoe trails using a portage 14 miles (23 km) below the Parks Highway put-in point. The Little Susitna

River is a very popular fishing river, there are so many power boats that caution is required and restrictions on their use have been initiated in the interests of safety.

The **Nenana River** runs right by the entrance to Denali National Park, floating this whitewater river in rafts has become extremely popular as more and more people visit the park. Operators are based near the park entrance and are easy to find. You can make arrangements at your campground if you are staying at one of the commercial ones outside the park. This is a good way to spend a day while waiting for a seat on a bus into the park.

Hiking and Mountain Biking

Hatcher Pass presents some of the best hiking opportunities north of Anchorage. The **Little Susitna Trail** climbs 8 miles (13 km) along the upper Little Susitna River to the foot of the Mint Glacier from about Mile 14 of the Fishhook-Willow Road. The **Reed Lakes Trail** climbs 4 miles (6 km) to Lower and Upper Reed Lakes with branches to the Snowbird Mine and Snowbird Glacier. This trail starts at Mile 2.4 of the Archangel Road which leaves the Fishhook-Willow Road at about Mile 14.5. From the **Independence Mine Historical Park** there are several short day hikes, the park is near Mile 17 of the Fishhook-Willow road. Mountain bikers will find the Fishhook-Willow Road to be a decent ride but automobile traffic can be a problem, particularly on weekends.

The Nancy Lake Recreation Area is known for its canoe trails but also has a good hiking trail. There is a 3 mile (5 km) **trail to Red Shirt Lake** with an 8-site tent-camping area at the lake. The trail runs along the tops of gravel ridges so it isn't as wet as most of the ground in the area. The trailhead is at the entrance of the South Rolly Lake Campground.

Denali State Park has several hiking possibilities. Most are on the mountain to the east of the highway, it's known as Kesugi Ridge. The **Kesugi Ridge Trail** (also sometimes called the Curry Ridge Trail) starts at the Upper Troublesome Creek Trailhead at Mile 138 of the Parks Highway. It climbs to the top of the ridge and runs 36 miles (58 km) north before descending to the Little Coal Creek Trailhead at Mile 164 of the Parks Highway. An intermediate access points is a 3.5 mile (5.6 km) trail from Byers Lake at Mile 147 of the Parks Highway. For shorter hikes you could do Troublesome Creek to Byers Lake (15 miles (24 km)) or Byers Lake to Little Coal Creek (27 miles (45 km)). A complicating factor is that during salmon season (middle of July to early September here) the Troublesome Creek portion of the trail is closed because there are too many bears for safety.

At **Byers Lake** there is also a pleasant trail around the lake, a distance of 4.1 miles (6.6 km). There's a walk-in tent campground on the east side of the lake, a distance of 1.8 miles (2.9 km) from the trailhead at Byers Lake Campground.

Also in Denali State Park is the **Lower Troublesome Creek Trail** leading from the road at the Lower Troublesome Creek Recreation Site (Mile 137, Parks Highway) to the Chulitna River, a distance of only half a mile.

Denali National Park really offers three kinds of hiking. First, there's climbs of Mt. McKinley, definitely outside the scope of this book. Second, there's hiking in the high country north of the Alaska Range near the access road, see Chapter 14 - *Camp-*

Short hikes near entrance

ing Away From the Road System for this. Finally, Denali National Park has several miles of trails near the park entrance. These are easy to access and do not require riding one of the park busses to reach them. The **Horseshoe Lake Trail** is .7 miles (1.1 km) long and starts near the railroad tracks about 1.2 miles (1.9 km) from the park entrance. **Mount Healy Overlook Trail** is 2.5 miles (4 km) long and starts at the Denali Park Hotel which is near the park entrance. The **Rock Creek Trail, Taiga Loop Trail**, and **Morino Loop Trail** are all trails in the entrance area connecting the Denali Park Hotel with nearby facilities. There's also a nice trail up the **Savage River** from the parking area on both sides of the bridge. This is as far as you can drive into the park without a special pass or a campground reservation, it's 15 miles (24 km) on the paved Park Road from the Parks Highway.

The 91 mile long (147 km) **Park Road** makes a wonderful mountain-bike ride. Vehicle traffic on the road is restricted largely to tour busses. A bicycle frees you to some degree from reliance on the busses for transportation yet you can use the special camper busses to transport your bicycle so you don't have to ride the whole road. In fact, it is wise to check with rangers about sections of the road that might be dangerous due to concentrations of bears, you can easily bypass these sections on a bus. Bicycles are not allowed off the road but campgrounds have bicycle racks where you can leave yours when you want to hike.

Wildlife Viewing

The **Nancy Lake Recreation Area**, particularly away from the roads on the canoe routes, is an excellent place to see loons (each lake has a pair), beaver, moose, and black bears.

Driving north on the Parks Highway you will pass through **Broad Pass** at about Mile 200. Watch for caribou, stop occasionally and glass the wide-open hillsides on each side of the road.

Denali National Park is definitely the easiest place to see wildlife in Alaska. Grab a window seat on one of the busses that go as far as Eielson Visitor Center, better yet, go all the way to Wonder Lake. No guarantees, but on an average trip you might see a moose or two, caribou, Dall sheep, and probably several grizzly bears. See the *Denali National Park* section of this chapter for more information.

THE ROUTES, TOWNS, AND CAMPGROUNDS

WASILLA, THE MAT-SU VALLEY, AND THE HATCHER PASS ROAD
Wasilla Population 7,800, Elevation 330 feet

The Matanuska-Susitna (Mat-Su) Valley is a huge mostly-flat area north of Anchorage. In the east (the Matanuska portion) the valley is oriented toward farming with Palmer the focal point of settlement (See Chapter 7 - *The Glenn Highway*). To the west is Wasilla which has grown rapidly since the Parks Highway was completed. Even farther west, in the Susitna Valley, there is less settlement with large areas west of the Parks highway and on the far side of the Susitna River having no road access at all.

The **Matanuska-Susitna Valley Visitor's Center** (907 746 5000) is located near the intersection of the Parks and Glenn Highways. Take the Trunk Road Exit at Mile 36 of the Parks Highway and then follow the frontage road north of the highway to the east for about .2 miles (.3 km). This is a good place to educate yourself about the valley's attractions and ask questions.

Wasilla is a spread out town. As real estate prices have increased in the Anchorage area many people have moved to the "Valley", and many of them are in or around Wasilla. There are large stores including Walmart, and Fred Meyer. All of these stores are strung along several miles of the Parks Highway east of the town center.

Wasilla does have a town center. It is located north of the Parks Highway at about Mile 42. The **Dorothy G. Page Museum** (907 373-9071) includes the **Old Wasilla Town Site Park** with historical buildings. Also interesting is the **Museum of Alaska Transportation and Industry** (907 376-1211) south of the Parks Highway near Mile 47. There's also a **farmers market** on Wednesdays in the afternoon and all day Saturday behind the Wasilla Library.

From Wasilla at Mile 42.2 of the Parks Highway you can drive south on the **Knik-Goose Bay Road** and then the **Point Mackenzie Road**, a distance of 30 miles (48 km) to the **Susitna Flats State Game Refuge**. There is a 40-site state campground there as well as a launch ramp for access to the Little Susitna River. Along the way you'll pass several camping locations (listed in this section) as well as the Iditarod

THE PARKS HIGHWAY

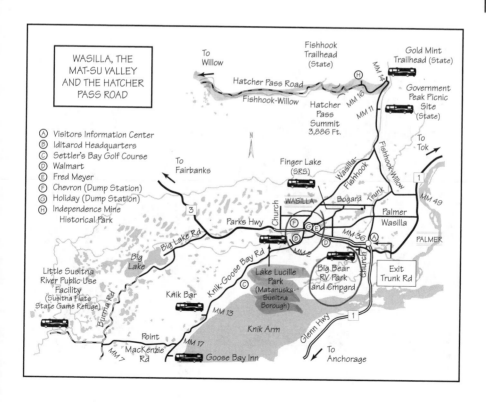

Sled Dog Race Headquarters (see below), **The Palmer Hay Flats State Game Refuge** at Mile 4, and the 18-hole **Settler's Bay Golf Course** at Mile 8 (907 376-5466).

Most visitors to Alaska are very familiar with the Iditarod Sled Dog Race. Held in March each year this 1,150 mile (1,856 km) race from Anchorage to Nome attracts entrants from all over the world. The Anchorage to Wasilla portion of the race is ceremonial, the race really starts in Wasilla. You'll find the **Iditarod Trail Sled Dog Race Headquarters** and visitor's center (907 376-5166) near Wasilla at about Mile 2 of the Knik Road. The Lake Lucille Campground is nearby.

From the intersection in Wasilla at Mile 42.2 of the Parks Highway you can drive north to reach the **Hatcher Pass Road** and **Independence Mine State Historical Park**. There is also access from Mile 49 of the Glenn Highway on the Fishhook-Willow Road. The road from the Glenn Highway and the road from Wasilla meet about 11 miles (18 km) north of Wasilla near Turner's Corner to form the Hatcher Pass Road which runs another 42 miles (68 km) to meet the Parks Highway at Mile 71 near Willow. The highway traverses the very scenic Talkeetna Mountains. At Mile 17 a side road leads to the **Independence Mine State Historical Park**. The park has old mining buildings and a visitors center, you can take guided tours of the buildings and there are hiking trails in the vicinity. Two miles past the park is Hatcher Pass Summit which has an elevation of 3,886 feet. There are two State of Alaska camping areas (one is really just a parking lot) along the Hatcher Pass Road in the section before it reaches Hatcher Pass State Historical Park. They are described in the *Wasilla*

WHAT FAMOUS POLITICIAN'S HOUSE IS THIS?

For us: Talkeetna - Willow - Wasilla - Kenai

and the *Mat-Su Valley Campgrounds* section immediately below. The section of the Hatcher Pass Road past the historical park is not suitable for large RVs.

Wasilla, the Mat-Su Valley, Hatcher Pass Road, and Knik-Goose Bay Road Campgrounds

BIG BEAR RV PARK

Address:	2010 S. Church St., Palmer, AK 99645
Telephone:	(907) 745-7445
Email:	bigbear@mtaonline.net
Website:	www.bigbearrv.net

GPS Location: 61.56137 N, 149.29307 W, 200 Ft.

This is a modern full-service big rig campground. The campground has 52 large RV sites and 7 small sites for tenters. There are full and partial hookup sites to 60 feet. Sites and roads are gravel, areas of grass separate them. Each has a picnic table. There's also a tent-camping area and some rental cabins. Other amenities include free showers, laundry, a dump site, and a gift shop. Firewood and propane are available.

To reach the campground take the Trunk Rd. exit off the Parks Hwy. near Mile 36. Go south and turn right on Fireweed which parallels the Parks Highway. In .8 mile (1.3 km) turn left on Church Rd. and you'll see the campground ahead on the right.

LAKE LUCILLE PARK (MATANUSKA-SUSITNA BOROUGH)

Location:	Mile 2 Knik-Goose Bay Road
Info:	(907) 745-4801

Area 2

GPS Location: 61.56822 N, 149.47982 W, 400 Ft.

This public campground near Lake Lucille's south shore is one of the best deals in the Matanuska Valley. The Iditarod Sled Dog Race Headquarters located along the entrance road may bring you near so take a quick look at the campground, you might decide to spend the night.

This basic campground is separated into two areas. Area #1 is a small loop near the entrance, area #2 is beyond. In area #1 there are 17 small sites (plus one long pull-thru) off a loop. Area #2 is 38 sites on a second loop nearby. Both areas have back-in public-campground-type sites set in natural vegetation with pretty good separation. There are picnic tables, fire pits, and vault toilets. Area #1 has small sites and old outhouses while area #2 (also called Bushnell Campground) has more modern vault toilets. Water is available in both areas. Area #1 has a hand pump, area #2 has a faucet that can be used to fill RVs. The sites in this campground are not really next to the lake which is just as well since this south side of Lake Lucille is very swampy and has plenty of mosquitoes at times. Fishing for land-locked silver salmon is possible in the lake and there are hiking trails.

If you follow Main Street (which becomes the Knik-Goose Bay Road) south from central Wasilla (near Mile 42 of the Parks Highway) you'll see the Iditarod Sled Dog Race Headquarters at about 2 miles (3 km) on the right. Just beyond turn right on Endeavor Street and drive .6 miles (1 km) to the park entrance.

THE PARKS HIGHWAY

GOVERNMENT PEAK PICNIC SITE (STATE OF ALASKA)

Location:	Mile 11 Hatcher Pass Road
Info:	(907) 345-3975
Website:	dnr.alaska.gov/parks/aspunits/matsu/govpeakcamp.htm

GPS Location: 61.74276 N, 149.23113 W, 1,500 Ft.

This small picnic site and campground is located right alongside the Hatcher Pass Road and Little Susitna River as they climb the valley toward the high country. The campground has 5 paved back-in RV or tent sites, some to 45 feet, and 3 picnic sites. Picnic tables and fire pits are provided. Tents can be pitched on grass. The restroom is a modern vault toilet.

GOLD MINT TRAILHEAD (STATE OF ALASKA)

Location:	Mile 14 Hatcher Pass Road
Info:	(907) 345-3975
Website:	dnr.alaska.gov/parks/aspunits/matsu/goldminttrl.htm

GPS Location: 61.77801 N, 149.19886 W, 1,800 Ft.

This campground is a very large paved lot for people heading up the Gold Mint Trail. In summer it's a popular hiking area, in winter a snow machine area. Overnight camping in vehicles is allowed, any size vehicle will fit. There are tables and fire pits and a modern vault toilet. Tent campers can pitch next to the tables and off the paved surface. Drinking water is available from a faucet. The campground is located at the sharp left turn just past the Mile 14 marker.

FINGER LAKE STATE RECREATION SITE (STATE OF ALASKA)

Location:	Off Bogard Road
Info:	(907) 746-4644 or (907) 345-3975
Res.:	(907) 746-4644 or www.lifetimeadventures.net
Website:	dnr.alaska.gov/parks/aspunits/matsu/fingerlksrs.htm

GPS Location: 61.61055 N, 149.26498 W, 400 Ft.

This state recreation site on Finger Lake is a popular fishing destination since the lake has rainbows, grayling, and silver salmon. There's a boat ramp at the campground.

There are 36 camping sites at this campground, most back-in wooded sites off two loops while the remainder are back-in slots in a gravel parking lot. All sites have picnic tables and fire pits and many are near the lake. Large RVs can find a place to park in both the lot and the sites in the trees, but maneuvering room is tight in some areas and some sites on the loops are short. There are vault toilets and limited water is available from a tank. This campground normally has a host and firewood is on sale. Stays are generally limited to fourteen days but are sometimes adjusted to seven days. Unlike most state campgrounds you can reserve a spot at this one.

The campground is located off Bogard Road, not exactly a major highway but still a fairly major arterial through the valley. You can reach the campground from many directions and via many routes. The one below is the most scenic. From about Mile 36 of the Parks Highway turn north on Trunk Road. Trunk meanders up past the University of Alaska's experimental farm, it intersects with the Palmer-Wasilla Highway after 3.1 miles (5 km). Drive straight across the intersection and continue to an intersection with Bogard Road after another 1.1 miles (1.8 km). Turn left on Bogard and you will see the campground entrance road on your left in another .8 miles (1.4 km).

🚐 KNIK BAR

Location: Near Mile 13 Knik-Goose Bay Road
Telephone: (907) 376-3818

     GPS Location: 61.46183 N, 149.72396 W, 100 Ft.

The Knik Bar overlooks Knik Lake. Across a parking lot on the lakeshore is a grassy area with scattered trees. Picnic tables are scattered around and tent camping is allowed on the grass. RVs are allowed to park next to the area in the parking lot so any size rig will fit. There is an electrical outlet that can be used. Other facilities include a portable toilet and the bar, which has Wi-Fi.

From near Mile 42.2 of the Parks Highway in Wasilla follow the Knik Goose Bay Road south for 13.3 miles (21.5 km). The bar is on the right.

🚐 GOOSE BAY INN

Location: Near Mile 18 Knik-Goose Bay Road
Telephone: (907) 376-5720
Email: info@goosebayinn.com

     GPS Location: 61.41251 N, 149.83003 W, 200 Ft.

The Goose Bay Inn is a local bar, restaurant, and liquor store. They have a grass lawn area next door that is a popular RV and tent camping area. Parking is on grass, there is room for about 10 rigs, but access for big rigs can be difficult if others are using the area. Amenities include picnic tables, a central fire area and a portable toilet, the restaurant/bar has Wi-Fi and pay showers and sauna.

From near Mile 42.2 of the Parks Highway in Wasilla follow the Knik-Goose Bay Road south for 18.4 miles (29.7 km). The bar is on the right.

🚐 LITTLE SUSITNA RIVER PUBLIC USE FACILITY (SUSITNA FLATS STATE GAME REFUGE)

Location: At Little Susitna River
Info: (907) 745-3975

     GPS Location: 61.43845 N, 150.16583 W, 100 Ft.

The Little Susitna River is a popular fishing destination. This facility offers a well-used boat ramp and camping area that allows easy access to the lower river.

The 40 campsites here are on the outer edges of two large parking lots, the center of the lots are occupied by parked boat trailers. Sites are all parking lot back-ins with no hookups, they can take large rigs. Picnic tables and fire pits are located behind the parking spaces, tenters pitch either on the gravel parking spaces or near the tables. There is a host and firewood can be purchased. Restrooms are vault toilets. There is fifteen day stay limit.

From near Mile 42.2 of the Parks Highway in Wasilla follow the Knik-Goose Bay Road south for 17.1 miles (27.6 km). Turn right on the paved Point Mackenzie Road and drive for 7.4 miles (11.9 km) to a T. The road now turns to gravel. Turn right and follow signs for 5.7 miles (9.2 km) to the campground.

THE PARKS HIGHWAY

Talkeetna

THE PARKS HIGHWAY

FROM THE MAT-SU JUNCTION WITH THE GLENN HIGHWAY TO DENALI PARK
202 Miles (326 Kilometers)

As you head west on the Parks Highway after leaving the Glenn Highway at Mile 35 you'll spot the exit for Trunk Road at Mile 36. If you exit here and then follow the frontage road on the north side of the highway back toward the east you'll soon come to the **Mat-Su Visitor's Center** (7744 East Visitors View Court, Palmer, AK 99645; 907 746-5000). If you are planning to spend any time in the valley you will probably find a quick visit quite useful.

Continuing westward, the highway soon enters the outskirts of Wasilla. At Mile 42 the Knik Road goes south. Follow it for 2 miles (3.2 km) and you'll see the **Iditarod Trail Sled Dog Race Headquarters** on the right.

After passing through Wasilla watch for the **Big Lake** road at Mile 52. This large lake and many smaller surrounding ones attract large numbers of visitors. Because they're shallow they get warm enough for swimming and water sports in the summer. Many people have cabins here, there are also two state campgrounds on the lake and another on a small lake nearby.

From Mile 57 to Mile 97 the Parks Highway crosses many **streams that are popular destinations for Alaskan fishermen**. These streams include: the Little Susitna at Mile 57, Lower Willow Creek at Mile 71, Little Willow Creek at Mile 75, the Kashwitna River at Mile 83, Caswell Creek at Mile 84, Sheep Creek at Mile 89, and Montana Creek at Mile 97. There are many camping areas along this stretch of road, expect them to be very full on weekends during the salmon runs.

At Mile 67 you'll find an access road to another popular lake area, the **Nancy Lake State Recreation Area**. Nancy Lake and many nearby lakes form a popular canoeing area complete with a 16 mile (26 km) canoe trail. There's also a large state campground here.

The small town of **Willow**, at one time an unsuccessful candidate to be Alaska's capital, appears at Mile 69. Almost in the middle of the somewhat spread-out area known as Willow, at Mile 71, is the junction for the gravel **Hatcher Pass Road**. This 42 mile (68 km) road climbs into a scenic mountainous region before dropping into the Matanuska Valley near Wasilla. It is not suitable for large vehicles in the middle section.

At Mile 99 a paved road leads north from the Parks Highway for 14 miles (23 km) to **Talkeetna**. Talkeetna is a friendly little country town that is accustomed to lots of visitors. There are two big reasons for this. Talkeetna serves as the base for air taxi operators specializing in flying Mt. McKinley climbers up to the Kahiltna Glacier. Most of this activity takes place during the early summer, the town is a beehive of activity during the climbing season. You can also book a sightseeing flight with one of these air-taxi operators.

Talkeetna also serves as the base for charter riverboats taking fishermen and sightseers up the Susitna, Chulitna, and Talkeetna Rivers. This is one of the most popular fishing charters in the state. Before driving in to Talkeetna you can stop and visit the **Talkeetna Visitor Center** located right at the junction with the Parks Highway.

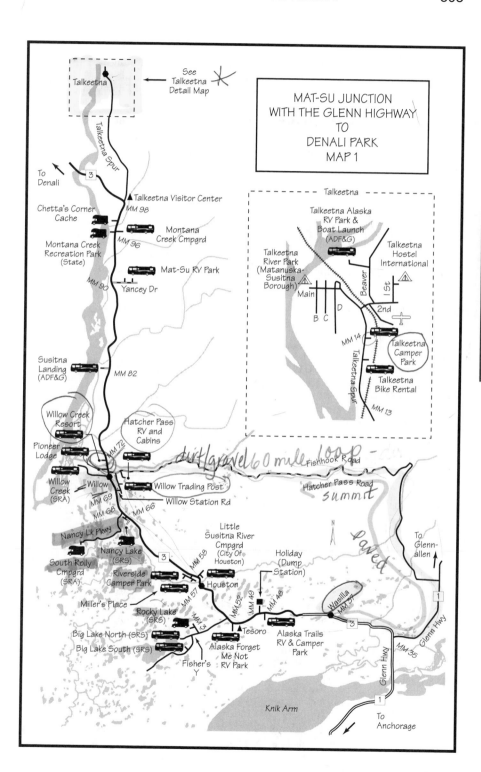

THE PARKS HIGHWAY

THE PARKS HIGHWAY

After passing the Talkeetna junction the highway curves west and crosses the Susitna River. Then it heads north again, up the Chulitna River and into high country at the foothills of the Alaska Range. You enter **Denali State Park** at Mile 133. It is largely undeveloped and offers great views of the Alaska Range. At Mile 135 there is an excellent viewpoint for looking at the south face of Mt. McKinley. Also visible are Mt. Foraker (17,400 ft.) and Mt. Hunter (14,573 ft.). There are trails along the ridges to the east of the highway, they are accessible at Troublesome Creek at Mile 137, Byers Lake at Mile 147, and at Little Coal Creek at Mile 164.

The highway soon enters **Broad Pass**. The name is accurate. You can often see caribou on the hillsides visible from the highway.

The junction with the **Denali Highway**, connecting with the Richardson Highway, is at Mile 210. The Denali Highway is unpaved but quite scenic. There are 113 miles (182 km) of gravel and 21 miles (34 km) of paved road before you reach Paxson on the Richardson Highway. Before the construction of the Parks Highway this was the access road for Denali National Park. See Chapter 6 for more about this highway.

After passing the junction with the Denali Highway the Parks enters a much narrower canyon, Nenana Canyon, and follows the Nenana River north to the Denali National Park access road at Mile 237.

Mat-Su Junction with the Glenn Highway to Denali Park Campgrounds

ALASKAN TRAILS RV AND CAMPER PARK

Address:	HC 34, Box 2095, Wasilla, AK 99654
Telephone:	(907) 376-5504
Email:	aktrails@mtaonline.net
Website:	www.aktrailsrvpark.com

GPS Location: 61.58123 N, 149.61690 W, 300 Ft.

The Alaska Trails is a relatively new and very large RV park. There are 121 full-hookup large sites in a gravel lot with no landscaping. About half are pull-thrus, there are sites to 60 feet. There is a large restroom building with coin-op showers and raised fire grills at some sites. They also sell propane.

The campground is on the south side of the Parks at Mile 48.2.

ALASKA FORGET ME NOT RV PARK

| Telephone: | (907) 892-3733 |

GPS Location: 61.57014 N, 149.71729 W, 250 Ft.

This is a small and very rustic campground located next to a small lake. There are 15 gravel sites with pull-thrus and back-ins to 35 feet set among trees and next to the reedy lakeshore. Restrooms are outhouses and there are no utilities. Cable spools serve as tables at some sites and there are a few fire pits. The campground is on the south side of the Parks at Mile 51.8.

ROCKY LAKE STATE RECREATION SITE (STATE OF ALASKA)

Location:	Near Mile 3 Of The Big Lake Road
Info:	(907) 317-9094
Website:	dnr.alaska.gov/parks/aspunits/matsu/rockylksrs.htm

GPS Location: 61.55771 N, 149.82233 W, 200 Ft.

Rocky Lake is a small but pleasant state campground, a good place to stop during the week when the area isn't full of Anchorage residents. The lake is stocked and offers small landlocked salmon and a few rainbows.

There are 11 sites, most are right next to the lake. These are back-in sites set in a grove of trees, the 1996 Big Lake forest fire didn't touch this immediate area. Sites are short, this campground is suitable for RVs to about 30 feet. The campground has picnic tables, fire pits, handicap accessible vault toilets, a hand-operated water pump, and a boat ramp. The camping limit here is 15 days.

To find the campground drive south on Big Lake Road from the intersection at about Mile 52 of the Parks Highway. Turn right on Beaver Lake Road at about 3 miles (5 km) and then left on Rocky Lake Road after another half-mile (.8 km), the campground entrance will be on your left.

BIG LAKE NORTH STATE RECREATION SITE (STATE OF ALASKA)

Location: End Of North Shore Drive Off Big Lake Road
Info: (907) 317-9094

GPS Location: 61.54498 N, 149.85471 W, 200 Ft.

Big Lake is a very popular summer and winter destination for Anchorage residents. The lake is large and shallow with many coves and islands, many cabins line the shore and even occupy some of the islands. The lake is plenty warm enough for swimming and is very popular with owners of recreational vehicles of all kinds, including those that float in the summer and snow machines in the winter.

If you don't own a cabin here then you can use two state recreation sites for access to the lake. The largest of the two is Big Lake North. Camping at Big Lake North means parking in a large paved lot, 32 of the sites in the lot are set aside for campers and some are as long as 40 feet. These offer a few picnic tables, a few fire pits, vault toilets, a paved boat ramp, a dock, a designated swimming area, a covered picnic area, and during the busy season a camp store. There is a walk-in area for tent campers with 8 sites, they have picnic tables and fire pits. The campground has a 7 day limit. There is also sometimes a host. Fishing in Big Lake is for rainbows, arctic char, and burbot.

To reach Big Lake North follow the Big Lake Road from Mile 52 of the Parks Highway. At 3.5 miles (5.6 km) you will come to a fork in the road known as Fisher's Y. Take the right fork (North Shore Drive) and in another 1.5 miles (2.4 km) you will come to the end of the road and the campground. The entire route is paved.

BIG LAKE SOUTH STATE RECREATION SITE (STATE OF ALASKA)

Location: Near Mile 5 Of The Big Lake Road
Info: (907) 317-9094

GPS Location: 61.53275 N, 149.83244 W, 200 Ft.

Big Lake South is much smaller than Big Lake North but offers much the same features. There is room for 23 RVs here in a gravel parking lot with sites to 40 feet. There are also 6 picnic/tent sites with tables and fire pits. This campground also has vault toilets, a dock, a boat ramp and a sandy beach area. Stays are limited to fifteen days unless otherwise posted.

To reach the campground just follow the Big Lake Road from about Mile 52 of the Parks Highway. Take the left fork at Fisher's Y at Mile 3.5. The campground is on the right in another 1.5 miles (2.4 km).

LITTLE SUSITNA RIVER CAMPGROUND (CITY OF HOUSTON)

Location: Mile 57 Of The Parks Highway
Telephone: (907) 892-6869 (City Hall)

GPS Location: 61.63035 N, 149.79885 W, 300 Ft.

This campground is a popular place when the salmon are running in the "Little Su". The river gets runs of kings, silvers, chums, reds, and pinks during May through August. The runs aren't totally predictable but you can tell when the fish are in, just watch for large numbers of fishermen. If there are no fish the campground will probably be almost deserted. This is also a put-in point for boating on the Little Susitna River.

The Little Susitna River Campground is much like other government campgrounds in Alaska. This one might be considered just a little more rustic, the location isn't very scenic. The river and fishing are the draw here, the campground sits in the middle of a stand of spruce trees. There are about 80 camping sites arranged off one large loop and 4 wagon wheel-type circles. Most sites are fairly short but a few will take RVs to 40 feet. Picnic tables and fire pits are provided, there are also vault toilets and a water house with hose for RV service. Other facilities include a playground, a covered picnic pavilion, and a dump station with potable water (fee is $5). The campground has a 10-day limit.

This campground is located north of the Parks Highway just west of the Little Susitna bridge at about Mile 57. There is also a large parking area and river access on the other side of the highway.

MILLER'S PLACE

Location: Mile 58 Of The Parks Highway
Telephone: (907) 892-6129

GPS Location: 61.62984 N, 149.81049 W, 200 Ft.

Behind Miller's Market near Mile 58 of the Parks is a basic RV park and boat launch where the river runs just south of the highway. It's an open lot next to the river, it is possible to get electricity here with a long cord. Showers and toilets are available at Miller's out front.

RIVERSIDE CAMPER PARK

Address: PO Box 940087, Houston, AK 99694
Telephone: (907) 892-9020
Email: aksalmon@mtaonline.net

GPS Location: 61.62975 N, 149.81296 W, 200 Ft.

Next to Miller's Place is a good alternative with full hookups. The Riverside offers a good selection of amenities and also access to the Little Susitna River.

The Riverside RV Park has 56 sites to 40 feet including a few pull-thrus arranged in an open field next to the Little Susitna River. Each site has 20 or 30-amp electricity, sewer, water and a picnic table. There are also several dry camp or tent sites on grass with fire pits. The campground offers restrooms with showers and a coin-op laundry. There is also a boat ramp, a covered picnic area, and an RV wash area.

The Riverside is on the south side of the Parks Highway near Mile 58. This is in the commercial center of the community of Houston.

⛺ NANCY LAKE STATE RECREATION SITE (STATE OF ALASKA)

Location:	Near Mile 67 Of The Parks Highway
Info:	(907) 745-3975
Website:	dnr.alaska.gov/parks/aspunits/matsu/nancylksrs.htm

GPS Location: 61.70212 N, 150.00544 W, 300 Ft.

This state campground has a pleasant location atop a small ridge next to Nancy Lake. It is close to the highway and often almost empty, a good place to spend the night. The lake has rainbows, Dollies, burbot, and northern pike.

The campground has 30 back-in sites arranged around three circles. These are decently-separated sites surrounded by natural vegetation and trees, they have picnic tables and fire pits and are suitable for RVs to about 30 feet. There is a host at this campground and firewood is available for purchase. Interior roads are gravel as are parking pads. The campground has vault toilets and a hand-operated water pump. There is also a boat ramp. Stays are limited to 15 days.

The campground is near Mile 66.7 of the Parks Hwy. on the south side of the highway. Turn south on a short access road to the old highway which parallels the new highway at this point. Turn left on the old highway (now called Buckingham Palace Road) and follow it for .2 miles (.3 km), the campground entrance is on the right.

⛺ SOUTH ROLLY CAMPGROUND (STATE OF ALASKA)

Location:	Nancy Lake Recreation Area, 6.6 Miles (10.6 Km)
	South From Mile 67 Of The Parks Highway
Info:	(907) 745-3975
Website:	dnr.alaska.gov/parks/aspunits/matsu/sorollylkcamp.htm

GPS Location: 61.66690 N, 150.14076 W, 200 Ft.

The Nancy Lakes Recreation Area is a huge area of popular lakes, most accessible only by canoe trail. The largest formal campground for vehicle campers in the recreation area is the South Rolly Lake Campground.

This is a large campground, there are about 100 sites, many overlooking the lake. The sites have the traditional picnic tables and fire pits. Interior roads and parking pads are gravel. These campsites are widely spaced and surrounded by trees, some are along the lake. Some will take large RVs to over 45 feet and there are some pull-thrus. The campground has a host so firewood is available for purchase, there are vault toilets and a hand-operated water pump. Canoes are sometimes available for rent and there is a boat launch (electric motors only). Stays are limited to 14 days.

This campground is located well off the highway. A paved road, 6.6 miles (10.6 km)

THE PARKS HIGHWAY

in length, provides access. The road leaves the Parks Highway at about Mile 67, the campground is at its end.

WILLOW TRADING POST

Address:	14345 N. Willow Station Rd., Willow, Alaska 99688
Telephone:	(907) 495-1695

GPS Location: 61.74748 N, 150.04001 W, 200 Ft.

The Willow Trading Post Lodge is located in Willow but off the main highway. Many people whiz by and don't even know it's there.

The lodge has 10 back-in spaces, 7 with electricity and water in a secluded area behind the main lodge. Sites will take RVs to 45 feet. There are restrooms, showers, a restaurant and a bar. The lodge also has a liquor store and gift shop.

To find the lodge turn east at Mile 69.5 of the Parks Highway. Turn left at .2 miles (.3 km) after crossing the RR tracks. The lodge will be on your right in another .2 miles (.3 km).

WILLOW CREEK STATE RECREATION AREA (STATE OF ALASKA)

Location:	At The End Of Access Road From Mile 71 Of Parks Highway
Info:	(907) 745-3975

GPS Location: 61.77441 N, 150.16147 W, 200 Ft.

The Willow Creek campground is another popular fishing destination. It offers access to the Susitna River at the mouth of Willow Creek. Willow Creek gets runs of kings, silvers, and pinks and also rainbows, Dollies, and grayling.

The campground is relatively new, it is one of the big parking-lot type with back-in parking for about 110 RVs, some to 45 feet. Picnic tables, fire pits, and vault toilets are provided. There is usually a host and firewood is available. Walking trails lead to the river and bank fishing. Rafters from upstream use this facility as a take-out point. Stays are limited to 7 days.

Access to this campground is via a wide paved 4 mile (6 km) road heading west from near Mile 71 of the Parks Highway.

HATCHER PASS RV AND CABINS

Address:	Mile 71 Parks Highway, ½ Mile Hatcher Pass Road, Willow, AK 99688
Telephone:	(907) 495-4955
Website:	www.hatcherpassrv.com

GPS Location: 61.76077 N, 150.04690 W, 200 Ft.

This is a 48-space RV park located off the Hatcher Pass Road near its intersection with the Parks Highway. Sites have 50 and 30-amp power, water and sewer and there is a dump and water-fill station. Their use is included in the camping price, otherwise the dump price is $10. There are no sanitary facilities, the campground is suitable only for self-contained units. Some sites have tables and there are fire rings. There are also four rental cabins.

To reach the campground head east on the Hatcher Pass Road from Mile 71 of the Parks Highway. In a half-mile you'll see a wide gravel road climbing to the right. Turn here, you'll pass the dump station and then turn left into the campground.

PIONEER LODGE

Address:	Mile 71.4 Parks Highway, Willow, AK 99688
Telephone:	(907(495-1000)
Email:	pioneerlodge@yahoo.com
Website:	www.pioneerlodge.webs.com

GPS Location: 61.76640 N, 150.06775 W, 200 Ft.

The old Pioneer Lodge was one of two campgrounds facing each other across Willow Creek. Willow Creek is one of the most popular and easily-accessible streams in the state for fishermen after kings, chums, pinks, and silvers. From early June until well into August you can expect this place to be hopping on weekends and active during the week. Unfortunately, the lodge burned down in 2009. It has been replaced by a small café, and the RV sites remain.

There are some 15 camping slots with 30-amp electric and water hookups, many along the banks of the river. RVs to 45 feet will fit in most of these sites. Many additional campsites are available for tents and self-contained RVs. There is a dump station although you must back into it. The fee is included in the overnight price, otherwise it's $10. Showers are available in the laundry building.

The campground is on the west side of the highway near Mile 71 of the Parks Highway. Just watch for the bridge over Willow Creek.

WILLOW CREEK RESORT

Address:	Mile 71.5 Parks Highway (PO Box 85), Willow, AK 99688
Telephone:	(907) 495-6343
Email:	theresacdean@yahoo.com
Website:	www.willowcreekresortalaska.com

GPS Location: 61.76806 N, 150.06832 W, 200 Ft.

This campground caters primarily to salmon fishermen. It is a modern camping area and modern lodge building with no bar or restaurant.

The campground has about 40 spaces with utility hookups. The 12 located right on the bank of the creek have electricity and water only, most of the remaining 27 are pull-thrus with 30-amp electricity, sewer, and water. There are also many dry sites extending down the river and also riverside cabins. There is plenty of maneuvering room for big RVs in the open gravel-surfaced lot and some sites are as long as 50 feet. There is also an easy-to-access dump station. The modern lodge building has restrooms, free showers, and a coin-op laundry. A small store in the lodge offers supplies and fishing tackle. Guided fishing trips and rental rafts are available or you can fish from the bank in front of the campground.

The Willow Creek Resort is located near Mile 71 of the Parks Highway, on the west side of the road and the north bank of Willow Creek.

⫶ SUSITNA LANDING (ADF&G)

Address:	14400 West Susitna Landing Road, Willow, AK 99688
Telephone:	(907) 495-7700
Email:	jbsbearcache@yahoo.com
Website:	www.susitnalanding.com

GPS Location: 61.91345 N, 150.09790 W, 200 Ft.

If you have a jet boat you probably know about Susitna Landing. If not you will probably enjoy watching the action as fishermen use this launch site at the mouth of the Kashwitna River on the Susitna River to embark and return from successful fishing trips.

The landing has 69 modern back-in vehicle camping sites off three loops. Nineteen sites have electricity, most of it is 50 amps. Sites extend to 50 feet. Sites have fire pits and there is a covered picnic area. Sanitary facilities are new handicapped-accessible vault toilets and a coin-op shower building. There's also the well-used boat ramp.

To reach Susitna Landing follow the good gravel road west 1 mile (1.6 km) from about Mile 82.5 of the Parks Highway.

⫶ MAT-SU RV PARK

Address:	Mile 90.8 Parks Highway (HC 89, Box 432), Willow, AK 99688
Telephone:	(907) 495-6300
Email:	matsurvpark@aol.com
Website:	www.matsurvpark.com

Location: 62.02609 N, 150.07083 W, 300 Ft.

This is an older campground that has been substantially upgraded. It has large sites and offers full hookups in a popular fishing region where they are sometimes difficult to find.

The campground has 46 sites. Sites are pull-thrus and back-ins to 70 feet. Most are full hookup sites. There are also tent sites. Parking is on gravel with some grass. One building houses the office, groceries and fishing tackle, restrooms, free showers, and a coin-op laundry. While not right next to a fishing stream they offer guided fishing charters.

To find the campground take the gravel road east from Mile 90.8 of the Parks Highway. The campground is the second driveway on the left.

⫶ CHETTA'S CORNER CACHE

Location:	Mile 97 Of The Parks Highway Next To Montana Creek

GPS Location: 62.10583 N, 150.06027 W, 400 Ft.

Montana Creek is one of the popular salmon fishing streams that cross the Parks Highway in this area. Montana Creek actually has three different campgrounds occupying quadrants formed by the crossing of the highway and the stream. Bank fishing for salmon is extremely popular on this river and this and the other nearby campgrounds are very crowded when the fish are running and practically empty when they are not.

Located on the north bank of the river on the west side of the highway is a very basic campground called Chetta's Corner Cache with about 60 smaller back-in sites suitable for tents and RVs to 30 feet and surrounded by natural vegetation. Some sites have picnic tables, there are fire rings, and vault toilets.

MONTANA CREEK CAMPGROUND

Location:	Mile 96.5 Of The Parks Hwy. Next To Montana Creek
Telephone:	(907) 733-8225, (907) 733-5267 or (877) 475-CAMP
Email:	mccreservations@mtaonline.net
Website:	www.montanacreekcampground.com/contact.html

GPS Location: 62.10334 N, 150.05946 W, 300 Ft.

The most sophisticated of the Montana Creek campgrounds is this one. It is the only one with electrical hookups. It is located on the south bank on the east side of the highway.

There are two types of campsites here. Toward the highway are a number of open back-in sites suitable for large RVs and surrounded by clipped grass. Eighteen of these have 50-amp and 30-amp electrical outlets. Farther back from the road are many smaller well-separated back-in campsites surrounded by natural vegetation. Most of the sites at this campground have picnic tables and fire pits. There is no dump station here but water is available. Portable toilets are provided and there is also a small store out front selling fishing tackle.

MONTANA CREEK RECREATION PARK (STATE OF ALASKA)

Location:	Mile 97 Of The Parks Highway Next To Montana Creek
Telephone:	(907) 345-5764
Website:	dnr.alaska.gov/parks/aspunits/matsu/montcksrs.htm

GPS Location: 62.10278 N, 150.06254 W, 300 Ft.

On the south side of Montana Creek on the west side of the highway is the Montana Creek Recreation Park. It is actually managed by the same folks who operate the campground located across the highway. This campground is a big gravel parking lot where camping is allowed with some picnic tables and fire pits. The 35 sites are back-ins for RVs to 35 feet and there are also some tent pads. There are vault toilets and a hand-operated water pump.

TALKEETNA CAMPER PARK

Address:	Box 221, Talkeetna, AK 99676
Telephone:	(907) 733-2693
Email:	talkeetnacamper@hotmail.com
Website:	www.talkeetnacamper.com

GPS Location: 62.31775 N, 150.10413 W, 400 Ft.

Talkeetna has a full-service RV park. It's located just outside the town along the main entrance road, it's very convenient.

There are 35 sites. Some are full hookup, others offer just electricity and water. Power is 50 or 30 amp. Parking is on gravel. Sites come in a variety of sizes but some are pull-thrus large enough for RVs to 40 feet. Restrooms have flush toilets and coin-op showers and there is a laundry and a dump station. Wi-Fi is only useable near the office. Day parking is available for RVs, it's easy to walk the half-mile into town.

You can't miss the campground, it's on the right just before you enter Talkeetna at Mile 13.7 of the Talkeetna Spur Road.

🚲 TALKEETNA BIKE RENTAL

Location: Mile 13.6 of the Talkeetna Spur Road

GPS Location: 62.31587 N, 150.10437 W, 400 Ft.

Talkeetna Bike Rentals has a big gravel lot. RVs can overnight with no hookups for a fee. The only facilities provided are portable toilets. The facility is on the right just before you reach Talkeetna, it's slightly farther out than the Talkeetna Camper Park described above.

🚐 TALKEETNA ALASKA RV PARK AND BOAT LAUNCH (ADF&G)

Address: PO Box 473, Talkeetna, AK 99676
Telephone: (907) 733-2604
Email: riveradv@alaska.net

GPS Location: 62.32553 N, 150.10799 W, 400 Ft.

North of Talkeetna at the boat launch for the Talkeetna River there is a large area operated as a campground by a subcontractor for the Alaska Department of Fish and Game.

There are about 50 camping sites arranged in a wooded area with gravel interior roads. There are no hook-ups but campsites have picnic tables and fire rings and

TALKEETNA IS A FRIENDLY LITTLE COUNTRY TOWN ACCUSTOMED TO LOTS OF VISITORS

THE PARKS HIGHWAY

there are vault toilets. Many also have rain shelters over the picnic tables. At the entrance gate is a small store and tackle shop which offers showers. Next door is the Swiss-Alaska Inn which has a restaurant and there is a short trail leading to central Talkeetna.

As you enter Talkeetna watch for signs marking a road to the right leading to the airport. Take this road, cross the railroad tracks, and turn left just on the far side of the tracks. Drive .7 mile (1.1 km), the campground entrance will be on your left.

TALKEETNA RIVER PARK (MATANUSKA-SUSITNA BOROUGH)

Location:	Just South Of Central Talkeetna
Telephone:	(907) 745-9690
Website:	www.matsugov.us/des/639-talkeetna-river-park

GPS Location: 62.32304 N, 150.11777 W, 400 Ft.

If you drive right through downtown Talkeetna on Main Street you'll spot this little city campground at the far side. There are 11 sites for tents only. There are picnic tables, vault toilets, fire rings, raised grills, and a food storage locker. Although there is a host it is not really possible to control access to this campground since the sites actually front on city streets.

TALKEETNA HOSTEL INTERNATIONAL

Address:	PO Box 361, Talkeetna, AK 99676
Telephone:	(907) 733-4678
Email:	talkeetnahostel@gmail.com
Website:	www.talkeetnahostel.com

GPS Location: 62.32464 N, 150.09693 W, 400 Ft.

As you might expect, Talkeetna has a hostel. There are tent sites here as well as rooms, a cabin, and even an old Volkswagen camper that's used as a small cabin. No other RV camping though.

There is room to pitch about ten tents on a grassy lawn. Picnic tables, hammocks, and a fire pit are provided. Other amenities include flush toilets and showers, Wi-Fi, a kitchen, and a lounge area.

As you enter Talkeetna watch for signs marking a road to the right leading to the airport. Take this road, cross the railroad tracks, and turn right on second street on the far side of the tracks. Proceed for two blocks to I Street, turn left, and the hostel is the third home on the right. The route is well signed.

HIS & HERS LAKEVIEW CAMPER PARK

Address:	HC 89 Box 616, Willow, AK 99688
Telephone:	(907) 733-2415
Email:	lakeview@mtaonline.net

GPS Location: 62.13998 N, 150.05586 W, 400 Ft.

The H & H is a traditional-style roadhouse offering gas, a restaurant, rooms and an RV park out back along the shores of a pleasant little lake.

The campground has 10 pull-thru sites with 30-amp electricity on a gravel surface with plenty of room to maneuver big RVs. There is also lots of room for dry campers and a tent-camping area. There is a wash house with coin-op showers and laundry.

Use of a dump station and water fill-up are available for an extra charge.

The H & H is located near Mile 100 of the Parks Highway.

🚐 TRAPPER CREEK INN AND RV PARK

Address: PO Box 13209, Trapper Creek, AK 99683
Telephone: (907) 733-2302 or (907) 440-4444
Email: reservations@trappercreekinn.com
Website: www.trappercrkinn.com

GPS Location: 62.31444 N, 150.23181 W, 400 Ft.

The Trapper Creek Inn is a roadhouse-style facility. Watch for the Tesoro station with the red-roofed building. They offer gas, groceries, gifts, rooms, a delicatessen, a laundry, a cash machine and an RV campground. There's even an airstrip out back. It's a nice campground, and the price is decent.

The campground here has 32 spaces. Nine are long full-hookup pull-thrus with 50-amp power. The rest are back-ins, some with full hookups, some with no utilities. There is a covered gazebo at the center of the campground and the sites are separated by trees and natural vegetation. The inn offers showers and a laundry. There's also a dump station with an extra fee for its use.

The Trapper Creek Inn is located in Trapper Creek at about Mile 115 of the Parks Highway.

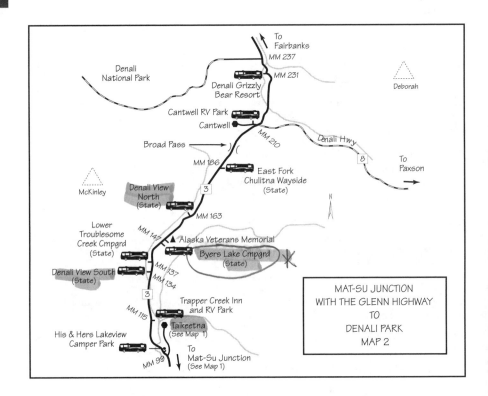

MAT-SU JUNCTION
WITH THE GLENN HIGHWAY
TO
DENALI PARK
MAP 2

THERE ARE GREAT VIEWS OF DENALI FROM THE PARKS HIGHWAY

THE PARKS HIGHWAY

🚐 DENALI VIEW SOUTH (DENALI STATE PARK)

Location: Mile 135 Of The Denali Highway
Info: (907) 345-3975
Website: dnr.alaska.gov/parks/aspunits/matsu/denaliviewso.htm

$$\$\$$

GPS Location: 62.59231 N, 150.23970 W, 700 Ft.

Like Denali View North, this is a large paved parking area with fantastic views of Denali. Overnight parking by RVs is permitted, some spaces are large pull-thrus. Amenities include vault toilets as well as some picnic tables, fire pits and a hand-operated water pump.

🚐 LOWER TROUBLESOME CREEK CAMPGROUND (DENALI STATE PARK)

Location: Mile 137 Of The Parks Highway
Info: (907) 345-3975
Website: dnr.alaska.gov/parks/aspunits/matsu/lrtrbckcamp.htm

$$\$\$$

GPS Location: 62.62581 N, 150.22760 W, 600 Ft.

The Troublesome Creek Campsite is little more than a large paved pull-off next to the highway as far as vehicle campers are concerned but overnight camping in RVs is allowed. There are also eight good walk-in tent sites with picnic tables, fire pits, and a bear-proof locker so it is a decent stopping place for tenters too. Unlike Denali View North and South there is no view from this parking area. The facility has vault toilets and a hand-operated water pump and there is a good trail to the Chulitna River. Fishing is for grayling. Stays are limited to 15 days.

◨ BYERS LAKE CAMPGROUND (DENALI STATE PARK)

Location:	Mile 147 Of The Parks Highway
Info:	(907) 345-3975
Website:	dnr.alaska.gov/parks/aspunits/matsu/byerslkcamp.htm

GPS Location: 62.74393 N, 150.12534 W, 800 Ft.

One of our favorite state campgrounds is Byers Lake. It is well-wooded, has some pull-thrus, and is seldom crowded. There are boats for rent to explore the lake (only electric motors are allowed) and several good hiking trails.

The campground has 73 campsites. The access road to the campground is paved, interior roads are gravel as are parking pads. The sites are well-separated and surrounded by trees and natural vegetation. A few of the back-ins and pull-thrus are as long as 40 feet but most are not. There are picnic tables and fire pits at the sites, a hand-operated water pump, a bear-proof food locker, and vault toilets. This campground usually has a host on site and firewood can be purchased. It also has a dump and water-fill site, one of the few in the area. Stays are limited to 15 days. There are good hiking trails from the campground around the lake and onto Kesugi ridge beyond. Overflow camping is available at nearby Alaska Veterans Memorial/POW-MIA Rest Area which is accessible from the highway, the entrances are north of the campground entrance and there is a walking trail between the two facilities.

The campground is located about a half-mile off the highway, far enough so that there is no highway noise but still easily accessible. The entrance road is on the east side of the highway at about Mile 147 of the Parks Highway.

◨ DENALI VIEW NORTH (DENALI STATE PARK)

Location:	Mile 163 Of The Parks Highway
Info:	(907) 345-3975
Website:	dnr.alaska.gov/parks/aspunits/matsu/denaliviewnocamp.htm

GPS Location: 62.88676 N, 149.78666 W, 1,300 Ft.

The outstanding feature of this campground is the fantastic view of Denali and the southern side of the Alaska Range. The camping area itself is not much more than a large paved parking lot shared with tour busses and other highway travelers. There are about 20 large pull-thru and back-in sites available for camping with picnic tables and fire pits as well as three walk-in tent sites. Some of the pull-thrus are very long. The wayside has vault toilets, a hand-operated water pump, and a telescope. There is also a park host. Stays are limited to 15 days. A paved nature trail loop runs off the south side of the campground and a reader board tells the fantastic story of the first ascent of Denali in 1910 by miners after a bet in a Fairbanks bar.

◨ EAST FORK CHULITNA WAYSIDE (STATE OF ALASKA)

Location:	Mile 186 Of The Parks Highway

GPS Location: 63.15142 N, 149.41065 W, 1,800 Ft.

This is a rest area that has formal camping sites. There are a variety of paved parking areas with adjoining picnic tables and fire pits or grills, also a few walk-in tent sites. There are 11 sites in all, some are long parallel spaces that will take any size RV, others are back-ins that will take only short RVs. Nearer the road is a large paved parking area which allows 8-hour overnight parking. Toilets are the modern vault type and there is also a water pump.

The campground is on the east side of the highway near Mile 186.

CANTWELL RV PARK

Address:	PO Box 210, Cantwell, AK 99729
Telephone:	(907) 768-2210 or (800) 940-2210
Email:	cantwellrvpark@ak.net
Website:	www.alaskaone.com/cantwellrv
	or www.cantwellrvpark.wordpress.com

GPS Location: 63.39242 N, 148.90949 W, 2,100 Ft.

Since it is located some 27 miles (44 km) south of Denali Park you might think that this RV park wouldn't get much business. Nothing could be farther from the truth. Apparently the friendly management and squeaky-clean restrooms and showers provide an adequate tradeoff for the half-hour drive north to the park.

The Cantwell is a large campground with 79 spaces, 68 of them are pull-thrus to 65 feet. Each site has 30-amp electricity, about half have water hookups too. This campground is basically a very large leveled gravel field so big RVs can easily maneuver. There is a tent-camping area at one end in a grove of trees. The campground has a dump station and water fill hose. The services building houses the office, a small gift shop with a few supplies, showers, clean restrooms, and a laundry. There are two community fire rings. Tours to the park as well as rafting, sightseeing, and berry picking can be arranged here. Pet sitting is available too.

This campground is located on the spur road to Cantwell. Turn west at the junction of the Denali and Parks Highways (about Mile 210 of the Parks), the campground is on the right after a short distance.

DENALI GRIZZLY BEAR RESORT

Address:	Mile 231 Parks Highway (PO Box 7),
	Denali National Park, AK 99755
Telephone:	(907) 683-2696 (Summer),
	(866) 583-2696, (907) 374-8796 (Winter)
Email:	info@denaligrizzlybear.com
Website:	www.denaligrizzlybear.com

GPS Location: 63.65446 N, 148.83423 W, 1,900 Ft.

For a campground that can handle big RVs (and small ones, and tents) near Denali Park the Denali Grizzly Bear Resort is a decent choice. They also have a small hotel and many rental cabins. The resort is located not far south of the park, just across the Nenana River.

This campground has about 50 sites, many of them are no-hookup RV or tent camping sites but some 40 have water and electricity hookups. Many of these are back-in sites to 40 feet, there are also two long pull-thrus. Other sites for smaller RVs are in a wooded area. Each site has a picnic table and there are community fire pits. Restrooms have flush toilets and coin-operated showers. There is a dump station and

looking at entrance p. 296

also a store with supplies, gifts, and a liquor store. Propane is available. Wi-Fi can be accessed in the office/store building, there is a fee. Reservations are recommended.

The campground is located about 6 miles (10 km) south of the Denali Park entrance near Mile 231 of the Parks Highway.

DENALI NATIONAL PARK

Denali Park is one of Alaska's prime attractions and is not to be missed. If you have come north to see wildlife, this is the place. The 6 million plus acre park encompasses the highest portion of the Alaska Range including Mt. McKinley, at 20,320 feet the highest peak in the northern hemisphere. It also includes a huge, mostly treeless alpine region of foothills to the north of the range that is prime habitat for grizzlies, caribou, wolves, and other wildlife. For information about the park see the www.nps.gov/dena which is the park's website or call (907) 683-9532.

The park contains several campgrounds. These are Riley Creek, Savage River, Sanctuary River (tents only), Teklanika River, Igloo Creek (tents only), and Wonder Lake (tents only). These campgrounds are popular, especially the one at Teklanika because it allows you to drive quite a distance into the park to get to your campsite.

One of the reasons for the abundant wildlife in the park is that the Park Service severely limits access. Very few vehicles travel the one road that leads far into the park. Most visitors entering must do so in busses. The difficult access is the price you pay

IF YOU'VE COME NORTH TO SEE WILDLIFE, DENALI PARK IS THE PLACE

THE PARKS HIGHWAY

Wildness Access Center - 1st

to see wildlife. Don't let the restrictions frustrate you. Instead plan ahead and relax, the park is well worth the effort you will expend to visit it. Shuttle busses run from about the middle of May through about the middle of September, most campgrounds are only open during the same period.

When you arrive at the park your first priority is a visit to the Wilderness Access Center near the park entrance. You can drive to the center in your RV if it is not too large, it has a large parking lot with RV slots. If you're towing you'll want to use the tow car, the lot doesn't have enough room for RVs with tow cars attached. There's also parking near the entrance of the Riley Creek Campground if the Wilderness Access Center lot doesn't have room. At the center you can find out about the park, arrange reservations, pick up shuttle tickets and sign in for campgrounds in the park. The park has an entrance fee of $10 per person in addition to charges for shuttle busses and campgrounds, you can visit the visitor center without paying this fee. Denali also honors the various national park passes.

A reservation system is used to ensure that most visitors are able to enjoy Denali. A similar system is used for bus and campground reservations. Over half of shuttle bus seats and all of campground spaces in Riley (except tent-only sites), Savage River, Teklanika, and Wonder Lake campsites can be reserved in advance. This can be done by fax, phone or internet. Fax reservations are accepted up to two days in advance of the planned visit and telephone and internet reservations the day before the planned visit but should be made as far in advance as possible since the available slots are likely to have been claimed by the time you call if you delay. The remaining bus and available unreserved camping slots are parceled out on a first-come, first-served basis at the park. Your best plan is to reserve far in advance for both bus and campground slots. Failing that, arrive early in the day and hope for the best. Keep in mind that June and July are the most popular months for visiting the park. The crowds begin to taper off by the middle of August. You can stay in a commercial campground just outside the park entrance if you are not able to get a site in the park. Those with large RVs will probably prefer one of the campgrounds outside the park because sites are larger and facilities better.

Phone numbers for reservations are (800) 622-7275 in the U.S. except Alaska, and (907) 272-7275 for international and local calls, the internet reservation site is www.reservedenali.com. Reservations can be booked from December 1 until September 15. The fax number is (602) 331-5258. It is easiest to pay by credit card; Visa, Master Card, and Discover Card are accepted. To insure that you enclose all the necessary information you can download a fax form from the Internet at www.reservedenali.com. This Website is also a good source of other information about the park.

There is a private tour operator, Kantishna Wilderness Trails (800 230-7275) offering bus trips along the park road to Kantishna. The price is higher than taking a government bus but the tour goes all the way to Kantishna (95 miles (153 km) into the park) and includes lunch.

The only exception to the shuttle or tour bus rule is the **Road Lottery** and subsequent shoulder season. For four days the winners of the Road Lottery can purchase a day-long permit allowing them to drive their own vehicles out as far as the road remains open. Some years this is all the way to Wonder Lake, in early winter years it may only be as far as Savage River. The lottery period is always the four days beginning the second Friday after Labor Day. Lottery submissions are accepted from May 1 to June 30, contact the park for instructions. After the Road Lottery dates private vehicles can drive in to the park up to 30 miles until snow closes the road.

Denali's season is determined by weather and when the road is open. The summer season lasts from late May until late September. All of the campgrounds except Riley Creek are only open in summer. The park busses also only run in summer since that's when the road is open. The winter season is late September until sometime in May when the park road opens. In winter the park road is only plowed to Mile 3.

In addition to the campgrounds inside the park there are also many private campgrounds near the park entrance. Most RV visitors to the park will find that these are much more convenient than facilities inside the park.

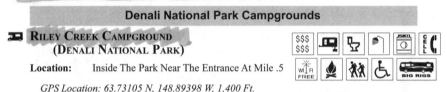

Denali National Park Campgrounds

🚐 RILEY CREEK CAMPGROUND
(DENALI NATIONAL PARK)

Location: Inside The Park Near The Entrance At Mile .5

$$$ $$$

GPS Location: 63.73105 N, 148.89398 W, 1,400 Ft.

Riley Creek is the largest of the park's campgrounds and one of the easiest to actually get into. This is the only campground in the park open all year long, facilities

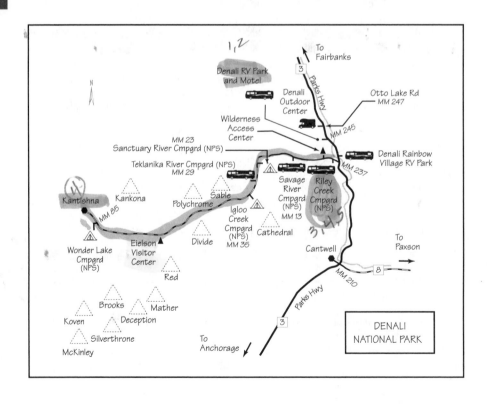

are limited in the winter. It is located near the Wilderness Access Center and the park entrance off the Denali Highway.

The campground has 147 campsites off three large loops, a few are pull-thrus. There is also a walk-in tent-camping area. The vehicle sites aren't large, most are suitable only for RVs to about 30 feet and they are narrow, although there are a very few 40-foot sites. Each site has a picnic table and fire pit. A maximum of 8 people and one vehicle is allowed at each site. Interior roads are paved or gravel, parking pads are gravel. There is a central food locker area where you can store food that might attract bears. The restrooms in the campground itself have no showers but they do have flush toilets. Riley Creek Mercantile offering a store, a coffee counter, free Wi-Fi access, pay showers and a laundry is near the campground. Next to it is a large dump station area. This campground has a host and there is a campfire circle. Reservations are recommended, check-in at the Wilderness Access Center is required before proceeding to the campground, see reservation information above. Note that the walk-in tent sites here cannot be reserved in advance. There is no fee in the winter (mid-September to May 15) for camping here.

SAVAGE RIVER CAMPGROUND (DENALI NATIONAL PARK)

Location: Mile 13 Of Park Road

GPS Location: 63.71724 N, 149.25761 W, 2.700 Ft.

Savage River is a 33-site vehicle campground with sites off two loops. This campground is open May 19 to September 16. Large RVs are OK, there are ten very long pull-thrus. Tents are also allowed. Sites have picnic tables and fire pits and there are bear boxes for food storage. Restrooms have flush toilets but not showers. A maximum of 8 campers are allowed in each space. Water is available from spigots in the campground but not at the sites. The campground has a host and firewood is available. Vehicles are allowed to Mile 15 of the park road so it is possible to drive to this campground without restriction in summer. Reservations are recommended, check-in at the Wilderness Access Center is required before travel into the park to the campground, see information about reservations above.

SANCTUARY RIVER CAMPGROUND (DENALI NATIONAL PARK)
Location: Mile 23 Of The Park Road

GPS Location: 63.72361 N, 149.47111 W, 2,500 Ft.

Sanctuary River is a very small 7-site tent campground. This campground is open May 20 to September 12. No vehicles are allowed. There is a vault toilet and bear-proof food storage lockers. No campfires are allowed, only stoves. Water is from the river so bring water purification equipment. Reservations for this campground are only available within two days prior to the night of your stay and they must be made at the Wilderness Access Center or Riley Creek Mercantile. Access is only by bus.

TEKLANIKA RIVER CAMPGROUND (DENALI NATIONAL PARK)

Location: Mile 29 Of The Park Road

GPS Location: 63.67007 N, 149.57948 W, 2,600 Ft.

Teklanika River Campground is a large vehicle campground with 53 sites for RVs to 40 feet. This campground is open May 20 to September 15. Each site has a fire pit

YOU'RE LIKELY TO SEE ALASKA'S STATE BIRD, THE WILLOW PTARMIGAN, IN THE PARK

and picnic table. The campground is set on a gravel riverbed floodplain and many sites can accommodate larger RVs. There are vault toilets but no showers. Water is available at faucets in the campground. Sometimes tents are allowed in the campground but at other times, due to wildlife activity, they are prohibited. The location of this campground inside the park on limited access road beyond the 15 mile (24 km) checkpoint makes it popular but imposes restrictions. Campers are given special permits to drive in and return, vehicles cannot be used otherwise. Tow vehicles not necessary to move the living unit must be left in the visitor center parking lots near the park entrance. In addition, vehicle campers must stay 3 days at the campground to limit road traffic. Tent campers who arrive by bus are not subject to this limitation and may stay for fewer days. For the price of one bus ticket campers may buy a Tek Ticket which allows unlimited use of the busses for the period they are staying in the campground. Campers can board the park shuttle busses to continue on into the park or return to the entrance area on day trips. Reservations are recommended for staying at Teklanika, check-in at the Wilderness Access Center is required, see information about reservations above.

▄ IGLOO CREEK CAMPGROUND (DENALI NATIONAL PARK)

Location: Mile 35 Of The Park Road

GPS Location: 63.60914 N, 149.58250 W, 3,000 Ft.

There are seven sites in this tent-only campground, no vehicles are allowed. These are wooded sites with some natural vegetation between sites, vault toilets are provided but there is no water provided except the creek. Bring purification equipment.

No fires are permitted. Bear-proof food storage lockers are on site. Reservations for this campground are only available within two days prior to the night of your stay and they must be made at the Wilderness Access Center or Riley Creek Mercantile. This campground is open from May 20 to September 12.

WONDER LAKE CAMPGROUND (DENALI NATIONAL PARK)
Location: Mile 85 Of The Park Road

GPS Location: 63.45721 N, 150.86367 W, 2,000 Ft.

The 28-site tent-only campground at Wonder Lake has a choice location with great views of the mountain, when it's out. This campground is open June 8 to September 12. Food is stored in lockers. No campfires are allowed, only stoves. A maximum of 4 campers (3 tents) are allowed in each site. There are flush toilets but no showers. Potable water is available. Reservations are recommended, check-in at the Wilderness Access Center is required, see information about reservations above. There are lake trout and grayling in Wonder Lake.

DENALI RAINBOW VILLAGE RV PARK
Address: Mile 238.6 Parks Highway (PO Box 30),
                 Denali National Park, AK 99755
Telephone: (907) 683-7777
Email: denalirainbow@mtaonline.net
Website: www.denalirv.com

GPS Location: 63.74679 N, 148.89807 W, 1,600 Ft.

The Denali Rainbow Village is the closest commercial RV park to Denali Park. Sites here are in a gravel lot behind a row of small stores.

For the present there are about 65 sites. Many are pull-thrus with electric and water to 55 feet but there are back-ins and full-hookups too. There are even some tent sites. Some sites have picnic tables and fire rings. The park is located on a flat gravel bench. A line of small buildings has been built between the road and the park, they serve to isolate it from the road and house various business establishments. Electricity is via 30 or 50-amp outlets and there is a dump station and water fill station. There are restrooms with pay showers, and a coin-op laundry. Restaurants, a gas station, and a small store are conveniently located in the immediate vicinity.

The Denali Rainbow Village RV Park is located on the east side of the Parks Highway at Mile 238.6, about 1.3 miles (2.1 km) north of the Denali Park entrance.

DENALI RV PARK AND MOTEL
Address: 245.1 Parks Highway (PO Box 155),
                 Denali National Park, AK 99755
Telephone: (907) 683-1500 or (800) 478-1501
Email: stay@denaliRVparkandmotel.com
Website: www.denaliRVparkandmotel.com

GPS Location: 63.82142 N, 148.98695 W, 1,700 Ft.

Not far north of the Denali Park entrance is a large well-established RV park and motel, the Denali.

This campground has some 90 sites, about half have full hookups with 30-amp electricity, most of the remainder have water and electricity although a few are electricity

only. A few are long pull-thrus to 60 feet. Sites have picnic tables. The campground also has a dump station. The restrooms have flush toilets and coin-op showers. There's also a large gift shop.

The campground is on the west side of the Parks Highway near Mile 245. It is 7.8 miles (12.6 km) north of the Denali entrance road.

DENALI OUTDOOR CENTER

Location:	Mile 1/2 Otto Lake Road, West From Mile 247 Of The Parks Highway
Telephone:	(907) 683-1925 or (888) 303-1925
Email:	docadventure@hotmail.com
Website:	www.denalioutdoorcenter.com

GPS Location: 63.84861 N, 149.03304 W, 1,800 Ft.

Denali Outdoor Adventures uses this campground as a base. They offer raft and kayak trips as well as mountain bike and other outdoor tours. They also have rental cabins and bike and kayak rentals.

The campground itself occupies a low gravel hill behind the entrance buildings. Many sites adjoin or overlook Otto Lake, a pretty little lake good for paddling, fishing, swimming, and birding. Sites are similar to those at government campgrounds with parking on gravel and natural vegetation separating them. Some are also walk-in tent sites near the lake. Picnic tables and fire rings are provided at some sites. There is a 30-foot limit on rig size at this campground. There are outhouses at the campground and flush toilets near the entrance. Fee showers and laundry are available there too. Boats can be rented and Wi-Fi is available at the entrance building. The campground fee here is on a per-person basis, the icon above shows the fee for two people.

Follow Otto Lake Road west from Mile 247 of the Parks Highway. The campground entrance is on the left in .5 mile (.8 km).

FROM DENALI PARK TO FAIRBANKS
121 Miles (195 Kilometers)

After passing the Denali Park Entrance the Parks Highway continues through the Nenana Canyon and soon passes Healy. **Healy** is the location of Alaska's largest open-pit coal mine, you can sometimes see the giant crane stripping overburden on the hilltop to the east of the highway. Without the crane you wouldn't know that it was there.

As the road descends out of the mountains you will begin to notice the dips and heaves that show that it was built on permafrost. This section of road from the mountains to Nenana on the Tanana River was one of the most difficult sections of the entire highway to build, even though the terrain is flat. At Mile 283 you pass the access road to **Clear**, a large radar site that is part of the ballistic missile early warning system.

At Mile 304 you will enter **Nenana** (population 400). Today this small village serves largely as a transfer point for fuel and other goods from the railroad to river barges

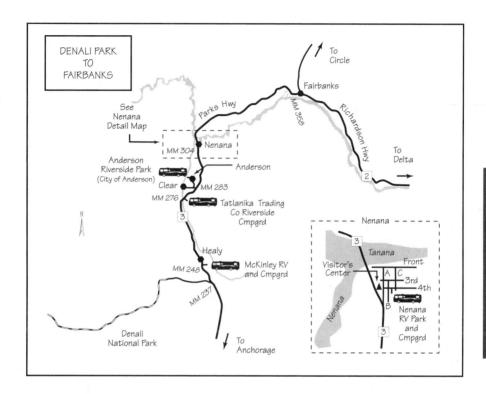

headed for villages on the Tanana and Yukon Rivers. It is best known as the site of the **Nenana Ice Classic**, an annual betting pool where hundreds of thousands of dollars are wagered by people trying to guess the exact time in the spring when the river ice will go out. The **Nenana Visitor Center** (907 832-5435) is at the corner at Mile 304 where A Street goes into Nenana. When the Alaska Railroad was completed in 1923 President Harding drove a golden spike in Nenana, today the **Alaska Railroad Museum** is in the renovated original **Nenana Railroad Depot** which is on the National Register of Historic Places.

After leaving Nenana the highway crosses the Tanana River and makes its way across rolling hills for 54 miles (87 km) before descending into Fairbanks.

Denali Park to Fairbanks Campgrounds

⛺ MCKINLEY RV AND CAMPGROUND

Address:	Mile 248.5 Parks Hwy, Healy, AK 99743
Telephone:	(907) 683-2379 or (800) 478-2562
Email:	reservations@mckinleyrv.com
Website:	www.mckinleyrv.com

GPS Location: 63.86557 N, 149.01834 W, 1,500 Ft.

This campground is showing its age and could use some attention. It's run in conjunction with a gas station and mini-market.

THE PARKS HIGHWAY

There are about 50 sites at the McKinley. Full-hookup and pull-thrus to 50 feet are offered as well as sites with only water and electric, electric only, and dry. Sites are big, suitable for any large RVs. There's also a tent-camping area. The campground has flush toilets, showers, a coin-op laundry, a gift and supplies shop, gas sales, an ATM, propane sales and a playground.

The campground is located in Healy, on the east side of the Parks Highway at Mile 248.5. This is 11 miles (18 km) north of the Denali Park entrance road.

▄▟ TATLANIKA TRADING CO. RIVERSIDE CAMPGROUND

Address:	Mile 276 Parks Highway
	(HC 66 Box 27625), Nenana, AK 99760
Telephone:	(907) 582-2341

GPS Location: 64.21774 N, 149.27506 W, 800 Ft.

One of the nicer places to stop along the Parks Highway and one of the best deals is the Tatlanika Trading Post. The gift shop here is outstanding, and there are also over 50 mounted animals on display.

The Tatlanika also has 21 camping sites, some are suitable for large RVs. Many of them are situated along the Nenana River. The sites have 20/30-amp outlets and water with picnic tables. They are well separated with natural vegetation. The campground has a dump station (extra charge), flush toilets, and showers (extra fee).

The Tatlanika Trading Co. is located at Mile 276 of the Parks Highway, just north of a bridge over the Nenana River.

▄▟ ANDERSON RIVERSIDE PARK (CITY OF ANDERSON)

| Address: | PO Box 3100, Anderson, AK 99744 |
| Telephone: | (907) 582-2500 |

GPS Location: 64.34320 N, 149.20229 W, 500 Ft.

This park, known as the home of the Anderson Bluegrass Festival on the last weekend of July each year, offers both hookup and boondocking facilities.

Campsites are located in two places. In a grove of trees near the Nenana River there are 17 back-in dry sites surrounded by trees, some have picnic tables and fire pits. Some distance away, on the far side of a large grassy field and next to a small bandstand, are 36 side-by-side sites with either 20 or 30-amp outlets. Nearby are a covered picnic area as well as a restroom building with flush toilets, and showers that require a token available at the campground and at a nearby business (see signs). Near the entrance of the park is a dump station and water fill station.

The road to Clear and Anderson leaves the Parks Highway at Mile 283.5. Drive westward on the paved highway for 1.2 miles (1.9 km) and then turn right following the sign for Anderson. You'll drive through Anderson and on the far side, at 6.3 miles (10.2 km) from the Parks Highway, enter the park. The hookup sites are to the left, the dry sites straight ahead. Watch for a pay station with payment envelopes as you enter the campground.

■ NENANA **RV PARK AND CAMPGROUND**

Address:	210 E. 4th Ave. (PO Box 207), Nenana, AK 99706
Telephone:	(907) 832-5230
Email:	nenanarv@gmail.com
Website:	nenanarvpark.wordpress.com

GPS Location: 64.56020 N, 149.09118 W, 400 Ft.

Among travelers Nenana is known for its very friendly and helpful visitor center located just south of the bridge over the Tanana River at the junction of the road into town. Now the Nenana RV Park is once again open, so you can spend some time here. The campground is located within a few blocks of central Nenana.

The park has about 40 pull-thru sites surrounded by a nice lawn. They are 40 to 45 feet long and there's lots of maneuvering room. There are electric and water, electric only, and dry sites, and a dump station. There's also a grassy area for tenters and two covered shelters for rainy days. All sites have picnic tables and there's a central campfire area. The modern restroom building has free showers and a laundry. Wi-Fi is included in the price and propane is available.

Take the road into the town of Nenana south of the Tanana River bridge and near the visitor center between Mile 304 and 305 of the Parks Highway. It's signed for Nenana. Almost immediately turn right on 4th Street, the RV park is on the right in .1 mile (.2 km).

PARKS HIGHWAY DUMP STATIONS

Many of the campgrounds in this chapter have dump stations or sewer hookups, see the individual entries for these. There is generally a fee charged for using them, particularly if you are not staying at the campground. Here are some additional possibilities:

In **Wasilla** the Holiday station in town at the intersection of the Parks Highway and Boundary (*GPS Location 61.58149 N, 149.43919 W*) has a dump station. There is also one behind the Chevron station across from Wendy's .7 mile (1.1 km) west of Main St. on the Parks Highway (*GPS Location 61.58245 N, 149.46622 W*). The dump station is actually behind Wasilla Auto, the metal building behind the Chevron. Access to both of these is difficult for larger RVs, however, because there's lots of traffic. A better choice might be the Holiday station about 5 miles (8 km) west of town near Mile 49 of the Parks Highway (*GPS Location 61.58310 N, 149.63779 W*) which charges a $5 fee.

At **Denali National Park** there is a dump station inside the park at the Riley Creek Mercantile (*GPS Location 63.73317 N, 148.89803 W*) which is not far from the highway. It can be used by folks not staying in the park. The fee is $5.00, but it's free if you're camping in the park.

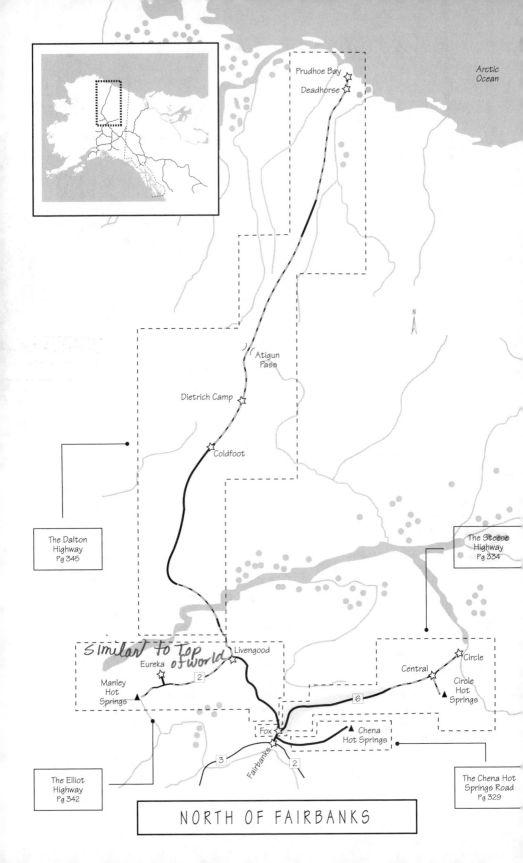

Arctic
Ocean

Prudhoe Bay
Deadhorse

N

Atigun
Pass

Dietrich Camp

Coldfoot

The Dalton
Highway
Pg 345

The Steese
Highway
Pg 334

Similar to Top
of World   Livengood

Eureka   Circle

Central   Circle
Hot
Springs

Manley
Hot
Springs

Fox   Chena
Hot Springs

Fairbanks

The Elliot
Highway
Pg 342

The Chena Hot
Springs Road
Pg 329

NORTH OF FAIRBANKS

Chapter 10

North of Fairbanks

INTRODUCTION

There are a surprising number of roads giving access to the country north of Fairbanks. Both RVers and tent campers will find much to interest them in this region.

Fairbanks and the area north to the Brooks Range have some of the best summer weather in the state. On many summer days you can expect blue skies with cumulous clouds building in the afternoon to produce a few showers that disperse in the evening. Daytime temperatures approaching 70° are not uncommon. During the middle of the summer you can also expect long days, in fact it will never get really dark during June and July.

The region is definitely not crowded. For a short time before the growth of Dawson City, Circle City was the largest city in the interior. The city served the Birch Creek mining district in the hills to the south. There were also many other mining areas along these roads. When the mining pretty much shut down in the 1940s most people left the area leaving interesting ghost towns and mining relics, and the roads to reach them.

Highlights

There are several developed and easy to reach hot springs north of Fairbanks. Closest and easiest with a paved road all the way, is **Chena Hot Springs** on the Chena Hot Springs Road. There is also a hot springs at **Manley Hot Springs** at the end of the Elliott Highway. On the Steese, unfortunately, Circle Hot Springs has been closed for several years.

The entire region was a mining area. Important strikes or mining areas include **Pedro Creek** and **Upper Goldstream Creek** near Fox, **Cleary Creek**, **Chatanika**, **Nome Creek**, **Birch Creek** and **Circle-Mastodon Creek** on the Steese Highway; **Tolovana** (Livengood), **Eureka** and **Tofty** on the Elliott Highway; and **Ruby** (Wiseman) and **Coldfoot** on the Dalton Highway. Many relics of these gold rushes remain within easy walking distance of the highways.

The 420 mile (677 km) long **Dalton Highway**, also long known as the Pipeline Haul Road, is a major destination in its own right. You'll find an entire section about this formidable but rewarding route below.

 Fuel

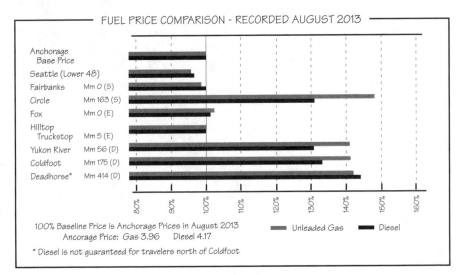

FUEL PRICE COMPARISON - RECORDED AUGUST 2013

100% Baseline Price is Anchorage Prices in August 2013
Ancorage Price: Gas 3.96   Diesel 4.17

■ Unleaded Gas   ■ Diesel

* Diesel is not guaranteed for travelers north of Coldfoot

Fishing

Fishing in the interior is primarily for grayling, whitefish, and northern pike. King, silver, and chum (also known as calico or dog) salmon do get far into the interior, but by the time they get this far up the river they are quite red and often no good for eating. Local fishermen do enjoy catching and releasing them, however.

The **Chena River**, which runs through Fairbanks, was a very good grayling stream at one time but the fish population crashed in the 80s. The upper reaches in the Chena River State Recreation Area are clear and fun to fish. The grayling are coming back, all grayling fishing in the Chena is catch-and-release. You might want to give it a try. There's easy access off the Chena Hot Springs Road in many places.

The **Chatanika River** is another clear-water river that has seen heavy fishing pressure for grayling. Check regulations. Access to the Chatanika is from the Steese

Highway at Mile 35 and 39 and from the Elliott Highway at Mile 11. The best access is by canoe, see below.

On the Steese Highway there are several **small lakes in the tailing piles at Chatanika** that are stocked with grayling. They're between Mile 29 and Mile 40 and are marked with signs on the road.

Beaver and Birch Creeks run north into the Yukon River, both have good grayling fishing. Access to Beaver Creek is very limited and along most of the river requires either a hike or airplane ride. The headwaters are road-accessible from Mile 57 of the Steese Highway on the Nome Creek Road. Access to Birch Creek is at Mile 94 and Mile 147 of the Steese Highway. Both of these rivers are popular canoe routes, they're designated Wild and Scenic Rivers, see below.

The **Tolovana River** joins the Chatanika River near Minto. The upper reaches of the river provide good grayling fishing, access is from bridges on the Elliott Highway at Mile 57 and Mile 75. Other creeks to try on the Elliott Highway are **Tatalina Creek** (Mile 45), **Hutlinana Creek** (Mile 129), and **Baker Creek** (Mile 137).

The **Dalton Highway** remains a wilderness road and fishing in the creeks it crosses can be good. These are mostly grayling streams but swampy areas with slow-moving water have northern pike. Try **Hess Creek** (Mile 24), the **Ray River** (Mile 70), **No Name Creek** (Mile 79), the **Kanuti River** (Mile 106), **Fish Creek** (Mile 114), **South Fork of Bonanza Creek** (Mile 125), the **North Fork of Bonanza Creek** (Mile 126), **Prospect Creek** (Mile 135), the **Jim River** (Mile 140, 141), **Grayling Lake** (Mile 151), the **South Fork of the Koyukuk River** (Mile 156), **Minnie Creek** (Mile 187), and the **Dietrich River** (Mile 207).

Boating, Rafting, Canoeing, and Kayaking

There are four popular canoe routes north of Fairbanks and accessible from the road. These are the Chena River, the Chatanika River, Beaver Creek, and Birch Creek.

The **Chena River** has excellent road access. The upper river is in the Chena River State Recreation Area. Short or long floats are available, from a few hours to almost 80 hours (all the way to Fairbanks) of float time. Tent camping on gravel bars along the river is allowed within the Recreation Area. Access points along the Chena Hot Springs Road are at Mile 48.9, Mile 44.0, Mile 39.5, Mile 37.8, Mile 31.6, Mile 28.6, Mile 28, Mile 27, and off the Grange Hill Road at Mile 20.8. There's also access from Nordale Road and at several places in Fairbanks. The river is rated as Class II and has sweepers and log jams so exercise caution. Lower sections of the river are slower and easier to negotiate.

The **Chatanika River** is navigable a distance of about 130 miles (210 km) but most canoeists float no more than the 60 river miles (97 km) between Sourdough Creek and the Elliott Highway which takes three to four days. This is a Class I and Class II river with log jams and sweepers so exercise caution. Access points are from the Steese Highway at Sourdough Creek (Mile 60), Cripple Creek (Mile 53), Long Creek (Mile 45), the Chatanika River Bridge (Mile 39), and on the Elliott Highway at Mile 11.

Birch Creek is a National Wild and Scenic River with road-accessible put-in and take-out points. The put-in is at Twelve Mile Creek on the Steese Highway (Mile 94), the take-out is at the Birch Creek Bridge at Mile 147 of the Steese Highway. Between the two are 126 river miles (203 km) for a 7 to 10 day float. Birch Creek does not run along the road, this is a wilderness float. The water is rated Class I and II with some Class III rapids so exercise caution. Much of the river is within the Steese National Conservation Area.

Beaver Creek is the most remote of these rivers. There is road access to the put-in point but it is necessary to arrange for an aircraft for take-out. This river is a National Wild and Scenic River. The put-in point is on Nome Creek which is accessible via the U.S. Creek Road from Mile 57 of the Steese Highway. From the put-in to take-out at a gravel bar at Victoria Creek is 127 river miles (205 km) and takes 7 or 8 days. This is a Class I river in remote country with log jams and sweepers, exercise caution.

Hiking and Mountain Biking

The high country north of Fairbanks is excellent hiking terrain with many designated trails. Most trails are within the Chena River State Recreation Area, the White Mountains National Recreation Area, the Steese National Conservation Area, or the Trans-Alaska Pipeline Utility Corridor.

The **Chena River State Recreation Area** has a good selection of trails. The **Granite Tors Trail** is a 15-mile (24-km) loop trail up a ridge on one side of Rock Creek to a region of rocky pillars in high treeless country, and then back to the starting point along the other side of Rock Creek. The trail has an elevation gain of 2,500 feet and takes from 4 to 8 hours. Access is from the Tors Trail Campground at Mile 39 of the Chena Hot Spring Road. An easier trail is the **Angel Rocks Trail,** a 3.5-mile (5.6-km) (round trip) hike to rock outcroppings above the river. Access is from a parking lot at Mile 48.9 of the Chena Hot Springs Road. Finally, the challenging **Chena Dome Trail** is a 30-mile (40-km) loop through high country following a chain of rock cairns that mark the trail. Altitude gain is over 3,000 feet. Plan on 2 to 4 days to make the loop. Access is from Mile 50.5 of the Chena Hot Springs Road. Of these three trails only the last is open to mountain bikes.

The White Mountains National Recreation Area has lots of trails, unfortunately almost all of them are designed for winter use, they are too wet to make good summer hiking trails. The **Summit Trail** is an exception. This ridge trail from Mile 28 of the Elliot Highway is a one-way day hike of 3.5 miles (5.6-km) to the north side of Wickersham Dome, a climb of 900 feet. It is also possible to follow this trail much farther to Birch Creek. The one-way distance to the creek is 20 miles (32.3 km).

A popular trail along the Steese Highway is the **Pinnell Mountain Trail**. It connects Eagle Summit at Mile 107 and Twelvemile Summit at Mile 85. The trail is 27 miles (44 km) long and follows mountain ridges with wonderful views in all directions. There are basic shelters at Mile 10 and Mile 17.5 as measured from the Eagle Summit trailhead, the BLM recommends walking the trail from Eagle Summit to Twelvemile Summit because it is slightly easier in that direction. Plan on two to four days to finish this hike. Water can be a problem, don't pass up a source. You may have to descend from the ridgeline to find it. Some sections of the trail are marked with cairns. Visiting the summits and walking the trail at the summer solstice has become very popular. From June 18 to June 24 the sun doesn't dip below the horizon at all from higher points on the trail, the solstice is June 20 or 21.

On the Elliott Highway near Manley Hot Springs is the trail to **Hutlinana Warm Springs**. The 8-mile (12.9-km) trail follows Hutlinana Creek north from near the east side of the bridge at Mile 129.

Along the **Dalton Highway** hiking options are limited except in the high country. Check at the Coldfoot Interagency Visitor Center at Mile 175 for information. Try the trail up Gold Creek from Mile 197 to **Bob Johnson Lake**. The distance is 13 miles (21 km) and the lake is known for its fishing (grayling, lake trout, and northern pike). Really ambitious hikers can also climb Sukakpak Mountain near Mile 204 for great views.

Wildlife Viewing

You are likely to run into a moose almost anywhere along the roads north of Fairbanks and there are often grouse and ptarmigan feeding along the shoulders. The **Dalton Highway** is in another class entirely. From Atigun Pass (Mile 245) to Galbraith Lake (Mile 275) you are almost sure to see Dall sheep. Also watch for caribou, arctic fox, muskoxen, and a long list of birds. The BLM even prints a booklet that serves as a checklist titled *Birds Along the Dalton Highway.*

FROM ATIGUN PASS TO GALBRAITH LAKE YOU'RE ALMOST SURE TO SEE DALL SHEEP

THE ROUTES, TOWNS, AND CAMPGROUNDS

STEESE HIGHWAY
162 Miles (261 Kilometers)

The Steese Highway was the first of the roads north of Fairbanks. Today it is not the busiest, the Dalton Highway claims that honor, but it is the only one of the roads that begins in Fairbanks. The others all branch off the Steese.

For the first 81 miles (131 km) the Steese Highway is paved. Then for another 64 miles (103 km) to Central the road is wide and generally in good shape but not paved. The remaining 35 miles (56 km) to Circle City on the banks of the Yukon River are not as wide or well-maintained but still easily good enough for RVs.

The Steese Highway starts as the Steese Expressway running just east of downtown Fairbanks. At Mile 5 the Chena Hot Springs Road cuts off to the east. There's a **pipeline viewing area** at Mile 7 and at Mile 11 the expressway reaches the Fox junction.

Fox is in the middle of an area of tailing piles from gold dredges that worked the region until WW II. There is a dredge located near Fox (Gold Dredge #8) that can be visited as part of a tour offered by the Binkley Family, the same folks who run the Riverboat Discovery on the Chena River.

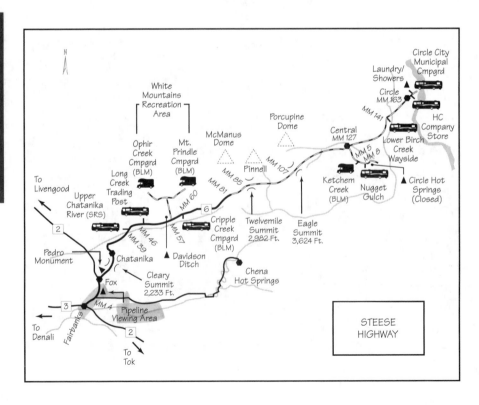

NORTH OF FAIRBANKS

THE PINNELL MOUNTAIN TRAIL IS A POPULAR HIKE ALONG THE STEESE HIGHWAY

At Fox junction the Steese Highway goes right while the Elliott Highway continues straight. After turning right you'll soon see the **Pedro Monument** on the left at Mile 16. Felix Pedro discovered gold near here, this was the strike that caused the founding of the city of Fairbanks.

The road climbs over the first of three summits, 2,233-foot **Cleary Summit**, at Mile 21 and descends into the **Chatanika River Valley**. This valley was another gold mining area, there are lots more tailing piles. The Chatanika Valley had two gold mining towns, Cleary and Chatanika. It also has the beautifully clear Chatanika River.

As the road continues northwest up the Chatanika Valley you may notice a large pipeline to the left. This is the **Davidson Ditch**, a system of ditches on the mountaintops and inverted siphons in the valleys that delivered water to the mining operations downstream. It is no longer in use but was only closed down after the 1967 Fairbanks flood.

At Mile 85 the road climbs up out of the trees to 2,982 foot **Twelvemile Summit.** The Pinnell Mountain National Recreation Trail, leading 24 miles (39 km) to Eagle Summit, leaves the road here. Note the scattered shiny pieces of airplanes that didn't quite make it over the summit.

The road takes a slightly lower route than the Pinnell trail to **Eagle Summit** at Mile 108. From there it descends to Central at Mile 127.

Central is a small town with a population of about 400 dating from the days of the Birch Creek strike in the early 1890s. Today there's a post office, an airstrip, and a museum. Gas was not available last time we visited.

In the middle of town is the junction with a gravel road that leads 8 miles (13 km) to Circle Hot Springs Resort. Unfortunately the resort has been closed for several years, hopefully it will reopen soon.

From Central the Steese Highway is narrower and not as straight. It continues another 35 miles (58 km) to **Circle City** on the Yukon River. Circle also dates from the Birch Creek Strike. It was known as the Paris of the north in the few short years before gold was found at Dawson City. Once that happened the miners abandoned Circle and headed upstream. Today you'll find a town with a population of about 100 people. Despite the name Circle is well south of the Arctic Circle, to cross it you'll have to drive up the Dalton Highway. Services in Circle include a small store, gas, a laundry, and a camping area on the south bank of the Yukon River.

Steese Highway Campgrounds

UPPER CHATANIKA RIVER STATE RECREATION SITE (STATE OF ALASKA)

Location:	Mile 39 Steese Highway
Info:	(907) 451-2695
Website:	dnr.alaska.gov/parks/aspunits/northern/upchatrvsrs.htm

GPS Location: 65.19197 N, 147.25644 W, 700 Ft.

The Upper Chatanika River campground is one of the nicest in this area. It offers some sites right on this beautifully clear wilderness river. This is a popular put-in point for canoeing the river.

There are 24 vehicle camping sites at this campground. They are well-separated by trees and natural vegetation and have picnic tables and fire pits. The best big-rig sites are off a clearing to the left as you enter. There are vault toilets and a hand-operated water pump. Firewood can be purchased. The campground is an access point for the Chatanika River Float Trail, a 19-mile (31-km) float to Mile 11 of the Elliott Highway at Whitefish Campground.

The campground is on the Steese Highway to Circle at Mile 39.

LONG CREEK TRADING POST

| Location: | Mile 45.5, Steese Highway |
| Telephone: | (907) 456-4104 |

GPS Location: 65.22036 N, 147.07521 W, 900 Ft.

The Long Creek Trading Post is a small store along the highway. They have three back-in RV sites (no size limit) with electricity. Water is available and also showers and a laundry. There is lots of room for tents to pitch on grass.

The campground is on the Steese Highway to Circle at Mile 45.5.

NORTH OF FAIRBANKS

🚐 MT. PRINDLE CAMPGROUND
(WHITE MOUNTAINS RECREATION AREA – BLM)

Location: U.S. Creek Road From Mile 57 of The Steese Highway
Info: (907) 474-2200
Website: www.blm.gov/ak/st/en/prog/nlcs/white_mtns/campgrounds.html

GPS Location: 65.36700 N, 146.59481 W, 2,500 Ft.

This is one of two campgrounds located off Nome Creek Road (also known as the White Mountains Gateway) in the White Mountains National Recreation Area. It is located in high country with few trees. The Quartz Creek Trail begins nearby and Nome Creek is just to the east.

The campground has 13 rather small sites off a loop, probably appropriately so since the access road is not suitable for really large RVs. Six are parallel parking sites so larger RVs could park if they successfully braved the road. There are vault toilets, and a hand-operated water pump. There is a 10-day limit at this campground.

The dirt and gravel U.S. Creek road goes north from Mile 57 of the Steese Highway. It is usually suitable for RVs up to about 35 feet. Just after leaving the Steese the road passes the Davidson Ditch water pipeline and then climbs across a pass to the Nome Creek watershed. After 7 miles (11 km) the road crosses Nome Creek and then comes to a T at Nome Creek Road, go right for Mt. Prindle Campground. You will reach the campground in another 4.2 miles (6.8 km).

🚐 OPHIR CREEK CAMPGROUND
(WHITE MOUNTAINS RECREATION AREA – BLM)

Location: U.S. Creek Road From Mile 57 Of The Steese Highway
Info: (907) 474-2200
Website: www.blm.gov/ak/st/en/prog/nlcs/white_mtns/campgrounds.html

GPS Location: 65.36886 N, 147.08422 W, 1,600 Ft.

This is the second of two campgrounds located off Nome Creek Road (also known as the White Mountains Gateway) in the White Mountains National Recreation Area. It is located in an area forested by small spruce trees. Ophir Creek meets Nome Creek here and they flow into the **Beaver Creek National Wild River** three miles (4.8 km) downstream. The campground provides the starting point for extended wilderness floats.

Ophir Creek Campground has nineteen campsites off two loops. These are mostly separated back-in sites with some parallel parking of larger RVs possible. Sites have picnic tables and fire pits, there are also raised grills at some sites. There are vault toilets and a hand-operated water pump. The stay limit here is 10 days.

The dirt and gravel U.S. Creek road goes north from Mile 57 of the Steese Highway. It is usually suitable for RVs up to about 35 feet. Just after leaving the Steese the road passes the Davidson Ditch water pipeline and then climbs across a pass to the Nome Creek watershed. After 7 miles (11 km) the road crosses Nome Creek and comes to a T at the Nome Creek Road, go left for Ophir Creek Campground. You will reach the campground in another 12.1 miles (19.5 km).

Cripple Creek Campground (BLM)

Location: Mile 60 Of Steese Highway
Info: (907) 474-2200
Website: www.blm.gov/ak/st/en/prog/nlcs/white_mtns/campgrounds.html

GPS Location: 65.27654 N, 146.64937 W, 1,200 Ft.

There are 12 back-in vehicle sites in a grove of mixed spruce and birch. Some sites will take RVs to 40 feet. Picnic tables and fire pits are provided. There are also 6 sites in a walk-in tent-camping area. There are vault toilets and a hand-operated water pump. The BLM also operates a recreational rental cabin at this campground. You must pre-register to use it, see our section about rental recreational cabins in Chapter 14 - *Camping Away From the Road System*. There's also a short walking trail along the river.

You will find this campground on the south side of the road near Mile 60.

Ketchem Creek

Location: Mile 5.7 Circle Hot Springs Road

FREE

GPS Location: 65.51023 N, 144.69273 W, 900 Ft.

This is a de-commissioned BLM campground. The 8 back-in spaces are still there in a grove of spruce but there are no other amenities; no toilets, no tables. Overhanging branches on the entry road and sites and short spaces make this a camping area with limited usefulness but there are few alternatives. It's OK for cars and vans, but anyone with something higher will have to cautiously enter the camping area and perhaps cut back a few branches overhead.

Watch for the campground on the side road that goes toward the old Circle Hot Springs Resort. It's between Mile 5 and Mile 6, on the right just before you cross the Ketchem Creek bridge.

Nugget Gulch

Location: Mile 8, Circle Hot Springs Road

GPS Location: 65.48450 N, 144.64330 W, 1,000 Ft.

Located right next door to the old Chena Hot Springs Resort, this small motel allows parking or tent camping on the large grassy field out front. There are picnic tables and fire pits, and pay showers are available.

From Central take the road toward Circle Hot Springs. You'll see the Nugget Gulch on the right at Mile 8.

Lower Birch Creek Wayside

Location: Near Mile 141 of the Steese Highway

GPS Location: 65.64119 N, 144.42311 W, 700 Ft.

This parking lot near Birch Creek is not an official campground but it's normally quiet and commonly used by RVers and tent campers visiting this area. It's also used for access to Birch Creek so make sure to park or pitch in a spot where you're not blocking others. That should be easy. It's a large gravel lot with a vault toilet, no other amenities.

NORTH OF FAIRBANKS

HC COMPANY STORE
Location: Circle City, Mile 163 of the Steese Hwy.

GPS Location: 65.82494 N, 144.06481 W, 600 Ft.

This is village land which is used for parking boat trailers. It's located on the river side of the HC Company Store. RVs can sometimes park there too overnight and it is really nicer than the boat ramp mentioned below. This RV parking area is not really part of the HC Company Store operation, but it's right next door and since no one else is usually around you might check at the store for permission to park. The store itself offers gas, diesel, a public phone, and supplies. The hours are very irregular. The coin-op village laundry across the street has water, pay showers, and toilets.

CIRCLE CITY MUNICIPAL CAMPGROUND
Location: Circle City, Mile 163 Of The Steese Hwy.

GPS Location: 65.82575 N, 144.06297 W, 600 Ft.

The town of Circle provides parking for RVs at the Yukon River boat ramp which forms the very end of the Steese Highway. There is room for about 5 RVs or tents with a few old picnic tables, fire rings, and a garbage bin. A barely usable outhouse is nearby, but back toward the entrance to town is a laundry which has toilets and hot showers. There can be a lot of activity here, make sure you park so that you aren't blocking the ramp.

To find this campground just follow the Steese Highway right to its end at the Yukon River, about Mile 163.

CHENA HOT SPRINGS ROAD
57 Miles (92 Kilometers)

The Chena Hot Springs Road is the most civilized of the routes north of Fairbanks. The road leads almost directly east from a junction at Mile 5 of the Steese Highway. The Chena Hot Springs Road is 57 miles (92 km) long and paved for its entire length. It generally leads up the valley of the Chena River. Along the way there are several campgrounds and access points for fishing or floating the Chena and also access to several good hiking trails into the surrounding hills.

Chena Hot Springs Road Campgrounds

ROSEHIP CAMPGROUND (CHENA RIVER STATE RECREATION AREA)
Location: Mile 27 Chena Hot Springs Road
Info: (907) 451-2695
Website: dnr.alaska.gov/parks/aspunits/northern/rosehipcamp.htm

GPS Location: 64.87717 N, 146.76481 W, 700 Ft.

This pleasant riverside campground has 37 vehicle camping sites. Many of the vehicle sites are long back-in sites suitable for any size RV. Trees and natural vegetation separate them. There are also four walk-in tent sites. The campground has picnic tables, fire pits, vault toilets, and a hand-operated water pump. Sites are off a circular drive so if you're towing you can drive in and take a look. There is often a host and

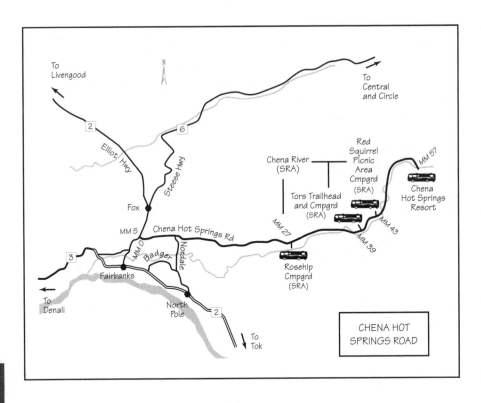

CHENA HOT SPRINGS ROAD

firewood is available. The Rosehip Campground is a popular access point for Chena River canoeists. There's also a nature trail.

The campground is located on the south side of the Chena Hot Springs Road at about Mile 27.

Tors Trailhead and Campground
(Chena River State Recreation Area)

Location:	Mile 39 Chena Hot Springs Road
Info:	(907) 451-2695
Website:	dnr.alaska.gov/parks/aspunits/northern/torstlcamp.htm

GPS Location: 64.90302 N, 146.36082 W, 700 Ft.

One of the most popular hikes in the Fairbanks area is to the Granite Tors, large granite rocks projecting from rounded hilltops. This campground makes a good base camp since it is where the trail starts.

The campground is located near the North Fork of the Chena River. There are 24 long back-in sites off a loop road. They are well separated with spruces and other natural vegetation and have picnic tables and fire pits. Grass covered pads are provided for tents. This campground has vault toilets, a hand-operated water pump, and a canoe launching area. Some sites are as long as 50 feet. There is often a host here, firewood is available.

You can't miss this campground since it sits on the north side of the highway near Mile 39 of the Chena Hot Springs Road. A bridge over the North Fork of the Chena helps mark the location.

RED SQUIRREL PICNIC AREA CAMPGROUND (CHENA RIVER STATE RECREATION AREA)

Location:	Mile 43 Chena Hot Springs Road
Info:	(907) 451-2695
Website:	dnr.alaska.gov/parks/aspunits/northern/rdsqrlcamp.htm

GPS Location: 64.93606 N, 146.28510 W, 800 Ft.

This is really just a picnic area with two covered picnic kiosks but camping is allowed in open parking areas. The campground is suitable for about 10 RVs to 40 feet and there are spots for tents too. If you're in a coach towing something and go in to take a look you'll probably have to unhitch to turn around. The place is attractive and is next to a small lake. There are picnic tables, fire rings, vault toilets, and a hand-operated water pump.

The campground is located on the north side of the Chena Hot Springs Road at about Mile 43.

CHENA HOT SPRINGS RESORT

Address:	PO Box 58740, Fairbanks, AK 99711
Telephone:	(907) 451-8104
Website:	www.chenahotsprings.com

GPS Location: 65.05471 N, 146.05888 W, 1,200 Ft.

At the end of a 57-mile paved highway Chena Hot Springs is the easiest to reach of the hot springs north of Fairbanks. The springs here were discovered in 1905, the water comes out of the ground at 165° F. The outdoor pool is a must-see (actually a must-swim).

Chena Hot Springs is a small resort offering campsites, hotel rooms, a restaurant and bar, an ice museum and ice bar, and an aircraft landing strip. The swimming area includes an indoor pool and hot tubs, outdoor hot tub, and an extremely impressive outdoor pool surrounded by rocks with a smooth gravel bottom and hot water. This pool itself is worth the trip out to the resort. The price for camping does not include swimming, there is an extra daily charge for that. Wi-Fi is available at the resort, but does not reach the camping areas. There is an extra charge.

There are two camping areas. One area has larger sites, both back-in and pull-thru, adjoining the parking lot on the north side. Also in this area is a loop in the trees with smaller sites. Together there are 24 sites north of the parking lot. The site's number signs even show site length so it's easy to pick one. There are no utility hookups but outhouses are provided. All sites have picnic tables and fire pits.

A second area is located west of the main area of the resort. Many sites here have rental yurts but there are also six sites for tents. Again, there are no hookups but outhouses are provided. These sites also have picnic tables and fire pits.

The resort also has a dump station with water fill and a laundry. Nearby cross-country skiing trails can be used as hiking trails in the summer. Other offered activities

CHENA HOT SPRINGS OUTDOOR POOL

include bike rentals, canoeing, a dog kennel tour and sled-dog rides, flight-seeing, horseback tours, ATV tours, and even ice carving classes.

Chena Hot Springs Resort is located at the very end of the Chena Hot Spring Road near Mile 57.

Elliot Highway
152 Miles (245 Kilometers)

If the Chena Hot Springs road is the most civilized of these routes north of Fairbanks the Elliot Highway is the quietest, at least once you pass the Dalton Highway Junction. The Elliot Highway leaves the Steese Highway at Mile 11 at the Fox junction. From there it leads northeast to Livengood. Just past Livengood the Dalton Highway turns north to the Arctic Ocean while the Elliot Highway heads westward to Manley Hot Springs.

The Elliot Highway is paved as far as the Dalton Highway Junction at Mile 73. After the Dalton junction the road is much narrower and often rough but still suitable for all RVs. The Elliott follows ridge tops west with vistas to the south across the extensive Minto Flats. It's actually very similar to the better known Top of the World Highway. Many people camp at an unofficial campground at Mile 75 at the Tolovana River Bridge and at other pull-offs and gravel pits along the road. A side road at Mile 110 leads 10 miles south to **Minto**, an Athabaskan Indian village. Another side road at Mile 131 leads north to the gold-mining district of **Eureka**.

Finally at Mile 152 the highway reaches **Manley Hot Springs**. The hot springs and town were developed in the early 1900s to service nearby gold fields at Tofty and Eureka. Access to the Tanana River made the town a supply center. Today there are some 100 residents. Dry camping is allowed at the small city park in town just west of the slough bridge. There are fire pits, picnic tables, and an outhouse. The Manley Roadhouse has a restaurant and bar, showers, and laundry. Ask at the roadhouse about the greenhouse run by Chuck and Gladys Dart, it has hot spring fed concrete baths.

From Manley Hot Springs an access road leads 16 miles (10 km) into the **Tofty** mining area. Mining continues in the district.

Elliot Highway Campgrounds

NORTHERN MOOSED RV PARK AND CAMPGROUND
  Location: Mile 0 Elliot Highway
  Telephone: (907) 451-0984

   GPS Location: 64.96226 N, 147.62087 WW, 800 Ft.

The campground name here is a play on words. They're proud to be the northernmost full-hookup campground in Alaska.

There are about forty sites including pull-thrus and back-ins for big rigs. Some sites have full-hookups but there are also partial hookup and no-hookup and tent sites. The central building houses the office, restrooms, and a laundry. There's also a dump site.

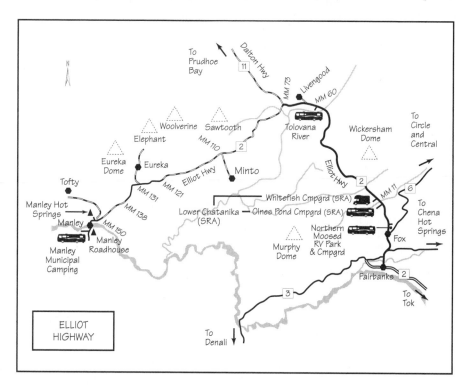

ELLIOT
HIGHWAY

To reach the campground follow the Steese Highway north from Fairbanks for 11 miles (18 km), then go straight ahead past the State of Alaska truck weighing station. You're now on the Elliott Highway and the campground entrance is on your right, just past the weight station.

OLNES POND CAMPGROUND (LOWER CHATANIKA STATE RECREATION AREA)

Location:	Mile 11 Elliot Highway
Info:	(907) 451-2695
Website:	dnr.alaska.gov/parks/aspunits/northern/olnespond.html

GPS Location: 65.07678 N, 147.74656 W, 500 Ft.

For several years Olnes Pond was one of the Alaska state campgrounds that was put on "passive management" status. That means it was not maintained to normal standards so there was no charge. This has changed and the campground is being refurbished, a fee may soon be reestablished.

This large gravel pit filled with a small lake is a good campground for folks with swimming-age children. Gravel pits are often popular central Alaska destinations since the good interior weather makes them warm enough for swimming by about the first of July. Make sure you take precautions against swimmers itch, however, there is a sign board explaining the phenomena and how to deal with it at the campground.

There are dedicated campsites dotted around the lake along the surrounding tree line. Some have picnic tables. There's quite a bit of room here, big RVs should have no problem finding a good spot to park. There are several vault toilets. The camping limit here is 15 days.

To reach the campground follow the road south from the Elliot Highway at about Mile 11. The good entry road is about 1.1 miles (1.8 km) long.

WHITEFISH CAMPGROUND (LOWER CHATANIKA STATE RECREATION AREA)

Location:	Mile 11 Elliot Highway
Info:	(907) 451-2695
Website:	dnr.alaska.gov/parks/aspunits/northern/whitefish.htm

GPS Location: 65.08617 N, 147.73139 W, 500 Ft.

This campground along the Chatanika River is a popular place to spearfish for whitefish in the fall, it is also the take-out point for canoeists on the Chatanika River. It, like nearby Olnes Pond which is described above, was "passively managed" but is being refurbished, a fee may soon be reestablished.

The campground has about 7 camping spots off two loops. Sites are suitable for RVs to about 35 feet. Picnic tables, fire pits and vault toilets are provided. There is a boat launch as well as a picnic shelter and group firepit.

The campground is located about a half-mile past the turnoff to Olnes Pond on the Elliott Highway at Mile 11. If you are coming from Fairbanks turn left just after crossing the bridge.

TOLOVANA RIVER

Location: Mile 60 Elliot Highway

GPS Location: 65.46623 N, 148.33200 W, 600 Ft.

This is really just an informal camping area next to the bridge over the Tolovana River. The state has formalized it in a way, there is a camping sign pointing to it as you approach from the Fairbanks side. There is enough room for two large RVs to park. There are no facilities except rock fire rings.

The camping area is on the Elliot Highway near Mile 60.

MANLEY MUNICIPAL CAMPING

Location: West Of The Bridge, Across From The Roadhouse

GPS Location: 65.00110 N, 150.63520 W, 300 Ft.

Manley has a municipal camping area with parking in a large dirt lot and a few short back-ins spaces next to the slough. They make decent tent locations. There is an outhouse and a few fire pits. At the roadhouse across the road you'll find a restaurant, bar, showers, and laundry. There's an extra charge for these facilities as the roadhouse is a privately owned business.

As you enter Manley you'll cross a metal bridge across a slough. The Manley Roadhouse is on the left, the camping area on the right. You pay for the camping at the roadhouse.

DALTON HIGHWAY
420 Miles (677 Kilometers)

The North Slope Haul Road, now called the Dalton Highway, is one of the few remaining highways in the U.S. through really remote country. It is open to tourist traffic all the way to Deadhorse. Along the highway you will find spectacular scenery as well as lots of opportunities for fishing, hiking, wildlife viewing, and just plain experiencing really empty country. Often you'll have nothing but the road and the pipeline to keep you company.

You should check road conditions before heading north. Call the Alaska Department of Transportation at (907) 456-7623 for recorded information or the Alaska Public Lands Information Center at (907) 456-0527.

The Dalton Highway demands preparation. The road surface is gravel and often in poor condition. Travelers should carry at least two mounted spare tires of each size required and any equipment necessary to change them. Your vehicle must be in excellent mechanical condition. Gasoline stops are few and far between, as are service facilities. If you do break down be prepared to pay a hefty price for tow service. Heavy trucks commonly travel the highway so tourists should exercise caution. Drive with your lights on at all times. In the event of a breakdown the truckers can relay messages, the commonly used CB channel is 19.

Mileages on the Dalton start at the southern end where the highway leaves the Elliott Highway at Mile 73. Gasoline and services are available at three locations: the **Yu-**

kon Crossing at Mile 56, **Coldfoot** at Mile 175, and **Deadhorse** at Mile 420. Note the 245-mile gap between Coldfoot and Deadhorse.

While not widely known a few sections of the road are paved and more is being completed each year. As you head north gravel starts at the junction with the Elliott Highway which is 84 miles north of Fairbanks. There are paved sections from Mile 19 to Mile 24, and between mile 36 and Mile 49 before you reach the Yukon River. Then there's a long section from about Mile 90 to Mile 198 which is 22 miles beyond Coldfoot. The section from Mile 258 to Mile 266 is paved and there are a few other short sections of seal-coated road, some badly worn, including a long section from Mile 334 near Happy Valley to Mile 362 just past Pump Station 2.

Much of the land that the Dalton Highway crosses is public lands. From the Yukon River crossing north to Mile 301 there is a 24-mile-wide utility corridor that is administered by the BLM. To the east along the Yukon River is the **Yukon Flats National Wildlife Refuge**. West of the highway at about Mile 115 is the **Kanuti National Wildlife Refuge**. West of the highway, this time in the Brooks Range, is the **Gates of the Arctic National Park and Preserve**. Finally, east of the highway through the Brooks Range and north to the ocean is the **Arctic National Wildlife Refuge**. Information and administrative offices are at the Yukon River Crossing Visitor Contact Station at Mile 56 and the Coldfoot Interagency Visitor Center at Mile 175. Both can provide lots of information about the road, the surrounding country, and recreational opportunities.

THE DALTON FOLLOWS THE PIPELINE NORTH ALL THE WAY TO DEADHORSE

There is a historic gold mining area on the Dalton too. The strike at Coldfoot was in 1900, everyone later moved to a new strike at Wiseman. You'll still find some mining activity there as well as a few tourist oriented businesses but no campground.

Once you get to Prudhoe Bay you will find that you cannot enter the oil fields and cannot drive to the Arctic Ocean. The only access is through an authorized tour company. You must call the tour company and make a reservation at least 24 hours in advance: Arctic Ocean Shuttle (888 474-3565 or 907 474-3565), operating out of Deadhorse Camp which also has hotel rooms that can be reserved at the same number. They also serve meals.

Dalton Highway Campgrounds

Formal camping facilities along the Dalton Highway are extremely limited. The only commercial campground is in Coldfoot at Mile 175. **Coldfoot Camp** has electrical hookups, water and showers. At Mile 60.7, five miles (8 km) north of the Yukon River, there is an old pipeline-camp gravel pad where camping is allowed, facilities include an artesian spring for water, and a dump station. There is also a BLM camping area near **Arctic Circle Wayside** in a revegetated gravel pit at Mile 115 with vault toilets but no water. The BLM has a formal campground near Coldfoot at Mile 179.5. This is called **Marion Creek Campground** and has pull-thru and back-in sites with picnic tables, fire pits, a well, and vault toilets. **Galbraith Lake** at Mile 275 is another old pipeline-camp gravel pad, there is a vault toilet but no water. A huge rest area is at the **Mile 355 Wayside** with a vault toilet. RVers tend to camp pretty much anywhere that looks good, make sure not to block the pipeline maintenance access roads and do not camp in the Toolik Lake Research Natural Area between Mile 278 and Mile 293. At Deadhorse, the end of the road for tourists, there are no facilities for RVs. Hotel rooms and meals are available with prior reservations at the Deadhorse Camp (www.deadhorsecamp.com, (907) 474-3565, (888) 474-3565) at Mile 413, just before you enter Deadhorse.

FIVE MILE CAMP CAMPING AREA (BLM)
Location: Mile 60.7 Of The Dalton Highway

GPS Location: 65.91867 N, 149.82850 W, 400 Ft.

Located 5 miles (8 km) north of the bridge over the Yukon, this camping area was the location of Five Mile Camp when the pipeline was under construction. Reader boards at the camping area describe the camps along the highway during the pipeline construction and their operation.

The camping area is a large gravel area, not completely flat but with lots of flat areas to park any size RV. There are a few picnic tables and also some fire pits as well as a vault toilet. A host is sometimes on site and firewood is available. There is a dump station just north of the parking area along the access road, one of only two available along the Dalton Highway. There is also an artesian well and sometimes a hose for water nearby. Just .3 mile (.5 km) south of the campground is a commercial roadhouse called the Hotspot Café with restaurant, gift shop, and restrooms.

The access road to the campground goes west from the Dalton Highway 5 miles (8 km) north of the Yukon bridge near mile 60.7. It's .2 mile (.3 km) from the highway to the camping area.

ARCTIC CIRCLE WAYSIDE CAMPING AREA (BLM)

Location: Mile 115 Of The Dalton Highway

GPS Location: 66.55825 N, 150.79314 W, 1,300 Ft.

Where the highway crosses the Arctic Circle there is a formal rest stop with parking, vault toilets, and some nice picnic areas with tables. From the north end of the rest stop a gravel road goes east for a half mile to a camping area. Gravel roads loop through an area of scattered birches. There is a vault toilet, a few picnic tables and some fire rings. Any size RV can access the camping area and park.

COLDFOOT CAMP

Telephone: (907) 474-3500
Website: www.coldfootcamp.com

GPS Location: 67.25128 N, 150.17347 W, 1,100 Ft.

Coldfoot Camp is the only hookup campground along the highway. There is a restaurant and gas station here, a small motel called the Slate Creek Inn, and the RV parking area. A small garage can fix flats. Across the highway is the federal Arctic Interagency Visitor's Center which has exhibits, a book store, and staff to answer your questions about the area.

The camping area has about twenty sites with 20-amp electrical outlets and water. It is located in an open gravel area about a hundred yards northeast of the restaurant and motel.

The campground is on the east side of the highway at Mile 175.

MARION CREEK CAMPGROUND (BLM)

Location: Mile 179.5 Of The Dalton Highway
Info: (907) 474-2200

GPS Location: 67.31608 N, 150.15944 W, 1,000 Ft.

This is a modern BLM campground designed for big RVs. There are 27 sites. Many are pull-thrus suitable for any size RV. A few of the smaller back-in sites have tent platforms and all have picnic tables and fire pits. Restrooms are vault toilets and there's a water pump. This campground has a host and a bear-proof storage bin. It is located on the east side of the highway at Mile 179.5.

GALBRAITH LAKE CAMPING AREA (BLM)

Location: Mile 274.7 Of The Dalton Highway

GPS Location: 68.45383 N, 149.48194 W, 2,800 Ft.

This camping areas is the former site of the Galbraith Camp. It's a large flat gravel area with vault toilets, fire rings, and bear-proof food lockers. Water is from the creek. Any size RV can park here. The campground is about four miles (6 km) off the highway to the west with an access road leading past the Galbraith airstrip. This is a rough slow road but passable in any rig, in an RV it is slow going.

355 MILE WAYSIDE

Location: Mile 355 Dalton Highway

GPS Location: 69.42200 N, 148.69133 W, 1,000 Ft.

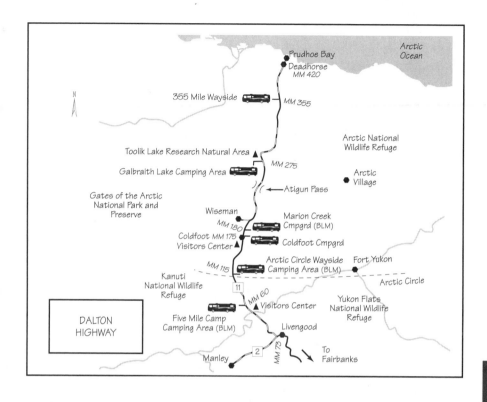

This is a very large gravel lot that is used as a wayside. There is lots of room to park well out of the way. There are vault toilets and bear-proof garbage bins.

NORTH OF FAIRBANKS DUMP STATIONS

There's a definite shortage of dump stations north of Fairbanks. There's one at Chena Hot Springs Resort (GPS Location 65.05471 N, 146.05888 W). The Dalton Highway also has one at Five Mile Camping Area at Mile 60.7 (*GPS Location 65.91867 N, 149.82850 W*). It's best to leave Fairbanks with your water tanks full and your waste tanks empty.

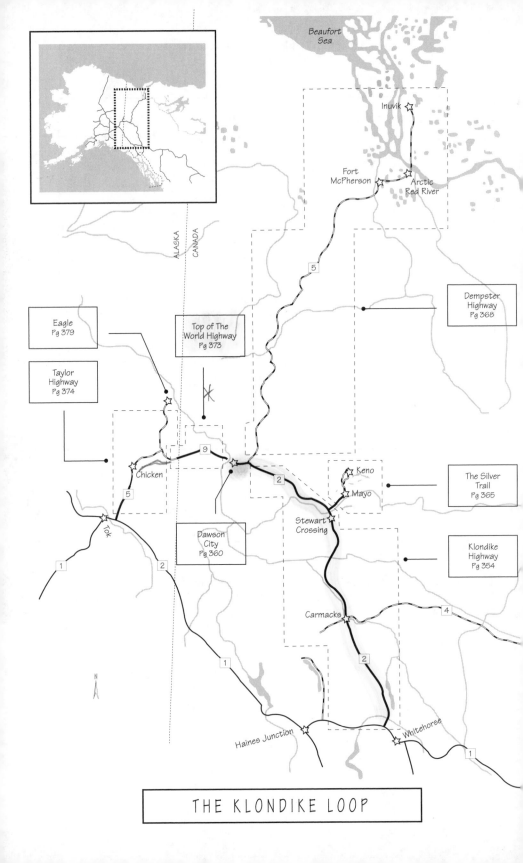

THE KLONDIKE LOOP

Chapter 11

The Klondike Loop

INTRODUCTION

A series of three different highways form a half-loop north of the Alaska Highway from Whitehorse to Tok. They are a not-to-be-missed alternate to the Alaska Highway. We recommend that travelers from the Lower 48 plan to drive the Klondike Loop one way and the Alaska Highway between Whitehorse and Tok the other. However, a warning is in order. When it's wet the 45 miles (73 km) of gravel, mud, and clay road between the Alaska border and the beginning of the pavement near Chicken can be difficult, perhaps even downright dangerous for large coaches and trailers. If the weather is wet and you're driving a big rig you should consider driving to Dawson City and then backtracking rather than making the loop. See the *Taylor Highway* section for more about this.

The Klondike Loop is really three highways. From Whitehorse north to Dawson City in the Yukon you follow the **Klondike Highway**, the distance is 527 km (327 miles). Then, from Dawson City west for 127 km (78 miles) and across the Alaska-Canada border there is the **Top of the World Highway**. Finally, in Alaska, the route follows a portion of the **Taylor Highway** 155 kilometers (96 miles) south. The Taylor really runs from the Alaska Highway near Tok north to Eagle, in this chapter we'll cover that entire highway since Eagle in an interesting destination in its own right.

The Klondike Loop visits true gold rush country. The 1896 Klondike strike was made in the creeks near Dawson City. Many of the Klondike Argonauts traveled on the Yukon River from Whitehorse to Dawson City. The Klondike Highway from Whitehorse to Dawson City follows this general route, although it follows the much straighter path that was historically a winter trail and gets you there much faster.

Highlights

Gold and the gold rushes are a big part of Alaska and the Yukon, past and present. There was no bigger or more famous rush than Dawson's Klondike rush. Even though the town is really in Canada no visit to Alaska would be complete without a visit to **Dawson City**.

A short but pleasant side trip is the **Silver Trail**. The big mines in the area are shuttered but a few of the people and the history are still there. It's a great chance to visit some small friendly towns off the main highway.

The **Campbell Highway** runs for 582 kilometers (361 miles) connecting the Alaska Highway in Watson Lake with the Klondike Loop near Carmacks. This is a mostly gravel route although there are some paved sections near the Carmacks end. The highway and its campgrounds are described in our Alaska Highway chapter but since the best road conditions are on the western end many travelers elect to visit Faro and Ross River from the Klondike Loop. See Chapter 4 – *The Alaska Highway* for more information.

The 742 km (460-mile) **Dempster Highway** heads north from a junction near Dawson City. This is one of only two opportunities in the Yukon and Alaska to drive north of the Arctic Circle and approach the coast of the Arctic Ocean. The Dempster ends at **Inuvik**, from there you can easily fly to other arctic destinations in the area.

A trip along the **Top of the World Highway** west of Dawson City isn't to be missed. It comes complete with a ferry crossing of the Yukon River.

Eagle, Alaska is like no other small town in the state. Eagle is truly at the end of the road, but at one time it was in the center of the action. There's lots of history to see and friendly folks to show it to you.

Fuel

See the following page for the *Fuel Price Comparison Table*.

Fishing

Along the Klondike Highway between Whitehorse and Dawson give these waters a try: **Lake Laberge** (Km 225) for lake trout, grayling, and northern pike; **Fox Creek** (Km 228) for grayling; **Fox Lake** (Km 248) for lake trout, grayling and northern pike; **Little Fox Lake** (Km 259) for lake trout, grayling, and northern pike; **Braeburn Lake** (Km 282) for lake trout, grayling, and northern pike; **Twin Lakes** (Km 308) for lake trout, grayling, northern pike; **Nordenskiold River** (Km 354) for grayling; **Tatchun Creek** (Km 382) for grayling; **Tatchun Lake** (take 6 km road at Km 382) for northern pike; **Crooked Creek** (Km 523) for grayling; **Moose Creek** (Km 560) for grayling; **McQuesten River** (Km 582) for grayling; **Klondike River** (Km 698) for grayling; and finally, the **Klondike River mouth** at Dawson City for grayling.

In Alaska the **Fortymile River** has grayling, try Mile 43, Mile 64, Mile 75, and Mile

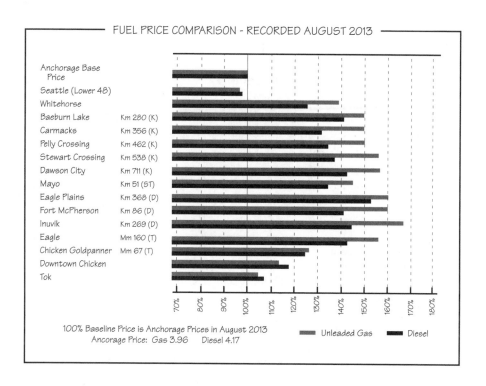

FUEL PRICE COMPARISON - RECORDED AUGUST 2013

Location	
Anchorage Base Price	
Seattle (Lower 48)	
Whitehorse	
Baeburn Lake	Km 280 (K)
Carmacks	Km 356 (K)
Pelly Crossing	Km 462 (K)
Stewart Crossing	Km 538 (K)
Dawson City	Km 711 (K)
Mayo	Km 51 (ST)
Eagle Plains	Km 368 (D)
Fort McPherson	Km 86 (D)
Inuvik	Km 269 (D)
Eagle	Mm 160 (T)
Chicken Goldpanner	Mm 67 (T)
Downtown Chicken	
Tok	

100% Baseline Price is Anchorage Prices in August 2013
Ancorage Price: Gas 3.96   Diesel 4.17

Unleaded Gas   Diesel

81 of the Taylor Highway. Also try **Four Mile Lake** at Mile 4 of the Taylor Highway for rainbows, it is reached along a 1-mile (1.6 km) trail.

Boating, Rafting, Canoeing, and Kayaking

The **Yukon River** was the original highway in this country and it continues to be an excellent float trip. It is actually possible to travel the river from the upper end of the Chilkoot Trail at Lake Bennett downstream all the way to the mouth of the river in far western Alaska. Most people limit their trip to the section from Marsh Lake or Whitehorse to Dawson City or Eagle. Access to the river and the logistics of the drop-off and pick-up are easiest on this route. The Whitehorse to Dawson City section is easily done in a canoe, they can be rented in Whitehorse and arrangements made for a pick-up in Dawson City. Plan on about 2 weeks to make the trip to allow plenty of time to explore old gold rush settlements and relics along the way. The river has little in the way of challenges other than a 51-kilometer (32-mile) crossing of Lake Laberge where it is best to stay near the west shore for safety in the event of sudden winds. See Chapter 14 for more about this.

The **Fortymile River** is a designated National Wild and Scenic River. It is rated Class II to Class III with rapids to Class IV. Experienced paddlers can float this river in canoes but inflatables are probably best. Put-in points include the four bridges along the Taylor Highway with the take-out near Clinton which is near the Yukon at the end of a 40 km (25-mile) road from Km 59 of the Top Of The World Highway.

THE KLONDIKE LOOP

For information including current river conditions contact: BLM, Eastern Interior Field Office, 1150 University Avenue, Fairbanks, AK 99709, (907) 474-2200 or (800) 437-7021.

Hiking and Mountain Biking

There is a hiking trail from the south end of the Yukon River bridge at Km 357 of the Klondike Highway near Carmacks. It follows the river to **Coal Mine Lake**. Across the river is **Tantalus Butte**, known for its coal seams that were mined for riverboat fuel.

From an overlook at Km 379 there is a good trail down the bluff to the **Five-Finger Rapids** of the Yukon River. Two hundred and twenty-one stairs from the highway down to the floor of the valley make this a short but challenging hike, particularly on the way back.

Around Dawson City there are several interesting walks. The **sternwheeler graveyard** is on the west bank of the Yukon River. The trail begins at the Yukon River Campground. Follow the campground loop road as far downstream as possible, then the riverbank. You'll find three abandoned and deteriorated riverboats pulled up on the bank.

There's a trail to the top of **Midnight Dome** where you will find excellent views over Dawson City and the Yukon River. The trail is on the left just after you start up the Old Dome Road at the east end of King Street. It is also possible to drive to the top of Midnight Dome, the New Dome Road cuts off the main highway just outside Dawson.

The "creeks" make an interesting place to explore on foot or mountain bike. Two long gravel loop roads (one off the other) and several access roads leading off them let you explore **Eldorado Creek, Sulphur Creek, Dominion Creek, and Hunker Creek**; all very historic ground although much of it has been dredged in the years since the original 98 rush. A hiking route called the **Ridge Road Trail** runs through the area.

THE ROUTES, TOWNS, AND CAMPGROUNDS

KLONDIKE HIGHWAY
520 Kilometers (322 Miles)

About 13 km (8 miles) west of Whitehorse Alaska-bound travelers have a choice. They can continue west on the Alaska Highway or turn right and head for Dawson City along what is called the Klondike Loop. If the road beyond Dawson City has been cleared of snow and is open you should consider visiting Dawson City on your way north, early fall snows could make a trip on the Top of the World Highway a real trial in September. On the other hand, if you plan to return south before September you can wait until then to visit Dawson, although some tourist attractions may have been closed by then.

The Klondike Highway (Yukon Highway 2) is an excellent paved highway. It is not difficult to drive the entire distance from Whitehorse to Dawson in one day in any rig. Don't be in a hurry, however, this is a historic route and there are some good places to do some exploring.

Because the Klondike Highway is in Canada it is marked in kilometers. The highway really starts in Skagway, so the kilometer marker at the beginning of this route near Whitehorse is the 192 km marker.

The first junction, at Km 198, will take you west to **Takhini Hot Springs**. There's a campground at the hot springs, it's described below. The hot springs are worth a stop even if you decide not to camp there.

After passing the Takhini Hot Springs cutoff the highway passes along the west side of **Lake Laberge**. You will probably recognize this lake as Lake Labarge from Robert Service's poem "The Cremation of Sam McGee". Unfortunately the big lake isn't really visible from the road. You can drive down to the lake and take a look at Lake Laberge Campground at Km 225. Lake Laberge was well-known to Klondike travelers since the big lake was the last part of the water route from Whitehorse to Dawson to thaw in the spring.

Like the Richardson Highway in Alaska the Klondike Highway had a series of road-houses to serve travelers in early days. The **Montague House** at Km 324 was one of these.

Carmacks at Km 357 was the location of a trading post founded by one of the three

A RED FOX STROLLS BY AT PELLY RIVER CROSSING

THE KLONDIKE LOOP

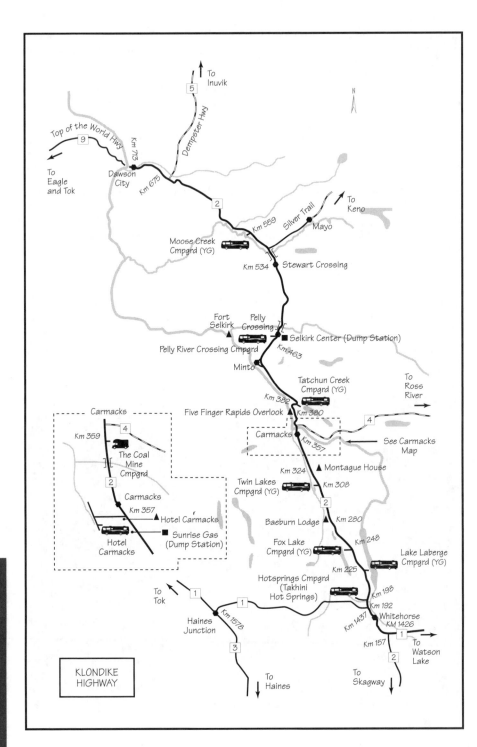

men who made the first gold discovery on the Klondike. George Carmack settled in Carmacks in 1892. Now there's an RV park at Carmacks, not to mention other services. It is sometimes possible to take a boat tour from there through Five Finger Rapids.

A large pull-off at Km 380 gives a great view of **Five Finger Rapids** far below. These rapids were run by huge sternwheelers. The riverboats didn't have enough power to pass through going upstream so they were winched up on a cable. There is a long stairway and a trail leading from the overlook down to the rapids.

Fort Selkirk was an important trading post along the Yukon. It is located at the confluence of the Pelly and Yukon Rivers, about 61 km (38 miles) downstream from Pelly Crossing (Km 463 of the Klondike Highway). It was originally founded for the Hudson's Bay Company in 1848. Now abandoned, the fort can only be reached by water or air. Boat transport may be available from Pelly Crossing.

Silver was also mined in this part of the world. Follow the **Silver Trail** east from Km 535 at Stewart Crossing. It will take you to Mayo, Elsa and Keno City, a distance of 111 km (69 miles) one way. The first 58 km (36 miles), to just beyond Mayo, are paved. There are several campgrounds on this routes, see the *Silver Trail* section in this chapter for information about them.

At Km 675 you'll reach the junction with the **Dempster Highway**. The Highway and its campgrounds are described in the *Dempster Highway* section in this chapter. Then, in just 37 more kilometers (23 miles) you'll reach the outskirts of Dawson City.

Klondike Highway Campgrounds

HOTSPRINGS CAMPGROUND (TAKHINI HOT SPRINGS)

Address:	Box 20423, Whitehorse, Y.T. Y1A 7A2
Telephone:	(867) 456-8004
Email:	camp@yukoncampground.com
Website:	www.yukoncampground.com/

GPS Location: 60.87873 N, 135.35745 W, 2,400 Ft.

For something different near Whitehorse you might try the city's favorite swimming hole: Takhini Hot Springs. They have a shallow but nice swimming pool that is kept comfortably hot, but not steaming, about 100° F and also a hot pool. The pools feel great and there's no smelly sulfur in them. There's also a café

A new campground, managed separately from the hotsprings, is partially open with further construction under way. It will have about 60 sites including very large pull-thrus and back-ins with 15, 30, or 50-amp power. Sites don't have water and sewer but there is a water fill and dump station (extra fee not reflected in rates shown in icon area above). There are also tent sites and toilet and shower facilities. Campers get a discount when using the hotsprings.

To find the campground follow the paved access highway from Km 198 of the North Klondike Highway westward for 9.0 kilometers (5.6 miles). The campground road goes to the right and the hot springs is directly ahead. The campground office is at the campground, not the hotsprings.

LAKE LABERGE CAMPGROUND (YUKON GOV.)

Location: Km 225 Northern Klondike Highway
Info: (867) 667-5648

GPS Location: 61.07508 N, 135.19817 W, 2,100 Ft.

The campground has 16 vehicle sites and additional tent sites off two loops and a gravel area near the lake adjoining a boat launch. Sites are back-ins to about 30 feet although the few sites opening onto the boat launch clearing will take any size RV. The campground is best for RVs to about 30 feet due to restricted maneuvering room. Sites have picnic tables and fire pits. The campground also offers vault toilets, a kitchen/picnic shelter, drinking water, and free firewood.

The mostly gravel entrance road, marked as Deep Creek Rd., leaves the highway near Km 225 and leads east for 2.9 km (1.8 miles) to the campground. Only the first 2 km (1.2 miles) of the road are paved.

FOX LAKE CAMPGROUND (YUKON GOV.)

Location: Km 248 Northern Klondike Highway
Info: (867) 667-5648

GPS Location: 61.24529 N, 135.46079 W, 2,700 Ft.

This popular campground has 43 sites, 3 are tent sites and the rest are separated vehicle sites. These are mostly back-ins, some are along the lakeshore, and several will take RVs to 60 feet. Sites are off a circular drive so even if you're towing you can go in and check for empty sites without fear of finding a dead end. All sites have picnic tables and fire pits. The campground also offers vault toilets, a playground, a kitchen/picnic shelter, a boat ramp, and a hand-operated water pump.

TWIN LAKES CAMPGROUND (YUKON GOV.)

Location: Km 308 Northern Klondike Highway
Info: (867) 667-5648

GPS Location: 61.70472 N, 135.93781 W, 2,200 Ft.

Twin Lake Campground offers two different camping areas. The first has 10 back-in sites. They are well separated by trees and vegetation. Another 9 sites are arranged around a gravel parking lot near one of the lakes. Some sites will take RVs to 45 feet. All have picnic tables and fire pits. The campground also offers a kitchen/picnic shelter, a hand-operated water pump, free firewood, a boat ramp, and a small dock.

HOTEL CARMACKS

Address: Box 160, Carmacks
            Y.T. Y0B 1C0
Telephone: (867) 863-5221
Email: info@hotelcarmacks.com
Website: www.hotelcarmacks.com

GPS Location: 62.08999 N, 136.28282 W, 1,700 Ft.

This is a modern campground, just a few years old. It sits behind the hotel and Chevron station but across a small road from the river. There's a nice boardwalk along the river and you can get a brochure with a walking tour when you check in. The RV park is in a relatively quiet location and is pleasant place to stay. The motel has a restaurant and lounge and the there is a laundry and restrooms with showers.

THE KLONDIKE LOOP

The campground has 15 sites. They're full-hookup sites, several are pull-thrus to 60 feet. Each site has a patch of grass and a picnic table, some of the back-ins have trees too. In the building out front are a gas station and a general store. Wi-Fi is free but only for the first 60 minutes. No-hookup camping is available if the campground is full. Check-in is at the motel office.

The hotel is located near Km 357 of the Northern Klondike Highway. This is in the community of Carmacks.

THE COAL MINE CAMPGROUND

Address:	PO Box 110, Carmacks, Y.T. Y0B 1C0
Telephone:	(867) 863-6363
Email:	coalminecampgroundcarmacks@yahoo.com
Website:	www.coalminecampground.com

GPS Location: 62.11082 N, 136.26778 W, 1,700 Ft.

This small campground along the shore of the Yukon River now has RV sites in addition to the tent-camping sites that have long been popular with folks floating the river. The tent sites are scattered in the trees along the river and the RV sites are back-ins in an area between the riverside tent sites and the highway. These RV sites are somewhat sheltered from the highway by a fence, but there's not much traffic anyway. They open into a gravel maneuvering area and can take RVs to 32 feet. Seven sites have electricity, another seven have no utilities. There are also a few smaller vehicle sites in trees. Tents sites have picnic tables and fire pits, RV sites have picnic tables only. A water fill station and dump station are provided and a small building has flush toilets, showers, and a laundry. A few rental cabins are available. An on-site snack bar has a large covered and screened seating area, it's very popular with the tent campers.

Watch for the campground on the east side of the highway near Km 359. This is north of the bridge over the Yukon and just south of the cutoff to Ross River on the Robert Campbell Highway, about 3 km (2 miles) north of Carmacks.

TATCHUN CREEK CAMPGROUND (YUKON GOV.)

Location:	Km 382 Of The North Klondike Highway
Info:	(867) 667-5648

GPS Location: 62.28335 N, 136.30651 W, 1,500 Ft.

The campground has 12 spaces, one is a double pull-thru and one a parallel-type pull-off. Several sites are along the river. Trees and natural vegetation separate the spaces. Each space has a picnic table and fire pit, there are vault toilets, a kitchen/picnic shelter, and free firewood. There's no pump, water is only available in the creek. Some sites will take a 40 foot RV and there are loops so even if you're towing you can go in and check for empty sites without fear of finding a dead end.

PELLY RIVER CROSSING CAMPGROUND AND SELKIRK HERITAGE CENTRE

Address:	Pelly Crossing, Y.T. Y0B 1P0
Telephone:	(867) 537-3031

GPS Location: 62.82576 N, 136.58118 W, 1,500 Ft.

If you don't feel the need for hookups but do like having other amenities handy Pelly River Crossing Campground is a decent choice. The campground is along the river south of the Pelly River bridge, you can't miss it. It's just about halfway between Whitehorse and Dawson City. Across the street is Selkirk Center with gas and groceries. Next to it is the Selkirk Heritage Centre, a replica of Big Jonathan House at Fort Selkirk, with exhibits explaining the First Nation history of the area. Many of the residents moved here from Fort Selkirk which is located downstream where the Pelly runs into the Yukon River.

The campground has about 20 sites with picnic tables and fire pits. Sites are ill-defined and there's generally no on-site management but drivers of any size RV should be able to find a place to park. Some picnic tables are available and some sites have fire rings. Electrical hookups as well as water and sewer have been installed at five sites near the entrance, but these are reserved for construction crews. Across the highway at Selkirk Centre is a gas station and store, it serves as a commercial center for the community. In addition to the small store there is a laundromat, showers, motel, and public telephone. You'll even find a dump station, free if you fill up on fuel.

The campground is near Km 463 on the south end of the bridge over the Pelly River.

▦ MOOSE CREEK CAMPGROUND (YUKON GOV.)

Location: Km 559 Of The North Klondike Hwy.
Info: (867) 667-5648

GPS Location: 63.50971 N, 137.02852 W, 1,500 Ft.

The campground has 36 sites off two loops. You can take a look without fear even if you're towing. Six are tent sites, 4 are pull-thrus, and the remainder are back-in spaces. Many are long sites up to 60 feet long. Aspens and natural vegetation separate the spaces. Each space has a picnic table and fire pit. There are vault toilets, a hand-operated water pump, a children's playground, and free firewood. A trail leads to fishing at Moose Creek.

DAWSON CITY
Population 1,300, Elevation 1,100 feet

There's lots to see and do in Dawson. You could reasonably say that the whole place is devoted to providing entertainment for visitors. This wasn't always the case, of course. When Skookum Jim, Tagish Charlie and George Carmack discovered gold on nearby Rabbit Creek in 1896 the Klondike River was best known as a good place to catch salmon. Two years later there was a population of 35,000 people in Dawson City and the surrounding creeks. A year later many of these prospectors had gone home or moved on to new strikes like Nome and the town settled into a long decline. When the Alaska Highway was built through Whitehorse, Dawson eventually became a virtual ghost town.

Today the population of Dawson City explodes in the summer when the tourists arrive and the Top of the World Highway opens.

While you're in Dawson there will be lots to keep you busy. Tours of the reconstructed **Palace Grand Theater** are available and there are also some presentations. At

Diamond Tooth Gertie's you can gamble in a saloon much like those of 1898. There are also many interesting historical sites to visit. You can get full information at the **Dawson Visitor Reception Centre** (PO Box 389, Dawson City, Yukon Y0B 1G0, Canada; 867 993-5566) on Front Street, they also have walking tours. Places you'll probably want to visit are the **cabins of both Jack London and Robert Service**, the **Dawson City Museum** in the old Territorial Administration Building, and the old **sternwheeler Keno** and **Danoja Zho Cultural Centre** down by the waterfront.

If you find the Keno interesting you might want to visit Dawson's **sternwheeler graveyard**, it's on the far side of the river just downstream from the campground. You can walk along the river to get there.

The gold didn't really come from Dawson, it came from the "creeks" located to the southeast. You can drive through the mining area by taking the **Bonanza Creek Road** at Km 712 of the Klondike Highway, just a kilometer or two from town. Twelve kilometers (8 miles) out this road is **Dredge #4** and at Km 15 is the **Original Discovery Claim** on Rabbit (now Eldorado) Creek. There's an area open to gold-panning here that is run by the visitor's association. Smaller vehicles or mountain bikers can make a 96-kilometer (60-mile) loop that takes them along Upper Bonanza Creek Road past **King Solomon Dome** and back down Hunker Creek to the Klondike Highway. There's also an additional loop for the truly adventurous who want to see Sulphur and Dominion Creeks. The total of the two loops is 164 kilometers (102 miles). While you're out exploring the creeks you might want to stop and see **Bear Creek Historical Site** at Km 705 of the Klondike Highway. The Canadian park ser-

IN DAWSON CITY YOU CAN VISIT THE GOLD CREEKS AND TOUR HISTORIC DREDGE #4

vice operates this Klondike National Historical Site that shows the way of life during the industrial era of the gold fields from 1905 to 1966 when the dredges replaced the original drift-mining techniques.

Also just outside town is the 8-kilometer (5-mile) road up to **Discovery Dome** for a view over the town.

Dawson City Campgrounds

🚐 **YUKON RIVER CAMPGROUND (YUKON GOV.)**

Location: Directly Across Yukon River From
                 Dawson City
Info: (867) 667-5648

GPS Location: 64.07216 N, 139.43837 W, 1,100 Ft.

This is a nice Dawson City campground with only one problem, it is a ferry ride away from the town. If you don't mind a short stroll there's no real problem. The ferry runs very frequently, it's free, and there should be no wait for walk-on passengers. From the campground you can easily walk downriver a short distance along the bank to the sternwheeler graveyard. You'll find three sternwheelers pulled up on the bank although they've deteriorated to the point that you might not recognize them as boats.

The campground has 98 spaces, about 75 vehicle spaces and the remainder tent sites.

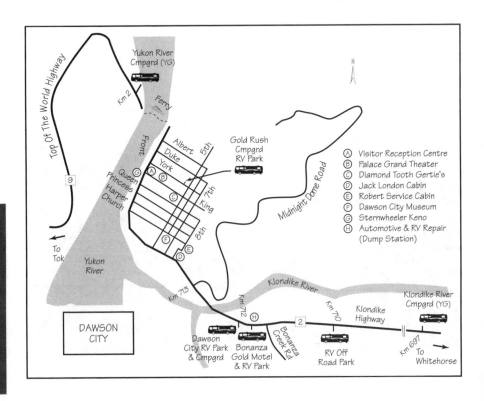

A Visitor Reception Centre
B Palace Grand Theater
C Diamond Tooth Gertie's
D Jack London Cabin
E Robert Service Cabin
F Dawson City Museum
G Sternwheeler Keno
H Automotive & RV Repair
   (Dump Station)

They are arranged in a long loop. Many of the spaces are pull-thrus, some to 55 feet and even longer, and some spaces are right along the river. The larger sites are on the north end of the campground, the upper sites (away from the river) tend to be sloped. Trees and natural vegetation separate the spaces. Each one has a picnic table and fire pit, there are vault toilets, hand-operated water pumps, a children's playground, a boat launch, a kitchen shelter, and free firewood. Since this is a busy place it often has an attendant to collect fees, unlike most Yukon Government campgrounds.

The campground is located about .3 kilometers (.2 miles) up the hill from the ferry landing area on the north side of the road.

⛟ GOLD RUSH CAMPGROUND RV PARK

Address:	PO Box 198, Dawson City, Y.T. Y0B 1G0
Telephone:	(867) 993-5247, (866) 330-5006
Email:	goldrushcampground@shaw.ca
Website:	www.goldrushcampground.com

GPS Location: 64.06307 N, 139.42684 W, 1,100 Ft.

The Gold Rush is the only campground located conveniently right in Dawson City.

There are 83 sites, back-ins and a few pull-thrus to about 50 feet. Sites are provided with 15 or 30-amp power, sewer hookups are also available. A dump station is provided and for a fee it is also available to those not staying at the campground. There are showers (token required) and a laundromat, There is free but limited Wi-Fi at the sites.

The campground is located at the corner of Fifth Ave. and York, about two blocks from Diamond Tooth Gertie's and near most other popular city destinations.

⛟ DAWSON CITY RV PARK AND CAMPGROUND

Address:	Box 750, Dawson City, Y.T. Y0B 1G0
Telephone:	(867) 993-5142
Email:	info@dawsoncityrvpark.com
Website:	www.dawsoncityrvpark.com

GPS Location: 64.04136 N, 139.40719 W, 1,100 Ft.

The second closest campground to town is this one (not counting the one on the far side of the river). It is located with two others on the dredge tailing piles just outside town. You can tell this is the place because there's a mammoth out front near the highway.

The campground has over 50 sites with electricity (15 or 30 amp) and water, some have sewer, and many more dry vehicle sites and tent sites. Some sites extend to 50 feet. The tent sites are in a tree-shaded area and one of the best places to stay in town for tent camping. There's a modern washroom building with individual shower rooms (extra fee). Other services include dump station, laundromat, coin-operated vehicle wash, a service station, and a small grocery store. There's a bike/hiking trail along the river in to town.

Dawson City RV Park is located near Km 712 of the North Klondike Highway, about 2.3 kilometers (1.4 miles) outside the city.

THE KLONDIKE LOOP

BONANZA GOLD MOTEL AND RV PARK

Address:	Box 5000, Dawson City, Y.T. Y0B 1G0
Telephone:	(867) 993-6789 or (888) 993-6789
Email:	bonanzagold.dawson@gmail.com
Website:	www.bonanzagold.ca

GPS Location: 64.04140 N, 139.40301 W, 1,100 Ft.

This campground is very popular, many caravans stay here and individual campers like it too. With 50-amp power and big sites it's a favorite of those with big rigs.

The campground is a large one with some 120 sites. They are set on a large gravel lot, really flattened tailing piles from the dredges that thoroughly scoured the area in their search for gold. Hookups vary with 50, 30, and 20-amp power available. Sites will take the largest RVs as roadways are wide and in many places rigs can extend quite a distance without getting in the way. Water hookups go to most sites and sewer is available if you want it. Some sites also have TV and telephone hookups. The central building houses handicapped accessible restrooms with coin-op showers. A computer with an internet connection is in the office and free Wi-Fi is available. This facility also has motel rooms, dump station, and a vehicle wash.

The campground is located near Km 712 of the North Klondike Highway, about 2.4 kilometers (1.5 miles) outside the city.

RV OFF ROAD PARK

Location: Km 711 Klondike Highway

GPS Location: 64.04054 N, 139.37700 W, 1,100 Ft.

This large gravel lot is the simplest campground near Dawson, and among the least expensive. You may have to share the place with a considerable amount of stored heavy equipment. There are no hookups or restrooms but water is available and there is a dump station.

Watch for the camping sign on the south side of the road near Km 711 of the North Klondike Highway.

KLONDIKE RIVER CAMPGROUND (YUKON GOV.)

Location:	Km 697 Of The North Klondike Highway, About 18 Km (11 Miles) From Dawson City
Info:	(867)-667-5648

GPS Location: 64.05122 N, 139.11254 W, 1,200 Ft.

This government campground is close enough to Dawson City to use as a base for visiting the city and there is no ferry to worry about like there is for the other nearby government campground, the Yukon River Campground.

The campground has 38 spaces off a loop road, one is a long double pull-thru. Some sites extend to 45 feet. Trees and natural vegetation separate the spaces. Each space has a picnic table and fire pit, there are vault toilets, a hand-operated water pump, a children's playground, and free firewood. A 1 km (half-mile) interpretive trail will take you to the Klondike River.

THE KLONDIKE LOOP

From Dawson City drive to Km 697 of the North Klondike Highway, a distance of 19 km (12 miles).

The Silver Trail
111 Kilometers (69 Miles)

From Stewart Crossing a highway heads east on the north side of the Stewart River. This is the highway leading to the old mining towns of Mayo, Elsa, and Keno City. It's officially called The Silver Trail, Yukon Hwy. 11.

The highway begins at the north end of the Stewart Crossing bridge near Km 535 of the Klondike Highway. This is 343 km (213 miles) north of the Klondike Highway intersection with the Alaska Highway and 176 km (109 miles) south of Dawson City. The Silver Trail leads eastward for 52 km (32 miles) to a T junction. If you turn right at that junction you'll reach Mayo in about 2 kilometers (1.2 mile). If you turn left the road continues on another 59 km (37 miles) to Keno City. The road is paved to a point about 6 km (4 miles) beyond the Mayo junction. Beyond that it's usually a well-maintained gravel road. Because this has been an active mining area there's a web of small roads throughout the region, many leading past small lakes offering decent fishing.

From the time of the gold rush until completion of the Silver Highway in 1955 made

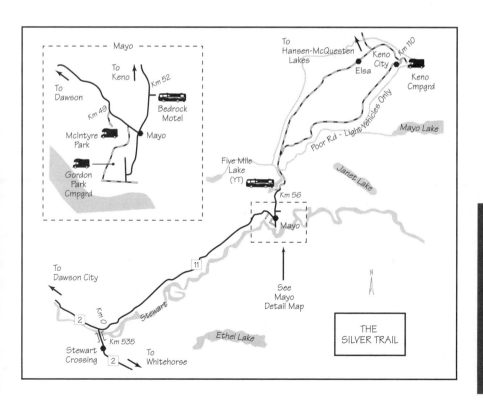

water transportation unnecessary Mayo was the port town for the mining district. It is the largest town in the area with a population of about 500. The riverboat Keno, now located on the dike on the waterfront in Dawson City, was one of the boats designed and built for this trade.

During the industrial production years of the silver mines in the area Elsa was the place most of the miners lived. Silver was discovered near Elsa in 1924 and large-scale production was closed down in 1989. Elsa is located 50 km (28.6 miles) beyond the junction at Mayo. It is private property and is now being watched by caretakers, visitors are not allowed and the road bypasses the town.

Keno, the town at the end of the road, is also a mining town. Unlike Elsa this some-what funky little town welcomes visitors and has quite a bit to see and do. There's an excellent museum documenting the history of the area as well as some restaurants and tourist shops, a community campground, and good hiking trails.

The Silver Trail Campgrounds

McINTYRE PARK   FREE 🔥
Location: Just Outside Mayo
Telephone: (867) 996-2317

GPS Location: 63.60425 N, 135.90114 W, 1,900 Ft.

This is a small local campground located along the Mayo River just outside the town of Mayo. The sign for this campground is the first one you'll see along the Silver Trail.

The campground has 8 sites. Two are pull-thrus. It is suitable for RVs to 30 feet. Sites have picnic tables and fire rings, firewood is provided. There is also a picnic shelter and outhouses.

To reach the campground start at the intersection of Hwy. 11 with the Klondike Loop. Follow Hwy. 11 for 49.2 km (30.5 miles). The short entrance road to the campground is on the right.

GORDON PARK CAMPGROUND   FREE 🔥
Location: At The Edge Of The Town Of Mayo
Telephone: (867) 996-2317

GPS Location: 63.59547 N, 135.90108 W, 1,900 Ft.

This is another small local campground. It's actually located at the edge of the town of Mayo although the entrance described below is from the road outside town. An-other entrance road leads from the waterfront in Mayo.

The campground has 8 back-in sites with picnic tables and fire pits. Some sites are suitable for RVs to 40 feet although maneuvering room for that size rig is limited and the road is pretty rough so this campground is best for RVs to 30 feet. There are outhouses and firewood is provided. The campground is in a grove of dense spruce so it tends to be a little dark.

To reach the campground start at the intersection of Hwy. 11 with the Klondike Loop. Follow Hwy. 11 for 49.5 km (30.6 miles). The entrance road to the campground goes right at this point. It's a long gravel road, you'll reach the first campground entrance at 1.3 km (.8 mile). The road continues another .6 km (.4 mile) to the waterfront in Mayo.

BEDROCK MOTEL

Address:	PO Box 69, Mayo, Y.T. Y0B 1M0
Telephone:	(867) 996-2290
Email:	bedrock@northwestel.net

GPS Location: 63.61039 N, 135.87972 W, 1,900 Ft.

The Bedrock Motel is the only campground with electrical hookups on the Silver Trail. It's also the best campground for big rigs. You can easily use it as a base and explore the area with a tow car.

The Motel has a large grassy area ahead and to the right as you enter the driveway. There are three hookup sites in one area and another four back-in sites offering electricity located next to one of the back buildings. Some electrical outlets are low amp. In addition to the hookup sites there's lots of room for dry camping. The hookup sites are good for RVs to about 35 feet, all of the others will take any size rig. There is a laundry room in the motel building as well as a bathroom with a shower. Breakfasts are available and canoes can be rented. Wi-Fi is a hotspot in the restaurant.

To reach the hotel start at the intersection of Hwy. 11 with the Klondike Loop. Follow Hwy. 11 for 50 km (31 miles) to a T junction. Mayo is to the right, you should turn left. The campground is on your right 1 km (.6 mile) from this turn.

FIVE MILE LAKE (YUKON GOV.)

Location:	Between Mayo And Elsa
Info:	(867) 667-5648

GPS Location: 63.65347 N, 135.87694 W, 2,000 Ft.

This is a nice territorial campground that is conveniently located for exploring the Silver Trail. There are 20 sites here, most are back-ins but three are pull-thrus. Some sites are suitable for the largest RVs. The campground has picnic tables and fire rings, vault toilets, a cooking shelter, and even a dock and swimming beach. A trail circles the lake. Firewood is provided.

The campground is located 8 km (5 miles) from Mayo. Start at the intersection of Hwy. 11 with the Klondike Loop. Follow Hwy. 11 for 50 km (31 miles) to a T. Mayo is to the right, you should turn left. The campground is on your left 6.6 km (4.1 miles) from this turn.

KENO CAMPGROUND

Location:	In Keno
Telephone:	(867) 995-3103

GPS Location: 63.90772 N, 135.30017 W, 2,100 Ft.

This community campground is pleasantly located on the far side of Keno but within a few minute walk of the center of the little town. Lightning Creek runs alongside. There are 16 spaces here, 3 are pull-thrus. Sites are suitable for RVs to 30 feet. Sites have picnic tables and fire pits, the campground has outhouses and water, and firewood is provided. There's a screened shelter and the access road has a turnaround at the end so you can take a look without unhooking. There's a Laundromat in town that has showers.

Entering Keno you'll come to a T, turn left and then immediately right and proceed .5 km (.3 mile) to the campground entrance on your right.

DEMPSTER HIGHWAY
734 Kilometers (455 Miles)

The Dempster is Canada's road to the region north of the Arctic Circle. Designated as Hwy. 5 it leaves the Klondike Loop at Km 675, about 26 km (16 miles) from Dawson City. In length it is similar to Alaska's Dalton Highway. It is gravel and has a reputation for being especially hard on tires. You can get lots of information about the Dempster at the **Dempster/Delta Visitor Information Centre** (867 993-6167) in Dawson City, it is just across Front Street from the Dawson Visitor Center. No one should attempt the Dempster without a visit there for first-hand information about road conditions and ferry availability and schedules (there are two of them along the route).

Kilometer markers start at the junction with the Klondike Highway, but they restart at 0 at the Northwest Territories border at Km 465. To try and avoid confusion most of our references below are from the intersection with the Klondike Highway, to get the real kilometer post number just subtract 465 once you get past the Northwest Territories border. Gas is available at Eagle Plains (Km 369), Fort McPherson (Km 551), and at Inuvik (Km 734). Your vehicle should be in good condition with good tires and at least one spare of each size needed, two would be much better. Flying rocks can be hard on windshields so slow way down and pull over when you meet someone or when someone comes up behind you. RVers, especially those pulling trailers, should take precautions to protect their rigs from flying gravel. See Chapter 2 - *Details, Details, Details* about doing this. Those pulling trailers should also stop very frequently to check their tires for flats or slow leaks.

There are 8 government campgrounds along the highway: **Tombstone Mountain Campground** at Km 72, **Engineer Creek Campground** at Km 193, **Rock River Campground** at Km 446, **Nitainilaii Campground** at Km 541, **Vadzaih Van Tshik Campground** at Km 685, **Gwich'n Territorial Campground** at Km 699, **Chuk Territorial Park** at Km 731 (with electrical hookups), and the **Happy Valley Territorial Campground** in Inuvik which has electrical hookups and a dump station. Additionally, there is a commercial RV campground at the **Eagle Plains Hotel** at Km 369 with electrical hookups and showers. All of these campgrounds are described in more detail below.

There's no question that driving the Dempster is something you'll never forget. Even more than on the Alaska Highway there are "miles and miles of miles and miles". The highway crosses true wilderness, also the Arctic Circle, the Yukon – NW Territories border, two mountain ranges, and two rivers on ferries. You'll find lots of opportunities to see wildlife, particularly birds, and spectacular scenery but more than anything you'll probably be impressed by the sheer size of the country and the solitude.

INUVIK'S UNUSUAL IGLOO CHURCH

Once you reach Inuvik (population 3,000) you might expect little to do in this isolated rainbow-colored but modern town but you just might be surprised. Inuvik was built only in 1955 when Aklavik, then the administrative center of the region, was flooded out. Inuvik's **Western Arctic Regional Visitor Centre** (276 Mackenzie Road, Inuvik, N.T. X0E 0T0; 867 777-4727) doubles as a museum for the Inuvialuit (Eskimo) and Gwich'n (Indian) cultures that share this region. Interesting places to visit include the **Igloo Church** and the huge **Inuvik Community Greenhouse**. The thing to do in Inuvik is to take an air-taxi trip to one of several possible destinations on the Mackenzie Delta or the Arctic coast. Check at the Northwest Territories Information Center in Dawson or the Inuvik Visitor Center for details about fly-out trips to **Hershel Island Yukon Territorial Park**, **Tuktoyaktuk**, and **Aklavik**.

An increasingly popular event in Inuvik is the 10-day **Great Northern Arts and Music Festival** held sometime during the latter half of July each year. It features artists and performers from across the Arctic. If you time your visit to catch this festival (and many RVers do) plan on lots of enthusiastic company.

Dempster Highway Campgrounds

TOMBSTONE MOUNTAIN CAMPGROUND (YUKON GOV.)

Location:	Km 71.5 Dempster Highway, Yukon
Info:	(867) 667-5652

GPS Location: 64.50614 N, 138.22094 W, 3,500 Ft.

This campground is situated inside the Tombstone Yukon Territorial Park next to

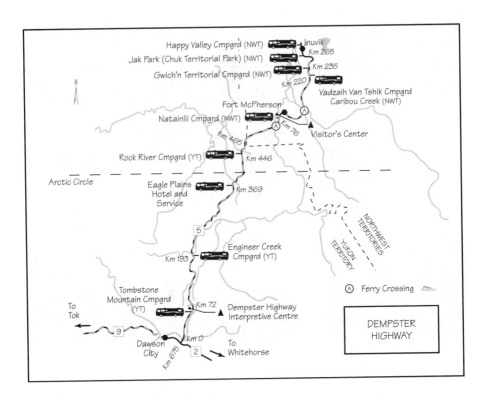

the confluence of Black Shale Creek and the North Klondike River. The highway is inside this mountain park from Km 54 to Km 100. The new Dempster Highway Interpretive Centre is located just up the road.

The campground has 31 sites for RVs and an additional 5 tent sites. They're back-in sites suitable for any size RVs and are located off a circular drive. Tent sites have platforms. Picnic tables, fire rings, and firewood are provided, there's also a shelter that is handy for tent campers. Water is from a faucet. There is a good short hiking trail along the river nearby, ask at the interpretive center about other routes.

The campground is located on the west side of the highway at Km 71.5.

ENGINEER CREEK CAMPGROUND (YUKON GOV.)

Location:	Km 193 Dempster Highway, Yukon	
Info:	(867) 667-5648	

GPS Location: 65.35264 N, 138.27133 W, 2,200 Ft.

This campground is located below Sapper Hill along Engineer Creek. The water in the creek has a lot of iron in it and as a result the rocks are colored red by the growth of mineral-loving algae.

There are 15 back-in sites, some are long enough for any size RV. A few of the sites are along Engineer Creek. Picnic tables and fire rings are provided. Firewood is available and there is a cooking shelter. Water is from the creek. The rock face of Sapper Hill visible across the river from the campground is well known as a good place to spot Peregrine falcons.

Engineer Creek Campground is on the east side of the highway near Km 193.

🚐 EAGLE PLAINS HOTEL AND SERVICE

Address:	Bag Service 2735, Whitehorse, Y.T. Y1A 3V5
Telephone:	(867) 993-2453
Email:	eagleplains@northwestel.net

GPS Location: 66.37239 N, 136.71950 W, 2,400 Ft.

Despite its name this hotel, gas station, and campground is located on a ridge at 2,360 feet with good views to the north and south. It's the only hookup campground along the highway other than those in Inuvik. The facility also has a restaurant, a bar, and a gift shop. Lots of people find the garage near the gas pumps to be a good place to get flats repaired.

The campsites are located at the north end of the motel building. Hookups consist of 20-amp electrical outlets mounted on a fence in a gravel lot with room for about 12 RVs. Rigs back up to the fence to plug in. There's room for any size RV. There are also a few tent-camping sites at the edge of the brush nearby. Picnic tables and fire rings are provided in these no-hookup sites. The ridge-top location can make this a pretty exposed place for tent camping but the frequent breeze is handy for keeping the bugs down. Restrooms are located at the end of the motel building near the camping area, they have coin-op showers. A water faucet is mounted on the building near the restrooms and laundry. Free Wi-Fi can be used in the motel lobby.

The campground is located at Km 369 of the Dempster Highway.

🚐 ROCK RIVER CAMPGROUND (YUKON GOV.)

| **Location:** | Km 446 Dempster Highway, Yukon |
| **Info:** | (867) 667-5648 |

GPS Location: 66.91186 N, 136.35583 W, 1,700 Ft.

The Rock River Campground has an isolated location on the west side of the Richardson Mountains. The campground is set in a grove of white spruce next to the river. The campground is in an area protected from the wind, it's known for its bugs.

There are 20 sites here, three are pull-thrus. Any size RV will fit in some of the sites. There are picnic tables and fire pits, firewood is provided. There's also a picnic shelter and vault toilets. Water is from the creek. The campsites are set off a loop drive so you can easily pull in and take a look.

🚐 NITAINLAII CAMPGROUND (NWT GOV.)

Location:	Km 76 Dempster Highway, Northwest Territory
	(Km 541 From Hwy. 2)
Info:	(867) 777-7353
Website:	www.nwtparks.ca

GPS Location: 67.35028 N, 134.85917 W, 100 Ft.

Just a kilometer or so after leaving the ferry over the Peel River you'll see the sign for Natainlii Territorial Park Campground on the left. There is also a visitor center

located at the entrance to the campground. A new building in the campground houses flush toilets and showers. Water is available from a faucet. You'll notice that the facilities here and at the Northwest Territorial campgrounds farther along are painted with a cheerful bright blue trim.

There are 24 sites in this campground. These are back-in sites with some suitable for RVs to 40 feet. Sites have picnic tables and fire pits, firewood is provided. There's a picnic shelter with a stove and vault toilets in addition to the new flush toilets.

VADZAIH VAN TSHIK CAMPGROUND (NWT GOV.)

Location: Km 220 Dempster Highway, NWT (Km 685 From Hwy. 2)
Info: (867) 777-7353
Website: www.nwtparks.ca

GPS Location: 68.08781 N, 133.49167 W, 200 Ft.

This campground was formerly known as Caribou Creek Campground, it is located in Gwich'n Territorial Park.

This small campground along the creek has 9 sites, two are pull-thrus. Just a few sites will take larger rigs to 40 feet. There are picnic tables and fire pits, firewood is provided. Water is from the creek.

GWICH'N TERRITORIAL CAMPGROUND (NWT GOV.)

Location: Km 234 Dempster Highway, NWT
(Km 699 From Hwy. 2)
Info: (867) 777-7353

GPS Location 68.20297 N, 133.42425 W, 200 Ft.

This is a newer campground set in a former gravel pit near Campbell Lake. There are about 18 vehicle sites here, some are very large pull-thrus suitable for any size RV. Sites have picnic tables and fire pits. There are also eleven tent sites, some with platforms, many with great views. Firewood is provided and there is a cooking shelter and vault toilets.

JAK PARK (CHUK TERRITORIAL PARK) (NWT GOV.)

Location: Km 265 Dempster Highway, NWT
(Km 730 From Hwy. 2)
Telephone: (867) 777-3613
Website: www.nwtparks.ca

GPS Location: 68.33083 N, W 133.64689 W, 100 Ft.

Set in an area of white birches on a ridge top this is a nice campground with hookups within easy driving distance of Inuvik. It's about 5 km from the center of town.

The campground has 37 sites. Many are pull-thrus to 55 feet. There are 20-amp electrical outlets at 5 sites. A faucet is available for filling water tanks. The campground has no dump station but there is one at the Happy Valley Campground in town. Restrooms have flush toilets and free showers. There's a tower that you can climb for the view.

The campground road is on the west side of the highway near Km 265, this is about 6 kilometers after the pavement begins if you are coming from the south.

THE KLONDIKE LOOP

HAPPY VALLEY TERRITORIAL CAMPGROUND (NWT GOV.)

Location: In Inuvik
Telephone: (867) 777-3652
Website: www.nwtparks.ca

GPS Location: 68.36050 N, 133.73697 W, 100 Ft.

Inuvik's in-town campground is a popular place. It has decent facilities and is within walking distance of the central area so it is often full. Still, unless you arrive during the Great Northern Arts Festival you'll probably find a place if you arrive in the early afternoon.

The campground has 28 vehicle sites. Some are pull-thrus, some back-ins. A few will take RVs to 40 feet. They have electrical hookups and there is a dump and water fill station. Sites have picnic tables and fire pits and firewood is available. The restrooms have flush toilets, free showers, and good coin-op washers and dryers. There are also six sites with tent platforms with good views, these have parking in a location near but not adjacent to the sites.

The campground is on the north side of town. As you arrive from the south you'll pass the Visitor's Center, zero your odometer here. You'll be coming in to town on McKenzie, .7 km (.4 mile) after leaving the visitor center you'll see the domed church on your right. At 1.4 km (.9 mile) after passing through the center of town turn left on Reliance. Drive a block to a T, turn right and you'll soon see the campground entrance on your left.

TOP OF THE WORLD HIGHWAY
126 Kilometers (78 Miles)

The Top of the World Highway connects Dawson City with the Taylor Highway. The section from Dawson to the border customs stations, 105 km (65 miles), was sealcoated at one time but the surface is now badly deteriorated although the roadbed itself is built to a higher standard than the first few miles in Alaska. The 13 miles (29 km) from the border to the Taylor Highway and the first part of the Taylor itself are unpaved and the condition can vary dramatically from year to year or day to day depending upon the weather. Kilometer markings start at the Yukon River and run to the border at Boundary. They then turn to mile markers (very scarce) and count down the 12 miles to the intersection with the Taylor Highway. Once you leave Dawson City or Tok fuel is only available in Chicken or Eagle, and it's very expensive so start out with a full fuel tank. This highway is only open when the Yukon Ferry operates and snow allows, from May to October.

Virtually all of the Top of the World Highway runs above the timber line with great views in all directions. The only civilization is at the border stations and at nearby Boundary where there is a historic roadhouse. At Km 57 a small unpaved side road runs 40 kilometers (25 miles) to **Clinton Creek**, an abandoned trading post and mining town near the mouth of the Fortymile River. Floaters on the Fortymile often use this as a take-out point although many just continue down the Yukon to Eagle.

Travelers on the highway should be aware that the customs stations are only open

THE KLONDIKE LOOP

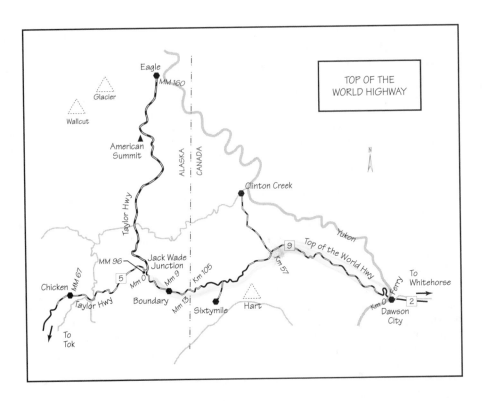

from 9 a.m. to 9 p.m. Yukon time (8 a.m. to 8 p.m. Alaska time). At the very beginning and end of the season the station may not be open at all, check in Dawson City or Tok before taking this route if you are very early or late in the season. You won't be able to pass if they aren't open. The ferry crossing the Yukon at Dawson City runs 24 hours each day except on Wednesdays when it is down for two hours from five to seven a.m. for maintenance. Lines to cross on the ferry can get long at the height of the season.

TAYLOR HIGHWAY
160 Miles (258 Kilometers)

If you are traveling the Klondike Loop you'll find that when you reach the Taylor Highway you intersect it near Mile 96 and mileposts count down as you head toward Chicken and Tok, up if you head toward Eagle. However, the section below starts at the beginning of the Taylor Highway at the Tetlin Junction and proceeds north.

The Taylor Highway, also called Alaska Route 5, runs 160 miles (258 km) through high rolling hills to Eagle, Alaska on the Yukon River. En route the gravel highway passes through the Fortymile mining district and also provides a connection to the Top of the World Highway to Dawson City in the Yukon. Mileposts along the Taylor start at the Tetlin Junction at the southern end of the highway. The Tetlin Junction is on the Alaska Highway 10 miles east of Tok. Much of the Taylor Highway is gravel although the southern-most 64 miles (103 km) are paved. The section from the end of the pavement to the Jack Wade Junction at Mile 96 is fine when dry but is narrow and must be driven very carefully, particularly by big rigs. The section from Jack Wade Junction to Eagle, a distance of 65 miles (105 km), is even narrower in spots and not as well maintained. Since camping for large vehicles is limited in Eagle anyway it might be best to make the side trip there as a day trip in your tow truck or car if you have a large rig. Large vehicles (RVs) should drive cautiously along the entire Taylor and Top of the World Highway. Road conditions deteriorate badly in rainy weather and can make the trip miserable and even dangerous for big RVs as the surface becomes slippery and the shoulders soft. Use extreme caution when passing other vehicles, large coaches have toppled over along here due to soft shoulders, even in dry weather. The Taylor Highway is closed during the winter by snow.

Services are very limited along the Taylor so start with a full tank and watch your gas gauge. You can get gas at Chicken near Mile 67 and also in Eagle at Mile 160.

For much of its length the highway passes near the **Fortymile National Wild, Scenic, and Recreational River**. For information including current river conditions contact: BLM, Eastern Interior Field Office, 1150 University Ave, Fairbanks, Alaska 99709; (907) 474-2200. There are many popular floats along this river, also lots of gold rush history. This was one of the interior's first large gold rush areas. Min-

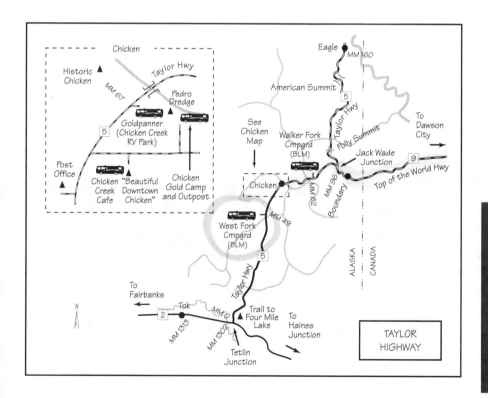

ers already working the Fortymile were among the first to reach the Klondike near Dawson when word of the strike there got out. Float trips on the Fortymile can be challenging and depend upon having adequate but not too much water. Check ahead if you plan to do one.

The town of Eagle and large portions of the Yukon River valley to the east and west are inside the **Yukon–Charley Rivers National Preserve**. A preserve visitor center is in Eagle and can be reached by telephone at (907) 547-2233.

As you head up the Taylor Highway the first point of interest is a trail leading in to Four Mile Lake at Mile 4. The lake offers good rainbow fishing, the trail is a little less than a mile long. The road soon begins climbing to its first summit on Mt. Fairplay at Mile 33.

The first campground is the BLM's West Fork Campground at Mile 49, it is in the valley of the West Fork of the Fortymile River. The nearby bridge is a popular put-in point for floating the river. Another popular access point is the bridge at Mile 64.

Historic **Chicken** is near Mile 67. It seems that everyone traveling the Taylor Highway is anxious to visit Chicken, you might as well stop too. The uninitiated find the whole place a little confusing. Chicken was one of the Fortymile-area gold camps. It is well-known because it was featured in the novel **Tisha** by Ann Purdy. This is a pretty good book, make sure you pick up a copy when you visit Chicken, paperback copies are readily available. The town is also known for its name. The original settlers apparently planned to call the place Ptarmigan, but none of them could spell

"BEAUTIFUL DOWNTOWN CHICKEN, ALASKA"

the word. They settled for Chicken instead. The original town site is abandoned, it is located along the west bank of Chicken Creek on the north side of the highway. Unfortunately, it is on private property and access is controlled. Across the highway is the Chicken Creek RV Park which offers tours of the site. Beyond the Chicken Creek RV Park the Airport Road cuts southeast and a short distance down it is "Beautiful Downtown Chicken Alaska", really a relatively modern saloon, café, and gift shop gussied up to look old. Many of the folk who visit Chicken actually think this is the old town site. It's not, but it's still worth a visit. There are three places to camp in Chicken, they are listed below. A dredge that was formerly located near Fairbanks and then later on the creeks nearby (the Pedro dredge) has been moved to a location in Chicken and can be toured.

Another Fortymile River access point is the bridge over the South Fork at Mile 75. The BLM has another campground, the Walker Fork Campground, at Mile 82.

At Mile 96 is the **Jack Wade Junction**. The Top of the World Highway swings east from here to Dawson City. The Taylor Highway goes left and continues to Eagle.

Continuing north the highway crosses Polly Summit and then descends to cross the Fortymile at Mile 113. This is a good put-in for floating the lower river out to where it meets the Yukon near Clinton Creek. The road continues, following O'Brien Creek and then ascends to cross American Summit. You'll get excellent views across the high country before the road descends along American Creek into Eagle.

Taylor Highway Campgrounds

WEST FORK CAMPGROUND (BLM)

Location:	Mile 49 Of The Taylor Highway
Info:	(907) 883-5121

GPS Location: 63.88696 N, 142.23499 W, 1,900 Ft.

There are few campgrounds in the Fortymile Country but this and the other BLM site (Walker Fork) are excellent. There are 25 camping sites at West Fork. They are off two loops. The loop to the right as you enter has seven pull-thrus and the one straight ahead has 18 back-ins, some very long. All sites are separated by natural vegetation and trees. There are picnic tables, fire pits, handicapped-accessible vault toilets, and water is available from a faucet. This campground sometimes has a host.

Watch for the West Fork Campground on the west side of the road near Mile 49 of the Taylor Highway.

CHICKEN GOLD CAMP AND OUTPOST

Address:	PO Box 70, Chicken, AK 99732
Telephone:	(520) 413-1480
Email:	chickenrvpark@gmail.com
Website:	www.chickengold.com

GPS Location: 64.06891 N, 141.94087 W, 1,700 Ft.

If you approach Chicken from the east you might miss this campground. It's a few hundred feet off the main road and you won't see the sign until you head west in the morning.

The campground has grown and become more sophisticated in recent years. There are now about 70 campsites. They include long pull-thru and back-in sites, many with 20 or 30-amp power. There are also wooded tent sites. A special large group area has 25 electric sites with a large pavillion and grill. Restrooms are vault toilets but there are showers. There is free gray water dump and water fill-up, there's a fee for dumping black water. There's free Wi-Fi and free firewood is provided.The modern main building here serves as gift shop, restaurant, and espresso bar. Recreational gold panning is available both on-site and on nearby mining claims. The Pedro gold dredge was relocated a few years ago and sits at the back of the campground. Tours cost $10. Grayling fishing is possible nearby.

This campground is a short distance off the main road. To reach it follow the gravel road south from about Mile 66.4 of the Taylor Highway on the airport road. In .1 mile you'll see "Beautiful Downtown Chicken" on your right with its café, gift shop, and bar. Just beyond is a left turn for the Chicken Gold Camp.

▄▄ CHICKEN CREEK RV PARK

Address:	Mile 66.6 Taylor Highway (PO Box 25), Chicken, AK 99732
Telephone:	(907) 505-0231
Email:	rvpark@townofchicken.com
Website:	www.townofchicken.com

GPS Location: 64.07222 N, 141.93474 W, 1,700 Ft.

The Chicken Creek RV Park (and Goldpanner Gift Shop) is located on the main road. It's a large gravel lot suitable for any size RV. Thirty electrical hookup sites (24-hour power), mostly large pull-thrus at the back of the campground, are available. There are also many no-hookup sites. The campground also has showers (extra charge) water fill station, and a dump station (substantial extra charge, not included in price icon amount above). A separate empty lot across the creek offers free boondocking if you fill up with fuel. A large souvenir store dominates the campground, there are also vault toilets, gold panning, and gas sales. The Chicken Creek RV Park offers tours of Historic Chicken, ask at the store for details. There's also a restaurant. Grayling fishing is possible nearby.

The Chicken Creek RV Park is located at Mile 66.6 of the Taylor Highway right next to the bridge over Chicken Creek.

▄▄ CHICKEN CREEK CAFÉ

FREE	🍴

Location: Beautiful Downtown Chicken

GPS Location: 64.07085 N, 141.94121 W, 1,800 Ft.

This café, part of a rustic complex which also includes a bar and gift ship, has started to allow one-day boondocking for rigs to 25 feet in the parking area to the north (right as you face the café). Facilities include the café, vault toilets, and of course a bar and gift shop. They limit this overnight parking to just a few rigs. We'd suggest you utilize the café to show your appreciation.

This cafe is part of the Beautiful Downtown Chicken complex. To reach it follow the gravel road south from about Mile 66.4 of the Taylor Highway on the airport road. In .1 mile you'll see "Beautiful Downtown Chicken" on your right, the parking area is on the far right. Check with the café before parking and make sure to park at the edge of the lot to allow maneuver room for the large vehicles that park and turn here.

WALKER FORK CAMPGROUND (BLM)

Location: Mile 82 Of The Taylor Highway
Info: (907) 883-5121

GPS Location: 64.07653 N, 141.63255 W, 1,700 Ft.

This is another excellent BLM campground. It offers 22 campsites, some 12 are pull-thrus. Sites are off a loop road and are separated by trees and shrubs. A few of the pull-thrus will take long RVs with sites to 40 feet. There are picnic tables, fire pits, and handicapped-accessible vault toilets. Some sites have tent pads. Water is available. There is also a host at this campground.

The campground is on the west side of the Taylor Highway near Mile 82 (Km 132).

EAGLE
Population 100, Elevation 850 feet

During the gold rush period Eagle was, for a short time, an important little place. Founded in about 1880 as Belle Isle, Eagle had a population of only thirty or so in 1897 but after the big influx of miners to Dawson City in 1898 some 1,700 people lived there. The first push toward growth was reaction against the control and tax-collection activities of the Mounties on the other side of the border. Eagle soon became the American trading center for the gold-seekers. This activity inevitably at-

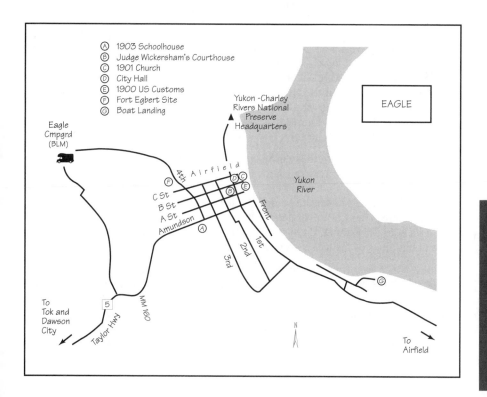

JUDGE WICKERSHAM'S COURTHOUSE IN EAGLE

tracted the U.S. government and the government activity definitely helped the town grow. As the first river town west of the border Eagle was a great place to collect customs duties and was the port of entry into Alaska for many miners as they abandoned Dawson City and headed for Nome and Fairbanks. Fort Egbert was established in 1889. A telegraph line, known as the WAMCATS line, running from Valdez to Eagle was finished in 1902. The Third Judicial District and Judge Wickersham set up shop in Eagle in 1900 although he soon threw it over for Fairbanks.

Interesting structures from those days survive. The **Eagle Historical Society** serves as the town visitor information source (PO Box 23, Eagle City, Alaska 99738; 907 547-2325) and runs daily tours. They meet at **Judge Wickersham's courthouse** at 9 a.m. each morning during the summer. The courthouse serves as a museum and gift/book store. There are several other interesting sights in Eagle visited by the tour. These include **Ft. Egbert**, the northern terminus of the WAMCATS telegraph line. Several buildings of the fort have been restored and house many interesting exhibits.

Eagle also is home for a visitor center for the **Yukon-Charley Rivers National Preserve** (PO Box 167, Eagle, Alaska 99738; 907 547-2233). The 2,260,000-acre preserve borders much of the Yukon River downstream almost as far as Circle. It also includes the waters of the remote Charley River which flows into the Yukon from the south about halfway between Eagle and Circle. Many people float the Yukon from Dawson City or from Eagle to Circle City. Canoes are available for rent in Dawson and sometimes in Eagle.

Eagle Campground

🚐 **EAGLE CAMPGROUND (BLM)**

| $$ | 🔥 | 👫 | 🛶 | ♿ |

Location: Just Northwest Of The Eagle Town Site
Info: (907) 883-5121

GPS Location: 64.79224 N, 141.22699 W, 1,000 Ft.

The BLM campground for Eagle is very nice. You're a ways from town but in a very pleasant woodland location. Town is an easy hike along the road or the old water pipeline trail.

The campground has 16 sites. They're set in spruce and are well-separated. Some will take RVs to 35 feet. Sites have picnic tables and fire pits and there are vault toilets. Water is available from a faucet. There's also an interesting old cemetery near the entrance. This campground sometimes has a host.

As you enter Eagle turn left on 4th. After .2 miles (.3 km) you'll pass Fort Egbert and the town's grass landing strip. Forge ahead and in another .5 mile (.7 km) you'll come to the campground entrance.

KLONDIKE LOOP DUMP STATIONS

There are a very limited number of dump stations along the Klondike Loop, most located in campgrounds. See the individual campground entries for information. Additional dump station locations:

Carmack – Sunrise Services – Km 356 of the Klondike Hwy (*GPS Location 62.08886 N, 136.28463 W*). Free with fill-up, otherwise a charge. **Pelly Crossing** – Selkirk Services – Km 463 of the Klondike Hwy (*GPS Location 62.82475 N, 136.57818 W*). Free with fill-up, otherwise $ 5.00.

Dawson City – Across highway from Bonanza Gold RV Park – Km 712 of the Klondike Highway (*GPS Location 64.04205 N, 139.40110 W*).

The **Dempster Highway** – Happy Valley Campground – Inuvik (*GPS Location 68.36050 N, 133.73697 W*).

It is best to make sure you empty your tanks before leaving Whitehorse, Dawson City, Tok, or Inuvik.

SKAGWAY AND HAINES

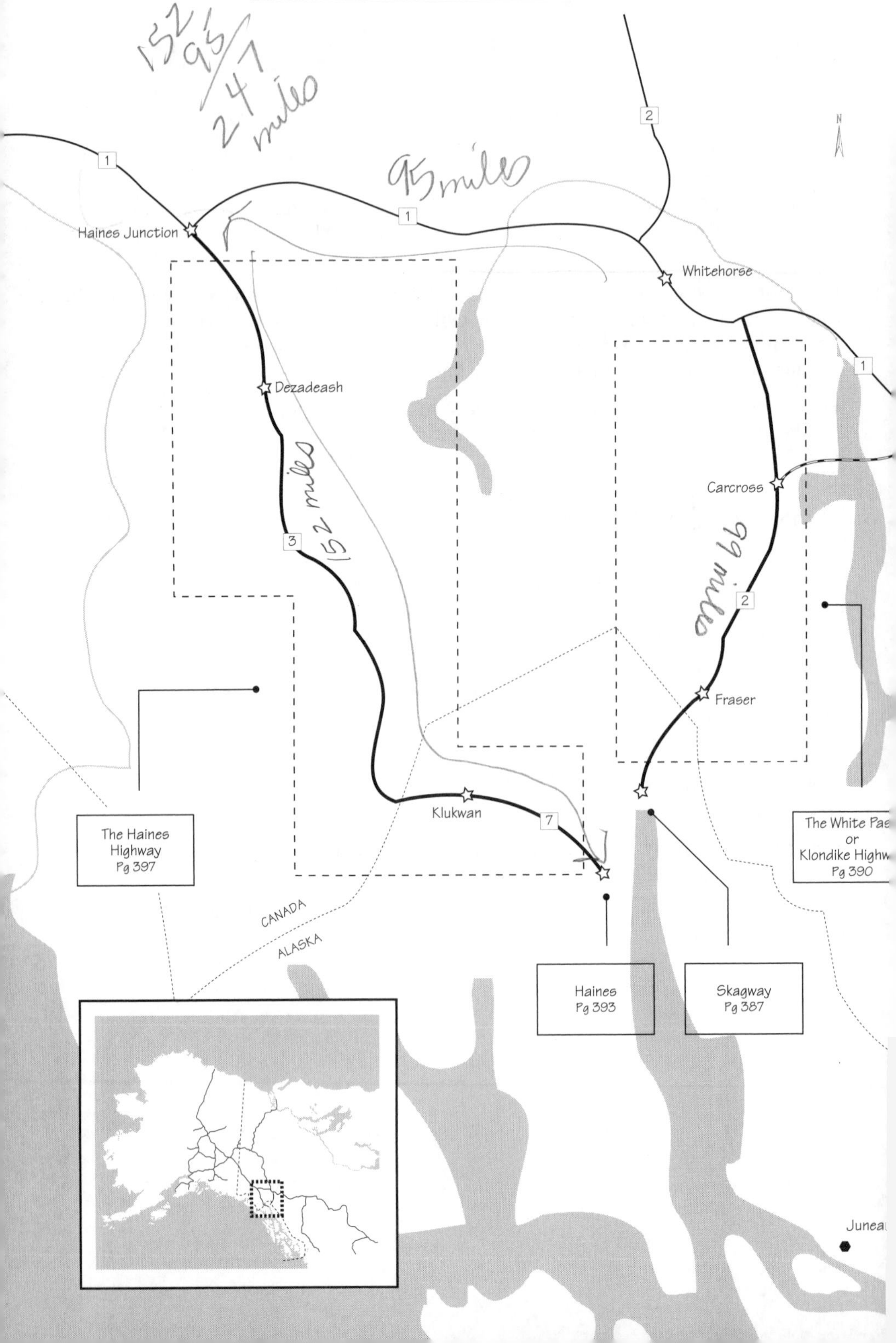

152
95/
247 miles

95 mile

1

2

1

Haines Junction

Whitehorse

Dezadeash

52 miles

3

Carcross

99 mile

2

Fraser

Klukwan

7

The Haines
Highway
Pg 397

The White Pas
or
Klondike Highwa
Pg 390

CANADA
ALASKA

Haines
Pg 393

Skagway
Pg 387

Junea

N

Chapter 12

Skagway and Haines

INTRODUCTION

Skagway and Haines, located at the far north end of Southeast Alaska and the Inside Passage, have always been gateways to the interior. In the early days the passes leading up and over the coastal mountains behind these two towns were used as trading routes between the coastal Tlingits and the Indians of the interior. Explorers and prospectors also used Skagway's White and Chilkoot Passes and Haines' Chilkat Pass. Today there are paved highways leading into the interior from both towns, they are now gateways to the Yukon and Alaska for ferry travelers and cruise ship passengers. There's also another little-known attraction to these towns, they receive far less rain than most of Southeast Alaska.

Highlights

When the prospectors headed for the Klondike most of them traveled through **Skagway** or nearby Dyea and then passed over either the **White Pass** or the **Chilkoot Pass**. Today Skagway attracts huge numbers of tourists, most arrive on cruise ships. From there you can ride the historic **White Pass and Yukon Route Railroad** over the White Pass or hike the famous **Chilkoot Trail**.

Many Alaska Highway travelers, those who do not plan to travel on the ferries, will appreciate the opportunity to see part of **Southeast Alaska.** In Skagway and Haines you will see steep mountains dropping into deep fiords with glaciers hanging above. You can easily get out on the water, there are tours, fishing charters, and even a walk-on ferry between the two towns. You can also use Haines as a base for an air-taxi flight over nearby **Glacier Bay**.

Many RVers take their RVs on the **Alaska State Ferry** between Haines and Skagway (or the reverse). That way they can visit both towns without driving many extra miles, and they get a ride on the ferry to boot. It's usually easy to get a reservation since most large RVs get off in Haines leaving lots of room on the car deck, and the rate can be cheaper than the cost of gas to make the loop from Haines to Skagway. Although they are usually not hard to get for this short run it is still wise to get reservations several weeks in advance.

If you are visiting Haines or Skagway with a vehicle you might also consider leaving the RV in a campground and making a walk-on ferry trip to Juneau or other ports in Southeast. Walk-on reservations are easy to get and the cost is reasonable. There are also smaller tour boats that make the trip and might fit your schedule better.

Fuel

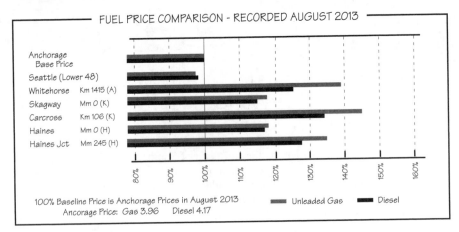

FUEL PRICE COMPARISON - RECORDED AUGUST 2013

Anchorage Base Price
Seattle (Lower 48)
Whitehorse Km 1415 (A)
Skagway Mm 0 (K)
Carcross Km 106 (K)
Haines Mm 0 (H)
Haines Jct Mm 245 (H)

100% Baseline Price is Anchorage Prices in August 2013
Ancorage Price: Gas 3.96   Diesel 4.17
Unleaded Gas   Diesel

Fishing

Skagway and Highway 2 to the north offer a few fishing opportunities. In Skagway there is a salmon hatchery, you can fish **Pullen Creek** or **the harbor** for kings in June, pinks in July and August, and silvers in September. Near Dyea the **Taiya River** has Dolly Varden in the spring and fall, also silvers and chum salmon in the fall. The **Dewey Lakes** (see hiking section), both upper and lower, have brook trout. The upper lake has smaller fish but they are easier to catch. In the salt water try **Taiya Inlet** for kings, silvers, pinks, dogs, Dollies and halibut. Charters are available.

Along Highway 2 the large lakes–**Tutshi, Tagish and Bennett**–all have lake trout and grayling, be aware that all or parts of some of these lakes are in British Columbia, not the Yukon, and a British Columbia fishing license is required in those areas. Farther north **Lewes Lake** (on a one-mile road from Km 136) has lake trout, grayling and northern pike.

Haines and the Haines Highway have more to offer. The salt water of **Chilkat Inlet**,

Chilkoot Inlet and **Lutak Inlet** have all species of salmon as well as sea-run Dollies and halibut. It is possible to catch Dollies and pinks from the shore in many places. The top fresh-water fishing spot has got to be the short (about a mile long) section of the **Chilkoot River** between Chilkoot Lake and Lutak Inlet. It is known for Dolly Varden in April and May, two runs of reds (June/July and August), pinks during the second half of August, and silvers in early October. Fishing is also possible in the lake, particularly for Dollies. On the other side of town the **Chilkat River** also has fish, but silty conditions in the summer limit fishing to clear-water tributary lakes and streams. In the fall it is possible to catch chum and silvers in this river near the airport. **Mosquito Lake** (Mile 27 Haines Highway) is known for both cutthroat trout and Dolly Varden.

Heading north on the Haines Highway try the **Takhanne River** (Km 159) for gray-ling, Dollies, rainbows, and salmon below the falls; **Dezadeash Lake** (Km 196) for lake trout, grayling, and northern pike; **Kathleen Lake** (Km 220) for lake trout, grayling, and rainbows; and **Kathleen River** (Km 221) for catch-and-release rain-bows, lake trout, and grayling. Be aware of where you are fishing, separate licenses are required for Alaska, British Columbia, the Yukon Territory, and Kluane National Park.

Boating, Rafting, Canoeing, and Kayaking

In Skagway the local float trip is down the **Taiya River** near Dyea and the Chilkoot Trail. Kayaks can be rented in Skagway for saltwater explora-tion.

In Haines commercial float trips and jet boat tours are offered on the **Chilkat River**. It is also possible to book trips here for extended trips to float the famous **Tatshen-shini and Alsek Rivers**. Haines is also a good place to go ocean kayaking, guided trips and kayak rentals are available.

Hiking and Mountain Biking

In Skagway the top hiking route has to be the **Chilkoot Trail**. See Chapter 14 - *Camping Away From the Road System* for information about this hike.

Much closer to town and less strenuous are the **Yakutania Point and Smuggler's Cove** waterfront trails. Just walk to the west end of 1st Avenue south of the end of the airport and cross the footbridge over the Skagway River.

From the east end of Third Avenue in Skagway cross the railroad tracks and you'll find the steep trail to the **Dewey Lake Trail System**. Destinations along the trails are Lower Dewey Lake (.7 mile, 1.1 km), Icy Lake (2.5 miles, 4.0 km), Upper Reid Falls (3.5 miles, 5.6 km), Sturgill's Landing (4.5 miles, 7.3 km), Upper Dewey Lake (3.5 miles, 5.6 km) and the Devil's Punch Bowl (4.2 miles, 6.8 km). There are some developed tent-camping sites along the trails as well as solitude and excellent views.

Another worthwhile hike in the Skagway area is really much more of a climb. The **Skyline Trail to AB Mountain** begins at Mile 3 of the Dyea Road. The climb and return should take four to five hours.

Haines also has a selection of trails. The **Seduction Point** trail starts at a trailhead parking lot at Chilkat State Park near the campground there. The trail leads 7 miles (11 km) south to the point at the end of the Chilkat Peninsula called Seduction Point. In several places the trail actually runs along the beach and is not passable at high tide so plan accordingly. There are several tent-camping sites along the way and near the point. Some do not have drinking water including the one at the point.

Another hike not far away is the trail to the top of **Mt. Riley**. This is a good place to head for on clear days for views of Haines, the Lynn Canal, and the surrounding glaciers. There are actually two routes to the top of Mt. Riley. From Mile 3 of the Mud Bay Road (the road out to Chilkat State Park) there is a 2.8 mile (4.5 km) trail that gains 1,500 feet to get to the top. From the end of Beach Road (the road that passes Portage Cove Campground) a four-mile (6.5 km) trail climbs 1,600 feet to the same summit. Of course you can treat this as a traverse if you can arrange for a pick-up at the end.

A tougher trail in the Haines area is the **Mt. Ripinsky** trail. The mountain is an especially good place for views on a clear day, it tops out at 3,560 feet! You don't have to climb all the way to the summit for good views, however. This is fortunate since there is likely to be snow on the trail well into the summer. There are actually a north and south peak, the round-trip hike to the farther north peak is 8 miles (12.9 km), expect a hike that far to take a good six hours. To find the trail, head north on 2nd Ave. or Lutak Road. When Lutak goes right continue on Young Street. Follow Young up the hill and then follow the road along a buried water pipeline for another mile to the trailhead.

HAINES' CHILKOOT RIVER IS A GOOD PLACE FOR BEAR WATCHING

Wildlife Viewing

Haines is home to the **Alaska Chilkat Bald Eagle Preserve**. The area is unique in southeast Alaska because the Chilkat River here stays ice-free and affords bald eagles from far and wide the best place to find a meal during the late fall and winter. At the time of their peak numbers in November there can be 4,000 bald eagles in the area. A few eagles can be seen year-round but the real viewing season is October to February. The preserve encompasses 49,000 acres, but the viewing area is between Mile 18 and Mile 22 of the Haines Highway. This area is known as the "Council Grounds". The only facilities are restrooms, some parking slots, and limited walking paths. Observers and photographers can conflict with the traffic along the highway, both drivers and those on foot should exercise caution. For information call (907) 465-4563.

In Haines, the **Chilkoot River** is a great place to watch brown bears when the salmon are running. The best time is the evening, if the bears are around you'll have lots of company trying to get pictures. Don't stray far from your car!

THE ROUTES, TOWNS, AND CAMPGROUNDS

SKAGWAY
Population 900, Elevation sea level

Today's Skagway is something of a shock to someone who hasn't seen it for a few years. Visits by over 300 cruise ships each year have turned a picturesque but sleepy historic gold rush town into a true tourist destination. Much of downtown Skagway is now part of the **Klondike Gold Rush National Historical Park** and the streets are lined with restored buildings housing restaurants, souvenir stores, and hotels. Today's Skagway has become a fascinating place to visit and it's especially convenient since there are two RV parks within just blocks of the center of town.

The large number of cruise boat tourists have given rise to an active tourism infrastructure. A good place to start is the **Klondike Gold Rush Historical Park Visitor Center** (PO Box 517, Skagway, Alaska 99840; 907 983-9200). It is located near the waterfront end of central Broadway Street in the old White Pass Railroad Depot. They have exhibits, films, and information about the Chilkoot Trail, Skagway, and the gold rush. They also have guided walking tours of Skagway. The **Skagway Visitor Center** (PO Box 1029, Skagway, Alaska 99840; 907 983-2855) is in the old Arctic Brotherhood Hall at Second and Broadway. That's the building with the driftwood-covered facade. Also worth a visit is the city's **Skagway Museum** (907 983-2420) in the McCabe College Building at 7th and Spring and the unusual **Corrington Museum of Alaskan History** (907 983-2637) at 5th and Broadway. You'll probably also want to visit the **Gold Rush Cemetery** where both Frank Reid and Soapy Smith are buried.

The historic **White Pass and Yukon Route** narrow-gauge railroad was finished in 1902. It was considered an engineering marvel as it climbed the precipitous White Pass and then continued on to Whitehorse. After the Klondike Highway to White-

THE WHITE PASS AND YUKON ROUTE NARROW GAUGE RAILROAD

horse was opened in 1982 the railroad eventually shut down. Today it is running again, but only along the first section up through the pass. On tour-ship-visit days you can ride from Skagway up to Fraser, there are also some runs up to Lake Bennett to pick up hikers who have hiked the Chilkoot Trail. Busses connect with the train to take some cruise ship passengers on to Whitehorse.

The **Chilkoot Trail** is once again very popular, although not quite as heavily traveled as during the gold rush. It is now part of the Klondike Gold Rush National Historical Park. So many people want to hike the 33 mile (53 km) trail over 3,739 foot Chilkoot Pass that access has been limited because there are limited camping sites. See the information in our Chapter 14 - *Camping Away From the Road System.*

Skagway Campgrounds

PULLEN CREEK RV PARK

Address:	501 Congress Way (PO Box 836), Skagway, AK 99840
Telephone:	(907) 983-2768 or (800) 936-3731
Email:	pullencreekrv@gmail.com
Website:	www.pullencreekrv.com

GPS Location: 59.45144 N, 135.31619 W, Near Sea Level

This is a city-owned campground managed by a subcontractor. It has an excellent location near the boat harbor and within easy walking distance of town.

There are 32 back-in vehicle spaces to about 35 feet with electricity (15, 30, and 50 amp) and water. There are also a few tent sites with pitching on grass. Spaces are surrounded by grass and a few trees. Some have picnic tables, there are no fire pits. The restroom buildings are adequate, they have coin-op showers and flush toilets. There is a dump station. There are also 12 large back-in sites on a paved parking area on the ocean side of the campground. These are probably the best-kept secret of the campground, the sites are nothing more than parking slots with 30-amp electric hookups but they offer fantastic views of the many cruise ships that dock in Skagway, the small boat harbor, and the surrounding mountains. They can handle any size RV.

To find the park follow 2nd Ave. east from State Street. It crosses the RR tracks and curves right, you will see the campground on your right. Note that this access route is often blocked by strolling cruise ship passengers and unloading train cars just at the wrong time, the early evening when you're likely to be trying to reach the park. Expect delays.

GARDEN CITY RV PARK AND LAUNDROMAT

Address:	PO Box 228, Skagway, AK 99840
Telephone:	(907) 983-2378 or (866) 983-2378
Email:	gcrv@aptalaska.net

GPS Location: 59.46219 N, 135.30565 W, Near Sea Level

The Garden City RV Park will undoubtedly be the first campground you see as you drive into town. That, and the price, is probably why it is often difficult to get into

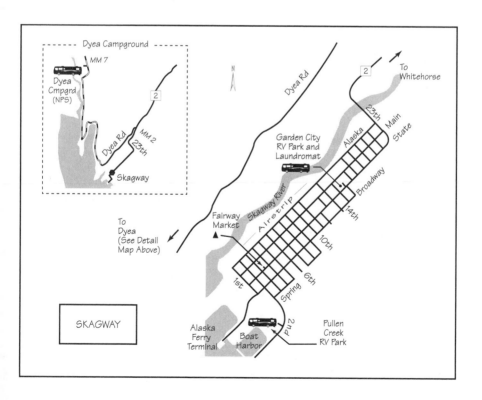

this campground during the height of the summer season. Other advantages RVers notice are large sites and full hookups.

The park has about 100 spaces, all have full-hookups (30 amp). Some pull-thrus to 50 feet are available and back-ins reach 40 feet. Parking is on good gravel. New modern restrooms have showers (extra cost) and there is a laundry that get lots of use by folks from both inside and outside the park.

The campground is located at the corner of State Street and 15th, right on your way in to or out of town. The walk to central Skagway takes only a few minutes.

DYEA CAMPGROUND (NATIONAL PARK SERVICE)

Location:	Mile 6.8 Of Dyea Road
Info:	(907) 983-2921
Website:	www.nps.gov/klgo/planyourvisit/campgrounds.htm

GPS Location: 59.50550 N, 135.34722 W, Near Sea Level

The Dyea Campground is some distance from Skagway on a minor dirt road so larger RVs must exercise caution. It is located close to the beginning of the Chilkoot Trail and hikers like to use it as a base camp. There is a parking area for the trail located at the campground.

This campground has 21 RV sites and 3 walk-in tent sites. They are set in an area of alders and cottonwoods near the Taiya River. Most are back-ins and they are well separated, a few are large enough for RVs to 45 feet. Each site has a picnic table and a fire pit. Bear-proof food vaults and a food-hanging frame are provided. There are vault toilets and the campground does have a host. From October to April camping here is free.

To get to the campground follow the Dyea Road. It leaves the Klondike Highway just outside Skagway at Mile 2. The first 1.8 miles (2.9 km) are paved, then the road narrows. Watch ahead carefully, there are several spots where the road is only one and a half lanes wide so big rigs might have to back up. The campground is at 6.8 miles (11.0 km).

WHITE PASS OR KLONDIKE HIGHWAY
99 Miles (160 Kilometers)

The South Klondike Highway, Yukon Highway 2, is the southern portion of the same Klondike Highway that runs from Whitehorse to Dawson City. This portion of the highway was completed in 1982 and runs from Skagway up the famous White Pass and then north along several long lakes to Whitehorse. The excellent highway is paved for the entire distance, mile markers run north from Skagway to the border, then they change to kilometer markers and continue north. This short road actually passes through parts of Alaska, British Columbia, and the Yukon. We'll cover the road from south to north.

After leaving Skagway the road passes the junction for the 8 mile (13 km) gravel road to **Dyea** at Mile 1.6 and begins climbing almost immediately. There are several places to pull off and look across the valley at the old gold rush trails and the railroad. The top of the pass is at Mile 14, the altitude is 3,292 feet. U.S. Customs is at Mile 6.7, the border at Mile 15, but Canadian Customs is located at Km 36 (Mile 22) at **Fraser**. It is manned from 8 a.m. to midnight, check at 907 983-3144 if you want to cross from midnight to 8 a.m. Fraser is the turn-around for most White Pass railroad excursions from Skagway. A few miles farther along is **Log Cabin** where the Chilkoot Hiking Trail connects with the road. A few trains also continue on to the south end of Lake Bennett to pick up Chilkoot Trail hikers. The countryside around Fraser and Log Cabin is glacier-scrubbed rock, very forbidding but beautiful.

Continuing north, the highway passes along the shores of Tutshi and Tagish Lake to **Carcross** at Km 105. The name Carcross is a shortened form of Caribou Crossing. The town is located at a point long used by Indians for caribou hunting. During the gold rush, especially after the railroad was built, the town grew. It became a supply center for riverboat accessible destinations on the surrounding lakes. A fleet of sternwheelers serviced these lakes for many years. There's a **Visitor Reception Centre** (867 821-4431) located in the old railway station. The town's cemetery has the graves of two of the men who made the original Klondike strike and the wife of the third: Tagish Charlie, Skookum Jim and Kate Carmack.

Just north of Carcross at Km 107 is another junction, this one for the Tagish Road (Yukon Highway 8) which leads east to the Alaska Highway at Jake's Corner. See Chapter 4 of this book for more information about this road and its campgrounds. Just north of the intersection is a pull-off for the **Carcross Desert**. Here a small region of sand dunes will make you do a double-take and probably stop for a photo.

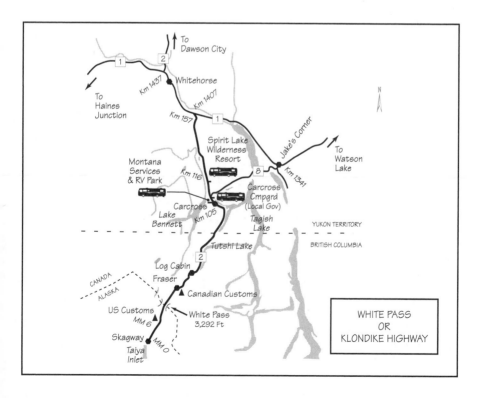

As the highway runs north it passes several lakes including Spirit, Emerald, Rat, Bear and Kookatsoon until meeting the Alaska Highway at Km 157. From there the Klondike and Alaska highways are the same road as they pass through Whitehorse and then split north of town as the Klondike Highway heads for Dawson City.

White Pass or Klondike Highway Campgrounds

Montana Services & RV Park

Address: Box 75, Carcross, Yukon. Y0B 1B0
Telephone: (867) 821-3708

GPS Location: 60.16983 N, 134.70519 W, 2,200 Ft.

This is a gas station and grocery store with 40 large pull-thru and back-in camping slots with full hookups in a gravel lot to the side of the main structure. You can have either 30 or 50-amp hookups. There's lots of maneuvering room. Also available are flush toilets, showers, a laundry, a grocery store, a dump station, a snack bar, and a car wash facility. Montana Services is located on the west side of the highway near Km 106.

Carcross Campground (Local Gov.)

Location: Km 106 Klondike Highway

GPS Location: 60.17361 N, 134.70222 W, 2,200 Ft.

This is a typical government campground. For tent campers and RVers not needing hookups it's a great alternative to the nearby Montana Services.

There are 14 long back-in camping sites. They are well-separated with trees and natural vegetation and have picnic tables and fire pits. The campground has vault toilets and water is available from a faucet. Firewood is provided for free.

Head east from the Klondike Highway at Km 106 just north of Carcross next to the airstrip, you'll soon see the campground entrance on your left.

Spirit Lake Wilderness Resort

Address: Km 115 Klondike Highway, Carcross, Yukon
Telephone: (867) 821-4337 or (866) 739-8566
Email: info@spiritlakeyukon.com
Website: www.spiritlakeyukon.com

GPS Location: 60.24997 N, 134.74563 W, 2,300 Ft.

This small campground make a convenient overnight stop. It also makes a good base for canoe trips on the Wheaton River to Lake Bennett, they provide drop-off and pick-up services and rent canoes.

The campground has 5 back-in spaces with 30-amp electric hookups in an open gravel lot behind the main buildings. Big RVs can fit in these sites, they have picnic table and fire pits. Farther back are about 5 more dry spaces in pine trees near the lake for small RVs and tents that also have picnic tables and fire pits. A restroom building provides flush toilets and showers. Other services include a dump station and water fill point, hiking trails, canoe rentals, and a restaurant and bar with Wi-Fi. Horseback, canoe, and fishing tours are offered. The campground is located at Km 115 of the Klondike Highway.

HAINES
Population 1,800, Elevation sea level

Haines is the "other" southeast town with a connection to the road system. In fact, Haines has had such a connection for many years. The Haines Road, now called the Haines Highway, was built in 1943 to connect with the Alaska Highway. The pass through the Coastal Mountains at Haines has been in use for centuries, first as a native trading route into the interior, then by Jack Dalton who pioneered a route here just before the Gold Rush and operated a toll road that was used to drive cattle into the Klondike.

Haines gets a few cruise ships so there are some tourist-oriented attractions in town. The helpful **Visitor Information Center** (Second Avenue and Willard Street; 907 766-2234 or 800 458-3579) is just down the hill from Main St. Several of the attractions in town are related to old **Fort William Henry Seward**. It was active from 1904 to 1946 and is now privately owned. The structures are in use as hotels, bed and breakfasts, restaurants, and shops. There is also a traditional Chilkat plank house and totem poles on the old parade grounds. The **Chilkat Dancers** often perform at **Alaska Indian Arts** (907 766-2160). A salmon bake is sometimes held at the Fort.

Haines is home to the **Alaska Chilkat Bald Eagle Preserve** which is discussed in detail under *Wildlife Viewing* at the beginning of this chapter. A related destination is the **American Bald Eagle Foundation** at the intersection of Second Avenue and the

CHILKOOT LAKE FROM THE NEARBY RECREATION SITE

Haines Highway. They have a huge diorama showing local wildlife and also an eagle display as well as a gift shop.

Haines has an outstanding museum, the **Sheldon Museum** (907 766-2366). It is located just above the small boat harbor in the old Presbyterian mission location. There you'll find displays about the local Chilkat Indian culture and local transportation including the ferry system and highway. You might also enjoy the Hammer Museum across the street, it features hammers.

There are two excellent state parks near Haines. **Chilkat State Park** is south of town a few miles, take Mud Bay Road. This shoreline park offers hiking trails and beach walking. North of town on Chilkoot Lake is **Chilkoot Lake State Recreation Site** with a campground located on the shore of Chilkoot Lake. A short river runs from the lake to tidewater.

Haines Campgrounds

🚐 CHILKOOT LAKE STATE RECREATION SITE (STATE OF ALASKA)

Location:	9.6 Miles (15.5 Km) From Haines On The Lutak Rd.
Info:	(907) 766-2292
Website:	dnr.alaska.gov/parks/aspunits/southeast/chilkootlksrs.htm

GPS Location: 59.33561 N, 135.56186 W, 100 Ft.

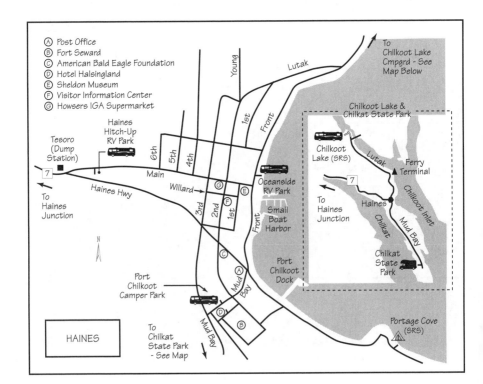

Ⓐ Post Office
Ⓑ Fort Seward
Ⓒ American Bald Eagle Foundation
Ⓓ Hotel Halsingland
Ⓔ Sheldon Museum
Ⓕ Visitor Information Center
Ⓖ Howsers IGA Supermarket

To Chilkoot Lake Cmpgrd - See Map Below

Chilkoot Lake & Chilkat State Park

Haines Hitch-Up RV Park

Tesoro (Dump Station)

Chilkoot Lake (SRS)

Ferry Terminal

Main

Oceanside RV Park

To Haines Junction

To Haines Junction

Haines Hwy

Willard

Small Boat Harbor

Chilkat State Park

Port Chilkoot Camper Park

Port Chilkoot Dock

Portage Cove (SRS)

HAINES

To Chilkat State Park - See Map

SKAGWAY AND HAINES

This is a beautiful state campground sitting in huge evergreens trees at the foot of Chilkoot Lake. The short Chilkoot River runs nearby and may be open for salmon fishing during your stay. The river is also a great place to see grizzlies during the fish runs.

There are 32 sites, a few are fairly long but narrow pull-thrus. Some back-ins reach 45 feet but limited maneuvering room makes this a campground best for rigs to 35 feet. Sites are well separated by giant trees and vegetation, the most popular ones are near the lake. All sites have picnic tables and fire pits with benches. The campground has vault toilets, a hand-operated water pump, and a boat ramp. There is also a host.

From Haines follow signs for the Alaska State Ferries Terminal. It's about 4 miles (6.5 km) east of town along Lutak Inlet. Zero your odometer at the ferry terminal and in another 4.8 miles (7.7 km) come to the Chilkoot River Bridge. Just before the bridge the unpaved campground access road goes left, follow it for .9 miles (1.5 km) along the Chilkoot River to the campground.

CHILKAT STATE PARK (STATE OF ALASKA)

Location:	Mile 6.8 Off Mud Bay Road Southwest Of Haines
Info:	(907) 766-2292
Website:	dnr.alaska.gov/parks/aspunits/southeast/chilkatsp.htm

GPS Location: 59.13881 N, 135.36936 W, 100 Ft.

This campground is out of the way and usually not too crowded. An excellent hiking route, the Seduction Point beach trail (12 to 14 miles (19 to 23 km) round trip) leaves from this campground. Big RVs need to be aware that the washboard entrance road, while it is a good wide gravel road, is also very steep. It's posted as 14 percent and the steep part of the hill is .4 mile (.7 km) long. If your RV lacks climbing power you might want to avoid it.

The campground has 32 vehicle camping sites, 17 are narrow pull-thrus about 50 feet long. There are also back-ins, a few to 40 feet. They are off a loop road. This campground is best for RVs to 35 feet due to the steep entrance and difficult to enter sites. There are also 3 tent sites below the campground next to the beach. Each site has a picnic table and fire pit. The campground has handicapped-accessible vault toilets, a hand-operated water pump, and, downhill from the camp, a boat ramp and a dock on a pretty beach.

To reach the campground start at the Post Office near the end of the Haines Highway (see map). Drive southeast on the Haines Highway and take the first road to the right heading up the hill. This is Mud Bay Road. From there follow frequent signs for both Mud Bay Road and Chilkat State Park approximately 6.7 miles (10.8 km) to the park entrance. The road is paved this entire distance. Turn right into the park and drive about .5 mile (.8 km) down a wide but rough and steeply winding entrance road to the campground.

HAINES HITCH-UP RV PARK

Address:	851 Main Street (PO Box 383), Haines, AK 99827
Telephone:	(907) 766-2882
Email:	info@hitchuprv.com
Website:	www.hitchuprv.com

GPS Location: 59.23547 N, 135.46086 W, 100 Ft.

The Hitch-Up is the largest and most polished campground in town. It will probably be the first you see when you arrive and it will look so nice that you'll probably turn right into the entrance.

There are 92 large sites with full hookups (30 or 50-amp outlets). Twenty are pull-thrus to 60 feet, back-ins reach 45 feet. Cable TV is available. So is Wi-Fi, for no charge, and it's a good system that reaches the sites. It's actually the city-wide service, but the park provides it for free. All parking is on well-clipped very green grass and all sites have picnic tables. The modern central services building houses the office with gift shop and tour booking assistance, restrooms with free showers, and a laundry. Central Haines is within easy walking distance on city sidewalks.

OCEANSIDE RV PARK

Address:	14 Front St., Haines, AK 99827
Telephone:	(907) 766-2437
Email:	greatview@oceansiderv.com
Website:	www.oceansiderv.com

GPS Location: 59.23530 N, 135.44173 W, Near Sea Level

Centrally located at the foot of Main Street and right on the water the Oceanside has a lot going for it. There are 23 back-in RV slots to 50 feet with full-hookups, tents can be pitched above the beach. There's an office at the park with showers and a laundry. The enthusiastic owners offer weekly crab or salmon potlucks and the location couldn't be more convenient since the campground is adjacent to restaurants, the boat harbor, and downtown shopping. Reservations are recommended. Wi-Fi is via the town's subscription service.

To reach the campground take the left fork at the Welcome to Haines sign as you enter town. Take a right at the next Y and you'll drive right into central Haines on Main Street. Drive all the way to the waterfront, take a jog to the left, and you're at the Oceanside RV Park.

PORT CHILKOOT CAMPER PARK

Address:	13 Ft. Seward Dr. (PO Box 1649), Haines, Alaska 99827
Telephone:	(907) 766-2000 or (800) 542-6363
Email:	reservations@hotelhalsingland.com
Website:	www.hotelhalsingland.com

GPS Location: 59.22858 N, 135.44569 W, 200 Ft.

The Port Chilkoot offers something a little different. This campground sits under towering Sitka Spruces on the hillside near Fort Seward. Even so it's within walking distance of town. Facilities here are definitely showing their age and management is not usually on-site.

The campground has about 45 spaces. Most are partial or dry spaces under the spruces but there are also a few full-hookup back-in spaces out front to 35 feet with quite a bit of maneuvering room. Some spaces have picnic tables. There is also lots of room to tent camp. Restrooms are OK but not great, they have flush toilets and coin-op showers. There's also a laundry and dump station. Wi-Fi is available for free in the lobby of the nearby associated Hotel Halsingland, or you can use the city-wide subscription Wi-Fi.

To reach the campground head uphill on Mud Bay Road from the Haines Highway near the post office. You'll see the campground almost immediately on your right. The office is a block to the south in the Hotel Halsingland.

🚐 PORTAGE COVE STATE RECREATION SITE

Location: On Beach Rd. Just Past Port Chilkoot Dock

GPS Location: 59.22583 N, 135.42497 W, Near Sea Level

Conveniently located about a mile from downtown Haines is a grass-covered campground only for tenters. It is located right along the shore of Portage Cove just southwest of town on the road to Battery Point. The campground has nine tent sites on a grass lawn with fire pits and picnic tables and there are water and handicapped accessible vault toilets. A rack is provided for hanging your food so it doesn't attract bears.

HAINES HIGHWAY
152 Miles (245 Kilometers)

The Haines Highway has as long a history as any highway in this part of the world. Originally this pass through the Coastal Range was an Indian "kleena" or "grease trail" trading route. Coastal Indians carried trading goods, including fish oil from candlefish (also called eulachon, smelt, or hooligan), inland to trade for products of that area. Later, when the Russians arrived it was a fur-trade route. Anticipating an

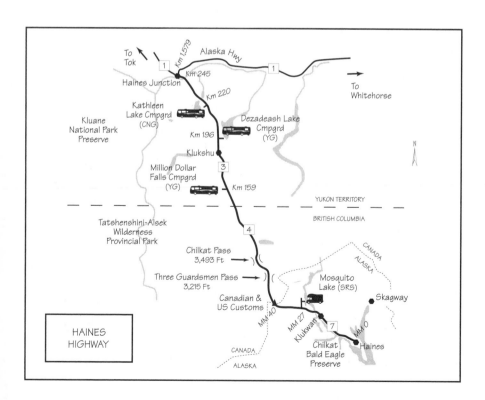

interior gold rush Jack Dalton scouted a route from Haines to Stewart Landing on the Yukon River. This route, which became a toll road, wasn't popular with gold seekers but was used during the Klondike Gold Rush to drive cattle inland. Gradually updated, the route became a gravel road during World War II and was connected to the new Alaska Highway. For many years this road was the only northern access to the Inside Passage and Alaskan ferry system in Southeast Alaska. It was heavily used by Alaskans who didn't want to drive the entire Alaska Highway when traveling to and from Alaska, not to mention state legislators moving to Juneau for the legislative session.

The Haines Highway is paved for its entire 152 miles (245 km) from Haines to Haines Junction at Km 1,579 of the Alaska Highway. The road is marked with mileposts starting in Haines and running to the border. There they change to kilometer posts for the Canadian section of the road.

The Haines Highway starts in Haines and follows the Chilkat River north. Border stations are at Mile 40. They are open from 7 a.m. to 11 p.m. Alaska Time, 8 a.m. to midnight Pacific (Canadian) time, you lose an hour as you travel north. The highway then climbs to cross Three Guardsmen Pass (3,215 feet) and Chilkat Pass (3,493 feet). It then descends to follow the Tatshenshini River into the lower lake country and finally hooks up with the Alaska Highway. As the road travels north it passes through or alongside several park areas: the **Alaska Chilkat Bald Eagle Preserve**, the **Tatshenshini-Alsek Wilderness Provincial Park,** and **Kluane National Park Preserve.**

Haines Highway Campgrounds

🚐 Mosquito Lake State Recreation Site (State of Alaska)

Location:	Mile 2.4 Of Mosquito Lake Rd., Junction At Mile 27 Of Haines Highway
Info:	(907) 766-2292

FREE 🏕️ 🚳 🔥 〜

GPS Location: 59.45444 N, 136.02878 W, 200 Ft.

This is a very small state campground sitting next to little Mosquito Lake. There's no fee, this is a passively managed park, that means there's little management at all. There are perhaps six poorly-defined small sites sitting under large trees at the lakeshore. More importantly, there are no restrooms so this park only works for self-contained rigs. Due to the steep entry road and soft ground the campground is appropriate only for RVs to 25 feet. Picnic tables, fire pits, a boat launch, and a small dock are provided. We suspect that eventually a toilet will be re-installed (it's badly needed) and that there will then be a fee to stay here.

Access is via a paved road leaving the Haines Highway at Mile 27. The campground is at 2.4 miles (3.9 km).

🚐 Million Dollar Falls Campground (Yukon Gov.)

Location:	Km 159 Of The Haines Highway
Info:	(867) 667-5648

$$$ 🏕️ 🔥 〜 🥾 🚌 BIG RIGS

GPS Location: 60.10808 N, 136.94503 W, 2,300 Ft.

This nice government campground has lots of room for big rigs although all 28 vehicle spaces are back-ins. Six walk-in tent sites are spaced around a clearing with three tables. Spaces are well separated with trees and natural vegetation, there are picnic tables and fire pits at each space. Sites are located off a loop road so you can drive in and take a look. The campground also has vault toilets, two picnic and cooking shelters, and a playground. There's an interesting half-mile trail into a rocky ravine to an overlook above Million Dollar Falls and another to a small lake.

➡ DEZADEASH LAKE CAMPGROUND (YUKON GOV.)

Location: Km 196 Of The Haines Highway,
52 Km (32 Miles) From The Haines Junction
Info: (867) 667-5648

GPS Location: 60.39742 N, 137.04236 W, 2,300 Ft.

This Yukon government campground occupies a small gravel point projecting into Dezadeash Lake. It is very pleasant if the wind isn't blowing. Several of the 20 back-in sites are along the shore. This campground is most suitable for rigs to 30 feet although a couple of the sites will take 40 footers and there is plenty of maneuvering room. There are picnic tables and fire pits and the campground has a cooking and picnic shelter and boat-launching ramp. Free firewood is provided.

➡ KATHLEEN LAKE CAMPGROUND ➥ (CANADIAN NATIONAL GOV.)

Location: Km 220 Of The Haines Highway,
27 Km (17 Miles) From Haines Junction
Info: (867) 634-7250

GPS Location: 60.57662 N, 137.21073 W, 2,500 Ft.

Kathleen Lake Campground is located in Kluane National Park so you will notice some differences from the Yukon Government campgrounds you've been staying in, but the differences are small. This campground has 39 large sites (good for RVs although all are back-ins) arranged on a small knoll in cottonwood and spruce. Sites have picnic tables and fire pits. There are vault toilets, food storage lockers, and a central water supply. Near the campground in a day-use area on the lake are a dock, a boat launch and a big fully enclosed cooking and picnic area. Fishing in the lake is said to be good and there is even a beach for a short stroll.

SKAGWAY AND HAINES DUMP STATIONS

Most dump stations in the area covered by this chapter are at campgrounds, see the individual campground descriptions for those. There is a station in **Haines** at the Tesoro at Mile 0 Haines Highway (*GPS Location 59.23566 N, 135.46455 W*).

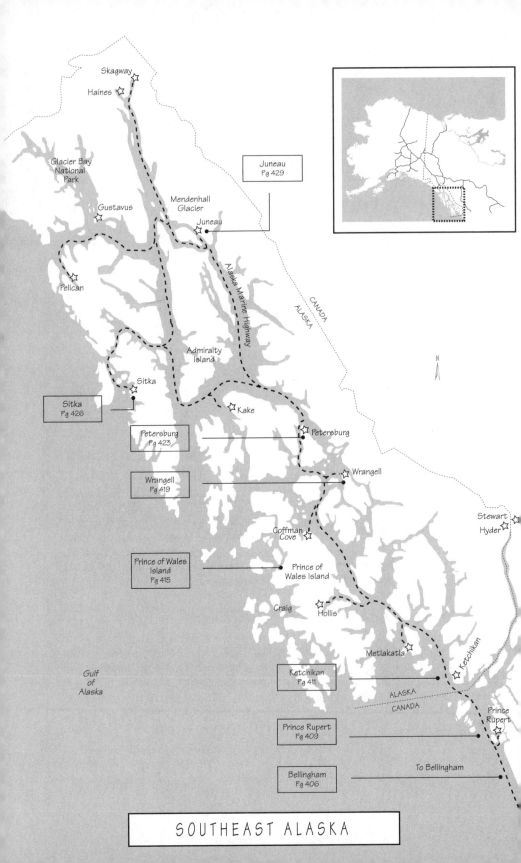

SOUTHEAST ALASKA

Chapter 13

Southeast Alaska

INTRODUCTION

Southeast Alaska, also called the Panhandle, is a different world from the other regions covered in this book. It's a land of water: deep fjords, green shorelines, glaciers, and rain. Travel in Southeast is almost entirely by boat or by air, there are very few roads.

Fortunately, there is a perfect answer to Southeast's transportation difficulties. The Alaska State Ferry System turns the water barriers into highways. The state's ferries dedicated to Southeast run frequently, and they can carry any RV. With proper planning you can travel through the Panhandle conveniently and comfortably, stopping occasionally to see the sights.

The Alaska Panhandle is famous for its weather, more specifically, its rain. However, it doesn't really rain in Southeast every day. The monthly rainfall statistics show an interesting pattern. First, it rains much more in the southern Panhandle than in the northern part. Ketchikan in the far south averages about 7¾ inches in June while Juneau averages under 4 inches. Second, the summer is much drier than the winter. The best month is June, followed by July and then May. Be aware–Juneau averages twice as much rain in August as it does in June! In truth, there are many summer days when there is no rain, but luck will have a lot to do with your personal experience when you visit.

Southeast, like the rest of the state, is sparsely populated. There are just seven towns of any size. These are Juneau, the largest and the state's capital, Ketchikan, Petersburg, Wrangell, Sitka, Skagway, and Haines. We've already talked about Skagway and Haines in Chapter 12. Another town, Prince Rupert in British Columbia, is also an important part of most visits to Southeastern Alaska. There are also some smaller towns and islands that are not on the mainline ferry route that make interesting stopping points, many are connected by smaller ferries. The most attractive of these to RVers is Prince of Wales Island.

Highlights

The real highlight of Southeast Alaska is the scenery. As your ferry glides along the shorelines and through the passages you'll probably find yourself spending a lot of time either on deck or in the observation lounge watching both the wildlife and the traffic along the "Inside Passage" marine highway. You're sure to see many bald eagles, as well as the occasional whale, porpoise, or even a bear.

Southeast Alaska has become cruise ship country. Some towns receive over 300 visits by the huge ships during the five-month-long May to September season. The **cruise ships** are themselves an interesting spectacle as they ghost through the fjords and pause to disgorge thousands of passengers for brief middle of the day visits to each port. A side benefit to the cruise industry is that most cities in Southeast offer a large number of tourist-oriented diversions and services. These include day tours, stage shows, scenic flights, museums, shops, and restaurants. As a vehicle traveler you can book many of the tours in Southeast destination ports directly with the providers, and sometimes get a much lower price than that paid by cruise ship passengers. A good place to explore each town's offerings is the ubiquitous visitor's center

MENDENHALL GLACIER IS ONE OF THE MOST POPULAR TOURIST SITES IN SOUTHEAST

sure to be located near the cruise ship docks. The most popular cruise ship destinations are **Ketchikan, Sitka, Juneau, Skagway**, and of course **Glacier Bay**. Some of the most popular sights include Juneau's **Mendenhall Glacier, Ketchikan's totem poles**, and **Sitka's Russian buildings and heritage**.

Those wanting to get away from civilization will find large areas of Southeast easily accessible. Kayakers, hikers, and assorted tent campers will enjoy **Misty Fiords National Monument Wilderness** near Ketchikan and **Glacier Bay National Park** near Juneau. For a place that is easier to access, even with a car or RV, try **Prince of Wales Island**. A separate ferry service provides service from Ketchikan to the island, details are provided below.

The Marine Highway

Since 1962 the State of Alaska has maintained a fleet of large ferries in lieu of a highway system in Southeastern Alaska. There are now eleven ships in the fleet. Not all operate in Southeast, there are also routes in South Central and Southwest Alaska. The following information is from the 2013 schedule. It applies to the summer schedule, winter sailings are similar but reduced.

The ferry system is very popular and reservations must be made far ahead for the summer season. Don't cast your plans in concrete until you have your reservations, you might be disappointed. You will need reservations for both your vehicle and each passenger. Staterooms are optional, many people travel the entire passage without one and sleep in airline-style recliners or on deck in tents. If you want a stateroom make sure to reserve one. You can save approximately 50% on a ticket through Southeast by beginning or ending your voyage in Prince Rupert instead of Bellingham. Many people do this, note the high frequency of sailings from Prince Rupert discussed below.

A word here about the cost of traveling on the ferry. For two people and a 21-foot RV to travel between Bellingham and Haines costs approximately $1,930. Between Prince Rupert and Haines the cost would be approximately $860. A stateroom would add about $340 between Bellingham and Haines or $160 between Prince Rupert and Haines. These costs would vary with the type of stateroom and stopovers cost extra. Larger RVs pay much more. You can see that driving the highway is the cheaper way to go even in a small RV, if you only consider fuel. On the other hand, if you factor in wear and tear, not to mention the scenery, the ferry may not be such a bad deal.

The ferries usually run pretty much a regular schedule on fixed routes during the height of the summer, the routes from the 2013 schedule are detailed below. During the early summer season and during the spring, fall, and winter the schedules are slightly different and ferries are substituted for each other as ships are taken out of service for a time for maintenance work.

The *Columbia*, at 418 feet long the largest and most luxurious ship in the fleet, runs between Bellingham, Washington and Skagway with stops in Ketchikan, Wrangell, Petersburg, Juneau, Haines and Skagway. Southbound only the ferry also stops in Sitka. The Columbia leaves Bellingham each Friday evening and returns each Friday morning having turned around in Skagway Monday afternoon.

The *Matanuska*, 408 feet long, make two round trips each week between Prince Rupert and Skagway with stops in Ketchikan, Wrangell, Petersburg, Juneau, and Haines.

The *Taku*, 352 feet long, also usually makes two round trips each week from Prince Rupert, but only as far as Juneau. Every run stops are made in Ketchikan, Wrangell, Petersburg and Kake, every other run a stop is also made in Sitka.

The *Malaspina*, 408 feet long, shuttles between Skagway and Juneau with a stop in Haines while traveling in each direction. This is done six days a week with the ship usually leaving Skagway at 3:00 PM and arriving back in Skagway about 1:30 PM.

The new fast ferry, the *Fairweather*, shuttles daily between Juneau and Sitka or Juneau and Petersburg. On Tuesday the run is to Petersburg and back. On all other days of the week it's to Sitka and back. This is a fast boat with speeds exceeding 30 knots. Scheduled time from Juneau to Sitka is 4.5 hours rather than the normal 9 hours on the other ferries. The Fairweather can carry RVs and can be a lot of fun, particularly as she barrels through Peril Straight en route to Sitka.

The *Kennicott* joined the fleet in 1999. She is 380 feet long and is designed with open-water capabilities that allows her to run across the Gulf of Alaska. Twice a month she starts in Bellingham and travels to Whittier with stops en route at Ketchikan, Juneau, and Yakutat; then she returns.

The *MV Stikine* and *MV Prince of Wales*, operated by the **Inter-Island Ferry Authority,** have replaced the State of Alaska service between Ketchikan and Hollis on Prince of Wales Island. There is one round trip daily with the ferry leaving from Hollis in the morning for Ketchikan and then returning to Hollis in the afternoon. It's a three hour run each way. In Ketchikan the ferries operate from a dock next to the State of Alaska ferry terminal, the company has a desk in the state terminal.

For information and reservations on the Inner-Island Ferry Authority Ferries call (866) 308-4848. For information and fares see the link from our website at www.rollinghomes.com.

If you have a ferry reservation it's a good idea to keep an eye on the news and check with the ferry system by phone several weeks and then a week before you are scheduled to depart. Each year it seems that one of the ferries is seriously damaged and the schedules are disrupted. The ferry administration tries to contact those with reservations when there are changes but isn't always successful. The sooner you know about problems the more likely that you'll be able to reschedule.

The ferries are nice but they aren't cruise ships. They have lounge areas, cafeterias, bars, and shower rooms. During the summer many ferries have a U.S. Forest Service interpreter on board to provide information about the area and the wildlife. This makes sense because most of Southeast is inside the Tongass National Forest. Most of the ferries, the larger ones, have staterooms, but many people do not use them. You can save a lot of money by sleeping either in reclining seats or spreading a sleeping bag in the solarium. The solariums are partially glassed-in areas on upper decks. They have overhead heat lamps but are open to the weather at the aft end. Many people actually pitch tents on the upper decks. Passengers are not allowed to stay on the auto decks while the ferries are underway so sleeping in your RV is not an option. Our advice is to book a stateroom on overnight runs if possible, but don't panic if there isn't one available. Occasionally while underway and also while in port you will be allowed to visit your vehicle. Pets must stay on the vehicle deck, you are allowed to walk them during the visits to the vehicle deck. Propane must be turned off and sealed while on the ferry so you will not be able to keep your refrigerator and freezer running in your RV. Most runs are short enough that things in the refrigerator or freezer of your RV will be fine if they are plenty cold before the propane is turned off and if the door is not opened during the voyage. If you're concerned you can place a block of ice in the refrigerator to keep things cool longer.

When the ferries dock it is often possible to get off and take a walk. Sometimes the stop will be for several hours. Layover time will be announced before docking and if the time of day is right there might be a bus into town or a tour available so that you can look around. Unfortunately it is not really possible to plan ahead for these layovers, if the ferry is running late or tides conflict the layover is likely to be shorter than expected.

It is possible to make reservations including stops at each port. There is a small extra cost for these stopovers and they must be planned and reserved in advance. It is well worth your time to sit down with a ferry schedule (see below for ordering address) and work out a schedule that will let you see and do all of the things you want.

For information about schedules and rates you can contact the Alaska Marine Highway, P.O. Box 112505, Juneau, AK 99811-2505. Their toll free telephone number is (800) 642-0066. They have an excellent website, you'll find a link to it on our website: www.rollinghomes.com.

British Columbia has its own system with a ferry that runs between Port Hardy on Vancouver Island and Prince Rupert. You might want to drive the length of Vancouver Island from Victoria or Nanaimo to Port Hardy, catch the new *MV Northern Expedition* to Prince Rupert, and then use the Alaska Marine Highway to travel the rest of the way north. The ferry only runs during daylight hours, north one day and south the next. The route is very scenic and this is the best way to see it since the Alaska state ferries run much of it after dark. For information about schedules and rates contact BC Ferries, 1010 Canada Place, Vancouver, Canada. Their telephone number is (888) 223-3779, and there is a link to their website on ours – www.rollinghomes.com.

Fuel

See the following page for the *Fuel Price Comparison Table*.

Fishing

Southeast Alaska offers some of the best saltwater fishing in the world. All of the towns with campgrounds have excellent fishing nearby but two locations stand out. Many RVers spend the summer in either Ketchikan or on Prince of Wales Island because they offer access to great fishing on a daily basis yet can be reached with fairly short (and less expensive) ferry trips.

Southeast Alaska

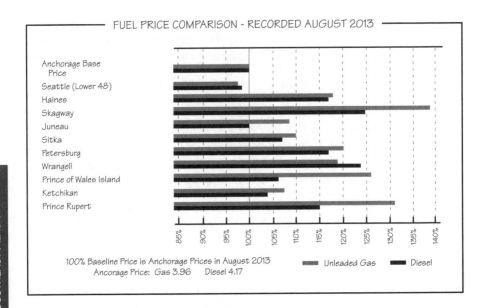

FUEL PRICE COMPARISON - RECORDED AUGUST 2013

100% Baseline Price is Anchorage Prices in August 2013
Anchorage Price: Gas 3.96   Diesel 4.17

Unleaded Gas   Diesel

Wildlife Viewing

The ferries offer a wonderful opportunity to see marine mammals and bald eagles. Whales, porpoises, and sea otters are common in Southeast and so are bald eagles. One nice thing about the ferries is that there are many eyes watching for wildlife, if you pay attention you'll know when something is spotted. You'll quickly find that there are two great places to position yourself for the best spotting. The first is the viewing lounge at the front of the superstructure on each ferry, big windows and comfortable chairs make it easy to spend hours watching the view go by. Even better, but less comfortable, is outside on the upper deck, if you stand just behind the open solarium you're sheltered from the wind, pretty comfortable unless it's raining.

THE ROUTES, TOWNS, AND CAMPGROUNDS

BELLINGHAM, WASHINGTON
Population 130,000, Elevation sea level

It may seem strange to include information about a town in Washington in a book about Alaska. You might consider Bellingham an honorary Alaskan town. After all, Bellingham is closer to Ketchikan than Anchorage is. Many people start their Alaska trip in Bellingham.

At one time the southern terminal of the ferry system was in Seattle, 90 miles (145 km) south of Bellingham. Moving to Bellingham cut several hours from the run north, a significant savings. Bellingham is also a lot less intimidating for RVers driving big rigs.

Bellingham has lots of good stores and is an excellent place to stock up on everything except perishables. Ferry rules require that you turn off the propane in your RV so if you depend upon a propane refrigerator you will want to make sure your freezer is empty for the long voyage to Ketchikan. You may be able to keep the refrigerator cool by putting a block of ice in it.

Bellingham Campgrounds

BIRCH BAY STATE PARK

Location:	20 Miles (32 Km) N. Of Bellingham
Info:	(360) 902-8844
Res.:	(888) 226-7688, www.parks.wa.gov/reservations/
Website:	www.parks.wa.gov

GPS Location: 48.90330 N, 122.76056 W, Near Sea Level

This state park campground occupies a ridge overlooking the beach at the south side of Birch Bay. Along the beach is a day-use area where it is possible to swim and a boat launch. Most of the 167 sites here are non-hookup but there is an area with 20 hookup sites (a few with sewer) in the North Campground for RVs to about 30 feet. There are larger sites, including some pull-thrus but no hookups, for RVs to 35 feet in the South Campground. Some sites reach 60 feet but maneuvering room limits accessibility.

From I-5 take Exit 266 and follow Grandview Road (SR-548) westward for 5.8 miles

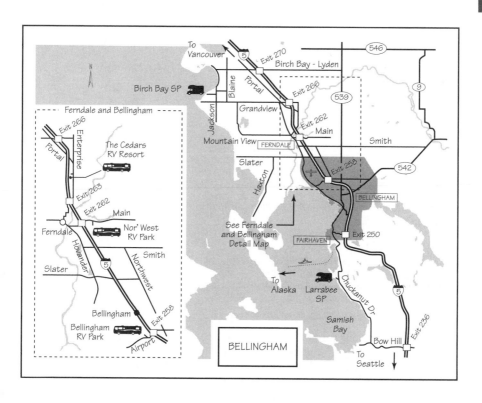

(9.4 km). Turn right onto Jackson Road and then in .8 mile (1.3 km) turn left into Helweg Road. The campground entrance is just ahead.

🚐 THE CEDARS RV RESORT

Address:	6335 Portal Way, Ferndale, WA 98248
Telephone:	(360) 384-2622
Website:	www.holidaytrailsresorts.com/thecedars

GPS Location: 48.87056 N, 122.58528 W, 100 Ft.

The Cedars is a very nice resort for tents and RVs conveniently located just north of Ferndale with easy freeway access. It's a pretty large park with about 260 sites. Most are pull-thrus of about 70 feet in length. Amenities include seasonal swimming pool, instant-on telephone at the sites, and Wi-Fi.

From I-5 take Exit 263 and drive north on Portal Way. The campground will be on your left in .9 mile (1.5 km).

🚐 NOR'WEST RV PARK

Address:	1627 Main St., Ferndale, WA 98248
Telephone:	(360) 384-5038
Email:	nwrvferndale@yahoo.com

GPS Location: 48.84600 N, 122.56972 W, 100 Ft.

This modern, small and tidy RV park is very popular. Reservations are necessary all through the summer months. The 27 sites are paved back-ins and pull-thrus to 60 feet.

From I-5 take Exit 262 and follow Main Street east for .3 mile (.5 km). The campground entrance is on the right.

🚐 BELLINGHAM RV PARK

Address:	3939 Bennett Dr., Bellingham, WA 98224
Telephone:	(888) 372-1224 or (360) 752-1224
Email:	bellrvpark@msn.com
Website:	www.BellinghamRVPark.com

GPS Location: 48.78750 N, 122.52000 W, 200 Ft.

The most convenient park to Bellingham is this modern big-rig park just off the freeway. All of the sites here are 65-foot pull-thrus. Restrooms are exceptionally nice.

Take Exit 258 from I-5 as it passes through Bellingham. You'll spot the park on the south side of the freeway.

🚐 LARRABEE STATE PARK

Location:	5 Miles (8 Km) S. Of Bellingham
Info.:	(360) 902-8844
Res.:	(888) 226-7688, www.parks.wa.gov/reservations/
Website:	www.parks.wa.gov

GPS Location: 48.65361 N, 122.49028 W, 100 Ft.

This 85 site state campground is located south of Bellingham at the north end of Chuckanut Drive. It's a venerable campground, in fact it was the first Washington state park. Sites here are arranged off a narrow loop. Although there are some pull-thrus here to 70 feet they are narrow and sloping. Limited maneuvering room makes this campground only suitable for RVs to 30 feet.

The campground must be approached from the north if you are in an RV because Chuckanut Drive to the south is very narrow and long RVs are restricted. From I-5 take Exit 250. Drive west on Old Fairhaven Parkway for 1.2 miles (1.9 km) until you reach Chuckanut Drive North. Turn south and you'll reach the campground in 5.1 miles (8.2 km).

Bellingham to Ketchikan (37 hours)

The ferry usually leaves Bellingham about 6 p.m. so you won't have much of an opportunity to sightsee until first thing the following morning. By then the ship will probably be passing through Johnstone Strait well up the east side of Vancouver Island. Most of the route north is in protected waters, the ferry is usually rock steady. There are a few places where the inside passage is open to the Pacific waves, and the run across Smith Sound to the north of Vancouver Island is one of the longest. You should get there in the early afternoon, the open passage shouldn't take more than two hours.

Once across Smith Sound you'll be in true inside passage country. The passages narrow and you'll see little civilization. Two towns, Namu and Bella Bella will pass by but you will probably see little other than perhaps some lights in the distance. During the night (your second on the ferry) you may notice a little rolling and pitching, that is your signal that the ferry is crossing Dixon Entrance near Prince Rupert and entering Alaska. You must set your watch back an hour to Alaska Time and get ready to dock in Ketchikan in the morning.

PRINCE RUPERT
Population 13,000, Elevation sea level

The northwest British Columbian city of Prince Rupert is the real gateway to Southeast Alaska. Prince Rupert is at the end of a good paved road and is much closer to Alaska than Bellingham. Even Alaskans living in Southeast use the city as a gateway, many think it well worth the effort to drive 900 or so miles (1,450 km) through Canada to reach the Lower 48. Incidentally, you can't get to Prince Rupert on the ferry from Bellingham, that boat doesn't stop here.

Prince Rupert is a very clean and well-organized little town with full services. It is the western terminus for one of Canada's few rail lines to the Pacific Ocean and dates from the early 1900s. Today the town continues to be an important port.

The town's **Visitor Info Centre** is located at 100 First Ave West, Prince Rupert, BC V8J 1A8 (250 624-5637 and 800 667-1994). Probably the most interesting area of Prince Rupert for visitors is **Cow Bay**. This small waterfront area has historical buildings now housing restaurants, pubs, and gift shops. Also interesting is the **Museum of Northern British Columbia** at First and McBride overlooking the water. Other sights include the **Kwinitsa Railway Museum** and the **North Pacific Cannery** in nearby Port Edward with displays about the salmon canning industry that was the lifeblood of Southeast for many years.

SOUTHEAST ALASKA

Prince Rupert Campgrounds

PRINCE RUPERT RV CAMPGROUND

Address: Box 612, Prince Rupert, B.C. V8J 3R5
Telephone: (250) 627-1000
Email: campgrd@citytel.net
Website: www.princerupertrv.com

GPS Location: 54.29958 N, 130.34103 W, 100 Ft.

This is the most convenient place to stay in Prince Rupert. It's just a kilometer (half-mile) or so up the road from the docks for both the B.C. and Alaska ferries. It can get full on ferry days since almost everyone uses it. The office also serves as a local information office.

The campground has spacious paved drives with about 110 RV camping sites spread down a gentle slope below the office. All sites are back-ins, most are full hookup sites with 20 and 30-amp power extending to about 45 feet. Most sites have fire pits and picnic tables and are separated by grassy areas. There are additional tent sites, some with wooden platforms. Restrooms are modern frame buildings and have showers. There are also a coin-op laundry and a dump station. Wi-Fi is available only in the office area. Reservations are recommended.

To find the campground just follow the signs toward the ferry. You'll find yourself on a wide highway called Park Avenue. The campground is well signed on the right,

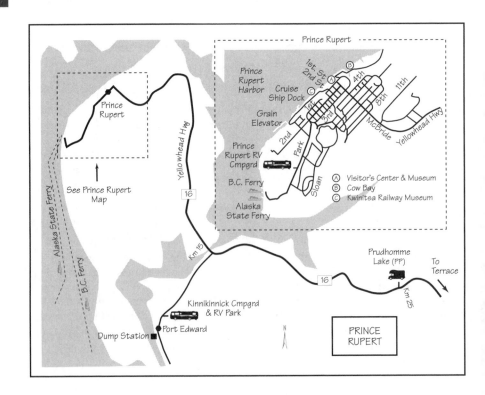

if you find yourself reaching the ferry parking area you've gone too far. The physical address is 1750 Park Avenue. The campground office stays open late for the convenience of ferry travelers.

KINNIKINICK CAMPGROUND AND RV PARK

Address:	Box 1107, Port Edwards, B.C. V0V 1G0
Telephone:	(250) 628-9449 or (866) 628-9449
Email:	rvpark@citytel.net
Website:	www.kinnikcamp.com

GPS Location: 54.22906 N, 130.29005 W, 100 Ft.

While not actually in Prince Rupert the Kinnikinick is nearby, and makes a good alternative to the Prince Rupert RV Campground. It's located in Port Edward, along the route to the North Pacific Fishing Village Museum.

The campground has back-in gravel sites to 50 feet. They are separated by vegetation and some have decent views. Full hookups are available and so are tent sites.

The road to Port Edward leaves Hwy. 16 about 11 km (6.8 miles) southeast of Prince Rupert and leads southwest. About 3.4 km (2.1 miles) from the junction you'll see the campground entrance on your left.

PRUDHOMME LAKE PROVINCIAL PARK

Location:	20 Km (12 Miles) East Of Prince Rupert On Highway 16
Info:	(250) 638-8490
Website:	www.env.gov.bc.ca/bcparks/explore/parkpgs/prudhomme/

GPS Location: 54.23994 N, 130.13290 W, 100 Ft.

If you prefer a government campground for your visit to Prince Rupert the closest one is at Prudhomme Lake, about 20 km (12 miles) from town but just off the main highway. There are 24 spaces. Some sites reach 40 feet and big rigs can access them with careful driving. Sites have the normal British Columbia government campground amenities: picnic tables, fire pits, and vault toilets. There's also a hand water pump. The adjacent Prudhomme Lake is said to have decent fishing for Dolly Varden and rainbows.

Prince Rupert to Ketchikan (6 hours)

The ferries leave Prince Rupert at widely varying times. The route up to Ketchikan is relatively short. It runs across Dixon Entrance so a couple of hours of somewhat rough water are possible.

KETCHIKAN
Population 8,000, Elevation sea level

The ferry doesn't usually stop long in Ketchikan. Since the ferry dock is 2.5 miles (4 km) north of town you aren't likely to have enough time to see much of the city except from the deck as you pass by.

Since Ketchikan is Alaska's seventh largest city it is a good place to pause for a while and look around. The town stretches for several miles along the waterfront, it's long and skinny because there isn't much flat building space. Some of the central downtown area is actually built on pilings. The airport for Ketchikan is located on the far side of the Tongass Narrows, you have to take a short ferry ride to get there. The Tongass Narrows are also used as a landing strip by the local float plane operators and there are several small boat harbors. All of this makes the waterfront an interesting and active place to explore. A new addition to town is a Walmart, located about 1.7 miles (2.7 km) north of the ferry docks.

Ketchikan's history is long and varied. The site was first an Indian fishing village, then a cannery town, a mining town, a cannery town for a second time, a timber town, and now something of a tourist town. As the largest town in the southern Panhandle Ketchikan is also a transportation hub and a supply center. If you plan to visit either **Misty Fiords National Monument** or Prince of Wales Island (see below) you'll be passing through Ketchikan or using it as a base.

Ketchikan has one of the four **Alaska Public Lands Information Centers (APLIC)** that have been placed in gateways to Alaska. This one, the **Southeast Alaska Discovery Center**, (50 Main Street; 907 228-6220) is near the cruise ship docks. Others are in Tok, Fairbanks, and Anchorage. This is the first place to go for information about any government-owned lands you are interested in, including state parks, national forests, national monuments, and national parks.

There's another visitor center in Ketchikan, the **Ketchikan Visitors Bureau** (131 Front St.; 907 225-6166 or 800 770-3300) very near the Southeast Alaska Visitor

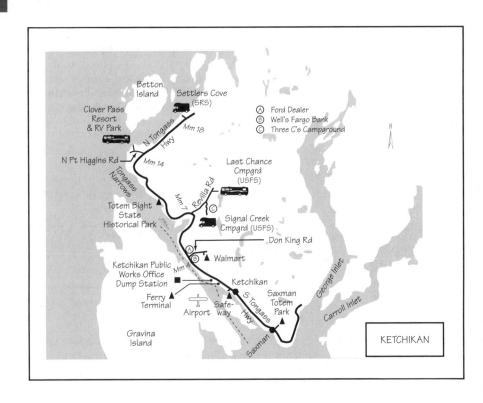

Center. This one specializes in information about Ketchikan itself. **Creek Street**, the town's former red light district seems to be the top attraction for cruise ship passengers. There are shops and a museum with wooden walkways built over a salmon spawning stream. Nearby is a tramway up to a hotel, the **Cape Fox Westmark**. Go on up to see the view and to take a look at some modern totem poles.

Ketchikan is known for its totem poles. The **Totem Heritage Center** is near the downtown area and has 33 of them. The **Saxman Totem Park**, located 2.5 miles (4 km) south of town has another 28 of them and the **Totem Bight State Historical Park** 9.9 miles (16 km) north of town has 14 totems and a model of a Tlingit community house. Along with all those totem poles you'll want to see the **Tongass Historical Museum** (629 Dock Street; 907 225-5600) to gain some perspective and see displays of Tlingit baskets and blankets.

Ketchikan Campgrounds

Ketchikan is pretty well equipped for campers. There are four campgrounds: one is private, two are USFS campgrounds, and one is a state campground. All of the campgrounds are north of town on either the North Tongass Highway or Revilla Road which branches off this highway about 6.5 miles (10.5 km) north of central Ketchikan. There is a **dump station** in town at the Ketchikan Public Works Office at (3291 Tongass Ave., *GPS Location 55.35712 N, 131.69610 W)*, two blocks north of the ferry terminal. The dump station is in the front parking lot of the building, access is difficult except after business hours.

CLOVER PASS RESORT AND RV PARK

    Address: PO Box 8331, Ketchikan, AK 99901
    Telephone: (907) 247-2234 or (800) 410-2234
    Website: www.cloverpassresort.com

    GPS Location: 55.47161 N, 131.81297 W, Near Sea Level

This campground is the only commercial campground in Ketchikan and is very popular. Not only does it have hookups but it has a very active dock area and is a popular destination for folks from outside Alaska who want to spend the summer fishing the very productive salt water of Southeast. Reservations are definitely recommended.

The campground has about 35 back-in sites. Most are full hookup back-in sites with 30 or 50-amp power on terraces on the hillside behind the buildings or along the water next to them. Some can take RVs of any size. Other amenities include motel rooms, a bar that serves some food, restrooms with free showers, a laundry, a dump station, a dock with boat rentals, fishing charters, and a small store.

To reach the campground drive north from the ferry terminal on the Tongass Highway for 11.9 miles (19.2 km) and turn left on N. Pt. Higgins Road. The entrance to the campground is on the right in another .6 mile (1.0 km).

SETTLER'S COVE STATE RECREATION SITE

    Location: Near Mile 18 Of The Tongass Highway
    Info: (907) 465-4563
    Website: dnr.alaska.gov/parks/aspunits/southeast/settlerscvsrs.htm

    GPS Location: 55.50889 N, 131.72800 W, Near Sea Level

This is a small state campground located next to a rocky beach in a quiet area quite a distance north of Ketchikan. There are 14 back-in sites arranged off a circular drive, three sites are large enough for RVs to 35 feet, the others are smaller. Sites have no hookups but do have picnic tables and fire pits. The restrooms are handicapped-accessible vault toilets and there is a hand water pump. The campground serves as a starting point for two nice trails, the circular waterfall trail is easy and worthwhile. The stay limit here is 7 days.

To reach the campground turn left from the ferry terminal and drive north on the Tongass Highway. At 15.8 miles (25.5 km) you'll see the entrance road to the campground on your left. Automobile access to the campground is closed in the evening from 10 p.m. to 6 a.m.

SIGNAL CREEK CAMPGROUND (U.S. FOREST SERVICE)

Location:	At Mile 1.3 Of Revilla Road
Info:	(907) 225-2148
Res.:	(877) 444-6777 or www.recreation.gov

GPS Location: 55.40953 N, 131.70064 W, 100 Ft.

The Signal Creek Campground next to Ward Lake is a modern Forest Service campground. The Ward Lake day use area is nearby and the Ward Lake nature trail runs for 1.3 miles around the lake.

There are 24 back-in sites arranged off a paved circular drive. A few are large enough for RVs to 35 feet. Each site has a picnic table and fire pit, there is a hand-operated water pump and handicapped-accessible vault toilets. There is also usually a host in this campground. There's a great hiking trail around the lake and another leading east to the Last Chance Campground.

To reach the campground turn left from the ferry dock and drive north on the Tongass Highway. After 4.8 miles (7.7 km) turn right on Revilla Road and drive another 1.3 miles (2.1 km). Turn right on the Ward Lake access road, you'll pass the entrance to the Ward Lake day use area on the right, the Three C's group campground on the left, and then reach the Signal Creek Campground.

LAST CHANCE CAMPGROUND (U.S. FOREST SERVICE)

Location:	At Mile 2.2 Of Revilla Road
Info:	(907) 225-2148
Res.:	(877) 444-6777 or www.recreation.gov

GPS Location: 55.43258 N, 131.68606 W, 200 Ft.

This is another modern Forest Service campground. There are 19 spaces off a paved circular drive. Many of these are long spaces, a few can take carefully driven RVs to 40 feet. Sites have picnic tables and fire pits and there is a hand-operated water pump as well as handicapped-accessible vault toilets. There is a 14-day limit at this campground. A trails leads down the valley to Ward Lake.

To reach the campground turn left from the ferry dock and drive north on the Tongass Highway. After 4.8 miles (7.7 km) turn right on Revilla Road and drive another 2.2 miles (3.5 km), you'll see the campground entrance on your right.

Side Trip to Prince of Wales Island from Ketchikan (3 hours)

The short run over to Hollis from Ketchikan on the Inter-Island Ferry Authority's *M/V Prince of Wale or M/V Stikine* has become quite popular. Make sure to secure reservations in advance if you plan to visit Prince of Wales Island.

PRINCE OF WALES ISLAND

Prince of Wales Island offers the best opportunity to explore an undeveloped region of Southeast in your vehicle. The island has been logged, most of the roads were built for that purpose. Now there are some 2,000 miles of roads, mostly unpaved logging roads but also paved highways on the most-traveled routes. This is a good place to go to see black bears. There are also many excellent fishing opportunities.

Hollis is near the ferry landing, there is little else there. **Klawock** (population 900), is 24 miles (39 km) west of Hollis on a paved road and has a good totem pole collection as well as a supermarket. **Craig**, 5 paved miles (8 km) south of Klawock, is a fishing port and probably would be considered the main service center of the island. The town (population 1,500) has supermarkets, gas, laundry, and restaurants. Hollis, Klawock, and Craig are in the central portion of the island.

South of the Klawock/Craig/Hollis axis is **Hydaburg** (population 500). This town of

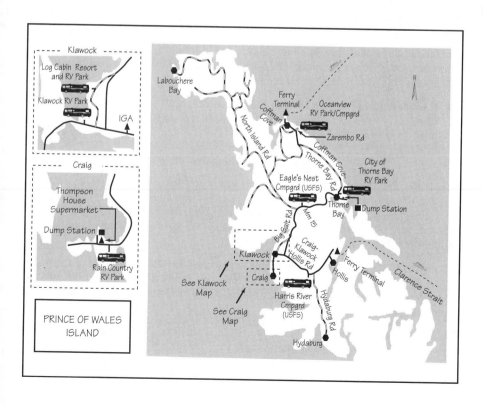

mostly Haida Indians has many totem poles and is an excellent departure point for kayaking the protected west coast of Prince of Wales Island.

To the north of the Klawock/Craig/Hollis axis are most of the logging roads and several smaller communities. **Coffman Cove**, north of Thorne Bay, has a campground and offers services to visitors to the north end of the island, there's also a ferry terminal. While formal campgrounds are scarce there are many places to park your RV and camp and also some interesting sights including **El Capitan**, a limestone cave which can be toured with a Forest Service guide.

For information about Prince of Wales Island contact the Craig Ranger District, 900 9th St, Craig, AK 99921 (907) 826-3271 or the Prince of Wales Chamber of Commerce (6488 Klawock Hollis Hwy. (PO Box 490), Klawock, AK 99925; 907 755-2626).

Prince of Wales Island Campgrounds

Camping facilities on Prince of Wales include a few commercial campgrounds and two modern developed USFS campgrounds. There are many spots on the miles of National Forest logging roads where you can free camp without services. Respect private land ownership.

There are two **dump stations** on Prince of Wales Island in addition to the drains at the commercial campgrounds. The first is in Craig next to the Craig City Shop on Cold Storage Road *(GPS Location 55.47826 N, 133.14000 W)*. It is kept locked, during work hours Monday through Friday the key is available next door at the shop, the rest of the time you can get it at the police station. There is no fee.

The second dump station is in Thorne Bay. You'll spot it on the left as you enter town from the west *(GPS Location 55.68517 N, 132.52601 W)*. It too is kept locked, the key is available at City Hall and there is a fee.

🚐 HARRIS RIVER CAMPGROUND (U. S. FOREST SERVICE)

Location:	Between Mileposts 19 And 20 Between Hollis And Klawock
Info:	(907) 826-3271
Res.:	(877) 444-6777 or www.recreation.gov

GPS Location: 55.46745 N, 132.85681 W, 300 Ft.

This is the first campground you'll reach when you leave the ferry at Hollis. It is a modern forest service campground with 14 camping sites off a loop access road. All are back-in and some are as long as 60 feet. The sites have picnic tables and fire pits, there are two hand-operated water pumps, and there are handicapped-accessible vault toilets. This campground is open all year.

Coming from the ferry landing in Hollis zero your odometer as you leave the parking lot. You'll see the campground on the left in 11 miles (17.7 km). From Klawock if you zero your odometer at the Klawock IGA supermarket you'll reach the campground at 12 miles (19.4 km).

🚐 KLAWOCK RV PARK

Telephone: (907) 755-4888 or (907) 755-2722

GPS Location: 55.55297 N, 133.08724 W, 100 Ft.

This is a very small RV park often full of permanently located units. Sometimes, however, there's room for a traveler. It's located next to the highway as it passes through Klawock.

The park is a gravel lot with back-in parking along one side for five units. There are full hookups and RVs to 40 feet can be accommodated. There are no restrooms or other services.

As you enter Klawock from the direction of Hollis zero you odometer at the IGA supermarket. At .1 mile (.2 km) you'll see the road to Thorne Bay go right. Don't turn. At .2 miles (.3 km) you'll see the Big Salt Lake Road go right, continue another .1 mile (.2 km) and the campground is on the right.

🚐 LOG CABIN RESORT AND RV PARK

Address:	PO Box 54, Klawock, AK 99925
Telephone:	(907) 755-2205 or (800) 544-2205
Email:	lcresak@aptalaska.net
Website:	www.logcabinresortandrvpark.com

GPS Location: 55.55739 N, 133.08458 W, 100 Ft.

The Log Cabin is a popular destination for fishermen. The waters off the west side of Prince of Wales Island offer excellent fishing, several of the campers here spend the whole summer, every summer. The resort is on the beach and has its own dock facility, charters are offered as well as boat rentals. There are also rental cabins.

There are 20 full-hookup spaces, a few along the road for larger RVs up to 40 feet and others for smaller units under and between old-growth hemlock and spruce nearer the water. Some sites are large and others aren't. Definitely walk down the narrow entrance road and look around before entering. Reservations are recommended. The campground has restrooms with showers and a laundry. The office is in the main house at the top of the hill to the right of the entrance drive.

As you enter Klawock from the direction of Hollis zero your odometer at the IGA supermarket. At .1 mile (.2 km) you'll see the road to Thorne Bay go right. Don't turn. At .2 miles (.3 km) you'll see the Big Salt Lake Road go right, turn right and you'll soon see the campground on the left.

🚐 RAIN COUNTRY RV PARK

Address:	510 JS Drive (PO Box 79), Craig, AK 99921
Telephone:	(907) 826-3632

GPS Location: 55.47528 N, 133.13428 W, 100 Ft.

The Rain Country is a modern RV park in the town of Craig. It has eleven large back-in sites suitable for the largest rigs, they offer 30 and 50-amp power and full hookups. There are also restrooms with free showers and a laundry.

To reach the campground zero your odometer in Klawock as you pass over the Klawock River. In 2.6 miles (4.2 km) you'll see the sign for the Craig city limits and at 5.6 miles (9 km) you'll see a sign for the campground and spot the RVs up the hill to the left. Check-in is at the JS True Value hardware store that is off to your right after you enter the park.

EAGLE'S NEST CAMPGROUND (U.S. FOREST SERVICE)

Location:	19 Miles (31 Km) From Klawock On the Thorne Bay Rd
Info:	(907) 826-3271
Res.:	(877) 444-6777 or www.recreation.gov

GPS Location: 55.70194 N, 132.83656 W, 400 Ft.

The second Forest Service campground on Prince of Wales Island is a little smaller than the one at Harris River and also more remote. It has twelve back-in spaces on an out and back road with a turnaround loop at the end. These are long spaces suitable for large RVs and they have the usual picnic tables and fire pits. The campground has handicapped-accessible vault toilets and also a hand-operated water pump. There is often a host. This campground is adjacent to Ball's Lake and there is a boardwalk trail through the marsh along the lake that is great for watching the lake's wildlife, particularly loons and bald eagles. There's a 14 day limit at this campground.

From the IGA store in Klawock drive west just .1 mile (.2 km) and you'll spot the road to Thorne Bay on the right. Zero your odometer and head north. At 16.6 miles (26.8 km) you'll reach an intersection, turn right toward Thorne Bay, and in another 1.9 miles (3.1 km) you'll see the campground entrance on the left.

CITY OF THORNE BAY RV PARK

Telephone: (907) 828-3380

GPS Location: 55.68703 N, 132.52764 W, 100 Ft.

This is primarily a residential park at the western entrance to Thorne Bay. There are 13 back-in sites for units to 40 feet and often one or two are available for travelers. Sites have full hookups but there are no facilities for those who don't have self-contained units.

Approaching Thorne Bay from the west you'll spot Sandy Beach Road heading left at a Y. Following it you'll spot the campground on the right in .2 mile (.3 km).

OCEANVIEW RV PARK/CAMPGROUND

Address:	PO Box 18035, Coffman Cove, AK 99918
Telephone:	(907) 329-2032
Email:	djeffrey@coveconnect.com
Website:	www.coffmancove.org/rvpark.html

GPS Location: 56.01569 N, 132.82583 W, Near Sea Level

The Oceanview has 14 back-in sites fronting on a rocky beach. All have full hookups with 30-amp power. Restrooms have flush toilets, showers, even a laundry.

Coffman cove isn't a large place so finding the campground isn't hard. Approaching town from the south you'll spot a campground sign pointing east on Zarembo Dr. Follow Zarembo for .1 mile (.2 km) to the campground. If you can't find it just ask, you're not likely to find anyone who lives in Coffman Cove and doesn't know where it is.

Ketchikan to Wrangell (6 hours)

The relatively short run up Clarence Straight to Wrangell offers views of Prince of Wales Island, third largest island in the U.S., to the west along much of the route. The ferry docks right in Wrangell. The layover is generally short but occasionally there are delays due to tide conditions in the Wrangell Narrows to the north which give time for a look around town.

WRANGELL
Population 2,400, Elevation sea level

Wrangell is strategically located near the mouth of the Stikine River. The mouth is on the mainland some 5 miles (8 km) distant. The Stikine has long been a highway into the interior of British Columbia, at one time the swift-flowing river was served by several steamboats. The Russians and British used the town as a fur-trading base and later Wrangell was a supply base for the Stikine (1861), Cassiar, and even the Klondike gold rushes. Today the economy is based on fishing, timber, and tourism, but the Stikine still provides access to mines in the interior.

Wrangell doesn't get nearly as many cruise ships as Ketchikan, Juneau or Skagway so the tourism here is oriented more toward ferry travelers. Sights are open when the ferry is in town, especially if the stopover is going to be long enough for passengers to spend some time ashore. There's a **Visitor's Information Center** (907 874-3901 or 800 367-9745) near the ferry terminal. In town you'll want to visit **Shakes Island** which has totem poles and a tribal house built by the CCC. There are interesting **petroglyphs** along the beach north of town. Wrangell also has a 9-hole golf course known as **Muskeg Meadows**.

SOUTHEAST ALASKA

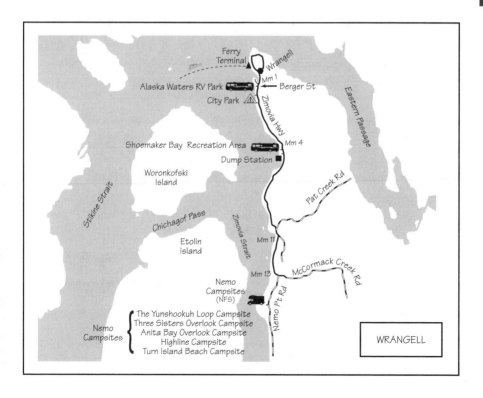

If you decide to stay for a while you'll find that **Wrangell Island**, like Prince of Wales Island, has lots of logging roads giving access to some interesting country. The U.S. Forest Service office at 525 Bennett St. (907 874-2323) has information about attractions, campgrounds, trails, and roads.

The **Stikine-LeConte Wilderness** Area is easily reached by boat from Wrangell. The Stikine is a popular float river, particularly the upper reaches near Telegraph Creek. The LeConte tidewater glacier to the north of the Stikine is probably more easily reached from Petersburg which is slightly closer. There are many Forest Service rental cabins along the Stikine as well as two hot springs. For information contact the Tongass National Forest Wrangell Ranger District at PO Box 51, Wrangell, AK 99929; (907) 874-2323.

Wrangell Campgrounds

Surprisingly, Wrangell is one of the better destinations for RVers in Southeast Alaska. There are two campgrounds offering hookups and many forest service campgrounds and recreation sites suitable for RVs. RVs to 30 feet can easily reach the Nemo campsites listed below and RVs to about 25 feet can travel the logging roads and reach many other remote National Forest recreation sites with parking areas that make excellent RV sites, many complete with picnic tables, fire pits, and outhouses. Tent campers with an automobile for transportation have an even wider selection because there are many hike-in locations. There is an easily-accessible **dump station** at the Shoemaker Bay boat harbor parking lot *(GPS Location 56.41684 N, 132.34716 W)*.

ALASKA WATERS RV PARK

Address:	241 Berger Street (PO Box 1978), Wrangell, AK 99929
Telephone:	(907) 874-2378 or (800) 347-4462
Email:	info@alaskawaters.com
Website:	www.alaskawaters.com

GPS Location: 56.46022 N, 132.38061 W, 100 Ft.

This is the commercial campground in Wrangell. It offers 7 back-in spaces, 4 have full hookups and 3 have electricity and water only. The spaces are large enough for RVs to 45 feet. The building on the site serves as storage and a part-time office for the tour and fishing-charter company operated by the same owners. Restrooms and showers are available a half-mile from the park at the Wrangell Public Swimming Pool.

To reach the campground head south on the Zimovia Highway. At Mile 1.1 turn right on Berger Street, the campground is on the right after the turn.

SHOEMAKER BAY RECREATION AREA

Location:	Mile 4.5 Zimovia Hwy.
Info:	(907) 874-2444
Website:	www.wrangell.com/recreation/ shoemaker-rv-park

GPS Location: 56.41900 N, 132.35161 W, Near Sea Level

For self-contained RVs Shoemaker Bay makes an excellent place to stay while you are in Wrangell. This is a boat harbor, but there are nice RV sites overlooking the harbor, RV parking is allowed in the harbor parking lot, and there is also a tent-camping area.

The 16 back-in (or pull-in) spaces overlooking the boat harbor are just off the high-way before you reach the harbor parking lot. Many of these spaces will take RVs to 45 feet, 30-amp power is available. A little farther along is the harbor parking lot. RV parking is allowed on the far left along the trees but there are no hookups. There is a tent camping area here along the creek, and restrooms with flush toilets but no showers are located across a small footbridge beyond the tent sites. Water is available next to the tennis courts nearby and there is a dump station next to the parking lot entrance. If you are staying at Shoemaker Bay you also may use the very nice city swimming pool facilities on Church Street in town including weight room and showers for no additional charge. You are allowed to stay in the RV campground for 10 days and this can be extended with permission. The maximum stay in the tent area is 5 days.

To reach the campground head south on the Zimovia Highway. You'll see the electric sites on the right at Mile 4.4 and the entrance to the harbor parking lot at Mile 4.5.

⊞ NEMO POINT CAMPSITES (U.S. FOREST SERVICE)   FREE [icons]
   Location: Mile 13.7 Zimovia Hwy.
   Info: (907) 225-3101

GPS Location: 56.30256 N, 132.34394 W, 400 Ft.

The Nemo Campsites are really designed for tent campers but some are suitable for RVs too. There are five different camping areas. All sit high on a mountainside and offer great views. Bald eagles like to perch on snags just below the campsites to enjoy the same views.

The **Yunshookuh Loop Campsite** is the best for RVs, some sites to about 30 feet. It has three places suitable for parking an RV, all with great views. Two have a picnic table and fire ring adjoining the parking pad. The other has a table and fire ring a short distance away. There is also a vault toilet at this camping area, as well as a sign naming the site.

Three Sisters Overlook Campsite has a parking area right on the main road that will accept several RVs to about 30 feet, there are no amenities at the parking area but the view is pretty good. The one tent-camping site is down a short boardwalk and has picnic table, fire pit, handicapped-accessible vault toilet, and great views. There's a sign identifying this site.

The **Anita Bay Overlook Campsite** has a parking area that could take several RVs to about 30 feet but the parking lot doesn't offer much in the way of amenities or views. There are two tent sites a short distance away with spectacular views, picnic tables, fire pits and a handicapped-accessible vault toilet. There's no name sign identifying this site, just a sign with a tent icon at the entrance.

Highline Campsite has four vehicle parking sites with two picnic tables and fire pits, also a vault toilet. It's suitable for tent campers, pickup campers, and vans only. A sign identifies the access road.

Finally, **Turn Island Beach Campsite** is a walk-in tent-camping site. The boardwalk

THE NEMO CAMPSITES SIT HIGH ON THE MOUNTAINSIDE AND OFFER GREAT VIEWS

trail descending from the road parking area to the site has 574 stairs, easy in and hard out. There are two sites with platforms, picnic tables, fire pits, and a vault toilet. A sign identifies the parking area and beginning of the trail.

To reach the Nemo Campsites head south on the Zimovia Highway to Mile 13.7. Turn right at the sign for the Nemo Point Recreation Area, zero your odometer, and follow the one-lane gravel road. In .5 mile (.8 km) you'll pass a host, the entrance to Yunshookun Loop goes right at .8 mile (1.3 km), the parking for Three Sisters Overlook is on the right at 1.5 miles (2.4 km), Anita Bay Overlook is at 2 miles (3.2 km), the access road to Highline goes right at 3.4 miles (5.5 km), and the Turn Island parking area is at 5 miles (8 km).

🚐 City Park

Location:	Mile 1.3 Zimovia Hwy.
Info:	(907) 874-2444
Website:	www.wrangell.com/recreation/city-park

GPS Location: 56.45397 N, 132.38239 W, Near Sea Level

The city park has picnic shelters and allows tent camping 48 hours. There are four covered sites and restrooms with flush toilets, but these were in very poor condition when we visited. RV camping is not allowed, in fact vehicles are not allowed to park overnight.

To reach the City Park head south on the Zimovia Highway, the City Park is on the right at Mile 1.3.

Wrangell to Petersburg (3 hours)

The ferry trip from Wrangell to Petersburg is one of the most interesting of the entire Inside Passage. Much of the route is through the **Wrangell Narrows** between Kuprenof and Mitkof Islands. This 21-mile (34 km) passage is often as narrow as 300 feet and quite shallow, there is a string of range markers showing the crew where to steer. The passage through the narrows is very impressive, you'll like the lights at night and the chance to see the intricate passage better during daylight passages. The ferries can only pass through at high tide and this is a big factor in scheduling the ferries. Most cruise ships don't get to go through the narrows because they're too big.

PETERSBURG
Population 3,000, Elevation sea level

Petersburg may be only a few miles from Wrangell but the atmosphere is entirely different. Petersburg is scrubbed and neat and shows its Norwegian heritage. Petersburg is a fishing town with just a little logging thrown in. Like Wrangell, few cruise ships stop in Petersburg.

Also like Wrangell, Petersburg has a local **Visitor Information Office** (907 772-3646) and a **U.S. Forest Service Office** (907 772-3841). Both are located near 1st and Fram and have information and maps of roads, trails, and campgrounds on **Mitkof Island** and other islands nearby.

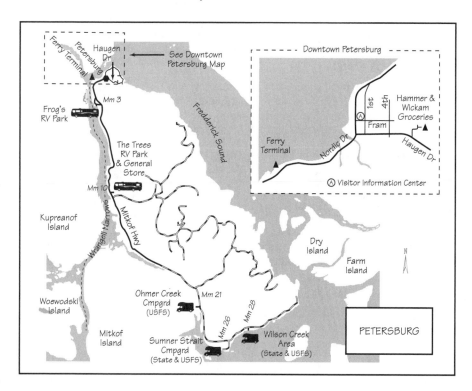

Sights in Petersburg are limited and show off the town's Norwegian heritage. Wander around town and admire the trim lawns and decorated buildings including the **Sons of Norway Hall**. A Viking boat, the **Valhalla**, sits next to the hall. There's also the **Clausen Memorial Museum** with exhibits on Petersburg's history.

Petersburg, like Wrangell, is used as an access point for the nearby **Stikine-LeConte Wilderness**. There are tours out to see the **LeConte Glacier** about 25 miles (40 km) east. You can also take jet boat tours up the Stikine River.

Petersburg Campgrounds

Petersburg is well supplied with campgrounds. South of town are two good commercial ones with hookups, a USFS campground, and some former campgrounds along the southern end of the island that make good boondocking sites. Like Wrangell, Petersburg (Mitkof Island) has a surprisingly large road system in the form of logging roads.

FROG'S RV PARK

Address:	126 Scow Bay Loop Road, Petersburg, AK 99833
Telephone:	(360) 482-8589
Email:	frogsrvpark@hotmail.com

GPS Location: 56.77836 N, 132.96744 W, Near Sea Level

This traveler park makes up a small part of a residential RV park area. The park is located above the beach south of town, it overlooks the narrows and a barge-dock facility. There are five 45-foot pull-thru sites with full hookups. There is also a tent camping site near the water. Restrooms have coin operated showers, and there is a laundry. There's a community fire pit and picnic table. Free Wi-Fi reaches the sites. The owners live on-site.

From the ferry dock head south. At .1 miles (.2 km) you'll pass the Mile 1 marker, at 2 miles (3.2 km) you'll pass the north junction for Scow Bay Loop Road, and at 2.2 miles (3.5 km) you'll reach the south junction with the Scow Bay Loop Road. Turn right here and you'll soon see Frog's RV Park on the left.

THE TREES RV PARK AND GENERAL STORE

Address:	PO Box 404, Petersburg, AK 99833
Telephone:	(907) 772-2502
Email:	thetrees@aptalaska.net
Website:	www.thetreesrvpark.com

GPS Location: 56.68596 N, 132.92681 W, 100 Ft.

This new campground has seven full hookup sites and six with water and electric. These are back-in gravel sites, some as long as 70 feet. They are separated by trees and other natural vegetation and off a loop road which runs behind a small store. Restrooms have showers and there is a laundry.

From the ferry dock head south. At 9.3 miles (15 km) you'll see the Twin Creek RV Park on the left.

OHMER CREEK CAMPGROUND (U.S. FOREST SERVICE)

Location: Mile 21.5 Mitkof Highway
Info: (907) 772-3841

GPS Location: 56.57733 N, 132.73978 W, 100 Ft.

This is a forest service campground with some sites suitable for RVs to 35 feet. There are ten back-in RV sites as well as additional tent sites. Sites have picnic tables and fire pits, there is a host, and vault toilets are handicapped-accessible. A large turn-around at the back end of the campground lets RVs turn around. There's a hand water pump and the campground has a 14-day stay limit. A handicapped-accessible trail leads from the highway near the campground to the nearby creek for fishing.

From the ferry landing head south. You'll see the campground entrance just before the 22 mile marker.

SUMNER STRAIT CAMPGROUND (GREENS CAMP)

Location: Near Mile 26 Mitkof Highway

GPS Location: 56.54071 N, 132.68148 W, Near Sea Level

There are about 30 back-in sites off a loop road. Some sites are very scenic water-front locations and some sites are as long as 35 feet. They have picnic tables, and fire pits and the campground has vault toilets.

From the ferry landing head south. The entrance road is on the right just after the 26 Mile marker.

WILSON CREEK AREA

Location: Mile 28 Mitkof Highway

GPS Location: 56.55373 N, 132.64472 W, Near Sea Level

A narrow road leads a short distance from the highway to a gravel parking area along the shore of Sumner Strait on the south shore of Mitkof Island. There is room for about four RVs to park in the lot. Facilities are limited to a couple of fire pits, a picnic table, and a vault toilet.

From the ferry landing head south. The entrance road is on the right just before the 28 Mile marker.

Petersburg to Sitka (10 hours)

If you look at your map you'll see that unlike other Southeast towns Sitka isn't really located along the Inside Passage. The town sits on the west side of Baranof Island and is quite remote from the normal protected shipping routes. To get to Sitka the ferry must negotiate the narrow and aptly named **Peril Strait**. Most ships must do this at slack water so the ferry is often delayed in Sitka giving visitors a chance to look around. Peril Strait is probably the best place along the entire ferry route to watch for wildlife, particularly bald eagles.

Not all ferries stop at Sitka when passing between Petersburg and Juneau. Those that don't go directly up Stephens Passage on the east side of Admiralty Island. This more direct route to Juneau takes about 8 hours. You might want to make sure yours is a Sitka ferry, even if you don't plan to stop over in Sitka the cost is the same and you

SOUTHEAST ALASKA

have the opportunity to see Peril Strait and perhaps take a quick tour of Sitka while the ferry is in port.

SITKA
Population 9,100, Elevation sea level

Sitka was the capital of Russian America. Long an Indian settlement, the Russians arrived in 1799, were kicked out by the Indians a few years later, and then re-established themselves after a major battle. Sitka is a popular cruise ship port so there are quite a few things to see. The cruise ships can't dock here, small boats are used to ferry the passengers to shore. This is nice since the ships don't overwhelm the town like in Juneau and Ketchikan. The **Visitor's Information Center** (907 747-5940) is located downtown near the Pioneer's Home.

The **Centennial Building**, located at the harbor's edge, is the center of cruise ship activities. Since there is no dock for them in Sitka tourists come ashore in small boats. The **New Archangel Dancers** perform traditional Russian dances and various tours leave from the Centennial Building. Nearby is the **Isabel Miller Museum**, the town's historical museum.

Many of the sights in Sitka are Russian and are located near each other. They include the reconstructed **St. Michael's Cathedral**. The original burned down in 1966 but the irreplaceable icons were saved and are in the new church. There's also the painstakingly restored **Russian Bishop's House**, a reconstructed **Russian blockhouse**,

VIEW OF MOUNT EDGECOMBE FROM SITKA

Castle Hill where Baranov's Castle was located before it burned in 1894, and a **Russian Orthodox cemetery** with graves dating from long before the U.S. purchase of Alaska.

The Russian and Indian cultures come together forcefully at the **Sitka National Historical Park**. It is located just southeast of town at the mouth of the Indian River. This is the site of the 1804 Tlingit-Russian battle. There is a Tlingit cultural museum and workshop and several totem poles along pleasant trails. Nearby **Sheldon Jackson Museum** has an excellent museum with artifacts representing many of Alaska's native cultures. Another popular site nearby is the **Alaska Raptor Rehabilitation Center**.

Finally, to get a good look at some grizzlies you'll want to visit **Fortress of the Bears**. It's located about 4 miles (6 km) out Sawmill Creek Road, near the intersection with Blue Lake Road.

Sitka Campgrounds

Sitka has four campgrounds, one is commercial, one is a city campground with electric and water hookups, and the other two are USFS campgrounds. A dump station *(GPS Location 57.04762 N, 135.35546 W)* is available at the wastewater treatment plant on Japonski Island (see the write-up below about Sealing Cove Boat Harbor Campground for more information).

STARRIGAVAN CAMPGROUND (U.S. FOREST SERVICE)

Location:	North End Of Halibut Point Road, Just North Of Ferry Dock
Info:	(907) 747-4216
Res.:	(877) 444-6777 or www.recreation.gov

GPS Location: 57.13291 N, 135.36651 W, Near Sea Level

This Forest Service campground is convenient to the ferry. From the landing just turn left and you'll be at the entrance gate in just .7 mile (1.1 km). This is about seven miles (11.3 km) from downtown Sitka.

When you enter this campground you have a choice. To the right is the Estuary Loop. Immediately after this turn (on the left) are six hike-in sites and if you continue straight there are 26 vehicle sites. Each site is marked with the maximum vehicle size allowed, they go up to 38 feet. However, many sites are longer than the signs say, and in fact when we visited many had longer vehicles in them than the signs directed. This side of the park also provides access to a boardwalk overlooking the nearby estuary, and three tent sites with vehicle parking nearby. Gates are locked from 10 p.m. to 7 a.m. each day, and the host is in the house to the left of the entrance as you enter. There's a 14 day limit on stays at this park.

To the left is the Bayside Loop which has three hike-in sites, a picnic area, and the trailhead for the very pleasant Mosquito Cove Trail.

SITKA SPORTSMAN'S ASSOCIATION RV PARK

Address:	5211 Halibut Point Rd, Sitka, AK 99835
Telephone:	(800) 750-4712
Website:	www.rvsitka.com

GPS Location: 57.12714 N, 135.38286 W, Near Sea Level

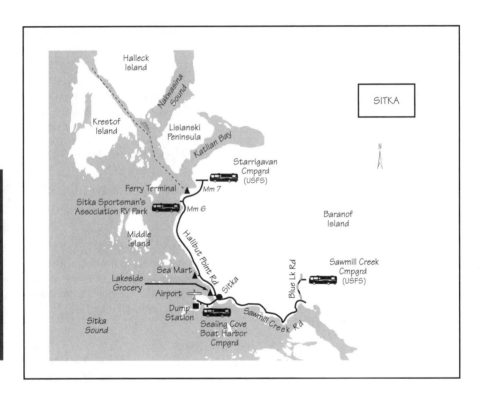

This little commercial campground is located right next to the ferry dock so it's an easy place to pull into if you are getting in late. It's a good idea to call and make a reservation if you plan to do that. The facility is located on the grounds of the Robert B Laguire Memorial Indoor Trap Range.

The campground has 16 back-in spaces on a paved or gravel surface. There are full and partial hookup sites with 30-amp outlets. There is also a dump station. A grassy tent camping area is near the water. A small handicapped-accessible restroom building has showers and flush toilets.

When you leave the ferry dock turn right. You'll see the campground entrance on the right in just a tenth of a mile (.2 km).

☲ SEALING COVE BOAT HARBOR CAMPGROUND

Location:	Japonski Island
Info:	(907) 747-3439
Website:	www.cityofsitka.com/government/departments/
	harbor/RVParking.html

GPS Location: 57.04925 N, 135.34928 W, Near Sea Level

The sites at this campground are essentially long slots in a parking lot overlooking the Sealing Cove Boat Harbor. There are 26 of them, and they offer 30-amp electricity and water hookups. Next door at the marina there is a bathroom with a flush toilet but no showers. There is a 30-day limit for stays here. There is a city dump station nearby. To reach it continue past the camping area toward the airport and take the first left onto Kruzov Ave. The dump station is next to the large gray building on the right ahead.

To drive to Sealing Cove Boat Harbor turn right when you leave the ferry dock. Drive 6.8 miles (11 km) to a major intersection with Lake Street. Turn right here and in .4 miles (.6 km) you'll drive up and over the bridge onto Japonski Island. Immediately after descending on the far side of the bridge you'll see the RV parking area ahead and on the left.

⛟ SAWMILL CREEK CAMPGROUND (U.S. FOREST SERVICE)

Location: 3.6 Miles (5.8 km) South Of Town Off Sawmill Creek Road
Info: (907) 747-4216

GPS Location: 57.06133 N, 135.20914 W, 300 Ft.

This Forest Service campground is closed for renovation through 2015. It has nine RV sites and additional walk-in tent sites. Several of the RV sites are arranged around a very large gravel opening in the trees so any size RV has plenty of room to park and maneuver. Camp sites have picnic tables and fire pits and there are vault toilets. A trail starts at the campground and climbs steeply to circle a lake high above on the hillside.

To reach the campground drive south from town on Sawmill Creek Road. If you zero your odometer as you pass the post office at Mile 1 you'll come to the intersection with Blue Lake Road at 4.2 miles (6.8 km). Turn left here and follow Blue Lake Road for 1.4 miles (2.3 km), the campground entrance is on your right. That last 1.4 miles is gravel and can be rough, it's not a great road for large RVs although some brave it. If you have a large RV and also a tow car you'll probably want to check the road before committing your big RV.

Sitka to Juneau (8 hours, 45 minutes)

The ferries leave Sitka the way they arrive, through Peril Straight. They then travel up Chatham Straight with Admiralty Island to the east and Chichagof Island to the west. At the north end of Admiralty Island the ferry rounds the Mansfield Peninsula and docks at Auke Bay 13 miles (21 km) north of downtown Juneau. If the stop is long enough (it often is) you can take a quick bus tour of Juneau even if you don't schedule a stopover.

JUNEAU
Population 31,000, Elevation sea level

Alaska's capital city is one of the most popular tourist destinations in Southeast, almost all of the cruise ships stop here. There are quite a few things to see and do in Juneau. Government and tourism are the mainstays of the economy here.

Juneau actually spreads over quite a large area for a Panhandle city. The downtown area is cramped, the buildings climb up the side of Mt. Juneau and Gastineau Peak. The population is spread out over neighboring Douglas Island which is connected by a bridge and north into the Mendenhall Valley where there is lots more room.

SOUTHEAST ALASKA

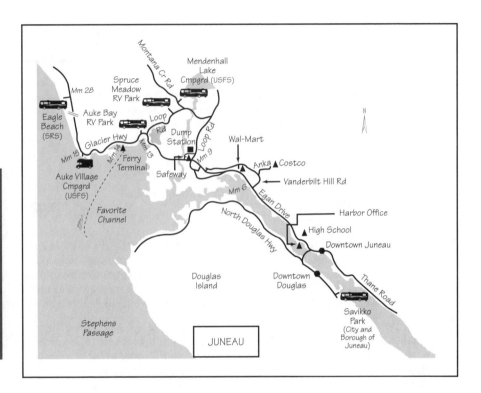

The **Visitor Information Center** (907 586-2201) in Juneau is in Centennial Hall at 101 Egan Drive. There's also a small one at the ferry dock. There is a Forest Service information office in Centennial Hall. Juneau is the usual jumping-off point for both Glacier Bay National Park and Admiralty Island's Pack Creek Bear Observatory, see Chapter 14 for more about both of these destinations.

Visitor-oriented sights and activities in Juneau include the **Alaska State Museum** and the **Juneau-Douglas City Museum** downtown. State buildings including the **Governor's Mansion**, **State Office Building** (SOB), **State Capitol Building**, and **House of Wickersham** are worth a look. The downtown area is interesting to explore, you can get walking tour maps at the visitor information center. A new attraction in Juneau is the **Mt. Roberts Tramway and Observatory**, the lower station is near the cruise ship dock. If you have come to appreciate the products of the **Alaskan Brewing Company** you might want to tour the brewery at 5429 Shaune Dr which is in Lemon Creek between Juneau and the Mendenhall Valley. Tours start every 30 minutes.

Probably the most-visited sight in Juneau is the **Mendenhall Glacier**. The glacier is actually inside the city limits, you can drive to the Mendenhall Visitor Center which offers excellent views. There are also hiking trails in the area.

Juneau Campgrounds

Juneau gets a lot of camping visitors and has the facilities to handle them. There are six campgrounds in town: two are commercial RV parks, two are USFS campgrounds, one is a state park, and there is a city-operated parking area. Downtown Juneau is quite cramped and parking is difficult. Try leaving your RV outside town and using the Capital Transit Bus System.

The ferry terminal is located off the Glacier Highway at Mile 13 north of downtown Juneau. All of the directions to campgrounds below are given from the ferry docks.

There is a dump station at the Valley Tesoro station near the Mendenhall Center Mall at about Mile 7.5 of the Glacier Highway. It is located behind the station and is difficult to access with large RVs *(GPS Location 58.37259 N, 134.58658 W)*. Many people use the dump sites at the Forest Service's Mendenhall Lake Campground *(GPS Location 58.41308 N, 134.59083 W)*, there is no charge. Both of these dump stations also have water.

SPRUCE MEADOW RV PARK

Address:	10200 Mendenhall Loop Rd., Juneau, AK 99801
Telephone:	(907) 789-1990
Email:	spruce@juneaurv.com
Website:	www.JuneauRV.com

GPS Location: 58.40329 N, 134.60414 W, 100 Ft.

This is Juneau's newest commercial RV park. There are about fifty back-in sites and they are suitable for RVs to 40 feet. One area is filled with long-term rigs but traveler sites are in a different area. Both full and partial hookups are available. Parking is on gravel and there are wide spaces of natural vegetation between most of the sites. There is also a tent camping area. Facilities include handicapped-accessible restrooms (individual rooms) with showers, a laundry, and a dump station. While the park is located in a country setting it is on the bus line and not far from the Mendenhall Glacier. Reservations are a good idea.

To drive to the park from the ferry landing turn right onto the Glacier Highway toward downtown Juneau. After 1.6 miles (2.6 km) turn left onto Mendenhall Loop Road. Drive another 2.1 miles (3.4 km) and you will see the campground sign and entrance on the left side of the highway.

MENDENHALL LAKE CAMPGROUND (U.S. FOREST SERVICE)

Location:	Off Montana Creek Road Near Mendenhall Glacier
Info:	(907) 586-8800
Res.:	(877) 444-6777 or www.recreation.gov

GPS Location: 58.41308 N, 134.59083 W, 100 Ft.

The Mendenhall Lake Campground in many ways is now the nicest campground in Juneau. Would you believe a Forest Service campground with 50-amp hookups and showers? Of course, the price for hookup sites reflects this.

The campground has 69 sites, a few are full-hookup (20, 30, and 50 amp), others

SOUTHEAST ALASKA

have electricity and water or no hookups. Three hookup sites are pull-thrus. Many sites, even those without hookups, are 40 feet long, the pull-thrus are 50 feet. There is a dump station and modern handicapped-accessible restrooms with flush toilets and free showers. Some of the sites at this campground are on the waterfront with tree-screened views of the Mendenhall Glacier, but not any of the sites with hookups. There is a 14 day limit here.

To drive to the park from the ferry landing turn right onto the Glacier Highway toward downtown Juneau. After 1.6 miles (2.6 km) turn left onto Loop Road. Drive another 2.6 miles (4.2 km) and you will see a road to the left marked Montana Creek Road and Mendenhall Lake. Turn left here and you'll reach the entrance to the campground in .6 miles (1 km), it's on the right.

AUKE BAY RV PARK

Location: 11930 Glacier Highway,
                   Auke Bay, AK 99821
Telephone: (907) 789-9467
Email: ABRV@gci.net
Website: www.rvjuneau.com/

GPS Location: 58.38775 N, W 134.65067 W, 100 Ft.

This RV park is conveniently located along the Glacier Highway not far from the ferry terminal. While it does have a number of semi-permanent residents there are also about five spaces for overnighters.

Most of these are back-in full hookups with 30-amp power. One is a pull-thru. They are suitable for RVs to 45 feet. A small modern building houses restrooms with flush toilets and showers and there is a laundry room.

From the ferry dock turn right and proceed for 1.4 miles (2.3 km), you'll see the campground on the left.

AUKE VILLAGE CAMPGROUND (U.S. FOREST SERVICE)

Location: Glacier Highway Mile 15
Info: (907) 586-8800

GPS Location: 58.37589 N, 134.72842 W, Near Sea Level

This is an older small U.S. Forest Service Campground located near the beach. It has 11 back-in sites. Most are small, the few largest ones would take RVs to about 25 feet. Sites have fire pits and picnic tables and there are vault toilets. Short trails lead down to the rocky beach. There is a two-week limit here and the campground is often full.

From the ferry dock turn left on the Glacier Highway. In .9 mile (1.5 km) turn left on a small road labeled Auke Village Rec Area and then in another .9 miles (1.4 km) turn left into the campground.

EAGLE BEACH STATE RECREATION SITE

Location: Glacier Highway Mile 28.5
Info: (907) 465-4563
Website: dnr.alaska.gov/parks/aspunits/southeast/eaglebeachsra.htm

GPS Location: 58.52658 N, 134.81619 W, Near Sea Level

This newly upgraded recreation site is far out of town near the mouth of the Eagle River and seldom used by RV visitors to Juneau.

There are two camping areas here. One is 17 traditional back-in sites set in trees and separated by vegetation. There are fire pits and picnic tables. While some sites would take 45 foot RVs the campground is best for RVs to 30 feet because the access roads are narrow and rough.

A second camping area is the paved parking lot beyond the visitor station. There are 13 spaces here where RVs are allowed to park and camp, four exceed 45 feet, the remainder are for vans and pickups.

Both areas have vault toilets and there are paved walking trails. There is a seven day limit in this campground.

From the ferry terminal turn left and proceed 13.8 miles (22.3 km), you'll see the campground on the left. When we visited the only marking was a P for parking sign, there was no indication that this was a campground. The gate is closed at night but usually not locked. If you arrive late be sure to check, it's probably open.

SAVIKKO PARK
(CITY AND BOROUGH OF JUNEAU)

| Location: | Douglas Island |
| Telephone: | (907) 586-5255 |

GPS Location: 58.27550 N, 134.39169 W, Near Sea Level

Savikko Park offers 4 back-in RV spaces. They're just paved parking spaces. Camping here is best for self-contained rigs because restrooms are quite a distance away and are really provided for users of the sports fields in the park. South of the play fields there are hiking trails passing by the old buildings of the Treadwell Goldmine. There's a three day limit here.

To camp at this park you must register at the harbor office over in Juneau. The following instructions describe the location of both the harbor office and the camping area. From the ferry terminal turn right and head for downtown Juneau. At 10.9 miles (17.6 km) you will see the large high school building to the left, the turn toward the boat harbor and harbor office is to the right just before the pedestrian bridge. Turn in and register. When you return to the main highway after signing in turn right and proceed another .2 miles (.3 km) to the Douglas Bridge. Turn right and pass over the bridge and then on the far side at the Y turn to the left. In 2 miles (3.2 km) the road to the park and camping goes left, the campsites are on the right. This road continues to a boat harbor and sports fields.

Juneau to Haines (4 hours, 30 minutes) and Skagway (1 hour more)

From Juneau ferries travel north up the Lynn Canal to Haines and then Skagway. Almost all of the ferries make both stops. Both towns provide access to the Alaska Highway in Canada and eventually to Alaska.

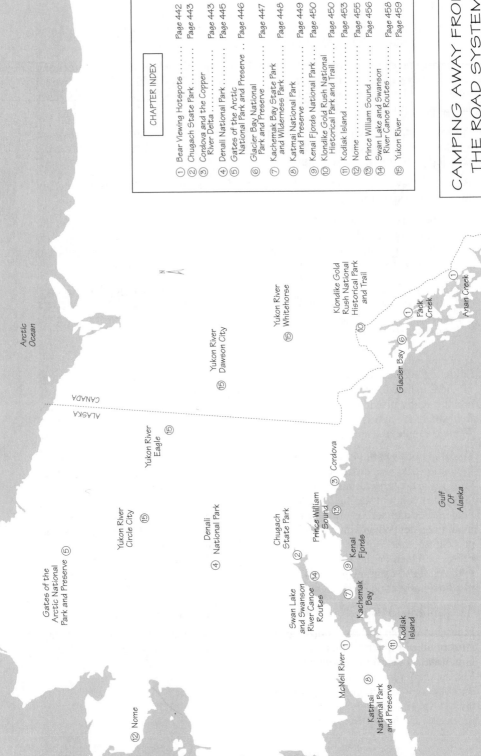

CAMPING AWAY FROM
THE ROAD SYSTEM

Arctic
Ocean

CANADA
ALASKA

Yukon River
Whitehorse ⑮

Klondike Gold
Rush National
Historical Park
and Trail
⑩

Glacier Bay ⑥

Pack
Creek ①

Anan Creek ①

Yukon River
Dawson City ⑮

N

Yukon River
Eagle ⑮

Cordova ③

Gulf
Of
Alaska

Yukon River
Circle City ⑮

Gates of the
Arctic National
Park and Preserve ⑤

Denali
National Park ④

Chugach
State Park ②

Prince William
Sound ⑬

Kenai
Fjords ⑨

Swan Lake
and Swanson ⑭
River Canoe
Routes

Kachemak ⑦
Bay

Kodiak ⑪
Island

McNeil River ①

Katmai ⑧
National Park
and Preserve

⑫ Nome

Chapter 14

Camping Away From The Road System

INTRODUCTION

A quick look at a map of Alaska will show you that highways reach only a small portion of the huge land area. In the west, the north, the southwest, and even in the central part of the state where the few roads are located there are thousands of square miles with tiny populations only accessible using air or water transportation. No visit to Alaska can really be considered complete if you don't make at least one trip into the true wilderness. It's the only way you can appreciate one of Alaska's truly outstanding features: miles and miles of country with no people.

There are several ways to get away from the highways. The least expensive is no doubt hiking. Several areas have excellent trail systems. But for quick access to really remote country there is no substitute for an aircraft. Alaska has an air transportation system like nowhere else, don't hesitate to use it. In a few areas boats provide the best access whether they are the state ferries of Southeast, Southcentral, and Southwest or a riverboat, kayak, raft or canoe.

Preparation for an Off-Highway Trip

Your first step should be thorough **research** of the planned trip. You need to know all about the destination, how to get there, what kind of weather to expect, and much more. The more information you have the more enjoyable and safer your trip will be. You can find a lot of information in books, magazines, and on the Internet. Alaska's Public Lands Information Centers are also a great place to find information. Contact the one in Anchorage at: Alaska Public Lands Information Center, 605 W. 4th Ave., Suite 105, Anchorage, AK 99501; (907) 644-3661 or (866) 869-6887.

Many Alaska off-road camping destinations will be on' government lands with a managing agency. Most of these agencies specialize in providing information to interested visitors. Internet research and follow-up phone calls can net you a lot of information including the names of some possible guides and transportation options.

It is important to have good maps of the area you will visit. These should be maps with good detail including terrain data. They're a great planning tool and will be a big help once you are in the woods. Never go into the wilderness without good maps.

Gear for an Off-Highway Trip

We'll assume that you are an experienced wilderness camper. If not, you should not consider venturing far into the wilderness without an experienced guide. You should outfit yourself for an Alaska trip much like you would elsewhere. The following information and ideas cover areas that may be unfamiliar to you because they are specific to Alaska.

You should, of course, carry good maps and a compass. Alaska is unusual, however, in that some areas have few useful features to allow you to place yourself on a map. Huge flat regions have no mountains for triangulation, and from the ground it is difficult to see the bodies of water that are the only real way of placing yourself. On some river floats it is very difficult to tell how far you have come and therefore to adjust the schedule of your trip. One oxbow bend looks much like another on the map. You may arrive days before your scheduled pickup or days late. Consider carrying a **GPS** (global positioning satellite) receiver. It will give you a lot of peace of mind.

Alaska camping requires a good **tent**. It must be waterproof and bug proof. It must also be very durable. High winds can tear a cheap tent apart and leave you with no protection from the weather and the bugs. Many people like to have a dark-colored tent in Alaska, it helps them to sleep when the sun continues to shine all night. Finally, a tent that can stand without stakes is very useful, particularly when you are camping on gravel bars or moss tussocks where pegs just don't hold well.

Even in the middle of the summer it is a good idea to have a **sleeping bag** that will keep you warm down into the low 30s (Fahrenheit). If it gets colder you can wear clothes in the bag to stay warm. The bag should be a synthetic so that it will be warm when wet and so that you can get it dry if it does get wet. You will need a **foam pad**, the ground can be cold when permafrost is just a few inches beneath the surface.

A **stove** of some kind is essential for camping in Alaska. Many areas do not even have firewood available since they are beyond the timber line. Others have only very wet wood. Many parks do not allow campfires at all. We like the stoves that will burn on a wide variety of fuels since it may be hard to find exactly what you need in a remote location. You can almost always find gasoline.

You will need some means of **water purification**. Giardia lamblia (the protozoan that causes beaver fever) is widespread throughout the state. Boiling water for an adequate period of time will kill it, but boiling uses fuel and leaves hot water—OK for cooking but not great when you are thirsty. Better is a backpacker's water filter or a Steripen portable ultraviolet light water purifier When you must use silty water you should let it sit in a pan until the suspended material has had a chance to settle, that will extend the life of your filter.

Normal **hiking boots** often don't work well in Alaska. They're fine in high well-drained terrain, but many Alaskan trails are very wet. If you think that your hiking area might be wet make sure to have some kind of rubber boots that will provide enough support to let you hike comfortably. Many hikes require repeated river crossings. These rivers can be cold, many come directly from glaciers. You will need some kind of easy-drying sandal or shoe to wear across them. Another alternative is neoprene booties like scuba divers wear. They keep your feet warmer than tennis shoes but aren't very good for wearing around camp.

When around the water in Alaska the footwear of choice is often **hip boots**. When you wear them in a boat never tie them to your belt, if you fall overboard they can kill you. Make sure you can kick out of them in an emergency. Chest waders are a real no-no in a boat unless they are the neoprene type that actually help you float.

When crossing rivers you will need a **hiking stick** or pole. Since such a stick can be hard to find above the tree line you may want to carry poles. The new collapsible walking poles can also be a big help when crossing moss tussocks and other unstable ground with a pack on your back.

Clothing must be warm and capable of keeping you warm when wet. This means wool or synthetics. Cotton is useless unless it is a dry sunny day. Why carry it along? Clothing that can be layered so that you are always comfortably dressed is best. Bring three changes of clothes: one that you will probably have gotten wet, one to wear, and a backup. You'll want synthetic long underwear, even in the summer bring at least one light pair for top and bottom. For rain gear forget ponchos, you want a durable coat and pant combination that will keep you dry. A waterproof hat with a brim will really be appreciated if the rain keeps coming and coming. A wool stocking cap is also very useful, it is light and will keep you warm in cooler temperatures and when sleeping. Finally, bring a mosquito head net that will fit over that wide-brimmed hat. You may not need it but when you do you will love it. Also bring gloves, they'll protect you from the weather and from the bugs.

Insect repellent is essential. See Chapter 2 for a discussion of this.

Many Alaska wilderness trips are float trips on rivers or remote kayak expeditions. Some of those require that you use a small aircraft for transportation. That means you can't use a hard-shell canoe or kayak since it is not legal to fly an aircraft with such a load tied to the float struts when passengers are being carried. Even with no passengers a special permit is required. Folding kayaks and canoes and inflatable rafts are very popular in Alaska. If you plan to do a lot of this type of travel and you want to purchase an expensive piece of gear for Alaska, these are just the ticket. On the other hand, rafts are often available for rent from air-taxi operators. Before allowing yourself to be dropped in the wilderness with a rental raft make sure that you know it is in excellent condition. Also make sure you have a repair kit in your gear.

Safety

There are some safety issues that are unique to Alaska. Even if you have extensive camping experience elsewhere you should be aware of them.

When traveling in the wilderness it is essential that a **reliable person** back home knows where you are. That person should know your exact planned route and schedule and the name of the charter operator responsible for picking you up, if there is one. If you don't show up at the expected time your reliable friend can raise the alarm. We do not feel that having an air taxi or charter boat operator know your plans is enough. Better to have someone who knows you well and who will not drop the ball. Actually, better to have two such people.

Never travel alone in the wilderness. If something happens–you break a leg, an axe slips–you will need help. Also never travel on an isolated river in only one raft or boat. You don't want to be stuck if your only boat is damaged beyond repair.

Almost all Alaskan wilderness areas are home to lots of **bears**. There are very few bear attacks, but there are some. Both black and brown bears are dangerous. It is absolutely essential that you use proper camping techniques in bear country. Pamphlets are distributed from many sources in the state with information about how to camp in bear country and how to react if you meet a bear. There is also a lot of information available about bear habits. The best way to stay safe is to know a lot about the subject.

Here are some of the essentials. Do not set your tent up on a game trail or in an area with bear sign like tracks and droppings. If a bear is attracted to your campsite and then leaves you should pack up and leave immediately, it may return. Bears are attracted by food odors and also by the smell of cosmetics and perfume. Cook well away from your tent. Store food well away from your tent (300 feet minimum) and suspend it high in a tree if there is one. You can throw a rope over a limb to do this. Wrap food in double plastic and seal it. Never cook or eat in your tent. If you ever have cooked in the tent it must be washed thoroughly or replaced. Garbage will attract bears. Double bag garbage in sealed plastic and keep it far from your tent. Clean fish well away from camp, preferably in the water and downstream. Don't wear your cooking or fish-cleaning clothes to bed, store them in a sealed double plastic bag away from your tent. Wash yourself before going to bed to remove food and fish odors.

It is now possible to buy or rent bear-proof containers for trips into bear country. These provide a place to store food that will not attract bears, or failing that, they will not allow the bear to get to the food. Denali and many other parks require their use by off-road campers.

When hiking it is important not to surprise a bear. This is easy to do, particularly when traveling up wind. Make noise, perhaps by talking or even the use of bells attached to your equipment or tin cans filled with pebbles. Most bears will get out of your way if they hear you coming. Mountain bikers should be particularly cautious, they travel quickly and can easily come up on a bear with little warning. Hikers must be alert and watch the trail ahead at all times. Be particularly cautious if your view is obstructed by underbrush or a turn in the trail.

If you do happen to meet a bear on the trail do not approach for a better look. Do not run. Any bear can outrun you over any terrain. Stay calm. Bears seldom attack unless threatened or provoked. Sows with cubs are particularly dangerous because they tend to be very protective. Slowly back away and leave the area. If the bear follows try dropping an item of clothing or even your pack to distract it. Again, do not run. If it continues to come talk in a calm but firm voice. You may try climbing a tree but be aware that bears are quick and can also climb trees, a tree-climbing strategy is not always successful.

If you are attacked try to protect your vital organs. Drop to the ground with your face down, knees drawn up to your chest and hand clasped tightly over the back of your neck. In most cases you want to keep still and not present a threat to the bear, hopefully he will soon leave.

Some experts, including the Yukon Government's bear pamphlet, advise fighting back if the attacking bear is a black bear without cubs. The pamphlet says to yell and fight back as hard as you can, with a rock, a tree branch, or your bare hands. Remember, this is for black bears only, not grizzlies.

Many Alaskans carry weapons in the wilderness. This is not allowed in some park areas but it is allowed in many others. Experts say that nothing less than a 30-06 rifle or shotgun is really useful and these are inconvenient and heavy. An alternative is pepper spray–the big bottles of it designed specifically for bears. The judge is still out on these. They are sometimes ineffective and even if driven off with spray bears often return. Definitely do not spray pepper spray on something as a repellent, bears may actually be attracted. A favorite story in the North is the one about the cheechako who sprayed himself with bear spray as he would have done with insect repellent. There have been cases of airplanes, rafts, and tents that have been chewed by bears attracted by the taste of the pepper.

Many people do not carry any bear protection, they rely on the statistics that show actual bear attacks are unusual.

Hypothermia can be a real danger in Alaska because temperatures are often in a range that is dangerous. Long days of even 40° to 50° temperatures can cause hypothermia, especially if there is moisture involved. Be aware and don't let yourself get chilled. Most rivers and lakes in the north are very cold, immersion even for minutes is life-threatening. Stay near shore and always wear a life preserver when you're in a boat.

There may be lots of wildlife in Alaska but it is foolish to think that you will be able to feed yourself with it during a camping trip. Most game is protected unless it is hunting season. The fish probably won't bite if you are depending upon them. Always **bring enough food** for your planned trip, plus several days extra rations for if you get lost or injured. If you are expecting pickup by a boat or airplane it is not at all unusual for weather to cause delays of up to a week in some areas. Plan accordingly.

Low Impact Camping

Responsible camping in the wilderness means low-impact camping. Try to leave as little sign of your passing as possible.

While you are on the move try to stay on existing trails. Wear boots with shallow treads. Hike single file to keep from widening the trail. When there is no trail try to stay on rocks and creek beds, stay off loose or wet terrain. If you must walk over delicate terrain like a meadow spread out and do not walk single file.

When camping find a place that won't be damaged by your campsite. Gravel is best.

Don't cut trees and brush. Wear light shoes instead of heavy boots in camp and avoid making paths. Avoid campfires if there is not a suitable site, use a stove instead. Gravel bars along rivers are good campfire sites since high water in the spring generally scours them. Carry out all garbage. Drain dishwater into a small hole well away from streams and lakes and cover with earth. Use only biodegradable soap and wash well away from lakes and streams. Dispose of human waste by digging a shallow hole well away from streams and lakes and then covering it with earth when you are done, burn or carry out toilet paper.

Air Transportation

Small aircraft are often used for transportation in Alaska. Even small villages usually have an airport and at least weekly-scheduled service. It is usually less expensive to travel on a scheduled carrier than to charter your own aircraft so check into this if you are heading into the bush. Travel to a transportation hub that is close to your final destination before you charter.

The final leg of your trip may require the actual charter of an aircraft. Most transportation hubs have several different outfits so rates are usually competitive. Before shopping you need to know exactly how much your gear weighs. The cost to you will depend upon several factors: the size aircraft required, type of aircraft required (floats or wheels), the flight time, and how busy the air taxi operator is. Check with several outfits and make sure that the one you choose is familiar with your destination. Many off-runway landing sites are not easy to use, actual experience in flying to the place you want to go is important.

Weather can greatly restrict a small aircraft. Depend upon your pilot to make weather decisions. Do not pressure a pilot to fly in questionable weather, that is the cause of many accidents. Weather may delay your departure or pickup. Always have enough food with you on a trip to allow you to comfortably wait out an extended period of bad weather.

Waiting for a pick-up can be a stressful experience. Sometimes weather en route is impassable even though the weather you can see seems just fine for flying. You will feel much better about it if you know that someone other than the air taxi operator knows you are out there. Make sure a reliable friend knows when you are to return and who you have contracted for your pickup. There have been a few cases where parties have been dropped off and not picked up as scheduled. There have even been fatal cases where people chartered into the wilderness and didn't set up any pick-up at all. Make sure your pickup arrangements are clear and unambiguous. You and the charter operator must know the exact location. It must be easy to identify from the ground and also from the air.

The Public-Use Cabins

One of the best ways to get out into the wilderness in Alaska is to rent a cabin from the government. Several different management agencies, both Federal and State, have a considerable number of cabins scattered around the state. These cabins are a good deal, most are available for under $50 per night and most are in very desirable locations.

Unfortunately each of the organizations has its own reservation system. Here's a quick rundown of what is available. The first place to go for further information is one of the four public lands information centers, they can tell you what is available and where to go to make reservations. The Anchorage Alaska Public Lands Information Center is at 605 W. 4th, Suite 105, Anchorage, Alaska 99501. The telephone numbers are (907) 644-3661 and (866) 869-6887.

US Forest Service in Tongass National Forest – The Tongass covers most of Southeast Alaska. There are about 150 cabins, almost all require boat, aircraft, or hiking access. All have wood or oil stove, table, chairs, beds without mattresses and outhouses. Some cabins have boats. For information call (907) 586-8751. Reserve at www.recreation.gov or call (877) 444-6777.

US Forest Service in Chugach National Forest - About 40 cabins in the Kenai Mountains and Prince William Sound. All except one require boat, aircraft, or hiking access. All have wood or oil stove, table, chairs, beds without mattresses and outhouses. Some cabins have boats. For information call (907) 586-8751. Reserve at www.recreation.gov or call (877) 444-6777.

Alaska Dept. of Natural Resources - They have 60 cabins in the Interior, Southcentral, and Southeast Alaska. A few are accessible by road, most require a boat, aircraft, or hiking. Cabins are similar to Forest Service cabins. Information about the cabins and making reservations for them is available online at http://dnr.alaska.gov/parks/cabins/index.htm.

Bureau of Land Management - The BLM has several cabins in the White Mountains near Fairbanks. For reservations call the BLM Public Lands Information Office in Fairbanks at (907) 474-2250.

Fish and Wildlife Service - The USF&W Service has seven cabins on Kodiak Island. For information and reservations contact Kodiak National Wildlife Refuge, 1390 Buskin River Road, Kodiak, AK 99615; (907 487-2600).

Kenai Fjords National Park has three remote coastal cabins on the south side of the Kenai Peninsula. For information contact the park in Seward at (907) 224-3175.

The cabins are nothing luxurious, really just a glorified form of camping. They do provide a roof over your head for protection from the weather, heat, and some protection from bears. Most require that you bring everything you will need: bedding, kitchen utensils, lanterns, and so on. You also must arrange your own transportation, most air and boat charter operators in the region will be familiar with the cabins and how best to access them.

A SELECTION OF OFF-HIGHWAY DESTINATIONS

In this section you'll find a quick summary of just some of the smorgasbord of off-the-road offerings available around the state. Each summary has information about location, attractions, and how best to get there. Since there is no room in this book for the many maps that would be necessary to show all of these places you should read them with a supplementary map in hand. The best would probably be the Alaska Atlas & Gazetteer, see the *Travel Library* in Chapter 2 for more information.

BEAR-VIEWING HOT SPOTS
McNeil River, Pack Creek, Anan Creek, and Others

When the salmon start running the bears soon appear. Coastal brown bears are the same animal as the smaller inland grizzlies, they just eat better. Several places in Alaska have become known as the best places to see bears, lots of bears.

McNeil River is the best of the bunch, and the hardest to get into. The river is located on the west side of Cook Inlet and flows into Kamishak Bay. Literally dozens (often over 50 at one time) of brown bears fish for salmon in the falls near viewing platforms. The presence of observers seems to make little difference to the bears, they just go ahead and mind their own business. Very few people are allowed to be there at one time. The season is from June through the middle of August. The best access is by small airplane from Anchorage, Homer or Kenai. Tent sites are designated and are located away from the river. Access is limited, visitors are selected by lottery, applications must be in by March 1. For more information and lottery applications contact the Alaska Department of Fish and Game, Wildlife Conservation, Attn: McNeil River State Game Sanctuary, 333 Raspberry Road, Anchorage, AK 99518; (907) 267-2253. There is a link to the McNeil River official web pages on our website, www.rollinghomes.com.

The McNeil River is not the only river with bears in that same area. Access to some of the others is less restricted. Floatplane operators in Homer specialize in bear-watching flights, check with them about the possibilities. There are also multi-day boat tours to the southern side of the Alaska Peninsula to watch bears. Homer is the place to check on that too.

Pack Creek is located on the east side of Admiralty Island, about 25 miles (40 km) from Juneau. Admiralty Island is known for its brown bears, there are thought to be some 1,700 of them on the island. Pack Creek is the easiest place to see them, there is a viewing platform but no overnight camping is allowed. Usually viewers see only a few bears at a time. The season lasts from the middle of July to the last part of August. Access is by boat or floatplane from Juneau. For information contact the Juneau Ranger District Office, 8510 Mendenhall Loop Road, Juneau, AK 99801; (907) 586-8800. They can give you a list of approved air-taxi guide services and then you make your own arrangements. Application forms are also available on the Internet. There is a link to the Pack Creek official web pages on our website, www. rollinghomes.com.

Anan Creek Bear Observatory is another Southeast location. This is primarily a viewing spot for black bears although a few browns do show up. The observatory is located about 30 miles (48 km) southeast of Wrangell near the mouth of Bradfield Canal. There is a viewing platform here also, usually several bears are visible. No camping is permitted in the area although there is a Forest Service rental cabin about a mile away. The season at Anan Creek runs from the first part of July through the first part of September while the pink salmon are running. For information contact the U.S. Forest Service, Wrangell Ranger District, 525 Bennett St. (PO Box 51), Wrangell, AK 99929; (907) 874-2323. There is a link to the Anan Creek official web pages on our website, www.rollinghomes.com.

Several good bear-viewing areas are mentioned in other places in this book: Fish Creek near Hyder, Alaska is covered in Chapter 5 and the Brooks River in Katmai National Park is discussed below. Kodiak Island also offers good bear-viewing opportunities, particularly at fly-out locations. And don't forget Denali National Park.

CHUGACH STATE PARK

The 490,000-acre Chugach State Park is a mountainous area that directly adjoins Anchorage to the east. Most of the park, in fact, is technically within the boundaries of the Municipality of Anchorage. Anchorage residents can literally be in the wilderness within minutes of leaving their homes. The park is popular with almost everyone interested in the outdoors and offers opportunities to hike, camp, climb rocks or mountains, mountain bike, kayak, fish, hunt, snow-machine, ski, float rivers, and even hang-glide. Accommodating all these uses means that the park has zones and restricted areas to keep incompatible uses separated. There is wildlife in this park even though it is part of the largest city in the state; you may see black and brown bears, mountain goats, Dall sheep, moose, wolves, bald eagles, and even beluga whales.

There are about 50 miles (81 km) of maintained trails within the park, and many more miles of excellent alpine hiking although alder thickets can be a problem. Popular hikes include **Flattop Mountain** (1.5 miles (2.4 km) one way), **Williwaw Lakes** (5 miles (8 km) one way), **Wolverine Peak** (6 miles (9.7 km) one way), **McHugh and Rabbit Lakes Trail** (7 miles (11.3 km) one way) and **Crow Pass** (26 miles (42 km) one way). There are also good trails from the Eklutna Lake Campground.

Camping in the park is mostly unrestricted. The park has three formal vehicle campgrounds: Eklutna Lake, (Chapter 7 of this book), Eagle River (Chapter 7) and Bird Creek (Chapter 8). Fires are not allowed in the park except in the fire pits at the few formal campsites. Use camp stoves instead.

Access to the park is from many points including the Seward Highway along Turnagain Arm, the upper hillside area of Anchorage, the Arctic Valley Road (from Mile 6 of the Glenn Highway), the Eagle River Road (from Mile 13 of the Glenn Highway) and the Eklutna Road (from Mile 26 of the Glenn Highway). Visitor centers are located at the end of the Eagle River Road (907 694-2108) and at the Potter Section House at Mile 115 of the Seward Highway near Potter Marsh and Turnagain Arm (907 345-5014).

CORDOVA AND THE COPPER RIVER DELTA

Cordova is one of two destinations in this chapter that is perfectly suitable for RVs. The other is Kodiak, see below. Access to this small south-central Alaska town is quite easy. The Alaska Marine Highway system connects Cordova frequently with both Whittier and Valdez. Cordova is a pleasant little town, but the town isn't the only attraction here. The **Copper River Highway** leads out of town to the east, crossing the **Copper River Delta**, one of Alaska's premier bird migration and nesting areas, and then turns northeast to dead-end after about 50 miles (81 km) just beyond Child's Glacier and the **Million Dollar Bridge.**

Unfortunately, getting to Cordova's attractions out the Copper River Highway is temporarily not possible. A bridge at Mile 36 has failed and new bridge construction is not expected until 2015 at the earliest. For more information call the USFS Cordova Ranger District at (907) 424-7661.

Cordova (population 2,400) today is primarily a fishing town but has good tourist facilities. It was originally the salt-water terminus of the Copper River and Northwestern Railway, which was built to transport copper ore from the Kennicott Mine and operated until 1938. For visitor information go to the **Chamber of Commerce** on First Street (907 424-7260). The **Cordova Historical Museum** at 622 1ˢᵗ Street is an excellent place to start your tour of the area, it has historical and art exhibits. Another important information site is the **USFS Cordova Area District Office** (907 424-7661) which has an interpretive center and information about local hikes, attractions, and wildlife viewing areas. Cordova hosts the **Copper River Shorebird Festival** during May and a **silver salmon derby** in August.

An important attraction is the Copper River Highway and its sights. Wildlife often seen along the road includes trumpeter swans, dusky Canadian geese, ducks, moose, bears and beavers. There are also several good fishing holes and viewpoints to watch spawning salmon. The road is paved as far as the airport at Mile 12, then turns to gravel. There is a bird-viewing boardwalk and picnic area at the end of a 3 mile (4.8 km) road from Mile 17 known as **Alaganik Slough**. There is also a formal viewing area for **Childs Glacier** at Mile 48 just before you reach the **Million Dollar Bridge**.

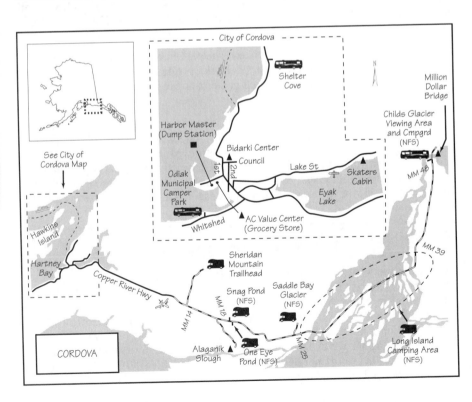

Be careful here, we know a woman who ended up in the hospital after a huge wave caused by ice falling from the nearby glacier swept over her–keep your eyes open! The bridge at the end of the road is open to traffic although it was severely damaged in the Good Friday Earthquake in 1964. The road beyond only goes a short distance.

Cordova has a municipal campground, the **Odiak Municipal Camper Park**, with 24 sites, electrical hookups, a dump station, and showers. Reservations are recommended, call (907) 424-6200. This park is full of summer-long residents but a few spaces are reserved for travelers. It is located at Mile .5 of the Whitshed Road to Hartney Bay which leaves the Copper River Highway at Mile 1.5. It's $25 a day. Sign in at Bidarki Rec Center on the corner of Council and 2nd Ave. The GPS location of the campground is 60.53653 N, 145.76734 W.

At **Shelter Cove** the municipality has 13 overnight parking lot style sites for any size RV with no hookups in a gravel lot across from the ocean. In the trees behind there are 3 tents sites with raised wooden platforms. Vault toilets are provided. There is a fee for staying here ($10 plus tax for RVs, $15 plus tax for tents) when we last visited). To find Shelter Cove turn left when you leave the ferry dock and drive .6 miles (1 km), the parking area is on the right. This is a very handy location if the ferry arrives late in the evening or early morning. The GPS location is 60.56394 N, 145.74302 W.

There is a beautiful National Forest Service campground near Childs Glacier and the Million Dollar Bridge. It is called **Childs Glacier Viewing Area and Campground**. It has 11 large vehicle camping sites and also a tent-camping area. This campground will take large RVs with no problem. There are vault toilets, picnic tables, and fire pits. The cost is $25 per night for RVs, $10 for tents. The glacier can be viewed from the waterfront near the campground and you'll probably hear it calving all night long if you stay here. It's at Mile 48 of the Glacier Highway, you reach it just before crossing the Million Dollar Bridge. The GPS location is 60.66441 N, 144.75842 W. Note that this is beyond the failed bridge at Mile 36 so staying here is not an option until the bridge repair is completed and the road opens.

The National Forest Service has several other small camping areas between town and the Million Dollar Bridge. These include the Sheridan Mountain Trailhead, Snag Pond, One Eye Pond, Saddle Bay Glacier, and Long Island Camping Area. Some have vault toilets and are OK for tents, others are best for self-contained vehicles only. Check at the Chugach National Forest Cordova Ranger District office at 612 2nd St. in town (907 424-7661) for more information and additional spots that might have developed, especially since the road has been closed past Mile 36.

There are showers available at the Bidarki Recreation Center on the corner of Council and 2nd Ave. and also at the Harbormaster's Office of the boat harbor. There is also a dump station behind the Harbormaster's Office, the GPS location is 60.54194 N, 145.76554 W.

DENALI NATIONAL PARK - ON FOOT

Denali National Park is one of the most popular destinations in Alaska. We've described the basics of a visit in Chapter 9–the way most people do it. Denali National Park is also an excellent place to wander around the backcountry. The alpine terrain along both sides of the park access road is relatively easy to hike, even without trails. Backcountry camping in the park is closely regulated. The park is divided into 87 units. Forty one of these have limits on the number of people who can camp in them each night. You must have a permit for the unit you camp in. Permits are only available at the Backcountry Information Center (BIC) near the park entrance. Once in the park, it is not unusual to wait for 2 to 4 days before you can get a permit. The permits are issued in person one day in advance and reservations are not accepted. The most popular zones are 8, 9, 10, 11, 12, 13, 15, 18, and 27; largely because they are easily accessible and have good terrain for hiking.

To get your permit go to the BIC. There you watch a video about backcountry traveling in the park and attend a safety briefing including information about bear safety. You then can see what is available in the way of backcountry openings and apply for your permit. Some zones are occasionally closed due to problems with curious or aggressive bears. Once you have your permit you will be issued a bear-proof food container for stays in most zones. Once you have your permit you can reserve space on a bus into the park.

GATES OF THE ARCTIC NATIONAL PARK AND PRESERVE

This park covers 8,090,000 acres of the Brooks Range to the west of the Dalton Highway and north of the Arctic Circle. The area encompassed is largely tundra-covered foothills and mountains to over 7,000 feet and includes the **Frigid Crags** and **Boreal Mountain** for which the park is named. There are six national wild and scenic rivers in the park: the **Alatna, John, Kobuk, Noatak, North Fork Koyukuk and Tinayguk.** This is completely undeveloped wild and empty country with wildlife including caribou, moose, grizzly and black bears, wolves, Dall sheep and a host of smaller animals and many birds.

Access to the park is usually by small aircraft charter from Bettles which gets scheduled air service from Fairbanks. Pick up supplies in Fairbanks since Bettles has little to offer. There is also some access for hikers and river travelers from the Dalton Highway near Wiseman and to the north.

Unrestricted camping is allowed throughout the park although there are no formal campsites. Firewood can be hard to find in treeless areas so bring along a camp stove. Fishing and guns are both allowed. Mosquitoes can be bad. Hiking in the park can be very slow and tedious, even areas free of trees have hard-to-penetrate alder thickets. One of the most popular activities is floating the many rivers in the park with occasional hikes away from the river.

The park is managed by the National Park Service. The Arctic Interagency Visitor Center at Mile 175 of the Dalton Highway has information for travelers using that access route. For information contact National Park Service, 4175 Geist Road, Fairbanks, Alaska 99709; 907 457-5752. There's also an Interagency Visitor Center in Coldfoot (907 678-5209) and a ranger station in remote Bettles (907 692-5494).

GLACIER BAY NATIONAL PARK AND PRESERVE

This 3,234,000-acre national park is located at the far north end of the inside passage and extends out along the open Gulf Coast as far as Dry Bay. Most visitor interest is in the southern portion of the park, the huge glacial inlets. These inlets–**Glacier Bay, Muir Inlet, Reid Inlet, Tarr Inlet** and others–have to be the best place in the world to see the effects of glaciation and the re-vegetation process. That is because this entire region was covered by glaciers in 1794 when visited by Captain Vancouver, today the glaciers have retreated as far as 65 miles (105 km). There are 12 tidewater glaciers in the park. The park is also an excellent place to view whales: there are minkes, humpbacks, and orcas. There are also black and brown bears, moose, mountain goats, harbor seals, sea lions and wolves. Whale watching is also very good in Icy Strait, just outside the entrance to Icy Bay.

There are no roads to the park. Access, however, is not difficult. **Gustavus** (pop. 400) is a gateway to the park. It has a good airport, stores, restaurants, scheduled jet service, and scheduled Alaska State Ferry service from Juneau. From Gustavus a 10 mile (16 km) road leads into the park terminating at **Bartlett Cove** where park headquarters are located as well as a lodge, a tent campground, nature trails, and a dock for boats making excursions into the park. Taxis and busses run between Gustavus and Bartlett Cover. From Bartlett Cove an excursion boat runs into the park

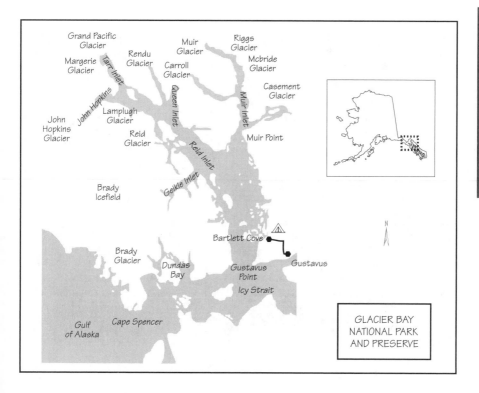

GLACIER BAY
NATIONAL PARK
AND PRESERVE

CAMPING AWAY FROM THE ROAD

and up Muir Inlet, they will drop kayakers and hiking parties and pick them up at an agreed time. Charter boats from Gustavus will do the same thing. Kayak rentals are available. Glacier Bay is also heavily visited by cruise ships, they tour the fjords but do not dock.

Campers (including those just using the campground) must attend an orientation session at Bartlett Cove and obtain a camping permit. Away from Bartlett Cove camping is not restricted although permits are required. In the park expect lots of rain and be prepared with wet weather gear. There are no formal trails but hiking is good along beaches and in open areas where the glaciers have recently retreated. Kayaking is very popular. Firearms are not allowed in the park, fishing is permitted.

Glacier Bay National Park is managed by the National Park Service. For more information contact the park headquarters at: Glacier Bay National Park Headquarters, 1 Park Rd., PO Box 140, Gustavus, AK 99826 (907 679-2230). Call (907) 697-2627 for information about recreational permits.

KACHEMAK BAY STATE PARK AND WILDERNESS PARK

A large part of the view that you see across Kachemak Bay from Homer is part of the 400,000-acre Kachemak Bay State Park. Encompassing much of the south side of Kachemak Bay, the park also stretches across the peninsula to take in the fjord country to the west of Kenai Fjords National Park. Across from Homer **Halibut**

TRAILS IN KACHEMAK BAY STATE PARK GIVE HIKERS ACCESS TO LAKES AND GLACIERS

Cove is the center of activities. There is a ranger station there as well as trailheads giving access to about 80 miles (129 km) of trails to mountain overlooks, glaciers, and lakes. There are also several campsites. Camping is unrestricted, campfires are permitted, as are hunting and fishing. The remote Gulf of Alaska side of the park is much less developed but is popular with kayakers and other boat-oriented visitors.

There is no road access to the park, many visitors catch a daily ferry to Halibut Cove. It swings by **Gull Island**, one of the best places in Southcentral Alaska for viewing seabirds including puffins. Many small boat operators in Homer will also shuttle you across and pick you up at a scheduled time and place. Floatplanes from Homer are also used to access the park, particularly the southern Gulf Coast portion.

For information about the park contact Alaska State Parks, PO Box 1247, Soldotna, AK 99669; (907) 262-5581.

KATMAI NATIONAL PARK AND PRESERVE

One of the oldest federal park areas in Alaska is 3,955,000-acre Katmai National Park and Preserve. It is also one of the most expensive to access since the location is fairly remote. There are many attractions in the park. **Brooks Camp** and the **Brooks River** are the most popular, many tourists visit on day trips to view brown bears fishing for red salmon from viewing platforms constructed for the purpose. The **Valley of Ten Thousand Smokes** is an ash-covered volcanic landscape with good hiking possibilities accessible along a 24 mile (39 km) road by daily van from Brooks Camp. Fishing is also extremely popular in the park, Brooks Camp was originally a fishing camp, today fishing there is limited but there are many other destinations in the park for fishermen. A national wild and scenic river, the **Alagnak**, and also the **Nonvianuk River**, are popular floats for fishermen. Kayakers and canoeists will find many routes on the huge lakes of the park including a 40 mile (65 km) round trip paddle from Brooks Camp to the **Bay of Islands** on Naknek Lake and a longer 75 mile (121 km) **circular trip on Naknek Lake, Lake Grosvenor, the Savonoski River and Iliuk Arm**.

The access gateway to the park is King Salmon which gets jet service from Anchorage. From King Salmon access into the park is usually by amphibian or float aircraft.

There is a 60-person tent campground at Brooks Camp with cooking shelters, bearproof food-storage caches, and an electric fence surrounding the campground. Reservations are required. For reservation call the national park reservation service at www.recreation.gov or (877) 444-6777. Brooks Camp also has other facilities including a ranger station, lodge, dining room, convenience store, and canoe rentals. Camping throughout the rest of the park is allowed although permits are required. Campfires are discouraged since wood is scarce and wet, bring a stove. Weather can be very wet. Grizzly bears can be thick and caution is required. Firearms are not allowed within the park although hunting is allowed in the preserve section in the far north at Kukaklek and Nonvianuk Lakes.

The park is managed by the National Parks Service, for information contact Katmai National Park and Preserve, PO Box 7, King Salmon, AK 99613; (907) 246-3305.

KENAI FJORDS NATIONAL PARK

Kenai Fjords National Park covers 588,000 acres of the southern coast and the ice-covered interior of the Kenai Peninsula near Seward. The **Harding Icefield** overlooks four major fjords and several offshore rookery islands in the park. The rough coastal waters at the mouth of the fjords and the hostile weather has kept development in the fjords to a minimum. This is great place to see glaciers, marine mammals, and seabirds. Visitors often see orcas, minke whales, humpback whales, gray whales, Dall porpoises, harbor seals, sea lions, sea otters, and seabirds including horned and tufted puffins, rhinoceros auklets, common murres, and marbled murrelets. Land mammals include black bears, mountain goats, and moose. Grizzly (brown) bears are uncommon except in Resurrection Bay near Seward.

One of the best features of the park is that access is not difficult. The town of Seward is near, there is actually road access to **Exit Glacier** just outside town. Access to the fjords is by charter boat or floatplane from Seward or floatplane from Homer. Most park visitors are day trippers on tour boats from Seward. Kayakers sometimes paddle into the park from Seward but it is a long paddle, it is easier to arrange for drop-off and pick-up by a charter boat.

There is a small tent-only **campground** at the Exit Glacier (see Chapter 8 of this book). Otherwise camping in the park is mostly unrestricted but there are no formal campsites. Hiking along the glacial fjords is very difficult and even for kayakers camping sites can be hard to find. Kayaking is popular, but only the experienced should venture into the park because the waters are open and often rough. Come prepared for wet weather. Campfires are allowed but bring a stove, wood is often wet. Fishing and firearms are allowed. Much of the shoreline of the park is owned by Native corporations. Check at the Seward visitor center before venturing into the park on a wilderness trip to see how this will affect your visit.

The park visitor's center is located in Seward near the small boat harbor. The park is managed by the National Park Service. For information contact the park headquarters at PO Box 1727, Seward, Alaska 99664; (907) 422-0500.

KLONDIKE GOLD RUSH NATIONAL HISTORICAL PARK AND TRAIL

The Klondike Gold Rush National Historical Park celebrates the 1897-1898 gold rush to Dawson City. Park units include the Chilkoot Trail, the White Pass Trail, much of downtown Skagway, Dyea, and even a visitor center in Seattle. The Chilkoot Trail is a 33-mile-long (53 km) hiking trail that starts at Dyea and ends at Lake Bennett in the Yukon Territory. It is jointly administered by Parks Canada and the National Park Service. The trail is extremely interesting to anyone with an interest in the gold rush, it is a sort of museum with ruins and hardware cast aside during the rush.

Some parts of the trail are difficult and the weather can turn on you so it is important to be prepared for cold weather, particularly along the alpine section between Sheep Camp and Deep Lake (about 10 miles, (16 km)). Snow in the pass means that it is not usually possible to do the hike except between late June and early September. The

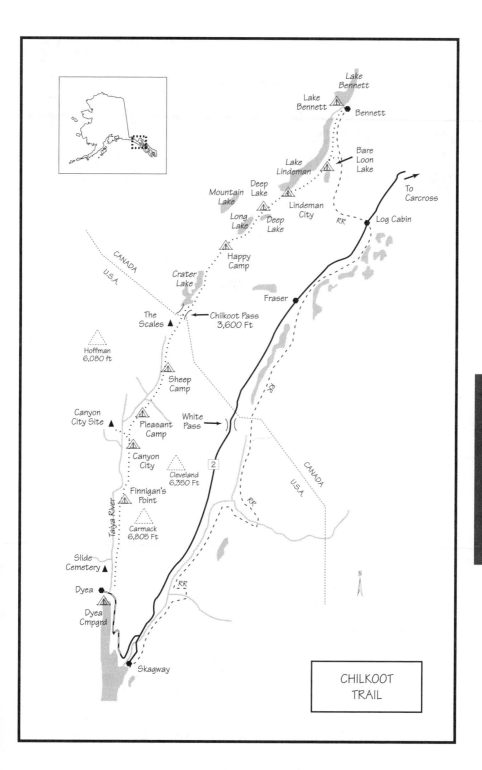

Lake Bennett

Lake Bennett

Bennett

Lake Lindeman

Bare Loon Lake

To Carcross

Deep Lake

Mountain Lake

Lindeman City

Long Lake

Deep Lake

RR

Log Cabin

Happy Camp

CANADA

U.S.A.

Crater Lake

Fraser

The Scales ▲

Chilkoot Pass 3,600 Ft

Hoffman 6,080 ft

Sheep Camp

RR

Canyon City Site ▲

Pleasant Camp

White Pass →

Canyon City

Cleveland 6,350 Ft

2

CANADA

U.S.A.

Finnigan's Point

RR

Taiya River

Carmack 6,805 Ft

Slide Cemetery ▲

Dyea

RR

Dyea Cmpgrd

N

Skagway

CHILKOOT TRAIL

CAMPING AWAY FROM THE ROAD

THE FOOT OF THE CHILKOOT TRAIL NEAR DYEA

Chilkoot is a three to five day hike with designated camping areas. Most people walk it from south to north but it is perfectly acceptable to do it in the opposite direction. The trail starts near the Taiya River bridge near the Dyea town site about 8 miles (12.9 km) outside Skagway. Campgrounds are **Finnigan's Point** at Mile 4.9, **Canyon City** at Mile 7.8, **Pleasant Camp** at Mile 10.5, **Sheep Camp** at Mile 13, **Happy Camp** at Mile 20.5, **Deep Lake** at Mile 23, **Lindeman City** at Mile 26, **Bare Loon Lake** at Mile 29, and **Lake Bennett** at Mile 33. From the Taiya River bridge the trail follows the Taiya River valley and then a canyon to Sheep Camp. From there the trail climbs across boulders (the golden stairs) to the top of the pass and the Canadian border. From the border the trail gradually descends to Lake Bennett. Once at Bennett hikers can catch a train back to Skagway or a previously arranged boat to Carcross. It is also possible to walk out to Log Cabin which is at about Km 44 of the Klondike Highway from Skagway. A daily shuttle bus returns to Skagway from Log Cabin.

The trail has become very popular so rules are in effect to limit the number of hikers. Only fifty hikers are now allowed to cross into Canada each day and this is administered through a reservation and Canadian hiking permit system. Reservations are highly recommended since 42 of the 50 slots are reserved leaving space for only 8 walk-ins each day. Call (867) 667-3910 or (800) 661-0486 for reservations. When you call be prepared with a credit card number, mailing address, number of people and names, preferred starting date and two alternates, and your itinerary including the camps you intend to use each night. There is an permit fee of approximately $50 per hiker. Detailed information will be mailed to you when you apply for your permit and there is a website at www.nps.gov/klgo/planyourvisit/chilkoottrail.htm.

KODIAK ISLAND

Kodiak Island is a very interesting destination for RV campers. It is connected to the road system by the Alaska Marine Highway. Service is from Homer by the ferry Tustumena. This ferry cannot take vehicles over 40 feet long. Kodiak is a very active fishing and fish processing port, but also has good tourist facilities. The island is probably best known for its huge population of very large brown bears.

The town of Kodiak (population 14,000) has a visitor center at 100 E. Marine Way #200, Kodiak, AK 99615; (907) 486-4782. Sights in town are limited, you may want to visit the **Baranov Museum** near the visitor center which is located in a Russian-built structure and is a designated National Historic Landmark. It covers the Russian period of Alaska's history. Another museum in town is the **Alutiiq Museum Archaeological Repository Center** which has articles from sites all around the island. You'll also want to visit the **Kodiak National Wildlife Refuge Visitor's Center** at the corner of Mission Road and Center Street (907 487-2626) near the downtown ferry terminal.

The Kodiak Area has several roads leading to quiet beaches and scenic outlooks. There are also many hiking trails in the area and fishing holes. Rezanof-Monashka Bay Road runs north and then northwest from town for 11 miles (18 km) to Monashka Bay. En route it passes **Fort Abercrombie State Park**. The Chiniak Highway

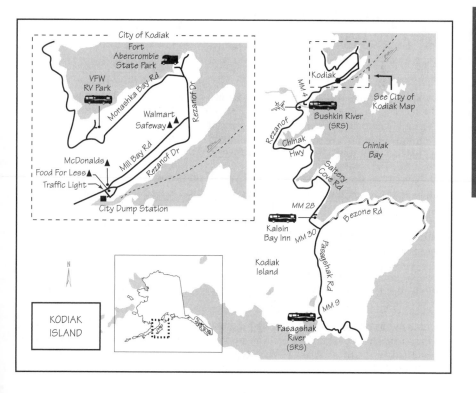

and Pasagshak Road go south for 43 miles (69 km) and reach the south shore of the island near Ugak Bay.

The road system really only reaches a small part of the island, many area attractions are accessible only by boat or aircraft. Shuyak Island is about 50 miles (81 km) to the north, it is a state park known for its kayaking waters, there are several rental cabins in the park. **The Kodiak National Wildlife Refuge** covers almost all of Kodiak Island itself. If you want to see bears it is best to get out into it. The air-taxi and tour operators in Kodiak know the places to go, many maintain cabins or campsites for bear-viewing trips.

Campgrounds are available in Kodiak. **Fort Abercrombie State Park** at Mile 4 of the Rezanof-Monashka Bay Road has a small campground with the normal state campground amenities: fire pits, picnic tables, a water pump, and vault toilets. The sites are small and will only take vans and pickup campers. An overflow area will take larger RVs to 30 feet. The GPS location is 57.82756 N, 152.35675 W.

Farther out on the same road at Mile 7 is the **VFW RV Park** which has electricity (30 amps), water, and sewer hookups. There are 12 back-in sites to 45 feet. It's a no-nonsense residential trailer park and has no restroom facilities so it's for self-contained rigs only. Reservations are recommended, call (907) 486-5816. The GPS location is 57.80964 N, 152.41652 W.

At Mile 4 of Chiniak Highway is the **Bushkin River State Recreation Site** which has 15 nice sites, The state managers recommend this campground for any big rigs wanting to camp near town, some sites are as long as 50 feet. Amenities include picnic tables, fire pits, firewood, a water spigot that will take a hose to fill RVs, and vault toilets. There are additional places to pitch tents on grass and there are bear-proof storage lockers. Nearby are a fish weir, an ADA accessible fishing platform, and the Audubon Bushkin View Trail. The GPS location is 57.75642 N, 152.49782 W.

The old **Kalsin Bay Inn** is near Mile 28 of the Chiniak Highway. It's a restaurant and bar with some hookup sites in the rear. Facilities here were in poor condition when we visited. There are perhaps five sites offering full hookups, laundry, showers, and flush toilets. Tenters are also accommodated. Call (907) 486-2659 for information. The GPS location is 57.59752 N, 152.47383 W.

Finally, there is the **Pasagshak River State Recreation Site.** This campground is located at Mile 9 of the Pasagshak Bay Road which leaves the Chiniak Highway at Mile 30. This camping area has a few walk-in tent sites with tables and fire pits and a large gravel parking lot next to the mouth of the Pasagshak River. Any size rig can park in the lot. Vault toilets are provided. This is a very popular fishing location. There is no fee to camp at this park. The GPS location is 57.46118 N, 152.45222 W.

Kodiak also has a small military campground with four full-hookup sites. It's the **Nemetz RV Park** and is located near the airport and Kodiak Coast Guard Station. GPS location is 57.76017 N, 152.50795 W.

There is a dump station in downtown Kodiak near the boat harbor. It's at the end of the harbormaster's parking lot off Marine Way and across the street from the Wells Fargo Bank in front of Alaska Fresh Seafoods. The GPS location is 57.78669 N, 152.40669 W.

NOME

Nome is the access point for another extensive Alaska road system that is not connected to the main highway system. You can't bring your RV here, there is no ferry connection, but it is possible to fly in to Nome and then rent a car or bicycle.

Nome (population 4,000) is a very important town in Alaska's history. The Nome gold rush of 1899 was the state's largest (Dawson City, of course, is in Canada). Mining in Nome during the gold rush was largely on the beaches, but later the area around Nome was heavily dredged, over 40 dredges remain near Nome, some occasionally active, and there are said to be about 100 of them on the Seward Peninsula. Nome is nationally known as the destination for the **Iditarod Sled Dog Race** and is also the center for an unusual industry, growing reindeer.

Despite its remote location Nome does get a lot of tourists. Most are traveling as part of a package tour included as part of their cruise, bus, train, and air tour of the state. The Visitor Center is on Front Street (Nome Convention & Visitors Bureau, 301 Front Street, Nome, AK 99762; 907 443-6555). Nome has lots of gift shops courtesy of the many tourists, ivory carvings are the hot item. Be sure to visit the **Carrie McLain Museum** at 223 Front Street to see the gold rush exhibits.

Three different gravel roads lead out of Nome like the forks of a trident. They make

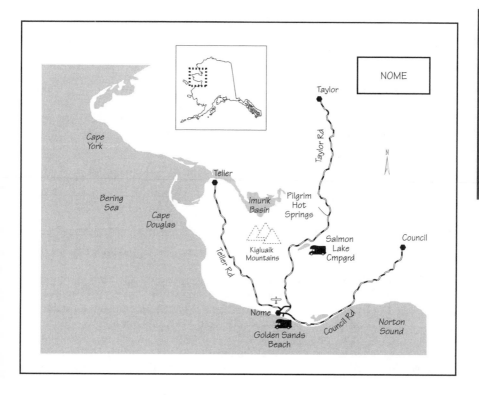

excellent bike or driving trips. It is probably best to bring your own mountain bike to Nome because you can cover a lot of miles here and will appreciate a good bike. Temperatures can be cool and there is often wind so come prepared.

The **Teller Road** is the left hand fork, it leads 73 miles (118 km) north to Teller. Along the way it passes King Island fish camp and through an area that is home to a 25,000-animal reindeer herd. The coast is often within view. Teller is a village with a population of about 300 people, you can stay at the school if you don't want to camp. Teller was the place where the dirigible Norge landed after the first crossing of the North Pole.

The center fork leading out of Nome is the **Kougarok** or **Taylor Road** which leads 86 miles (139 km) northeast past the eastern edge of the **Kigluaik Mountains**. The Kigluaik Mountains are managed by the Bureau of Land Management and are an interesting hiking area. There is a BLM campground, the **Salmon Lake Campground**, at Mile 38, see below. Hike-in destinations in the area include the Wild Goose Pipeline, Crater Lake, and the Mosquito Pass area. For information contact the BLM, Northern Field Office, 1150 University Avenue, Fairbanks, AK 99709; (907) 474-2200 or the BLM Nome Field Office, PO Box 952, Nome, AK 99762; (907) 443-2177. Another point of interest is **Pilgrim Hot Springs**, located on an eight mile (12.9 km) road leaving the Kougarok Road 13 miles (21 km) north of Salmon Lake Campground. This place was a resort of sorts during the gold rush, later it was a Catholic orphanage. Today it is on the National Register of Historic Places.

The third fork is the **Council Road** which leads 72 miles (116 km) east. Much of the road is along the coast. Sights along the way are Safety Sound at Mile 25 with a bird-watching boardwalk and the Last Train to Nowhere at Mile 33. You have to ford the Bear River to reach Council, it is not recommended unless you have local knowledge.

There are two camping options in the area. The most convenient to town is **Golden Sands Beach** which stretches east of Nome. You can tent camp along the beach and will have the company of gold prospectors who spent the summer here. There is one vault toilet in a small park across the road. The approximate GPS location is 64.49258 N, 165.37517 W.

More formal but harder to reach is the BLM's **Salmon Lake Campground**. It has six sites with picnic tables, fire pits, bear-proof food lockers, and a vault toilet near Salmon Lake. That's about 40 miles from town on the Taylor Highway. There is no charge, the GPS location is 64.91570 N, 164.96140 W.

PRINCE WILLIAM SOUND

Prince William Sound (PWS) has become a well-known Alaskan place name. Bruised but not beaten by the Exxon Valdez oil spill PWS remains a jewel. A huge jewel, but a jewel. The Sound covers some 25,000 square miles and has an estimated 2,500 miles of shoreline. This shoreline is almost all wilderness, the only towns are Whittier, Valdez, Cordova, Chenega Bay and Tatitlik. The entire sound with the exception of Port Valdez is within the boundaries of the Chugach National Forest which is administered by the U.S. Forest Service. For information contact USFS,

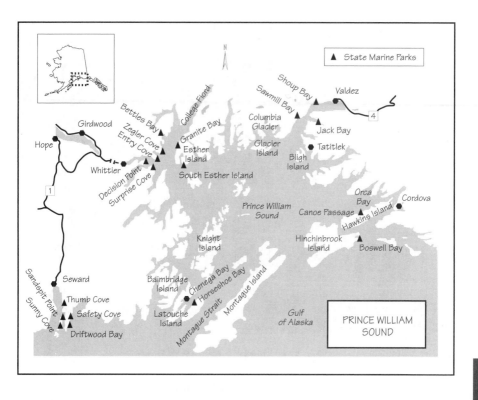

Chugach National Forest, 3301 C Street, Suite 300, Anchorage, AK 99503-3998; (907) 743-9500.

Wildlife viewing opportunities in the Sound are very good. Marine mammals include orcas, gray whales, humpback whales, sea lions, sea otters, and harbor seals. On shore you'll find black and brown bears, mountain sheep, moose, and Sitka black-tailed deer. Over 3,000 bald eagles are said to frequent the Sound, as well as marine seabirds and shorebirds.

Many of the visitors to the Sound travel on cruise ships, ferries, or excursion boats. Many cruise ship schedules now include a visit to **College Fiord**, an excellent place to see a lot of glaciers all in one place. Many excursion cruises also visit College Fiord, usually from Whittier. Excursions from Valdez generally visit **Columbia Glacier** instead, this largest of Alaskan glaciers was the source of the ice that caused the Exxon Valdez to shift course and go aground. State of Alaska Marine Highway ferries also run across the Sound; from Valdez to Cordova, from Whittier to Cordova, and from Whittier to Valdez. The ferries don't get really close to the glaciers but there are plenty of great views from their decks anyway.

A sailboat, power boat, or a kayak gives you the freedom to really explore Prince William Sound. Access is from Whittier, Valdez, Cordova, or Seward. It is also perfectly feasible to charter a boat or aircraft to deliver you pretty much anywhere in

CAMPING AWAY FROM THE ROAD

SEA LIONS IN PRINCE WILLIAM SOUND

PWS. The State of Alaska has 14 marine parks in the Sound and 5 more near Seward with scenic anchorages, camping sites on shore, and recreational opportunities. Most are clustered around Whittier, Valdez, or Cordova. For more information including individual maps contact Alaska State Marine Parks, Kenai / PWS Area Office, PO Box 1247, Soldotna, AK 99669; (907) 262-5581. There are also many rental cabins located around the sound, managed by the USFS. Camping in Chugach National Forest is mostly unrestricted, campfires are allowed but dry firewood can be difficult to find. There are private lands throughout the Sound, particularly the eastern Sound, respect private property.

SWAN LAKE AND SWANSON RIVER CANOE ROUTES

The Kenai National Wildlife Refuge has two excellent canoe routes. They are both accessed off the same road. Follow the Swanson River Road which becomes the Swan Lake Road at Mile 17–it leaves the Sterling Highway at Mile 83, just west of Sterling. Mileages given here are from the Sterling Highway. Vehicle-accessible campgrounds along these roads are listed and described in the *Tern Lake Junction to Soldotna* section of Chapter 8 of this book. The canoe routes run through an area that has many moose, beavers, loons, bald eagles, and swans. There are also a few black and brown bears, otters, and wolves. Fishing can be good for Dolly Varden, silver and red salmon, and rainbows. Registration at trailheads is required, parties are limited to 15 people. Camping is unrestricted but you should use established campsites if you find them. Fires are usually allowed but it can be difficult to find mineral soil to build one, bring a stove. The area is managed by the USF&W Service. For information contact Refuge Manager, Kenai National Wildlife Refuge, Ski Hill Road, PO Box 2139 MS 519, Soldotna, AK 99669; (907) 262-7021.

The shortest and easiest of the two routes is the **Swan Lake Route**. It starts from either of two trailheads: the West Entrance at Canoe Lake (Mile 21), and the East Entrance at Portage Lake (Mile 27). From either entrance the routes pass through several lakes connected by portages and then reach the Moose River which flows into the Kenai near Sterling. These routes take from three days to a week and cover a distance of about 60 miles (97 km). Many additional lakes are accessible by making side trips from the main routes and there's no reason you can't just paddle out for a day or two and then return to your starting point.

The **Swanson River Route** begins at Paddle Lake (Mile 30). You travel north through a series of lakes until reaching the Swanson River. You then travel down the Swanson with no portages to either a take-out at the Swanson River Landing (19 river miles, 31 km) near Mile 17 or to a take-out at Captain Cook State Recreation Area (43 river miles, 69 km) off the North Kenai Spur Highway. This trip also takes up to a week.

YUKON RIVER

The Yukon River is one of the longest navigable waterways on the North American Continent. It is actually possible to canoe or kayak from the headwaters near the head of the Chilkoot Pass all the way to the Bering Sea. En route you would have to make a portage at Whitehorse around a dam, run rapids at the outlet of Lake Lindeman and below Carmacks, and paddle across 5 rather large lakes, but otherwise your trip would be very uncomplicated.

As a practical matter most people travel the upper river from near Whitehorse to Circle City in Alaska. Distance and approximate time to complete are as follows: Whitehorse to Dawson City, 460 miles (742 km), 2 weeks; Dawson City to Eagle, 100 miles (161 km), 4 days; Eagle to Circle City, 150 miles (242 km), 1 week.

Canoes can be rented in Whitehorse, Dawson City, and Eagle. The rental companies can help you work out the logistics. Many people do this so the support structure is in place.

Below Eagle the river runs through the Yukon-Charlie Rivers National Preserve. For information contact: National Park Service, Yukon-Charlie Rivers National Preserve, PO Box 167, Eagle, AK 99738; (907) 547-2233.

CAMPING AWAY FROM THE ROAD

Text INDEX

MAP INDEX

Campground INDEX

474

477

478

TERRI AND MIKE ON THE BEACH IN WRANGELL

ABOUT THE AUTHORS

For the last twenty years Terri and Mike Church have traveled in Alaska, Mexico, Central America, Europe, Canada, Australia, and the western U.S. Most of this travel has been in RVs, a form of travel they love. It's affordable and comfortable; the perfect way to see interesting places.

Over the years they discovered that few guidebooks were available with the essential day-to-day information that camping travelers need when they are in unfamiliar surroundings. *Traveler's Guide to Alaskan Camping, Pacific Northwest Camping Destinations, Southwest Camping Destination, Traveler's Guide to Camping Mexico's Baja, Traveler's Guide to Mexican Camping, Traveler's Guide to European Camping, and RV and Car Camping Vacations in Europe* are designed to be the guidebooks that the authors tried to find when they first traveled to these places.

Terri and Mike now live full-time in an RV: traveling, writing new books, and working to keep these guidebooks as up-to-date as possible. The books are written and prepared for printing using laptop computers while on the road.

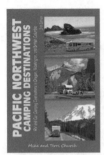

Pacific Northwest Camping Destinations
6" x 9" Paperback, 720 Pages,
Over 180 Maps
ISBN 978-0982310120
3rd Edition - Copyright 2012

Companion to Alaska Camping

Pacific Northwest Camping Destinations makes a great companion for our **Traveler's Guide to Alaskan Camping**. The books were designed to complement each other. The Pacific Northwest book guides you through Oregon, Washington, and southern British Columbia, right up to the southern end of the Alaska and Cassiar Highways. Then the Alaska book takes over with the information you'll need through northern British Columbia, the Yukon Territory, and Alaska.

A new feature of this edition is complete coverage of the campgrounds convenient to the Interstate highway corridors – from the Canadian border in the north to the California border in the south. Now it's easy to cruise along the main artery of travel with the confidence that when you want to stop for the night you can make a good decision. No more relying on billboards and hard to decipher catalog-style guides. Each campground along the corridor is described and also depicted on easy-to-follow maps, you'll always know what to expect and where you're going, even after dark.

In addition to being the gateway to Alaska, the Pacific Northwest is itself an RVers paradise. It offers everything an RV vacationer could desire: seashores, snow-topped mountains, old growth forests, visitor friendly cities, and national parks. In fact, the Pacific Northwest is one of the most popular RVing destinations in North America.

Pacific Northwest Camping Destinations provides the camping traveler with all the information needed to visit the Northwest without missing any of its top destinations. It combines the functions of a campground directory and a sightseeing guide directing the way to more than 140 destinations and over 1,300 campgrounds throughout Oregon, Washington, and southern British Columbia. Each entry describes a vacation spot and its attractions and recommends good camping sites in the area, including privately owned, federal, state, provincial and local government campgrounds.

Each campground is described in detail including a recommendation for the maximum size RV suitable for the campground. Written driving instructions as well as a map are provided showing the exact location of each campground. Tourist destinations are described and several itineraries are proved for driving on scenic routes throughout the region.

Stop and visit the Northwest on your way to Alaska or spend the entire summer, the choice is yours! Here are some of the top attractions:

* The Oregon Coast	* Mount Rainier	* Victoria
* The Columbia Gorge	* The Olympic Peninsula	* Banff and Lake Louise
* Mount St. Helens	* The Oregon Trail	* Hells Canyon
* Portland	* Seattle	* Vancouver
* The Okanagan Valley	* Crater Lake National Park	* Rainier National Park
* Vancouver Island	* Coeur d'Alene	* And Lots More!

Traveler's Guide To Mexican Camping
6" x 9" Paperback, 576 Pages, Over 250 Maps
ISBN 978-0982310106
Fourth Edition - Copyright 2009

Mexico, one of the world's most interesting and least expensive travel destinations, is just across the southern U.S. border. It offers warm sunny weather all winter long, beautiful beaches, colonial cities, and excellent food. Best of all, you can easily and economically visit Mexico in your own car or RV.

The fourth edition of *Traveler's Guide To Mexican Camping* is now even better! It has become the bible for Mexican campers. With this book you will cross the border and travel Mexico like a veteran. It is designed to make your trip as simple and trouble-free as possible. In addition to camping and campground information the guide also includes information about important cities, tourist destinations, roads and driving, trip preparation, vehicle care, shopping, entertainment and sports opportunities. It will help you plan your itinerary and enjoy yourself more while you are on the road. Some features are:

❑ Instructions for crossing the border including detailed information about every important crossing and recommendations for the best places to cross with large RVs.

❑ Detailed descriptions of over three hundred Mexican campgrounds.

❑ Information about camping in Belize and Guatemala including border-crossing details and campground descriptions.

Traveler's Guide To Camping Mexico's Baja
6" x 9" Paperback, 256 Pages, Over 65 Maps
ISBN 978-0982310137
Fifth Edition - Copyright 2012

Sun, sand, and clear blue water are just three of the many reasons more and more RVers are choosing Mexico's Baja as a winter destination. The Baja is fun, easy, and the perfect RVing getaway.

With the right information crossing the border onto the Baja is a snap. Only a few miles south you'll find many camping opportunities–some on beaches where you'll park your vehicle just feet from the water.

The Transpeninsular Highway extends all the way to the tip of the peninsula in Cabo San Lucas. This two-lane paved highway gives access to some of the most remote and interesting country in the world, including lots of desert and miles and miles of deserted beaches. RVers love this country for boating, fishing, beachcombing, and just plain enjoying the sunshine.

Traveler's Guide To Camping Mexico's Baja starts by giving you the Baja-related information from our popular book *Traveler's Guide To Mexican Camping*. It also covers nearby Puerto Peñasco. We've added more campgrounds, expanded the border-crossing section, and given even more information about towns, roads, and recreational opportunities. Like all our books, this one features easy-to-follow maps showing exactly how to find every campground listed.

Traveler's Guide To European Camping
6" x 9" Paperback, 640 Pages, Over 400 Maps
ISBN 978-0965296885
Third Edition - Copyright 2004

O ver 350 campgrounds including at least one in virtually every important European city are described in detail, directions are given for finding them, and in many cases information about convenient shopping, entertainment and sports opportunities is included.

The book features campgrounds in Paris, London, Rome, Lisbon, Amsterdam, Munich, Madrid, Athens, Istanbul, Oslo, Germany's Romantic Road, France's Loire Valley, the Swiss Alps, the Greek Islands, and many more great destinations.

This guide will tell you how to rent, lease, or buy a rig in Europe or ship your own from home. It contains the answers to questions about the myriad details of living, driving, and camping in Europe.

In addition to camping and campground information *Traveler's Guide To European Camping* gives you invaluable details about the history and sights you will encounter. This information will help you plan your itinerary and enjoy yourself more when you are on the road.

Use the information in this book to travel Europe like a native. Enjoy the food, sights, and people of Europe. Go for a week, a month, a year. Europe can fill your RV or camping vacation seasons for many years to come!

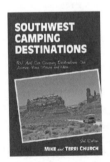

Southwest Camping Destinations
6" x 9" Paperback, 544 Pages, Over 100 Maps
ISBN 978-0974947198
Second Edition - Copyright 2008

B ryce Canyon, Carlsbad Caverns, the Grand Canyon, and Mesa Verde are among the 100 destinations covered in this travel guide for RVers and car campers. Native American sites and desert habitats are also of interest in this region, making it a great vacation destination for families with children. Maps are provided for each destination along with descriptions of tourist attractions and listings for more than 600 traveler campgrounds in Arizona, New Mexico, Utah's Canyon Country, California's desert southeast, and Mexico's nearby seaside resort cities. You'll find campsites here of every type including private, state, local, and federal campgrounds as well as desert boondocking sites. Several itineraries are provided for scenic tours throughout the region.

For those who want to escape to a warm climate in the winter there is a special "snowbird" chapter which gives details on top snowbird destinations in the southwest. Over 275 campgrounds are compared in destination like Palm Springs, Las Vegas, Lake Havasu and Parker, Needles and Laughlin, Yuma, Quartzsite, Phoenix, Mesa, Apache Junction, Casa Grande, Tucson, and Benson. This analysis is accompanied by maps showing the exact locations of campgrounds in these favorite destinations.

RV and Car Camping Vacations in Europe
6" x 9" Paperback, 320 Pages, Over 140 Maps
ISBN 978-0965296892
First Edition - Copyright 2004

People from North America love to visit Europe on their vacations. One great way to travel in Europe is by RV or car, spending the night in convenient and inexpensive campgrounds. It's a way to travel inexpensively and get off the beaten tourist trail. It's also a great way to meet Europeans. Many of them travel the same way!

Most of us lead busy lives with little time to spend on planning an unusual vacation trip. With this book a camping vacation in Europe is easy.

❑ It tells how to arrange a rental RV or car from home.

❑ When to go and what to take with you.

❑ It explains the process of picking up the rental vehicle and turning it back in when you're ready to head for home.

❑ There's also information about shopping, driving, roads, and other things that you should know before you arrive.

❑ Then it describes a series of tours, each taking from a week to two weeks. The ten tours cover much of Western Europe and even the capitals of the Central European countries. The book has details about the routes and roads, the campgrounds to use while visiting each destination, and what to do and see while you are there.

HOW TO BUY BOOKS
PUBLISHED BY ROLLING HOMES PRESS

Rolling Homes Press is a specialty publisher. Our books can be found in many large bookstores and almost all travel bookstores. Even if such a bookstore is not convenient to your location you can buy our books easily from Internet bookstores or even directly from us. Also, most bookstores will order our books for you, just supply them with the ISBN number shown on the previous pages or on the back cover of this book.

We maintain a Website – **www.rollinghomes.com**. If you go to our Website and click on the tab labeled *How To Buy* you will find instructions for buying our book from a variety of Web and storefront retailers as well as directly from us. The instructions on the Website change periodically, they reflect the fact that we are sometime out of the country for long stretches of time. When we are not available we make arrangements to be sure that you can obtain our books quickly and easily in our absence.

Retailers and individuals can always obtain our books from our distributor:

Independent Publisher's Group
814 North Franklin Street
Chicago, Illinois 60610

(800) 888-4741 or (312) 337-0747

www.ipgbook.com